LAND LAW AND POLICY IN PAPUA NEW GUINEA

Second Edition

LAND LAW AND POLICY IN PAPUA NEW GUINEA

Second Edition

John T Mugambwa
LLB (Hons) (Makerere); LLM (Yale); PhD (ANU)
Former Head of Department of Law, University of Papua New Guinea
Senior Lecturer, Program Chair, Murdoch University,
Western Australia

Harrison A Amankwah
BA, LLB (Hons) (Ghana); LLM (Cornell); LLM,
SJD (New York University)
Former Dean, Faculty of Law, University of Papua New Guinea
Associate Professor of Law, James Cook University,
Townsville, Queensland

Routledge
Taylor & Francis Group
LONDON AND NEW YORK

Second edition first published in Great Britain 2002 by Cavendish Publishing Limited, The Glass House, Wharton Street, London WC1X 9PX, United Kingdom

The first edition of this title was entitled *Land Law and Policy in Papua New Guinea – Cases, and Materials*, and was published by Pacific Law Press.

This edition published 2014 by Routledge
2 Park Square, Milton Park, Abingdon, Oxon OX14 4RN
711 Third Avenue, New York, NY 10017, USA

Routledge is an imprint of the Taylor & Francis Group, an informa business

First edition 1996
Second edition 2002

British Library Cataloguing in Publication Data

Amankwah, HA
Land law and policy in Papua New Guinea
1 Real property – Papua New Guinea 2 Land use – Papua New Guinea
I Title II Mugambwa, JT
346.9'53'043

ISBN 13 : 978-1-876905-14-9 (pbk)

To Juliet and Gwenneth and our intellectual guru Professor Thomas M Franck

FOREWORD

This is the second edition of a book that was first published in 1996 on issues relating to land law and policy in Papua New Guinea. It marked the first substantive statement on the subject since Professor Rudi James' work in land law and policy in Papua New Guinea, which was published by the Law Reform Commission in 1985. The authors of the book are eminently qualified to write on the subject, a subject which is so close to hearts of all Papua New Guineans. Both have taught at the former Faculty of Law at the University of Papua New Guinea. The second edition of this book marks both an important contribution to the availability of textbooks on Papua New Guinea law and the authors' continuing interest in the interplay of land law principles, use and development of land, and government policies on land.

This edition is particularly significant because it complements the authors' most recent publication titled *Land Law in Papua New Guinea*; a publication which was one of a series prepared under the auspices of the AusAID funded Access to Laws project. They wrote that book with Mr George Muroa, Senior Lecturer at the School of Law, University of Papua New Guinea.

Papua New Guinea has continued a process of examining its laws, most of which have been introduced from England and Australia, over the years to make them more appropriate to the requirements of the country as it develops and changes. Some of these laws have received severe criticism from lawyers, academics, politicians and ordinary people. The inclusion in this book of articles and other related commentaries which indicate a divergence of views on different aspects of land law by persons other than the authors to augment the text confirm, to some extent, this continuing process. Most major legal principles regarding land law are technical and therefore difficult to understand, unless one is trained to understand and appreciate their significance. While some of the criticisms that have been made against land law principles are valid, others owe their origins to a genuine lack of an understanding of these complex principles.

However, a lack of written materials on the subject only compounds the problem. This edition addresses this and the related wider issue of accessibility to written materials on land law in this country in a concise, authoritative and accurate manner. I especially commend them for the additional material they have included in this edition, material which they were not able to include in the first edition.

The first edition was sold out almost immediately after it was released. This probably explains why the Michael Somare Library of the University of Papua New Guinea does not have a copy of that edition. I am sure that the second edition will, as it truly deserves, receive similar acclaim and popularity. And, this time, the Michael Somare Library will be at the front of the race to get an appropriate number of copies.

I warmly congratulate the authors and commend it as being an indispensable tool for the teaching of land law principles and policies at the School of Law, University of Papua New Guinea, and for providing a useful reference for lawyers, magistrates, judges, law reformers, policy makers and landowners.

We do not own land, we hold it in trust for future generations.

John Y Luluaki
Associate Professor of Law
School of Law
University of Papua New Guinea

PREFACE

Last year, through the assistance of the Australian government PNG Access to Laws Project, Papua New Guinea was blessed with a rich dividend of scholarly legal texts. The legal texts include *Land Law in Papua New Guinea* (Lawbook Co, Sydney, 2001), which we wrote with George Muroa. In writing the new text, we drew inspiration from the first edition of this casebook. However, due to the publishers' constraint on the length of the former text, we were forced to compress the content.

Cases and Materials on Papua New Guinea Land Law and Policy appropriately furnishes the missing details and serves as a companion text, thus providing a fuller picture of PNG land law. The first edition of this book proved to be a very popular and useful work on PNG land law. It sold out almost immediately upon its release from the press. We hope that the second edition with its augmented new materials will prove to be even more popular and useful.

John Mugambwa
Harrison A Amankwah
2002

Preface to the first edition

Since the establishment of the Faculty of Law within the University of Papua New Guinea (UPNG) in 1967, land law and policy has been an important component of the basic LLB curriculum. However, due to the predominantly expatriate composition of the University's academic staff, this course has been taught by many scholars, some of whom in their determination to leave something permanent for their students had put together teaching materials. The most prominent of these law teachers was Dr CEP Haynes whose pioneer compilation *Land Law and Land Policy in Papua New Guinea: Text, Cases and Materials Parts I, II, III, IV and V* (UPNG Printery, Port Moresby, 1983) still provides basic materials on the course for both lecturer and student. Mention must be made also of Prof RW James' work, *Land Law and Policy in Papua New Guinea* (Land Reform Commission, Port Moresby, 1985) commissioned by the PNG Land Reform Commission.

During our tenure of office as Dean and Head of Department respectively, The Asia Foundation (USA) acceded to our request for some funding for the production of a text on Papua New Guinea land law and policy. It was our considered opinion that English and Australian texts on land law needed considerable doctoring to render them suitable for the needs of Papua New Guinea students. The Asia Foundation's assistance in this regard provided a unique opportunity for us to assemble and integrate a conglomerate of teaching materials which had been employed by various law teachers over the years in the teaching of land law at UPNG.

Chapter 1 is a summary of materials on pre-colonial land policy which may be found elsewhere. Chapter 2 is a summary of material on post-colonial land policy. Chapter 3 is an exposition of basic principles of land law. Chapters 4–8 represent a consolidation of ideas and material on the basic law. It is hoped that in subsequent editions all the materials on land policy would similarly be consolidated by amalgamation of existing materials and the newer or additional materials herein. It is our own firm belief that the younger generations of Papua New Guineans should understand and appreciate the sacrifice their forebears invested in the acquisition of the fatherland and the factors which nurtured it and ensured its continued existence.

It is easy to allow the national patrimony to be fretted away like some perishable commodity through its indiscriminate alienation instead of regarding it as a sacred or ancestral trust which the living share with the dead. Our aim is to drive this lesson home without the use of expensive foreign texts of doubtful relevance to the Papua New Guinea situation.

As Papua New Guinea enters the 21st century, advancement in technology and science and galloping population growth would exert additional pressures on land, its resources and environment. But no one should lose sight of Goal No 5 of The Constitution of Papua New Guinea (1975) that development (whatever that means) shall be pursued via Papua New Guinea's own forms of social, political and economic organisations. Foreign prescriptions, experience has demonstrated, have not fared too well on Papua New Guinea terrain. We acknowledge with sincere gratitude the secretarial assistance we have received from Ms Kerrie Thompson, Helen Stokes, Dale Montgomery of our respective Law Schools and Mr Rupert Johnson our research assistant; also the moral and financial help from our said institutions.

JT Mugambwa
School of Law
Murdoch University
Perth WA
Australia

HA Amankwah
School of Law
James Cook University
Townsville QLD
Australia

ACKNOWLEDGMENTS

We gratefully acknowledge permission to reproduce material from the following persons and companies. For permission to reproduce extracts from English cases: the Incorporated Council of Law Reporting for England and Wales. For permission to reproduce extracts from Papua New Guinea cases: Council of Law Reporting for Papua New Guinea. For permission to reproduce extracts from Queensland cases: the Incorporated Council of Law Reporting for the State of Queensland. For permission to reproduce extracts from New South Wales cases: the Incorporated Council of Law Reporting for New South Wales. For permission to reproduce extracts from Victoria cases: the Council of Law Reporting for Victoria. For permission to reproduce extracts from Western Australia cases: the Council of Law Reporting for Western Australia. For permission to reproduce extracts from New Zealand cases: the Council of Law Reporting for New Zealand. For permission to reproduce extracts from Australian cases: the Law Book Co Ltd and Butterworths. For permission to reproduce material from legal periodicals: Professor RW James, University of Papua New Guinea and the Melanesian Law Journal; The Sage Publications Inc and the Annals of the American Academy of Political and Social Science. For permission to reproduce extracts from books: Professor RW James and the Law Reform Commission of Papua New Guinea; Professor PG Sack and the Australian National University Press; Mr J Millet and the Papua New Guinea Institute of National Affairs.

While every care has been taken to trace and acknowledge copyright, the publishers tender their apologies for any accidental infringement where copyright has proven unascertainable. They would be pleased to come to a suitable accommodation with the rightful owners in each case.

CONTENTS

Foreword *vii*

Preface *ix*

Acknowledgments *xi*

Table of Cases *xvii*

Table of Legislation *xxxvii*

Table of International Legislation *xlvii*

CHAPTER 1: INTRODUCTION: LAND POLICY IN PAPUA NEW GUINEA 1

I The land policy in the protectorate period in British New Guinea (Papua) 1884–1906 1

II Land law and policy in German New Guinea 1885–1914 18

III Land law and policy in Papua New Guinea 1906–45 28

IV Land law and policy in New Guinea 1914–21 29

V Land law and policy in Mandated New Guinea 1921–45 32

VI Land law and policy in Papua New Guinea 1945–62 36

VII Land law and policy in Papua New Guinea 1962–73 37

CHAPTER 2: NATIONHOOD AND DEVELOPMENT POLITICS: TOWARDS LAND USE MAXIMIZATION 53

I Introduction 53

II The basic principles of the CILM Report 54

III Restoration of land to the indigenous people 59

IV Securing State land 68

V Land and the economy of PNG 71

VI Land reform and land use: lessons from some Third World nations 86

VII Conclusion 99

CHAPTER 3: LAND: LEGAL CONCEPTION AND NATURE OF INTERESTS 103

I What is land? The statutory and underlying law position 103

II Definition and concept of land at customary law 116

III Classification 117

IV The doctrines of estate and tenure 119

V Interests at customary law: allodial and usufruct 128

VI Nature of interests in land: the legal-equitable interest dichotomy 133

CHAPTER 4: CO-OWNERSHIP OF LAND **151**

I Introduction 151

II Types of co-ownership 151

II Creation of joint tenancy and tenancy in common 155

IV Right of enjoyment amongst co-owners 165

V Determination of co-ownership 176

CHAPTER 5: MORTGAGES **197**

I Introduction 197

II Nature and effect of mortgage 197

III Creation of mortgage 200

IV Rights and remedies of a mortgagee 201

V Rights of the mortgagor 254

CHAPTER 6: LEASES **275**

I Leases and licences distinguished 275

II Essential features of a lease 277

III Creation of leases 296

IV Rights and duties of landlord and tenant 311

V Remedies for breach of covenants 334

VI Termination of leases 352

CHAPTER 7: STATE LEASES **359**

I Classification of leases 359

II Grant of State lease 360

III Purposes for which a State lease may be granted 378

IV Termination of a State lease 387

CHAPTER 8: EASEMENTS AND RESTRICTIVE COVENANTS **399**

I Introduction 399

II Easements 399

III Restrictive covenants 413

CHAPTER 9: REGISTRATION OF TITLES 421

I Introduction 421

II Essential characteristics 421

III Protection of unregistered interests 487

IV Remedies for wrongful deprivation of an interest in land 501

V National lands registration 507

Index 515

TABLE OF CASES

AG Securities v Vaughan and Others [1988] 3 All ER 1058; reversing [1988] 2 All ER 173 .... 151, 152

ANZ v Bangadilly Pastoral Co Pty Ltd and Others (1978) 139 CLR 195 222

Abbeyfield (Harpenden) Society Ltd v Woods [1968] 1 WLR 374; [1968] 1 All ER 352(n) 287

Abela v Public Trustee [1983] 1 NSWLR 308 192

Abigail v Lapin [1934] AC 491 .... 247, 493, 497, 499

Addiscombe Garden Estates Ltd v Crabbe [1958] 1 QB 513; [1957] 3 All ER 563 .... 153, 294

Administration of the Territory of Papua and New Guinea v Daera and Guba (Newtown case) (1973) 130 CLR 353; (1973) 47 ALJR 621 .... 1, 6, 9, 88, 92, 120

Administration of the Territory of Papua and New Guinea v Guba and Doriga (1973) P&NGLR 603; (1973) 130 CLR 353, HC (Aus) 87, 123, 128, 129, 142

Administration of the Territory of Papua and New Guinea v Blasius Tirupia and Others (In Re Vunapaladig and Japalik Land) [1971–72] P&NGLR 229 .... 121, 148, 425, 506

Advisory Opinion on Western Sahara [1975] 1 ICJR 12 4

Advocate General (Bengal) v Ranee Surnomoye Dossee (1863) 2 Moo NS 22; 15 ER 811; 9 Moo Ind App 391; 19 ER 786 5

Agevu v The Government of Papua New Guinea [1977] PNGLR 99 87

Ahern v LA Wilkinson (Northern) Ltd [1929] St R Qd 66 .... 302, 303

Aldin v Latimer Clark Muirhead & Co Ltd [1894] 2 Ch 437 315

Allan v Liverpool Overseere (1874) LR 9 QB 180 291

Amicable Society v Bolland 1830) 2 Dow & Cl 1; 6 ER 630; 4 Bli NS 194; 4 ER 70 193

Amodu Tijani v The Secretary, Southern Nigeria [1921] 2 AC 399 .... 6, 87, 108, 120, 129, 131

Ankar Pty Ltd v National Westminster Finance (Australia) Ltd (1987) 162 CLR 549; 70 ALR 641 335

Anning v Anning (1907) 4 CLR 1049 178

Application of Heather Joan Hutchinson, Re [1984] PNGLR 71 159

Application of Moge Enga and Kuipi Group in the Matter of the Decision of the Minister of Lands Concerning Section 30 Allotment 7 Mount Hagen [1995] PNGLR 31, National Court of Papua New Guinea 360, 365, 373, 376, 377

Application of the National Capital District Interim Commission [1987] PNGLR 339 369

Arlesford Trading Co Ltd v Servansingh [1971] 1 WLR 1080 333

Arthur Agevu and Others v The Government of Papua New Guinea [1977] PNGLR 99 11
Ashburn Anstalt v Arnold [1988] 2 All ER 147 280
Assets Co Ltd v Mere Roihi [1905] AC 176 .... 429, 430, 442, 447–50, 453
Associated Provincial Picture House v Wednesbury Corporation [1948] 1 KB 223 368
Attorney General v Brown (1847) 1 Legge 312 .... 119, 121, 133
Attorney General of Ontario v Mercer (1883) LR 8 App Cas 767 119
Austerberry v Corporation of Oldham (1885) 29 Ch D 750 414
Austotel Pty Ltd v Franklins Selfserve Pty Ltd [1989] 16 NSWLR 582 135
Australia and New Zealand Banking Group v Kila Wari (1990) unreported judgment of the National Court of Papua New Guinea, 16 February 1990, N801 .... 220, 229, 231
Australian Conservation Foundation v The Commonwealth (1980) 146 CLR 493 132
Australian Hi-Fi Publications Pty Ltd v Gehl [1979] 2 NSWLR 618 470
Australian Provincial Assurance Co Ltd v Coroneo (1938) 38 SR (NSW) 700 .... 113, 115
Avia Aihi v The State [1981] PNGLR 81 395

Bahr and Another v Nicolay and Others (No 2) (1988) 164 CLR 604; (1988) 78 ALR 1, HC (Aus) 450, 453, 475, 482, 485
Bailey v Barnes [1894] 1 Ch 25 225
Bain v Brand [1876] App Cas 762 109
Bank of Papua New Guinea v Muteng Basa [1992] PNGLR 271 243
Bannister v Bannister [1948] 2 All ER 133 .... 454, 483
Barbour, deceased, Re [1967] Qd R 10 158
Barrow v Isaacs & Son [1891] 1 QB 417, CA 327
Barrowcliff, Re [1927] SASR 147 .... 193, 194
Barry v Hasseldine [1952] Ch 835 407
Barry v Heider and Another (1914) 19 CLR 197 487
Bates v Donaldson [1896] 2 QB 241; [1895–99] All ER Rep 170 .... 325, 326
Beaman v ARTS Limited [1948] 1 All ER 465 368
Beck v Auerbach [1986] 6 NSWLR 454 470
Bedson v Bedson [1965] 2 QB 666 167
Belgrave Nominees Pty Ltd and Others v Barlin-Scott Airconditioning (Aust) Pty Ltd [1984] VR 947 115
Bickel v Duke of Westminster [1976] 3 All ER 801; [1977] QB 517 .... 326, 327
Biggs v Hoddinott [1898] 2 Ch 307; [1895–99] All ER 625, CA 260, 263, 266

Blasius Tirupia and Others v Administration of the Territory of Papua and New Guinea [1973] PNGLR 34 . . . 426
Bonner (Deceased), Re [1963] Qd R 488 . . . 127
Booij Bros Pty Ltd v BMH Co Pty Ltd (1974) unreported judgment N795, Supreme Court of Justice . . . 202
Booker v Palmer [1942] 2 All ER 674 . . . 281, 291, 293
Booth v Booth (1935) 53 CLR 1 . . . 126, 127
Bosca Land Pty Ltd's Caveat, Re [1976] Qd R 119 . . . 493
Bourne, Re, Bourne v Bourne [1906] 2 Ch 427 . . . 159, 160
Boyd v Mayor & C of Wellington [1924] NZLR 1174 . . . 428, 430, 431
Boyd v Shorrock (1867) LR 5 Eq 72 . . . 115
Bradley v Carritt [1903] AC 253 . . . 256, 268, 270
Bradshaw v Toulmin (1784) Dick 633; 21 ER 417 . . . 154
Brand v Chris Building Co Pty Ltd [1957] VR 625, Supreme Court of Victoria . . . 110, 112
Breskvar and Another v Wall and Others (1971) 126 CLR 376, HC (Aus) . . . 247, 248, 422, 427, 428, 432, 438, 441, 450, 462, 463, 475, 476, 484, 493, 504
Breskvar v White [1978] Qd R 187, SC (Qld) . . . 504
British Anzani (Felixstow) Ltd v International Marine Management (UK) Ltd [1980] QB 137 . . . 338
Bromley Park Garden Estates Ltd v Moss [1982] 2 All ER 890; [1982] 1 WLR 1019 . . . 326, 327
Brunker v Perpetual Trustee Co (Ltd) (1937) 57 CLR 555 . . . 178
Buchanan v Byrnes (1906) 3 CLR 704 . . . 355
Buckby v Coles and Price (1814) 5 Taunt 311; 128 ER 709 . . . 410
Budd-Scott v Daniell [1902] 2 KB 351 . . . 313
Bull v Bull [1955] 1 QB 234 . . . 166
Burgess v Rawnsley [1975] Ch 429; [1975] 3 All ER 142, CA . . . 185, 189, 191
Burns Philip (PNG) Ltd v The State and Others (1989) unreported, N769 . . . 366
Bursill Enterprises Pty Ltd v Berger Bros Trading Co Ltd (1971) 124 CLR 73, HC (Aus) . . . 457
Busin v Havini (1957) unreported judgment N102, Supreme Court . . . 36, 37
Butler v Fairclough (1917) 23 CLR 78, HC (Aus) . . . 452, 494–97, 499

Caffoor v Commissioner of Income Tax, Colombo [1961] AC 584 145
Calder v Attorney General of British Columbia
(1973) 34 DLR (3d) 145 Supreme Court of Canada 6, 123
Callaghan v The Queen (1952) 87 CLR 115 194
Calverley v Green (1984) 155 CLR 242 165
Campbell v Bank of New South Wales
16 NSWLR (Eq) 285; 11 AC 192 208
Campbell v Holyland (1877) 7 Ch D 166 .... 202, 205, 208
Canning v Temby (1905) 3 CLR 419 335
Capital and Counties Bank Ltd v Rhodes [1903] 1 Ch 631 209
Carl Zeiss Stiftung v Rayner & Keeler Ltd (No 2) [1967] 1 AC 853 145
Carter v Carter (1857) 3 K & J 617 139
Case of Mines, The (1567) 1 Plowd 310 107
Cave v Cave (1880) 15 Ch D 639 136
Caveat No 774 ex p Hodgson, Re (1873) 3 SCR 142 .... 491, 492
Charles Clay & Sons Ltd v British Railways Board
[1971] 1 All ER 1007; [1971] Ch 725 .... 279, 280
Cheshire Lines Committee v Lewis & Co (1880) 50 LJQB 121 279
Cityland and Property (Holdings) Limited
v Dabrah [1968] Ch 166 270
Clarke v Japan Machines (Australia) Pty Ltd [1984] 1 Qd R 404 220
Clem Smith Nominees Pty Ltd v Farrelly and Farrelly;
Adelaide International Raceway Pty Ltd and Mallala
Motors Racing Co Pty Ltd (1978) 20 SASR 227 415
Clements v Ellis (1934) 51 CLR 217 .... 433, 462
Cleaver v Mutual Reserve Fund Life Association
[1892] 1 QB 147 193
Coatsworth v Johnson (1886) 55 LJQB 220, CA 302
Codelfa Construction Pty Ltd v State Rail Authority of
New South Wales (1982) 149 CLR 337 287
Comissioner for Railways v Valuer General
[1973] 3 All ER 268; [1974] AC 328 105
Congleton Corporation v Pattison (1808) 10 East 130 328
Connellan Nominees Pty Ltd v Camerer [1988] 2 Qd R 248 470
Consolidated Trust Company Limited
v Naylor (1936) 55 CLR 423 199
Cooper v Stuart (1889) 14 App Cas 286 4–6
Corin and Another v Patton (1990) 92 ALR 1,
High Court of Australia 177, 180, 185

Council of the Civil Service Union v Minister for the
Civil Service [1984] 3 All ER 935 373
Cox v Bishop (1857) 8 DM & G 815 140
Crabb v Arun District Council [1976] Ch 179; [1975] 3 All ER 865 .... 147, 148, 166, 276
Crane v Morris [1965] 1 WLR 1104 354
Croft v Lumley (1858) 6 HLC 672 346
Crossley & Sons Ltd v Lightowler (1867) 2 Ch App 478 411
Cruse v Mount [1932] All ER Rep 781, Ch D 316, 317, 442
Cuckmere Brick Co Ltd and Another v Mutual Finance Ltd
[1971] Ch D 949; [1971] 2 All ER 633, CA 226, 231, 233, 236
Custodian of Expropriated Property, The v Commissioner of
Native Affairs (Re Jomba Plain) (1971–72) P&NGLR 501 27
Custodian of Expropriated Property and Another, The
v Tedep and Others (1964) 113 CLR 318, HC (Aus) 36, 121, 422, 426

Dadzie v Kokofu (1960) GLR 90 116
Danga Mondo v Korugl Goi (1987) unreported judgment,
Kundiawa District Land Court 116
Darvell v Auckland Legal Services [1993] NZLR 111 368
David Lambu v The Independent State of Papua New Guinea
[1988] PNGLR 121 321
Davis v Pitzz (Secretary for Lands and Physical Planning) and
the Independent State of Papua New Guinea
[1988–89] PNGLR 147, NCJ 390
De Soysa v De Pless Pol [1912] AC 194 335
Dennis v McDonald [1981] 2 All ER 633 171
Dent v Kavali [1981] PNGLR 488 391
Di Masi v Piromalli [1980] WAR 57 470
Diamond v Moore (1931) 45 CLR 159 337
Direct Food Supplies (Vic) Pty Ltd
v DLV Pty Ltd [1975] VR 358 350
Dockrill v Cavanagh (1944) 45 SR (NSW) 78 300
Dodson v Downey [1901] 2 Ch 620 208
Doe d Ambler v Woodbridge (1829) 9 B & C 376 346
Doe d Phillip and Walters v Benjamin
(1839) 9 Ad & E 644; 112 ER 1356, KB 307, 308
Doe d Thomson v Amey (1840) 12 A & E 476; 113 ER 892 299
Doe d Warner v Browne (1807) 8 East 165 279
Dolphin's Conveyance, Re [1970] 1 Ch 654 418

Downie v Lockwood [1965] VR 257 471
Drape's Conveyance, Re [1969] 1 Ch 486.... 185
Dyke v Walford (1846) 5 Moo PCC 434; 13 ER 557.... 128
Dyson v Forster [1909] AC 98.... 329

ER Eves Investment Ltd v High [1967] 2 QB 379 148
EXPO International Pty Limited (Receivers and Managers Appointed) (In Liquidation) and Another v Chant and Others [1979] 2 NSWLR 820 217
Edge v Boileau (1885) 16 QBD 117.... 313
Ellenborough Park, In Re [1955] 3 All ER 667, CA 399
Ellis v Loftus Iron Co (1874) LR 10 CP 10; [1874–80] All ER Rep 232 105
Elliston v Reacher [1908] 2 Ch 374.... 416, 418
Emas Estate Development Pty Ltd v John Mea and Another [1993] PNGLR 215.... 434, 440–42, 444–46, 451, 485
Emile Erlanger and Others v New Sombrero Phosphate Co (1878) 3 App Cas 1218.... 149
English Scottish and Australian Bank Ltd, The v Phillips (1937) 57 CLR 302 .... 198, 199
Errington v Errington and Woods [1952] 1 KB 290; [1952] 1 All ER 149.... 281, 293, 294
Espin v Pemberton 3 De G & J 547 136
Esther Investments Pty Ltd v Cherrywood Pty Ltd [1986] WAR 279 331
Evigeniou v The Queen (1964) 38 ALJR 508 194
Ex p Karynette Pty Ltd [1984] 2 Qd R 211 112
Ex p Van Achterberg [1984] 1 Qd R 160 112

Facchini v Bryson [1952] 1 TLR 1386.... 293, 294
Fairclough v Swan Brewery Co [1912] AC 565 259
Farrar v Farrars Limited (1889) 40 Ch D 395, CA.... 221, 224, 229
Federated Homes Ltd v Mill Lodge Properties Ltd [1980] 1 WLR 594.... 415
Fink v Robertson (1907) 4 CLR 864, High Court of Australia 204, 205, 207
Fisherman's Island, Re [1979] PNGLR 202.... 11
Flexman v Corbett [1930] 1 Ch 672 318
Foley (Deceased), Re; Public Trustee v Foley and Others [1955] NZLR 702, Supreme Court of New Zealand 164
Forbes v Cochrane (1824) 2 B & C 448; 107 ER 450.... 4

Forsyth v Blundell (1973) 129 CLR 477 .... 245, 250
Four-Maids Ltd v Dudley Marshall (Properties) Ltd [1957] Ch 317 198
Francis v Ibitoye (1936) NLR 11, judgment of the Divisional Court of Nigeria 110
Frazer v Walker [1967] 1 AC 569 .... 428, 432, 433, 441, 450, 462, 481
Freed v Taffel [1984] 2 NSWLR 322 185
Freeth v Burr (1874) LR 9 CP 208 337
Friedman v Barrett ex p Friedman [1962] Qd R 498 .... 200, 451
Frimpong v Poku (1973) 2 GR 1 101

G & C Kreglinger v New Patagonia Meat and Cold Storage Co Ltd [1914] AC 25 .... 202, 260, 262, 264, 270
Garrick v Lord Camden; Paton v Jones (1807) 14 Ves 372; 33 ER 564 125
Gaskell v Gosling [1896] 1 QB 669; [1897] AC 575 218
Gathomo v Murito (1921) EAPLR 102 (Kenya) 6
Gaudron v Mackay (1936) 60 (NSW) WN 11 305
Gaya Nomgui and Others v The Administration of the Territory of Papua and New Guinea (Re Lae Administration Case) [1974] PNGLR 349, SC of Papua New Guinea 9, 27, 32, 34
Gegeyo, Re; Gegeyo v Minister for Lands and Physical Planning [1987] PNGLR 331 .... 369, 370, 375
Geita Sebea v The Territory of Papua (1940) unreported judgment, Central Court of Papua, 12 6
Geita Sebea v The Territory of Papua (1941) 67 CLR 544, HC of Australia 108, 113, 116
Genrich v Maitland Holdings Pty Ltd [1982] Qd R 58, SC (Qld) 491
George Livanos, deceased, Re [1955] St R Qd 362 159
George Routledge & Sons Ltd, Re; Hummel v George Routledge & Sons Ltd [1904] 2 Ch 474 208
Gibbs and Houlder Brothers and Company Limited's Lease, In Re; Houlder Brothers and Company Limited v Gibbs [1925] Ch 198; [1925] All ER Rep 128, Ch D 324, 326
Gifford v Dent [1926] 1 WN 336 104
Giles, Re [1972] Ch 544 195
Gill and Another v Lewis and Another [1956] 2 QB 1, CA 348
Glenwood Lumber Co Ltd v Phillips [1904] AC 405 285
Goodman v Gallant [1986] 1 All ER 311, CA 158
Goodwin v Phillips (1908) 7 CLR 1 .... 479, 480

Graham v KD Morris & Sons Pty Ltd [1974] Qd R1 107
Grangeside Properties Ltd v Collingwood Securities Ltd and Others [1964] 1 All ER 143 254
Green v Sevin (1879) 13 Ch D 589 336
Griffiths v Pelton [1958] Ch 205 330
Guba and Doriga v The Administration (1969) unreported judgment N548, Supreme Court 36
Guba and Doriga v The Administration (1973) P&NGLR 603; affirmed (1973) 130 CLR 353, HC 36
Guerin v The Queen (1984) 13 DLR (4d) 321 131
Gutheil v Ballarat Trustees, Executors and Agency Co Ltd (1922) 30 CLR 293 125

Hamerton v Stead (1824) 3 B & C 478; 107 ER 811 299
Hannaford v Hunn (1825) 2 C & P 148; 1723 ER 68 145
Harman Gawi v PNG Ready Mixed Concrete Pty Ltd [1984] PNGLR 74 .... 149, 277, 298, 303, 343
Harmer v Jumbi (Nigeria) Tin Areas Ltd [1921] 1 Ch 200 316
Harrison v Wells [1966] 3 All ER 524 .... 309, 310
Hart v Windsor (1844) 12 M & W 68; 152 ER 1114 317
Hatfield v Alford (1846) 1 Legge 330 309
Havini, Re (1959) unreported judgment N139, Native Land Appeal Court 36
Hawkesley v May [1956] 1 QB 304 185
Haywood v The Brunswick Permanent Benefit Building Society (1881) 8 QBD 403 415
Hemmings and Wife v The Stoke Poges Golf Club and Another [1920] 1 KB 720 340
Henderson v Eason (1851) 17 QB 701 166
Hey v Moorehouse (1839) 6 Bing NC 52 170
Hi Lift Company Pty Ltd v Secretary for Agriculture and the State of Papua New Guinea (2000) unreported, N2004 .... 360, 440, 443, 449, 451, 480, 481, 485
Highlands Produce Buyers Ltd v Minister for Lands [1988] PNGLR 39, NCJ 388, 392
Hill v Tupper (1866) 2 H & C 121; 159 ER 51 .... 404, 405
Hitchcock, In Re (1900) 17 WN (NSW) 62 491
Hodson v Deans [1903] 2 Ch 647 236

Holland v Wiltshire (1954) 90 CLR 409 335
Holland and Another v Hodgson and Another (1872) LR 7 CP 328 .... 114, 115
Hoole v Smith (1881) 17 Ch D 434 219
Houghton, Re [1915] 2 Ch 173 193
Howard v Fanshawe [1895] 2 Ch 581 .... 348, 350, 351
Howard v Harris (1681) 1 Vern 33; 2 Ch Cas 147 266
Hua Chiao Commercial Bank Ltd
v Chiaphua Industries Ltd [1987] AC 99 330

Idewu Inasa v Oshodi [1934] AC 99 132
In the Land and Goods of Doa Minch (aka Doa Mints)
(1973) P&NGLR 558, Supreme Court of Papua New Guinea 40
In the Matter of an Application by Rose Tarere et al
v Australia and New Zealand Banking Group (PNG) Ltd
[1988] PNGLR 201 .... 239, 240, 512
In the Matter of Luabar Logging Pty Ltd and in the Matter of
the Companies Act (Ch No 145) [1988] PNGLR 124 .... 303, 304, 307
Independent State of Papua New Guinea
v Kapal [1987] PNGLR 417 376
Independent State of Papua New Guinea
v Lohia Sisia [1987] PNGLR 102 .... 241, 242, 511
Indian Chief, The (1801) 3 C Roc 12; 165 ER 367 5
Industrial Properties (Barton Hill) Ltd v Associated Electrical
Industries Ltd [1977] 2 All ER 293 310
International Drilling Fluids Ltd v Louisville Investments
(Uxbridge) Ltd [1986] 1 All ER 321 325
Inwards v Baker [1965] 2 QB 29; [1965] 1 All ER 446 .... 148, 166
Isaac v Hotel de Paris Ltd [1960] 1 All ER 348; [1960] 1 WLR 239 294

J & H Just (Holdings) Pty Ltd v Bank of New South Wales
(1971) 125 CLR 546, HC (Aus) 476, 496, 501
Jackson, Re; Smith v Sibthorpe (1887) 34 Ch D 732 161
Jacobs v Seward (1872) LR 5 HL 464 .... 169, 171
James v Registrar General [1967] 69 SR (NSW) 361, SC (NSW) 468–70
James v Stevenson and Others [1893] AC 162, PC 410
James Fairclough v Swan Brewery Company Ltd [1912] AC 565 258
Jefferys v Dickson (1865–66) 1 Ch App 183 216
Jennings v Ward (1705) 2 Vern 520; 23 ER 923 .... 260, 261, 266
Jivetuo and Another v The Independent State of Papua
New Guinea [1984] PNGLR 174 340

Jobson v Nankervis (1943) 44 SR (NSW) 277 468
Johns, Re [1971–72] P&NGLR 110, Supreme Court of Papua New Guinea 124
Johnson v McIntosh (1823) 8 Wheat 586 131
Jones, Re; Farrington v Forrester [1893] 2 Ch 461 173
Jones (AE) v Jones (FW) [1977] 1 WLR 438, CA 148, 166

Kaporonovski v The Queen (1973) 133 CLR 209 194
Keeves v Dean [1924] 1 KB 685 324
Keimbun Keindip v The Independent State of Papua New Guinea and Others [1993] PNGLR 28, NCJ 434, 459, 506
Kekedo v Burns Philip (PNG) and Others [1988–89] PNGLR 122 376
Kelsen v Imperial Tobacco Co (of Great Britain and Ireland) Ltd [1957] 2 QB 334; [1957] All ER 343 . . . . 103, 104
Kemp v Public Curator of Queensland [1969] Qd R 145 . . . . 193, 194
Kennedy v de Trafford [1896] 1 Ch 762; [1897] AC 180 227–29
Kenny v Preen [1963] 1 QB 499, CA 312
Knightsbridge Estates Trust Limited v Byrne and Others [1939] Ch 441, CA 258
Knockholt Pty Ltd v Graff [1975] Qd R 88 338
Kok Hoong v Leong Cheong Kweng Mines Ltd [1964] AC 993 146
Kumar v Dunning [1987] 3 WLR 1167 . . . . 328, 330
Kuper and Kuper v Keywest Constructions Pty Ltd [1990] 3 WAR 419 . . . . 477, 493

Lace v Chantler [1944] 1 All ER 305, CA 277–80
Lake v Craddock (1732) 3 P Wms 158; 24 ER 1011 159
Landale v Menzies (1909) 9 CLR 89 286
Lapin and Another v Abigail [1930] 344 CLR 166; [1934] AC 491 . . . . 495, 498
Latec Investments Ltd v Hotel Terrigal Pty Ltd (In Liquidation) (1964–65) 113 CLR 265 . . . . 223, 247, 250
Laurinda Pty Ltd and Others v Capalaba Park Shopping Centre Pty Ltd (1989) 85 ALR 183, High Court of Australia 334
Lavender v Betts [1942] 2 All ER 72 . . . . 314, 334
Law Guarantee and Trust Society v Bank of England (1890) 24 QBD 406 153
Leathes ex p Leathes, Re (1883) 3 Deac & Ch 112 201
Leeward Securities Ltd v Lilyheath Properties Ltd (1984) 271 EG 279 326

Leigh v Dickeson (1884) 15 QBD 60;
[1881–85] All ER Rep 1099, CA. 167, 173, 175, 176
Leitz Lee Holme Stud Pty v Robinson [1977] 2 NSWLR 544 . . . . 300, 303
Leros Pty Ltd v Terara Pty Ltd and Another
(1992) 106 ALR 595, HC (Aus) 474, 478, 488, 501
Lewis v Bell (1985) 1 NSWLR 731, CA, New South Wales 284, 289
Lewis v Frank Love Ltd [1961] 1 All ER 446 257
Lisle v Reeve [1902] 1 Ch 53; [1902] AC 461. . . . . 256, 257
Liverpool City Council v Irwin [1977] AC 239 287
Loke Yew v Port Swettenham Rubber Co Ltd [1913] AC 491. 452–55
London and South Western Railway
v Gomm (1882) 20 Ch D 562 140
London City Council v Allen and Another
[1914–15] All ER Rep 1008. . . . . 415, 416
Lord Advocate v Balfour (1907) SC 1360 120
Lord Bernstein of Leigh (Baron) v Skyviews & General Ltd
[1977] 2 All ER 902. 103
Louinder v Leis (1982) 149 CLR 509 . . . . 335, 336
Luabar Logging Pty Ltd, Re [1988] PNGLR 124. 135
Luke v Luke (1936) 36 SR (NSW) 310 167
Luxmoore-May v Baverstock [1990] 1 WLR 1009. 463
Lyons v Lyons [1967] VR 169, Supreme Court of Victoria 186, 189, 198
Lyus v Prowsa Developments Ltd [1982] 2 All ER 953 . . . . 483, 484

McCall v Abelesz and Another [1976] QB 585, CA 314
McCosker and King v Kuster [1967–68] PNGLR 182 . . . . 135, 305, 307
McHugh v Union Bank of Canada [1913] AC 299 228
McKean v Maloney (1988) 1 Qd R 628 250
McKee, In Re; Public Trustee v McKee [1931] 2 Ch 145. 125
M'Mahon v Burchell (1846) 2 Ph 127 . . . . 166, 172
McMahon v Public Curator of Queensland [1952] St R Qd 197. 195
Mabo et al v The State of Queensland (No 2)
(1992) 175 CLR 1, HC (Aus) 1, 6, 17, 119, 123, 130, 160
Madaha Resena and Others v The Independent State
of Papua New Guinea [1990] PNGLR 22. . . . . 110, 112, 113
Maddison v Alderson [1881–85] All ER Rep 742 301
Maip Pty Ltd v Ambra Coffee Estates Pty Ltd [1995] PNGLR 25 133
Maki v Minister for Land and Others (1995) unreported, N1568 434
Maki v Pundia & PNG Motors Pty Ltd [1993] PNGLR 337 . . . . 451, 455

Malayan Credit Ltd v Jack Chia-MPH Ltd [1986] AC 549 161
Malzy v Eichholz [1916] 2 KB 308 314
Mamun Investments v Ponda [1995] PNGLR 1 434
Mancetter Developments Ltd v Garmanson Ltd and Others
[1986] QB 1212, CA 116
Mander v Falcke [1891] 2 Ch 554 140
Marchioness of Huntly v Gaskell [1905] 2 Ch 656 146
Marcroft Wagons Ltd v Smith
[1951] 2 All ER 271; [1951] 2 KB 496 .... 292, 293
Marks v Jolly (1938) 38 SR (NW) 351 305
Marsden and Another v McAlister and Others
(1887) 8 LR (NSW) 300 466
Martinali v Ramuz and Others [1953] 1 WLR 1196 354
Massart v Blight and Another (1951) 82 CLR 423 327
Matthews v Smallwood [1910] 1 Ch 777 345
Maybury v Plowman (1913) 16 CLR 468 480
Mayer v Coe [1968] 2 NSWR 747 .... 433, 462
Mayhew v Suttle (1854) 4 E & B 347; 119 ER 137 291
Maynard v Goode (1926) 37 CLR 529 336
Mears v Callender [1901] 2 Ch 388 116
Medical Benefits Funds of Australia Ltd
v Fisher [1984] 1 Qd R 606 465
Menday, Re (1916) 16 SR (NSW) 442 125
Mercantile Credits Ltd v Shell Co of Australia Ltd
(1976) 136 CLR 326 .... 300, 459, 475, 478
Mersey Steel and Iron Co (Ltd) v Naylor Benzon & Co
(1884) 9 App Cas 434 337
Meye v Electric Transmission Ltd [1942] Ch 290 352
Midland Railway Company v Miles (1886) 33 Ch D 632 408
Milirrpum and Others v Nabalco Pty Ltd and Another
[1971] 17 FLR 141 (Aus) 6, 34, 123, 130
Miller v Davy (1889) 7 NZLR 515 .... 462, 463
Mills v Stokman (1967) 116 CLR 61 476
Milmo v Carreras [1946] KB 306 323
Milroy v Lord (1862) 4 De GF & J 264; 45 ER 1185 .... 177, 178
Mitchell v Cowie (1962) 5 West Indian Reports 409 115
Monroe v Kerry (1710) 1 Bro Parl Cas 67 309
Moore v Diamond [1929–30] 43 CLR 105, High Court of Australia 298, 300
Morley v Bird (1798) 3 Ves 629; 30 ER 1192 .... 156, 158

Mortlock Island, Re [1971–72] P&NGLR 621, Central Court of the Territory of New Guinea . . . 34
Moses v Parker [1896] AC 245 . . . 146
Moule v Garrett and Others (1872) LR 7 Ex 101 . . . 331, 334
Mudge and Mudge v Secretary for Lands and Others [1985] PNGLR 387, SCJ . . . 431, 434, 438, 440–46, 449, 451, 460–64, 487
Murdoch and Barry, Re (1975) 64 DLR (3d) 222 . . . 185
Muller v Trafford [1901] 1 Ch 54 . . . 330
Murray v Brown River Timber Co Ltd [1964] P&NGLR 167 . . . 127

NTN Pty Ltd v Post and Telecommunication Corporation [1987] PNGLR 70 . . . 391
Nana Ofori Atta II and Another v Nana Abu Bonsra II [1958] AC 95 . . . 144, 147
National Bank of Australasia v United Hand-in-Hand and Band of Hope Co (1879) 4 App Cas 391 . . . 228
National Capital District Interim Commission v Crusoe Pty Limited (1989) unreported, N836 . . . 369, 442
National Trustees Co v Hassett [1907] VLR 404 . . . 467
Neeta (Epping) Pty Ltd v Phillips (1974) 131 CLR 286; 3 ALR 151 . . . 335, 336
Neilson-Jones v Feddon [1975] Ch 222 . . . 185
New Brunswick Railway Company v British and French Trust Corporation Ltd [1939] AC 1 . . . 146
Newbolt v Bingham (1895) 72 LT 852 . . . 349
Nielson-Jones v Fedden [1974] 3 All ER 38 . . . 191
Ningiga v Koavea [1988–89] PNGLR 312 . . . 135, 307
Nireaha Tamaki v Baker [1901] AC 561 . . . 120
Nisbet and Potts' Contract, Re [1905] 1 Ch 391; affirmed [1906] 1 Ch 386, CA . . . 140
Noakes & Co Limited v Rice [1902] AC 24 . . . 256, 262, 268–70
Norris v Wilkinson (1805) 12 Vea 192; 33 ER 73 . . . 201
Norton v Kilduff [1974] Qd R 47 . . . 419

O'Keefe v Malone [1903] AC 365 . . . 286
Oil Tool Sales Pty Ltd, Classified Pre-Mixed Concrete Pty Ltd, Caveator, Re [1966] QWN II . . . 491
Onus v Alcoa of Australia Ltd (1981) 149 CLR 27 . . . 132
Osborne Park Co-operative Society Ltd v Wilden Pty Ltd Supreme Court of Western Australia [1989] 2 WAR 77 . . . 471, 476

Owen v Gadd and Others [1956] 2 QB 99, CA 313, 315
Oyekan v Adele [1957] WLR 880 87

P & A Swift Investments (A Firm) v Combined English Stores
Group plc [1988] 2 WLR 313, HL 328
PLAR No 1 of 1980 [1980] PNGLR 326 243
PNG Ready Mixed Concrete Pty Ltd v The Independent
State of Papua New Guinea and Utula Samana
and Sampson Kiamba [1981] PNGLR 396 .... 112, 147, 275, 277
Padfield v Minister of Agriculture,
Fisheries and Food [1968] AC 997 368
Papua New Guinea v Lohia Sisia [1987] PNGLR 102 391
Parker v Webb (1822) 3 Salk 4 329
Partriche v Powlet (1740) 2 Atk 54; 26 ER 430 185
Partridge v McIntosh & Sons Ltd (1933) 49 CLR 453 .... 198, 199
Pascoe v Turner [1979] 1 WLR 431 148
Patzak v Lytton and The Registrar of Titles [1984] WAR 353 192
Peacock v Newtown Marrickville and General Co-operative
Building Society No 4 Limited (1943) 67 CLR 25 146
Pechar, Re [1969] NZLR 574 194
Pembery v Lamdin [1940] 2 All ER 434 200
Penton v Barnett [1898] 1 QB 276 346
People of California v Nogarr
(1958) 330 P (2nd) 858; 67 Am LR (2nd) 992 .... 187, 188
Pickering v Rudd (1815) 4 Camp 219 .... 104, 105
Pilcher v Rawlins (1870) 11 LR Eq 53; (1872) 7 Ch App 259 138
Pimms Ltd v Tallow Chandlers in the City of London
[1964] 2 All ER 145; [1964] 2 QB 547 326
Pioneer Gravels (Qld) Pty Ltd v T & T Mining
Corporation Pty Ltd [1975] Qld R 151 350
Pitts, Re [1931] 1 Ch 546 194
Placer Holdings Pty Ltd and the Land Act (Ch 185)
[1982] PNGLR 326 .... 391, 393
Plaister, Re (1934) 34 SR (NSW) 547 .... 193, 194
Pole-Carew v Western Counties and
General Manure Co [1920] 2 Ch 97 109
Post Office v Estuary Radio Ltd [1968] 2 QB 740 2
Power v Grace [1932] 2 DLR 793 187
Progressive Mailing House Pty Ltd v Tabali Pty Ltd
(1985) 157 CLR 17; 57 ALR 609 336

Property & Bloodstock Ltd v Emerton [1968] 1 Ch 94 248
Proposed Appeal by Constantinou, In Re [1977] PNGLR 1 393
Proprietor of the Centre Building Units Plan No 343
v Bourne [1984] 1 Qd R 613, Supreme Court of Queensland 169
Proudfoot v Hart (1890) 25 QBD 42, CA 319, 321
Prudential Assurance Co Ltd v London Residuary
and Others [1992] 3 All ER 504 278
Public Trustee v Evans [1985] 2 NSWLR 188 .... 194, 195
Pullback Colliery Co Ltd v Woodman [1915] AC 634 409

Queen's Club Gardens Estates Ltd v Bignell
[1924] 1 KB 117, KBD 353

R v Bevan ex p Elias and Gordon (1942) 66 CLR 452 145
R v Cox ex p Smith (1945) 71 CLR 1 145
R v Mullen (1938) 59 CLR 124 194
R v Secretary for State ex p Fire Brigades Union
[1995] 2 All ER 244 368
R v Symonds (1847) NZPCC 390 131
Radaich v Smith and Another (1959) 101 CLR 209,
High Court of Australia 275, 281, 284–89, 295
Rahonamo v Enai and Another (Re Hitau)
[1971–72] P&NGLR 58 .... 8, 122
Ramsden v Dyson (1866) LR1 HL 129 111
Rasmanis v Jurewitsch (1968) 88 WN (Pt 1) (NSW) 59 .... 193, 194
Raz v Matane [1986] PNGLR 38 241
Reeve v Lisle
See Lisle v Reeve—
Regione v Palms Tavern Pty Ltd [1988–89] PNGLR 150 341
Registrar of Titles (WA) v Franzon (1975) 132 CLR 611 450
Reliance Permanent Building Society
v Harwood-Stamper [1944] Ch 362 227
Remon v City of London Real Property Co Ltd
[1921] 1 KB 49 352
Reva Mase v The Independent State of Papua New Guinea
unreported judgment, N296 .... 17, 18
Rice v Rice (1883) 2 Drew 73; 61 ER 646 .... 464, 493, 494, 497
Richardson v Landecker (1950) 50 SR (NSW) 250; 67 WN 149 287
Rigden v Vailler 2 Ves Sen 252 156

Riggall v Muirhead and Others (1911) 13 CLR 436 203
Roads v Overseers of Trumpington (1870) LR 6 QB 56 283
Robertson v Fraser (1871) 6 Ch App 696 156
Robinson v Kilvert [1888] 41 Ch D 88, CA 315
Robinson v Preston (1858) 4 K & J 505; 70 ER 211 158
Rogers v Hosegood [1900] 2 Ch 388 .... 140, 328
Rolland v Hart Law Rep 6 Ch 678 136
Russell v Registrar General of Land [1906] 26 NZLR 1223 .... 462, 463
Ryan v O'Sullivan [1956] VLR 99 253

SCR No 1 of 1984; Re Default Penalties [1984] PNGLR 418 241
SCR No 1 of 1984; Re Minimum Penalties Legislation
[1984] PNGLR 314 240–42
SCR No 2 of 1981; Re s 19(1)(f) of the Criminal Code
[1982] PNGLR 150 395
SCR No 5 of 1985; Raz v Matane [1985] PNGLR 329 .... 241, 242
Safe Lavao v The Independent State of Papua New Guinea
(In Re the Kerema Town and Airstrip Land) [1978] PNGLR 15 8
Sammon, Re (1979) 94 DLR (3d) 594 185
Samuel v Jarraj Timber & Wood Paving
Corporation Limited [1904] AC 323 .... 255, 269
Santley v Wilde [1899] 2 Ch 474 .... 263, 268
Sarson v Roberts [1895] 2 QB 395 317
Saunders v Smith (1838) 2 Jur 491 105
Schebsman, In Re; Official Receiver v Cargo Superintendents
(London) Ltd [1944] Ch 83 483
Schobelt v Barber (1967) 69 DLR 519 194
Scoones v Galvin and the Public Trustee [1934] NZLR 1004 179
Seaman v Vawdrey (1810) 16 Ves 390; 33 ER 1032 412
Segal Securities Ltd v Thoseby [1963] 1 QB 887, QBD 345
Selwyn v Garfit (1888) 38 Ch D 273 225
Shanley v Ward (1913) 29 TLR 714 326
Shaw and Another v Applegate [1978] 1 All ER 123 418
Sheppard v Hong Kong and Shanghae Banking Corp
[1872] 20 WR 459 326
Shevill v Builders Licensing Board
(1982) 149 CLR 620; 42 ALR 305 336
Shiloh Spinners Ltd v Harding [1973] AC 691 .... 348, 350–52
Shropshire Union Railways and Canal Co
v The Queen (1875) LR 7 HL 496 498

Sidebottom v Holland [1895] 1 QBD 378 354
Smith v Jones [1954] 1 WLR 1089.......... 141
Smith v Marrable (1843) 11 M & W 5; 152 ER 697 .... 316, 317
Smith v Registrar of Titles, The State and Duna People's Association Inc (1996) unreported, N1739 464
Smith v Seghill Overseers (1875) LR 10 QB 422; [1874–80] All ER Rep 373 291
Smith and Snipes Hall Farm Ltd v River Douglas Catchment Board [1949] 2 All ER 179 413
Snowlong Pty Ltd v Choe and Others [1991] 23 NSWLR 198 455
Soape and Others v Wesiki and Others, Supreme Court (1960) unreported judgment N159.......... 29
Society of Medical Officers of Health v Hope (Valuation Officer) [1960] AC 551.......... 146
South-Eastern Drainage Board (South Australia), The v The Savings Bank of South Australia (1939) 62 CLR 603 479
Southern Rhodesia, Re [1919] AC 211.......... 6, 86, 130
Sovmots Investments Ltd v Secretary of State for the Environment [1976] 3 All ER 720; [1976] 3 WLR 597.......... 105
Spackman v Plumstead District Board of Works (1885) 10 App Cas 229.......... 146
Spencer's case (1582) 5 Rep 16a; 15 MLC.......... 140
Squire v Rogers [1979] 39 FLR 106 (Aus) 173, 176
St Catherine's Milling & Lumber Co v The Queen (1887) 13 SCR 577; (1888) 14 App Cas 55.......... 131
Standards Chartered Bank Ltd v Walker [1982] 1 WLR 1410.......... 218
State v Bonga [1988–89] PNGLR 360.......... 479
State v Tulong [1995] PNGLR 329 .... 479, 480
Steamship Trading Company Limited v Minister of Lands and Physical Planning and Others (1999) unreported, N1959.......... 360, 366, 440, 445, 446, 449, 452, 480, 481, 485
Stedman v Smith 8 E & B 1 170
Stevens v Hoberg (No 2) [1952] QWN 13.......... 204
Stone, Re [1989] 1 Qd R 251, Supreme Court of Queensland 193
Strathblaine Estates Ltd, Re [1948] 1 All ER 162 160
Street v Mountford [1985] 2 All ER 289 .... 281, 290, 296
Stuart v Kingston (1923) 32 CLR 309.......... 453
Stuy v BC Ronalds Pty Ltd [1984] 2 Qd R 578.......... 470
Suffield v Brown (1864) 4 De GJ & SM 185; 46 ER 888.......... 407
Summer v Salford Corporation [1943] AC 283 317
Sylvanus Goria v National Parks Board [1982] PNGLR 364.......... 390

Tarere v ANZ Bank Group (PNG) Ltd [1988] PNGLR 201 . . . . . 243, 244
Telex (Australasia) Pty Ltd v Thomas Cook & Son (Australasian) Pty Ltd [1970] 2 NSWLR 257 316
Tessmann v Costello [1987] 1 Qd R 283, Supreme Court of Queensland 198
Thomas v Sorrell (1673) Vaugh 330; 124 ER 1098 . . . . . 275, 281
Thompson v Cartwright 33 Beav 178; 2 DJ & S 10 . . . . . 136, 137
Thomson v Richardson (1928) 29 SR (NSW) 221 499
Thomson Mortgage Trusts, In Re [1920] 1 Ch 508 251
Thorp, Re (1961) 80 WN (NSW) 61 193
Thurgood, In Re (1986) unreported judgment of the Supreme Court of Queensland, 8 October 172
Thursby and Others v Plant (1670) 1 Wms Saund 230; 85 ER 254 328
Tietyens v Cox (1916) 17 SR (NSW) 48 307
Tiltwood Sussex, Re [1978] Ch 269 418
Timano v Timano [1993] PNGLR 334 434
Toare Karakara v The Independent State of Papua New Guinea [1986] PNGLR 186 . . . . . 70, 513
Tomlin v Luce (1889) 41 Ch D 573; (1889) 43 Ch D 191 . . . . . 227, 229
Toomes v Conset 3 Atk 261 256
Tramway Advertising Pty Ltd v Luna Park (NSW) Ltd (1938) 38 SR (NSW) 632 335
Treweeke v 36 Wolseley Road Pty Limited (1972) 128 CLR 274, HC of Australia 410
Trust & Agency Co v Markwell (No 2) (1874) 4 QSCR 50 197
Tse Kwong Lam v Wong Chit Sen and Others [1983] 3 All ER 54 . . . . . 222, 233
Tucker v Coleman (1885) 4 NZLR 128 184
Tulk v Moxhay [1843–60] 3 All ER Rep 9; (1848) 2 Ph 774; 41 ER 1143 . . . . . 140, 333, 414
Twentieth Century Banking Co Ltd v Wilkinson [1976] 3 All ER 361 219
Tylee v Webb (1843) 6 Beav 552; 49 ER 939 205

Ulelio and Others v Nelulu Land Group and Others (1996) unreported, N1699 485

Vassos v State Bank of South Australia [1993] 2 VR 316 450
Viscount Tredegar v Harwood and Others
[1929] AC 72; [1928] All ER Rep 11 .... 324, 327
Vyvyan v Arthur (1823) 1 B & C 410 329

Wadman v Calcroft (1804) 10 Ves Jun 67; 32 ER 768 350
Waimiha Sawmilling Co Ltd (In Liquidation)
v Waione Timber Co Ltd [1926] AC 101 454
Wakefield Corporation v Cooke [1904] AC 31 146
Walsh v Lonsdale (1882) 21 Ch D 9 .... 301–03, 308
Walton Stores v Maher (1988) 164 CLR 387 .... 134, 135
Wandaki v Minister for Lands and Another
[1996] PNGLR 116, NCJ 365, 375
Wandsworth Board of Works v United Telephone Co
(1884) 13 QBD 904 .... 104, 105
Ward v Ward (1852) 7 Ex 838; 155 ER 1189 412
Waring (Lord) v London and Manchester
Assurance Co Ltd [1935] 1 Ch 310 248
Warmington and Another v Miller [1973] 2 All ER 372 302
Warner v Jacob (1882) 20 Ch D 220 246
Warren v Keen [1954] 1 QB 15 323
Waterlow v Bacon (1866) LR 2 Eq 514 410
Watson v Gray (1880) 14 Ch D 192 170
Weg Motors Ltd v Hales and Others [1962] Ch 49 331
Wells, Re [1933] 1 Ch 29 255
West Australian Fresh Foods and Ice Company
v Freecorn (1904) 7 WALR 22 466
West Layton Ltd v Ford [1979] 2 All ER 657; [1979] QB 593 327
West London Commercial Bank v Reliance Permanent
Building Society (1885) 29 Ch D 954, CA 251
Westpak Bank (PNG) Limited v Maxwell Forbes
Henderson and Henderson [1990] PNGLR 112 216
Whalley's Caveat, In Re [1975] Qd R 111 491
Wheeldon v Burrows [1874–80] All ER Rep 669, CA 406
Wheeler v Baldwin (1934–35) 52 CLR 609 .... 491, 492
White v City of London Brewery Company
(1889) 42 Ch D 237, CA 214
White v Metcalf [1903] 2 Ch 567 .... 213, 216, 218
Whitehead v Bennett (1958) 27 LJ Ch 474 109
Wilken v Young (1895) 41 NE 68 187

Williams v Hensman (1861) 1 J & H 546; 70 ER 862 .... 176, 190–92
Willmott v Barber (1880) 15 Ch D 96 .... 148, 276
Wilson v Darling Island Stevedoring & Lighterage Co Ltd
(1956) 95 CLR 43 483
Wine v Giglmai [1990] PNGLR 462 .... 149, 301–03, 306, 348
Wolff v Vanderzee (1869) 20 LT 353 228
Wollerton and Wilson Ltd v Richard Costain Ltd
[1970] All ER 483; [1970] 1 WLR 411 107
Wong v Beaumont Property Trust Ltd [1965] 1 QB 173, CA 408
Woodall v Clifton [1905] 2 Ch 257 330
Wright and Another v Gibbons
(1948) 78 CLR 313, High Court of Australia 180, 184, 189
Wytcherley v Andrews (1871) LR 2P & D 327 147

Yared v Spier and Others [1979] 2 NSWLR 291 327
York Buildings Co v MacKenzie (1795) 3 Cr S & P 378 235
Young v Rydalmere Credits Pty Ltd (1963) 80 WN (NSW) 1463 493

TABLE OF LEGISLATION

Bodies Corporate (Joint Tenancy) Act (Ch No 143) 153
s 1 153
s 2 154

Business Groups Incorporation Act (Ch No 144) 89
Preamble 89

Civil Aviation (Aircraft Operators' Liability) Act (Ch No 292)—
Sched 1 107

Colonial Boundaries Act 1895 2

Commissions of Enquiries Act—
s 15 368

Communal Land Rights (Vesting in Trustees) Law (Western Nigeria) 42

Companies Act (Ch No 146) 99

Constitution of the Independent State of Papua New Guinea 1975 (Ch No 1) 63, 145, 311
Pt VIA 310
s 41 .... 239–44, 438, 511, 512
s 41(1) 240, 243
s 53 58
s 53(1) 507
s 53(4) 68
s 53(5) 68
s 54(a) 507
s 56(2)(b) 93
s 58 240
s 155 .... 442, 511, 512
s 155(2)(b) 388
s 155(4) 394, 395, 511
s 158(2) 310
Sched 2.1 .... 147, 276
Sched 2.2 .... 309, 348

Conveyancing Act 1881 122

Co-operative (Companies) Act 99

Co-operative Societies Act 1965 99

Co-operative Societies Act 1967 99

Co-operative Societies Act (Ch 389 of 1982) 99

Courts and Laws Adopting Ordinance 1889—
s 4 .... 126, 127

Criminal Code (Ch No 262)—
s 275 340

Crown Grants Ordinance 1889 .... 11, 122

Crown Lands Ordinance 1890 .... 9, 12, 13
Pt I 1
Pt IV 122
Pt V 122
s I 122
s III 122

Directions Regarding the Procedures for the Acquisition of Land by the Neu Guinea Kompagnie, of 10 August 1887 .... 23, 27
ss 1–3 23
ss 4–6 24
s 5ff 23
ss 7–11 25

Disaster Management Act (Ch No 403) 362

Distress Replevin and Ejectment Act 1867 .... 339, 351
s 58 339
s 118 .... 351, 352
s 119 .... 351, 352

District Courts Act (Ch No 40)—
s 21 342

Electricity Commission Act (Ch No 78)—
s 25 107
s 30(3) 406

Evidence (Land Titles) Ordinance 1969 (No 59 of 1969) 51

Fisheries Act 1994 486

Forestry Act 1991 304

Frauds and Limitations Act
1988 (No 3) . . . 296
ss 2–5 . . . 189
s 2 . . . 296, 297
s 3 . . . 297
s 3(2) . . . 307
s 5 . . . 297

Imperial Charter for the New Guinea Kompagnie, of 17 May 1885 . . . 18, 19, 22, 23

Imperial Charter for the New Guinea Kompagnie, of 13 December 1886 . . . 19

Imperial Laws Replacement Act 1975 . . . 331, 332

Imperial Ordinance Regarding the Acquisition of Ownership and the Charging of Land in the Protectorate of the Neu Guinea Kompagnie, of 20 July 1887 (RG B1, 1887, 379) . . . 21
ss 1–4 . . . 21
ss 5–11 . . . 22
s 5 . . . 23
s 7 . . . 23
s 9 . . . 23

Imperial Ordinance Regarding the Assumption of Local Sovereignty over the Protectorate of German New Guinea by the Reich, of 27 March 1899 . . . 20
s 1 . . . 20
s 2 . . . 20, 21
s 4 . . . 21

Imperial Ordinance Regarding the Rights to Land in the German Protectorate, of 21 November 1902 . . . 26
ss 3, 5, 6, 19 . . . 26

Implementation Order for the Imperial Ordinance Regarding the Assumption of Local Sovereignty over the Protectorate of German New Guinea by the Reich, of 1 April 1899 . . . 21
s 1 . . . 21

Implementation Order for the Imperial Ordinance Regarding the Rights to Land in the German Protectorate, of 22 July 1904 . . . 26

Insolvency Act (Ch No 253) . . . 355

Interpretation Act (Ch No 2)—
s 3 . . . 103

Interpretation Act (Ch No 3)—
s 5 . . . 230

Interpretation (Interim Provisions) Act (No 91 of 1975) (Cap 2) . . . 118

Intestates Estates Act 1884—
s 4 . . . 126

Land Acquisition Act 1914 . . . 92

Land Acquisition Act 1952 . . . 92

Land Acquisition Act 1974
(Ch No 66 of 1974) . . . 61, 64, 67, 78
s 1 . . . 61
s 3 . . . 61
s 3(2), (3) . . . 62
s 4 . . . 62
s 5A . . . 61

Land Acquisition (Development Purposes) Act 1983
(Ch No 192) . . . 59, 61, 363
s 1 . . . 509
s 7 . . . 271

Land Acquisition Ordinance 1952 . . . 38
s 7 . . . 38
s 83(1) . . . 38

Land Act 1962 (No 6 of 1963) . . . 60, 92, 307
s 7 . . . 7
s 17 . . . 61
s 75 . . . 65
s 84 . . . 61

Land Act 1962–73 . . . 73, 78

Land Act 1963 . . . 62

Land Act 1968 (Ch No 185) . . . 96, 310, 311, 374, 432, 433, 439, 462, 464

Land Act 1968 (Ch No 185) (contd)—
Pt VIII 8
Pt IX 8
s 1 509
s 1(1) 480
s 4 118
s 4(1) 7
s 8(1), (2) 376
s 9 376
s 9(a) 376
s 9(2) 431
s 9(9) 432
s 11 . . . . . 373, 377, 435
s 11(1) 376
s 12(1) 376
s 12(2) 375, 376
s 12(2)(a) 376, 377, 439
s 15 80
s 15(3) 80
ss 26–28 94
s 29(3) 431, 432
s 33 376
s 33(b) 376
s 46 459
s 46(1) 435
s 46(2) 390, 435, 436
s 48 113
s 57(5) 435
ss 68–72 8
s 69 . . . . . 160, 303–06, 310, 311
s 69(1) 307
s 69(2) 307
s 69(3)(a) 307
ss 73–78 8
s 84 460
s 87 460
s 88 460
s 112(2) 393–95

Land Act 1996 (Ch 45) 68, 116, 271, 311, 323, 355, 359, 360, 365–68, 370–75, 387, 389, 396–98, 431, 441, 442, 445, 446, 479–81, 486
Pt VI 360
Pt VIII 365
Pt IX 370, 441, 480
Pt XVII 303

Land Act 1996 (Ch 45) (contd)—
s 2 68
s 2(1) 359
s 4 69
s 10(4) 359
s 11 . . . . . 383, 384
s 12 271
s 29(1) 360
s 46(2) 388
s 49 . . . . . 382, 383
s 55 360
s 55(5) 361
s 57 . . . . . 360, 371, 372, 376
s 58 . . . . . 361, 366, 371, 376
s 58(5)(c) 371
s 58(9)(b), (c) 362
s 58(10) 362, 365
s 58(11) 362
s 62 . . . . . 365, 373, 376
s 63 . . . . . 365, 376, 381
s 63(2) 375
s 64(1) 360, 441, 445, 480
s 65 . . . . . 360, 370, 378, 480
s 67 . . . . . 359, 371, 378, 444, 480
ss 68–76 . . . . . 364, 382, 383
s 68 . . . . . 362, 363, 366, 371, 379, 384, 440, 444, 480
s 69 . . . . . 362, 366, 381, 383, 384, 480
s 69(2) 366, 371, 372, 382, 440, 444
s 69(2)(d) 371, 372
s 69(2)(f)–(j) 363
ss 70–73 363
s 70 386
s 71 371
s 72 371
s 73 381
s 73(3)–(5) 364
s 74 364
s 75 . . . . . 364, 388
s 76 364
s 79 364
s 81 378
s 82 . . . . . 378, 382, 383, 386
s 82(2) 386
s 83 . . . . . 378, 382, 383
s 83(3)–(8) 379
s 84 . . . . . 379, 383
s 85 . . . . . 379, 380
s 85(3), (4) 380

Land Act 1996 (Ch 45) (contd)—
ss 86–90 380
ss 91–97 381
s 95 .... 364, 371
s 98 271
s 98(5) 273
s 98(6), (7) 272
ss 97–100 382
s 99 .... 363, 442
s 99(7) 359
ss 100–03 271
s 100 .... 272, 379
s 100(2)–(7) 383
s 101 .... 272, 364, 383
s 102 .... 363, 379, 383
s 102(6) 364
s 103 384
s 103(1) 271–73
s 103(2), (3) 273
ss 104–06 273
s 104 384
s 105 384
s 106 385
s 106(2) 386
s 107 .... 274, 385
s 107(c) 396
s 107(3) 386
s 108 386
s 109(3) 396
s 110 .... 363, 396
s 111 363
s 112 391
s 113 389
s 116 379
s 119 396
s 119(3)–(9) 397
s 119(3) 398
s 119(4) 398
s 119(5) 398
s 119(6) 398
s 119(8) 388, 398
s 119(10)–(13) 398
s 119(13) 397, 398
s 120 379
s 122 .... 382, 383, 387, 388, 395
s 122(2) 388, 390
s 122(5), (6) 388
s 124 395

Land Act 1996 (Ch 45) (contd)—
s 125 478
s 127 .... 303, 311
s 128 303
s 128(2)–(7) 304
s 130 363
s 131 363
s 142 .... 388, 392
s 142(3) 388
s 145 382

Land Compensation Act 78, 79

Land Disputes Settlement
Act No 25 1975 (Ch No 45) 29, 36, 73, 75, 79, 117, 487
s 2 117
s 76 36

Land Groups Act 1974
(No 64 of 1974) 64, 67, 77

Land Groups Incorporation
Act 1974 (Ch No 147) 59, 61, 62, 89, 97
Preamble 89

Land Ordinance 1887 18

Land Ordinance 1899 .... 9, 12, 14–16
s 11 9–11

Land Ordinance 1903 .... 18, 28

Land Ordinance 1906 .... 92, 125

Land Ordinance 1911–40 .... 28, 29, 36, 92
s 9 .... 36, 37
s 10 29
s 24 28
s 33 29

Land Ordinance 1911–53—
s 6 144
s 8 142–44
s 9 142–46

Land Ordinance 1922–27 .... 35, 425
s 8 35
s 13 122
s 16 35

Land Ordinance 1922–41 .... 32, 35
ss 6–8 35

Land Ordinance 1962 . . . . . 37, 359
Pt VII 274
s 6 37
s 7 37
s 7(3) 38
s 75 305

Land (Ownership of Freeholds) Act (Ch No 359)—
s 3 93
ss 16–24 93

Land Redistribution Act 1974 (No 62 of 1974) 64, 67

Land Redistribution Act 1974 (Ch No 190) 59–61
s 1 60
s 5 60
s 5(1)(a) 61
s 5(2) 61
s 15 61

Land Registration Act, of 5 May 1872 21

Land Registration Act 1924 (New Guinea) 155, 202
s 69 148
s 113(2) 203

Land Registration Act 1981 (Ch No 191) 164, 197, 198, 201, 211, 220, 239, 240, 243, 244, 250, 254, 271, 275, 297, 301, 318, 319, 333, 359, 366, 372, 382, 386, 410, 418, 421–23, 431, 432, 434, 441–43, 445–50, 460, 462, 464, 467, 480, 481, 487, 501
Pt IV 432
Pt VIII 488
s 2(1) 197, 359
s 11 . . . . . 423, 501
s 11(1) 422
s 11(2) 424
s 17(1) 200, 297, 302, 421, 487
s 17(2) 297, 298, 487
s 17(4) 487
s 18(1) 298
s 26 421

Land Registration Act 1981 (Ch No 191) (contd)—
s 26(1)(b) 200
s 28 . . . . . 424, 447, 470, 471
s 28(2) 471
s 28(3) 300, 423, 471, 472, 488
s 28(3)(A) 459
s 33 . . . . . 303, 422, 424, 432, 433, 438, 440, 447, 450, 453, 457, 460, 462, 464, 482, 487, 501
s 33(1)–(9) 471
s 33(1) 460, 464, 481
s 33(1)(a) 438, 447
s 33(1)(b) 198, 457
s 33(1)(c) 459, 464, 467
s 33(1)(d) 410, 468, 470
s 33(1)(e) 465, 467
s 33(1)(f) 457, 470, 471
s 33(1)(g) 471
s 33(1)(h) 478
s 33(1)(i) 479
s 34 . . . . . 164, 165
s 36 . . . . . 359, 433
s 36(1) 432
s 36(2) 421, 432
s 37 432
s 38 423
s 38(1)(c) 432
s 39 . . . . . 388, 423, 432
s 45 . . . . . 424, 453
s 45(1) 447, 450
s 46 424
s 49 297
s 49(1) 280, 307, 470
s 49(2) 298, 300
s 50(b) 339
s 51 323
s 51(1)(b) 323
s 52 312
s 54 333
s 54(1) 297
s 54(2) 198
s 54(4) 334
s 54(5) 334
s 54(6)(a) 334
s 55 333
s 57 355
s 62 . . . . . 197, 200

Land Registration Act 1981
(Ch No 191) (contd)—
s 63. . . . 197
s 63(a) 189
s 66. . . . 198
s 67 . . . . 219, 230, 238, 253
s 67(1) 220
s 67(1)(a). . . . 219, 230, 231
a 67(1)(b). . . . 219
s 68 . . . . 219, 220, 230, 244, 245, 253
s 68(1) 220
s 68(1)(a), (b) 219
s 68(5) 222
s 68(6) 251, 253
s 69. . . . 244
s 70. . . . 219
s 71. . . . 253
s 72. . . . 219
s 73(1) 219
s 74. . . . 212
s 74(1)(c) 243
s 74(3) 202
s 75. . . . 213
s 76. . . . 213
s 77. . . . 253, 254
s 78. . . . 254
s 79. . . . 254
s 80. . . . 161
s 81. . . . 201, 487
s 81(2) 488
s 81(3) 478
s 82 . . . . 487, 488, 491
s 82(a) 488–90
s 82(b) 489, 490
s 83. . . . 489
s 86. . . . 488
s 88. . . . 490, 491
s 89. . . . 490
s 90. . . . 493
s 91. . . . 489
s 92. . . . 488, 490
s 93. . . . 490
s 94. . . . 489
s 95. . . . 410
s 96. . . . 410
s 98. . . . 470
s 100. . . . 318, 339
s 104 . . . . 418, 481, 487

Land Registration Act 1981
(Ch No 191) (contd)—
s 108. . . . 481, 487
s 111. . . . 159, 204
s 118. . . . 161
s 120. . . . 161
s 137. . . . 504
s 138. . . . 504
s 146 . . . . 450, 468, 501, 502
s 146(2) 357
s 146(2)(c) 356
s 146(2)(d). . . . 450
s 146(2)(e) 450
s 146(2)(f) 466
s 146(2)(g). . . . 464
s 146(3) 450, 466
s 146(4)(a) 447
s 146(4)(b). . . . 466
s 148. . . . 355, 356
s 148(2)–(5). . . . 356
s 149. . . . 502
s 150 . . . . 502–04, 506
s 150(2) 505
s 150(3) 505
s 150(7) 505
s 151. . . . 504–07
s 153. . . . 489, 490
s 160. . . . 433, 466
s 161. . . . 433, 466
s 163. . . . 488
s 283. . . . 474
s 560. . . . 465
Sched 2 410
Sched 3 . . . . 312, 324

Land Registration (Communally Owned Land) Act 1963 (No 10) 96

Land Registration (Communally Owned Land) Ordinance 1962. . . . 38

Land Registration (Communally Owned Land) Ordinance 1963. . . . 39

Land Registration Ordinance 1924–39 . . . . 33, 35, 248, 422, 423, 425, 426, 432, 480
ss 21–27. . . . 35
s 22. . . . 425
s 24. . . . 425

Land Registration Ordinance
1924–39 (contd)—
s 26(3) 423
s 38. 423
s 39. 423
s 53. 122
s 57. 426
s 68 . . . . . 422, 423, 426

Land Registration Regulations—
reg 11. 297
Sched 1 . . . . . 200, 297

Land Regulation Ordinance 1888 . . . . . 7, 8, 92

Land Settlement Schemes Act
(No 45) 59

Land Settlement Schemes (Prevention
of Disruption) Act
(No 53 of 1974) 59, 509
s 3. 59
s 7. 59

Land Settlement Schemes (Prevention
of Disruption) Act (Ch No 358) 69
s 1. 69

Land (Tenure Conversion)
Act 1963–83
(No 15 of 1964) 274, 421, 456, 485
s 11(1)(a), (b) 421
s 26. . . . . 79, 96, 274
s 26(a), (b). 274
s 26A 274

Land (Tenure Conversion) Act 1967. 52

Land (Tenure Conversion)
(Amendment) Act 1987—
s 12. 79

Land (Tenure Conversion)
(Amendment) Ordinance 1967. 40

Land (Tenure Conversion)
Ordinance 1963
(No 15 of 1964) 38–40, 52
Preamble. 51
s 9(2) 51
s 26. 40
s 26(1)(a)(i) 52
s 26A 40

Land (Tenure Conversion)
Ordinance 1967. 40

Land Titles Commission Act 1962. 73

Land Titles Commission
Ordinance 1962–71 . . . . . 38, 39
s 16. 426
s 44. 36

Land Titles Restoration
Ordinance 1951 . . . . . 422, 423

Land Trespass Act 1974
(No 53 of 1974) 64, 67

Land Trespass Act
(Ch No 271 of 1974) 59
s 1. 59
s 5. 60
s 6. 59
s 7(1)(b). 60
s 8. 59
s 8(2)–(6) 60
s 9. . . . . 59, 60

Land (Underdeveloped Freeholds)
Act 1969 (Ch No 193). 62, 94
s 9. 271
s 13. 94

Land (Underdeveloped Freeholds)
Ordinance 1970 (No 13 of 1970). 51

Landlord and Tenant (Miscellaneous
Provisions) Act (Ch No 189)—
s 3. . . . . 331, 333
s 3(5) 332
s 4. 332

Laws Repeal and Adopting
Ordinance 1921–33. 425
s 16. . . . . 126, 127

Laws Repeal and Adopting
Ordinance 1921–39. 34
s 6. 32
ss 68, 69. 34

Laws Repeal and Adopting
Ordinance 1921–52—
s 9. 35
s 10. 35

Local Government Act (Ch No 57)—
s 76(6), (7) 479

Mining Act 1992 (Ch No 195) 304
s 7 101
s 25 478

Mining (Amalgamated) Act (Ch No 195)—
s 7 107

National Court Rules (Ch No 38) 196
Ord 8 442
r 1 442
r 8 456
r 30 456
Ord 14 211
r 33 196
r 34 196
Ord 16 391
r 4(1), (2) 391

National Land Registration Act 1977 (Ch No 357) 69–71, 78, 79, 94, 507, 510, 513
s 1 507
s 3 .... 69, 509
s 6 511
s 7 .... 69, 508
s 8 .... 508, 509, 511
s 9 .... 508, 510–12
s 10 .... 69, 511
s 11 .... 509, 510
s 12 510
s 13 .... 510, 513
s 14 510
s 15 510
s 19 .... 69, 510, 511, 513
s 22 510
s 23 .... 510, 513
s 34(4) 70, 512
s 39 .... 69, 512
s 40 .... 69, 512
s 43 70
s 44 .... 70, 513
s 45 .... 70, 513
s 45(4) 70, 513

National Land Registration Act 1977 (Ch No 357) (contd)—
s 52 .... 508, 510, 511
s 53 .... 69, 509
s 55 51
s 57 511
Sched 2 .... 70, 513

National Seas Act (Ch 361) 486

Native Administration Regulations 1924 32

Native Board Regulation No 2 1894 (Planting Coconuts Regulation) 16

Native Customs (Recognition) Ordinance 1963 35

Native Land Registration Act 1952 73

Native Land Registration Ordinance 1952 36

Native Land Registration Ordinance 1962 39

Native Plantation Ordinance 1913 16

Native Plantation Ordinance 1918 16

Native Plantation Ordinance 1925 29

Native Plantation Ordinance 1928 16

Native Regulations 1939 29
s 132(b) 29
s 133(1) 29

New Guinea Land Titles Registration Ordinance 1951 36

New Guinea Ordinance 1920 32

Ordinance Regarding the Jurisdiction of the Neu Guinea Kompagnie over the Natives in its Protectorate, of 15 October 1897 20

Organic Law on Provincial Government (Ch No 1) 310, 311
Pt VIII 311

Papua Act 1905 . . . 28
s 5 . . . 28
s 20(1) . . . 29

Papua and New Guinea Ordinance 1949 . . . 36

Partnership Act (Ch No 148)—
s 21 . . . 159, 160
s 21(2) . . . 159
s 22 . . . 160
s 23 . . . 160

Petroleum Act (Ch No 198) . . . 304
s 9 . . . 107

Physical Planning Act 1989 . . . 369–71, 378, 384
s 4 . . . 369
s 5 . . . 369, 370
s 6 . . . 384
s 7 . . . 369
ss 77(3)(e) . . . 370
s 97 . . . 370

Physical Planning Regulations—
Sched 1 . . . 370

Probate and Administration Ordinance 1913–40 (Papua) . . . 124, 125
s 4 . . . 125
s 20 . . . 125, 128
s 21 . . . 125, 128
s 31 . . . 126
s 58 . . . 124

Probate and Administration Ordinance 1951 . . . 124
s 4(2) . . . 124

Protectorates Act 1900 (RG B1, 1900, 813)—
s 3 . . . 26

Real Property Act 1889 (Papua) . . . 480

Real Property Act 1913 (Papua)—
s 52 . . . 203

Real Property Ordinance 1889 . . . 14, 432

Registration of Titles Act (Cap 191) . . . 464

Simultaneous Deaths Act (Ch No 332) . . . 154
s 2 . . . 154
s 3 . . . 154
s 7 . . . 154
s 11 . . . 155

Statute Regarding Consular Jurisdiction, of 7 April 1900
s 21 . . . 26

Statute Regarding the Acquisition of Ownership and the Charging of Land, Mines and Independent Land Rights, of 5 May 1872 (PG, 1872) . . . 21
s 2 . . . 21

Statute Regarding the Revenue and Expenditure of the Protectorates, of 30 March 1892, RG B1, 1892, 369 . . . 20

Succession Act 1867—
s 25 . . . 126

Summary Ejectment Act (Ch No 202) . . . 341–43, 345
s 3 . . . 340, 342
s 3(4) . . . 341, 342
s 3(5) . . . 341
s 4 . . . 339–43, 345
s 4(3)–(7) . . . 344
s 4(4) . . . 351
s 5 . . . 339–45
s 5(2) . . . 351
s 5(3), (4) . . . 345
s 6 . . . 341, 342

Supreme Court Act—
s 14(1) . . . 438

Supreme Court (Full Court) Ordinance 1968—
s 34(2) . . . 393

Supreme Court of Justice Rules—
Ord 6 r 9 . . . 203
Ord 6 r 11 . . . 203
Ord 19 r 1 . . . 203
Ord 19 r 4 . . . 203

Torres Strait Treaty 1978 486

Town Planning Act (Ch No 204) 369, 432

Transfer of Land Control
Ordinance 1951—
s 3 305

Trustees and Executors Act
(Ch No 289)—
s 29(1)(f), (h) 159

Village Courts Act (Ch No 441) 117
s 1 117

Wills Act 1827—
s 28 122

Wills Probate and Administration
Act (Ch No 291)—
s 44 159

TABLE OF INTERNATIONAL LEGISLATION

ALGERIA

Proclamation No 78 of 1976 95

ARGENTINA

Act No 17253, April 1967 95

AUSTRIA

Basic Law on Agricultural Land Settlement Bundesgesetzblatt No 22, 7 March 1967 95

AUSTRALIA

Building Units Titles Act 1965 (Qld) 169

Coast Islands Act 1879 (Qld) 6

Community Services (Torres Strait) Act 1984 (Qld)—
- s 41(2)(b) 132

Conveyancing Act (Cth)—
- s 24 185

Conveyancing Act 1919—
- s 89(1)(b) 411

Conveyancing Act 1919–54 (NSW)—
- s 109 225
- s 110 225
- s 111 225
- s 164 458

Conveyancing Act 1919–61 (NSW)—
- s 112(3)(a) 225

Criminal Code (Qld)—
- s 23 194
- s 27 .... 194, 195
- s 289 194
- s 291 194
- s 300 194
- s 304A 194, 195

Crown Lands Act (NSW) 282

Land Transfer Act (Vic) 467

Property Land Act 1974–89 (Qld)—
- ss 182–94 112
- s 196 112
- s 197 112

Property Law Act 1974–90 (Qld)—
- s 99(2) 211

Property Law Act—
- s 43 195

Real Property Act 1900 (NSW) 177, 179, 223, 307, 493, 496
- s 27 492
- s 32(1) 500
- s 37 457
- s 40 500
- s 41 307
- s 42 .... 224, 457, 458, 469
- s 42(b) 468
- s 42(d) 468, 469
- s 43 .... 224, 458
- s 43(2) 499
- s 44 470
- s 46 468
- s 49 457
- s 54 457
- s 58 225
- s 59 225
- s 111 498
- s 135 .... 468, 469

Real Property Act 1861 (Qld) 451
- s 44 .... 200, 450
- s 60 .... 197, 199, 203
- s 65 199
- s 98 491
- s 99 491
- s 109 .... 200, 451

Real Property Act 1980 (Qld)—
- s 98 491
- s 99 491
- s 126 504–06
- s 127 .... 505, 506

Real Property Act 1862–1935 (Tas) 180–84
- s 3 181
- s 34(3) 181

Real Property Act 1862–1935 (Tas) (contd)—
s 35(2) 181
s 37.......... 181, 457
s 39.......... 180, 184
s 39(1) 181
s 42 .... 180, 181, 184, 457
s 49.......... 457
s 54.......... 457
s 87.......... 181, 184
s 88.......... 181

Real Property Ordinance 1925–61 (ACT)—
s 93(1) 247
s 94.......... 250
s 94(1) 249
s 94(2) 248–50
s 94(3) 248, 249
s 94(5) 248–50

Residential Tenancies Act 1975 (Qld)—
s 7(a)(ii).......... 317

Stamp Act (Qld) 427

Statute of Uses (Tas) 183

Transfer of Land Act 1890 (Vic).......... 207–10
s 74.......... 208
s 95.......... 209
s 129.......... 207
s 130.......... 207–09
s 188.......... 209
s 230.......... 209

Transfer of Land Act 1915 (Vic).......... 494

Transfer of Lands Act 1958 (Vic)—
s 42(2)(e).......... 471

Transfer of Land Act 1893 (WA) 466, 475
s 68 .... 450, 453–55, 466, 471–76, 478, 482, 484
s 129A 419
s 129C 418
s 134 .... 453–55, 482
s 137 .... 474, 477, 478

CAMEROON

Decree No 64-8/COR, January 1964.......... 93

CHILE

Act No 16, 640 16 July 1967 96

EAST SEPIK

Customary Land Registration Act 86

EUROPE

Treaty of Versailles 1919 32
Art 120 33
Art 438 33

GERMANY

Civil Code, Third Book.......... 26

Missions Ordinance 1926 33

Prussian Statute Implementing the Civil Code—
s 40.......... 26

Statute Regarding the Legal Condition in the German Protectorates (RG B1, 1888, 75).......... 20
s 3.......... 21

GHANA

Constitution 1960—
Art 4(1) 101

Constitution 1969—
Art 4(1) 101

IVORY COAST

Decree No 57-243, February 24 1957 (French Decree) 91, 92

JAPAN

Land Reform Law (No 43)
21 October 1964 . . . . . 95, 100

KENYA

Land Control Act 1967 (No 34) 93

NEW ZEALAND

Land Transfer Act 1870 448

Land Transfer Act 1952 . . . . . 186, 429, 431, 449
s 2 430
s 42 . . . . . 428, 429
ss 61–64 165
s 61 . . . . . 164, 165
s 62 . . . . . 165, 429
s 63 . . . . . 165, 429–31
s 64 165
s 74(2) 188
s 75 429
s 80 430
s 81 430
s 85 430
s 100 430
s 157 . . . . . 428, 429
s 164 . . . . . 428, 429
s 182 430
s 183 430
s 189 451

Land Transfer Regulations 1948—
reg 24 429

Maori Affairs Act 1953 77

Native Land Act 448

Transfer of Land Act 1885 . . . . . 449, 450
s 55 450
s 56 450
s 189 450

MALAWI

Customary Land Development
Act 1967 (Act No 5) 95

Customary Land (Development)
Act 1967 (No 34) 93

NIGERIA

Administration of Lands Act 1962
(No 123) 100

Constitution 1979 100

Land Reform Law of 1978 . . . . . 90, 99

Land Use Act 1978 (No 6) 99–101
s 1 . . . . . 93, 101
s 6(2) 96
s 23(1) 96
s 24(b) 96

Lands (Kila Kila Aerodrome)
Acquisition Order 1939 (No 19) 109
s 3 108

State Lands Act 1962 (No 125) 100

Stool Land Act 1960 (No 27) 100

TUNISIA

Loi No 58–63, 2 June 1958 96

Loi No 60–6, 26 July 1960 96

UNITED KINGDOM

Administration of Estates Act 1925—
s 45 126

Air Navigation Act 1920—
s 9(1) 104

British Settlements Act 1887—
s 3 10

Civil Aviation Act 1949 105
s 40(1) 103, 104, 106, 107

Conveyancing Act 1882 141

Forfeiture Act 1982—
s 2(2) 196

Grantees of Reversions Act 1540
(c 34) (32 Hen 8) 331

Judicature Act 1873 308

Landlord and Tenant Act 1954 279

Law of Property Act 1925 . . . . 351, 484
s 1 290
s 36(2) 185, 191
s 40 190
s 91 211
s 146 . . . . 346, 347
s 184 155
s 199(1) 141
s 205(1)(xxvii) 290

Law of Reform (Miscellaneous
Provisions) Act 1962 154

Legacy Duty Act (36 Geo 3, C 52) 157

Married Women's Property Act 127

Mortuaries Act 1529 (Ch 6)
(21 Hen 8) 290

Rent Act 290, 292, 295, 326, 327

Royal Mines Act 1688 107

Royal Mines Act 1693 107

Statute of Frauds 300, 484

Statute of Gloucester 1278
(6 Edw I) 290

ZAMBIA

Land (Conversion of Title)
Act 1975 (No 20) 93

INTRODUCTION: LAND POLICY IN PAPUA NEW GUINEA

The reasons for the complexity of PNG land law have been outlined in *Land Law in PNG*.[1] A brief historical exposition on British acquisition of PNG has also been presented there.[2] PNG is not immune from the problems associated with the acquisition of new territories. As far as the legal profession is concerned however, the most salient issue in this regard is the effect of the acquisition on the legal system.

I THE LAND POLICY IN THE PROTECTORATE PERIOD IN BRITISH NEW GUINEA (PAPUA) 1884–1906

Papua New Guinea was not treated as settled territory such as Australia but annexed as a form of conquest short of full-scale war.

Acquisition of native land by individuals before annexation

Because individual land purchases had preceded the annexation of New Guinea, the Imperial government was faced with the dilemma of regularising such transactions, although they flew in the face of Commodore JE Erskine's proclamation: 'no acquisition of land, whensoever or howsoever acquired, within the limits of the Protectorate hereby established, will be recognised by Her Majesty.'[3] The Crown Lands Ordinance 1890 provided machinery for dealing with such cases. Under Part I of that Ordinance, private purchasers from indigenous Papuans were given the opportunity to apply *for the recognition* of their grants within six months of the publication of the notice in the *Gazette* inviting claims in that regard. It must be noted that land purchased before the proclamation was not caught by Erskine's proclamation.

In *The Administration of the Territory of Papua and New Guinea and Another v Daera and Guba*,[4] the High Court of Australia made a judicial pronouncement on the theory of acquisition of territory and the legal effect of such acquisition. In *Mabo v Queensland*[5] the High Court again revisited the issue. Extracted below are some relevant observations of the court.

MABO ET AL v THE STATE OF QUEENSLAND (NO 2) (1992) 175 CLR 1, High Court of Australia

[In 1879, Australia annexed the Murray Islands thereby proclaiming them subject to English law. These Islands, located in the Torres Strait, were home to the Meriam people, the

1 HA Amankwah and JT Mugambwa (with G Muroa), *Land Law in Papua New Guinea* (Lawbook Co, Sydney, 2001), p 2.

2 *Ibid.*

3 *Ibid.*

4 (1973) 130 CLR 353; 47 ALJR 621.

5 (1992) 175 CLR 1.

plaintiffs in this case. They brought an action against the Queensland government seeking a declaration that they were the owners by custom of, the holders of traditional rights in, and holders of usufructuary rights over, the Murray Islands. The plaintiffs proposed a legal theory that upon annexation of a territory by the Crown, the pre-annexation rights of the indigenous people continue and become a dimension of the 'common law native title'. Consequently, they argued that they enjoy those land rights enjoyed by their ancestors over the Murray Islands, though the Crown has not made a grant or recognition of these rights. The defendants argued that if the plaintiffs' traditional land rights claimed ever existed, they had not survived annexation of the territory. Upon annexation, the Crown acquired absolute beneficial ownership of all land, so that the colony became the Crown's demesne to the exclusion of any other rights. In consequence, any land rights of the native people must be derived from the Crown by grant or express recognition.]

BRENNAN J (at p 30): ... In the present case, the defendant's chain of argument contains several links, each of which must be separately considered although, as we shall see, a common theme or thread runs through them. Some of these links are unchallenged. We start with the proposition that the Imperial Crown acquired sovereignty over the Murray Islands on 1 August 1879 and that the laws of Queensland (including the common law) became the law of the Murray Islands on that day – or, if it be necessary to rely on the Colonial Boundaries Act 1895, is deemed to have become the law of the Murray Islands on that day. Next, by the common law, the Crown acquired a radical or ultimate title to the Murray Islands. The plaintiffs accept these propositions but challenge the final link in the chain, namely, that the Crown also acquired absolute beneficial ownership of the land in the Murray Island when the Crown acquired sovereignty over them.

... the proposition that, by the common law, the Sovereign acquired absolute beneficial ownership of all land in the Murray Islands rests on a number of bases. In the first place, it is said that the Crown is absolute owner because 'there is no *other* proprietor'. This basis denies that the indigenous inhabitants possessed a proprietary interest. The negative basis is then buttressed by three positive bases to show why it is necessary to attribute absolute beneficial ownership to the Crown. One basis is that, when English law was brought to Australia with and by British colonists, the common law to be applied in the colonies included the feudal doctrine of tenure. Just as the Crown acquired or is deemed to have acquired universal ownership of all land in England, so the Crown became the owner of all land in the Australian colonies. We may call this the feudal basis. Another basis is that land in a colony is 'the patrimony of the nation' and, on this basis, the Crown acquired ownership of the patrimony on behalf of the nation. A third basis is the prerogative basis ... In order to determine whether, on any or all of these bases, the Crown acquired beneficial ownership of the land in the Murray Islands when the Crown acquired sovereignty over them, we must first review the legal theories relating to the acquisition of sovereignty and the introduction of the common law.

> The acquisition of territory by sovereign State for the first time is an act of State which cannot be challenged, controlled or interfered with by the courts of that State.

This principle precludes any contest between the executive and the judicial branches of government as to whether a territory is or is not within the Crown's Dominions. The Murray Islands were annexed by an exercise of the prerogative evidenced by the Letters Patent; a mode of acquisition recognised by the common law as a valid means of acquiring sovereignty over foreign territory. The recognition is accorded simply on the footing that such a prerogative act is an act of State the validity of which is not justiciable in the municipal courts ... In *Post Office v Estuary Radio Ltd*, Diplock LJ said [1968] 2 QB 740 at p 753:

> It still lies within the prerogative power of the Crown to extend its sovereignty and jurisdiction to areas of land or sea over which it has not previously claimed or exercised sovereignty or jurisdiction. For such extension the authority of Parliament is not required.
>
> Although the question whether a territory has been acquired by the Crown is not justiciable before municipal courts, those courts have jurisdiction to determine the consequences of an acquisition under municipal law. Accordingly, the municipal courts must determine the body of law which is in force in the new territory. By the common law, the law in force in a newly-acquired territory depends on the manner of its acquisition by the Crown. Although the manner in which a sovereign State might acquire new territory is a matter for international law, the common law has had to march in step with international law in order to provide the body of law to apply in a territory newly acquired by the Crown.
>
> International law recognised conquest, cession, and occupation of territory that was *terra nullius* as three of the effective ways of acquiring sovereignty. No other way is presently relevant. The great voyages of European discovery opened to European nations the prospect of occupying new and valuable territories that were already inhabited. As among themselves, the European nations parcelled out the territories newly discovered to the sovereigns of the respective discoverers ... provided the discovery was confirmed by occupation and provided the indigenous inhabitants were not organised in a society that was united permanently for political action ... To these territories the European colonial nations applied the doctrines relating to acquisition of territory that was *terra nullius*. They recognised the sovereignty of the respective European nations over the territory of 'backward peoples' and, by State practice, permitted the acquisition of sovereignty of such territory by occupation rather than by conquest ... Various justifications for the acquisition of sovereignty over the territory of 'backward peoples' were advanced. The benefits of Christianity and European civilisation had been seen as a sufficient justification from medieval times ... Another justification for the application of the theory of *terra nullius* to inhabited territory – a justification first advanced by Vattel at the end of the 18th century – was that new territories could be claimed by occupation if the land were uncultivated by the indigenous inhabitants ... It may be doubted whether, even if these justifications were accepted, the facts would have sufficed to permit acquisition of the Murray Islands as though the Islands were *terra nullius*. The Meriam people were, as Moynihan J found, devoted gardeners. In 1879, having accepted the influence of the London Missionary Society, they were living peacefully in a land-based society under some sort of governance by the Mamoose and the London Missionary Society. However that may be, it is not for this court to canvass the validity of the Crown's acquisition of sovereignty over the Islands which, in any event, was consolidated by uninterrupted control of the Islands by Queensland authorities ...

The enlarging of the concept of *terra nullius* by international law to justify the acquisition of inhabited territory by occupation on behalf of the acquiring sovereign raised some difficulties in the expounding of the common law doctrines as to the law to be applied when inhabited territories were acquired by occupation (or 'settlement', to use the term of the common law). Although Blackstone commended the practice of 'sending colonies [of settlers] to find out new habitations', he wrote (*Commentaries on the Laws of England,* 17th edn (1830), Bk II, Ch 1, p 7):

> ... so long as it was confined to the stocking and cultivation of desert uninhabited countries, it kept strictly within the limits of the law of nature. But how far the seising on countries already peopled, and driving out or massacring the innocent and defenceless natives, merely because they differed from their invaders in language, in religion, in customs, in

> government, or in colour; how far such a conduct was consonant to nature, to reason, or to christianity, deserved well to be considered by those, who have rendered their names immortal by thus civilising mankind.

As we shall see, Blackstone's misgivings found a resonance in international law after two centuries (*Advisory Opinion on Western Sahara* [1975] 1 ICJR 12). But he was unable to declare any rule by which the laws of England became the laws of a territory which was not a 'desert uninhabited' country when the Crown acquired sovereignty over that territory by discovery and occupation as *terra nullius*. As the British acquisition of sovereignty over the Colony of New South Wales was regarded as dependent upon the settlement of territory that was *terra nullius* consequent on discovery (see *Cooper v Stuart* (1889) 14 App Cas 286), and as the law of New South Wales is the source of the law applicable to the Murray Islands, we must next examine the basis on which the common law was received as the law of the Colony of New South Wales.

Reception of the common law

The means by which the municipal laws of England, including the common law, became the law of the country that had been outside the King's dominions were stated by Blackstone (*Commentaries*, Bk I, Ch 4, pp 106–08; accord: *Forbes v Cochrane* (1824) 2 B & C 448, at p 463 [107 ER 450, at p 456]) as follows:

> Plantations or colonies, in distant countries, are either such where the lands are claimed by right of occupancy only, by finding them desert and uncultivated, and peopling them from the mother-country; or where, when already cultivated, they have been either gained by conquest, or ceded to us by treaties. And both these rights are founded upon the law of nature, or at least upon that of nations. But there is a difference between these two species of colonies, with respect to the laws by which they are bound. For it hath been held, that if an uninhabited country be discovered and planted by English subjects, all the English laws then in being, which are the birthright of every subject, are immediately there in force. But this must be understood with very many and very great restrictions. Such colonists carry with them only so much of the English law, as is applicable to their own situation and the condition of an infant colony ... What shall be admitted and what rejected, at what times, and under what restrictions, must, in case of dispute, be decided in the first instance by their own provincial judicature, subject to the revision and control of the king in council: the whole of their constitution being also liable to be new-modelled and reformed by the general superintending power of the legislature in the mother-country. But in conquered or ceded countries, that have already laws of their own, the king may indeed alter and change those laws; but, till he does actually change them, the ancient laws of the country remain, unless such as are against the law of God, as in the case of an infidel country. Our American plantations are principally of this latter sort, being obtained in the last century either by right of conquest and driving out the natives (with what natural justice I shall not at present inquire) or by treaties. And therefore the common law of England, as such, has no allowance or authority there; they being no part of the mother-country, but distinct (though dependent) dominions. They are subject, however, to the control of the Parliament.

According to Blackstone, English law would become the law of a country outside England either upon first settlement by English colonists of a 'desert uninhabited' country or by the exercise of the Sovereign's legislative power over a conquered or ceded country. Blackstone did not contemplate other ways by which sovereignty might be acquired. In the case of a conquered country, the general rule was the laws of the country continued after the conquest until those laws were altered by the conqueror. The Crown had a prerogative power to make new laws for a conquered country although that power was subject to laws enacted by the Imperial Parliament ... The same rule applied to ceded colonies, though the prerogative may have been limited by the treaty of cession ... When 'desert uninhabited countries' were colonised by English settlers, however, they brought with them 'so much of the English law as [was] applicable to their own situation and the condition of an infant colony' ... English colonists were, in the eye of the common law, entitled to live under the common law of England which Blackstone described as their 'birthright' ... The tender concern of the common law of England for British settlers in foreign parts led to the recognition that such settlers should be regarded as living under the law of England if the local law was unsuitable for Christian Europeans ... This rule was applied even to English residents in Eastern countries which were not under British sovereignty (The *'Indian Chief'* (1801) 3 C Rob 12, at pp 28–29 [165 ER 367, at pp 373–74]).

When British colonists went out to other inhabited parts of the world, including New South Wales, and settled there under the protection of the forces of the Crown, so that the Crown acquired sovereignty recognised by the European family of nations under the enlarged nation of *terra nullius*, it was necessary for the common law to prescribe a doctrine relating to the law to be applied in such colonies, for sovereignty imports supreme international legal authority ... The view was taken that, when sovereignty of a territory could be acquired under the enlarged notion of *terra nullius*, for the purposes of the municipal law that territory (though inhabited) could be treated as a 'desert uninhabited' country. The hypothesis being that there was no local law already in existence in the territory ... the law of England became the law of the territory (and not merely the personal law of the colonists). Colonies of this kind were called 'settled colonies'. *Ex hypothesi*, the indigenous inhabitants of a settled colony had no recognised sovereign, else the territory could have been acquired only by conquest or cession. The indigenous people of a settled colony were thus taken to be without laws, without a sovereign and primitive in their social organisation. In *Advocate-General (Bengal) v Ranee Surnomoye Dossee* (1863) 2 Moo NS 22, at 59 [15 ER 811, at p 824]; 9 Moo Ind App 391, at p 428 [19 ER 786, at p 800] Lord Kingsdown used the term 'barbarous' to describe the native state of a settled colony:

> Where Englishmen established themselves in an uninhabited or barbarous country, they carry with them not only the laws, but the sovereignty of their own State; and those who live amongst them and become members of their community become also partakers of, and subject to the same laws.

In *Cooper v Stuart* Lord Watson proffered the absence of 'settled inhabitants' and 'settled law' as a criterion for determining whether inhabited territory had been acquired by 'settlement' under English law ((1889) 14 App Cas 286, at p 291):

> The extent to which English law is introduced into a British Colony, and the manner of its introduction, must necessarily vary according to circumstances. There is a great difference between the case of a Colony acquired by conquest or cession, in which there is an established system of law, and that of a Colony which consisted of a tract of territory practically unoccupied, without settled inhabitants or settled law, at the time when it was peacefully annexed to the British dominions. The Colony of New South Wales belongs to the latter class. In the case of such a Colony the Crown may by ordinance, and the Imperial

> Parliament, or its own legislature when it comes to possess one, may by statute declare what parts of the common and statute law of England shall have effect within its limits. But, when that is not done, the law of England must (subject to well established exceptions) become from the outset the law of the Colony, and be administered by its tribunals. In so far as it is reasonably applicable to the circumstances of the Colony, the law of England must prevail, until it is abrogated or modified, either by ordinance or statute.

As the settlement of an inhabited territory is equated with settlement of an uninhabited territory in ascertaining the law of the territory on colonisation, the common law which the English settlers brought with them to New South Wales could not have been altered or amended by the prerogative – only by the Imperial Parliament or by the local legislature ... In a settled colony in inhabited territory, the law of England was not merely the personal law of the English colonists; it became the law of the land, protecting and binding colonists and indigenous inhabitants alike and equally. Thus the theory which underpins the application of English law to the Colony of New South Wales is that English settlers brought with them the law of England and that, as the indigenous inhabitants were regarded as barbarous or unsettled and without a settled law, the law of England including the common law became the law of the Colony (so far as it was locally applicable) as though New South Wales were 'an uninhabited country ... discovered and planted by English subjects'. (See *Cooper v Stuart* (1889) 14 App Cas 286, *per* Lord Watson at p 291.) The common law thus became the common law of all subjects within the Colony who were equally entitled to the law's protection as subjects of the Crown ... As the laws of New South Wales became the laws of Queensland on separation of the two Colonies in 1859 ... and, by the terms of the Queensland Coast Islands Act 1879 and the Governor's Proclamation, the Murray Islands on annexation became subject to the laws in force in Queensland, the common law became the basic law of the Murray Islands. Thus the Meriam people in 1879, like Australian Aborigines in earlier times, became British subjects owing allegiance to the Imperial Sovereign entitled to such rights and privileges and subject to such liabilities as the common law and applicable statutes provided. And this is so irrespective of the fact that, in 1879, the Meriam people were settled on their land, the gardens were being tilled, the Mamoose and the London Missionary Society were keeping the peace and a form of justice was being administered.

The effect of annexation on customary or indigenous land rights

Several cases decided in other Commonwealth jurisdictions considered the issue of the ramifications of colonisation on customary title. The most important decisions are: *In Re Southern Rhodesia* [1919] AC 211; *Amodu Tijani v The Secretary, Southern Nigeria* [1921] 2 AC 399 (Nigeria); *Gathomo v Murito* (1921) EAPLR 102 (Kenya); *Milirrpum v Nabalco Pty Ltd* [1971] 17 FLR 141 (Australia);[6] *Calder v Attorney General of British Columbia* (1973) 34 DLR (3d) 145 (Canada).

In *Geita Sebea v The Territory of Papua*[7] Gore J said:

6 This case was overruled in *Mabo v Queensland.*

7 (1940) unreported judgment, Central Court of Papua, 12. See also *The Administration of The Territory of Papua and New Guinea and Another v Daera and Guba* (1973) 130 CLR 353, High Court of Australia. Barwick CJ, at pp 396–97, assumed without deciding that the declaration of the Protectorate or the annexation of British New Guinea did not vest in the Crown the ultimate title to all the land in the territory. The relevant portion of this decision has been extracted below.

> In the Territory of Papua, which was acquired by settlement, there was no importation of the Common Law of real property with respect to Native lands, nor have Native lands been brought under the Torrens system. It has been suggested that the lands held by natives are allodial but I do not think that there is such a thing as an allodium existing in modern times. The conception of the term here is that the title to native lands is higher than a fee simple and has no derivative fountain. In my judgment it is not so but on constitutional grounds the radical title is in the King and whatever estate the Natives have is the recognition of the security promised by Commodore Erskine's proclamation. It was argued that it is a statutory freehold either in plain words or by implication ...
>
> In Papua the position is very much like that. While there is a restriction on the disposal of land contained in the Lands Ordinance ... the government does not interfere with the rights of the natives amongst themselves, except that the court for Native Matters has power to decide who has the right to occupy. The Kila Kila land belongs to Kila Kila village, that is, to the community, and what they have is the possessory title to the usufruct ...

In 1962 a major change to the common law position was effected. Section 7 of the Land Act[8] provided that 'All land in Papua New Guinea other than customary land is the property of the State subject to any estates, rights, titles or interests from time to time in force under any law in force in Papua New Guinea or part of Papua New Guinea'. Was this tantamount to the State's disclaimer of allodial title to customary land? If so, what is the legal significance of the disclaimer? Does it, for example, mean that anyone is free to establish and assert ownership rights to such land?[9]

Private dealings in customary land

All dealings in land were governed by legislation. These could be private or public. Private dealing in native land was governed by the Land Regulation Ordinance of 1888. The relevant sections read:

> I No person shall either by himself or his agent, nor shall any person acting as or purporting to act as the agent of any other person, directly or indirectly, negotiate for purchase or acquire or contract or agree to purchase or acquire from any native, or from any person on behalf of any such native, any land, or any right, title, or interest in any land or in the usufruct of any land, within the Possession.
>
> Any person offending against any provision of this section shall be liable on summary conviction to a penalty not exceeding one hundred pounds, or to imprisonment not exceeding twelve months.
>
> II No native shall, except as is hereinafter provided, contract or agree with any person or persons, directly or indirectly, for the sale or purchase or acquisition or use of any estate, or for any right, title, or interest in any land or in the usufruct of any land within the Possession.
>
> III Any contract, agreement, or instrument made, signed, or executed contrary to the provisions of this Ordinance shall be void, and any monies, value, or consideration paid, or purporting or agreed to be paid thereunder, shall not be recoverable, and no person shall have any right, claim, or demand under or in respect of any such contract,

8 Now s 4(1).

9 See also material on the doctrine of tenure.

> agreement, or instrument, or any covenant, agreement, or instrument, or any covenant or agreement therein contained or implied.

Observe that these provisions were wide enough to embrace all land whether customary or not. It is doubtful whether they could operate to prevent indigenous Papuans from entering into land transactions *inter se*.

In 1906 the provisions were amended to except 'land which has been alienated by the Crown' and which the native had acquired 'under a will or an intestacy'; a native could sell or otherwise dispose of such land with the consent of the Curator of Intestate Estates. In 1911 these provisions were further widened to allow Papuans to deal with alienated land irrespective of how it was acquired, subject to the consent of the government Secretary.

The current law on such matters is embodied in the Land Act (Ch No 185) Part VIII (ss 68–72) and Part IX (ss 73–78).

Public dealings in customary land

Public dealing in native land was governed by the Land Regulation Ordinance of 1888. The relevant sections read:

> IV Nothing in this Ordinance contained shall preclude the Administrator from negotiating, on behalf of Her Majesty, direct with the ascertained native owners of any land within the Possession, for the purchase in perpetuity or for the lease or any other use of any such land, or of the usufruct of any such land, which such native owners may wish to dispose of upon such terms and conditions as may be agreed upon between the Administrator and the owners aforesaid.
>
> V It shall not be lawful for the Administrator to acquire under the last preceding section any land or any interest, right or title in any land until by sufficient inquiry he has become satisfied that such land, or the use or usufruct thereof, is not required nor likely to be required by the native owners.

These provisions were tested in *Safe Lavao v The Independent State of Papua New Guinea (In Re The Kerema Town and Airstrip Land)*[10] where a purported transfer of land was voided because the instrument of transfer 'contains no suggestion that any one had even bothered to ask if the vendors had considered whether they would possibly have a need for their land in the future'.[11]

Early 'waste and vacant' declarations contained a similar provision, ie, whether land was required by the native owners. In the Supreme Court in the case of *Administration v Guba and Doriga*[12] (Coram Minogue CJ Frost SPJ Prentice dissenting) only Frost SPJ addressed the issue whether an inquiry whether the land was 'used or required or reasonably likely to be required by native-born Papuans for building, agricultural or other industrial purposes' was made in respect of the subject land. But provided an

10 [1978] PNGLR 15. See also *Rahonamo v Enai and Another (Re Hitau)* [1971–72] P&NGLR 58.

11 *Per* Pritchard J at p 21.

12 Unreported judgment No FC 18 (1968) p 85.

enquiry was made an appellate court will not inquire into a finding based on such enquiry.[13]

Acquisition of waste and vacant

It was generally believed that in order to protect the land of the indigenous people, the Administration should bring under its control as much land as it possibly could.[14] In order to achieve this, resort was had to 'waste and vacant land' declarations. The first legislation to provide for this mechanism was the Crown Lands Ordinance 1890 which was superseded by the Land Ordinance 1899. Section 11 of the 1899 Ordinance provided:

> XI The Administrator in Council may from time to time by Order in Council published in the *Gazette* declare that any land which has never been alienated by the Crown and not being land used or required by native-born Papuans for building agricultural or other industrial purposes will unless cause be shown to the contrary within the period specified in such order become Crown land.
>
> Every such Order in Council shall set forth the name or names (if any) by which such land is known with a description thereof made from an actual survey or a diagrammatic sketch of the same the position of the land, an estimate of its area and a statement showing as far as known how long it has been unused by natives.
>
> From and after the expiration of the time limited by such Order in Council the lands referred to therein shall be and be deemed to be absolutely vested in Her Majesty and to be Crown Land:
>
> Provided that the Administrator in Council shall at any time before the expiration of the time so limited and may at any time thereafter take into consideration any claim to such land or any interest therein made by or on behalf of any alleged owner thereof and if he allows such claim may either by another Order in Council published in the *Gazette* declare that the Crown disclaims its title to such land in which case the land shall not then vest in Her Majesty or become Crown Land or if it has so vested shall be divested from Her Majesty and cease to be Crown Land; or he may acquire the right of such owner in which case an instrument of title shall be executed, sealed and recorded in manner hereinbefore provided

In *The Administration of the Territory of Papua and New Guinea and Another v Daera and Guba* (1973) 130 CLR 353 the substance of s 11 of the Land Ordinance 1899 was expounded.

> **GIBBS J** (p 442): A further submission made on behalf of the applicants is that s XI on its proper construction applied only to ownerless land and that *ex hypothesi* the subject land was not ownerless. Alternatively it was submitted that if the section applied to land in native ownership its provisions were invalid. These contentions are insupportable. The opening words of the section describe the land in respect of which an Order in Council may be made and the proviso to the section makes it clear that such land may in fact be owned by a native. It is quite impossible on ordinary principles of construction to imply words, inconsistent with the proviso and not suggested by anything in the section, restricting the operation of the provisions to ownerless land. Of course the protection intended to be given to an owner of land in respect of which an Order in Council was made was that provided

13 See *Gaya Nomgui and Others v The Administration of The Territory of Papua and New Guinea* [1974] PNGLR 349.

14 See James, 'The role of the courts in an attempt to recover alienated land' (1974) 2 MLJ 270.

> by the proviso, under which, if the owner established his claim to ownership within the time provided, the Administrator in Council was bound either to disclaim the Crown's title or to acquire the right of the owner – which of course meant acquired by lawful means. Even if the owner's claim was made out of time the Administrator in Council was permitted to consider it, and if he allowed it the same consequences followed. The submission that the Order in Council was invalid rested on the proposition that when applied to land the subject of native ownership it would have been in conflict with Art XXXI of the Instructions passed under the Royal Sign Manual and Signet, to the Administrator of British New Guinea, dated 8 June 1888, which read (*inter alia*) as follows: 'The Administrator is to the utmost of his power to promote religion and education among the native inhabitants of the Possession; and he is especially to take care to protect them in their persons and in the free enjoyment of their land and other possessions ...' This article was a direction to the Administrator; it was not a limitation on the power of the Legislative Council. The powers of the Legislative Council depended upon the Letters Patent of 8 June 1888, by which the Queen, in pursuance of s 3 of the British Settlements Act of 1887 (UK) delegated to the Legislative Council (*inter alia*) 'full power and authority to establish all such laws and institutions ... as may be necessary for the peace, order, and good government of Our subjects within the Possession .... Subject, nevertheless to all such conditions, provisions, and limitations as We shall see fit to prescribe from time to time by Our Order in Our Privy Council, or by this or any other Instrument under Our said great Seal, or by the Instructions under Our Sign Manual and Signet ....' (Art X). The Instructions contained provisions as to the form of Ordinances and provided that the Administrator should not assent to Ordinances of certain classes (including Ordinances authorizing the purchase of land by private persons, except from the Administrator or purchasers from him Art XX.III (11) and required that all Ordinances be transmitted to the Queen 'for Our final approval, disallowance, or other direction thereupon' (Art XXV). There was no relevant condition, provision or limitation to which the law-making power delegated to the Legislative Council was subject and s XI of the Land Ordinance of 1899 was plainly within the power of the Legislative Council to make. It follows that an Order in Council made in pursuance of the power given by the section would not be invalid for non-compliance with Art XXXI. In any case, having regard to the provisions in s XI designed to protect the rights of owners, the Order in Council could not properly be said to amount to a failure to protect the natives in the free enjoyment of their land assuming that those words could ever be applied to an Order in Council made under an Ordinance.

On the issue of the validity of an Order in Council once made after the appropriate enquiry, his Honour said the following:

> **GIBBS J** (p 658): The next objection to the validity of the Order in Council was that the land to which it applied was not of the description which under s XI, as properly construed, alone can be the subject of an Order in Council under that section. The section applies to 'land which has never been alienated by the Crown and not being land used or required or reasonably likely to be required by native-born Papuans for building agricultural or other industrial purposes'. It was submitted that on the evidence it should be held that in 1901 some of the land within the boundaries contained in the Schedule to the Order in Council, including parts of Era Taora if they fell within those boundaries, was land which was either used or required or reasonably likely to be required by native-born Papuans for agricultural purposes and that the Order in Council could not validly apply to that land. There is certainly evidence that at various times there were native gardens on different parts of Era Taora. I have already referred to the evidence of Daera Guba to that effect and to the documentary evidence that shows that in 1886 and again in the 1920s there were gardens on part of that land. Moreover, there were some gardens on the neighbouring land acquired by

> the Koitapuans on 5 October 1900. There is, however, no evidence that any of the land within the boundaries in the Schedule to the Order in Council, however construed, was used for gardens at the time when the Order in Council was made. It is quite probable that as a result of the transactions in 1886 the natives had ceased gardening in the area and that they did not resume gardening there again until after Governor Murray had given them permission to do so, that is, after 1907. There is, further, no evidence that in 1901 the lands were either required, or reasonably likely to be required, for agricultural purposes. The applicants in effect suggested that any land on which gardens could be made should be held to be land likely to be required for agricultural purposes, but it must be remembered that in 1901 the pressures of population and the demand for land that exist today had not become manifested, particularly in British New Guinea. The following words of Sir Hubert Murray, quoted by Prentice J, which were written a decade after 1901, show that an able and sympathetic Administrator could well have believed in 1901 that lands suitable for agriculture, but not in fact so used, were not reasonably likely to be required for that purpose: 'Papua is sparsely populated, and there is far more land than is ever likely to be wanted either for natives or for Europeans, so that the land problems which have caused so much trouble elsewhere are not likely to arise.' However, the short answer to the contention that the Order in Council is invalid on this ground is that if it is permissible to establish that the land was at the date of the Order in Council not a kind to which s XI extended (question as to which I express no opinion) the burden of establishing that fact lies on those attacking the validity of the Order in Council and the burden has not been discharged ...

Another perplexing issue was whether the Crown could claim ownership of land on the basis that it was 'vacant and waste' in the absence of a declaration to that effect. In 1889 and before the enactment of the Crown Grants Ordinance 1889 the Crown took possession of Fisherman's Island leading to the development of a coconut plantation on it. Although enquiries were made in relation to the Island's status no formal declaration was made in that regard. Many indigenous people and groups had laid claim to the Island. The two cases *Arthur Agevu and Others v The Government of Papua New Guinea* and *Re Fisherman's Island*[15] deal with this problem.

The development of alienated land

The effort to establish the foundation for the economic development of the new territory was symbolised by the legal backing of Sir William MacGregor, the Lieutenant Governor gave the involvement of the London based British New Guinea syndicate. Established in 1897, the syndicate encourages the flow of capital into there. Sir William passed a law to allow the syndicate to acquire 250,000 acres of land in the territory to cultivate rubber and other tropical crops. Joyce commented on this development thus:[16]

> MacGregor derived many of his colonial ideas from his experience in Fiji, thus he tried to apply to the Papuans the tenets that their land should be secured to them; their lives should be as little disturbed by government or other whites as possible; they should follow the traditional, usually agricultural economies and they should not be forced to supply labour for white planters. Each of these tenets was revised during his governorship better to suit what MacGregor felt were the needs of the Papuans and New Guinea.

15 [1977] PNGLR 99; [1979] PNGLR 202, 205.

16 See RB Joyce, Sir William MacGregor (Oxford University Press, Melbourne, 1971), pp 196–99, 208–13; also Amankwah *et al*, *op cit*, note 1, at p 6.

> Such general statements are important in bringing together the various facts of his policy. MacGregor was a governor of a British colony and as such was expected to develop it. Every step he took in the interests of the Papuans had to be compatible with such an end. In arriving at a verdict on his administration this point must be kept clearly in mind. He was not an independent leader with freedom to choose his own policies; he had neither adequate funds nor sufficient staff to carry out the policies he desired; and he did not have the benefit of anthropological analyses of New Guinea's many cultures, nor even the opportunity to obtain much insight into their ideas he was restricted by the 19th century boundaries of knowledge and by the fact that his own time was overcrowded ...

Perhaps it is necessary to reproduce the relevant sections of the two most important pieces of legislation of the era under consideration: Crown Lands Ordinance 1890 and Lands Ordinance 1899.

CROWN LANDS ORDINANCE OF 1890

XXXV The Administrator in Council may alienate by private bargain any Crown Lands for agricultural pastoral fishing or trading purposes or for the planting of coconut trees or may cause any such land to be sold by public auction. Notice of any intended sale by auction shall be notified for at least three months in the *Gazette* together with a description of the land and a statement of the upset price thereof which shall be fixed by the Administrator in Council in each case.

XXXVI When Crown land is alienated by private bargain under the last preceding section for agricultural purposes and the sale is made conditional on the introduction of some new industry into the Possession or into some district of the possession and on the further condition that an extent of improvement of a kind to be specified in the conditions of sale shall be carried out within a time to be fixed by the Administrator in Council. The Administrator in Council may fix the price to be paid therefor at any sum not less than two shillings and sixpence an acre.

XXXVII When land is alienated by private bargain for agricultural pastoral fishing or trading purposes or for the planting of coconut trees under section thirty-five hereof and when no improvement conditions are attached to the sale the Administrator in Council may fix the prices to be paid therefor at any sum not at a less rate an acre than:

(1) For agricultural land ten shillings;

(2) For pastoral land two shillings;

(3) For land for trading or fishing purposes five pounds;

(4) For land for planting of coconuts five shillings.

XLIII The Administrator in Council may lease to any applicant any Crown lands or any lands in which the Crown possesses a leasehold estate for agricultural or pastoral purposes or for planting coconuts or as trading or fishing stations subject to the following provisions:

(1) Agricultural land shall not be leased if without any conditions as to improvement at a less rate of yearly rent than one shilling an acre.

(2) Agricultural land may be leased subject to conditions of improvement to be imposed by the Administrator in Council on a graduated scale of rent under

which nothing may be payable for any term not exceeding three years but not less than sixpence a year shall be payable for each acre after the first three years.

(3) Leases of agricultural land shall not be issued for any period exceeding twenty-five years but they may be issued with a purchasing clause under which a Crown Grant may be issued to the lessee on the completion of such improvements as may be specified in the lease on payment of any sum inclusive or otherwise as may have been determined by the Administrator in Council of any rent that have been paid by the lessee in respect of such land.

(4) Pastoral land shall not be leased for a term exceeding fifteen years or at a less annual rate of rental than two pence an acre. No such lease shall contain any purchasing clause.

(5) In issuing any lease for land to be used for trading or fishing purposes the Administrator in Council may take care that such lease does not grant any right or privilege which would confer on any lessee exclusive rights as to anchorage or the procuring of fresh water or firewood or which would prevent vessels traders or fishermen from obtaining shelter ashore or afloat in case of need. No lease for any land to be used for trading or fishing purposes shall be given at a less annual rate than ten shillings an acre or part of an acre. No lease under this sub-section shall be for a period exceeding five years.

(6) Land may be leased for the planting of coconut trees for any term not exceeding sixty years. The conditions of any such lease may not require the payment of any rent for the first five years but for the second five years shall fix an annual rent for each acre at a rate not less than six pence and for the remainder of the lease not less than one shilling an acre. Every such lease shall contain an improvement condition which shall require that not less than one-fourth of the land so leased which is fit to grow coconut-trees shall be planted therewith during the first five years.

(7) Any lease granted under the last preceding sub-section shall be issued subject to such reservations as the public interest may require with due regard for shelter for vessels and travellers the procuring of wood and water by vessels and any other right or convenience which the Administrator in Council may deem it necessary to preserve. Any such lease as aforesaid may contain a purchasing clause or such conditions as the Administrator in Council may impose: provided that the price to be paid shall not be at a less rate than five shillings an acre irrespective of any rent that may have been paid to the Crown for the use of such land.

LIV Every Crown Grant or Lease or Provisional Grant or Lease issued under this Ordinance shall contain a reservation of all gold and silver in or under the land comprised in such Crown Grant or Lease or provisional Crown Grant or Lease and of full right of access to the Crown or its licensees to enter upon the land and dig for and remove the gold and silver therefrom.

LAND ORDINANCE OF 1899

XIV The Administrator in Council may in the name of Her Majesty and under and subject to the provisions of this Ordinance grant fee simple in any Crown Land within the Possession.

XXIV The Administrator in Council may from time to time in manner provided by this Ordinance sell any Crown Lands either by private contract or by public auction.

XXXI The Administrator in Council may not any time without any such notice as last hereinbefore provided and on such conditions as he thinks fit to prescribe sell to any applicant therefor any Crown Land not exceeding one square mile (six hundred and forty acres) in any part of the Possession: provided that no land included in any such notice as aforesaid shall be sold under this section until the period limited by notice has expired.

XXXII The Administrator in Council may at any time without any notice as aforesaid and on such conditions as he thinks fit to prescribe sell to any person in the Possession who has actually visited examined and selected the same any available Crown Land not exceeding five thousand acres in area: provided that no land included in any such notice as aforesaid shall be sold under this section until the period limited by such notice has expired.

XXXIII When Crown Lands are sold under this Ordinance subject to conditions of improvement and the introduction of some new industry a provisional Grant in such form as may be directed by the Administrator in Council may be issued to the purchaser.

Every such Provisional Grant shall be prepared in duplicate one copy of which shall be recorded by the Registrar General in a special register in the manner in which instruments are directed to be recorded under The Real Property Ordinance of 1889 and the other copy shall be delivered to the purchaser on the payment of the fees payable upon the issue of a Crown Grant other than any fees payable in respect of the Assurance Fund.

When all the conditions of sale have been complied with the Administrator in Council shall on the surrender and cancellation of the Provisional Grant order a Crown Grant to issue for the land and such Grant shall issue accordingly. No fees shall be payable upon the issue of such grant other than any fees payable in respect of the Assurance Fund which shall be paid before the issue of such Grant.

XXXV The Administrator in Council may subject to the following provisions lease to any applicant any Crown Land or any lands in which the Crown possesses a leasehold estates:

(1) The annual rent of agricultural land leased without any conditions as to improvement shall not be less than six pence an acre;

(2) Agricultural land may be leased subject to conditions of improvement to be imposed by the Administrator in Council and upon a graduated scale of rent by which the rent shall be payable for any part of the term not exceeding three years and an annual rent of not less than six pence an acre shall be payable for the remainder of the term;

(3) No lease of agricultural land shall be granted for any period exceeding twenty-five years;

(4) Pasturage land shall not be leased for any term exceeding twenty-five years or at a less annual rent than one penny an acre;

(5) A lease of agricultural land or pasturage land may contain a purchasing clause under which a Crown Grant may issue to the lessee upon the completion of such improvements as are specified in the lease and upon payment of a sum of money which sum may be stated to be inclusive or exclusive of any rent paid by the lessee in respect of such land;

(6) No lease of land to be used for trading or fishing purposes shall grant any right or privilege which may confer on the lessee exclusive rights as to anchorage or the procuring of fresh water or firewood or which may obstruct or prevent vessels traders or fishermen from obtaining shelter ashore or afloat in case of need. No such lease shall reserve a less annual rent than ten shillings an acre or part of an acre. No such lease shall be for any period exceeding ten years;

(7) Land may be leased for the planting of coconut trees for any term not exceeding sixty years;

The conditions of any such lease may specify that no rent shall be payable for the first five years that for the second five years an annual rent of not less than six pence an acre shall be payable and that for the remainder of the term an annual rent of not less than one shilling an acre shall be payable.

Every such lease shall contain an improvement condition which shall require that not less than one fourth of the land so leased which is fit to grown coconut trees shall be planted therewith during the first five years of the terms.

Every lease shall be granted subject to such reservations in the public interest with respect to affording shelter for vessels and all other rights and conveniences which the Administrator in Council may deem it necessary to preserve.

Any such lease may contain a purchasing clause upon such conditions as the Administrator in Council may impose: provided that the purchasing price shall not be less than five shillings an acre exclusive of any rent paid by the lessee in respect of such land.

XLVII Every Crown Grant Lease Provincial Grant and Provincial Lease granted under this ordinance shall be deemed to contain a reservation of all mines and minerals other than coal in the land comprised therein and of the right of access for the purpose of searching or working any such mines or minerals in any part of the land whether such or any reservation is expressed in the instrument itself or not and generally shall be subject in every respect to the ordinance in force for the time being relating to mining. Every such grant or lease shall be subject to all the reservations and conditions prescribed by this Ordinance and also to any reservation or condition which the Administrator in Council may deem it advisable to prescribe therein.

In introducing the Land Ordinance 1889 the Lieutenant Governor outlined in his speech in the Legislative Council the policy to govern the allocation of land to new immigrants:

(1) The government will advertise in Australia, New Zealand, and England that lands in specified districts or parts of the Possession are open for application.

(2) The applications will not be dealt with until six months have elapsed from the last advertisement in England so as to give a fair chance to all.

(Applications for areas of 50,000 acres and over will be notified to the contributing Colonies, and not finally dealt with until they have had an opportunity of expressing their views.)

(3) Applications for areas not exceeding 6,400 acres (ten square miles) for settlers who have actually selected land, and not exceeding 640 acres (one square mile) in the case of small holders, can be dealt with at any time if the land has not been included in any advertised area.

(4) To guard against lands being obtained from the Crown for a nominal sum and not further utilized, provision is made for minimum conditions as to price and improvements:

(i) The minimum prices for agricultural or pasturage lands have been reduced respectively to 2s 6d and 6d per acre for freehold, and to 1s and 1d per acre for leasehold.

(ii) The minimum improvements to be effected within five years will be to the extent of not less than 2s 6d per acre for agricultural land, and 2s per acre for pasturage lands.

(5) The government is not bound to give priority to any application, and will, as a rule, only deal with applicants, or their representatives, in the Possession. It is not expedient to deal with large blocks of land on paper, as to the existence or nature of which neither the government nor the applicant have any precise knowledge.[17]

Improving customary land

Agriculture was considered the backbone of the colony's economic well being, and the policy on this was pressed home to the inhabitants by draconian methods backed by legislation, the Native Board Regulation No 2 1894 also known as the Planting Coconuts Regulation. The marriage MacGregor fostered between the Western money economic system and traditional land tenure was expressed in the policy of encouragement of cash crop farming among Papuans albeit enforced coercively under. The supervision of the planting of coconuts was assigned to magistrates although the law made no provision for a marketing mechanism. Progress was slow and the area covered unnecessarily small because there were not enough magistrates to supervise the scheme. Nevertheless, progress in cash crop farming had been initiated to expand later and to engulf other economic trees such as cocoa and coffee. The policy was advanced by later legislation: the Native Plantations Ordinances 1913, 1918, and 1928.

However, it must be noted that this policy did not sweep away the perennial problem of subsistence agriculture and shifting cultivation to usher in the millennium of mechanised farming. Notwithstanding the cash crop farming legislations, most Papuans continued to acquire, retain and use their land in accordance with time honoured traditional precepts and norms.

17 Annual Report, 1888–89. See Amankwah *et al*, *op cit*, note 1, at pp 6–7.

Notes and questions

1 Is it clear from the materials what mode of acquisition applies to Papua: settlement, conquest or annexation? How, if at all, did the manner of colonisation influence colonial land policies in Papua?

2 There had been some ambivalence in British colonial policy. Sometimes they spoke of the paramountcy of native interests: PNG for example; at other times it was just the reverse: the paramountcy of the settler's interest – Kenya, Zimbabwe, Malawi and Zambia. What are the possible reasons for this ambivalence? Do you think that the congenial climatic conditions and other natural factors might have something to do with it?

3 Can you reconcile the ostensible policy of protecting native lands from unscrupulous land-hungry mongers, and the policy of waste and vacant declarations of the Australian Administration?

4 Where did the Crown derive the power to appropriate so called waste and vacant land? Was it by virtue of the Royal Prerogative? If proper enquiries were made before such declarations were made, would cases such as Agevu have arisen?

5 Note the colonists' conception of natives: epithets such as uncivilised, barbaric, primitive were used to describe natives. Referring to the situation of the Australian Aborigines in the *Mabo v Queensland* case, Brennan J said: 'The facts as we know them today do not fit the 'absence of law' or 'barbarian theory' underpinning the colonial reception of the common law' (at p 39). Was the 'barbarian theory' a result of ignorance of the Aboriginal people's way of life or was it merely an excuse to deprive them of their land?

6 Is it clear where colonialism (politics) begins and policy ends? See the views of James and Narakobi below.

7 Consider the act of State doctrine: the act of the sovereign can stand no scrutiny. Why must this be applied to outsiders among whom the doctrine is unknown?

8 In Canada and the USA perhaps, it seems Indian lands were purchased from them. Australia is currently coming to grips with the problem of recognising Aboriginal land rights with the handing down of the High Court decision in *Mabo v Queensland* (1992) 175 CLR 1. What do you make of Narakobi's view in the *Reva Mase* case? (See overleaf.)

9 Can land be sold in a culture in which a money economy had not been inaugurated? What are the requirements for the validity of a contract of sale of land?

10 If land is acquired compulsorily, does the common law require the payment of adequate compensation?

11 On the part of the natives, can it be argued that they sincerely did not understand the nature of the transactions? See Barwick CJ's view in *Administration v Guba* that a culture of sale existed in PNC at this time.

12 RW James states: 'The High Court's decision in the *Newtown* case is undoubtedly of interest to students of Colonialism and is best explicable in the context of imperialism.' (1974) 2 MLJ 270. Discuss.

13 'The whole history of land acquisition by Europeans of indigenous races is shrouded with legal positivism, resource exploitation and Euro-centricism; dressed in legal

technicality and military dominance.' *Per* Narakobi AJ, *Reva Mase v The Independent State of Papua New Guinea* (unreported judgment N296). Assess the validity of this statement.

14 *In Reva Mase v The Independent State of Papua New Guinea* (unreported judgment N260), Narakobi AJ said: 'I look to trends in Australia, New Zealand, Canada and the United States where native rights and titles rest on statute or even on treaties or on sovereign proclamations and find that the native people have not always done well.' Elaborate on this statement.

15 'In my humble view, there should be a fresh review of all the written evidence, the decisions and fresh evidence should be taken by an administrative type tribunal or a Permanent Parliamentary Committee.' *Per* Narakobi AJ, *Reva Mase v The Independent State of Papua New Guinea* (unreported judgment N296). Is this the right way of resolving with finality the perennial problem concerning title to disputed land, such as Newtown land? What difficulties do you envisage would confront a tribunal assigned to engage in the task of determining title to the land in question?

II LAND LAW AND POLICY IN GERMAN NEW GUINEA 1885–1914

Officially German New Guinea was annexed on 17 May 1885, however, as was the situation of Papua, the annexation was preceded by an influx of settlers among whom numbered Hernsheim and the notorious Queen Emma who purported to have 'purchased' vast tracts of the land of New Guinea. This acquisition occurred before the Imperial Charter of 17 May 1885 conferred on the New Guinea Kompagnie the sole monopoly of acquisition of ownerless and native land in New Guinea. The Land Ordinance 1887 which regulated land dealings was replaced by the Land Ordinance of 1903. The New Guinea Company issued Directions to its agents to supplement the law. These directions were a set of instructions to be followed by the Company's agents in their dealings with the land of the indigenous people to ensure that their customary interests were not violated. Under the Land Ordinance of 1903 the Governor had more power than under the 1887 Ordinance to deal with so called ownerless or 'waste and vacant' land.[18]

Imperial land legislations: a selected few

Because of the massive destruction of official documents during the Japanese invasion of New Guinea in World War II most of the legislations reproduced below, are not easily accessible and may be reached only in some foreign libraries. It is important therefore to set out in this work a few of the most relevant legislations of this period.

18 For an appropriate background information on the legal position in German New Guinea at this time, see Peter and Bridget Sack, *The Land Law of German New Guinea – A Collection of Documents* (ANU Press, Canberra, 1975) pp viii–xii; also R Crocombe and R Hide, 'New Guinea: unity in diversity' in *Land Tenure in the Pacific*, R Crocombe (ed) (OUP, Melbourne, 1971) pp 311–12; Sack, 'Land law and land policy in German New Guinea', Second Waigani Seminar, The History of Melanesia (UPNG, Port Moresby, 1969); P Sack, *Land Between Two Laws* (ANU Press, Canberra, 1973) pp 127–36.

PETER AND BRIDGET SACK, THE LAND LAW OF GERMAN NEW GUINEA – A COLLECTION OF DOCUMENTS (ANU PRESS, CANBERRA, 1975)

Imperial Charter for the New Guinea Kompagnie, of 17 May 1885 (p 2)

We also herewith grant the said Company, in return for its undertaking to create and maintain the administrative institutions for which it has taken responsibility and to bear the costs of an adequate administration of justice, the corresponding rights of local sovereignty as well as the exclusive right to occupy and to dispose of ownerless land in the Protectorate and to conclude contracts regarding land and land rights with the natives, all this under the supervision of our government which will enact those regulations necessary to protect the natives and to preserve rights of ownership, which were duly acquired at an earlier date.

PUBLIC NOTICE, OF 19 FEBRUARY 1886 (p 4)

In pursuance of the Ordinance which was proclaimed here on 22 May of last year, according to which:

> ... new land acquisitions in the German Protectorate are invalid without the approval of the German authorities and only rights which have been previously acquired in good faith shall be protected.

I herewith bring to public notice as instructed, that:

> ... all those who acquired rights of ownership to land in the Bismarck Archipelago before the said Public Notice (22 May of last year), are to submit their titles to me for the purpose of examination and possible registration.

The titles are to be submitted before 1 May of this year. Sketch maps of the land acquired are to be attached, together with German translations, if the documents have been drawn up in another language.

In the case of competing claims the parties are to postpone either settling on or cultivating the land in question until a decision has been made about the titles.

Mioko, 19 February 1886

The Imperial Commissioner

(signed) GV Oertzen

CONTRACT BETWEEN THE REICH AND THE NEU GUINEA KOMPAGNIE, OF 7 OCTOBER 1898 (pp 5–7)

The following contract is made between the Chancellor of the Reich on behalf of the Reich and the Neu Guinea Kompagnie, represented by its board of Directors:

> Clause 1
>
> The Reich resumes and shall itself exercise the local sovereignty granted to the Neu Guinea Kompagnie by the Imperial Charters of 17 May 1885 and 13 December 1886, as well as by subsequent Imperial Ordinances, over the Protectorate in the Pacific described therein, including all rights and duties appertaining thereto.

Clause 2

The Neu Guinea Kompagnie renounces in favour of the Reich the special property rights for the whole area of the Protectorate described in Clause 1 which were granted to it by the Charters and which it possesses by virtue of the same, to wit:

(a) the exclusive right to occupy and to dispose of ownerless land, as well as to conclude contracts with the natives regarding land and land rights,

(b) the right to make the following commercial undertakings dependent on its permission and subject to certain conditions, in particular the payment of fees: fishing for pearl shell, pearls and trepang, exploiting deposits of guano or other fertilisers, mining for ores, precious stones and combustible minerals, exploiting coconut groves, not in the possession of natives or otherwise privately owned, for copra, coastal fishing and felling timber for commercial or trading purposes in all areas which are not privately owned.

Clause 7

The Neu Guinea Kompagnie is also entitled to take into possession, without payment to the Reich, 500,000 hectares of land of its choice in Kaiser Wilhelmsland and the islands belonging thereto within three years from 1 April 1899 without prejudice to duly acquired rights of third parties with the proviso, however, that the selection of land along the coast and river banks on the two main islands named above is limited to a total sea and river frontage of 100 kilometres. The land to be selected along the sea or rivers must extend at least one kilometre inland unless the natural topography of the area in question makes an adjustment necessary. Land thus acquired is subject to the provisions of an expropriation ordinance to be enacted regarding the transfer of land for public purposes. The Neu Guinea Kompagnie is obliged to inform the representative of the Reich in the Protectorate in each case of the land it has selected and to prove within one year that the selected land was, in accordance with existing laws, either occupied as ownerless or acquired from natives.

IMPERIAL ORDINANCE REGARDING THE ASSUMPTION OF LOCAL SOVEREIGNTY OVER THE PROTECTORATE OF GERMAN NEW GUINEA BY THE REICH, OF 27 MARCH 1899 (p 11)

We, Wilhelm, by the Grace of God German Emperor, King of Prussia etc order by virtue of the Statute Regarding the Legal Condition in the German Protectorates (RG B1, 1888, 75) in the name of the Reich as follows:

Section 1

The Reich shall assume local sovereignty over the Protectorate of German New Guinea as from 1 April 1899.

Our Charters granted by us to the Neu Guinea Kompagnie on 17 May 1885 and 13 December 1886, as well as our Ordinance Regarding the Jurisdiction of the Neu Guinea Kompagnie over the Natives in its Protectorate, of 15 October 1897 shall become ineffective.

Section 2

Those special property rights and other privileges which the Neu Guinea Kompagnie held by virtue of the Charters and other statutory provisions shall as from 1 April 1899 pass to the Treasury of the Protectorate of German New Guinea (Statute Regarding the Revenue and Expenditure of the Protectorates, of 30 March 1892, RG B1, 1892, 369), except where specifically reserved to the Company by way of agreement.

IMPLEMENTATION ORDER FOR THE IMPERIAL ORDINANCE REGARDING THE ASSUMPTION OF LOCAL SOVEREIGNTY OVER THE PROTECTORATE OF GERMAN NEW GUINEA (p 13) BY THE REICH, OF 1 APRIL 1899

By virtue of section 4 of the Imperial Ordinance of 27 March 1899, I order for the Protectorate of German New Guinea as follows:

Section 1

In accordance with section 2 of the said Imperial Ordinance in particular the following property rights hitherto exercised by the Neu Guinea Kompagnie shall pass to the Treasury of the Protectorate of German New Guinea:

(a) the exclusive right to occupy and to dispose of ownerless land, as well as to make contracts with the natives regarding land and land rights;

(b) the right to make the following commercial undertakings dependent on permission from the authorities: fishing for pearl shell, pearls and trepang, exploiting deposits of guano or other fertilisers, mining for ores, precious stones and combustible minerals, exploiting coconut groves, not in the possession of natives or otherwise privately owned, for copra, coastal fishing and felling timber for commercial or trading purposes on all lands which are not privately owned.

ORDINANCE REGARDING THE ACQUISITION OF OWNERSHIP AND THE CHARGING OF LAND IN THE PROTECTORATE OF THE NEU GUINEA KOMPAGNIE, OF 20 JULY 1887 (pp 15–17)

We, Wilhelm, by the Grace of God German Emperor, King of Prussia etc, by virtue of section 3 of the Statute Regarding the Legal Conditions in the German Protectorates in the wording of the Statute of 7 July 1887 (RG B1, 307), order in the name of Reich as follows:

Section 1

The acquisition of ownership and the charging of land in the Protectorate of the Neu Guinea Kompagnie, in so far as the following does not provide otherwise, shall be governed by the rules of Prussian law, in particular by the Statute Regarding the Acquisition of Ownership and the Charging of Land, Mines and Independent Land Rights, of 5 May 1872 (PG, 1872, 433–45).

Section 2

The declarations by which the registered owner and the new acquirer transfer ownership (section 2 of the Statute Regarding the Acquisition of Ownership, of 5 May 1872) can also be made in writing. The declarations do not have to be made contemporaneously.

Section 3

The provisions regarding land charges and the ownership of mining rights in the Statute Regarding the Acquisition of Ownership, as well as the Land Registration Act, of 5 May 1872 are not applicable.

The requisite regulations in lieu of the latter for the implementation of this Ordinance will be issued by the Chancellor of the Reich after hearing the Neu Guinea Kompagnie's Board of Directors.

Section 4

The preceding sections apply neither to the acquisition of ownerless land nor to the land belonging to the natives. However, land which has been entered into the Ground Book remains governed by sections 1 to 3, even if it becomes the property of a native.

Section 5

The principles governing the acquisition of land by means of contracts with the natives or by occupying ownerless land, which is by virtue of the Imperial Charter of 17 May 1885 the exclusive right of the Neu Guinea Kompagnie, shall be laid down by the Neu Guinea Kompagnie with the approval of the Chancellor of the Reich.

Land acquired by the Neu Guinea Kompagnie in this way shall be registered in the Ground Book by virtue of an acquisition certificate issued by the Administrator or an official authorised by him.

Section 6

Other persons can only claim rights based on the occupation of ownerless land or on contracts with natives regarding the acquisition or charging of land, if the acquisition took place prior to 21 May 1885.

Section 7

The following rules shall apply to the acquisition of ownership as defined in section 6. In the case of the occupation of ownerless land the claim to ownership is valid only if the ownerless land was in fact occupied before 21 May 1885 and if its possession has not since been relinquished or otherwise lost.

In the case of acquisition based on contracts with natives, it shall be required that prior to 21 May 1885 a contract was concluded in writing or orally between the owner and the acquirer with the intention of transfering and acquiring ownership and that possession has been transfered and not since relinquished or otherwise lost.

Section 8

Section 7, sub-section 3 is correspondingly applicable to a transfer of land which took place between non-natives before this Ordinance comes into force.

Section 9

For the islands of the Solomons Group which belong to the Protectorate, the 28 of October 1886 shall take the place of the date set in sections 6 and 7.

Section 10

Persons wishing to claim ownership of land in the Protectorate of the Neu Guinea Kompagnie on the basis of acquisition titles of the kind defined in section 6 must apply to have their ownership registered in the Ground Book no later than 1 March 1888. Any claims to ownership which have not been lodged with the application described above by this date becomes *ipso iure* invalid.

This does not apply to claims to ownership based on titles which were registered before this Ordinance comes into force in the 'Ground Book or Register of Land Acquisition', established by the Imperial Commissioner.

Such claimants can however, on application by the Station Manager in whose district the land is situated, be summoned by the competent Ground Book Office to apply for the registration of their ownership in the new Ground Book. In such cases each claimant must be given by special order at lease three months' notice and be notified that his claims will become invalid if he fails to apply in time.

Section 11

In cases falling under section 10 a copy of the application for registration of ownership with enclosures must be sent to the Manager of the Station in whose district the land is situated, together with the request that any objections to the acquisition which might arise out of the Neu Guinea Kompagnie's exclusive right to acquire land be lodged within a set period of not more than three months.

If such objections are lodged within the set period, the applicant has to be notified and informed that he must assert his claims against the Neu Guinea Kompagnie by taking court action within a prescribed period of six months.

If the New Guinea Kompagnie does not lodge any objections within the set period the land will be registered, provided the examination of the acquisition title of the applicant and any predecessors (sections 7 and 9) shows that it is otherwise valid.

In order to supplement the evidence, the Ground Book Office can make appropriate investigations and issue a public summons that it is to be notified of all claims impairing the application. A period of at least three months is to be set for the notification. The summons is to be made public by displaying it on the court notice-board.

The Ground Book Office can dispense with the measure described in the preceding sub-section if the applicant and any predecessors have been in undisturbed possession of the land in question for at least the three preceding years.

DIRECTIONS REGARDING THE PROCEDURES FOR THE ACQUISITION OF LAND BY THE NEU GUINEA KOMPAGNIE, OF 10 AUGUST 1887 (pp 19–22)

By virtue of section 5 of the Imperial Ordinance of 20 July 1887 (RG B1, 1887, 379) and with the approval of the Chancellor of the Reich, the following directions are given for the occupation of ownerless land and for the acquisition of land from the natives, which, by virtue of the Imperial Charter of 17 May 1885, is the exclusive right of the Neu Guinea Kompagnie.

I Regarding ownerless land

Section 1

Occupation is to be preceded by a thorough investigation as to whether the land which is to be occupied is cultivated or otherwise used by natives, or whether it is marked in a customary way as belonging to an individual or a community and whether ownership is consequently claimed by certain persons.

Section 2

If inspection reveals such signs, the persons making claims must be ascertained by questioning the natives living nearby, especially the heads of families, communities or other groupings, if they exist. If possible an interpreter, speaking the language of the person involved, should be called in for the questioning and subsequent discussions, which are to be recorded in a way which shows the course of the investigations and in particular the questions and answers relating to the establishing of the claims.

Land thus claimed is, for the time being, to be excluded from occupation and directions must be obtained as to whether or not negotiations for transfer of the land should be opened with the persons allegedly entitled to the land. In the former case the rules laid down in section 5ff are to be applied.

Section 3

If no signs can be found that the land is in the possession of natives, or if it is impossible to determine the significance of existing signs, because no natives live in the vicinity or because no explanation can be obtained from them, the observations made as well as attempts to obtain an explanation are to be recorded in detail, whereupon the land should be forthwith occupied.

Section 4

The occupation shall take place by positioning boundary posts, stones, fences or other signs which show that the land has been taken into possession for the Neu Guinea Kompagnie, and to what extent. This process is to be recorded and the record must show:

(a) the position of the occupied land, indicating any natural boundaries, the natural condition of the soil or the extent of any cultivation, and its approximate size;

(b) the number, type and kind of markings which have been used to signify that it has been occupied.

This record must carry the signature of the authorised official. A sketch map is to be attached, showing as precisely as possible the position of the land, if possible in relation to fixed points, and the boundary marks which have been erected.

II Indirect acquisition of native land

Section 5

If land is to be acquired which is in the possession of natives or which individual natives or native communities claim as belonging to them, and if the possessor(s) is (are) prepared to transfer it, the transfer is to be certified in a written contract. This is to be preceded by investigations as to which person(s) is (are), in the opinion of the natives involved, entitled to decide on the permanent disposal of the land, which procedures for such a transfer are customary among them and must be followed to render the transfer valid, and to which persons the purchase price must be paid in order to discharge the acquirer from his stipulated obligations.

If the investigation reveals that the right of disposal or the right to receive the purchase price is held by several persons, or that the disposal on the part of an individual private possessor is valid only with the approval of other persons, who belong to the possessor's family, community or a similar grouping, then all persons involved are to be included in the negotiations; if possible in the form of a meeting with them; or, if this is not possible, a date is to be fixed by which the transferor is to procure the approval of all other rightholders.

Section 6

Once agreement has been reached regarding the object of the acquisition and the price payable for it, as well as regarding the persons who hold the right of disposal and the right to receive the price, two identical copies of the contract are to be drawn up with the entitled persons in the German language.

This contract must include everything which, according to German law, is essential for a contract of purchase and sale or exchange, to wit in particular: a precise description of the block of land to be transfered, indicating position, size, condition and boundaries, in such a way that it can be easily located and distinguished from the blocks; the intention of one party to transfer the ownership and the intention of the other to accept this transfer; the statement of the purchase or exchange price and the determination as to when and to whom it shall be paid or has been paid; the declaration that the land has been or shall be delivered, and in what time.

The contract must also show that the significance of the transfer has been made clear to the transferor, ie, that by the transfer he renounces for himself and his family for all time all rights to the land, and that he accordingly cannot transfer it again to any other person, whereas the new acquirer is entitled to use it or to dispose of it as he wishes.

Section 7

The contract has to be signed by the representative of the Neu Guinea Kompagnie. The native party (parties), so long as they cannot write, must affix their marks, and it must be explained to them that by doing so they make their consent final and binding. Care must also be taken that any possible co-owners, usufructuaries as well as persons whose approval is required for the transfer, sign the contract after receiving the same explanation and in the same way.

Section 8

Wherever possible, an interpreter who knows the language of the transferor(s) is to be called and his participation must be indicated in the document. There must also be a witness, who must be present during the negotiations and who must, in particular, certify that, in his opinion, the significance of the transfer has been brought to the knowledge of the transferor. If for any reason the transferor(s) object to the affixing of their marks, although there is no doubt that they agree in substance, the reason for their objection must be stated and shown in the document. Nevertheless the contract is valid if the witness present confirms that the objection to the execution has grounds other than the lack of agreement, and that, according to his observation, agreement had been reached.

Section 9

The delivery of the acquired land must be effected in such a way that it actually takes place as soon as agreement on the contents of the contract has been reached. This and in what way it was brought about must be shown in the contract. In the exceptional case of delivery taking place at a later date, this must be recorded in writing in a separate document for which the same form as for the contract of transfer must be observed.

Section 10

As a rule the payment of the purchase price in money or goods shall take place immediately after the delivery of the land. It is the strict duty of the Company's representatives to make sure that the price is paid without any deductions and in full accordance with the previous agreement to those persons who are entitled to it, as shown by the preceding investigations. If there are several persons so entitled, the dividing up of the purchase price is to be left to them. The contract is to indicate that payment has been made, the persons who received it, acknowledgment of receipt and the fact that all claims against the acquirer have been satisfied. If, for special reasons, the payment of the purchase price takes place at a date later than that of the execution of the contract, this is to be recorded in a separate document for which the same forms as for the contract must be observed.

Section 11

Once the contract has been executed, one of the two copies is to be handed over to and remain with the transferor(s).

Berlin, 10 August 1887

Neu Guinea Kompagnie

The Board of Directors

A v Herzog

Chairman

Imperial ordinance regarding the rights to land in the German protectorates, of 21 November 1902 (pp 35–36)

We, Wilhelm, by the Grace of God German Emperor, King of Prussia etc order by virtue of section 3 of the Protectorates Act (RG B1, 1900, 813) in connection with section 21 of the Statute Regarding Consular Jurisdiction, of 7 April 1900, 213 for the German Protectorates in the name of the Reich as follows:

I General provisions

Section 5

The Chancellor of the Reich and, with his approval, the Governor shall determine the conditions for the acquisition of rights to ownerless and crown land. The relevant regulations in force at present in the individual Protectorates shall remain in force until they are repealed in accordance with the above provisions. No rights can be acquired contrary to existing regulations, or those to be issued.

Section 6

The following rules shall apply in respect of land belonging to natives or other coloured persons:

(1) If and in so far as appears necessary in the public interest the Chancellor of the Reich and, with his approval, the Governor are authorised to either prohibit the acquisition of ownership or other real rights to such land and also its use by third parties, or to make it subject to special conditions or administrative approval. The same applies to the acquisition and the charging of such land by way of compulsory auction. Section 5, Sentences 2 and 3 are correspondingly applicable.

(2) Otherwise this Ordinance only applies to such land if a folio in the Ground Book has been established for it, or if it has been entered into a Land Register (section 19). To what extent natives or other coloured persons are entitled or can be requested to have their land registered in the Ground Book shall be determined by the Chancellor of the Reich and, with his approval, by the Governor.

(3) The Chancellor of the Reich and, with his approval, the Governor can direct in favour of natives or other coloured persons:

   (a) that forms for the charging of such land other than those contained in the Third Book of the Civil Code and section 40 of the Prussian Statute Implementing the Civil Code, shall be admissible,

   (b) that Ground Book folios can be established for certain rights of usufruct, even if they are not inheritable or are non-transferable, and that the law regarding land belonging to natives shall continue to apply to them.

Order by the Governor of German New Guinea for the Protectorate of German New Guinea, excluding the Island territory of the Carolines, Palaus and Marianas, in implementation of the imperial ordinance regarding the rights to land in the German Protectorates, of 21 November 1902 and the order issued thereto by the Chancellor of the Reich on 30 November 1902, of 22 July 1904 (pp 43–44)

Section 3

(to sections 5 and 6 of the Imperial Ordinance)

1 The right to occupy and to dispose of ownerless land as well as the right to conclude contracts with the natives regarding the acquisition of ownership or real rights to land or the use thereof shall be exclusively held by the Treasury which can be represented in any relevant legal actions by persons other than officials at the

discretion of the Governor. Land required by the natives for their sustenance, in particular dwelling places, garden land and palm groves, is excluded from acquisition.

2 The deed to be drawn up when ownerless land is occupied, must show how the 'appropriation' took place, contain a precise description of the boundaries and state the manner in which the given boundary points have been marked.

At his discretion the Governor shall issue further directions regarding the contents of the contracts with the natives and of the contracts regarding the re-transfer of land which the Treasury has acquired from natives or occupied as ownerless, either generally by drawing up appropriate contract forms, or from case to case.

3 To what extent natives are entitled or can be requested to enter their land in the Ground Book or the Land Register shall be determined in each individual case by the Governor.

4 The Directions Regarding the Procedures for the Acquisition of Land by the Neu Guinea Kompagnie, of 10 August 1887 as well as the supplements issued thereto for the District of Northern New Ireland on 24 January 1902 and for Kaiser Wilhelmsland on 28 July 1903 are repealed.

The administration and judicial application of the regulations

Administrative policy and the regime of the law are not always identical, for while administrators are driven by political considerations, judges and lawyers aim at the prevalence of a fair, equitable and just environment. The law is one thing. The process of its administration is another thing.[19] Ian Willis points out the injustice and inherent contradictions in the application of European law to transactions concluded by Europeans with indigenous and dependent people.[20]

The validity of a purchase depended on whether the appropriate legal procedures prescribed in the Regulations and Instructions had been complied with. The difficulty in making that determination is illustrated by the case of *Gaya Nomgui and Others v The Administration of the Territory of Papua and New Guinea (Re Lae Administration case)*.[21]

Students are invited to consider carefully the differences in the attitude of the German Administration in German New Guinea towards native land rights and that of the British in British New Guinea (Papua). They should observe also German recognition of the natives' allodial title, and compare that phenomenon with the British attitude to same in Papua. Students must notice also that in German New Guinea the German Administration pursued a policy of 'monopoly' in the acquisition of native lands first in favour of the New Guinea Company and later the Imperial government. This policy was executed through the imposition of very stringent conditions which should be met before a valid acquisition could be said to have been effected.

---

19 For materials on such problems, see PG Sack, *The Land Between Two Laws*, *op cit*, note 18, pp 176–86. PG Sack, 'Early land acquisitions in New Guinea: the native version' (1969) 3(2) J of P&NG Soc, p 7. *Custodian of Expropriated Property v Commissioner of Native Affairs (Re Jomba Plain)* (1971–72) P&NGLR 501. The Central Court of the Territory of New Guinea deals with the difficult problem of proof that the indigenous people actually sold a piece of their land to European purchasers.

20 Ian Willis, 'Lae's land grabbers: white man's justice – but who can afford it?' (1972) 6 New Guinea 4.

21 [1974] PNGLR 349 (Supreme Court of Papua New Guinea).

Questions

1 How could it be ascertained authoritatively whether or not the *Directions* and *Instructions* on land dealings were always observed by public officials?

2 After 1888 and especially after the promulgation of the Land Ordinance 1903, why did the indigenous people not vie with the German Administration in the appropriation of 'waste and vacant' land?

3 Note carefully how the German New Guinea Company dealt with pre-annexation acquisitions. Was this approach just and fair in your view as between the natives and settlers?

4 Did German colonial law define 'ownerless land'? How did the concept of 'ownerless land' under German Colonial law differ from the notion of 'waste and vacant' land under English law in Papua?

5 In your view, which colonial law German or English accorded customary land law and tenure greater respect?

6 How did German annexation or declaration of protectorate affect customary land rights?

7 Discuss the changes which the 1903 land legislation brought about in the law.

III LAND LAW AND POLICY IN PAPUA NEW GUINEA 1906–45

New constitution

The most important single legal development in this period was the promulgation of a new constitution, the Papua Act 1905. The territory of British New Guinea was renamed Papua by s 5 of the Act. An Australian Royal Commission was established to look into the issue of the formulation of a policy appropriate for the administration of the territory. It saw the land issue, that is, insecurity of title to land in the territory as inimical to the territory's economic progress.[22] The lack of progress in agriculture was attributed by the Commission to Administration's delay in granting land title, and lack of reliable information on suitable settlement areas for intending settlers.

Laying the foundation for securing title to land

Security of tenure is a *sine qua non* of a viable agrarian policy.[23] The Land Ordinance 1911–40 therefore inaugurated the Torrens system of land registration under s 24 and

22 Royal Commission Report, 1907, p 2.

23 For materials which provided the setting for a policy for making land title secure in Papua New Guinea, see WA Lalor, 'Land law and registration' in *Fashion of Law in New Guinea* (BJ Brown (ed)) (Butterworths, Sydney, 1969) 137 at pp 142–44, the Papua Act 1905 which prohibited the granting of freehold interests by the Crown in favour of leasehold grants, the Royal Commission of 1907 which made important policy recommendation especially on the need for the Administration to arm itself with the power of compulsory acquisition of land for public purposes and F West, *Hubert Murray – The Australian Pro-Consul* (OUP, Melbourne, 1968), pp 122, 124–31.

proclaimed in s 10 that only leaseholds not exceeding 99 years could be granted thus fortifying s 20(1) of the Papua Act 1905 which outlawed freehold grants. The Ordinance made provision for the establishment of a Land Board to carry out functions which hitherto had been performed by the Administration-in-Council. The Land Ordinance Act 1911–40 also made provisions for compulsory acquisition of land for public purposes.[24]

Native agriculture and the economy

Administration policy on indigenous agricultural input in the economy of the territory was further buttressed by legislative measures. Several Native Plantation Ordinances were passed beginning from 1894 culminating in the Native Plantation Ordinance 1925. The regulation of agricultural produce (cocoa, coffee and oil palms) were delegated to a Board under the Native Board Regulations administered by local magistrates.[25]

Customary land and the judicial system

The distinction between civil and criminal wrongs has long been established. Wrongs of the first order are the concern of ordinary citizens. Wrongs of the second category affect the society as a whole and, therefore, invite State sanction and intervention. In the case of civil wrongs, however, in PNG a further distinction was maintained in respect of land use claims and land ownership claims. Land ownership claims have potential for violence, so a policy was maintained that they should be dealt with 'administratively' taking them out of the realm of the judiciary. The Native Regulations 1939 ensured that land ownership claims did not get to the courts.[26] Since 97% of the total land mass is held under customary tenure this situation has had serious repercussions in the past.[27] The Land Disputes Settlement Act[28] it seems has gone some way to rectify the situation.

Question

How does a nation develop a corpus of jurisprudence on any matter in the absence of litigation?

IV LAND LAW AND POLICY IN NEW GUINEA 1914–21

German New Guinea was seized by Australian forces under Colonel William Holmes at the beginning of World War I. A proclamation was issued by the colonel and was followed by German capitulation.

24 Section 33.

25 See Amankwah *et al*, *op cit*, note 1, p 36.

26 While a claim by any person that 'he is entitled to the exclusive right to the use of any land, water or reef'; was a civil claim under s 132(b) of the Regulations, a claim by any person 'to the ownership of any land, water or reef'; was not under s 133(1).

27 The anomaly which the policy of determining land ownership claims administratively entailed is depicted by *Soape and Others v Wesiki and Others, Supreme Court* (1960) unreported judgment N159.

28 Ch No 45 1975.

For ease of reference, we reproduce below extracts of the Proclamation and Terms of Capitulation.

REPORT ON THE MILITARY OCCUPATION OF THE GERMAN NEW GUINEA POSSESSIONS (CANBERRA, COMMONWEALTH GOVERNMENT PRINTER 1922), pp 5–6

(i) Proclamation of military rule in New Guinea

Whereas the forces under my command have occupied the Island of New Britain; and whereas upon such occupation the authority of the German government has ceased to exist therein; and whereas it has become essential to provide for proper government of the said colony, and for the protection of the lives and property of the peaceful inhabitants thereof.

Now I, William Holmes, Companion of the Distinguished Service Order, Colonel in his Majesty's Forces, Brigadier Commanding the aforesaid Expeditionary Force, do hereby declare and proclaim as follows:

1 From and after the date of these presents the Island of New Britain and its dependencies are held by me in military occupation in the name of His Majesty the King.

2 War will be waged only against the armed forces of the German Empire and its allies in the present war.

The lives and private property of peaceful inhabitants will be protected, and the laws and customs of the colony will remain in force so far as is consistent with the military situation.

3 If the needs of the troops demand it, private property may be requisitioned. Such property will be paid for at its fair value.

4 In return for such protection it is the duty of all inhabitants to behave in an absolutely peaceful manner, to carry on their ordinary pursuits so far as is possible, to take no part directly or indirectly in any hostilities, to abstain from communication with His Majesty's enemies, and to render obedience to such orders as may be promulgated.

5 All male inhabitants of European origin are required to take the oath of neutrality prescribed, at the garrison headquarters, and all firearms, ammunition, and war material in the possession or control of inhabitants are to be surrendered forthwith, as is also all public property of the late government.

6 Non-compliance with the terms of this Proclamation, and disobedience of such orders as from time to time may be promulgated, will be dealt with according to military law.

7 It is hereby notified that this Proclamation takes effect in the whole Island of New Britain and its dependencies from this date.

Given at Government House, Rabaul, this twelfth day of September 1914.

(Sgd) WILLIAM HOLMES

Brigadier Commanding

REPORT ON THE MILITARY OCCUPATION OF THE GERMAN NEW GUINEA POSSESSIONS

(COMMONWEALTH GOVERNMENT PRINTER, CANBERRA, 1922), pp 6–8

(ii) The terms of capitulation

[According to international law, a military occupant is not the sovereign of a territory, and thus lacks the power to alter its legal and administrative system, except to maintain and safeguard his army. This explains the retention of 'local laws and customs' during the occupation. The retention of some German officials and the decision to allow all planters to stay arose from practical considerations: without them the administration and the economy of the colony would have collapsed.]

WHEREAS the principal centres of Deutsch Neu Guinea have been occupied by an overwhelming force under the command of the said Colonel Holmes;

AND WHEREAS the said Acting Governor has no authority to surrender any portion of the German Possessions under his Administration, but in view of the said occupation by the said overwhelming force, the said Acting Governor is prepared to give an assurance that all military resistance to such occupation in Deutsch Neu Guinea shall cease forthwith.

NOW, the following terms and conditions are solemnly agreed upon between the said contracting parties:

(1) The name Deutsch Neu Guinea (German New Guinea) includes the whole of the German Possessions in the Pacific Ocean lately administered from Rabaul by the said Acting Governor on behalf of the Imperial German government, and the said possessions are hereafter referred to as 'The Colony'.

(2) All military resistance to the said Military Occupation of the Colony shall cease forthwith ...

(8) As the administration of the Colony during the military occupation will be conducted by the British Military Commander, all monies and properties of the late administration are to be handed over to the said Colonel Holmes, Brigadier Commanding.

(9) During the said military occupation the local laws and customs will remain in force so far as is consistent with the military situation.

In witness whereof the said contracting parties of this first and second parts have hereunto set their hands this 17th day of September, 1914, at Herbertshohe, New Britain.

E HABER,

WILLIAM HOLMES

Land policy of Australian military administration in New Guinea

The land policy of the military administration in German New Guinea, was underpinned by economic development considerations.[29] Colonial administrations were enjoined to

29 See CD Rowley, *The Australians in German New Guinea, 1914–21* (Melbourne University Press, Melbourne, 1958), pp 87–98.

submit to the Colonial Office Annual Reports which were designed to determine the success or failure of the administration of a colonial power.[30]

The effect of the military occupation was considered in *Gaya Nomgui v The Administration of The Territory of Papua and New Guinea (Re Lae Administration Land)*.[31]

V LAND LAW AND POLICY IN MANDATED NEW GUINEA 1921–45

The Peace Treaty of Versailles 1919 resulted in the confiscation of German assets by the Allied Forces, which assumed them as a 'sacred trust' under the League of Nations Mandate System. The Commonwealth of Australia took possession of German New Guinea and administered it in the name of the British government. The New Guinea Ordinance 1920 clothed the new arrangement with legality.

The restoration of civil administration

The restoration of civil administration was not an easy task. J Leyser[32] offers an account of the legal quagmire, which a new civilian administration had to grapple with.

Securing title to land

We have noted that security of tenure is a *sine qua non* policy of economic development based on the exploitation of land and its resources. In former German New Guinea, the German Administration pursued a land policy based on allodial ownership. In this respect the land policy there differed from the British policy in Papua. The consequences of German land policy for the new Australian civil administration was analysed by WA Lalor.[33] His summary of land ownership is reproduced below.

Summary of land ownership in the Territory of New Guinea as at 1942

(1) All land in the Territory was allodial.

(2) Native title to land was recognized by Ordinance but no system of registration of such land existed. Disputes as to ownership could be decided by the court for native affairs under the Native Administration Regulations 1924.

(3) Administration land comprised those lands listed in s 6 of the Laws Repeal and Adopting Ordinance 1921 together with purchases, leases and land proclaimed waste and vacant or compulsorily acquired under the Land Ordinance 1922–41.

30 For some statistics on land holding and a summary of land policy in German New Guinea, see *1922 Year Book of the Commonwealth of Australia* (Canberra, 1922, pp 891–983) (No 15).

31 [1974] PNGLR 349.

32 'Title to land in the trust territory of New Guinea', JG Starke (ed), *The Australian Year Book of International Law 1965* (Butterworths, Sydney, 1966), p 105.

33 'Land law and registration' in *Fashion of Law in New Guinea, op cit*, note 23, pp 137–45.

(4) Portion of such land had been registered under the Land Registration Ordinances 1924 and had indefeasible title.

(5) The Custodian of Expropriated Property had succeeded to the property of German private persons other than missions and had sold these properties. Many of them were under contract of sale as a term purchase.

(6) Portion of this land had been registered under the Land Registration Ordinance 1924.

(7) Enemy mission property had been revested in the missions by order of the Administrator.

(8) British national mission and private property remained in the owners.

(9) Comparatively little mission or private property other than Custodian appears to have been registered.

(10) Administration leases were held and these were registered under the Land Registration Ordinance.

(11) Granted applications for leases were held under the Land Ordinance and a Register maintained in the Lands Department.

Expropriation of alien enemy property

By virtue of the provision of Art 120 of the Treaty of Versailles all assets of the German authority in German New Guinea devolved on the Australian Administering Authority. The Expropriation Ordinance established the mechanism for dealing with such assets.

There were three categories of German property: (1) the property of nationals; (2) that of companies; and (3) that of religious missions. JA Spicer throws more light on the situation.[34]

German missions

German religious assets were differently treated by virtue of Art 438 of the Treaty of Versailles. This position was given local legal content by the German Missions Ordinance 1926. The preamble of the Ordinance provided the reason for differentiation thus:

> Whereas by Article four hundred and thirty-eight of the Treaty of Peace between the Allied and Associated Powers and Germany signed at Versailles on the twenty-eighth day of June, 1919, the Allied and Associated Powers agreed that, where Christian religious missions were being maintained by German societies or persons in territory belonging to them, or of which the government is entrusted to them in accordance with the said Treaty, the property which such missions or missionary societies possessed, including that of trading societies whose profits were devoted to the support of missions, should continue to be devoted to missionary purposes;

34 'The expropriation and sale of German plantations in the mandated territory' in FW Eggleston (ed), *The Australian Mandate for New Guinea* (MacMillan Publishers, Melbourne, 1928), p 35.

> And whereas by the said Article it was further agreed that in order to ensure the due execution of that undertaking the Allied and Associated governments would hand over such property to boards of trustees appointed by or approved by the governments and composed of persons holding the faith of the mission whose property is involved ...

Forging a uniform land policy

The Laws Repeal and Adopting Ordinance 1921–39 was passed to provide a coherent land policy throughout New Guinea. The difficulties inherent in the effort were exemplified by *Re Mortlock Island*,[35] *Re Ratavul Land*[36] and *Re Lae Administration*[37] cases.[38]

Protection of customary rights in land

In New Guinea the courts have consistently upheld the principle that the British Crown's assumption of sovereignty over the territory did not operate to extinguish indigenous land interests and rights, a legal position diametrically opposed to that of Australia with respect to the land interests and rights of Australia's indigenous inhabitants.

In *Gaya Nomgui and Others v The Administration of the Territory of Papua and New Guinea (Re Lae Administration Land)*,[39] Kelly J said:

> The legal effect of the existence of customary ownership by native groups in New Guinea is beyond doubt and the legislative provisions in force in that Territory lead to a different result from that reached by Blackburn J in the Supreme Court of the Northern Territory in *Milirrpum & Others v Nabalco Pty Ltd and Another* (1971) 17 FLR 141 which concerned claims to land on behalf of aboriginal tribesmen of the Gove Peninsula in Arnhem Land. Although his Honour found against the plaintiffs on the fundamental question of fact which arose he also dealt at length with the question of 'communal native title', that is, whether communal occupation of land by the aboriginal inhabitants of a territory acquired by the Crown is recognized as a legally enforceable right. There being no applicable statutory provision his Honour considered the position at common law and after an extensive review of authority at p 244 of his judgment he expressed his conclusion in these words: 'The question whether English law, *as applied to a settled colony*, included, or now includes, a rule that communal native title where proved to exist must be recognized, is one which can be answered only by an examination of what has happened in the laws of the various places where English law has been applied. I have examined carefully the laws of various jurisdictions which have been put before me in considerable detail by counsel in this case, and, as I have already shown, in my opinion no doctrine of communal native title has any place in any of them, except under express statutory provisions. I must inevitably therefore come to the conclusion that the doctrine does not form, and never has formed, part of the law of any part of Australia.'
>
> The position in New Guinea is otherwise. In the first place New Guinea was at the relevant time a mandated territory administered by the Commonwealth of Australia and the weight of authority is that it did not thereby become part of the Dominions of the Crown ...

---

35 [1971–72] P&NGLR 621, Central Court of the Territory of New Guinea.

36 See ss 68, 69 for the import of public purpose.

37 [1974] PNGLR 349.

38 For a more detailed discussion of the subject see Amankwah *et al*, *op cit*, note 1.

39 [1974] PNGLR 349.

In the statute law of New Guinea there are to be found specific provisions which require recognition of communal native title. For instance, there is s 9 of the Laws Repeal and Adopting Ordinance 1921–52 which remains in the form in which it was originally enacted, namely:

> Nothing in this Ordinance shall affect the right, title, estate or interest, vested, possessory or contingent, of any aboriginal native or tribe of aboriginal natives to any land within the Territory, whether such land has been proclaimed as a native reserve or not, or any customary user by aboriginal natives of market-places and landing-places, or any existing right, privilege or custom of aboriginal natives in relation to cultivation, barter, hunting and fishing.

Section 10 of that Ordinance provides that native customs and usages shall be permitted to continue in existence in so far as they are not repugnant to the general principles of humanity, while the Native Customs (Recognition) Ordinance 1963 although of more recent origin, requires this court to recognize and enforce native custom, part of which is of course a system of ownership of land by native custom. The Land Ordinance 1922–27, although less explicit, certainly appears to contemplate communal native title when it refers in s 8 to the purchase of land by the Administrator from native owners and again in s 16 which, subject to certain exceptions, forbids the occupation of land owned by natives by any person other than a native.

The consequence is that in the Territory of New Guinea customary ownership of land by native groups was and is recognized as a legally enforceable right.

To prevent the inhabitants from unwittingly disposing of their patrimony to unscrupulous land speculators, the Land Ordinance 1922–41 was passed. Sections 6–8 allowed alienation of customary land, however to the Administration only. Additionally, provision was made for the introduction of Torrens land registration into the territory by the passage of the Land Registration Ordinance 1924–39. Provision was made however, to prevent bringing under Torrens customary land.[40]

Questions

1. Consider the necessity of introducing Torrens into a culture in which literacy rate among the indigenous population is infinitesimal. Whose interest does the system serve?
2. Has a fusion of the German and English legal systems been really achieved in Papua New Guinea?
3. What benefit(s) accrued to Papua New Guinea from its tutelage under the League of Nations/United Nations? (See also Section VI, below.)

40 Sections 21–27.

VI LAND LAW AND POLICY IN PAPUA NEW GUINEA 1945–62

New Guinea came under the United Nations Trusteeship system after the inauguration of that body. The Papua and New Guinea Ordinance 1949 provided local content for the consequence of that arrangement.

The restoration of land registers

The devastation which World War II wrought on New Guinea included the destruction of land registers in the Rabaul Land Registry. This necessitated the reconstruction of the land registers. This was accomplished by the passage of the New Guinea Land Titles Registration Ordinance 1951 which established the necessary apparatus for this purpose. It has been held that land registers did not operate to revive customary title previously held in land duly registered.[41]

Customary land, security of title and economic and social development

The viability of the traditional land tenure system continued to receive Administration's attention. The panacea of the problem, it was thought was to formalise customary tenure by making provision for the registration of customary title. To this effect, the Native Land Registration Ordinance 1952 was passed.

One of the issues which arose in respect of native land registration was the effect of the decisions and findings (cf s 44, Land Titles Ordinance 1962, Native Land Registration Ordinance 1952 and s 76, Land Disputes Settlement Act No 25, 1975) of the Native Land Commission. The cases *Guba and Doriga v The Administration*,[42] *Re Havini*[43] and *Busin v Havini*[44] provide some rather interesting answers.

GUBA AND DORIGA v THE ADMINISTRATION
(1969) unreported judgment N548,
Supreme Court

> **CLARKSON J**: Counsel for the Tubumaga clan submitted that the Land Board had no standing because s 9 of the Land Ordinance 1911 under which it was purportedly appointed had been impliedly repealed by the Native Land Registration Ordinance 1952. Alternatively he stated the Land Board was neither a judicial body nor did it exercise judicial power, with the consequence that its decision could not be a judgment *in rem* nor could it give rise to an estoppel ...
>
> The argument for the implied repeal of s 9 of the Land Ordinance was founded on the proposition that jurisdiction which could formerly have been conferred on a Land Board was by the 1952 Ordinance conferred on the Native Land Commission and that to avoid the absurdity of permitting an unsuccessful applicant to go from one tribunal to the other the 1952 Ordinance should be read as impliedly repealing the power to appoint a Land Board

41 *The Custodian of Expropriated Property and Others v Tedep* (1964) 113 CLR 318.
42 (1973) P&NGLR 603; affirmed (1973) 130 CLR 353 HC.
43 (1959) unreported judgment N139, Native Land Appeal Court.
44 (1957) unreported judgment N102, Supreme Court.

under s 9 of the 1911 Ordinance. The decision of Gore J in *Busin v Havini* (1957) unreported judgment N102 was cited as supporting this conclusion.

In my view this submission is unsound. Firstly, it is by no means unusual for concurrent jurisdiction to be held by two different courts and if such a situation had existed here it would not necessarily have followed that there had been a repeal by implication. But in any event the two tribunals had quite different jurisdictions. As I have already indicated, the jurisdiction of Native Land Commission was concerned only with native land while the jurisdiction of the Land Board when appointed embraced the disputes as to ownership between the Administration and Papuans which were expressly referred to it. Even if some basis exists for arguing a *pro tanto* repeal by implication where the dispute before the Land Board was between natives concerning native land such was not the case here where one question was whether the land was native land ...

As to the possibility of an unsuccessful claimant doing what coincidentally the Tubumaga clan did here, namely going from one tribunal to another in search of a favourable decision, it is against this possibility that the doctrine of judicial estoppel operates.

[Application dismissed.]

VII LAND LAW AND POLICY IN PAPUA NEW GUINEA 1962–73

Alienated land

The Land Ordinance 1962 set the stage for land reform in Papua New Guinea by bringing under the State's jurisdiction all non-customary land. P Lalor[45] spells out in more detail the purpose, function and achievement of the legislation. He says:

> This Ordinance repeals the Land Ordinances of both Papua and New Guinea and introduces substantial change. It is an Ordinance applicable to both Territories and attempts to achieve a unity in land law for the separate Territories in the Administrative union.

Section 7 states that all land other than native land in the Territory is, subject to any estates, etc, the property of the Administration. The Administration is defined in the Ordinance Interpretation Ordinance as 'The Administration or Government of the Territory' and by s 6 to include in relation to land, in the Territory of Papua, the Crown. Previously ownership of land, where it existed, vested in the Crown in Papua and New Guinea, in the Commonwealth as Mandatory.

The effect of the section appears to be to transfer the radical title of the Crown to 'The Administration' in Papua and to create an artificial radical title to former German freeholds in New Guinea. For this latter a 'deemed' sub-section is introduced by which all estates in land are deemed to be held under the Administration.

45 P Lalor, 'Land law and registration' in BJ Brown (ed), *Fashion of Law in Papua and New Guinea, op cit*, note 23, pp 137, 152–53.

Sub-section 3 of s 7 states that nothing in the earlier sub-sections shall be construed to deprive the Crown, the Commonwealth, the government of a Commonwealth or the Administration of any estate, right, title or interest in the land. On the other hand, native customary rights in land are expressly excluded from being deemed to be held under the Administration. The result appears to be that the doctrine of tenure has been introduced in New Guinea in relation to land other than native land.

Acquisition of land by agreement continues generally the provisions of previous Ordinances. Provisions as to compulsory acquisition are consolidated and the Land Acquisition Ordinance 1952 is repealed.

The provisions as to waste and vacant land are not reproduced. Instead, by virtue of s 7, all land not native land is the property of the Administration. This changes the previous law of both Territories by which certain conditions were required to be fulfilled before land of which there appeared to be no owner could vest in the Crown or the Administration. Section 83(1) provides machinery whereby the Administrator by notice in the *Gazette* can declare that the land which appears to him not to be native land is, after three months, conclusively deemed not to be native land, unless claims in the land are lodged. In that case, the matter is referred to the Land Titles Commission for decision.

Division 4 is concerned with dealings by and with persons under a disability and certain limited owners. The intention appears to be to facilitate and put beyond doubt transactions in which a person seised of, or possessed of, or entitled to, land or having the management of land of a person under a legal disability, deals with the Administration. To date there have been no decisions of the courts regarding these sections.

Further provisions specifically relating to native land are included. A native is deemed always to have had power to dispose of native land according to native custom and the Land Titles Commission is empowered to appoint an agent who has wide powers to act on behalf of the native owners, on the acquisition of land by the Administration. The sections appear designed to ensure the acquisition of a valid title by the Administration and to relieve the Administration of any obligation to the vendors other than to pay over the monies due to the agent. The Administrator is empowered to declare any Administration land to be native land and may conclusively declare the owner of such land by native custom.

Power is given to the Administrator to grant leases of Administration land and the procedures, types and conditions of such leases are set out in detail. There is no 'conclusive evidence' clause as contained in the earlier Ordinances.

Unalienated land

Development in PNG between 1956–59 coupled with the revelation in Austrian House by representatives by Mr Paul Hasluck in April 1960, that the government of Australia considers the Australian Torrens type of registered title as the solution to PNG's agrarian problems,[46] three laws were passed in succession, namely: the Land Titles Commission Ordinance 1962, the Land Registration (Communally Owned Land) Ordinance 1962 and the Land (Tenure Conversion) Ordinance 1963 were passed. The Land Commission was

46 Hansard, *House of Representatives* (Australia) 1960, Vol 26, 1019.

to adjudicate on and determine customary titles considered appropriate for conversion to and registration as individual titles. Some years of operation of the legislations revealed several difficulties. To obviate those difficulties that a land tenure expert, Mr Rowton S Simpson, was invited to advise the government on the land issue.

(i) Registration of customary land

Following the submission of the *Report on Land Problems in PNG* (Port Moresby, 1971) four Land Bills were prepared for passage into law, namely: Customary Land Adjudication Bill, Land Control Bill, Registered Land Bill and Land Titles Commission Bill. Amankwah *et al* say:

> The Bills never became law due mainly to opposition to them from the people's representatives in parliament and the general public. The view generally expressed was that the people had not been consulted adequately on such grave and important national issue as 'agrarian reform'. That consultation took the form of the *Commission of Inquiry into Land Matters* (CILM) 1973. Simpson's work necessitated a visitation to Kenya by a group of PNG government officials to acquaint them with land reform measures in a Third World setting. From all indications, members of the group were quite impressed by what they witnessed in Kenya. They recommended on their return the adoption of Simpson's Land Bills fashioned after Kenyan legislations in similar circumstances.

(ii) Tenure conversion

To give substance to the policy of land reform spelt out in Hasluck's speech, a land tenure conversion program was embarked upon. The Land Title Commission was set up under the Land Title Commission Ordinance 1962–71 to administer the scheme. The Land Registration (Communally Owned Land) Ordinance 1963 was passed to enable the registration of land owned by communities and groups. The idea was to clothe customary interest in the garment if indefeasibility.[47] That legislation was buttressed by the Native Land Registration Ordinance 1962.

Finally, the Land (Tenure Conversion) Ordinance 1963[48] was passed to enable people to opt for the registration of their customary holdings.

Being an Ordinance **'Relating to the Conversion of the Tenure of Native Land into Individualized Tenure, and for other purposes'**, the Preamble set out the reason and purpose of the Ordinance. It read in part:

> WHEREAS it is generally considered that a most efficacious method of promoting the agricultural development of a country and the economic well being of its people and especially of its agricultural population lies in the provision of a method whereby guaranteed individual titles to land may be given to the owners thereof;
>
> AND WHEREAS it is the fundamental policy of the government of the Commonwealth of Australia and the Administration of the Territory of Papua and New Guinea that the interests of the native peoples of the Territory in land held in accordance with native custom should be guaranteed and protected, and that, subject to that fundamental policy, there

47 T Bredmeyer, 'The registration of customary land in Papua New Guinea' (1975) 3 MLJ 267.

48 No 15 of 1964. See also DJ Whalan, 'Torrens and tropic tenure – a non-resident's non-expert view', UPNG Third Waigani Seminar (1969), pp 4–16.

should be provision whereby those peoples may acquire such guaranteed individual titles to that land;

AND WHEREAS it is also considered that it is essential that the rights of the peoples of the Territory of Papua and New Guinea to land held in accordance with native custom should, subject to the laws of the Territory, continue to be guaranteed to them, save insofar as they freely and in accordance with the law desire to exchange those rights for the benefits of such guaranteed individual titles;

AND WHEREAS it is further considered that such rights to land held in accordance with native custom and the right freely and in accordance with law to exchange such rights for guaranteed individual titles as aforesaid can best be promoted and safeguarded by an independent judicial tribunal charged with the duty of ensuring that those rights are so promoted and safeguarded and that any persons who might otherwise be injuriously affected are given adequate and proper recompense or other compensation ....

The Land (Tenure Conversion) Ordinance 1963 was amended by the Land (Tenure Conversion) Amendment Ordinance 1967 by the addition of a new section – s 26A – which provided as follows:

26A(1) In the case of any land which is the subject of a limitation referred to in paragraph (b) of section 26 of this Ordinance and which the registered proprietor desires to deal with in a manner contrary to that limitation or in a manner or with an intent which is rendered wholly or partly ineffective by reason of that limitation, if –

(a) where the proposed dealing consists of or includes a transfer of the fee simple in the land, the Minister; or

(b) in any other case, the Administrator in Council, is satisfied after due inquiry that the proposed dealing will not adversely effect the interests of the registered proprietor (and, where the interests of a native kinship group, native descent group or native local group or community are or are likely to be affected, the interests of that group or community), the Minister or the Administrator in Council (as the case may be) may direct the Registrar of Titles to cancel the registration of the limitation and Registrar shall act accordingly.

(2) The provisions of sub-section (1) of this section apply to and in respect of land registered in pursuance of this Ordinance whether before or after the date of commencement of the Land (Tenure Conversion) Ordinance 1967.[49]

It has been held in *In the Land and Goods of Doa Minch* (also known as *Doa Mints*)[50] that registration of customary land does not necessarily remove such interest from the regime of customary law. Some academics disagree with the decision in *Doa Minch*.[51]

The *Simpson Report*[52] triggered off the establishment of the *Commission of Inquiry into Land Matters*.

49 T Bredmeyer explains the mechanism of the legislation: 'The registration of customary land in Papua New Guinea', *op cit*, note 47.

50 (1973) P&NGLR 558 (Supreme Court of Papua New Guinea).

51 See FM Kassam, 'Laws of succession in Papua New Guinea: some reflections' (1974) 2 MLJ 5, 25–32 and C Haynes, 'Succession to land in Papua New Guinea: choice of law' (1981) 9 MLJ 74, 91–96.

52 SR Simpson, 'Land problems in Papua New Guinea' in *Land Tenure and Economic Development: Problems and Policies in Papua New Guinea and Kenya* (ANU, Canberra) New Guinea Research Bulletin, No 40 (1971) pp 3–36; House of Assembly Debates – Land Registration. Official Statement by the Director of Lands, Surveys and Mines – Mr DS Grove, MHA House of Assembly (12 March [contd]

(iii) Is customary tenure inimical to economic development?

The argument that customary land tenure is not conducive to economic development can be rebutted from different perspectives – factual, sociologic, philosophic[53] and even economic.[54] We extract below the economic rebuttal.

IRVING GERSHENBERG: 'CUSTOMARY LAND TENURE AS A CONSTRAINT ON AGRICULTURAL DEVELOPMENT: A RE-EVALUATION' (1971) EAST AFRICA JOURNAL OF RURAL DEVELOPMENT, pp 51–61

Credit and tenure arrangements

Much of the criticism regarding customary land law has been directed towards the inability, under customary arrangements, to use land as a security to obtain loans. The shortage or unavailability of credit has often been noted as constituting one of the most important obstacles to agricultural development and this credit constraint has, as noted above, been attributed to a lack of freehold tenure. This criticism can be discussed at two levels, one being the validity of the assertion that a lack of credit has constituted a serious obstacle to African agricultural progress and the other being the contention that customary land tenure has operated as an obstacle to the flow of credit to the agricultural sector.

In discussing the role of credit in African agriculture, de Wilde writes that 'There are instances where liberal credit has obviously acted as a disincentive, an invitation or opportunity to the farmer to work less hard and to save less'. He goes on to note that:

> It is surprising how much development has taken place in tropical Africa with comparatively little or no credit ... In Kenya the phenomenal development of arabica planting by smallholders during the fifties was financed almost entirely from the farmer's own resources; and although government credit has been available for the establishment of smallholder tea in more recent years, there is little doubt that tea planting could have made rapid progress even in the absence of government credit for plant material ... In Nyeri District ... coffee planting were virtually all self-financed, and coffee profits had in turn financed development of dairying. Similarly, in Elgeyo-Marakwet we encountered quite a few farmers in the uplands who had first earned some money from growing potatoes, had used this to start the cultivation of pyrethrum, and had finally purchased dairy cattle with their pyrethrum profits ... In West Africa the expansion of such tree crops as robusta coffee and cocoa has not been significantly assisted by credit.

De Wilde concludes his analysis with the statement that 'Africans' disposition to save has often been under-estimated'. This suggests that given markets for cash crops, agricultural development in Africa will not long be hindered by any lack of adequate credit.

The other part of this criticism, relating to the inverse relationship between customary tenure and the availability of agricultural credit, is based on the observation that profit-making organizations require some form of security before they make advances and that farmers who do not have freehold title to their land cannot pledge their land as security. In fact, even where freehold title has been established, the anticipated flow of credit to agriculture has still failed to take place. In Kenya, for example, it was hoped that once title

52 [contd] 1970). DS Grove, 'Land use and land tenure – the new legislation' in MW Ward (ed), *Change and Development in Rural Melanesia* (Fifth Waigani Seminar, Port Moresby, 1972), pp 67, 73 *et seq*.

53 See for example AD Ward, 'Agrarian revolution: handle with care' (1972) 6(1) New Guinea 25.

54 I Gershenberg, 'Customary land tenure as a constraint on agricultural development: a re-evaluation' (1971) East Africa Journal of Rural Development, pp 51–61.

to the land has been issued, commercial banks would become important sources of credit, land having been made mortgageable. Such credit, at least in the volume anticipated, has not been forthcoming. Oluwasanmi states that 'lending institutions, particularly commercial banks, are always reluctant even where there is clear title to land to make long term loans ... Land cannot be easily turned into cash. Even in countries where the farmers have clear titles to their land the illiquid nature of landed assets makes lending agencies cautious in mortgage financing'.

The lack of private interest in extending credit to African farmers has suggested to many African agriculturalists the need to develop lending institutions that would work through co-operatives. There is no reason to think that freehold titles to the land will be required in such a scheme. The primary difficulty for the creditor in extending loans involves the certainty of repayment. Credit can, therefore, best be extended to the co-operative (marketing and/or farming) in which arrangements exist for all of the members to be responsible for the repayment of a loan. This would ensure the use of any loan for its indicated purpose and that individuals receiving such loans would be helped and pressured to insure their repayment. Such a scheme is currently being implemented in Nigeria. In Western Nigeria, the Communal Land Rights (Vesting in Trustees) Law allows land holding communities to obtain juristic personality and, therefore, to be held responsible as a corporate aggregate for defaulting debts.

Obviously there can be no winners in the debate on customary tenure, whether it is a hindrance to economic development or promotes it. In conclusion, we examine the prospects for the future of customary tenure. The material which follows provides some food for thought.

KG KRISHNA, 'SMALLHOLDER AGRICULTURE IN AFRICA: CONSTRAINTS AND POTENTIALS' (1977) 432 ANNALS, pp 12–22

Abstract: Peasant farming is the backbone of the African rural economy. In the predominantly agrarian societies of Africa, smallholder farming plays a major role in producing food for both rural and urban populations and in providing incomes, employment, and export earnings. However, these farmers have received a disproportionately small amount of available developmental resources. Few people in Africa live in wholly subsistence economies. Peasant farmers are steadily increasing their share of marketed output and, in the process have belied the myth that rural societies are stagnant. Extending effective support to widely dispersed farming populations requires financial and manpower resources on a scale which few African countries can afford. Few technical packages exist, extension services are scanty, and marketing and credit services are deficient. These are formidable problems the resolution of which will take much time, effort, and resources. But the potential for improvement is so considerable, and the social implications so immense, the national agricultural policies should articulate the needs of smallholders far better than they have so far. Given proven and comprehensible technical packages and advice, and attractive prices for their products, peasant farmers have shown a capacity to increase their contribution to the economy in a quick and efficient manner.

Smallholder or peasant farming is the backbone of the African rural economy. It concerns the manner in which about 280 million people in sub-Saharan rural Africa, 50–55 million families, earn their living from year to year. The overwhelming majority of these people (about 85–90% of the total population of this area) are peasant farmers. Their activities – crop production and livestock herding – play a major role in feeding the rural and urban populations, acting as the main source of employment and earnings, and providing the principal basis of exports and often of government revenues as well. Because of the quiet and unobtrusive way in which these activities take place from year to year, the role of peasant farmers is seldom the focus of much attention and their activities are more or less taken for granted. What is even less apparent is that the very significant contribution of peasant farmers to the economy often takes place within a framework of primitive techniques, low levels of productivity, and much uncertainty concerning production levels attained from one crop season to the other. More than anything else, this situation reflects the fact that the majority of the rural population has tended to receive only a meagre share of the resources available for development and that it has largely been ignored in the plans and programs which are periodically formulated in their capitals.

Contrary to popular belief, there are no wholly subsistence economies in Africa in the sense of people leading self-contained lives. In fact, living in a wholly subsistence economy has, for many years, been neither feasible nor practical in most countries since the breakdown of complete isolation and the steadily growing requirement to pay taxes. Having been forced initially to participate in the market economy at least to a small extent, peasant farmers have actively sought to enlarge their role both as consumers and producers, often encountering much frustration in the latter role. In fact, given the difficulties in participating actively in producing for the market, what is surprising is the extent of progress already achieved in this regard. In the few situations where governments actively sought to encourage smallholder production – either or political or socio-economic reasons – through a combination of incentives and support services, there has been an amazing degree of responsiveness from the latter, thereby belying the myth that rural societies are stagnant and fatalistic or devoid of ambition and initiative. It has been a hard struggle, however, since there continues to be much skepticism, and some ignorance, among governmental authorities with regard to the potential role of smallholder agriculture.

PAST POLICIES

The colonial period

Past policies with regard to smallholder agriculture have tended to be influenced by the number of considerations depending on whether they were formulated within the framework of colonial governments or the independent governments which succeeded them. During the colonial period, policies tended to vary as between situations where there was an active attempt to introduce expatriate capital and enterprise to develop the economies and those where the focus was on promoting market-oriented production, but strictly within the framework of traditional peasant agriculture. Policies varied further depending on whether overseas settler-farmers were to be encouraged and assisted in developing modern agriculture or whether overseas initiative would be limited to plantation companies. Where a settler element was involved, as in the Highlands of Kenya, not only did it entail concessions and privileges to settlers out of proportion to their number, but it became apparent before long that there was a clear dichotomy between the role envisaged for the settlers and the potential role of traditional peasant agriculture.

This dichotomy is most vividly brought out in the experience of Kenya which had a, active and influential settler community that, despite its small numbers, succeeded within a relatively short period in becoming the major source of market-oriented production, whether for exports or for the domestic market. During the period 1950–60 for example, the large-farm sector, comprised of settler-farmers and the plantation companies, accounted for as much as 90% of the total marketed output. Not only were traditional farmers hopelessly ill-equipped to share in producing for the growing market, but also there were no government policies at the time which were consciously aimed at enlarging opportunities for the traditional sector comprised of millions of African peasant farmers. On the contrary, where some smallholders displayed initiative in producing cash crops – notably tea and coffee – which had been monopolized by settler-farmers, the latter put enough pressure on the government to seek a restriction of prohibition on such production, on the ground that the products of peasant farmers could not satisfy and maintain quality standards of the export and, on occasions, even the domestic market. The imposition of such restrictions seriously jeopardized and delayed the development of smallholder production. It was not until the late 1950s that this policy was modified and an attempt was made to promote a policy for the advancement of African smallholders in cash crop production. This policy, which was elaborated in the 'Plan for the Advancement of Africans in Cash Farming' (Swynnerton Plan), began in and became a widely known success story. The plan cleared the way for significant smallholder – African – participation in market-oriented production. The share of such production which was as low as 10% in 1950 rose to about 30% in 1962, the last year before the independence of Kenya.

In some African countries where there was no expatriate settler-farmer element, overseas-based plantation companies were quite prominent. These companies, which were drawn principally from the former metropolitan power – France, Belgium, United Kingdom – created the first modernized agricultural sectors in these countries. Their production was based on a system of obtaining low-cost land from the governments, hiring low cost labour which ostensibly was underemployed, and combining these with foreign investment and modern technology to produce crops principally, but not exclusively, for the export market. While these companies dominated the production of certain crops – rubber, tea, coffee, and palm oil – they were not generally averse to sharing production with smallholder farmers whom they, in fact, encouraged and assisted on occasions. Their role in exemplifying market-oriented production was an important factor in stimulating smallholder participation in the market economy.

Post-independence period

Since attaining independence, many African governments have endeavoured to encourage and assist large-scale participation by their nationals in all types of economic activity. As the largest sector of most African economies, agriculture has naturally been the focus of much attention and has received a substantial allocation of finance and manpower. The thrust of government policies has been twofold. In the first place, where African economies had for many year been dominated by foreign entrepreneurs, there was an understandable desire to Africanize or nationalize various enterprises as an initial step in promoting domestic enterprise. Since agriculture was in most cases – except where expatriate settler-farmers or overseas plantation companies played an important role – in the hands of native African farmers, the need here was not so much nationalization as giving an impetus to the sector so that it would begin to undergo a transformation with beneficial effects on yields and output. This was done through a combination of measures including improved and expanded extension, marketing and credit, and a better determination and improved deliver of suitable inputs. An important, although not spectacular, transformation has been achieved in the process.

Policies with regard to agricultural transformation or modernization have varied a lot among African countries. Three main types of policies may be identified in this regard. In the first place, there were those which were directed principally toward expanding the range and output of crops, but which did not reveal much preoccupation either with issues of a nationalistic nature or with considerations of equity. The main consideration behind this policy appears to have been to attain rapid progress in self-sufficiency in food or the expansion and diversification of export crops. Whether the enterprise which engineered progress was local or foreign or whether the government was actively involved or not was irrelevant for this policy.

The second policy emphasizes the importance of assigning a growing role to nationals but did not exclude a continuing role for foreign enterprise, particularly if it already existed and had performed an important role. The objective appears to have been the creation of conditions under which the participation of nationals would be phased in smoothly and in an orderly fashion, while the role of non-nationals would be phased out in an equally smooth, non-disruptive manner. In both the above cases, there was no particular emphasis on expanding the role of smallholders, but only on helping them in whatever way was found feasible to participate in the market economy.

The third policy clearly aimed at the earliest possible assumption by nationals of responsibility for both food and cash crop production on the clear further assumption that large companies, large individual entrepreneurs, absentee landlords, and others who were not directly involved in agricultural activities would be speedily replaced by peasant farmers who would be the government's principal target groups.

It is perhaps premature to determine which among the three policies noted above has been the most or least successful. Moreover, any determination which is based on physical measures of progress may not stand the test of social factors, particularly the aspects relating to equity and income distribution. It is difficult to dispute the claim of the Ivory Coast that it has created the basis of an efficient agricultural system or of Kenya and Malawi that they have speedily opened up opportunities for African participation in production directed both to the domestic and export markets. It is equally difficult to prove that, despite their declared concern for smallholders, Tanzania or Somalia have really improved their lot. But these are short-term perspectives, and the experiences of the countries to date cannot be regarded as conclusive proof that any given policy has been particularly successful in raising levels of productivity and maximizing opportunities for raising living standards of large numbers of people.

Large-scale farming after independence

While the existence of large-scale farming in the pre-independence period of some African countries can be seen in retrospect in the context of expatriate companies or individual farmers, there is little rational explanation for its continuation – particularly of individual large-scale farming – in the post-independence period. Typically, many of these post-independence large farmers have been drawn from the ranks of government officials, professional politicians, and senior executives from private or parastatal organizations. Few, if any, have any legitimate claims to own land. The motivation is one of social prestige and few have demonstrated their capability in farming. And yet, because of their influential position, they have managed to obtain for themselves a disproportionate share of the available resources, particularly credit and the agricultural services. However, because of their lack of direct involvement in agricultural operations (often resulting from their being absentee landlords), the productivity of land has suffered and has resulted in substantial economic waste, which is indefensible particularly in situations where the growing pressure of population on the soil has caused land hunger, shrinking opportunities in rural areas, and consequent exodus to the towns and cities.

The case for and against large-scale farming

In recent years, the case for and against large-scale farming has again become the subject of vigorous debate, although it should be recognized in the African context that nowhere is large-scale farming the dominant mode of agriculture at present, nor is it likely to become dominant in the foreseeable future. Nevertheless, although large-scale farming was either a straightforward adoption of an alien-inspired system which prevailed prior to independence or the result of the pre-eminent social and political position of the privileged few, some claims have been advanced in its favour. Among these are: (1) the responsiveness of large-scale farming to market opportunities; (2) its ability to keep up with, and take advantage of, improvements in farming technology; (3) the usual claims relating to economies of scale; (4) its ability to withstand fluctuations in prices, particularly of items destined for export markets; and (5) its ability to provide leadership to smaller scale producers.

However, barring the role of large international companies, there is little evidence that large-scale private or individual farming has, in fact, met the above criteria or that it has at least a potentially critical role to play. On the contrary, and again excluding plantations companies, there is evidence that large-scale farming is wasteful in terms of capital investment and managerial skills, that because of its frequent dependence on mechanized farming it promotes a pattern of development which conflicts with the prevailing resource endowment – particularly the availability of labour – and that it acts as a drain often on scarce foreign exchange resources available to the governments. Each of these factors is of vital significance for many African countries in view of the acute scarcity of precisely those items which large-scale farming demands in substantial quantities. Moreover, the development of farming which depends on varying degrees of mechanization would, if encouraged and actively assisted, hamper the growth of rural employment, thereby causing an urban drift. It makes demands on scarce capital and even scarcer foreign exchange and adds to the burden of growing recurrent expenditures, much of it in foreign exchange, for imports of spares, fuel, and technical services. The case for large-scale mechanized farming, which was already weak prior to the steep increase in fuel prices, has since become weaker still. Its continued encouragement would, therefore, be contrary to the overall economic interests of many African economies unless its advantages could be established clearly and conclusively.

Past policy towards smallholder farming

Despite the many disadvantages of large-scale farming and its unsuitability to the agro-social environment of Africa, this sector has continued to receive much encouragement, often at the cost of small farming. It is well known that when the production of crops is being undertaken in the large-scale farming sector this very fact often militates against these crops being grown by smallholders on grounds such as scale economies or sophisticated management. But the point here is not that large-scale farming has received too much attention, but that small farming has perhaps received too little. Given the fact that small farming is by far the dominant mode of farming in Africa and, hence, it is obviously important to improve its overall performance, why do agricultural policies in many countries fail to reflect an adequate concern for smallholders? And again, assuming that there is no lack of desire on the part of governments to assist smallholders, are there any major and indeed insuperable problems in assisting them? Has it been established beyond doubt that smallholders either cannot produce certain crops at all or only produce them at such high cost that it cannot be justified in terms of its benefits? And finally, has the actual performance of smallholder agriculture – with or without assistance from the governments – been such that only negative conclusions can be drawn from it, or are there cases where it has proved to be sufficiently imaginative and adaptable as to record significant achievements? These are important questions which should have an important bearing on the scope and thrust of future policies with regard to smallholder farming in the years to come.

Smallholder agriculture: some fallacies

Lack of initiative

Among the most persistent fallacies pertaining to smallholder farming is the one that, by and large, these people are unwilling and often unable to take advantage of new technical packages, agricultural services, and innovation generally. Apart from the fact that this is without foundation, it has in it the dangerous implication – often evidenced in government policies – that assistance provided to small farmers has justification more socially and politically than strictly economically, and hence that it represents only a desirable transfer from the more to the less privileged classes. It also assumes that small farming cannot be depended upon in the realization of objectives such as greater food self-sufficiency and expansion and diversification of agricultural exports and, by implication, that large-scale farming constitutes the main element not only of stability in agriculture, but also of its orderly growth.

Although, as noted above, much of the better publicized and documented modernization and growth of African agriculture has taken place in the organized, large-scale sector, including the private plantations, there is much (relatively much more in overall terms) that has taken place in the smallholder sector. One need only recall the role of peasant farmers who produce cocoa in Nigeria and Ghana, coffee and cotton in Uganda, and tobacco and cotton in Tanzania – just a few of the dozens of examples which may be drawn from all over Africa – to demonstrate how well and how much these people have responded to opportunities provided to them. It is to be noted, however, widespread participation by smallholders generally occurred in situations where either the governments felt, for political or socio-economic reasons, that the activities concerned should be spearheaded by small farmers or there was no initiative on the part of individual large farmers – either expatriate or local – to undertake these activities. The absence of large farmers was a significant factor insofar as the governments were not only not distracted by the belief that quick increases in production could be accomplished by encouraging large farmers or by pressures emanating from them, but also geared their policies towards assisting the smallholders in whatever way they could. The result was that smallholders responded very well to the opportunities which became available to them. In the process, production for the market was expanded, cash incomes grew, the domestic economies as a whole were strengthened, and government revenues became more firmly based.

There were, however, other situations where smallholder participation in production for the market had been artificially held back for various reasons, the principal reason being the pressure of large growers, including plantation companies, who did not relish the prospect of opening the floodgates of competition from peasant farmers. The example which most vividly brings home this point is smallholder tea production in Kenya. It was not until the mid-1950s that the Kenya government, with financial and technical assistance from the British government, established a scheme for enabling smallholders to cultivate tea. From small beginnings the scheme expanded rapidly, so that by 1963, when the country became independent, smallholder tea was already well established. Since then there has been considerable progress with the result that today over 100,000 peasant farmers grow tea, each with an average of less than one acre of tea. The scheme which is being implemented by the Kenya Tea Development Authority has been a major source of cash earnings for participants and has brought about a number of supplementary benefits, including a significant contribution to export earnings and some wage employment. The quality of *smallholder* tea compares favourably with that of the estates. In retrospect, there is no doubt that, in the absence of a special effort and appropriate institutional arrangements, smallholders would not have made a successful entry into tea cultivation. Given the needed encouragement, smallholders demonstrated both their responsiveness to economic opportunity and their willingness to allocate their land and labour to a new and untried activity.

High cost of servicing small farmers

It is often claimed that it is difficult to assist large numbers of smallholders because of their widely scattered location, limited numbers of government personnel, lack of suitable institutions, poor governmental organization, and the shortage of funds. These are, of course, real problems, but they are by no means overwhelming. The danger is that these problems are often used as an excuse for the rather limited efforts to assist the rural population in breaking away from there isolation and participating in the market economy, with the result that the situation is perpetuated. None of the problems noted above is insoluble in the long run if there is a firm commitment on the part of governments and remedial measures are being taken. The delay in assisting smallholders often stems not from a lack of the answers to the problems in this regard, but from the elaborate solutions worked out which, in the end, exceed both the financial and manpower resources available to governments.

A further factor which often limits the efforts of governments with regard to smallholder farming is the feeling that programs designed to assist them may not be cost effective, particularly by comparison with large-scale farming. While this may be true in some cases, failure to assist those who may now be difficult and expensive to serve would result in their always being less cost effective and hence possibly never being worthy of support. In that event, two situations could result. The first is that support to small farming may be motivated purely by political considerations, for example, by selecting an area which happens to be the constituency of an influential politician. The second is that, when schemes designed to assist smallholders are formulated, they may tend to be so overdesigned to make them foolproof that benefits accrue to only a small number of people. Some of the successful smallholder schemes are characterized by their rather limited impact in terms of the number of beneficiaries. While the success of these projects is no doubt commendable, it also serves as a reminder of the task yet to be under taken in assisting those who have still not enjoyed the fruits of development.

The spill-over effect

The argument is sometimes advanced that the interest of smallholders is better served not by explicitly recognizing them as a target group, but by enabling them to benefit indirectly from schemes directed at those – mainly large-scale farmers – able and willing to take advantage of new opportunities. It is claimed that, as the latter break new ground, take risks, and open up markets, some opportunities will accrue to smallholders who could then be introduced into market-oriented production in a manner which minimizes risks. There are two problems with this reasoning. The first is that it implies that small farmers would be unable to make any headway except under the protective cover of the government. The second is that it makes them dependent on a spill-over effect, which may not materialize for a long time and sometimes never at all. Any assumption either that a spill-over effect would automatically occur or that its impact would be sufficient when it materialized is over-simplistic and often unrealistic.

Small farming – some real constraints

While the case for maximizing assistance to smallholder farming is both strong and urgent in all African countries, it is also true that much patient effort is required to prepare the ground well for this assistance to both maximize its impact and make it a steady and orderly process. What is needed is not a single dramatic gesture, but a series of modest and well considered initiatives which reflect a long term commitment on the part of authorities and which also recognize that there could well be initial set-backs. There is not doubt that programs aimed at providing massive assistance to smallholder agriculture face some real constraints. Some of these are examined below.

Technical packages

Perhaps the most important type of assistance to smallholders, but often not recognized as such, is the offer of technical packages which actually work under the agronomic and sociological conditions which the farmer confronts. It is both uneconomical and counter productive to ask the farmer to use seed, fertilizers, or insecticides if these have not been previously tested. The small farmer cannot afford to let himself be used as a guinea pig. If what is offered to farmers fails to work, it will create a mistrust on their part and will seriously jeopardize programs intended to help them. It is most important, therefore, that the combination of inputs and agronomic practices which are recommended to him are proven in the specific areas where they are to be introduced, that the small farmers both comprehend the advantages of using them and specifically agree to do so, and that there is a prompt follow-up which will ensure that the farmers could obtain guidance and assistance when needed. It is particularly important that the emphasis should be on the improvement of what already exists rather than on the introduction of systems, inputs, and techniques which are wholly alien to the farmers. In any program, the fact should not be lost sight of that the land and labour available to smallholders is limited, that food production for their own needs constitutes an important claimant on land and labour, that most smallholders are without any kind of cushion which will enable them to take risks, and hence, that the groundwork be properly prepared before they are ushered into competitive production for the market.

Delivery systems

The second major constraint facing smallholder production in Africa is the absence of the existence only in a rudimentary form of systems to deliver support services for agriculture. For example, the benefits from the promotion of modern inputs in smallholder agriculture would be severely constrained if extension services are deficient. Moreover, the recommended inputs should be available at the right time and locations in order to foster a sustained interest in their use by smallholders. Similarly, the creation of efficient marketing is critical to ensure the prompt handling of marketable surpluses produced by farmers. There is nothing more damaging to the morale of small farmers than the failure on the part of authorities to ensure an efficient disposal of production increases. The provision of credit is the third vital link, extension and marketing being the other, in the process of rural transformation, and its absence seriously inhibits the participation of smallholders in market-oriented production. The improvement of the delivery system is, therefore, vital for the success of smallholder farming.

Government policies

The advancement of smallholder production is often handicapped either by the absence of government policies supportive of it or the existence of some policies which clearly militate against it. The most glaring example of the latter is the policy still pursued in many African countries with regard to the pricing of agricultural commodities, particularly food. In general, governments have tried to keep producer prices for food as low as possible, principally in order to safeguard urban consumers, who tend to be better organized and informed and hence carry more political weight. However, by pursuing a policy of paying low prices for rural products but, at the same time, not protecting the rural population against a steady increase in the prices of urban products, including those imported from abroad, governments are causing a deterioration in the terms of trade for the rural areas. It is becoming increasingly clear that small farmers not only resent this, but simply cannot afford to continue to participate in an exchange which is heavily weighted against them. The best evidence of this is the growing crisis in many countries over food supplies caused, among other factors, by the farmers' unwillingness either to produce marketable surpluses at prevailing official prices or to deliver surpluses to official agencies a these prices.

Accessibility of small farmers

Any major program which aims to assist peasant farmers should in the first place, be able to reach the intended groups effectively. This is largely but not exclusively a function of transport and communications. In many African countries, a significant proportion of the rural population simply cannot be reached through the existing transport links. Even routine administrative links are weak and undependable. Hence, even where a commitment to support rural development programs exists, progress is limited since there is often a need to start from scratch. In the circumstances, rural roads, farmer training centres, and generally a more effective governmental presence should all be regarded as essential parts of agricultural development programs

Widely scattered peasant populations seriously restrict the ability of governments to provide effective assistance not only in fields such as health and education, but even for agriculture. It is the concern that the existing situation may forever prevent governmental assistance to the isolated and less privileged rural people that prompted the Tanzania government to regroup its rural population into Ujamaa villages. The actual implementation of the Ujamaa program has not been without snags – including wrong siting of villages with regard to soil types and water and the coercive measures employed by overenthusiastic officials – but it is highly probable that the basic objectives would prove to be sound and wholly defensible in the long run.

Smallholder agriculture – the future

Despite the very many problems and constraints inherent in smallholder agriculture, it is indisputable that it should receive far more attention and specific supportive measures than in the past. The case for this is not only social and political but, equally important, economic. Smallholder agriculture is so basic to the economies of African countries that failure to raise its productivity would constitute a grave deficiency in the resource allocation process. While the support to smallholder agriculture is justified on grounds of equity, this is not the only or even the main justification. There is a strong economic justification for this assistance which is to be seen in its appropriateness to the pattern of resource endowment in most African countries.

A major review of the policies toward smallholder agriculture is needed in most African countries. The main theme of such a policy should regard peasant farmers as the major source of production and the major object of support. In the long run, the efficient development of this type of farming would also tend to be the most economically advantageous one.

Experience with assisting smallholders has been limited, but it has proved encouraging. Peasant farmers have displayed initiative and responded well to opportunities which came their way. Active support to these people constitutes not only the most efficient method of accomplishing broad-based progress, but also the best hope of ensuring social and political stability in most African countries.

There are views in official circles in developing nations plagued presumably by the spectra of customary tenure that a way out of the conundrum is for government to bring as much land as possible under State jurisdiction. In many ways, this can be achieved through compulsory acquisition of land.[55] In PNG a new strategy was employed. The Evidence (Land Titles) Ordinance 1969[56] formulated a set of presumptions in favour of Administration land and then threw on persons with claims adverse to the government's presumed title or right to the land the onus to rebut those presumptions, an insurmountable obstacle for most claimants.[57]

Accelerated development often result in the emergence of the phenomenon of speculation in land. The Land (Underdeveloped Freeholds) Ordinance 1970[58] was passed to ensure that land speculation was kept under control. It empowered government to take away land not put to development purposes by the owner within a specified period and give it to those who were ready willing and able to do so. The preamble to the legislation summed that policy up rather aptly:

> To encourage the better development, in the public interest, of freehold. Those who cannot develop their land should yield it to those who can.

Questions

1 Critically examine the premise that customary land tenure is a constraint on economic development.

2 Hasluck said, 'customary tenures were suitable for subsistence agriculture ... But they are not suitable for any system of agriculture which results in substantial and permanent improvements to the land' (see p 38). And the Preamble to the Land (Tenure Conversion) Ordinance 1963 (No 15, 1964) says 'It is generally considered that a most efficacious method of promoting the agricultural development of a country and the economic well being of its people and especially of its agricultural population lies in the provision of a method whereby guaranteed individual titles to land may be given to the owners thereof'. Is it correct to assert that the problem lies in the system rather than the human operators? Does individualisation of tenure guarantee the millennium of economic prosperity and well being?

3 Discuss the rationale behind s 9(2) of the Land (Tenure Conversion) Ordinance 1963 which provides: 'The commission shall not make a conversion order over land which should, in order to meet the need for the production of food for their own consumption by some or all of the owners of the land, remain native land.'

4 Could tenure conversion proceed if one person who has a minor interest in the land objects to the conversion application? Would your answer be different if the applicant agrees to pay adequate compensation for the abolition or reduction of that customary interest?

---

55 HA Amankwah, 'Eminent domain and land use control in West Africa and Papua New Guinea: the political and social implications' (1988) 16 MLJ 52.

56 No 59 of 1969.

57 This legislation however was repealed by the National Land Registration Act 1977 s 55. See also JF Hookey, 'Customary title and the State', Third Waigani Seminar (Port Moresby, 1969).

58 No 13 of 1970.

5 If as a result of of a conversion order a customary interest is abolished or reduced, must compensation be paid to the people concerned?

6 What is fragmentation? How did the Land (Tenure Conversion) Ordinance 1963 seek to prevent fragmentation of land by transactions? By devolution?

7 Explain the meaning of s 26(1)(a)(i) of the Land (Tenure Conversion) Ordinance 1963.

8 What changes to the Land (Tenure Conversion) Ordinance 1963 were effected by the Land (Tenure Conversion) Act 1967?

NATIONHOOD AND DEVELOPMENT POLITICS: TOWARDS LAND USE MAXIMIZATION

I INTRODUCTION

PNG national leaders understood the importance of putting on an even keel the land issue in the country as independence approached. Mugambwa highlights the dilemma, which the country faced in this regard. He says:[1]

> At the time of Papua New Guinea's self-government in 1972, the land dispute issue had reached its climax. Already there were reports of widespread protests and violence in some regions. A solution had to be found to arrest a potentially violent situation. Nationalist politicians had helped to inflame the issue in their campaign for independence by calling for the restoration of all alienated land 'stolen' from its traditional owners. (JS Fingleton, 'Land policy in Papua New Guinea' in Weisbrot *et al* (ed), *Law and Social Change in Papua New Guinea* (Butterworths, Sydney, 1982), p 105).
>
> ... in a desperate attempt for quick results, the first self-government established a special *'ex-gratia'* payments fund. The purpose of the fund was to make payments to traditional landowners who were 'unfairly' deprived of their land though legally there was no obligation upon the government to pay them. Payment from the fund was made almost at random depending on, as one writer put it, whoever made most noise. (*Ibid*, p 118.) It was naively assumed that the government would thereby buy itself out of trouble. Predictably, the scheme backfired. Claims escalated in number and the amount demanded. Indeed even some of those groups, which received *ex-gratia* payment, were dissatisfied with the amount paid and claimed for more money. (For example, in 1975 the government after winning an appeal in the case of *The Administration v Guba and Doriga*, gave K160,000 in *ex-gratia* payment to the Tubumaga and Geakone clans as a final settlement of their claim over Eranese and Newtown. Soon thereafter, their clan leaders made fresh demands for more compensation. By 1983 they were demanding K60 million, *Post Courier*, PNG, 4 September, 1981, p 19.) The scheme was subsequently quietly abandoned.

The government met this challenge by setting up the Commission of Inquiry into Land Matters (CILM) to investigate the land issue especially the canker of land disputes and to make appropriate remuneration to the government. Commenting on the dilemma which the CILM faced of balancing indigenous interests against expatriate ones Mugambwa says:

> Although the CILM held the colonial administration responsible for the land disputes, it realised that history could not be re-written completely. On pragmatic grounds it recommended that the government should not accede to the demands to return all alienated land. Such a move in its view was impractical and was a cause for disaster as it would encourage more land claims and inter-group land disputes. Moreover, the government could not afford the huge cost of rectifying the situation. Furthermore, the CILM feared that such a policy was bound to cause anxiety amongst the expatriates

1 'Land disputes in PNG: a colonial legacy and post-Independence solutions' (1987) 15 MLJ 94, 108–17.

especially plantation owners who were already targets of intimidation. In the circumstances, the CILM opted for a compromise between the interests of the land claimants and those of the nation. It sought to achieve its objective mainly through a complicated formula which entailed returning some land to its original owners; payment of a limited compensation to some (but not all) aggrieved claimants; acquisition by the government of some alienated land (if necessary by compulsory process); and securing the government's title to select land from any legal challenge. The CILM strongly felt that land disputes should be dealt with by a permanent Commission rather than ordinary courts which it said were slow and expensive.[2]

In order to appreciate the policy considerations which inform the land restoration programme we set out below the relevant portions of the CILM Report.

II THE BASIC PRINCIPLES OF THE CILM REPORT

COMMISSION OF INQUIRY INTO LAND MATTERS (Port Moresby, 1973), pp 10–16

BASIC PRINCIPLES

2.1 Our approach to the problem

This report is the product of the continuous effort of ten Commissioners assisted by three full-time advisory staff and two visiting consultants, over a period of nine months. It is equivalent to the work of one man for eight years. Every District has been visited and indeed every Sub-District but three. Thousands of miles have been traveled; millions of words have been heard and read. The work has been intensive and continuous but unhurried. Each chapter has been drafted and discussed at least three times before the final draft has been approved. Where appropriate the draft chapters have been shown to people experienced in the subject of the chapter and their comments have been taken into account. None of the opinions or recommendations presented is presented lightly.

2.2 Alternatives considered

The first paragraph of our terms of reference required us to investigate fully and report to Cabinet and to the Administrator on the major land questions facing Papua New Guinea today. The paragraph then continues:

You should consider and evaluate alternative solutions to the problems you identify in order to provide a sound basis for the formulation of government policies in relation to these questions; and to enable Members of the House of Assembly to debate any land legislation introduced by the government following reports by the Commission, with a full appreciation of the problems involved and of alternative solutions.

In our Report we have tried to meet these requirements. We have set out the land problems of Papua New Guinea. We have recommended solutions to these problems and we have discussed alternative ways of solving the problems whenever there have been real alternatives to our recommendations.

2 *Ibid*, p 116.

2.3 Land is a basis of social relations

We have been conscious throughout our work that land is the basis of economic and social relations for most of Papua New Guinea. We are unable to regard land as simply a commodity or a tool. Our Report is affected not only by such questions as how to increase production, although this is a most important consideration; it is deeply concerned about what changes in society will result from changes in land tenure and the laws on land transfer. We assume that government and the House of Assembly will also consider our Report according to what kind of society they want in this country.

2.4 We have concentrated on setting out principles of policy

After government and the House of Assembly have considered the Report, the fine details must be worked out to implement the recommendations that are adopted. However, we have worked our recommendations out in enough detail, with due appreciation of the realities of the situation in which they would operate, to demonstrate that they are workable. We have also looked at land policy as a whole, and tried to make the recommendations of the various sections consistent with one another. We believe we are offering for consideration the basis of a new national land policy. We trust that Cabinet and the House of Assembly will give it early consideration, as we believe the country is in urgent need of a clear land policy.

2.5 Follow-up work required

We are happy to learn that Cabinet has directed that a special section be set up in the Department of Lands, Surveys and Mines to draft legislation and work out detailed administrative proposals on our Report insofar as it is adopted by the government and House of Assembly. We understand that this section will also be responsible for research into the effects of policy as it begins to work, and will recommend adjustments where necessary.

2.6 Urgent matter

There is an urgent need for better provision to recover more alienated land promptly, but in an orderly way, in some places where Papua New Guineans are genuinely short of land. We draw particular attention to Recommendations 20–28 in Chapter 4 'Alienated Land'.

BASIC PRINCIPLES

2.7 Land policy is closely connected to economic, social and political relations

Land policy will deeply affect the whole social, political and economic relations of the Papua New Guinea people. Registration, tenure change and transfer are not merely technical questions. Where a choice of policies is still open, the choice will have to be made by the elected representatives of the people, according to the kind of society they want. In theory this could range from a system of individual small farms as in Kenya or Taiwan to a system of co-operative or communal farms as in Israel or Tanzania. In practice the choice is more limited.

2.8 The government has indicated the kind of society it wants

The Eight Point Programme includes 'decentralization of economic activity ... with an emphasis on agricultural development', 'more equal distribution of economic benefits, including movement towards equalisation of incomes among people' and reliance, where possible, on typical Papua New Guinean forms of organisation. It refers to government control and involvement in those sectors of the economy where control is necessary to assure the desired kind of development. In addition, Item 5 of our Terms of Reference asks us to consider:

(a) ways of maximising the range and spread of benefits from land development to all members of local communities;

(b) minimising social dislocation arising from land development, while actively promoting better utilisation of Papua New Guinea land resources.

2.9 Building on a customary base

The balance between community and individual rights differs between various Papua New Guinea societies but is always complex and delicate. Within limits individual members of kinship groups can compete and do business on their own. The individual must accept restraints from his group but in return he is given its support and is entitled to basic rights, including land rights as a member of the group. Although this system has its limitations it also has many great strengths. We recognise the need to alter some customary practices to promote greater productivity from the land. But we do not think that the basic social structure of the people has to be destroyed to do this. We do not recommend a sweeping agrarian revolution and a total transformation of Papua New Guinean society. We do not recommend either collective or individualistic extremes. Our approach is rather to encourage evolution of certain existing features of our society in order to strengthen opportunities for commercial farming and permit freer transfer of rights to those who most need land. We believe our recommendations meet the request of the Eight Point Program for reliance, where possible, on Papua New Guinean forms of organisation.

2.10 Policies leading to great inequality must be avoided

This Eight Point Programme must rule out a policy which aims at a few people becoming rich from renting land while others become landless labourers. This kind of policy is often introduced with the justification that the people who are able and strong will get control of the land and use it wisely, while the others will become labourers in agriculture or industry. This is supposed to lead to general development and prosperity. But, in much of Asia and Latin America it has led to misery and poverty. Land is concentrated in fewer and fewer hands – not necessarily the hands of able and creative people, but of rich absentee landlords and speculators. A large class of landless people emerges who find only low-paid work or remain unemployed and prone to malnutrition, illness and crime. Political conflict emerges between the landowning and the tenant and labouring classes.

2.11 Private landlordism must be checked

There is a strong desire throughout the country to assert traditional clan rights against the holders of alienated land. This is a natural element of tribal feeling and we have had great regard to it, particularly where it leads to the recovery of land for land-short Papua New Guineans. But care must be taken that it does not lead to too much private ownership, based on ancient claims, against the Papua New Guinea government – an assertion of private interests against the interests of the people of the new Papua New Guinean national community as a whole. For this reason we have recommended that the government retain or acquire title to land for public purposes for town growth and for leasing to those who have greater need of it. The alternative is that many Papua New Guinean individuals and small groups will become landlords and that colonial exploitation will be replaced by exploitation of one class of Papua New Guineans by another. Direct leasing, which creates landlord and tenant classes, must be used sparingly. It should be introduced only in special circumstances and under careful control.

2.12 The law should favour those who need land most and will use it

In many situations there will be several claimants to land. We feel that, all else being equal, preference should be given to those who have little land and are in need of it, and those who will live on it and use it rather than leave it idle. We believe that the law should assist customary claimants to get secure title and develop their land. But we feel that people who get registered titles have an obligation to use the land well, or it should be transferred to someone who will use it well.

2.13 Most land transfer should be through government but some direct dealing in small lots allowed

(a) Some land transfer is needed to ensure that those who want to use land can get a reasonable amount with as little difficulty as possible. We do not think that a completely free trade in land should be allowed, however, because that would soon lead to some people having a lot of land and some people having no land. When land is to be transferred it is best if government can buy or lease the land in the first instance because it can then distribute the land fairly. It can also keep the value down at the time of the first lease or purchase and the increased value after registration and improvement can go to the community as a whole through the government collecting the rents and periodically revaluing them. There have been objections in the colonial period to the government buying land cheaply and making a profit on the rent or resale. This was mainly rented to foreign settlers. We feel that this objection is much less valid when a Papua New Guinean government is in control, and where the purpose is not to grant the land to settlers from overseas but to make it available at low cost to Papua New Guineans.

(b) It is indeed arguable that *all* land transfers should be through the government. Land gets its *monetary* value (as apart from any other value) mainly according to the amount buyers are prepared to pay. If government is the only buyer the cost of acquiring land can be kept down. A very free market in land, especially with overseas companies buying land, pushes prices up, with the result that only the wealthiest Papua New Guineans, if any, will be able to buy land. It will also make it very difficult for the government to get land cheaply to distribute at low cost to other Papua New Guineans. This is the sort of difficulty which could arise, for example, if Japanese buyers were allowed freely into the Gazelle Peninsula at a time when the government wants to buy back alienated land for Papua New Guineans. The problem may not be generally serious at first, but over time, free market trading in land opens up an increasing gap between the fortunate ones who can afford land (and go on profiting from it) and those who cannot.

(c) Or these reasons we have recommended throughout the Report that government remain the main buyer or lessee of land, and that all major transfers have to be through government. Where registration of title is recommended, restrictions on its transfer are usually made part of the title.

(d) However, we are very worried about the ability of government in the near future to transfer enough land quickly and easily enough to satisfy the needs of Papua New Guineans who want it and can develop it. This is largely because swift land registration and transfer needs good machinery and skilled staff to run it.

The past record of government in this regard is very poor and though we have stressed the need for a programme of land management training, we are not confident that the government's ability to transfer land smoothly will improve rapidly enough to meet local demand. For this reason we have recommended direct dealings between Papua New Guinean citizens over small lots of five hectares in rural areas and 0.10 hectares in urban areas, provided that a person can hold only one registered house site and one registered farm or business site. We have also recommended direct trading in government leaseholds provided the first option is given to the government. Even this amount of direct dealing will push up land values, but we feel this is a disadvantage that must be accepted in case the government cannot supply land quickly enough to meet the needs of Papua New Guineans who want house sites and small business or farm sites.

(e) We recommend a close study of the effects of the policy and a review of it after five years.

Recommendation 1

Basic principles

(a) Land policy must be concerned with increasing production but even more concerned with the kind of society Papua New Guinea should become.

(b) It follows from the Eight Point Program that land policy should be an evolution from a customary base, not a sweeping agrarian revolution; collective and individualistic extremes should be avoided.

(c) Very unequal distribution of land rights must be avoided.

(d) Private landlordism must be checked.

(e) The law should favour those who need land most and use it well.

(f) Most land transfer should be through government but some direct dealing in small lots allowed.

Recommendation 2

The basic choice of the government and house of assembly will be how much to open land to direct trading. It could help development in some ways, but have the disadvantages of pushing up prices and widening social division. More government control could give more equal distribution of land and wealth, but may slow transfer too much because government does not have enough skilled staff to handle all transactions. We have thought very deeply about this and believe we have recommended the best possible balance in the circumstances. Amankwah *et al* say:[3]

> The recommendations of the CILM were grounded on the Eight Point Plan of the Self-Governing State of PNG formulated by the government of Prime Minister Somare in 1972. The Basic Principles of lands as formulated in the *Report* of the CILM are thus based on the Eight Point Plan and Principle No 5 of the National Goals and Principles of the Constitution which implicitly recognises that Papua New Guinea's destiny lies in the utilisation of the nation's indigenous culture and institutions. By contrast, s 53 of the Constitution of the Independent State of Papua New Guinea (1975)[4] however, would seem to be antithetical to the egalitarian and self-reliance philosophy underlining the Eight Point Plan in its overt recognition of the sanctity of private property rights which can only be abrogated in law under very stringent conditions.

3 *Land Law in PNG* (Lawbook Co, Sydney, 2001), p 23.

4 Ch No 1.

III RESTORATION OF LAND TO THE INDIGENOUS PEOPLE

To counteract the exploitative aspects of foreign capital symbolised by the plantation system in parts of the country, the government responded to the recommendation of the CILM that some of the plantations should be returned to 'the traditional right-holders'. In the government's legislative armory were the Land Settlement Schemes Act,[5] the Land Trespass Act,[6] the Land Redistribution Act,[7] the Land Acquisition (Development Purposes) Act[8] and the Land Groups Incorporation Act[9] which were enacted to facilitate the task of the government in implementing the CILM recommendations relating to plantations and related matters.

Commenting on these Acts, Amankwah *et al* say: 'The Land Settlement Schemes (Prevention of Disruption) Act[10] was an Act to ensure that disruptive conduct on the part of an individual leaseholder does not endanger a land settlement scheme of which his lease forms part.'

Section 3 defines disruptive conduct as acts of a criminal nature or other reprehensible conduct. Curiously the Act prescribes no punishment for the offender; s 3 only confers on the District Court, on application by the Minister for Lands to declare that a conduct comes within the purview of the law and the person responsible. The Minister is then authorised under s 4 to compulsorily acquire the land from the holder and to deport him under s 7 to his original home province.

The Land Trespass Act[11] was an Act to provide for a summary method of ejecting unauthorized persons from certain land. Section 1 states the purpose of the Act. It reads:

> The purpose of this Act is to prevent the disruption of the orderly redistribution of land under the Land Redistribution Act 1974, or under any other scheme approved by the National government for the redistribution of non-customary land, that would occur if people attempted to anticipate decisions under that Act, or to influence such decisions, by the occupation or attempted occupation of such land, or of land that may be intended for redistribution under that Act, whether or not the occupation is made or attempted under a claim of right.

The Land Trespass Act made provision for appropriate punishment to be meted to persons who occupy land illegally. Sections 8 and 9 provide:

> **8 Illegal occupation, etc, of land to which this Act applies**
>
> (1) Subject to sub-sections (3) and (4), a person who, otherwise than as allowed by section 6, occupies, uses or enters on land to which this Act applies is guilty of an offence.
>
> Penalty for a first offence – a fine not exceeding K200.00 or imprisonment for a term not exceeding six months.

---

5 Ch No 45.

6 Ch No 271.

7 Ch No 190.

8 Ch No 192.

9 Ch No 147.

10 No 53, 1974.

11 Ch No 271, 1974.

For a second or subsequent offence – a fine not exceeding K400.00 or imprisonment for a term not exceeding 12 months.

(2) Where a person occupies, uses or enters on land in contravention of sub-section (1), a person authorised by the Minister for the purpose may, and shall if so directed by the Minister, remove, with such force as is necessary, the person and his movable property from the land.

(3) It is not an offence against sub-section (1) if –

(a) the occupation or use was continuous and commenced, or the entry in respect of the continuous occupation or use by the person entering commenced, before the date of publication of the relevant notice under section 5, and was continuous, and

(b) all action that was reasonable in the circumstances was being taken to end the occupation or use.

(4) It is a defence to a charge of an offence against sub-section (1) if the accused person proves that he did not know, and could not reasonably have been expected to know, that the land was land to which this Act applies.

(5) It is not a defence that the possession, use or entry was under a claim of right.

(6) This section does not prevent a Village Court from exercising jurisdiction under any other Act in respect of an action that is or may be an offence under sub-section (1).

9 Obstruction, etc

A person who –

(a) hinders or obstructs a member of the Police Force or a person authorized under section 8(2) in the exercise of his powers or the performance of his functions under this Act; or

(b) without lawful and reasonable excuse (the burden of proof of which lies upon him), destroys, tears down, defaces or in any way obscures a copy of a notice or exemption displayed under section 7(1)(b),

is guilty of an offence.

Penalty: a fine not exceeding K200.00 or imprisonment for a term not exceeding six months.

The Land Redistribution Act[12] was an Act to provide for the redistribution of certain land previously alienated from the customary owners and for the peaceful and certain settlement of claims concerning such redistribution.

Section 1 states: 'The purpose of this Act is to provide, by administrative and not judicial process, for the fair redistribution of certain areas of land that are to be returned to the people in accordance with their needs, to be held in accordance with this Act.'

The Act applies only to the State or government. Section 5 provides:

5 Land to which this Act applies

(1) Subject to sub-section (2), this Act applies to any land that is –

(a) government land as defined in the Land Act 1962 other than land that is the subject of a lease from the customary owners; or

12 Ch No 190.

(b) the subject of a declaration under section 84 of the Land Act 1962; or

(c) the subject of a notice to treat under section 5A of the Land Acquisition Act 1974 or under section 17 of the Land Act 1962,

that the Minister, by notice in the *National Gazette*, declares to be land to which this Act applies.

(2) Land other than government land within the meaning of sub-section (1)(a) that –

(a) has been the subject of a vesting order under section 15; or

(b) has been the subject of a notice under section 84 of the Land Act 1962 and is owned by virtue of that section by a group that is an incorporated group within the meaning of the Land Groups Incorporation Act 1974,

is not land to which this Act applies.

The Land Acquisition Act[13] empowered the government to acquire the plantations for redistribution under the Land Redistribution Act.[14] It provides, however, for the payment of compensation to those who would be affected. The acquisition was limited to cocoa, coconut, and coffee. Tea and cattle farms were excepted.

This legislation was later supplemented by an amending legislation, the Land Acquisition (Development Purposes) Act 1983.[15]

The Land Acquisition Act[16] was an all-purpose legislation intended being an Act to provide for and in relation to the acquisition of land by the State for development purposes. Section 1 states the purpose of the Act. It reads:

(1) The purpose of this Act is to enable the government to acquire land by agreement or by compulsory process in accordance with this Act –

(a) making land available to non-overseas persons –

(i) for subsistence farming where other land for that purpose is insufficient in any area; or

(ii) for economic development so that they may share in the economic progress of Papua New Guinea; or

(b) for the resettlement of residents of urban areas; or

(c) for any educational, social welfare or community development purpose where other suitable land is either unavailable or insufficient,

so as to implement the policies of the government to develop rural areas and to assist, where necessary, the non-overseas residents of the urban areas of Papua New Guinea to achieve a better standard of living.

Section 3 delineates the purview of the Act. It states:

(1) This Act applies to all land in the country that, in the opinion of the Minister –

(a) is undeveloped; or

(b) is used, or is normally used, wholly or partly for primary production or for any other prescribed purposes,

other than customary land or any other prescribed land.

13 Ch No 66.

14 Ch No 190.

15 Ch No 192.

16 *Ibid.*

(2) This Act does not apply to land acquired by any person from the State by lease or otherwise after the date of commencement of the pre-Independence Lands Acquisition Act 1974.

(3) The provisions of this Act are in addition to and do not derogate the provisions of the Land Act 1963, as in force from time to time.

Section 4 says:

> The Land (Underdeveloped Freeholds) Act 1969 does not apply to land acquired or to be acquired under this Act.

The Land Groups Incorporation Act[17] was an Act:

(a) to recognize the corporate nature of customary groups; and

(b) to allow them to hold, manage and deal with land in their customary names, and for related purposes.

The purpose was to encourage and facilitate the application of corporate principles to ownership of land. The materials which follow furnish a clue to a better appreciation of the legal mechanism which was inaugurated to tackle the land problem.

PETER EATON, 'MELANESIAN LAND REFORM: THE PLANTATION ACQUISITION SCHEME' (1980) 8 MLJ 134

Plantations were established during the colonial period in Papua New Guinea on land which had been alienated from customary tenure. In both Papua and German New Guinea, land dealings were controlled by the government and the official policy was that indigenous land interests should be protected. Commander Erskine's proclamation of the British protectorate in 1884 included an assurance to the local people that 'evil disposed people will not be permitted to occupy your countries, to seize your lands', and that 'your lands will be secured to you'. (C Lyne, *New Guinea: An Account of the Establishment of the British Protectorate over the Southern Shores of New Guinea* (London, 1885), pp 5–6.) Purchases of land could only be made by the government, or in the case of New Guinea from 1885 to 1899 by the New Guinea Kompagnie, and then it might be leased or sold to individuals or companies for plantations. Initially freehold titles were granted but this ceased in Papua in 1911 and in New Guinea after the 1914–18 war when most of the German plantations were expropriated and sold to Australians.

There had generally been more alienation of land in German New Guinea than Papua, 700,000 acres compared to 300,000 acres in 1914. The largest number of plantations was established on the Gazelle Peninsula on the island of New Britain, along the coast of the New Guinea mainland especially around Madang, and on some of the smaller islands. These were mainly coconut plantations for producing copra, but later cocoa was often grown on them also. In Papua, the plantations were generally for growing either coconuts or rubber. Later when the Highlands were opened up, they proved suitable for the development of coffee and tea plantations.

When Papua New Guinea became self-governing in 1973, there were about 1,200 plantations. These were expatriate owned and managed. They employed approximately

17 Ch No 147.

50,000 workers; in the case of the coastal plantations these workers often came from other areas such as the Highlands. At that time cash crops grown on the plantations provided much of the country's exports, 56% in 1972 (value of exports for 1972 from *Papua New Guinea Report for 1972–73* (Government Printer, Canberra, 1973), p 279) although later copper was to become more important. The plantations had also been responsible for the development of infrastructure, especially roads, in many areas. For many Papua New Guineans they represented their first contact with the monetary economy and commercial agriculture.

By 1973, however, the plantations had also become a source of resentment among the people where they were established. Some of the grievances expressed were due to the way in which the land for them had been acquired. Early purchases had been made with trade goods such as cloth, tobacco and axes; these payments were now regarded as inadequate in view of the high monetary value of the plantations. In some cases also it appears that the wrong people were paid, or that the payments were not distributed fairly among the landowning group. In other cases, the government acquired land without payment because it was considered 'ownerless' or 'waste and vacant' although in fact it was the territory of groups who, although they were not farming it, used the land for hunting or were keeping it for future use.

In addition to these complaints about the unfairness of the early acquisitions, there was often a problem of land shortage in areas where plantations had been established. This was partly due to population increase and also because of the greater need for land for growing both food and cash crops. Examples of areas where land alienation had resulted in the people being left without enough land were the Gazelle Peninsula, the Duke of York Islands and Enuk Island off the New Ireland coast. In the latter case, all 800 hectares of the islanders' traditional land was alienated and they were left with a 'reserve' of 18 hectares. (During the latter part of the German administration areas on alienated land were designated 'native reserves' in an effort to ensure that the indigenous people had enough land left for their villages and gardens.)

In 1973, a Commission of Inquiry into Land Matters was established to investigate land problems and make recommendations for policy and legislation. They travelled throughout the country, held public meetings and received submissions. They received a great many requests that alienated land should be restored to the descendants of the clans who originally held rights to them. In some cases, the people were already threatening to take action, and move onto the plantations. This had already happened on Enuk Island where the people had started to harvest coconuts from the plantation land.

In making its recommendations, the Commission of Inquiry was guided by certain principles; a belief that land should be distributed to those who needed it and would use it, a desire to discourage speculation, and a wish to achieve good relations between different communities.

They were also influenced by the Eight Point Plan which summarised government development policy. The aims relevant to policy on plantations stated that there should be greater participation by Papua New Guineans in the economy, more equal distribution of economic benefits, and government control and involvement in the economy where necessary. (See also the second and third National Goals and Directive Principles set out in the Constitution.)

In its Report, the Commission recommended:

> Where freeholds and leaseholds have been granted and the land developed but the traditional right-holders are acutely short of land, the government should recover the land, and return it to them and pay compensation to the present titleholder. (*Report of the Commission of Inquiry into Land Matters* (Government Printer, Port Moresby, 1973), p 66.)

Legislation on alienated land was introduced the year after the publication of the *Report of the Commission of Inquiry*. In his address to the House of Assembly, the Minister for Lands, Mr Kavali, emphasised that its basic purpose was 'the relief of Papua New Guinea land pressures', and he stated his belief that 'the plantation industry is one which can eventually be run by Papua New Guineans'. (*House of Assembly Debates*, Vol 3, No 2 (Government Printer, Port Moresby, 1974), p 3536.) He added that it was the government's long term policy 'to bring all aspects of plantation production under the ownership of Papua New Guinean individuals and groups'. He also stressed that the legislation was 'confined to properties at present held by expatriate interests' and that it would not affect future foreign investment.

There were four statutes in the legislative package. The Land Acquisition Act 1974 (No 66 of 1974) gave the government the power to acquire land by agreement or compulsory process. It also included provisions for compensation which would be based on average annual profits over a five year period or the value of improvements, in each case multiplied by a prescribed factor. The Land Redistribution Act 1974 (No 62 of 1974) provided for the establishment of Distribution Authorities composed of representatives of local groups whose main function was to decide on the way the land should be redistributed. The Land Groups Act 1974 (No 64 of 1974) gave recognition to the corporated nature of customary groups and enabled them to hold, manage and deal in land. The Land Trespass Act 1974 (No 53 of 1974) provided for the ejecting of unauthorised people from land that was to be redistributed in order to prevent people from anticipating decisions made by the Distribution Authority, or trying to influence them by illegally squatting on the land.

A special branch of the Department of Lands was established to deal with plantation redistribution. It was known as the Alienated Lands Redistribution Branch and it had Field Redistribution Officers in the provinces most likely to be affected.

The procedure is that when groups express an interest in taking over a plantation, this is reported by field officers to the Department of Lands headquarters who then instruct the Redistribution Officer to investigate and advise the group of government requirements under the scheme.

The Redistribution Officer makes a report and if this is satisfactory, the plantation owner is informed and negotiations begin. A valuation to determine compensation is made although this may be later subject to reappraisal. At the same time the Distribution Authority is formed, gazetted and finalises the proposed redistribution. Its proposals are submitted in a report to the Department of Lands and if this is satisfactory a land group can be formed and registered for the purpose of taking over the plantation. Following the receipt of the valuation report, an offer is made to the plantation owner and, usually after some negotiation, a contract of sale is drawn up and executed. Once the plantation has been acquired by the government, it is then handed over to the land group.

Payment for the plantations is made from a special fund known as the Alienated Land Trust Fund Account. The group taking over the plantation are also expected to pay a deposit, originally about 10% of the total cost although efforts have since been made to have it increased. The balance is then repaid by the group from the profits of the plantation over the next few years.

From 1974 to 1979, seventy-five plantations were purchased. These acquisitions have been confined to coconut, cocoa, coffee and rubber plantations established before 1974. Tea plantations and cattle farms have not been included, with one exception. (This was Takoa in Central Province where 480 hectares of pasture land were acquired from the Takoa Pastoral Company. The land has not yet been redistributed or developed.)

The problem of defining the land group's title to the land is still one that has not been finally solved. When the plantation is purchased, the group is given a licence to cultivate it, and then when they have finished repaying the total cost, they are given a lease and pay a nominal rent, originally one toea per year. Generally, the land is kept as a whole unit; only in one case, Malapau in East New Britain, has the land been sub-divided into blocks, and this has been mainly due to dissensions within the Vadirai land group. Whether more redistributed plantations will be sub-divided or revert to subsistence agriculture is uncertain. Some have been neglected, while others have continued to work as effective economic units. Sometimes the group themselves have worked the plantations, in other cases they have continued to employ labourers from elsewhere.

Management has been a problem, as many of the Papuan New Guineans taking over plantations lacked the experience and skills to organise and supervise them. In an attempt to solve this problem, the National Plantation Management Agency was established in 1977. This is a government company which gives advice, assistance and training in the management of plantations until the land group has paid off the original cost. At the beginning of May 1980, they were managing fifty plantations, of which twenty-seven were acquired under the redistribution scheme and twenty-three purchased by local groups with the help of commercial or Development Bank loans. Although the plantations in this latter group have not been purchased as part of the scheme, their acquisition is subject to government control and approval under s 75 of the Land Act 1962 (No 6 of 1963).

The period from 1974 to 1979 was generally a poor one for the plantation industry. To some extent this was a result of unstable commodity prices. Costs also increased; rises in the price of oil affected fuel and transport; increases in rural minimum wages raised wage bills. There was little replanting and investment in the plantations during the uncertain period before self-government. The plantation redistribution scheme itself caused plantation owners who expected their plantations to be taken over to allow them to run down – the methods of valuation used in calculating compensation often did not give enough weighting to the effects of depreciation and reinvestment.

There has been a tendency for some interested bodies such as the Planters' Association to blame the redistribution scheme for falls in production and the lack of security felt by plantation owners. This seems to ignore the fact that reduction in new planting had often started before the scheme was in force. It reflected the fact that many plantation owners initially found it difficult to accept the concept of Papua New Guinean self-government and were uncertain about their future in the newly independent State.

In August 1979, a committee was set up by the government to review the plantation redistribution scheme. It contained representatives of relevant government departments and the plantation industry. They were generally critical of the working of the scheme and expressed concern with the deterioration in the plantations, the lack of replanting, and poor standards of husbandry and maintenance. They were critical of the financing of the scheme, and were also worried that land groups were usually not in a good position to borrow and obtain capital to effect the development of the plantations that was now needed.

The committee felt that the four statutes concerned with redistribution should be repealed as they were considered too complex and difficult to work. They suggested that 'the transfer of plantations should be conducted on a freely competitive basis without coercion, and as far as possible, national groups should be assisted to buy valuable and fully maintained properties in preference to deteriorated plantations' (Report, p 9). Redevelopment of the latter would be done through a government company that could put the management and redevelopment of these properties up to competitive tenders.

The committee recommended that local land groups acquiring plantations should be encouraged to obtain finance from commercial banks and the Development Bank. They should also be given assistance under the National Investor Scheme. The committee also suggested that the Plantation Management Training Programme should be strengthened and should include provision for apprenticeships.

The committee believed that there should be a distinction made between expatriate owners willing to sell their plantations and those who were unwilling. The latter should not be forced to sell if their plantations were being well maintained. Instead, national involvement in them should be encouraged by the purchase of shares.

The committee also recommended changes in the method of plantation valuation, which would be based on sales over the last five years but give more weighting to the most recent years. Account would be taken of commodity price projections and of recent investment in the plantations.

Whether any of the committee of review's recommendations are accepted depends on the future of the plantation redistribution scheme. Since the middle of 1979 there has been a slowing down of the scheme with the emphasis on completing negotiations for transfers that had already been started. When a change of government occurred early in 1980, one of the first policy statements made by the new Prime Minister, Sir Julius Chan, was that the scheme would be abolished and replaced by land development projects. Since then, this early statement has been moderated and there are indications that the scheme will be allowed to continue. There is still a demand for redistribution, especially in areas of population pressure and land shortage such as the Gazelle Peninsula, and parts of the Highlands. Problems still exist on many of the smaller islands where privately owned plantations occupy much of the land and living space.

Any evaluation of plantation redistribution is still difficult. The scheme seems to have suffered from bad public relations with publicity given to the problems rather than the achievements. Some plantations have been neglected and there have also been quarrels among customary groups as to who are the rightful owners. There have been instances of political interference as in the case of Raniola plantation in East New Britain. (An article under the heading 'Government Slammed on Land Deal' in the Port Moresby *Post Courier*, 13 February 1979, contains a report on complaints by a group of Tolai villagers in the Totem Land Group against alleged interference by Mr Oscar Tamur, the local Member of Parliament and at that time, Minister of Education, in the purchase and redistribution of the Raniola Plantation.) Other plantations have been run successfully, either by the land groups or the National Plantation Management Agency. In many cases, the new owners are trying hard to develop plantations that had been run down, but need assistance in the form of both capital equipment and help from extension services.

Some indication of the productivity and efficiency of the redistributed plantations can be obtained from examining the extent to which the original purchase prices have been paid back by the new owners. In fifteen cases the cost of the plantation has been completely repaid: five of these were in the Highlands and seven in East New Britain. On many other plantations a considerable proportion has been paid off. On others, very little or nothing has been paid: some of these have only been repurchased recently but others seem to have made no profit over a period of several years. The worst figures are for Central Province. These statistics provide some indication of the successes and failures of the scheme, although there still remains a need for more information on the productivity of individual plantations.

Many of the criticisms of the scheme have been concerned with declines in cash crop exports and 'investors confidence'. If one looks at plantation redistribution as an attempt at land reform then it can be seen that it has achieved some of its original aims of encouraging Papua New Guinean participation in the plantation economy and promoting greater equality. It has succeeded in giving land to those who need it. What still has to be proved and what is likely to be crucial to the role of redistribution in rural development, is that the new owners can utilise this land effectively and get the maximum benefit from the management of its resources.

JOHN MUGAMBWA, 'LAND DISPUTES IN PNG: A COLONIAL LEGACY AND POST-INDEPENDENCE SOLUTIONS' (1987) 15 MLJ 94, pp 110–11

THE OUTCOME OF CILM REPORT

The report of the CILM became the basis of most of the post-colonial government's land disputes settlement. Some of its proposals that have been implemented are summarised below.

(i) The Plantation Redistribution Scheme

One of the first major outcomes of the CILM's report was the establishment of the Plantation Redistribution Scheme. Essentially the scheme involved acquisition of plantations by the government and subsequently sell [sic] them to the people identified as the original owners of the subject land. The scheme was implemented by a package of four statutes enacted in the 1974 House of Assembly: the Land Acquisition Act empowered the government to acquire any land by agreement or compulsory process, subject to compensation of the owners; the Land Redistribution Act provided for the establishment of distribution authorities charged with a duty to determine how the land acquired was to be redistributed; the Land Groups Act made provision for the incorporation of land owning groups, with power to hold and deal in land; finally, the Land Trespass Act, provided for the ejectment of trespassers from land. The later Act was intended to deter self-help before the land was officially redistributed. (Act Nos 66, 62, 64 and 53 of 1974.)

The Plantation Redistribution Scheme went into full gear almost right from its inception. At the time of self-government, there were about 1,200 plantations, most of which were located on the Gazelle Peninsula on the Island of New Britain. Between 1974 and 1979, 75 of these plantations were acquired under the scheme and redistributed to enthusiastic claimants. (P Eaton, 'Melanesian land reform: the plantation scheme in Papua New Guinea' (1980) 8(1) MLJ 137.) However, thereafter it apparently lost its momentum. Part of the reason was that the scheme run [sic] short of funds. The government was not prepared to commit more funds into the scheme. Expectation of financial assistance from the Australians, who everybody held responsible for the problem of land disputes, did not eventuate. Secondly, some sectors of the government were beginning to have second thoughts about the wisdom of redistributing plantations. Many of the redistributed farms were not performing according to expectation; indeed some were on the verge of collapsing. A report of the Committee of *Review Into the Plantation Redistribution Scheme*, 1979, was very critical of the scheme and it recommended that it had to be scraped. This report is reproduced in Monograph No 15, 'What do we do about plantations?' (Waigani, Institute of Applied Social and Economic Research, 1981).

However, the results of the scheme should not only be assessed in economic terms. The scheme had a social-political role: the return of land to the indigenous people many of whom felt were unfairly deprived of their land. Under the scheme, some land has been returned and this must have helped to defuse the tension. Fingleton reckons that if plantations had not been returned in some areas the government would have had to maintain them with riot squads. (Fingleton, 'Plantation Redistribution Scheme', p 44.) Hence, the scheme acted as a 'safety valve' to what was an explosive situation soon after the country's independence. The scheme made another indirect contribution. It provided a stimulus to Papua New Guineans to purchase plantations using their own funds outside the Plantation Redistribution Scheme. It is submitted that in the circumstances, irrespective of its economic performance, the exercise was worthwhile. Presently the scheme's future is in doubt mainly because of lack of funds and the government's indecision.

Questions

1 With the advantage of hindsight, would you say that the plantation redistribution scheme was doomed to fail?

2 What are the constitutional limits on compulsory acquisition? The constitutional requirements are: (i) public purpose; and (ii) payment of compensation.

Section 53(4) and (5) of the PNG Constitution (1975) proscribes acquisition 'by forfeiture or the extinction or determination otherwise than by way of a reasonable provision for limitation, of actions or a reasonable law in the nature of prescription or adverse possession'. Do you consider this another limitation on compulsory acquisition?

3 Review the recommendation of the *Commission of Inquiry into Land Matters* (1973) in respect of plantations in Papua New Guinea. How was the recommendation effected?

IV SECURING STATE LAND

There was the realisation that a registry of State lands was necessary in order to have a clear idea of the extent of the State's stake in the mass of the national territory. Some confusion has been experienced in the past due to a lack of uniform designation and nomenclature.

The usages 'State land'; 'government land' and 'land the property of the State' appear in several pieces of legislation dealing with land in PNG. It is not altogether clear whether they mean the same thing or different things. The Land Act 1996, for instance, provides a definition of 'government land'. The definition provided in s 2 says this means land other than:

(a) customary land that is not leased by the customary owners to the State; or

(b) land held by a person other than the State for an estate greater than an estate for a term of years; or

(c) land that is the subject of a State lease or a lease from the State under any other Act; or

(d) land reserved from lease or further lease under this Act.

However, s 4 of the Act vests in the State all land not held under customary tenure. It states that 'all land other than customary land is the property of the State', ie, State land. The Land Settlement Schemes (Prevention of Disruption) Act[18] which was enacted to promote the land settlement programme was aimed principally at land which the government owned but could afford to give back to those in need of land. Section 1 defines 'government land' as 'government land as defined in the Land Act'.

The material which follows provides a background material about the National Land Register.

JOHN MUGAMBWA, 'LAND DISPUTES IN PNG: A COLONIAL LEGACY AND POST-INDEPENDENCE SOLUTIONS' (1987) 15 MLJ 94, pp 112–15

(ii) National land registration

The second major outcome of the CILM's proposals was the policy for registration of select government land. The CILM recommended that where any government land was required for public purposes, it should be declared 'National land' and registered in a special register. Its proposition was prompted by the numerous disputes over the government's title, especially in urban areas. The CILM felt that government land which was required for public purposes needed to be protected beyond dispute in any courts of law. To implement this recommendation the National Land Registration Act was enacted in 1977 (Chapter 357). The preamble to the Act stipulates that its object, *inter alia*, is to make provision for the recognition of the State's title over land required for public purposes, the title to which is doubtful or appears to be so; and to settle grievances in relation thereto by providing for certain settlement payments. The Act empowers the Minister to declare any government land acquired prior to the independence day of Papua New Guinea, national land provided the land is required for a public purpose as defined thereunder. (Sections 3 and 7. Any aggrieved person may appeal to the Minister whose decision is final (s 10). Section 53 of the constitution makes provision for the government to declare any State land as 'National land' if required for a public purpose.) Once the land has been registered in the National Land Register, the government acquires an indefeasible title. Thereafter persons disputing its title have to lodge their claims with the National Land Commission (established under the Act) for compensation payment (ss 19 and 39).

Before any compensation is paid, claimants must comply with certain conditions. In the first place, the subject land must have been declared national land and registered in the national land register. Secondly, the claim must be made within six months of the declaration in the *Gazette*. Thirdly, the claimants must prove that before independence a previous claim to the land was made under a law by virtue of which a claim to the land might have been made. Finally, they must not have received any payment (including *ex-gratia* payment) whether in cash or not by a pre-independence administration (s 40).

These provisions were intended to deter fresh claims from springing up, and to ensure that those, which had previously been settled, however imperfectly, were not brought up again. Nevertheless, apart from the first condition the rest are flexible. The Commission at its discretion may allow claims that do not comply with these requirements. For example, if there are special reasons for not lodging a claim before independence and the Commission is of the opinion that non-enforcement would be unfair, it may admit the claim. In addition, if the purchase price that was originally paid was, in its view, insignificant, it may allow the claim.

18 Ch No 358.

In its proceedings, the Commission is not bound by technical rules of procedure and evidence. Section 34(4) of the Act states that the Commission shall investigate and inform itself on any matter before it in such manner as it thinks proper and admit and consider such relevant information as is available for purposes of determining the matter. Its only obligation is to comply with the rules of natural justice. Where the Commission is satisfied that the claimants are the owners of a customary right in the subject land, if it had not been acquired by the colonial administration, it must make an order for the payment by the State of a settlement payment. The amount of compensation payable is limited as prescribed in the Schedule to the Act (ss 44 and 45, and Sched 2). The scale ranges from a minimum of 500 to a maximum of 28,300 kina for urban areas and between 100 and 750 kina (plus 10 kina per hectare in excess of 10 hectares) for rural areas. The Minister may at his discretion increase the payment in individual cases by up to 50% (s 45(4)). Unlike proceedings before the Land Titles Commission, there is no right of appeal to the court except on the grounds of denial of natural justice. (*Toare Karakara v The Independent State of Papua New Guinea* [1986] PNGLR 186.)

Has the National Land Commission made a substantial contribution towards resolving land disputes? Since its establishment, very few claims have been admitted for compensation. For example, between 1979 and 1983, out of a total of 103 claims, only 17 were admitted, the government paying a total of 145,8000 kina (information obtained from the National Land Commission). Moreover, successful claimants are usually left dissatisfied with the sum paid, especially, after it is distributed amongst several members of the group. The result is that many groups immediately make fresh claims against the government running into millions of kina. (Between 1981 and 1982, the total claims for compensation made against the government exceeded 182 million kina, *Post Courier*, PNG, 1 February 1982, p 2.) Some officials of the National Land Commission privately concede that the Commission's contribution has been minimal, if at all. They attribute this to a number of grounds. In the first place, contrary to the political rhetoric at the time of the enactment of the National Land Registration Act, its main object was not so much to provide a mechanism for resolving land disputes as to protect the government's title to land. Because of the manner the Act was projected it created a false hope in the minds of the land claimants that all of them would be generously compensated. Secondly, many claimants do not meet the stringent conditions imposed under the Act. In the opinion of the present National Land Commissioner, the discretion to waive these conditions must only be used in exceptional circumstances. Thirdly, many claimants have been frustrated by the delay the Commission takes to resolve the disputes. Part of this delay is attributed to the presence of lawyers who tend to drag the hearings with 'technical' arguments. The other main reason for the delay is the requirement under s 43 that in the event of rival claims over the subject land, the matter should first be referred to the local Land Court to determine which group is the rightful claimant, before the claim against the government can be considered. This in most cases means several years of delay before the matter is settled. In the meantime, the tension builds, as the claimants get increasingly frustrated.

In spite of the foregoing, it is submitted that the Act provides a balanced solution between the interests of the grieved customary groups and the public. The Act makes it clear to the customary claimants that certain land, irrespective of the circumstances of its acquisition, in the interests of the public cannot be returned to its alleged traditional owners. Secondly, whilst the Act recognises that there might be a need to compensate those whose land was acquired in an unfair manner, it limits the amount of compensation that is payable and the circumstances under which claims would be admitted. Inevitably, some people miss out and others get much less than what they think they deserve. However, it is submitted that there must be a cut-off point somewhere otherwise there will be perpetual claims. Finally, the scope for judicial intervention is much more restricted than under the Land Titles Commission Act. Experience shows that these disputes involve more than legal consideration, hence the courts are in the worst position to resolve them.

Questions

1 Do you agree with the writer that the National Land Registration Act provides a balanced solution between the interests of customary groups, land claimants and public interest?

2 The National Land Registration Act does no more than legalise land illegally acquired. Do you agree?

3 Discuss the concept of State land and how State land is acquired.

V LAND AND THE ECONOMY OF PNG

Land *per se* has no value unless it can be put to some economic use. Land today has become a marketable commodity just as any species of property. However, the market theory of property when applied in its pristine state to land in nations where corporate or communal ownership is the rule rather than the exception, this is bound to create serious social and political problems.

The material which follows deals with this issue.

MICHAEL J TREBILCOCK AND JACK L KNETSH, 'LAND POLICY AND ECONOMIC DEVELOPMENT IN PAPUA NEW GUINEA' (1981) 9 MLJ 102

PART I: INTRODUCTION

Unquestionably, land occupies a complex social, economic, cultural, religious, psychological, and therefore legal role in Papua New Guinea society, which precludes it being analysed in straightforward economic terms as simply a factor of production. The unique characteristics of land in traditional Papua New Guinean society are well captured in the following statement by Burton-Bradley:

> In the course of my work in Papua New Guinea, I have become aware that the indigenous person has psychological attachment to his land transcending the purely economic and legal arrangements of the superimposed alien culture, however liberal the latter might be. I find that he may go along with the formal arrangements in order to please, but in his thinking and at a deeper level his basic attitude to what is his land remains substantially unchanged throughout life, independent of any transactions and exchanges which have taken place. His land is the place where he was born, where he was subjected to primary enculturation, where he has lived the most important aspects of his life, where the values of his cultural-linguistic group have been constantly reinforced, and where, in most instances he may die. As he grows up he learns that it is the place where his ancestors preceded him, and to which they may return, thus giving the attachment a magico-religious sanction. It is the place where his children and his children's children will follow. At the psychological level it is clearly an extension of the concept of self. (BG Burton-Bradley, 'The psychological dimensions', in Peter G Sack (ed), *Problems of Choice*, ANU Press, 1974, p 32.)

While recognising the complexity of the role of land in Papua New Guinea society, economic analysis remains relevant in two respects: first, a substantial and increasing amount of customary land in Papua New Guinea (97% of the land in Papua New Guinea is held in customary ownership) is being utilized for the production of saleable surpluses and in this respect its use can be rationally analysed in efficiency terms as an economic factor of production. Conservative estimates suggest that at least eight times the area of land presently being utilized for any form of agricultural production (including subsistence) could be utilized for commercial agricultural production. An emerging crisis in unemployment – the World Bank estimates (*World Bank Report on Papua New Guinea*, December 1982) that only 10–20% of the projected 250,000 net citizens additions to the work-force during the 1980s will be able to find formal employment despite rising levels of education and concomitant expectations – makes more effective utilization of this land an urgent imperative. Secondly, as Posner has recently argued (Richard A Posner, 'A theory of primitive society, with special reference to law' (1980) 2 J Legal Studies 1) even the traditional functions of land in a purely subsistence society can be viewed as having an economic rationale. In the absence of extensive information networks predicated upon literacy and in the absence of an effective government machinery to enforce contracts, group ownership of land can be conceived of as a kind of informal mutual insurance company which permitted members of a group opportunities for greater diversification of risk and to that extent enhanced economic security. With the emergence of alternative mechanism which provide insurance or social security such as self-insurance through diversified market and contractual activities, explicit insurance through insurance institutions, and minimum guarantees of social welfare through State-sponsored social security programs, the changing role of land as a source of economic security can be subjected to rational analysis.

In considering possible lines of evolution from the customary status quo in land matters, several factors are placing an increasing strain on the existing system and make rational and ordered policy responses an urgent imperative if the present system is not simply to collapse over time in the face of these shocks. First, one can predict that as land acquires increased economic value as a source of income generation in the money economy, pressures for increased opportunities for acquisition and alienation will mount. Similarly, one can predict that as land assumes increased economic value, and as population growth further increases its scarcity value, the potential for land disputes (already pervasive) will increase reflecting the enhanced values attached to assertions of territorial imperatives. Finally, one can predict that population mobility, reflecting higher levels of education, improved transportation infrastructures, and increased opportunities to participate in the development of the country, will render composition of landowning groups less stable. Thus, the environment in which a new land policy for Papua New Guinea must be fashioned must deal with the prospect of more direct dealings in customary land, more land disputes, and less stable group structures, all in the context of a country with no written history generally and no customary land records specifically. This scenario suggests the need for the introduction of a regime that permits, without over-bearing formality, limited direct dealings in customary land, a frontal attack on the task of designing effective dispute resolution mechanisms, a new regime governing group decision rules, and a feasible set of measures that will ensure a progression towards a documentary customary land law system. In the case of alienated land (ie, the tiny percentage of private freeholds, or land previously acquired by government from customary landowners and held in its own right or leased to other parties), the detailed administrative procedures presently in place regulating the issuance, transfer, mortgaging, and amendment of leasehold interests have created inordinate delays in the effectuation of land transactions in this sector. The necessity for such detailed regulations also calls for searching review.

PART II: CUSTOMARY LAND: ALIENATION AND REGISTRATION

Two abiding issues of debate with respect to land policy in Papua New Guinea have been: first, whether individualisation of land tenure is a pre-condition to greater economic productivity in activities involving land; and second, whether a comprehensive system of registration of ownership and perhaps occupation interests in customary land is necessary to induce a greater rate of investment, especially in the rural economy. On the first issue, the importance of individualisation of land tenure to enhanced economic productivity is easily exaggerated. Even in developed economies, most major economic resources are owned by groups, whether corporations, co-operatives, insurance companies, pension funds, mutual funds, etc. What is distinctive about the Papua New Guinea concept of communal ownership is the inability of a group to alienate interests in its land in most circumstances, except to the government. Even where alienation is permitted ie to the government, the rule of unanimity amongst group members which generally prevails generates formidable transaction costs in effectuating and maintaining agreements. With respect to the second issue (registration), past attempts (the Native Land Registration Act 1952 and the Land Titles Commission Act 1962) to determine and register interests in customary land have completely failed. This in large part seems explicable by reference to the excessive ambitiousness of the proposals, which aspired to register all customary land in Papua New Guinea (ie, involved 'systematic' rather than 'sporadic' registration). In a country lacking a written history, comprising 700 separate tribes speaking 700 different languages, espousing many different customary laws, recognising ownership as largely a function of the vicissitudes of tribal war, mostly defining individual ownership rights by reference to membership in often very large and ill-defined lineage groups, and recognising a multiplicity of different ownership and occupation interests in land the problems of developing, implementing, and maintaining a documentary title system (with a State guaranteed registry of all ownership interests) are nothing short of immense.

In dealing with the question of alienability of interests in customary land, Ward points out (Alan Ward, 'Customary land, land registration and social equality in Papua New Guinea', *History of Agriculture Discussion Paper No 20*, UPNG, 1978) that there has been a rapid growth in informal and often non-customary dealings in customary land, including clan land usage agreements permitting an individual member of a clan exclusive use of given land for agricultural production for a certain period of time, group projects involving inter-clan agreements as to common working and development of both groups' land, leasing and outright sale of land (often to migrants from other regions of the country), contrived disputes under the Land Disputes Settlements Act 1975 designed to produce binding declarations of title to land in order to facilitate development projects, and unofficial transfers of government leasehold interests in land settlement schemes. Part of the explanation for the growth in non-customary, direct dealings (of dubious legality) in customary land appears to be a chronic inability on the part of the Department of Lands to develop flexible and expeditious procedures to govern the intermediation role assigned to the central government by the existing provisions of the Land Act 1962–73. These provisions prohibit dealings in customary land otherwise than in accordance with custom except in favour of the government and essentially require any party seeking to acquire an interest in customary land to approach the central government through the offices of the Department of Lands to buy or lease the land from the customary owners and then in turn lease it to the party interested. Delays of two to three years in completing this process are the rule; much longer delays are common. Apparently at the present time a backlog of the order of 8,000–10,000 lease applications await processing by the Department of Lands. We agree with Ward's conclusion –

> ... that there is widespread popular support for direct dealing, and the attempt of the Committee of Inquiry into Land Matters 1973 to uphold a near-monopoly for the government is breaking down, as straight commercial transactions are elaborated under the guise of 'customary' dealing (Ward, *ibid*).

We propose that limited direct dealings in customary land be permitted and formalised. These dealings would be restricted to the creation of leasehold interests (absolute alienation would not be permitted) and would be subject to review where non-automatic citizens or significant tracts of land or investments are involved to ensure their basic fairness to the customary landowners in the light of the following guidelines:

(1) No lease should normally exceed X years in lengths.

(2) Where the customary landowners are guaranteed significant participation in the project planned for the leased land, a lease may be granted for up to Y years. Highly participatory, joint venture type arrangements with sources of development capital and management expertise should be strongly promoted.

(3) Where a lease is being granted to a public authority (eg, any level of government) for public purposes (eg, schools, police stations), a lease may be granted for up to Z years.

(4) No lease should be approved if the terms do not reflect a fair return to the customary owners.

(5) No lease should be approved if it would create a serious risk that the remaining land of the customary owners may prove inadequate for subsistence food production.

(6) No lease should be granted unless the applicants for approval can demonstrate that the agreement reflects the consent of those authorised to act by the decision-rule applicable to the group of customary owners in question.

Mortgages of interests in customary land in favour of government lending institutions and the major trading banks should also be permitted, subject to a mortgagee not being able to foreclose or sell the land on default, but instead be limited to working the land either directly or through an assignee for a period (eg, up to ten years). Mortgages would not be subject to the review process.

In our original study, we proposed that the vetting function for leases be vested in local Land Courts. Further consideration of this question now suggests to us the need for a more expert body drawing on legal, agricultural, business and sociological skills. Such a body would need to be specially constituted. In addition, we now see a need for a further body to play a pro-active, promotional role in agricultural development, ie, identifying development opportunities, presenting these to customary landowners, helping mobilize land groups, assisting in making applications to Land Courts for declarations of land rights, identifying and negotiating with possible sources of finance and management expertise on behalf of landowning groups. We believe that such a body could be built on a reconstituted and restructured National Plantation Management Agency (re-named, eg, the National Rural Land Management Agency), especially if current proposals to place the agency under the aegis of the Development Bank (the principal source of rural credit) are proceeded with. Such an agency would, because it is widely decentralised, provide one-stop service for customary landowners seeking assistance with problems of security of title, finance, and management and technical assistance in developing their land.

With respect to the issue of the security of title to interests in customary land (to which previous registration regimes attempted to respond) we propose adaptations to the existing Land Disputes Settlement Act, focusing on present land disputes, prospective (or apprehended) land disputes, and agreements with third parties. These proposals are all refinements and extensions of practices that have recently been evolving under this Act.

In the case of present land disputes, we recommend a strengthening of the existing informal mediation process under the Act by better training and vetting of mediators and the statutory codification of local customary land-laws by provincial governments in order to establish some parameters within which mediation can take place. In the event of failure of the mediation process, the study proposes a restructuring of local Land Courts whereby the disputants each nominate a qualified mediator (not previously involved in the dispute) and the two mediators agree on the appointment of a specialised, full-time, Land Court magistrate as Chairman of the Court. The parties would be encouraged and assisted to retain legal assistance in the preparation and presentation of their cases. The process suggested would hopefully offer an appropriate combination of local knowledge, acceptability, specialised expertise, and a measure of discipline in the isolation of the issues in dispute and the presentation of evidence and argument on those issues. Appeals from local Land Court decisions to Provincial Land Courts would lie only in respect of errors of law and procedural irregularities (not findings of fact). Provincial Land Courts would be staffed by senior, legally accomplished and highly experienced magistrates and parties would normally be represented by local legal advisors. An organised system of reporting important Land Court decisions should be instituted to improve the consistency of, and weight attached to principle in, Land Court decisions. Consideration should also be given to requiring parties to a land dispute to post a compliance bond before the adjudication process begins which would be returned say a year after the issuance of an order, if the order has been respected.

In the case of prospective land disputes, where a group fears that if it invests resources in enhancing the productivity of their land, another group may subsequently press an adverse claim to the land (especially if the first group's venture proves successful), the study proposes a procedure whereby the first group can apply to a local Land Court magistrate for a binding declaration of its rights. Following appropriate public notice of the application (by local radio broadcasts, etc) and in the absence of objections to the declaration sought, the local Land Court magistrate can proceed to make the declaration, which then binds all parties. If objections are received, then the procedure outlined above for present disputes is triggered. Where customary landowners wish to enter into leasing or mortgage arrangements with third parties, they would first obtain a declaration of their land rights from a local Land Court as described above. Thereafter, in the case of leases, they would be subject to a 'fairness' review by the vetting agency described above. If they satisfy this review, they would then be filed, as would mortgages, with the relevant office of the Provincial Land Court magistrate which would check, in the case of mortgages, that necessary consents to the transactions had been obtained (the vetting authority would perform this function in the case of leases) and then forward the agreement for registration in the customary land register proposed below.

By facilitating lending against the security of land and joint-venture leasing arrangements utilizing equity capital, a major infusion of additional development capital into the customary land segment of the agricultural sector should be encouraged.

Details of mediated agreements and Land Court orders in present disputes, declarations in prospective disputes, and agreements involving third parties would be entered in a proposed new centralised customary land titles registry in Port Moresby and in regional land registries maintained (probably) by Provincial Land Court officials. This registry system would form the beginnings of a documentary system for customary land titles. Once registered, Land Court orders would be come binding on all parties. Non-enforcement by the government of registered orders against parties seeking to defy an order would result in government compensation awards to any part relying on the order to his detriment. The mechanics of such a system might work roughly as follows.

A local Land Court, on issuing an order declaring rights in land, would forward it to the Provincial Land Court Magistrate's Office for filing, pending expiration of appeal periods or proceedings. Appeal periods would need to be somewhat shorter than at present to expediate the process. In the case of uncontested applications for declarations of land rights, this should create little injustice. When appeal periods or proceedings expire, the original Land Court order would be forwarded to the Registrar of Titles at Port Moresby for entry into the proposed register of customary land. A copy of the order would be retained by the Provincial Land Court Magistrate's Office. On receipt of the order, the Registrar of Titles would prepare a standardized abstract of the order, identifying the landowning group, and describing the location, area, and demarcation of the land and the nature of the landowning group's interest therein (typically base title only would be registered). Registrable Land Court orders would have to embody low-quality, chain and link surveys of boundaries. A copy of the Registrar's standardized abstract would be remitted to the Provincial Land Court Magistrate's Office for filing in a regional duplicate register. Where leasing or security (mortgage) transactions are entered into by landowners following a declaration of their rights by the Land Court, lessees and mortgagees would bear responsibility for filing the agreement with a Provincial Land Court Magistrate's Office. The agreement would then be forwarded to the Registrar of Titles who would abstract it as above and forward a copy of the abstract to the relevant Provincial Land Court Magistrate's Office for duplicate regional filing. Non-registration would render an agreement unenforceable by the third party. The Registrar of Titles would, on entering an abstract in the central customary land register, in all cases also send a copy of the abstract to representative(s) of the landowning groups named to act in that capacity in the Land Court order and to third parties involved in agreements.

PART III: TRANSACTION COSTS

In order to mitigate the substantial and sometimes crippling transaction costs often associated with land dealings in Papua New Guinea, a number of strategies warrant consideration.

Bargains for lesser interests

Negotiating agreements for lesser interests than have been historically involved in outright purchase or long term (99 year) leasing of customary land (typically through the government) probably involves fewer problems in securing agreement amongst members of a landowning group than to the alienation of more substantial interests. Permitting limited term direct leasing his consistent with this consideration.

Greater specification of gains and costs

Where feasible, agreements with customary landowners (eg, leases, sales of timber rights) should attempt to specify fully the allocation of gains, costs and risks so as to minimise future uncertainties and possible disenchantment and breach.

Showcase effects

Strategic location of demonstration projects involving the use of customary land may reduce uncertainties and inhibition in the minds of other customary landowners about the wisdom of entering into transactions or arrangements involving their land.

Compensation in kind

In the case of land required for government projects, compensation in kind, by the provision of alternative blocks of land, may sometimes be seen as a superior substitute to money for the land surrendered and facilitate negotiations over the acquisition.

Modifying group decision rules

In place of the rule of unanimity that seems typically to govern group decisions over land dealings, serious consideration needs to be given to the adoption of majoritarian or representative decision rules if the increasingly fluid nature of group composition is not to paralyse decision-making governed by unanimity rules. The land corporations provided for under the New Zealand Maori Affairs Act 1953 which operate through an elected committee of management under court supervision offers an attractive precedent. Third parties dealing with the committee of management can legally treat the committee as duly authorised to enter into agreements on behalf of the corporation. The existing Land Groups Act 1974 goes some distance in this direction and could be modified to permit limited direct dealings by customary landowning groups with third parties.

More forward-looking bargaining strategies

In negotiating with customary landowners over land required for public projects, government often finds itself in a position where having begun a project, it requires a particular tract of land almost at any price. More forward-looking bargaining strategies, involving the identification of alternative routes or projects and the negotiations of options to purchase with respect to land required for the alternatives may avoid the government being 'held up' for extortionate amounts of compensation.

Contract enforcement and renegotiation

Many contracts with long term impacts involving customary land tend to unravel. The incidence of contract breach seems high in many contexts (eg, compensation agreements, sales of timber rights). The law needs to specify very clearly the circumstances in which renegotiation or adjustment will be permitted; otherwise the government has to be prepared to see that contracts are strictly enforced. An economic environment in which contracts can be breached with impunity whenever it is expedient to do so is likely to generate substantial investor uncertainty and ultimately disinvestment.

PART IV: COMPENSATION CLAIMS

Land compensation claims against the government have been a particularly acute and disruptive issue in Papua New Guinea. Some concerns are directed at earlier pre-Independence acquisitions where no or inadequate compensation is alleged to have been paid. Other concerns are directed at more recent acquisitions where, in some cases, inadequate compensation is said to have been paid, and in other cases, excessive compensation is said to have been paid either by way of political favouritism or in response to the extortionate bargaining position of groups in a position to disrupt or obstruct a major project.

The study proposes that the Land Act (or any separate Land Compensation Act that might be enacted) should specify as exhaustively as possible all compensable interests including those that have no direct market value (loss of sacred places, ancestral burial grounds, etc) and that schedules be developed and revised from time to time setting out rates of compensation for these various interests. Compensation awards would be determined in all contexts by a political tribunal, such as modified National Land Commission, with appeals therefrom to the courts only with respect to legal or procedural irregularities. Compulsory acquisition and compensation provisions in the Land Act, the National Land Registration Act 1977, and the Land Acquisition Act 1974 would be consolidated in a single statute and administered by a single tribunal.

Compulsory acquisitions under the Plantation Redistribution Scheme appear to have had a detrimental impact on the productivity of the plantation sector. In some cases, uncertainty as to which plantations would be acquired and what compensation payments would be likely to be forthcoming in that event has induced disinvestment in the sector and falling productivity. In other cases, poor management of the plantations following acquisition and distribution to local groups has had a similar effect. The study proposes that remaining expatriate plantation owners be permitted to retain (or convert to) long term leasehold interests in their plantations and be able to transfer or mortgage these interests freely, including effecting transfers to non-nationals. (We understand that the government has recently adopted a similar policy.) The government should seek to make available other alienated but undeveloped land to local groups for development.

PART V: ALIENATED LAND (GOVERNMENT LEASEHOLDS)

In the case of alienated land (3% of the land in Papua New Guinea), specifically government-owned leasehold interests, the procedures in place under the Land Act and administered by the Department of Lands for the issuance, transfer, amendment, and mortgaging of leasehold interests have created lengthy delays in processing land dealings involving government leasehold interests and have contributed to the scarcity of developable land, especially in urban centres. Few offsetting benefits seem to be associated with these detailed regulatory controls. A better strategy would seem to be to establish some general constraints on urban development through Town Planning and construction specification requirements, building permit requirements reflecting the availability of water, sewerage, and other amenities, and survey requirements. Within these constraints, a relatively free market in land in urban centres should be permitted with the government auctioning off leasehold blocks for development to the highest bidders, and direct long term leasehold dealings in customary land in urban centres being permitted by way of extension to the proposals on direct dealings outlined above.

Concerns over distributional questions, such as the availability of low-income urban housing, should be met by separate programmes designed specifically to this end rather than by policies that disrupt the entire market on this account. These programmes might be financed, in part, by land taxes that reflect the development potential of land (which would create incentives to realise that potential) and/or a capital gains tax on the purchase and re-sale of urban properties.

PART VI: CONCLUSION

The proposals we advance are highly incremental in nature and do not involve cataclysmic (and unattainable) agendas of reform. The proposals on alienation and registration of interests in customary land recognise evolving practices in the field (in the case of alienation) and involve some relatively straightforward refinements and extensions to the

Land Dispute Settlement Act (in the case of registration). They are readily amendable to trial in a pilot scheme in one or more provinces. The proposals for dealing with land compensation claims would again involve relatively straightforward adaptations and extensions to aspects of the National Land Registration Act and to the role of the National Land Commission (probably in the form of a new Land Compensation Act and Land Compensation Board, as exemplified in many other jurisdictions).

The proposals for reducing the legal and administrative impediments to the supply of leasehold land in urban centres would involve establishing some broad parameters for development but drastically reducing case-by-case review and approval of all individual legal transactions.

In order to think discretely and practically about land reform issues, it might be useful to set in train policy development strategies that focus sharply and to some extent separately on the following issues:

(a) what to do about alienability and registration of interests in customary land, and related questions of land dispute resolution, especially in the rural sector;

(b) what to do about land compensation claims;

(c) what to do about facilitating transactions involving alienated (leasehold) land, especially in urban centres, and how to ensure greater availability of land, including customary land, in these centres;

(d) whether pilot schemes in particular regions or centres might be a productive path to follow in testing out new approaches to each of the first three questions.

As Aaron Wildavsky, a distinguished American political scientist and policy analyst, once remarked: 'Policy analysis is an activity creating problems that can be solved.' (Aaron Wildavsky, *Speaking Truth to Power: The Art and Craft of Policy Analysis*, Boston, Little, Brown and Co, 1979, p 17.) Decomposing land problems in Papua New Guinea into discrete issues and identifying some incremental moves that might be made with respect to each issue seems to respect the force of this observation. More global conceptualisations of the problems and more ambitious agendas of reform are likely to leave the severe land problems presently being encountered in Papua New Guinea unresolved for many years to come.

RD COOTER, 'ISSUES IN CUSTOMARY LAND LAW' (PORT MORESBY: INSTITUTE OF NATIONAL AFFAIRS, DISCUSSION PAPER No 39, 1989), pp 43–50

THE CASE AGAINST GOVERNMENT MONOPOLY IN CUSTOMARY LAND DEALS

In many nations, government is the only supplier of certain kinds of goods such as hospitals, piped water, schools, universities, military security, mail, telephones, trains, airports, and electricity. In addition, government sets the prices or terms of sale on many goods that are privately supplied, such as medicine, health care, alcohol, guns, airplane tickets, unskilled labour, and legal services. Thus government exercises monopoly control over many goods as sole supplier or regulator of the terms of sale.

Papua New Guinea has created a government monopoly over many land deals. Customary land that has been converted to freehold and registered cannot be transferred or leased for more than 25 years without approval of the Land Board. (See s 12 of Land (Tenure Conversion) (Amendment) Act of 1987 that replaced s 26 of the Land (Tenure Conversion) Act of 1963. In lease-back, the annual value of the lease is ordinarily set at 5% of the unimproved capital value of the land.) Land remaining under customary law cannot be sold or leased to anyone other than customary groups except through the State (Land Act, Ch No 185, s 15). Before a customary group leases land to the State, the Minister for Lands and Physical Planning must be:

> ... satisfied, after reasonable inquiry, that the land is not required or likely to be required by the owners or by persons on whom the land will or may devolve by custom (Land Act, Ch No 185, s 15(3)).

The other face of this paternalism is that government cannot acquire native land by compulsion except for a public purpose. See 'Compulsory acquisition', CEP Haynes, *Land Law and Land Policy in Papua New Guinea: Text, Cases and Materials* (UPNG Printery, 1986, section 2 (ii), pages 7–9).

Most transactions in land, however, are between customary owners. The formalization of customary law by the Land Courts has not proceeded far enough to eliminate many of the uncertainties and risks attending these transactions. In the meantime, while customary owners await such developments, their attempts to legally bind themselves to the terms of a sale or lease are imperfect, so sales and leases of customary land are unnecessarily risky. ('The principal rationale for a system of registration of interests in customary land in Papua New Guinea revolves around the need to reduce uncertainty and therefore risk associated with economic activities involving land', *Task Force on Customary Land Issues*, Report, presented to Minister for Lands, 1983, p 8.)

The effect upon development is stifling. To overcome this risk, East Sepik Province has enacted legislation to register land titles in the names of the clans that are its customary owners and to facilitate its lease to others for use. This legislation, which is the model for national legislation that is currently being drafted, requires all deals involving customary land to be vetted by a government committee. (The East Sepik Province Land Act defines a sale or lease to anyone but the government as a 'controlled dealing', which requires the approval of the 'appropriate authority'.) The 'appropriate authority' is the Provincial or District Land Management Committee, possibly as reported to and approved by the Provincial Secretary. The procedure is for the acquiring party to forward the instrument to Assistant Secretary (Lands), who forwards it to the appropriate authority, who establishes that eleven conditions are satisfied, the most important being:

(i) the transaction 'is generally agreed to by the customary owners of the subject land and has been entered into in the manner provided for by the custom applying to the land';

(ii) adequate reason for sale or lease is given;

(iii) the boundaries are adequately identified;

(iv) adequate provision is made for road access to the property;

(v) appropriate authority is satisfied that the dealing is in the interest of customary land owners.

Thus government's monopoly power will extend to formal dealings in land under customary ownership.

Economists have developed theories over the years to predict the behaviour of government monopolies. This note applies these theories to dealings in customary land. I argue that government monopoly is too cumbersome and creates a grave risk of corruption. A more promising approach would rely more on Land Courts to safeguard customary land dealings.

Rationale for government monopoly

What characteristics distinguish goods whose supply is best monopolized by government? government monopolies serve a variety of needs such as health, education, safety, and communications, but these needs are also met by goods produced privately in relatively unregulated markets, such as food for health, books for education, guard dogs for safety, and private radios for communications. Thus the boundary between private and public sectors cannot be drawn on the basis that each serves different needs.

So how is the boundary to be drawn? After struggling with this problem for many years, economists developed a theory based upon the production characteristics of different goods. (A clear formulation of the market failures theory is found in Charles Schultze, *The Public Use of Private Interest*, Brookings, 1977.) The synthesis in theory explained by Schultze developed from two important strands of economic theory. First, general equilibrium theory produced a deep understanding of perfect competition. See, for example, KJ Arrow and F Hahn, *General Competitive Analysis* (1971). Second, the concept of public goods was given a rigorous formulation by Paul Samuelson in 'The pure theory of public expenditure' (1959) 36 *Rev of Econ & Stat 387–89*. A synthesis of thinking about public goods is found in Richard Musgrave's *The Theory of Public Finance* (1959). When a market works well, buyer and seller both benefit from exchange to the maximum possible extent. (Thus mathematical economists routinely prove that perfect competition is Pareto efficient. See Arrow and Hahn cited in preceding footnote.) When a market fails, however, the benefits of exchange fall short of the maximum, or one of the parties may even be harmed by exchange. One tradition in economic theory holds that government should intervene when markets fail. The basic rationale for government monopoly is that it provides the best remedy for failures in private markets caused by the production characteristics of certain goods.

I will discuss several forms of market failure that are relevant to land deals in Papua New Guinea. One significant form of market failure occurs when the cost of producing a good falls as the producer grows larger. To illustrate, the cost of telephone calls in Papua New Guinea will probably fall as the telephone network expands. (Networks usually have a central switch and there are large economies of scale in switching equipment.) Such an industry is said to have 'increasing returns to scale' because productivity increases with the scale of production. Increasing returns to scale characterize goods supplied through networks, such as telephones, electricity grids, water pipes, and railroads.

When production is characterized by increasing returns to scale, competing firms can produce more efficiently by merging into a single large firm. The gain in efficiency, however, is accompanied by risk to consumers. The single firm created by such mergers is a private monopolist who can maximize profits by keeping prices high and restraining production. To protect consumers, government may regulate prices and terms of sale for goods produced by a private monopolist. Thus government takes monopoly power away from the private producer and retains it for itself, ostensibly to protect consumers. Alternatively, the private monopoly may be nationalized and the good supplied directly by a government monopoly. The existence of increasing returns to scale thus provides a rationale for government's monopoly control over some of the goods listed above. (A more complete discussion would cover several important qualifications of this proposition. For example, natural monopoly explains why government may be the only supplier of a good, but it does not explain why the law should forbid private suppliers from competing with government. Similarly, there are ways to handle natural monopoly other than by government monopoly, such as auctioning production rights and selling them to the highest bidder.)

Another form of market failure occurs when a private transaction significantly affects people who are not parties to it. To illustrate, I may purchase cigarettes for my own enjoyment, but my smoking may bother you. Similarly, I may purchase a car for my private use, but my bad driving may endanger you. I may dump sewerage into the river when you wash your clothes. Guns or alcohol sold to one person may enable the buyer to harm others. In each of these cases, an economic transaction harms people who are not parties to it. Since harm is not the purpose of the transaction, but only an accidental by-product, it is called an 'external effect' or an 'externality'.

Some externalities, unlike the ones listed in the preceding paragraph, are beneficial rather than harmful. To illustrate, if I put a light in front of my house to deter thieves, the light may also make the street safer for pedestrians. Improved safety for pedestrians is an incidental by-product of my installing the light. Similarly, if I hire a private guard to protect my house at night, pedestrians walking in front of my house may also be safer. Another example is education, which is widely believed to benefit society as whole, not just the recipients of it, by making people better citizens.

In private market transactions, the parties look to their own benefits and pay little heed to external effects. Left to itself, the private market will, consequently, supply too many goods that cause harmful externalities and too few goods that cause beneficial externalities. To illustrate, without government there will be too much pollution and too few street lights. There is thus a potential advantage from government supplying or regulating the supply of goods that have significant external affects.

The third, and final, form of market failure that I will discuss occurs when one party to a transaction has far more knowledge than the other party about the quality and value of the product. To illustrate, the consumers of medical drugs, who usually know little about them, must have confidence that the drugs are effective and safe when used according to directions. If unscrupulous sellers, who know far more than consumers about drugs, were allowed to dump dangerous and ineffective drugs on the market, consumers might lose confidence in the industry and manufacturers might be discouraged from producing safe and effective products. (Declining sales due to loss of buyers' confidence and discouragement of high quality suppliers is called 'adverse selection'.) There are many economic models of adverse selection. The first such model was George Akerlof's 'The market for lemons: quality, uncertainty, and the market mechanism' (Aug 1970) QJ Econ. Government regulation allegedly provides uninformed consumers with a guarantee of the safety and effectiveness of drugs. (There are, of course, many devices other than government regulation for supplying such a guarantee. Manufacturer's warrantees and liability laws may have the same effect.)

Medical drugs are just one example in which the consumer knows far less about the product than the seller. There are many examples, such as used cars or the services of physicians and lawyers. In some cases the reverse situation arises in which consumers know far more than the sellers. For example, consumers who purchase life insurance policies know far more about their own health than the life insurance company who writes the policy.

In general, if one of the parties to a transaction does not understand the characteristics of the good, the benefits from market exchange will not be maximized, or one of the parties may even be harmed. 'Asymmetrical information' between buyer and seller can cause private markets to fail. Government regulation can protect the uninformed party and thus increase the scope for exchange.

Of the three forms of market failure – increasing returns to scale, externalities, and asymmetrical information – two are directly relevant to deals involving customary owners of land in Papua New Guinea. The fundamental rationale for government vetting of land deals is that customary owners do not understand or appreciate fully the consequences of leasing or selling their land. They might, consequently, fall prey to hard-bargaining or unscrupulous buyers. This is an argument based upon asymmetrical information, much like the argument for regulating the sale of medical drugs.

A second argument for government vetting of land deals is that sales and leases of customary land affect a whole network of kinsmen, including future generations. By protecting the integrity of the kin group and strengthening it, government can diminish social problems associated with the loosening of social bonds, such as rascalism and drunkenness. Thus a government monopoly on deals in customary land can be defended on the grounds that government is responsible for protecting the interests of people affected by the transaction who are not parties to it. This is an argument based upon externalities.

Critique of government monopoly

The preceding section developed an economic rationale for government vetting of customary land deals based upon two types of market failure – asymmetrical information and externalities. Market failure theory casts government in the role of public benefactor who, like the wise clan elder, intercedes to prevent private transactions from causing harm. Market failure theory, however, is just the first of two accounts of government monopoly that I will develop. The second theory depicts government very differently. Rather than viewing government monopoly as public benefactor, the second theory views it as a device by which politicians and civil servants extract private advantage at the expense of the general public. The second theory thus provides a critique of government monopoly, not a rationale in favour of it.

The starting point for a critique of government monopoly is the realization that civil servants and politicians, like businessmen, have their own ambitions and private goals. government is not wholly benevolent because it is staffed by human beings. Faced with a conflict between the best interests of the public and their own best interests, civil servants and politicians often look to their own interests first. Monopoly control can be used by government to correct market failure, which benefits the public, but it can also be used to benefit civil servants and politicians.

The private goals of politicians have a characteristic form. Just as businessmen try to maximize profits, so politicians try to maximize their own political power. In so far as politicians are in control, monopoly power in economic life will be directed at maximizing the political power of reigning politicians.

A similar argument applies to civil servants. Just as politicians try to maximize their own political power, so civil servants try to increase the size and influence of the agencies that they staff. Insofar as civil servants are in control, monopoly power in economic life may be directed, not at the public good, but at maximizing the size and influence of government agencies.

I have discussed the possibility that the monopoly power of government will be used to benefit civil servants and politicians, rather than benefiting the public. There is another possibility that must be mentioned. Competition between businessmen keeps prices low and profits down. If businessmen can stop competing with each other and agree to keep prices high, their profits will increase. It is thus in the interest of businessmen, but not the public interest, to conspire together to keep prices high. This fact was noted earlier when I said that high prices and high profits are a characteristic of unregulated private monopolies.

When businessmen agree to keep prices high and not to compete with each other, their agreements often break down. The breakdown occurs because any business that cuts its price will attract customers away from other businesses that stick to the agreed price. Thus, individual businesses have an incentive to sell below the agreed price, even though business as a whole enjoys higher profits by observing it. In brief, agreements not to compete are unstable because cheaters win.

To illustrate, nations belonging to the Organization of Petroleum Exporting Countries (OPEC) periodically negotiate an agreement to keep oil prices high. Conforming to the official OPEC price increases the profits of all the oil producing nations. Each individual country that produces oil, however, can make even more profit by undercutting the official OPEC price and attracting extra customers. Thus, OPEC has great difficulty preventing its members from cheating on the agreement. The nations of OPEC are, in this respect, just like businesses who have difficulty enforcing an agreement not to compete with each other.

To solve this problem, businessmen often try to get government to enforce high prices. Businesses in an industry may give donations, gifts, or bribes to induce politicians to pass a law that sets a minimum price for a certain good and ask government to prosecute anyone who sells below the legal price. Thus, businesses can prevent competition and avoid price cutting by getting government to enact monopoly prices. In the preceding section I explained that private monopolies keep prices high and that government regulation may be needed to protect consumers. The opposite possibility is contemplated here. Instead of lowering prices to protect consumers, government price regulation is often a device for raising prices and exploiting consumers.

In this section, I have discussed three possible objectives: (i) maximizing the power of reigning politicians; (ii) maximizing the size of government agencies; and (iii) maximizing the profits of private businesses. The history of government regulation in countries like the United States provides examples of each. To illustrate, the Civil Aeronautics Board kept air fares high for many years and stopped competition among airlines, as assumed by objective (iii). The Civil Aeronautics Board was described by its critics as the 'captive' of the airline companies. The Interstate Commerce Commission, in contrast, imposed a vast array of cumbersome regulations whose main effect was probably to create more work for itself, as assumed by objective (ii). Finally, many of the internal rules that govern regulatory agencies in America appear to increase the political power of Congressmen, as assumed by objective (i). Congressional power is increased because the existence of the regulations makes it possible for Congressmen to do favours and perform valuable services for constituents. No wonder that deregulation has been so popular among Americans recently.

Application to land in Papua New Guinea

These three accounts of the objectives of government monopolies have immediate application to land deals in Papua New Guinea. Assume that a prerequisite for making deals in customary land is registering title and obtaining approval from a government committee. There is always a line in the post office, there are always cases waiting for months to be tried in courts, there are applications for land conversions awaiting action at the Land Titles Commission ('an estimated 8,000 to 10,000 lease applications are now stalled in the Department of Lands', *Task Force on Customary Land Issues*, Report, presented to Minister for Lands, 1983, p 26) and there will assuredly be a backlog of customary land deals awaiting vetting.

It is not hard to see some reasons why a backlog will develop. Officials never have enough staff to monitor the full range of market transactions. Besides insufficient resources, officials seldom have the motivation needed to stay abreast of the market. Dedicated civil servants proceed with caution for fear of making a mistake that will harm their careers. The benefit of proceeding with caution on land deals accrues to civil servants, whereas the cost of delay falls upon private parties. If civil servants control the pace, their caution (not to mention their sloth) will impose excessive delays upon land deals.

With a backlog of land deals awaiting approval, costly delays can be avoided by moving to the front of the queue. Powerful people will be tempted to use their influence to do so. To get to the front of the queue, businessmen will enlist the support of politicians. The power of politicians will be increased because of their role in getting valuable approvals for land deals. Finally, some people who own land may realize that they can keep the prices of leases very high by restricting the number of deals actually completed. Thus they will try to influence government to approve their own deals and to obstruct deals involving their competitors. In this way government will create monopoly profits for favoured businessmen.

Proposed solution

I began this note by acknowledging that there is a market failure in customary land deals due to the ignorance of formal law on the part of some customary land owners (asymmetrical information) and due to the effects of land deals on clan discipline and future generations (externalities). A government monopoly might pursue the public interest and try to correct these market failures, or a government monopoly might be used to increase the power of politicians, the importance of civil servants, and the wealth of favoured businessmen. Even if the government monopoly proceeds with the best of intentions in all cases, it is unlikely to have enough resources for the task.

The two problems of diversion of objectives and insufficient resources might be overcome by streamlining processes and reducing government's monopoly power. The key to streamlining is enabling owners to do much of the work of vetting deals themselves, and putting more faith in mediators and courts to protect the clans. I suggest three steps that might help to achieve these goals.

First, the land mobilization officers should draft standard forms which land owners can use to make deals. The forms must direct owners to consider and make provision for the contingencies that give rise to disputes. To illustrate, customary land leases often fail to make provision for increases in the value of the land or the arrival of additional relatives of the people leasing the land. Thus the customary agreements tend to break down when land appreciates and more relatives join the original squatters. The standard form for leases should invite the parties to specify how they will handle such contingencies. The parties should be directed by the registration form to contemplate in advance the contingencies that cause most disputes.

Second, the government committee charged with vetting land deals, such as the Land Management Committee in East Sepik Province, should give preliminary approval automatically for all deals that use standard forms. Instead of civil servants scrutinizing every deal, detailed examination should be restricted to cases involving disagreement. When disputes arise, the vetting committee such as East Sepik's Land Management Committee would be well advised to limit itself to making a recommendation to mediators or the Lands Court. After all, Papua New Guinea does not need yet another judicial body besides mediators, Village Courts, Land Courts, and Local Courts.

Third, a central file should be established containing a card describing the boundaries of each registered clan, and recording any disputes or deals. Boundaries could be traced upon a master map as the file grows. Much hope is held out by East Sepik officials for establishing a computer system to record such information. Most computer systems have a software package with a name like 'Filebox' or 'Filecard' that provides an electronic method for recording and sorting file cards. Thus the file cards could be entered into a computer when the technology becomes available. My inspection of land records at courthouses around Papua New Guinea found them to be uneven in quality and quantity. It seems that many officials just cannot be bothered to record and file information promptly. The actual filing system must be devised with these human failings foremost in mind.

In East Sepik Province the legislation is already in place to proceed with these proposals. East Sepik's Customary Land Registration Act may be copied by other provinces or it may become the basis for national legislation. In any case, the changes that I recommend are primarily matters of administration, not legislation. Customary land deals are already being made throughout Papua New Guinea with little legal support. Land officials can develop standardized forms and procedures to assist these deals, while remaining within the scope of their power, even without new legislation. The Land Courts can proceed to develop standards for enforcing these deals as part of its responsibility for formalizing customary law.

There have been too many legislative daydreams among politicians and administrators in Papua New Guinea who delude themselves into thinking that they can direct the efforts of the nation by their commands. Many of the laws, directives, rules, and regulations concerning lands are, fortunately, ignored at the local level. The most important thing that national politicians can do for smallholders is to provide the legal framework and infrastructure for marketing agricultural products, and not burden smallholders with taxes. Agricultural development, including the improvement of property law, will proceed on a pace set by clans and families themselves, according to their interest in its various aspects, not according to a master plan set by a government monopoly.

Question

1 Discuss the validity or otherwise of the assertion that only a vigorous policy of individual tenure would usher in the millennium of prosperity which political independence presaged.

VI LAND REFORM AND LAND USE: LESSONS FROM SOME THIRD WORLD NATIONS[19]

We reproduce below extracts from Amankwah's earlier work on the issue:

Although the British claimed that respect for indigenous legal, political and social institutions was a hall-mark of their colonial policy[20] yet a close scrutiny of British colonial

19 Ref HA Amankwah, *The Legal Regime of Land Use in West Africa* (Pacific Law Press, Hobart, 1989), pp 131–40.

20 The Privy Council stated the judicial position thus in *Re Southern Rhodesia* [1919] AC 211, at p 233: 'Some tribes are so low in the scale of social organisation that their usages and conceptions of rights and duties are not to be reconciled with the institutions or ideas of civilized society ... On the other hand, there are indigenous peoples whose legal conceptions, though differently developed, [contd]

> policy reveals an ambivalence on the issue of land rights of indigenous peoples of British colonial territories. Sometimes the primary consideration was the paramountcy of native rights. At other times it was that of settlers' interests. Nowhere was contradiction in British colonial policy more vividly demonstrated than in the area of operation of the plantation system. While British colonial policy in West Africa frowned on the inauguration of the plantation system as a means of protecting the land of the natives from ruthless exploitation by foreign capital, in East Africa on the other hand it vigorously encouraged the establishment of plantations in places such as Kenya, Zimbabwe, Tanzania and Malawi. The congenial climatic conditions in these places may not be unconnected with this contradiction in British colonial policy.[21] Even where indigenous law and custom was recognised as applicable to a certain situation, resort was had to English legal doctrines and principles quite unintelligible to colonial subjects to defeat native rights.[22] While for example, 'waste and vacant land' declarations were directed ostensibly at the protection of native land rights, they were in fact a strategy designed to take away from the domain of customary law as much land as possible and placing same under the regime of the received English common law and statutes.

Though it is plausible to argue that a policy aimed at bringing more land under State control ensured land use control as well, yet it is also arguable that the same policy resulted in land shortage as large tracts of State land remained unutilised the while those who needed land for even subsistence farming could not find it. This fostered the growth of the phenomenon of landlessness and its appurtenance of social vices, a situation accentuated by increase in population and extreme pressure on the land in certain areas. Such was the situation at least in Papua New Guinea on the eve of independence, which forced the government to release State land to settle land-short groups of the populace.[23]

Our thesis is that a land policy which is not geared towards ensuring an efficacious use of land only compounds the land problem. A landless class is a political time-bomb which a government can ignore only at its own risk. In Papua New Guinea the inauguration of a land use policy took a long time.

What land use policy for PNG?

Successive administrations in Papua New Guinea have pursued one form of land policy or other. Professor James identifies at least four, namely the status quo, transformation, amelioration or improvement and corporate title registration.[24] It must be pointed out, however, that the fourth policy in so far as it complements or even enhances the achievement of the third, may be considered ... an integral part of it, and not a separate policy by itself.

---

20 [contd] are hardly less precise than our own. *When once they have been studied and understood they are no less enforceable than rights arising under English law.'* (Emphasis added.) See also, TO Elias, *British Colonial Laws* (Stevens & Sons, London, 1962), p 101.

21 See RK Udo, 'Sixty years of plantation agriculture in Southern Nigeria' (1965) Economic Geography Vol 41, p 356.

22 For example, the constitutional law doctrines of act of State, political sovereignty as opposed to possessory sovereignty etc. See *Amodu Tijani v Secretary, Southern Nigeria* [1921] 2 AC 399; *Administration of the Territory of Papua v Guba and Doriga* (1973) P&NGLR 603; *Agevu v The Government of Papua New Guinea* [1977] PNGLR 99 and *Oyekan v Adele* [1957] WLR 880.

23 *Report, Commission of Inquiry into Land Matters* (CILM) *supra*, see p 54; see also RW James, *Land Law and Policy in PNG*, PNG Law Reform Commission, Monograph No 5 (1985), p 78.

24 James, *ibid*, p 42ff.

The status quo policy was really a political gimmick designed to impress on colonial subjects the concern of the imperial power for their interests. It was malleable and depending on the political vicissitudes could be shelved to make room for the accommodation of other competing interests especially the interests of the settlers.[25]

The transformation policy was initiated by the Australian administration which proceeded on the assumption that respect for indigenous custom 'will not meet the needs of a society in which, to an increasing extent as a result of rapid economic progress, the native people are planting tree crops such as coffee, cocoa and copra and engaging in cash farming'.[26] It was also assumed that 'native customary tenures, were suitable for subsistence agriculture in which the land was required only for short term cropping or food gathering'.[27] The ultimate and long term objective of the Australian administration from 1962 was therefore, the introduction throughout the Territory of 'a single system of land holding regulated by the Central government by statute, administered by the Department of Lands of the Central government, and providing for secure individual registered titles after the pattern of the Australian system'.[28] This policy it was hoped would 'facilitate *the better use by the native people of the available land,* the more orderly handling of all land transactions, and the *better use of the natural resources of the Territory*'.[29]

The thesis that individual ownership of land is the panacea to the land use problem is not a new one. It has also been hotly contested by many. Dr Asante, for example, doubts if a robust policy of individual holding as advocated by some Western observers can lead to the millennium of efficacious land use system in Africa.[30] Noting that in the Middle East and South America, gross inequality in land holding had thrown certain countries in these areas into violent social convulsion, he prescribes for Ghana, where he believes such gross disparity in land ownership does not yet exist, the purging of corporate ownership of its more pernicious aspects which make nonsense of the trusteeship concept (instead of an out and out system of individual ownership) so that those who administer landed property for and on behalf of others and themselves could be held strictly, accountable for their stewardship. This, the learned author believes, will ensure a wider sharing of the wealth of the society. The learned author says that although he is not opposed to individual ownership *per se* (indeed he urges a limited type of individual ownership as

---

25 Thus for example, in *The Administration of the Territory of Papua and New Guinea and Others v Daera and Guba* (1973) 130 CLR 353 the High Court of Australia after finding that land matters were governed by native custom, then took the case out of the domain of customary law by holding that the land in issue fell within 'waste and vacant' declaration and was therefore, governed by English law. It however did not address the question of the validity of the transaction which according to English principles had to be evidenced by writing. Professor James appropriately said of this case, also called the *Newtown* case:

The High Court's decision in the *Newtown* case is undoubtedly of interest to students of colonialism and is best explicable in the context of imperialism ('The role of the courts in an attempt to recover alienated land' (1974) 2 MLJ 270).

26 P Hasluck, 'Ministerial statement on land tenure in Papua New Guinea', *Hansard, House of Representatives (Australia)* 1960, Vol 26, 1019, 1020–21.

27 *Ibid,* p 3.

28 *Ibid,* p 4.

29 *Ibid.* Emphasis supplied.

30 Asante, *Property Law and Social Goals in Ghana* (Ghana Universities Press, Accra, 1976), p 240, hereinafter cited *Property Law;* also Jegede, *Land Law and Development,* An Inaugural Lecture; delivered at the University of Lagos, 17 January 1980, p 34.

conducive to personal development and initiative), a thorough-going system of individual property leads to the concentration of wealth in the hands of a few, and this with its attendant incidence of the right to abuse property, selfishness, acquisitiveness and a callous and cynical unconcern for the public weal.[31]

This situation has afflicted with terrible consequences the Western countries, he says, and in a bid to avert further exacerbation of this condition of life, resort has been had to elaborate social security systems.[32] The type of limited private ownership which Dr Asante envisages is one which is impressed with the stamp of trusteeship.[33]

In Papua New Guinea, the CILM took a similar view of the policy of individualisation of land tenure; noting that this policy had led to misery, poverty and landlessness in much of Asia and Latin America, it recommended a *mid via* between extreme collectivism and unrestrained individualism.[34]

The amelioration or improvement policy was given a new lease of life with the appointment of the CILM. It was diametrically opposed to any sudden and drastic change in the country's land policy, and preferred instead a gradual and steady change based on the employment of indigenous institutions and concepts as vehicles for change. The CILM said specifically:

> We do not recommend a sweeping agrarian revolution and a total transformation of Papua New Guinean society. We do not recommend either collective or individualistic extremes. Our approach is rather to encourage evolution of certain existing features of our society in order to strengthen opportunities for commercial farming and permit freer transfer of rights to those who most need land.[35]

The most important single vehicle for this policy of unaccelerated change is the institution of corporate or communal ownership of land. The Land Groups Incorporation Act[36] and the Business Groups Incorporation Act[37] were passed to effect the desired change. The first is an Act 'to recognise the corporate nature of customary groups, and to allow them to hold, manage and deal with land in their customary names'.[38] The second is an Act to provide for 'the incorporation of customary groups for business and other economic purposes; and the control and regulation of the conduct of business by such groups'.[39] Together, both legislations provide the advantages of incorporation – an alien concept while at the same time preserving the application of customary law in the relationship of members *inter se*.

It is, therefore, clear that until 1973, ie, before the completion of the work of the CILM, there was no articulate State policy on the efficacious use of land. Land proprietorship *per se* is meaningless unless it is related to the use to which land can be put, for as Pollock pointed out: '[W]hat we call the law of property is in the first place the systematic

31 *Ibid*, p 286.
32 *Ibid*, p 232.
33 *Ibid.*
34 *Report, supra*, see p 54, para 2.9.
35 *Report, supra*, see p 54, para 2.9.
36 Ch No 147.
37 Ch No 144.
38 Preamble, Ch No 147.
39 Preamble, Ch No 144.

expression of degrees of control forms of use and enjoyment of land recognised and protected by law.'[40]

Land reform: issues and problems

Land reform aims at the extirpation of perceived iniquities in the land rights distribution pattern of society and the inaugurating in its stead a more equitable system of distribution. Professor Udo says: 'All land reform involves changes, while drastic land reforms usually involve revolutionary changes in the ownership or control of land and sometimes in the type and efficiency of land use.'[41] The more familiar methods of land reform include settlement, redistribution, consolidation and the formation of co-operatives. Our examples are mainly those from developing nations because PNG's circumstances are akin to those of other developing countries and the lessons from these examples would no doubt be beneficial to policy makers in PNG.

Land reform issues very often have political under-currents and have to be approached with caution. A programme of land reform could arouse discontent of local people where it involves the resettlement of strangers. This discontent may take the form of hostility and opposition to development schemes designed for the comfort of the new occupants of the land.

Yet history is replete with evidence that disparity in land ownership had led to violent upheavals in many parts of the world. It is true that land distribution pattern in some developing nations today has not reached the stage where a violent confrontation between the landed and the landless can be said to be imminent but it is also equally true that usable land is getting scarce in many places of high population density and that unless measures are taken immediately to check and perhaps reverse the trend of things, a violent cataclysm is inevitable in the long run.

In any programme of land reform perhaps the most difficult task is how to convince those who will be affected (invariably the illiterate local peoples) that the proposed change in the pattern of proprietorship of land will inure to their benefit. In plain language this means, for example, satisfying citizen X whose portion of land is being taken and given to citizen Y, a total stranger to X, that Y's new proprietorship will benefit X. One way of doing this is to provide appropriate compensation for X for the land he has lost. Another way is to give X a substitute land of the same acreage as that which he has lost. Most compulsory acquisition laws make provision for the two types of remedies. But ultimately, political ideology becomes a necessity. Appeal has often been made to concepts such as equality, justice, egalitarianism, development, etc.

The 17th Session of the FAO Conference on the State of Food and Agriculture, held in Rome, 10–29 November 1973 reviewed the state of agriculture in the developing countries of Africa. Significant growth rates were noted in Algeria, Ghana, the Ivory Coast, Kenya,

40 *Jurisprudence and Legal Essays* (OUP, London, 1961), p 93.

41 'Implementation of the Nigerian Land Reform Law of 1978: lessons from the Japanese Experience' Tokyo, *Institute of Development Economies Visiting Research Fellow Monograph Series* No 76 (1980), p 1.

Morocco, Tanzania, Tunisia, and Zambia.[42] In the case of Ghana, 'Operation Feed Yourself' was cited as the sole contributing factor to the nation's growth rate.[43]

The food production in 1975 fell by 25% over the 1974 level and was only slightly higher than the figure of 1963 while total population had increased by 37% since 1963.[44] Given favourable climatic conditions – ie, good rainfall – the 1973 increase in food production was not unexpected.

In the case of the rest of the African nations the recorded growth increases in agriculture were said to be attributable to reform in the land tenure systems, particularly in the area of title registration which boosted investment in the agricultural sector and sensible redistribution of land. In the Ivory Coast a colonial law, a French Decree,[45] which applied to several French overseas territories enabled the government to take over certain unexploited lands for redistribution.[46] In the other countries it was noted that projects in agriculture, livestock, etc were undertaken by individuals with extension services and credit facilities provided to farmers by government institutions.

In Morocco, quite apart from the prosperity which the phosphate industry has generated, government policy focussed on agriculture. The Moroccan government, it was noted, promoted the diffusion of high-yielding varieties. It also controlled the prices of agriculture inputs.

The importance of agriculture to Africa can hardly be over-emphasised. The continent is the least urbanised of the world's regions. In recent times, however the large-scale under-employment which exists in the rural areas has triggered off migration to urban areas where unemployment is already a major problem. According to United Nations projections the high rates of urban growth of the 1960s were likely to be accelerated over the period 1970–85.[47] While urban population will continue to provide expanding market for food, it will at the same time create shortage of labour in the farming communities. One way to arrest this trend of development is to create favourable agrarian conditions so that the rural population would not be attracted by urban life.

Our contention, therefore, is that if significant growth rates in agriculture is attributable to land reform measures in the African countries indicated, the possibilities are that land reform in other developing nations similarly situated would usher in a period of increased agricultural growth rate.

We have noted that in Papua New Guinea, Simpson's agrarian reform measures were rejected. The CILM which was set up following the rejection of the Simpson Land Bills recommended a cautious rather than a sweeping approach to the land problem.

---

42 See C 73/2 August, 1973.

43 This was part of the national self-reliance policy propagated by the military regime of the National Liberation Council of General IK Acheampong in 1972.

44 See P Cheshire, 'The Institutional Framework for Maximising Agricultural and Economic Productivity', Kumasi: Land Research Administration Centre, University of Science and Technology, July 1977, p 14.

45 *Decree* No 57-243, Feb 24 1957. See further FM Mifsud, *Customary Land Law in Africa,* Rome: FAO Legislative Series, No 7, p 48 (1967).

46 Mifsud, *ibid,* 48. See also FAO, *Agricultural Development in Nigeria 1965–80,* Rome 331–47 (1966).

47 *UN Monthly Bulletin of Statistics,* No 25(11) 160, November 1971.

At the approach of independence about 3% of the total land mass of the country was under foreign control as alienated land, 97% being still held by the natives under customary tenure. The holders of the 3% of land in the country acquired their title either through the government's compulsory acquisition scheme[48] or private purchases; and while it could be correct to assert that some of the land transactions at this time were unfair bargains from the point of view of the natives, and were therefore subsequently repudiated by them, there would seem to be nothing manifestly illegal about the acquisitions.[49] It must, however, be noted that the 3% land which came under foreign control, a portion of which consists of plantations happened incidentally to comprise the most cultivable and agriculturally most productive of the country's land, a situation which was to generate a lot of resentment and anger against plantation owners on the eve of independence. In the view of the nationalists the indigenisation of the plantations was a condition precedent to the achievement of political independence and nationhood.

This was the prevailing situation, which led to the inauguration of the Commission of Inquiry into Land Matters (CILM) in 1973. The abuses inherent in the extant land tenure system, which the CILM unearthed are a matter of history and need not be rehashed here.[50] The CILM recommended to the government that land should be taken and returned to 'the traditional right-holders' in return for payment of compensation to those who would lose their title.

Land redistribution and land use

The phenomenon of people holding on to unwieldy estates, while others have nothing on which to make even gardens accentuates class cleavage in a society – the privileged and wealthy landlords on the one hand, and the dispossessed and poverty-stricken on the other. Governments can sometimes not escape blame themselves for indulging in 'land hoarding' as where land under government control remains unutilised while citizens are in need of land.

A necessary pre-condition for a successful land reform programme is that the State should be armed with the necessary legal authority to bring under its control the lands required for redevelopment and to impose conditions on such development. In the Ivory Coast example that we have referred to, it transpired that while fertile land was becoming increasingly scarce, large tracts of land granted under concession contracts remained unexploited.[51] Under the legislation, the government is empowered to take over any land over which concession had been granted but which for five years preceding had remained unexploited. Another law provides for the payment of compensation, which is not based on the market value of the property but on the price paid for the concession compounded by a price index factor.[52] In the Cameroon, legislation, which has the same

48 See the Land Regulation Ordinance (1888), the Land Ordinances 1906, 1911, the Land Acquisition Acts 1914, 1952 and the Land Act 1962.

49 *The Administration of the Territory of Papua and New Guinea and Others v Daera and Guba, supra,* note 22.

50 See P Eaton, 'Melanesian land reform: the plantation acquisition scheme', *supra,* p 62; M Trebilcock and J Knetch, 'Land policy and economic development in Papua New Guinea', *supra,* p 71 and Mugambwa, 'Land disputes in PNG', *supra,* p 53.

51 *Decree* No 57-243, Feb 24 1957 *supra,* note 45.

52 *Arrete* No 8868, October 28 1958, cited in Mifsud, *supra,* note 45, at 49.

effect, enables the government to take unexploited land held under customary tenurial system.[53] In Malawi under the Customary Land (Development) Act, the government may determine customary rights in lands, which are adjudged inconsistent with development.[54] Under Kenya's Land Control Act,[55] the Minister responsible for land may refuse to grant his consent to land dealings if the grantee is unlikely to farm the land well, or to develop it adequately; if he is unlikely to use the land profitably for the intended purpose of the transfer owing to the nature of the land; and importantly, if the grantee already has sufficient agricultural land. Zambia's Land (Conversion of Title) Act[56] now vests in the President absolutely in perpetuity all lands in Zambia. He holds the lands for and on behalf of the people and no grants made without his consent shall be valid. He holds the lands for redistribution in the manner which the public interest shall dictate. The Nigerian Land Use Act[57] vests all land in the territory in each State in the Federation in the Governor of that State which shall be held in trust and administered for the use and benefit of all Nigerians. Under the Zambian law an individual can acquire only a leasehold interest. Under the Nigerian law only a right of occupancy can be granted by the State.

The freehold/leasehold controversy is an old one. The oft-quoted aphorism of Arthur Young runs thus:

> The magic of property turns sand into gold ... Give a man the secure possession of a bleak rock and he will turn it into a garden. Give him a nine year lease of a garden and he will convert it into a desert.[58]

Yet the absolute right to property implies the right to use and misuse property; and whatever truth lies in Young's *dictum* is not altogether incontrovertible, as the reverse form of it could well be true also. Much, it would seem depends on the ingenuity or lack of it on the part of the title holder whether the freehold or the leasehold. What perhaps is unassailable is the fact that a lease affords a greater opportunity for control than would have been possible under a freehold, hence the apparent predilection of the new states for the lease. In PNG, however, several years after independence, the recommendation of the CILM to the effect that a machinery be inaugurated for the voluntary conversion of freehold interests into leaseholds is yet to be effected.[59] The refusal or neglect on the part of the law makers to effect the necessary change may be due to a lack of commitment to overhaul a colonial legacy or lack of political will to effect changes or a case of conflict of interest situation, since it is plausible to argue that some legislators may be affected if the required change were effected.

In Papua New Guinea, the first articulate exposition of a State land use policy found expression in the *Report* of the CILM. It reads:

53 *Decree* No 64-8/COR, January 1964.

54 Act No 34 (1967).

55 Act No 34 (1967).

56 No 20 (1975).

57 No 6 1978, s 1.

58 Quoted in HW West, *The Mailo System in Buganda* (Government Printer, Entebe, 1964), p 60.

59 Section 3 of the Land (Ownership of Freeholds) Act (Ch No 359) merely defines freehold interests for the purposes of s 56(2)(b) of the Constitution of Papua New Guinea. Sections 16–24 deal with the question of conversion, but to date there is no record of this having been accomplished in fact.

> In many situations there will be several claimants to land. We feel that, all else being equal, *preference should be given to those who have little land and are in need of it, and those who will live on it and use it rather than leave it idle.* We believe that the law should assist customary claimants to get secure title and develop their land. *But we feel that people who get registered titles have an obligation to use the land well, or it should be transferred to someone who will use it well.*[60] [Emphasis added.]

Security of tenure, it would seem would be dependent upon land use. Of course, it can be argued that registration of title which confers indefeasibility of title is perhaps the law's best method of assuring security of tenure, and that, in the absence of title registration economic circumstances which promote land development and the provision of agricultural extension services could vie equally with land use as a means of securing tenure.[61]

Then, it transpired that many freeholds had remained either under utilised or simply undeveloped, a situation which posed problems not only for the development of urban centres, but also aggravated land shortage in the rural areas. To counteract the phenomenon of underdevelopment, the device of 'development condition' was instituted by which a lessee could continue to hold his lease if he complies with the condition attached to the lease;[62] default worked forfeiture enabling the State to repossess the land.[63] This strategy, it was hoped, would free more lands for redistribution to those in need. The policy of efficacious use of land was to be extended to inherited land also. The CILM recommended that where a beneficiary is not living on or near land devolving on him under the will of a deceased family member he must either return to the land and begin putting it to use or arrange to do so within 12 months of the death of the testator or else the land would devolve as on intestacy.[64]

The government, while acknowledging the need to hold a pool of land for national development purposes was also prepared to release at the same time unutilised State lands for redistribution to those who need land. The government therefore promulgated the National Land Registration Act[65] under which all national or State land or government lands would be registered. This would facilitate the identification of State land not required for public purposes or which remains undeveloped for redistribution as recommended by the CILM. Additionally the government has power to declare customary land 'native reserve' and place same under trusteeship.[66] This would enable the State to acquire land for redistribution without any obligation to pay compensation.

---

60 *Supra,* p 54, para 2.12.

61 See James, *Land Law and Policy in PNG, supra,* note 23, p 165.

62 Land (Underdeveloped Freehold) Act, Ch No 193.

63 *Ibid.* Section 13; see also James, *Land Law and Policy in PNG, supra,* note 23, p 121.

64 *Report, supra,* p 54, para 7.29.

65 Ch No 357.

66 Sections 26–28 of the Land Act, Ch No 185.

Land reform techniques and measures

It is proposed next to discuss some land reform measures. Our examples which are by no means exhaustive are intended to highlight the more familiar modes and how Third World nations have fared in their experimentation with them.

- Settlement

This involves the twin objectives of providing a group of people with a new home as well as agricultural land for development. An Austrian legislation depicts settlement operations as surprising the following: setting up of new farms, resiting of farm dwellings and out-buildings in more suitable positions for farming purposes; transfer of ownership of holdings to persons capable of running farms; conversion of farm holdings that have ceased to enjoy autonomy to autonomous units; conversion of tenancy to ownership, assignment of existing farms worked by their owners to others and demarcation of property fictitiously or actually divided.[67] By these criteria then, the law of Argentina which permits the conversion of rural leases and share cropping contracts into sale; the Ethiopian Proclamation providing for the utilization of idle lands,[68] the Algerian legislation transferring title in land to those who actually till it,[69] the Malawian law dividing the country into development areas for the purposes of a more efficient agricultural exploitation of the country,[70] the Japanese legislation empowering the government to purchase farmlands from non-operating owners at equitable rates for redistribution to the landless and which provided also for the transfer of land ownership from absentee land owners to land operators[71] are all settlement measures.

State regulated settlements in PNG may be traced to the high-cost Cape Hoskins Oil Palm Project[72] and the low-cost Gavien and Popondetta Schemes.[73] The CILM, however, recommended low-cost settlements because, as it reasoned:

> ... government has not got enough money for many high cost resettlements and small low-cost ones will be necessary in many places to help people in isolated mountain areas to come closer to roads, markets, etc. Government should watch for the beginnings of these and help them with services and secure land titles as they show signs of becoming permanent and settling down.[74]

The CILM's position is reminiscent of the admonition of the FAO in respect of settlement schemes in the former Eastern and Western Nigeria. The FAO warned:

> In order to keep costs of the required-scale settlement within manageable proportion, it must be the energy and initiative of the individual farmer that develops the land and constructs the buildings, while the role of the government is confined to the creation of the

67 Federal Act on Land Settlement, Basic Law on Agricultural Land Settlement Bundesgesetzblatt No 22, 7 March 1967.

68 Act No 17253, April 1967.

69 Proclamation No 78, 1976.

70 The Customary Land Development Act 1967, Act No 5.

71 Land Reform Law, Law No 43 21 Oct 1946; also, Udo, 'Implementation of the Nigerian Land Reform Law of 1978: lessons from the Japanese experience', *supra*, note 41, p 53.

72 *Report, supra*, p 54, para 9.15.

73 *Ibid*, para 9.19.

74 *Ibid*, para 9.1.

> environmental conditions (eg, eliminating the tsetse and flood control), the allocation of land to farmers (together with the granting of land titles), as well as the provision of essential services (roads, water supply, electricity etc) institutional facilities (ie, credit) and advice through the extension service, which are all basic preconditions for successful settlements.[75]

This is particularly desirable if only to keep to the barest minimum the resentment of local people who may feel aggrieved and alienated because in their view government is discriminating against them by lavishing on the new settlers amenities which they lack themselves.[76]

- Land consolidation

A programme of land consolidation aims at the creation of continuous regular plots where excessive fragmentation tends to inhibit efficacious use of land. Where a holding is so small that it cannot be put effectively to any economic use, the dictates of common sense and sound business would require its merger with other plots in the interest of the economic viability of the whole area. In Tunisia where rural development zones (*aires de mise en valeur rurale* – AMVR) are a feature of the land reform programme there are irrigation zones where development schemes are projected and within which peasants are settled and taught the techniques of modern farming. The creation of the zones entails a programme of land consolidation and acreage limitation. In these areas, formerly characterized by extreme degree of fragmented holding, the law now prohibits sub-division of holdings.[77]

The law also places a limitation on individual holdings which shall not exceed 50 hectares.[78] This is similar to a Chilean legislation which grants the State power to expropriate rural holding in excess of 800 hectares held by an individual.[79]

The Nigerian Land Use Act[80] prohibits the grant of a sub-lease without the consent of the Governor. It similarly proscribes the sub-division of a statutory right of occupancy on the death of the occupier without the consent of the Governor.[81]

In the case of Papua New Guinea the Land Act[82] prohibits the sub-division of a State lease. The Land Registration (Communally Owned Land) Act,[83] it may be argued, enhances land consolidation because since the philosophy being pursued is corporate ownership, by implication, the law frowns on fragmentation of land. Consequently it becomes legitimate to ask whether the Land (Tenure Conversion) Act[84] does not advocate a policy contrary to land consolidation.

75 FAO, *Agricultural Development in Nigerian 1965–80, supra*, note 46, p 437.

76 CILM *Report, supra*, p 54, para 9.16.

77 Mifsud, *Customary Land Law in Africa, supra*, note 45, p 55.

78 *Loi* No 58-63, 2 June 1958, amended by *Loi* No 60-6, 26 July 1960.

79 Act No 16, 640 16 July 1967. See also the Nigerian Land Use Act s 6(2) for the 500 and 2,000 hectares delimitation on agricultural and pastoral land use purposes respectively.

80 No 6, 1978, ss 24(b), 23(1).

81 *Ibid*, s 24(b).

82 Ch No 185, 1968.

83 No 10, 1963.

84 No 15, 1964.

A corollary of land consolidation is acreage delimitation. No one should be allowed to wield an unwieldy estate while some people have nothing on which to make even gardens. The CILM states the position quite clearly:

> Another control should be strict limits on the number of pieces of registered land, or the size of land, which a person can hold, or lease or sell to others.[85]

The CILM also advocates the 'one man one plot' philosophy in respect of agricultural holding and building site.[86]

- Co-operative efforts

Co-operation is a familiar concept in every human society. Man on earth having always had an eye to the avoidance of misfortune has endeavoured throughout the ages somehow to insure himself, to take out a 'policy' of some sort on which he paid regular premiums in some form of self-denial or sacrifice.[87] Co-operation is one form of the structure that provided security through complex inter-personal relations. Modern insurance, it would seem has replaced this relations with a cash nexus.

Writing on the *huza* system among the Krobo of Ghana's Eastern Region who purchased land as a group in other regions of the country to share thereafter according to the contribution of each member of the group, Dr Asante says among the group: 'there was coordination of farming policy, organization of mutual help, and a general attempt to relate the cultivation to meaningful pattern. Furthermore, the *huza* became a mechanism of social security in a strange land. Individual initiative was thus blended with social solidarity and group interest in a most effective manner.'[88] It must be noted that the *huza* is a voluntary association of farmers. Indeed, the co-operative system in Ghana involves two distinct but related factors; there is on the one hand the fostering of individual interest, a necessary ingredient in the provision of incentive for individual attainment; and on the other hand the cultivation of an attitude of dependence on the community in time of need. It is puzzling that while individual initiative tends to loosen traditional ties, it should thus be pressed into the service of dependence on the community. The *noboa* system among the centralized Akan also has the same effect.

In Papua New Guinea the idea of pulling resources together for trading purposes has been in vogue since time immemorial.[89] Indeed the Land (Groups Incorporation) Act[90] was designed to buttress this kind of group effort. While it may be argued that this kind of legal recognition of group identity accentuates group cleavage and is inimical to national cohesion there can be no doubt about the authenticity of the system.

85 *Report, supra,* p 54, para 3.51.

86 *Ibid,* para 3.53.

87 See generally EA Hoebel, *Man in the Primitive World* (2nd edn, McGraw-Hill Co, New York, 1949), *passim.* Also, B Summer and S Keller, *The Science of Society,* Vol 2 (West Publishing, St Paul, 1927), p 749.

88 *Property Law and Social Goals in Ghana, supra,* note 30, p 283.

89 This was called in Pisin language *bungim moni,* which literally translated is 'pull money'. See S Singh, 'Co-operatives in Papua New Guinea', *New Research Bulletin,* No 58, ANU, Canberra, 1974, *passim,* and Fitzpatrick and Southwood, 'The Community Cooperation in Papua New Guinea', unpublished seminar paper, Port Moresby IASER, 14 October 1976, p 14.

90 Ch No 147.

The CILM also preferring indigenous concepts to foreign contraptions saw it fit to recommend 'self-help housing schemes on a co-operative basis' as a means of solving the nation's housing problem.[91]

Government intervention in the affairs of co-operatives may sometimes be necessary to ensure efficiency in their management and also accountability. In Ghana for example, with the attainment of independence, however, the State took an active role in the formation of co-operative societies which were intended 'to remedy the short-comings of small-scale farming, and to make available to the small holder the facilities for obtaining capital and credit, the benefit of technical know-how and managerial skill which would otherwise be beyond his reach – as well as bolstering his economic position, which would otherwise be extremely vulnerable'.[92] Dr Asante is apparently unhappy about the State's involvement in the co-operative movement. It is true that the government of the First Republic being based on a mass-mobilization Party brought under its fold farmers' co-operatives as a wing of Dr Nkrumah's Convention People's Party (CPP). But this instilled in the farmers an awareness of the power they wielded as a group, a thing which was unimaginable in the colonial regime. A measure of the popularity of the farmers' co-operative movement under the CPP is the current clamour for the 'unionization' of the farmers. A drive is going on at this time to unite the farmers into one solid 'interest block', for they realize that they will never again be able to wield the political power they had under the government of the First Republic unless they are united as they were under the CPP.[93] The wielding of property *per se* does not ensure participation in the political process or indeed in a wide sharing of power. Dr Asante says:

> The fact that the social and political organization was interwoven with the distribution of resources under a scheme which assured to every individual access to participate in the resources of the family, and to every family had access to participation in the resources of the State, meant that every family had access to participation in the resources of the State, meant that every individual, every family, or other social group was guaranteed a distinct role in the power process. No Chief, however powerful, could disrupt this proprietary scheme by arbitrary divestiture ... The greater incidence of corporate holdings gave additional security to the individual. For the Chief could not encroach upon the individual's holding without invading the whole of the family property which encompassed such individual's holding, and the invasion of the family property meant the violation of the preserve of the family head who was also an elder of the preserve of the family head who was also an elder serving on the Chief's council.[94]

With the greatest respect, what the learned author says is true only in theory, for ordinary people felt generally betrayed because they did not know what happened when their representatives went to Parliament. Farmers' co-operatives on the other hand enabled

91 *Report, supra,* p 54, para 5.17.

92 Mifsud, *Customary Land Law in Africa, supra,* note 45, p 57. For Ghana, see *Co-operative Societies Decree,* 1968 (NLCD 252) as amended.

93 *The Ghanaian Times,* 9 January 1979.

94 Asante, *Property Law, supra,* note 30, p 287.

farmers to participate more fully in the political process under the government of the First Republic and effort should be made to reactivate the farmers' co-operative movement.[95]

In Papua New Guinea, it would seem there was no conscious government effort to politicise the co-operative movement apart from the hint that the Australian administration launched the co-operative movement in 1947 partly as a strategy to guide potential 'political forms of resistance into proper channels' following the acquisition of greater political awareness by colonial subjects, which was a necessary adjunct of the Second World War.[96]

VII CONCLUSION

Whatever measure of land reform a nation adopts, the paramount consideration is that its complete implementation must be ensured. Professor Udo observes that the Japanese experiment at land reform was a gigantic success because a few years after the inauguration of the programme, it had been implemented throughout the country.[97] He attributes the miraculous recovery of the Japanese industrial apparatus so soon after the ravages of World War II to the prompt implementation of Japan's land reform measures. One cannot however be over-sanguine about the level of implementation thus far attained under the Nigerian Land Use Act 1978 – several years after its promulgation.

The problem of inadequate implementation of the Land Use Act of Nigeria for example can be attributed to the opposition wealthy land owners and traditional chiefs, whose power of jurisdiction over community land has now been taken away from them, initially mounted against the Act. One of the purposes of the Act was to obliterate the phenomenon of scarcity of building land which was brought about by the practice of the wealthy who buy land on the periphery of towns and cities at cheap prices, hold on to them and then sell them at exorbitant prices when infrastructural facilities in these areas lead to an appreciation in their value. Apart from tying up land development, this practice of speculation in land creates a class of landless people.

Secondly, since land is vested in the separate States and not in the Federal government at the centre, State governments controlled by political parties not in power at the Federal level refused to co-operate with the Federal government when it needed land for public purposes.

95 The people's disappointment at the performance of their civilian political leaders explains in a large measure the popular support and euphoria which often greet military takeovers in West African States.

96 See Fitzpatrick and Southwood, *supra*, note 89. For Papua New Guinea, the situation is a little complex. The co-operative movement was regulated by the Co-operative Societies Acts of 1965 and 1967 but were repealed in 1975. The repeal of these Acts effectively killed the co-operative movement. In an attempt to revive the movement the Co-operative Societies Act, Ch 389 of 1982 was passed. Meanwhile, the Co-operative (Companies) Act which repealed the 1965 and 1967 legislations and was incorporated in the Companies Act, Ch No 146 as Division 5 of this Act makes provision for the incorporation of co-operative societies. A co-operative society in PNG therefore is a hybrid made of a society which is operated on the basis of co-operative principles which at the same time has all the attributes of an incorporated entity.

97 'Implementation of the Nigerian Land Reform Law of 1978: lessons from the Japanese experience', *supra*, note 41, p 85.

Thirdly, since government is far removed from ordinary people, the successful implementation of the law can be assured only by involving the people at grass-root level in the implementation process. The task of implementation is presently left to two bodies: viz, the Land Use Allocation Committee which is to advise the State Governor on land matters and to determine the quantum of compensation when land is acquired for public purposes, and the Land Allocation Advisory Committee which is to advise the Local government on land matters. The Village or Town Land Use Committee would be required to ensure the involvement of local people in the implementation of the Act, and possibly as Professor Udo suggests, a National Land Commission at the Federal level which should be responsible for overall policy decisions on land use.[98]

Finally by entrenching the Land Use Act in the Constitution of 1979 thus making it a part of the Constitution which cannot be repealed, amended or abrogated except in the manner a provision of the Constitution can be repealed or amended, it has become impossible to review and amend the law in the light of experience gained from its implementation thus far. Writing of the Japanese experience, Professor Udo says that the Japanese Land Reform Law of 1946 was propped up by several amending laws, viz, 31 Ordinances, 51 Ministerial Regulations and 120 Circulars, 'all of which were meant to clarify or even modify certain aspects of the original enactment'.[99]

A necessary precondition for a successful land reform programme is the commitment of the ruling elite to the programme. Tragically this commitment was lacking in the Shagari administration which succeeded the Military government of Obansanjo which promulgated the Land Use Act. Also the fact that no time limit was set for the realisation of a complete implementation of the law throughout Nigeria was one of the factors which affected the successful implementation of the law.

Needless to say the insufficient implementation of the Nigeria Act is antithetical to the achievement of the objectives of the Act, and the overall national economic development.[100]

In the case of Ghana one of the causes of economic stagnation in the nation arises from the under use of land. Most lands which ostensibly are fallow suddenly have 'owners' as soon as someone begins to put the land to some use. Since individuals are powerless in circumstances such as this, the government had to pass legislation to arm itself with power to take unoccupied stool land and put it to use.[101] In this way all unoccupied stool lands or lands which are not being put to any immediate use in areas where the concept of stool land does not exist would come under the State's jurisdiction for redistribution in a manner which the State may deem conducive to the nation's economic progress. This was what the infamous Lands Bill sought to do in the colonial past.

---

98 *Ibid*, 71.

99 *Ibid*, 72.

100 See RK Udo, 'Land Policy for effective management of the national economy', an Inaugural Lecture delivered at the University of Ibandan, Nigeria, 10 March 1977, pp 9, 20–21.

101 See State Lands Act (Act 125), 1962; Stool Lands Act (Act 27), 1960 and Administration of Lands Act (Act 123, 1962). See also HC Dunning, 'Law and economic development in Africa: the law of eminent domain' (1968) 68 Col LR, p 1968.

Again, there appears to be a logical inconsistency about the notion that although Ghana is a unitary State,[102] a citizen should be put to a disadvantage or given preferential treatment by virtue of his relationship to the stool on whose land he happens to be. If he is a subject of such a stool he may put up a house on the stool's land without difficulty; and with regard to farm lands, he may, according to precepts of archaic customs, cultivate as much land as he is physically capably of appropriating. But if he is not a subject of that stool, he is considered a stranger and denied the right to do those things which his fellow citizen is capable of doing with respect to the stool land. This certainly smacks of discrimination.[103] With the introduction of mechanised farming it cannot be argued too strongly that this state of affairs is inimical to the nation's overall economic advancement. Agricultural land must be redistributed on a basis which takes into account the nation's social and technological advancement rather than on a person's relationship with a stool. And building lands must be allocated on a basis which in the context of planning regulations enhances the economic value of urban property rather than on a person's connection with the owner of the allodial title.

In Nigeria, the Land Use Act[104] dealt a blow to this top of ethno-centricism by vesting all lands in every State in the respective State Governors 'for the benefit of *all Nigerians*'.

Fortunately for Papua New Guinea, the nation has not promulgated a nationalising legislation of the type such as the Nigerian Land Use Act and land continues to be preponderantly owned by clans and groups. State ownership is limited to a fragment of the 3% of alienated land. The nation appears to favour gradual change in land policy through the utilisation of indigenous institutions. The adverse effect of the amelioration land policy however is the stark reality that the State has no control over its natural resources. For, in spite of the provisions of s 7 of the Mining Act,[105] no one is certain where all the wealth from gold currently ends.

Again, clan or group ownership of land as presently constituted fosters parochialism at the expense of nationalism, and the observations made about the right of stool subjects in Ghana in respect of their stool land apply *mutatis mutandis* to group ownership in Papua New Guinea.

It will be naivety at its apogee for anyone to assume that anyone or combination of land reform methods discussed in the foregoing pages will *per se* make for land use maximization. Much depends also on the proper management of available resources and facilities.

102 Art 4(1) Constitution of Ghana, 1960; Art 4(1) Constitution of Ghana, 1969.

103 On the position of the so called stranger, Dr Asante says: 'To give proprietary significance to ethnic differences by assigning a different and inferior type of a landed interest to strangers, runs counter to the current drive to integrate the various ethnic groups in Ghana into a united nation. Nothing is more discriminating against Ghanaian citizens on the basis of ethnic origin.' *Property Law, supra*, note 30, p 218. Notice, however, the affect of *Frimpong v Poku* (1973) 2 GLR 1 on the stool subject's unlimited right of appropriation of stool land.

104 Section 1.

105 Ch No 195. The section reads: 'All gold and minerals in or on any land in the country are the property of the State.' See also RW James, *Land Law and Policy in Papua New Guinea, supra*, note 23, pp 190–202.

Questions

1. Of the three land policies that have been pursued by successive administrations in PNG, only one holds a promise of success because it approximates a traditional concept of land tenure. Which policy is this? Do you agree?
2. Two principles of land use are discernible from the Report of the CILM (1973): these are: (1) land use; and (2) the law must favour those who need land most and are ready to utilise it. How do these principles ensure land use maximization?

LAND: LEGAL CONCEPTION AND NATURE OF INTERESTS

I WHAT IS LAND? THE STATUTORY AND UNDERLYING LAW POSITION

The common law conception of land is summed up in the Latin maxim: *cujus est solum ejus usque coelum et ad inferos* which translated literally means that the person to whom the soil belongs owns also the space above it and everything below it.

The statutory definition of land is provided in s 3 of the Interpretation Act[1] and includes messuages, tenements and hereditaments, corporeal and incorporeal of any tenure or description whatever may be the estate or interest therein.[2]

Rights above the surface

Thus, to invade the airspace above another person's land by intrusion of any kind constitutes proprietary trespass. In *Kelsen v Imperial Tobacco Co (of Great Britain and Ireland Ltd)*,[3] it was held that an advertising sign fixed on the defendant's building which projected about eight inches over the plaintiff's shops constituted trespass to the plaintiff's land.

The extent of a landowner's interest in the space above the property is demonstrated by the case extracted below.

LORD BERNSTEIN OF LEIGH (BARON) v SKYVIEWS & GENERAL LTD [1977] 2 All ER 902

[The plaintiff was the owner of and resident at premises comprising a country house and surrounding land in Kent. The defendants, whose business was to take aerial photographs of properties and then offer them for sale to the owners, took a single aerial photograph of the plaintiff's premises from a height of several hundred feet. The plaintiff objected to the photograph being taken without his permission and demanded that the defendants hand over or destroy all negatives and prints of the photograph. The defendants did not do so. The plaintiff brought an action against the defendants alleging that they had wrongfully entered the airspace above the plaintiff's premises to take the photograph and were guilty of trespass and actionable invasion of the plaintiff's right to privacy. The plaintiff claimed damages for trespass and injunctions to restrain the defendants from entering the airspace and from invading the plaintiff's right to privacy. The plaintiff further contended that the defendants were not entitled to rely on the statutory defence under s 40(1) of the Civil

1 Ch No 2.

2 Corporeal refers to the physical soil and structures thereon. Incorporeals are the legal rights over the land, eg, easements, rent charges, etc.

3 [1957] 2 QB 334.

Aviation Act 1949 (UK), since that section was limited to a bare right of passage over land and did not permit the use of airspace for the purpose of photography.]

GRIFFITHS J: I turn now to the law. The plaintiff claims that as owner of the land he is also owner of the airspace above the land, or at least has the right to exclude any entry into the airspace above his land. He relies on the old Latin maxim, *cujus est solum ejus est usque ad coelum et ad inferos*, a colourful phrase often on the lips of lawyers since it was first coined by Accursius in Bologna in the 13th century. There are a number of cases in which the maxim has been used by English judges but an examination of those cases shows that they have all been concerned with structures attached to the adjoining land, such as overhanging buildings, signs or telegraph wires, and for their solution it has not been necessary for the judge to cast his eyes towards the heavens; he has been concerned with the rights of the owner in the airspace immediately adjacent to the surface of the land.

That an owner has certain rights in the airspace above his land is well established by authority. He has the right to lop the branches of trees that may overhang his boundary, although this right seems to be founded in nuisance rather than trespass ...

In *Gifford v Dent* [1926] 1 WN 336 Romer J held that it was a trespass to erect a sign that projected four feet eight inches over the plaintiff's forecourt and ordered it to be removed. He invoked the old maxim in his judgment. The report reads:

> ... *the plaintiffs were tenants of the forecourt and were accordingly tenants of the space above the forecourt* usque ad coelum, *it seemed to him that the projection was clearly a trespass upon the property of the plaintiffs.*

That decision was followed by McNair J in *Kelsen v Imperial Tobacco Co Ltd* [1957] All ER 343, [1957] 2 QB 334, in which he granted a mandatory injunction ordering the defendants to remove a sign which projected only eight inches over the plaintiff's property. The plaintiff relies strongly on this case, and in particular on the following passage when, after citing the judgment of Romer J to which I have already referred, McNair J continued [1957] 2 All ER 343 at 351; [1957] 2 QB 334 at 345:

> That decision, I think, has been recognised by the textbook writers, and, in particular, by the late Professor Winfield (*Winfield on Tort*, 6th edn, 1954, p 379), as stating the true law. It is not without significance that in the Air Navigation Act 1920, s 9(1), which was replaced by s 40(1) of the Civil Aviation Act 1949, the legislature found it necessary expressly to negative the action of trespass or nuisance arising from the mere fact of an aeroplane passing through the air above the land. It seems to me clearly to indicate that the legislature were not taking the same view of the matter as Lord Ellenborough in *Pickering v Rudd* (1815) 4 Camp 219, but were taking the view accepted in the later cases, such as *Wandsworth Board of Works v United Telephone Co* (1884) 13 QBD 904, subsequently followed by Romer J in *Gifford v Dent* [1926] 1 WN 336. Accordingly, I reach the conclusion that a trespass, and not a mere nuisance, was created by the invasion of the plaintiff's airspace by this sign.

I very much doubt if in that passage McNair J was intending to hold that the plaintiff's rights in the airspace continued to an unlimited height or *ad coelum* as counsel for the plaintiff submits. The point that the judge was considering was whether the sign was a trespass or a nuisance at the very low level at which it projected. This to my mind is clearly indicated by his reference to *Winfield on Tort* (6th edn, 1954, p 380) in which the text reads: 'it is submitted that trespass will be committed by [aircraft] to the airspace if they fly so low as to come within the area of ordinary user.' The aùthor in that passage is careful to limit the trespass to the height at which it is contemplated an owner might be expected to make use of the airspace as a natural incident of the user of his land. If, however, the learned judge was by his reference to the Civil Aviation Act 1949, and his disapproval of the views of Lord Ellenborough in *Pickering v Rudd* (1815) 4 Camp 219, indicating the opinion that the flight of an aircraft at whatever height constituted a trespass at common law, I must respectfully disagree.

I do not wish to cast any doubts on the correctness of the decision on its own particular facts. It may be a sound and practical rule to regard any incursion into the airspace at a height which may interfere with the ordinary user of the land as a trespass rather than a nuisance. Adjoining owners then know where they stand; they have no right to erect structures overhanging or passing over their neighbours' land and there is no room for argument whether they are thereby causing damage or annoyance to their neighbours about which there may be much room for argument and uncertainty. But wholly different considerations arise when considering the passage of aircraft at a height which in no way affects the user of the land.

There is no direct authority on this question but as long ago as 1815 Lord Ellenborough in *Pickering v Rudd* (4 Camp 219 at 221) expressed the view that it would not be a trespass to pass over a man's land in a balloon; and in *Saunders v Smith* (1838) 2 Jur 491 at 492 Shadwell VC said:

> Thus, upon the maxim of law *cujus est solum ejus est usque ad coelum*, an injunction might be granted for cutting timber and severing crops: but, suppose a person should apply to restrain an aerial wrong, as by sailing through the air over a person's freehold in a balloon; this surely would be too contemptible to be taken notice of.

In *Comr for Railways v Valuer General* [1973] 3 All ER 268 at 277, 278; [1974] AC 328 at 351, 352 Lord Wilberforce had this to say of the maxim:

> There are a number of examples of its use in judgments of the 19th century, by which time mineral values had drawn attention to downwards extent as well as, or more than, extent upwards. But its use, whether with reference to mineral rights, or trespass in the airspace by projections, animals or wires, is imprecise and it is mainly serviceable as dispensing with analysis (cf *Pickering v Rudd* (1815) 4 Camp 219, *Ellis v Loftus Iron Co* (1874) LR 10 CP 10; [1874–80] All ER Rep 232). In none of these cases is there an authoritative pronouncement that 'land' means the whole of the space from the centre of the earth to the heavens: so sweeping, unscientific and unpractical a doctrine is unlikely to appeal to the common law mind.

In *Sovmots Investments Ltd v Secretary of State for the Environment* [1976] 3 All ER 720 at 728; [1976] 3 WLR 597 at 608 Browne LJ said of counsel's submission that land in its ordinary legal sense meant from the centre of the earth to the sky:

> We therefore do not think it necessary to consider whether counsel's contention as to the 'ordinary legal meaning' of 'land' is right: we will only say that what Lord Wilberforce said in giving the opinion of the Privy Council in *Comr for Railways v Valuer General* [1973] 3 All ER 268; [1974] AC 328 seems to us to throw great doubt on it.

I can find no support in authority for the view that a landowner's rights in the airspace above his property extend to an unlimited height. In *Wandsworth Board of Works v United Telephone Co* (1884) 13 QBD 904 Bowen LJ described the maxim *usque ad coelum* as a fanciful phrase, to which I would add that if applied literally it is a fanciful notion leading to the absurdity of a trespass at common law being committed by a satellite every time it passes over a suburban garden. The academic writers speak with one voice in rejecting the uncritical and literal application of the maxim: see, by way of example only, *Winfield and*

Jolowicz on Tort (10th edn, 1975), p 305; *Salmond on Tort* (16th edn, 1973), p 44; *Shawcross and Beaumont on Air Law* (3rd edn, 1966), Vol 1, p 536; *McNair on the Law of the Air* (3rd edn, 1964), p 97 and *Halsbury's Laws of England* (2 *Halsbury's Laws* (4th edn), paras 1422–1500). I accept their collective approach as correct. The problem is to balance the rights of an owner to enjoy the use of his land against the rights of the general public to take advantage of all that science now offers in the use of airspace. This balance is in my judgment best struck in our present society by restricting the rights of an owner in the airspace above his land to such height as is necessary for the ordinary use and enjoyment of his land and the structures on it, and declaring that above that height he has no greater rights in the airspace than any other member of the public.

Applying this test to the facts of this case, I find that the defendants' aircraft did not infringe any rights in the plaintiff's airspace, and thus no trespass was committed. It was on any view of the evidence flying many hundred of feet above the ground and it is not suggested that by its mere presence in the airspace it caused any interference with any use to which the plaintiff put or might wish to put his land. The plaintiff's complaint is not that the aircraft interfered with the use of his land but that a photograph was taken from it. There is, however, no law against taking a photograph, and the mere taking of a photograph cannot turn an act which is not a trespass into the plaintiff's airspace into one that is a trespass ...

My finding that no trespass at common law has been established is sufficient to determine this case in the defendants' favour. I should, however, deal with a further defence under the Civil Aviation Act 1949, s 40(1) of which provides:

> No action shall lie in respect of trespass or in respect of nuisance, by reason only of the flight of an aircraft over any property at a height above the ground, which, having regard to wind, weather, and all the circumstances of the case is reasonable, or the ordinary incidents of such flight so long as the provisions of Part II and this Part of this Act and any Order in Council or order made under Part II of this Part of his Act are duly complied with.

It is agreed that all the statutory provisions have been complied with by the defendants, nor is there any suggestion that the aircraft was not flying at a reasonable height; but it is submitted by the plaintiff that the protection given by the subsection is limited to a bare right of passage over land analogous to the limited right of a member of the public to pass over the surface of a highway, and my attention has been drawn to a passage in *Shawcross and Beaumont on Air Law* (3rd edn, 1966), Vol 1, p 561 in which the editors express this view: I see nothing in the language of the section to invite such a restricted reading which would withdraw from its protection many very beneficial activities carried on from aircraft ...

It is, however, to be observed that the protection given is limited by the words 'by reason only of the flight', so although an owner can found no action in trespass or nuisance if he relies solely on the flight of the aircraft above his property as founding his cause of action, the section will not preclude him from bringing an action if he can point to some activity carried on by or from the aircraft that can properly be considered a trespass or nuisance, or some other tort. For example, the section would give no protection against the deliberate emission of vast quantities of smoke that polluted the atmosphere and seriously interfered with the plaintiff's use and enjoyment of his property; such behaviour remains an actionable nuisance. Nor would I wish this judgment to be understood as deciding that in no circumstances could a successful action be brought against an aerial photographer to restrain his activities. The present action is not founded in nuisance for no court would regard the taking of a single photograph as an actionable nuisance. But if the circumstances were such that a plaintiff was subjected to the harassment of constant surveillance of his house from the air, accompanied by the photographing of his every activity, I am far from saying that the court would not regard such a monstrous invasion of his privacy as an actionable nuisance for which they would give relief. However, that question does not fall for decision in this case and will be decided if and when it arises.

On the facts of this case even if contrary to my view the defendants' aircraft committed a trespass at common law in flying over the plaintiff's land, the plaintiff is prevented from bringing any action in respect of that trespass by the terms of s 40(1) of the Civil Aviation Act 1949.

For these reasons the plaintiff's action fails and there will be judgment for the defendants.

Judgment for the defendants.

Notes and questions

1 What does Griffith J mean when he says that the landowner's rights must be restricted to such height as is necessary for the ordinary use and enjoyment of his land? Is the test subjective or objective? Suppose A flies a kite over his neighbour's land. Is that interference with his neighbour's land?

2 X erects a crane on his land, which adjoins Y's land for purposes of construction of a building. When the crane is not in use its jib is left free to rotate so that occasionally when the wind blows it hovers and encroaches 30 metres above the plaintiff's house where it remains suspended until the wind changes direction and blows it back. Y sues X for trespass to land. Advise Y. (See *Wollerton and Wilson Ltd v Richard Costain Ltd* [1970] All ER 483; [1970] 1 WLR 411. Cf *Graham v KD Morris & Sons Pty Ltd* [1974] Qd R1.)

3 An owner's right to the superjacent air space may be limited by statute, see, for example, s 25 of the Electricity Commission Act,[4] and Sched 1 of the Civil Aviation (Aircraft Operators' Liability) Act.[5]

Rights below the surface

A landowner similarly does not have unlimited rights to things below the surface of the land.

At common law, ownership of the surface land does not include gold and silver in mines. These minerals (so called Royal metals or minerals) at common law belong to the Crown.[6] By legislation, ownership of all minerals on or below the surface of any land in Papua New Guinea are the property of the State.[7]

4 Ch No 78.

5 Ch No 292.

6 The Pleadings in *The Case of Mines* (1567) 1 Plowd 310; Royal Mines Acts 1688, 1693 (1 Will & Mar c 30) (5 Will & Mar c 6).

7 Section 7 of the Mining (Amalgamated) Act Ch No 195; and s 9 of the Petroleum Act Ch No 198 vests in the State all petroleum and helium in PNG. For an interesting recent review of the *cujus est solum* doctrine, see AJ Bradbrook, 'The relevance of the *cujus est solum* doctrine to the surface landowner's claims to natural resources located above and beneath the land' (1988) 11 Adel LR, p 462.

Fixtures

A logical extension of the *cujus est solum* principle is that, whatever becomes attached to land is regarded as having been integrated into it and is summed up in another maxim, namely: *quicquid plantatur solo, solo cedit.* This principle has been held to be applicable to land in PNG as the case extracted below illustrates.

GEITA SEBEA AND OTHERS v THE TERRITORY OF PAPUA
(1941) 67 CLR 544, High Court of Australia

[In 1937 certain natives in the Territory of Papua who possessed a communal usufructuary right to occupy certain unimproved land with perpetual right of succession in their community, leased the land to the Crown for a term of 10 years at a yearly rental. The Crown transformed the land into an aerodrome, leveling, draining, and making runways, and the Crown and private firms erected buildings thereon. In December 1939, an Ordinance was enacted providing for the compulsory acquisition of the said land by the Crown subject to the payment of compensation to the indigenous owners. One of the issues in the litigation was whether structural improvements to the land by the Crown and private business firms should be taken into account in assessing compensation payable to the native owners of the land.]

STARKE J: The compensation under the Ordinance is payable on the footing that an estate in fee simple freed and discharged from all trusts and encumbrances whatever is being transferred from the natives or people of Kila Kila to the Crown: see Ordinance 1939 No 19, s 3; *Amodu Tijani v Secretary, Southern Nigeria* [1921] 2 AC 399. The persons entitled to the compensation are the people or natives of Kila Kila, and it is distributable among the members of the community through the headmen or representatives of the Iduhu, which controlled the lands acquired. And no objection has been taken to the form of the action or to the parties thereto.

The value of the land is necessarily one of difficulty. It is situated in an uncivilised country and can at best be only roughly estimated. The learned judge fixed the value of the land for agricultural purposes at six pounds per acre for a block of 71 acres upon which there was an aerodrome, and 28 pounds for another block of 18 acres, or 454 altogether. And he held that this sum represented the true value of the land with all its potentialities. But he declined to consider as affecting the value of the land certain improvements and structures which existed upon the land at the date upon which the value of the land had to be assessed. These improvements and structures had been made by the government of the Territory or by business firms who were licensees of the government. They were aerodrome improvements such as the runways, drainage, roads, parking areas, and fencing, a building for housing the power plant erected on a concrete base with walls of fibrocement sheets, a building for a radio station and meteorological office and laboratory erected on heavy cement blocks, a customs and quarantine office, and there were also other buildings erected by business firms under the licence of the government. The learned judge was of opinion that these structures were not fixed to the land so as to become part of it, but remained chattels.

'The meaning of the word [fixtures] is anything annexed to the freehold, that is, fastened to or connected with it, not in mere juxtaposition with the soil. Whatever is so annexed becomes part of the realty, and the person who was the owner of it when it was a chattel loses his property in it, which immediately vests in the owner of the soil ... But an exception has long been established in favour of a tenant erecting fixtures for the purposes of trade, allowing him the privilege of removing them during the continuance of the term' (*Bain v Brand* [1876] App Cas 762 at p 772). And in determining whether or not a chattel becomes a fixture, the intention of the person affixing it to the soil is material only so far as it can be presumed from the degree and object of the annexation ...

The learned judge was unable to draw the inference that the improvements and structures were part of the land, because they would be useless to the natives and because he could not think that buildings erected in connection with a public utility were to remain attached to the land. Here I think the learned judge was in error. All he had to consider in connection with the structures on the land was the degree of annexation, which was very considerable, and the object of annexation, which was patent for all to see, namely their use as part of an aerodrome. Moreover, the improvements on the land in the way of runways, drainage, parking areas, and so forth were inherent in the land itself and did not depend upon annexation or affixation.

But the value of the land might, however, be affected and diminished if the structures and buildings upon the land upon the day for the assessment of its value were 'trade fixtures' removable by the government. The land did not vest in the government until 7 February 1940, when the *Gazette* notice of vesting was published pursuant to the *Lands (Kila Kila Aerodrome) Acquisition Ordinance* 1939 No 19, but on 1 January 1939, when the assessment had to be made, the government's rights under the lease from the natives subsisted, including the right to remove trade fixtures upon the land during the continuance of its term. This latter right was a relaxation in favour of the tenant for the encouragement of trade.

But whether they are or are not trade fixtures is a question of fact depending upon the circumstances of the case. In some cases, the size and permanence and the general character and object of the structures and buildings may lead one to the conclusion that they are not tenant's fixtures but something permanently annexed to the land (see *Pole-Carew v Western Counties and General Manure Co* [1920] 2 Ch 97; *Whitehead v Bennett* (1958) 27 LJ Ch 474); for the removal must be capable of being effected without material injury to the land or the destruction of the fixture: cf Foa, *Landlord and Tenant* (4th edn, 1907), p 697.

It is for the learned judge to determine whether the structures and buildings upon the land were or were not trade fixtures upon the land upon 1 January 1939. If they were, then in my opinion the value of the land should be assessed upon the footing that the government had a right to remove them from the land and would, rather than pay compensation therefor, remove them from the land during the continuance of its term. I do not of course refer to the improvements upon the land such as runways and so forth already mentioned, inherent in the land.

The question remains how the land should be valued, if these improvements and structures or any portion thereof form part of the land. It is useless to consider what the land with the improvements and structures upon it would bring in the open or any other market, for there was no market. Some artificial method must be adopted, and the most satisfactory, to my mind, is to take the agricultural value of the land as fixed by the learned judge plus an addition measured by what it would cost to make or establish the improvements and structures existing upon and forming part of the land at the date of valuation but taking into account a proper deduction for obsolescence or depreciation.

Appeal allowed [Rich ACJ and Williams J's judgment omitted].

Question

It is ironical that the government paid the indigenous people compensation in respect of improvements carried out by the government. Would you say that the judgment was over-generous? See *Madaha Resena and Others v The Independent State of Papua New Guinea* [1990] PNGLR 22.

The principle has been embraced in other common law jurisdictions as the next two cases below indicate.

FRANCIS v IBITOYE (1936) NLR 11,
Judgment of the Divisional Court of Nigeria

[The plaintiff and the defendant were negotiating for the sale of land by the defendant to the plaintiff. Before the negotiations were concluded the plaintiff, without knowledge or leave of the defendant, proceeded to construct a house on the land at a cost of 120 pounds. When the negotiations for the sale of the land fell through, the plaintiff sued the defendant for compensation for the erection of the building.]

GRAHAM PAUL J: In these circumstances I am asked to hold that the plaintiff can recover from the landowner the cost of the building. I know of no authority for such a claim ... It is trite law that a building erected in the circumstances I have indicated becomes the property of the landowner without any obligation to re-compensate the builder. The maxim *quicquid plantatur solo, solo cedit* applies without qualification.

The claim for the 120 pounds is obviously without justification and is dismissed.

Questions

1 Was the plaintiff's claim 'obviously' without justification? Is this a fair decision?

2 If this case were decided under your customary law, what would be the result?

3 Suppose the defendant was aware that the plaintiff was constructing the house before the negotiations were concluded, would the court have a different decision? See *Brand v Chris Building Co Pty Ltd* [1957] VR 625.

BRAND v CHRIS BUILDING CO PTY LTD [1957] VR 625,
Supreme Court of Victoria

[The defendant, Chris Building Company Pty Ltd, entered into a contract whereby it agreed to build a residential house for Mr and Mrs Pulis on the Pulis' land. Mr Pulis pointed out to the defendant's representative the land on which the house was to be built, but in error, he indicated the adjoining lot, which in fact belongs to Brand, the plaintiff. The house was erected thereon. When the mistake was discovered, the defendant offered to Brand to remove the almost completed house and to put the land back into its previous state. Alternatively, the defendant offered to accept 2,145 pounds from the plaintiff being the cost without profit of the labour and materials. The plaintiff declined both offers. He brought these proceedings to restrain the defendant from entering his land and demolishing the house. The main defence was acquiescence and unjust enrichment.]

HUDSON J: The position therefore is this, that the plaintiff as the owner is entitled to possession; the defendant under an honest mistake which was not contributed to by the plaintiff entered upon the land without any authority or licence of the plaintiff, became a trespasser and proceeded to build a house on it; and when the plaintiff found out, he took immediate steps to prevent the continuance of the trespass.

What does the law say about such a position? I think the correct statement of the position is as set out in *Halsbury's Laws of England* (3rd edn) Vol 14, para 1179, p 639: 'When A stands by while his right is being infringed by B, the following circumstances must as a general rule be present in order that the estoppel may be raised against A: (1) B must be mistaken as to his own legal rights; if he is aware that he is infringing the rights of another, he takes the risk of those rights being asserted; (2) B must expend money, or do some act, on the faith of his mistaken belief; otherwise, he does not suffer by A's subsequent assertion of his rights; (3) acquiescence is founded on contract with a knowledge of one's legal rights, and hence A must know of his own rights; (4) A must know of B's mistaken belief; with that knowledge it is inequitable for him to keep silence and allow B to proceed on his mistake; (5) A must encourage B in his expenditure of money or other act, either directly or by abstaining from asserting his legal right.'

The authorities for these propositions regarding estoppel have been referred to in argument. Perhaps the most important is *Ramsden v Dyson* ... [(1866) LR1 HL 129]. Those authorities, I think, amply support the propositions set out in *Halsbury* I have read, and in the absence of the requirements there set forth, the defence of acquiescence must fail. In my opinion, the last three requirements have not been satisfied. In other words, it has not been shown that there was knowledge by the plaintiff of his own rights for the simple reason that he did not know his rights were being infringed. It follows that he could not know of the mistaken belief of the defendant. The plaintiff did not know what was going on, and therefore, there was nothing he could do until he found out on 30 November. Therefore, it is amply clear that the plea of acquiescence upon which the defence and counter-claim are based fails. Mr Hewitt, in support of his argument for the defendant, relied on the maxim of equity: 'He who seeks equity must do equity.' This does not mean that in every action where a party seeks equitable relief that that relief will be refused if some injustice will be produced. The maxim must be applied having regard to the principles established by the cases. In cases such as the present, it must be shown that the plaintiff was guilty of something in the nature of a fraud, and there is nothing of that kind here and I can find no ground which could raise an equity in favour of the defendant.

Mr Hewitt also sought to call in aid the doctrine of unjust enrichment which has been the subject of much writing of recent years, but he was not able to point to any case where it had been applied in circumstances such as the present, and to apply it would be to fly in the face of the highest authority. It is quite impossible to apply it in the face of these authorities. I think, therefore, that the claim should succeed and the counter-claim must fail. The plaintiff is therefore entitled to judgment and the defendant's counter-claim must fail. It has appeared in evidence that inside the house, which had reached a stage where it could be locked up, some doors and other loose building materials were present, but the plaintiff makes no claim to them, and through his counsel has given an undertaking that they may be removed by the defendant. There will therefore be judgment for the plaintiff, for the declaration sought in paragraph (b) of the statement of claim and for the injunctions claimed in paragraphs (c) and (d). There has been no suggestion that the claim for damages has been made out or that the property has been injured. The plaintiff having intimated that he is not asking for costs, there will be no order as to costs.

> On the face of it, the result of the case seems very hard on the defendant and he may well feel that the decision is unjust; but he must realise that the court must be guided in its decision by principles of law. It has been said that the plaintiff is hard in insisting on his strict legal right, but it does appear that there were certain negotiations made in an effort to settle the matter. What the offers were that were made I am not concerned to inquire, nor can I say whether either side is reasonable or unreasonable.

Questions

1. Why did the court not apply the principle of estoppel in the case? See *PNG Ready Mixed Concrete Pty Ltd v The Independent State of Papua New Guinea* [1981] PNGLR 396, below.
2. Would it not have been fairer to force the plaintiff to pay some compensation to the defendant or at least let the defendant dismantle the building and take away whatever he could to minimise his loss? See note below.
3. Suppose your neighbour or stranger mistakenly carried out improvement on your land. Would you under customary law be entitled to the improvement with or without compensation? See *Madaha Resena and Others v The Independent State of Papua New Guinea* [1990] PNGLR 22.

Note

In some states in Australia legislation has been enacted to protect persons in a similar position as the defendant in *Brand v Chris Building Co* who mistakenly construct buildings or carry out permanent improvements on other people's lands or whose buildings encroach upon their neighbour's land. For example in Queensland, s 196 of the Property Land Act 1974–89 provides:

> Where a person makes a lasting improvement on land owned by another in the genuine but mistaken belief that:
>
> (a) such land is his property; or
>
> (b) such land is the property of person on whose land the improvement is made or intended to be made,
>
> application may be made in the court for relief under this Division.

Section 197 gives the court wide powers to grant such relief as it deems to be just and equitable. These include the power to order the landowner to pay compensation to the developer, to order the landowner to give the land or part of it on which the improvement is made to the developer; to order the developer to remove the structure etc.[8] With reference to encroaching buildings over the neighbour's land, ss 182–94 of the Act give the court the power to grant either to the owner of the encroaching building or the owner of the land such relief as it considers just and equitable.[9]

8 For a discussion of these provisions, see *Ex p Karynette Pty Ltd* [1984] 2 Qd R 211.

9 See, for example, *Ex p Van Achterberg* [1984] 1 Qd R 160.

There is no corresponding statutory provision in PNG. However, under s 48 of the Land Act the Minister in certain circumstances is required to pay compensation to an outgoing lessee for improvements made by him on the land.

It appears that customary law also favours the payment of compensation for improvements. In *Madaha Resena and Others v The Independent State of Papua New Guinea* (*supra*) Bredmayer J said (pp 38–39):

> In awarding this compensation, I have endeavoured to apply the customary law, but as no customary law was cited to me or discovered by me which was directly relevant, I have endeavoured to fashion a rule which is applicable and appropriate to the circumstances of the country in accordance with the matters set out in Sched 2.3 of the Constitution ... I can think of two analogies from custom which may be relevant. The first is that I believe under Motuan custom, and under many other customs in Papua New Guinea, when a wrong has been committed against a group, it can be put right by compensation and it is usual for the payment of that compensation to be marked by a feast at which speeches are made and food and drink is consumed. The compensation is handed over in a ceremony and the feast helps reconcile the hitherto opposed parties. I would like to award a sum to the plaintiffs for this purpose but, as I have heard no argument on it, will not.
>
> The second analogy I draw from custom is this. Mr Shepherd vigorously argued that the buildings on the land erected by the Department of Civil Aviation became the property of the plaintiffs following the Chief Commissioner's decision in April 1985 and hence should not have been removed by the Department of Civil Aviation in February 1989.
>
> I consider that under the relevant Motuan custom, these buildings did not pass to the plaintiffs and that Mr Tom Jones's evidence to the contrary was not convincing and is not to be believed. I remind myself that the airstrip and these ancillary buildings were not a blatant act of trespass by the government. When the airstrip and these buildings were constructed, the government honestly believed that it was the owner of the land. According to its records, it had taken possession of the land in 1889 and had treated it as its land ever since. Hence the establishment of the State plantation and of the quarantine station and the 1907 *Gazette* notice reserving it from sale or lease. Of course, the Chief Commissioner found in 1985, after 21 years of litigation, that the government did not own the land, but, up until that time I consider that the government did not own the land, but, up until that time. I consider that the government believed in good faith that it owned the land.

Because of the maxim *quicquid plantatur solo, solo cedit*, the question whether or not a thing is a fixture is crucial. Generally, the courts employ two tests to determine this question: the degree of annexation and the object of annexation. The degree of annexation is determined by the means by which the thing is attached to the land, for example by nails, bolts, mortar or own weight. Generally, an item, which is attached to the land by some means other than by its own weight *prima facie*, is deemed a fixture. In that situation, the burden of proof is upon the person alleging otherwise to discharge. Conversely, if the thing is resting on the ground by its own weight, *prima facie*, it is not a fixture and the onus of proof is on him who alleges that it is a fixture.[10]

The leading English authority on the principle is reproduced below.

10 See *Geita Sebea v The Territory of Papua, supra*, p 108. See also *Australian Provincial Assurance Co Ltd v Coroneo* (1938) 38 SR (NSW) 700.

HOLLAND AND ANOTHER v HODGSON AND ANOTHER (1872) LR 7 CP 328, Court of Exchequer Chamber

[George Mason owner in fee simple of a worsted mill, at which he carried on business of a worsted spinner and stuff manufacturer, mortgaged the mill and all fixtures to the plaintiffs. Subsequently, Mason in bankruptcy assigned all this property to the defendants in trust for the benefit of Mason's creditors. The defendants seized 436 looms in the mill and sold them. The plaintiffs sued in conversion claiming that the looms were fixtures and therefore part of their mortgage. These looms were attached to the store floors of the rooms of the mill by means of nails driven through holes in the feet of the looms, in some cases into beams which had been built into the stone, and in other cases into plugs of wood driven into holes drilled in the stone for the purpose. It was impossible to remove the looms without drawing out the nails; but this could be done and without causing any serious damage to the floor. The defendants contended that the looms were attached to the floor to make them steadier and more capable of convenient use as chattels. The trial judge held that the looms were fixtures. On appeal the issue turned on whether the looms were fixtures or remained as chattels.]

BLACKBURN J: There is no doubt that the general maxim of the law is that what is annexed to the land becomes part of the land; but it is very difficult, if not impossible, to say with precision what constitutes an annexation sufficient for this purpose. It is a question which must depend on the circumstances of each case, and mainly on two circumstances, as indicating the intention; viz, the degree of annexation and the object of the annexation. When the article in question is no further attached to the land then [sic] by its own weight it is generally considered to be a mere chattel ... But even in such a case, if the intention is apparent to make the articles part of the land, they do become part of the land ... Thus blocks of stone placed one on top of another without any mortar or cement for the purpose of forming a dry stone wall would become part of the land, though the same stones, if deposited in a builder's yard for convenience sake stacked on the top of each other in the form of a wall, would remain chattels. On the other hand, an article may be very firmly fixed to the land, and yet the circumstances may be such as to show that it was never intended to be part of the land, and then it does not become part of the land. The anchor of a large ship must be very firmly fixed in the ground in order to bear the strain of the cable, yet no one could suppose that it became part of the land, even though it should chance that the shipowner was also the owner of the fee of the spot where the anchor was dropped. An anchor similarly fixed in the soil for the purpose of bearing the strain of the chain of a suspension bridge would be part of the land. Perhaps the true rule is that articles not otherwise attached to the land than by their own weight are not to be considered as part of the land, unless the circumstances are such as to show that they were intended to be part of the land, the onus of showing that they were so intended lying on those who assert that they have ceased to be chattels, and that, on the contrary, an article which is affixed to the land even slightly is to be considered as part of the land, unless the circumstances are such as to show that it was intended all along to continue as a chattel, the onus lying on those who contend that it is a chattel ... This, however, only removes the difficulty one step, for it still remains a question in each case whether the circumstances are sufficient to satisfy the onus. In some cases, such as the anchor of the ship or the ordinary instance given of a carpet nailed to the floor of a room the nature of the thing sufficiently shows it is only fastened as a chattel temporarily, and not affixed permanently as part of the land. But ordinary trade or tenant fixtures which are put up with the intention that they should be removed by the tenant (and so are put up for a purpose in one sense only temporary, and certainly not for

> the purpose of improving the reversionary interest of the landlord) have always been considered as part of the land, though severable by the tenant. In most, if not all, of such cases the reason why the articles are considered fixtures is probably that indicated by Wood VC, in *Boyd v Shorrock* [(1867) LR 5 Eq 72 at p 78], that the tenant indicates by the mode in which he puts them up that he regards them as attached to the property during his interest in the property. What we have now to decide is as to the application of these rules to looms put up by the owner of the fee in the manner described in the case.
>
> It is established that where an article is affixed by the owner of the fee, though only affixed by bolts and screws, it is to be considered as part of the land, at all events where the object of setting up the articles is to enhance the value of the premises to which it is annexed for the purpose to which those premises are applied ... We think therefore that the judgment below should be affirmed.

Notes

As the case of *Holland v Hodgson* illustrates, the second test, ie, the object of annexation, does not lend itself to easy application. The courts employ many different guidelines to assist them to determine whether the thing was attached to the land with a view to permanent improvement of the land. The courts will for example, look at how firmly the thing is held to the land. If it is so firmly held that its removal would entail its destruction or cause substantial damage to the land, it is strong evidence that a permanent fixing was intended. Then the fact that the thing is only slightly attached to the land may support the inference that it was intended to be permanent. Again, the courts may look at the use to which the thing is put in relation to the principal use of the land. If the thing has a great connection with the main purpose of the land, the chances are that it will be held to be a fixture.[11] Finally, the capacity in which the fixer brought the thing onto the land is another relevant consideration. Where a proprietor of the land attaches a chattel to his land, he is more likely to intend it as a permanent improvement of the land than if a mere lessor or other temporary occupant did so.[12]

Questions

1 A number of UPNG members of staff (nationals and expatriates) have TV antennas fixed with bolts and screws onto the roof of the University houses rented to them. Advise the Registrar whether the antennas are fixtures or chattels.

2 Without prior permission, X built on Y's land a dwelling house of hollow clay blocks standing upon concrete pillars covered with galvanised iron sheeting. Y claims that the house is a fixture and is, therefore, his property. Advise. See *Mitchell v Cowie* (1962) 5 West Indian Reports 409, cited in James, *Land Law and Policy in Papua New Guinea*, Port Moresby, Law Reform Commission (1985), p 24.

---

11 For example, looms in a mill (see *Holland*); chairs fastened together in rows and fixed on the floor of a cinema hall (see *Australian Provincial Assurance* (1938) 38 SR (NSW) 700).

12 *Belgrave Nominees Pty Ltd and Others v Barlin-Scott Airconditioning (Aust) Pty Ltd* [1984] VR 947, 951; see also Amankwah *et al*, *Land Law in PNG* (Lawbook Co, Sydney, 2001), p 40.

The right to remove fixtures

(a) General law

One common law exception to the *quicquid plantatur solo, solo cedit* maxim, is the right of a tenant to remove domestic, ornamental and trade fixtures. These are considered as tenant's fixtures in contrast to landlord's fixtures (*Geita Sebea v The Territory of Papua*).[13] Fixtures used for agricultural purposes are not tenant's fixtures.[14] The right to remove fixtures arose under the common law independently of contract, though the right may be limited or excluded by agreement of the parties or by statute.[15] A tenant who wishes to exercise the right to remove his fixtures must do so during the currency of the lease. If his lease expires and he leaves the premises without first removing the fixtures he is deemed to have abandoned them and cannot thereafter remove them. Where a tenant or any person acting under his authority he/she removes fixtures must make good any damage caused in the process of removing the fixtures and leave the premises in a reasonable and tenantable condition.[16]

(b) Statutory right to remove fixtures and or to compensation

Under the Land Act 1996, provision is made for payment of compensation to an outgoing State lessee for improvements made on the land. For a detailed treatment of the subject see Chapter 6 (Leases) below.

II DEFINITION AND CONCEPT OF LAND AT CUSTOMARY LAW

The meaning of land at customary law is not very easy to determine. Undoubtedly in a given case one would need to study the relevant customary law of a particular group to decide what the term means legally. However, generally, customary law recognises the dichotomy between the soil and things on or forming a part of the soil. Thus, ownership of crops on land can be distinguished from ownership of the soil itself. Therefore if a landowner revokes his tenant's permission to the occupation and use of land granted him, the tenant is entitled to payment of compensation for improvement that he made to the land: *Danga Mondo v Korugl Goi*.[17] The principle of *quicquid plantatur solo, solo cedit* it would seem has no application at customary law.

For purposes of jurisdiction of Village Courts over land held under customary law, land is defined to include a reef or bank and a house or other structure, built on or over

---

13 See *supra*, p 108.

14 Note that fixtures used for market gardening were regarded as trade fixtures hence they could be removed by the tenant, see *Mears v Callender* [1901] 2 Ch 388.

15 *Mancetter Developments Ltd v Garmanson Ltd and Others* [1986] QB 1212 (CA).

16 *Ibid.*

17 Unreported judgment, Kundiawa District Land Court decision handed down on 27 November 1987, *per* RJ Giddings (Magistrate). In a Ghanaian case *Dadzie v Kokofu* (1960) GLR 90, the Supreme Court held that ownership of cocoa trees was distinguishable from ownership of the land itself.

water, but does not include things growing on land.[18] In contrast for purposes of the Land Disputes Settlement Act,[19] 'land' means customary land, and includes:

(a) a reef or a bank; and

(b) a house or other structure built on land or over water; and

(c) things growing on land or in water over land, earths and minerals on or under land; and

(d) an interest in land;

Questions

1 A stranger without permission constructs a building and grows crops on your customary land. Discuss how the matter is likely to be dealt with in accordance with your customary law.

2 Customary law is said to be dynamic and not static. Would you advocate that the customary law meaning of 'land' should move closer to the common law definition or away from it?

3 Why is land defined differently under the Village Courts Act and the Land Disputes Settlement Act?

III CLASSIFICATION

Land in Papua New Guinea is classified according to whether it has been *alienated* by the original native owners and, therefore, taken out of the regime of native law and custom or remains in the possession and control of the native owners and, therefore, *unalienated* and subject to native law and custom. Several consequences flow from this classification and are indicated below.

RW James, *Land Law and Policy in PNG,* Port Moresby, Law Reform Commission (1985), pp 33–34

Unalienated and alienated lands

The principles and rules of land tenure in Papua New Guinea are best discussed in the context of the divisions recognised in the legal system. The main categories are unalienated and alienated lands, as shown in Table 1 below:

18 Section 1, Village Courts Act, Ch No 441.

19 Section 2, Ch No 45.

TABLE 1

Total Land Area = 47,615,700 hectares	
Unalienated	**Alienated**
46,310,419 hectares	1,305,281 hectares
97.25%	2.75%

Unalienated land is that which is owned and controlled by the indigenous peoples according to their customs. The expression 'customary land' is normally used in legislation to refer to this category of land. 'Customary land' has been defined to mean land which is owned or possessed by an automatic citizen or community of automatic citizens by virtue of rights of a proprietary or possessory kind which belong to that citizen or community and arise from and are regulated by custom. (See Interpretation (Interim Provisions) Act, No 91 of 1975 (Cap 2).) This category forms just over 97% of the total land area.

Alienated land is largely land alienated from the traditional sector either voluntarily or by compulsory process. It comprises two basic sub-divisions: state land and privately-owned freeholds. Although it is only just under 3% of the total land area, it accounts for prime urban and agricultural land in the country. For example, alienated land accounts for over 40% of the arable land in the Gazelle area, which is a very fertile area of Papua New Guinea.

This broad division between unalienated and alienated land carries the implication of the contrast of unwritten and written laws. It also expresses diverse theoretical basic principles of the Papua New Guinea land tenure system, ie, the radical title to alienated land is in the State (Section 4, Cap 185; see also P Lalor, 'Land law and registration', *Fashion of Law in New Guinea*, p 137) whilst the ultimate ownership of unalienated lands is vested in the traditional groups. Whilst at customary law land is intended to provide a shelter and security for the group owners, at common law it is a marketable commodity. These different objectives are reflected in the controls and restrictions on dispositions apparent in both law and land policies ...

The colonial Administration adopted a long term policy to convert all unalienated land into alienated land, thus creating a unified land tenure system. The implementation of this policy was opposed by the nationalist government and has presumably been abandoned. On the other hand, the latter has resisted continuous pressures to adopt a policy of retransfering title of all alienated lands, including government lands, to the original owners or their descendants. A limited land redistribution programme has, however, been adopted. The Constitution of Vanuatu has effected a re-conversion of all alienated lands to traditional tenure. The arguments in favour of this demand have been mainly historical ones, eg, the original alienation was involuntary and/or resulted from trickery by officials during the colonial Administration. It was also contended that the original landowning groups should be able to share in the benefits that flow from the use of their land and that the share should be a continuing one in the form of rents from the occupiers of land. (See *Hansard*, 26 June 1969, p 1377.)

Though similar arguments found support in the *Report of the Special Select Committee on Lands and Mining for the Solomon Islands* (Honiara, March 1976, see Parts 1 and 2), and the indigenous landlord class has long been a feature of the land tenure system in Fiji, they were conclusively rejected by the Commission of Inquiry into Land Matters (CILM) for Papua New Guinea. That Commission recommended the passage of legislation to strengthen the government's title to its land which is needed for public purposes (National Lands) and to give greater power for further acquisitions to meet national needs, eg, urban development, land settlements, etc. Apart from the theoretical merits of the arguments, the experience of the limited redistribution programme in Papua New Guinea points to the confusion in and difficulty of determining who were the original owners, in the face of conflicting claims.

IV THE DOCTRINES OF ESTATE AND TENURE

These are discussed in detail in *Land Law in PNG*.[20]

In the case extracted below the High Court of Australia in a recent epoch-making decision examined anew the doctrine of tenure.

MABO AND OTHERS v THE STATE OF QUEENSLAND (NO 2) (1992) 175 CLR 1, High Court of Australia

BRENNAN J (pp 46–49): A basic doctrine of the land law is the doctrine of tenure, to which Stephen CJ referred in *Attorney General v Brown* [(1847) Legge 312] and it is a doctrine which could not be overturned without fracturing the skeleton which gives our land law its shape and consistency. It is derived from feudal origins.

The feudal basis of the proposition of absolute Crown ownership

The land law of England is based on the doctrine of tenure. In English legal theory, every parcel of land in England is held either mediately or immediately of the King who is the Lord Paramount; the term 'tenure' is used to signify the relationship between tenant and lord (*Attorney General of Ontario v Mercer* (1883) LR 8 App Cas 767 at 771–72), not the relationship between tenant and land. The characteristic of feudalism 'is not *tenere terram*, but *tenere terram* de X' (Pollock and Maitland, *The History of English Law*, 2nd edn, 1898, reprinted 1952, Vol 1, p 234n). It is implicit in the relationship of tenure that both lord and tenant have an interest in the land: 'The King had *'dominium directum'*, the subject *'dominium utile'* (at p 773; Co Litt 16). Absent a *'dominium directum'* in the Crown, there would be no foundation for a tenure arising on the making of a grant of land. When the Crown acquired territory outside England which was to be subject to the common law, there was a natural assumption that the doctrine of tenure should be the basis of the land law. Perhaps the assumption did not have to be made. After all, as Holdsworth observed (*op cit*, Vol ii, p 199), the universal application of the doctrine of tenure is a purely English phenomenon. And Pollock and Maitland may be correct in saying (*op cit*, Vol 2, p 236; accord: Holdsworth, *op cit*, Vol ii (1923), p 75, fn 8) that the notion of universal tenure 'perhaps was possible only in a conquered country'. In Scotland, the King was not Paramount Lord of all land: some allodial lands remained in the Orkney and Shetlands Islands, though most land that had been held allodially became subject to feudal tenure (Bell, *Lectures on Conveyancing* (Edinburgh, 1867), Vol 1, Ch I, pp 531–32; Stair, *The Institutions of the Law of Scotland* (4th edn, 1826), pp 219, 222; Craigie, *Scottish Law of Conveyancing* (Edinburgh, 1899), pp 27–28; *Lord*

20 Amankwah *et al*, *op cit*, note 12, pp 42–52.

Advocate v Balfour (1907) SC 1360 at 1368–69). However, the English view favoured a universal application of the doctrine of tenure (Pollock and Maitland, *op cit*, pp 232–33):

> Every acre of English soil and every proprietary right therein have been brought within the compass of a single formula, which may be expressed thus: Z *tenet terram illam de ... domino Rege*. The king himself holds land which is in every sense his own; no one else has any proprietary right in it; but if we leave out of account this royal demesne, then every acre of land is 'held of' the king. The person whom we may call its owner, the person who has the right to use and abuse the land, to cultivate it or leave it uncultivated, to keep all others off it, holds the land of the king either immediately or mediately.

It is arguable that universality of tenure is a rule depending on English history and that the rule is not reasonably applicable to the Australian colonies. The origin of the rule is to be found in a traditional belief that, at some time after the Norman Conquest, the King either owned beneficially and granted, or otherwise became the Paramount Lord of all land in the Kingdom (*Bacon's Abridgement* (6th edn, 1807), Vol V, 'Prerogative', B, 1). According to Digby's *History of the Law of Real Property* (1897), p 34, William I succeeded to all rights over land held by the Anglo-Saxon kings; he acquired by operation of law and land of those who had resisted his conquest and a vast quantity of land was deemed to have been forfeited or surrendered to William and regranted by him. He may have become the proprietor of all land in England so that no allodial land remained. Or it may be, as Blackstone asserts, that in England, as in France, the allodial estates were surrendered into the king's hands and were granted back as feuds, the only difference being that in France the change 'was effected gradually, by the consent of private persons; [the change] was done at once, all over England, by the common consent of the nation' (*Commentaries*, Bk II, Ch 4, pp 50–51). But, whatever the fact, it is the fiction of royal grants that underlies the English rule. Blackstone says (at pp 50–51) that:

> ... it became a fundamental maxim, and necessary principle (though in reality a mere fiction) of our English tenures, that the king is the universal lord and original proprietor of all the lands in his kingdom; and that no man doth or can possess any part of it, but what has, mediately or immediately, been derived 'as a gift from him, to be held upon feudal services'. For this being the real case in pure, original, proper feuds, other nations who adopted this system were obliged to act upon the same supposition, as a substruction and foundation of their new polity, though the fact was indeed far otherwise.

It is not surprising that the fiction that land granted by the Crown had been beneficially owned by the Crown was translated to the colonies and that Crown grants should be seen as the foundation of the doctrine of tenure which is an essential principle of our land law. It is far too late in the day to contemplate an allodial or other system of land ownership. Land in Australia which has been granted by the Crown is held on a tenure of some kind and the titles acquired under the accepted land law cannot be disturbed.

Accepting the doctrine of tenure, it was an essential postulate that the Crown have such a title to land as would invest the Sovereign with the character of Paramount Lord in respect of a tenure created by grant and would attract the incidents appropriate to the tenure, especially the Crown's right to escheat (Wright, *Introduction to the Law of Tenures* (4th edn, 1792), p 5). The Crown was invested with the character of Paramount Lord in the colonies by attributing to the Crown a title, adapted from feudal theory, that was called a radical, ultimate or final title: see, for example, *Amodu Tijani v Secretary, Southern Nigeria* [1921] 2 AC 399 at 403, 404, 407; *Nireaha Tamaki v Baker* [1901] AC 561 at 580; cf *Administration of Papua and New Guinea v Daera Guba* (1973) 130 CLR 353 at 396–97. The Crown was treated as having the radical title to all the land in the territory over which the Crown acquired sovereignty. The radical title is a postulate of the doctrine of tenure and a concomitant of sovereignty. As a sovereign enjoys supreme legal authority in and over a territory, the sovereign has power to prescribe what parcels of land and what interests in those parcels should be enjoyed by others and what parcels of land should be kept as the sovereign's beneficial demesne.

By attributing to the Crown a radical title to all land within a territory over which the Crown has assumed sovereignty, the common law enabled the Crown, in exercise of its sovereign power, to grant an interest in land to be held of the Crown or to acquire land for the Crown's demesne. The notion of radical title enabled the Crown to become Paramount Lord of all who hold a tenure granted by the Crown and to become absolute beneficial owner of unalienated land required for the Crown's purposes. But it is not a corollary of the Crown's acquisition of a radical title to land in an occupied territory that the Crown acquired absolute beneficial ownership of that land to the exclusion of the indigenous inhabitants. If the land were desert and uninhabited, a truly a *terra nullius*, the Crown would take an absolute beneficial title (an allodial title) to the land for the reason given by Stephen CJ in *Attorney General v Brown* (see pp 13–14 above (1847) 1 Legge, at 317–18): there would be no other proprietor. But if the land were occupied by the indigenous inhabitants and their rights and interest in the land are recognised by the common law, the radical title which is acquired with the acquisition of sovereignty cannot itself be taken to confer an absolute beneficial title to the occupied land. Nor is it necessary to the structure of our legal system to refuse recognition to the rights and interests in land of the indigenous inhabitants. The doctrine of tenure applies to every Crown grant of an interest in land, but not to rights and interest which do not owe their existence to a Crown grant. The English legal system accommodated the recognition of rights and interests derived from occupation of land in a territory over which sovereignty was acquired by conquest without the necessity of a Crown grant ...

THE ADMINISTRATION OF THE TERRITORY OF PAPUA AND NEW GUINEA v BLASIUS TIRUPIA AND OTHERS (IN RE VUNAPALADIG AND JAPALIK LAND) [1971–72] P&NGLR 229, Full Court of the Supreme Court (Minogue CJ, Clarkson and Kelly JJ)

[Pages 244–45] Paragraph 10 was explained by Mr Endery as being an assertion of law that prior to the enactment of the Land Ordinance of 1962 there was no power in the Territory of New Guinea to grant an estate in fee simple. All land acquired from the German Administration was allodial land and the German law did not recognise any doctrine of estates. Any land held had to be allodial and the concept of allodial land was essentially different from that of tenure of estates in land. This would seem to involve the proposition that no land in the former German Land Registrar could be brought under the provisions of the Land Registration Ordinance for an estate in fee simple. This proposition is we think untenable. Whilst the legislature did not expressly deem all German private title to be fee simple it dealt with land so held as if it were. The interests dealt with were translated by registration into an estate in fee simple. Their Honours of the High Court assumed without question that the prior German title was converted by registration into an estate in fee simple. See *The Custodian of Expropriated Property and Another v Tedep* (1964) 113 CLR 318 at p 328. Mr Hogg in his work *Australian Torrens System Statutes* regards the most important characteristic of the Torrens system as a system of real property law as being that it exhibits the nearest approach in form which has yet been made to allodial ownership of land by any system based on the principles of feudal tenure. In his view the most prominent feature in the Torrens system, ie, the necessity for registration to the due creation or transfer of any interest in land, causes the system to approximate to one of allodial ownership and he regards the system as technically consistent only with allodial ownership. It is to be noted that s 13 of the Land Ordinance of 1922 empowered the Governor General in the name of the Administration to grant convey or otherwise dispose of estates in fee simple of Administration lands, and s 53 of the Land Registration Ordinance with its accompanying Fifth Schedule provides for a certificate of title to an estate in fee simple being issued.

RAHONAMO v ENAI AND ANOTHER (RE HITAU) (1971) unreported judgment N612, Supreme Court of Papua New Guinea

[In 1890 and 1891, the Administration purchased some land known as Hitau, situated on the Western shore of Port Moresby harbour from the Roku clan. In 1892, it made a Crown Grant of the land in favour of Robert Hunter. The land then remained in private hands until 1951 when it was compulsorily acquired by the Administration. In 1958, the appellant applied to the Land Titles Commission for the land to be 'registered in the name of the Laurina clan'. Several arguments were advanced by the appellant in support of his claim. One of the submissions was that the grant to Hunter, 'his administrators and assigns for ever' was, in the absence of words of limitation referring to heirs, a grant of a life estate only.]

CLARKSON J: I refer now to the argument that Hunter held only a life estate because of the omission from the Crown Grant of the words of limitation 'and his heirs'. It is true that at common law the use of these words was essential to create *inter vivos* an estate in fee simple and that the only relaxation of this rule which occurred at the time of this grant was the use of the alternative expression 'in fee simple' permitted by the Conveyancing Act 1881. These formalities were not required in wills. See s 28 of the Wills Act 1827.

But this transaction was not an ordinary conveyance *inter vivos*. It was an alienation of Crown lands by Grant issued under the Crown Grants Ordinance 1889 to give effect to a purchase made by Hunter from the Crown pursuant to Part IV of the Crown Lands Ordinance 1890. I think it is beyond doubt that the 'purchase' of the land for 25 pounds referred to in the minutes of the Executive Council of 1 June 1892 was intended to be a purchase of an estate in fee simple. The only provisions in the Crown Lands Ordinance for alienation of interests in land by the Crown were those relating to the alienation in fee simple following sale in Part IV and leases in Part V. No provision was made for the granting of life estates in Crown lands.

Similarly the Crown Grants Ordinance contemplated a 'grant in fee simple' of Crown lands within the Possession (ss I and II). Section III of that Ordinance read: 'Every Crown Grant shall be made out in such form as the Administrator in Council may from time to time determine and being so made out and issued to the person therein named shall be valid and effectual to convey to and vest in such person subject to law the lands therein described for such estate as shall be set forth therein.'

There is nothing before me to show whether or not any form of grant was specified, but I think I am entitled to assume, in the absence of any indication to the contrary, that a form had been specified, that the use of the form of this Grant was itself a determination made from time to time of the appropriate form. The grant recites that in conformity with the laws and regulations in force for the alienation of Crown lands Hunter had become the purchaser of the land for 25 pounds. It then sets out that in consideration of this payment and the quit rent reserved a grant is made to 'Robert Hunter, his administrators and assigns' of the land 'to hold unto the said Robert Hunter his administrators and assigns for ever'.

The grant is sealed with the seal of the Possession witnessed by the Administrator.

That the Crown intended to make a grant of an estate in fee simple is put beyond doubt by an endorsement on the Crown Grant, which the parties appear to have overlooked, recording that pursuant to a transfer registered in January 1917 'Alfred John Hool ... is now seised of an estate in fee simple in the whole of the within land'.

I think that on the proper construction of the relevant legislation and the grant the grant was effective to convey an estate in fee simple. But in any event the issue to Hool in 1917 of a certificate of title to a fee simple estate in the land effected a rectification of the register which before that time the court would have made to carry out the intention of the parties to the purchase by Hunter from the Crown. Any doubts as to the nature of the estate granted by the Crown Grant were removed by the issue of the Certificate of Title for an estate in fee simple.

A logical application of this doctrine would deny the indigenous inhabitants of Australia any legally enforceable proprietary interests in Australian land.[21] The High Court of Australia in *Mabo v The State of Queensland*[22] however, reversed this position.

For PNG that position of the law had long been recognised as the case below demonstrates.

THE ADMINISTRATION OF PAPUA NEW GUINEA v GUBA AND DORIGA (1973) 130 CLR 353, High Court of Australia

BARWICK CJ: Finally, in connection with the identity of the land purchased I should perhaps observe that we do not certainly know if all the land suitable for an eastern section of the town of Granville was claimed in 1886 to be owned by the Papuans. It is said, however, by Rev Lawes that there was little if any land in the Port Moresby district which could be said to be ownerless. But there is, as I have said, insufficient evidence given by or on behalf of the Papuan claimants to establish their title to or any right to the subject land. No doubt Musgrave and Hunter assumed that there were such claims to ownership of all the land in question in the Port Moresby district and dealt with the clansmen, whether Motuans or Koitapuans, accordingly. I have made the same assumption in what I have written. I have also assumed, without deciding, that the declaration of the Protectorate or the annexation of the Protectorate or the annexation by the British government did not vest in the Crown the ultimate title to all the land in Papua subject only to any usufructuary or other rights of the Papuans, these to be determined by native custom. Whatever the traditional views in this connection (as to which see generally *Milirrpum v Nabalco Pty Ltd* (1971) 17 FLR 141, and more recently *Calder and Another v AG for British Columbia* in the Supreme Court of Canada, 31 Jan 1973 (unreported)), the title of the Papuans whatever its nature according to native custom was confirmed in them expressly by legislative acts from time to time on the part of the Territorial Administration. I find no need to detail these or to discuss further that matter.

21 See the *Milirrpum* case, below.

22 (1992) 175 CLR 1.

It is enough for present purposes that from the inception the law applicable in the Territory by virtue of the Protectorate and of the Colony, recognised a right in the Papuans to sell or surrender to the Crown whatever right they had communally or individually in the land. Commodore Erskine by his Proclamation of the Protectorate announced that no acquisition of land from Papuans would be recognised by Her Majesty, referring, of course, to acquisitions by others than Her Majesty or by persons on her behalf. Early Ordinances prevented the acquisition of land from Papuans and they were forbidden to sell land except to the Administration.

But none of this activity on the part of the Crown was inconsistent with the traditional result of occupation or settlement, namely, that though the indigenous people were secure in their usufructuary title to land, the land came from the inception of the colony into the dominion of Her Majesty. That is to say, the ultimate title subject to the usufructuary title was vested in the Crown. Alienation of that usufructuary title to the Crown completed the absolute fee simple in the Crown. Whether the subsequent legislative history of the Territory denies that traditional position is a matter with which I am not presently concerned.

Appeal allowed. (Menzies, Gibbs and Stephen JJ's judgment omitted.)

Thus, the doctrine of tenure it seems is limited in its application to PNG because native title is superimposed on it. However, for PNG one of the incidents of tenure, ie, escheat, appears to be quite important. Consider for instance the case below.

RE JOHNS [1971–72] P&NGLR 110, Supreme Court of Papua New Guinea

[A testator died in 1933. At the date of his death, the principal asset in his estate was the unexpired term of a Crown lease. The Supreme Court granted an order to administer the estate with the will annexed. The testator's widow was given possession of a life interest in the lease, which she took under the terms of the will and this interest was registered. The original will was destroyed by fire, and no evidence of its contents was available. At the date of death of the testator, as far as could be ascertained, there were no next of kin. The tenant died.]

KELLY J: In this case I regard it as a remote possibility that evidence of sufficient cogency to satisfy a court as to the contents of the destroyed will would ever be forthcoming, having regard to the enquiries which have been made, the time which has elapsed and the deaths which have occurred in the interim. In these circumstances I do not consider that I would be justified in allowing the residue of this estate to remain undistributed any longer. I think it is so improbable that the contents of the will will never now be known that I should proceed as though the Public Curator were administering an estate in which there was an intestacy as to the reversionary interest which comprises the residue of the estate. I do not consider that there is any purpose to be served by further advertising or that it is necessary to order the making of enquiries of any other persons.

The applicable Ordinance is the Probate and Administration Ordinance 1913–40 (Papua). Although this Ordinance was repealed by the Probate and Administration Ordinance 1951 of the Territory of Papua and New Guinea it continues to apply to the estates of persons who died before the commencement of the latter Ordinance (s 4(2)). Section 58 of the former Ordinance authorises the court to make such order with reference to the distribution or application of any moneys which the executor or administrator or curator may have in hand or as to the residue of the estate as it may think fit.

Section 20 of the Probate and Administration Ordinance 1913–40 provides:

> Any husband or wife shall be entitled on the death of the other as to the estate as to which he or she dies intestate after the commencement of this Ordinance to the following shares only:
>
> (a) where there is issue surviving to one-third share of such property;
>
> (b) where there is no issue surviving and in case of total in testacy;
>
> (i) where the net value of the property of the deceased does not exceed the sum of five hundred pounds to the whole of such property;
>
> (ii) where the net value of such property exceeds the sum of five hundred pounds to the sum of five hundred pounds absolutely and exclusively which sum with interest thereon from the date of the death until payment at the rate of four pounds per centum per annum shall be a charge upon the whole of such property; and in addition thereto to one-half share of the residue of such property after the payment of such sum of five hundred pounds and interest if any;
>
> (c) where there is no issue surviving and in case of partial intestacy to one-half share of such property.

I am satisfied that there is no issue surviving the deceased, but I do not consider that I am entitled to proceed as though there had been a total intestacy. There was no intestacy as to the life interest which the widow had already enjoyed so that the intestacy is only as to the reversionary interest and is therefore a partial intestacy (see *In Re McKee; Public Trustee v McKee* [1931] 2 Ch 145 at p 149). The applicable provision is therefore paragraph (c) of s 20 and the widow became entitled on the death of her husband to one-half share of the reversionary interest. The fact that this interest could only become an interest in possession after her own death is not to the point, as what she became entitled to by the operation of s 20 is one-half share of the estate as to which her husband died intestate, that is, the reversionary interest.

The balance of the estate as to which the deceased died intestate is then divisible among the next-of-kin pursuant to s 21. For the purpose of that section the widow is not included amongst the next-of-kin. The widow is not in the ordinary sense one of the next-of-kin (*Garrick v Lord Camden; Paton v Jones* (1807) 14 Ves 372, at p 385; 33 ER 564, at p 568). When used *simpliciter* in a will the primary meaning of the expression 'next-of-kin' is 'the nearest blood relation of the testator at the date of his death' (*Gutheil v Ballarat Trustees, Executors and Agency Co Ltd* (1922) 30 CLR 293, *per* Knox CJ, at p 299). In *Gutheil*'s case (1922) 30 CLR, at p 305 Isaacs J refers to the natural and obvious meaning of the words as 'nearest in proximity of blood'. There is nothing in s 21 which would require these words to be given any other meaning.

There are no known next-of-kin discoverable after due enquiry so that the property which under s 21 would otherwise be divisible among the next-of-kin should be dealt with on the assumption that there are no next-of-kin (*Re Menday* (1916) 16 SR (NSW) 442).

The property now under consideration, namely the one-half share in a reversionary interest in a lease for 99 years under the Land Ordinance of 1906 is 'real estate' for the purpose of the Probate and Administration Ordinance 1913–40 (see the definition of 'real estate' in s 4) and this is not affected by the fact that since the death the property has under the authority of an order of the court been converted into money. If escheat to the Crown were applicable in Papua, I am by no means certain that it could properly be applied to a share in a reversionary interest in a lease from the Crown. However, I do not find it necessary to go into that aspect as I do not consider that escheat now applies in the Territory of Papua. Escheat is a common law concept, the operation of which prior to its abolition in England by statute had been affected by such statutes as the Intestates Estates Act of 1884, by s 4 of which it was provided that from and after the passing of that Act, where a person dies without an heir and intestate in respect of any real estate consisting of any estate or interest whether legal or equitable in any incorporeal hereditament, or of any equitable estate or interest in any corporeal hereditament, whether devised or not devised to trustees by the will of such person, the law of escheat shall apply in the same manner as if the estate or interest above mentioned were a legal estate in corporeal hereditaments.

The operation of escheat in Papua is assumed, for instance, by s 31 of the Probate and Administration Ordinance 1913–40 (which limits its operation in the case of a person dying intestate and without heirs or next-of-kin to the residue remaining after the payment of debts) and by s 25 of the Succession Act of 1867 (Queensland, adopted), but so far as I can discover its operation is nowhere expressly provided for in any Ordinance of the Territory or in any adopted legislation which is or has been in force in Papua. Escheat therefore would only apply in Papua by reason of s 4 of the Courts and Laws Adopting Ordinance of 1889 which is as follows:

> The principles and rules of common law and equity that for the time being shall be in force and prevail in England shall so far as the same shall be applicable to the circumstances of the Possession be likewise the principles and rules of common law and equity that shall for the time being be in force and prevail in British New Guinea.

Escheat to the Crown was abolished in England by s 45 of the Administration of Estates Act 1925.

The extent to which regard is to be had to English statutory law in determining what are the principles and rules of common law and equity that are for the time being in force in England and, subject to its applicability to the circumstances of the Territory, consequently in force in Papua or New Guinea as the case may be, has been considered both by the High Court and by this court. In *Booth v Booth* (1935) 53 CLR 1, s 16 of the Laws Repeal and Adopting Ordinance 1921–33 (New Guinea) was under consideration.

That section provided that:

> The principles and rules of common law and equity that were in force in England on the ninth day of May, one thousand nine hundred and twenty-one, shall be in force in the Territory so far as the same are applicable to the circumstances of the Territory, and are not repugnant to or inconsistent with the provisions of any Act, ordinance, law, regulation, rule, order or proclamation having the force of law that is expressed to extend to or applied to or made or promulgated in the Territory.

Rich and Dixon JJ said (1935) 53 CLR, at p 30:

> It is so evidently the intention of the ordinance to introduce, subject to local ordinances and to the specified enactments of Queensland and Papua, the whole content of English law applicable to the circumstances of New Guinea that a very wide meaning should be given to s 16 in spite of the difficulties which its language presents. Probably the principles and rules of common law must be taken subject to and together with the statutory modifications in their application which had been made in England before 9 May 1921.

Starke J (1935) 53 CLR, at p 32 said:

> The development of the rules of English law relating to the proprietary rights of husband and wife has been continuous, and the rules of the common law, the doctrines of equity, and statutes, have all played a part in this development. The provisions of the Married Women's Property Acts in force in England on 9 May 1921 may therefore be regarded as part of 'the principles and rules of common law and equity' referred to in s 16 of the Laws Repeal and Adopting Ordinance.

In *Murray v Brown River Timber Co Ltd* [1964] P & NGLR 167, Mann CJ had to consider s 4 of the Courts and Laws Adopting Ordinance and he concluded that the common law adopted in the Territory of Papua by virtue of s 4 includes the common law in England at the present time as it would appear if unaffected by statutes which the Territory's courts would not be prepared to regard as incorporated into the general structure of the common law applicable to the Territory.

At this point of time a definite pronouncement by an appellate court on the meaning of s 4 of the Courts and Laws Adopting Ordinance is lacking and the wide statement by Rich and Dixon JJ in *Booth v Booth* (1935) 53 CLR 1 in relation to the comparable provision of the Laws Repeal and Adopting Ordinance is clearly *obiter*. However, I consider that it is correct to regard s 4 as going at least as far as incorporating in the law of Papua such of the principles and rules of the common law of England as had not been abrogated by statute from time to time, and provided that they are applicable to the circumstances of the Territory, so that in the present case where what was a rule of the common law has been abolished by statute in England and consequently is no longer in force there, then that common law rule is no longer in force in Papua. On this view it follows that escheat did not operate in Papua at the date of death of the deceased.

It next becomes necessary to consider whether the statutory provision in force in England which has replaced the abrogated common law rule is thereby in force in Papua as then being part of the principles of common law and equity referred to in s 4. In present case the same English statute which abolished escheat to the Crown provided by a subsequent section (s 46(1)(vi)) that the residuary estate of an intestate to which no person took an absolute interest in accordance with the provisions of the statute should belong to the Crown or to the Duchy of Lancaster or to the Duke of Cornwall for the time being, as the case may be, as *bona vacantia*, and in lieu of any right to escheat. In effect what was done was to preserve the principle of the property going to the Crown but to substitute for the method of escheat and the procedural requirements involved (as to which see the discussion of the history of escheat by Wanstall J in *Re Bonner (deceased)* [1963] Qd R 488) as the means of achieving this, the simple procedure of the property passing to the Crown as *bona vacantia* as was already the common law rule in relation to personalty which had no other owner. This may be regarded as a statutory modification in the application of a principle or rule of the common law to the extent that having abolished one common law principle, namely, that of escheat to the Crown in the case of realty another principle, that of ownerless property passing to the Crown as *ultimus haeres* was extended to cover interests in realty. Without finding it necessary to consider the limits of the dictum of Rich and Dixon JJ in *Booth v Booth* (1935) 53 CLR 1, I would consider that the common law in force in Papua as at the date of death of the deceased included a rule that interests in realty which had no other owner passed to the Crown as *bona vacantia*, there being no basis on which it could be said that such a rule would not be applicable to the circumstances of Papua.

In applying this principle to the present case I do not consider that the restricted meaning of *bona vacantia* as meaning the residuary estate of a person dying intestate without husband or wife should be adopted (see *Dyke v Walford* (1846) 5 Moo PCC 434; 13 ER 557) in view of the provisions of s 20 of the Probate and Administration Ordinance 1913–40 to which regard must be had and which in this instance limits the wife's entitlement to one-half share of the property, and the situation which arises whereby, by the joint operation of ss 20 and 21 of that Ordinance, there is property which has no other owner. The remaining one-half share of the property as to which the deceased must be treated as having died intestate should therefore be paid to the Treasurer on behalf of the Crown.

Question

Can it be argued then that the doctrine of tenure is part of the jurisprudence of the legal system of PNG? See *The Administration of Papua New Guinea v Guba and Doriga, supra,* p 123.

V INTERESTS AT CUSTOMARY LAW: ALLODIAL AND USUFRUCT

Amankwah *et al* write:[23]

> The admixture of English law and customary law has had the effect of generating for PNG legal dualism or pluralism in which two entirely different systems of law had to be administered within the same jurisdiction. Customary law had undergone a long period of experimentation. It was at first regarded as foreign law and had to be proved by evidence. The Constitution today recognises it as part of the underlying law which the judiciary is enjoined to develop.[24] However, it is not easy in a country of the size of PNG and with over 700 language groups to set out clearly the juristic notions of real property. Nor do we subscribe to the view that on account of language difficulties, the people had no conception of property;[25] disputes were however decided on a case by case basis. We agree with Dr Richard Scaglion's conclusion:
>
>> While the specifics of land law vary widely from culture to culture, there are certain similarities. In general, land is communally owned. In such cases, there is rarely total alienation of land; usufruct rights may be granted in virtual perpetuity as long as users hold to the original terms of agreement. Alienation of customary land should be discouraged, and long term leases should be negotiated.
>>
>> In general, multiple rights in land are recognised in customary law: firewood gathering rights, fishing or hunting rights, rights of thoroughfare, etc. Such rights should be recognised in law and should be clearly specified in lease agreements. The Customary Law Project is presently investigating the specifics of land law.[26]

The policy of successive administrations of curbing land ownership litigations by providing for the settling of disputes relating to land user only at district level has had the effect of preventing the development of a *corpus juris* by the superior courts. Currently the superior courts only have the power to review land cases.

---

23 *Land Law in PNG, op cit,* note 12, p 50.

24 See Law Reform Commission Report No 7 (1977).

25 See H Reynolds, *The Law of the Land* (2nd edn, Penguin Books, Ringwood, 1987).

26 *Law Reform Commission of PNG:* Monograph No 2: *Customary Law in Papua New Guinea: A Melanesian View,* Port Moresby, 1983, p viii.

What is clear however is that in most areas of the nation, ownership of land is a group or corporate affair (allodial?). Individuals have the right of user akin to the usufruct. Perhaps it may be instructive to observe the situation in other jurisdictions with similar patterns of land rights.[27]

The constitutional aspects of the problem are also indicated there.[28]

Questions

1 'While the specifics of land law vary widely from culture to culture, there are certain similarities. In general, land is communally owned. In such cases, there is rarely total alienation of land; usufruct rights may be granted in virtual perpetuity as long as users hold to the original terms of agreement. Alienation of customary land should be discouraged, and long term leases should be negotiate.'

Customary Law in Papua New Guinea (Richard Scaglion (ed)), Port Moresby, Law Reform Commission Monograph No 2, 1983, p viii.

With reference to the above statement, identify the nature of *interests* in land in your locality or clan. Address yourself specifically to the following issues:

(a) Who is the owner of the allodial or radical title?

(b) What is the extent and content of the individual title?

(c) Who inherits the property (real and personal) of a deceased clansman?

Offer your suggestion for improving your system.

2 'I conceive that land belongs to a vast family of whom many are dead, a few are living and countless host are still unborn.'

Per Chief Gboteyi, the Elesi of Odogbolu, Western Nigeria.

How far is this *dictum* true of the Papua New Guinea's customary tenure of land?

3 The Privy Council said in *Amodu Tijani v The Secretary, Southern Nigeria* [1921] 2 AC 399, p 404:

> The next fact which it is important to bear in mind in order to understand the native land law is that the notion of individual ownership is quite foreign to native ideas. Land belongs to the community, the village or family, never to the individual. All the members of the community, village or family have an equal right in the land, but in every case the Chief or Headman of the community or village or the head of the family, has charge of the land, and in loose mode of speech is sometimes called the owner.

Does the principle of community ownership of land enunciated here in respect of former British West Africa have any relevance to the land tenure system in Papua New Guinea?

4 Although a great deal of misconception surrounds interests in land at customary law, one principle stands out as the polar star: land ownership is a communal affair.

Do you agree with this view?

---

27 See *The Administration of PNG v Guba and Doriga*, *supra*, p 123.

28 *Ibid*, pp 51–52.

5 'I think that property, in its many forms, generally implies the right to use or enjoy, the right to exclude others, and the right to alienate. I do not say that all these rights must co-exist before there can be a proprietary interest, or deny that each of them may be subject to qualifications. But by this standard, I do not think that I can characterise the relationship of the clan to the land as proprietary.'

Per Blackburn J *Milirrpum and Others v Nabalco Pty Ltd and the Commonwealth of Australia* (1971) 17 FLR 141, p 272.

Assess the validity of this statement in relation to group title to land under the customary law of your area.

MABO v QUEENSLAND (1992) 175 CLR 1, High Court of Australia

BRENNAN J (pp 429–31) THE NATURE AND INCIDENTS OF NATIVE TITLE: Native title has its origin in and is given its content by the traditional laws acknowledged by and the traditional customs observed by the indigenous inhabitants of a territory. The nature and incidents of native title must be ascertained as a matter of fact by reference to those laws and customs. The ascertainment may present a problem of considerable difficulty, as Moynihan J perceived in the present case. It is a problem that did not arise in the case of a settled colony so long as the fictions were maintained that customary rights could not be reconciled 'with the institutions or the legal ideas of civilised society' (*In Re Southern Rhodesia* [1919] AC at 233), that there was no law before the arrival of the British colonists in a settled colony and that there was no sovereign law-maker in the territory of a settled colony before sovereignty was acquired by the Crown. These fictions denied the possibility of a native title recognised by our laws. But once it is acknowledged that an inhabited territory which became a settled colony was no more a legal desert than it was 'desert uninhabited' in fact, it is necessary to ascertain by evidence the nature and incidents of native title. Though these are matters of fact, some general propositions about native title can be stated without reference to evidence.

First, unless there are pre-existing laws of a territory over which the Crown acquires sovereignty which provide for the alienation of interests in land to strangers, the rights and interests which constitute a native title can be possessed only by the indigenous inhabitants and their descendants. Native title, though recognised by the common law, is not an institution of the common law and is not alienable by the common law. Its alienability is dependent on the laws from which it is derived. If alienation of a right or interest in land is a mere matter of the custom observed by the indigenous inhabitants, not provided for by law enforced by a sovereign power, there is no machinery which can enforce the rights of the alienee. The common law cannot enforce as a proprietary interest the rights of a putative alienee whose title is not created either under a law which was enforceable against the putative alienor at the time of the alienation and thereafter until the change of sovereignty or under the common law. And, subject to an important qualification, the only title dependent on custom which the common law will recognise is one which is consistent with the common law. Thus, in *The Case of Tanistry*, the Irish custom of tanistry was held to be void because it was to be founded in violence and because of vesting of title under the custom was uncertain (1608) Davis [80 ER]; 4th edn, Dublin (1762) English translation, at pp 94–99). The inconsistency that the court perceived between the custom of tanistry known to the Brehon law of Ireland and the common law precluded the recognition of the custom by the common law. At that stage in its development, the common law was too rigid to admit recognition of a native title based on other laws or customs, but that rigidity has been relaxed, at least since the decision of the Privy Council in *Amodu Tijani*. The general principle that the common law will recognise a customary title only if it be consistent with the common law is subject to an exception in favour of traditional native title.

Of course, since European settlement of Australia, many clans or groups of indigenous people have been physically separated from their traditional land and have lost their connection with it. But that is not the universal position. It is clearly not the position of the Meriam people. Where a clan or group has continued to acknowledge the laws and (so far as practicable) to observe the customs based on the traditions of that clan or group, whereby their traditional connection with the land has been substantially maintained, the traditional community title of that clan or group can be said to remain in existence. The common law can, by reference to the traditional laws and customs of an indigenous people, identify and protect the native rights and interests to which they give rise. However, when the tide of history was washed away any real acknowledgment of traditional law and any real observance of traditional customs, the foundation of native title has disappeared. A native title which has ceased with the abandoning of laws and customs based on tradition cannot be revived for contemporary recognition. Australian law can protect the interests of members of an indigenous clan or group, whether communally or individually, only in conformity with the traditional laws and customs of the people to whom the clan or group belongs and only where members of the clan or group acknowledge those laws and observe those customs (so far as it is practicable to do so). Once traditional native title expires, the Crown's radical title expands to a full beneficial title, for then there is no other proprietor than the Crown.

It follows that a right or interest possessed as a native title cannot be acquired from an indigenous people by one who, not being a member of the indigenous people, does not acknowledge their laws and observe their customs; nor can such a right or interest be acquired by a clan, group or member of the indigenous people unless the acquisition is consistent with the laws and customs of that people. Such a right or interest can be acquired outside those laws and customs only by the Crown. (This result has been reached in other jurisdictions, though for different reasons: see *R v Symonds* (1847) NZPCC, at 390; *Johnson v McIntosh* (1823) 8 Wheat, at 586 [21 US, at 259]; *St Catherine's Milling & Lumber Co v The Queen* (1887) 13 SCR 577 at 599.) Once the Crown acquires sovereignty and the common law becomes the law of the territory, the Crown's sovereignty over all land in the territory carries the capacity to accept a surrender of native title. The native title may be surrendered on purchase or surrendered voluntarily, whereupon the Crown's radical title is expanded to absolute ownership, a *plenum dominium*, for there is then no other owner (*St Catherine's Milling & Lumber Co v The Queen* (1888) 14 App Cas, at 55). If native title were surrendered to the Crown in expectation of a grant of a tenure to the indigenous title holders, there may be a fiduciary duty on the Crown to exercise its discretionary power to grant a tenure in land so as to satisfy the expectation (see *Guerin v The Queen* (1984) 13 DLR (4d) 321 at 334, 339, 342–43, 356–57, 360–61), but it is unnecessary to consider the existence or extent of such a fiduciary duty in this case. Here, the fact is that strangers were not allowed to settle on the Murray Islands and, even after annexation in 1879, strangers who were living on the Islands were deported. The Meriam people asserted an exclusive right to occupy the Murray Island and, as a community, held a proprietary interest in the Islands. They have maintained their identity as a people and the observe customs which are traditionally based. There was a possible alienation of some kind of interest in two acres to the London Missionary Society prior to annexation but it is unnecessary to consider whether that land was alienated by Meriam law or whether the alienation was sanctioned by custom alone. As we shall see, native title to that land was lost to the Meriam people in any event on the grant of a lease by the Crown in 1882 or by its subsequent renewal.

Secondly, native title, being recognised by the common law (though not as a common law tenure), may be protected by such legal or equitable remedies as are appropriate to the particular rights and interests established by the evidence, whether proprietary or personal and usufructuary in nature and whether possessed by a community, a group or an individual. The incidents of a particular native title relating to inheritance, the transmission or acquisition of rights and interests on death or marriage, the transfer of rights and interests in land and the grouping of persons to possess rights and interests in land are matters to be determined by the laws and customs of the indigenous inhabitants, provided those laws and customs are not so repugnant to natural justice, equity and good conscience that judicial sanctions under the new regime must be withheld: *Idewu Inasa v Oshodi* [1934] AC 99 at 105. Of course in time the laws and customs of any people will change and the rights and interests of the members of the people among themselves will change too. But so long as the people remain as an identifiable community, the members of whom are identified by one another as members of the community living under its laws and customs, the communal native title survives to be enjoyed by the members according to the rights and interests to which they are respectively entitled under the traditionally based laws and customs, as currently acknowledged and observed. Here, the Meriam people have maintained their own identity and their own customs. The Murray Islands clearly remain their home country. Their land disputes have been dealt with over the years by the Island Court in accordance with the customs of the Meriam people.

Thirdly, where an indigenous people (including a clan or group), as a community, are in possession or are entitled to possession of land under a proprietary native title, their possession may be protected or their entitlement to possession may be enforced by a representative action brought on behalf of the people or by a sub-group or individual who sues to protect or enforce rights or interests which are dependent on the communal native title. Those rights and interests are, so to speak, carved out the communal native title. A sub-group or individual asserting a native title dependent on a communal native title has a sufficient interest to sue to enforce or protect the communal title (*Australian Conservation Foundation v The Commonwealth* (1980) 146 CLR 493 at 530–31, 537–39, 547–48; *Onus v Alcoa of Australia Ltd* (1981) 149 CLR 27 at 35–36, 41–42, 46, 51, 62, 74–75). A communal native title enures for the benefit of the community as a whole and for the sub-groups and individuals within it who have particular rights and interests in the community's lands.

The recognition of the rights and interests of a sub-group or individual dependent on a communal native title is not precluded by an absence of a communal law to determine a point in contest between rival claimants. By custom, such a point may have to be settled by community consensus or in some other manner prescribed by custom. A court may have to act on evidence which lacks specificity in determining a question of that kind. That is statutorily recognised in the case of the Murray Islands. The jurisdiction conferred on the Island Court by s 41(2)(b) of the Community Services (Torres Strait) Act 1984 (Qld) includes a jurisdiction which must be exercised in accordance with the customs of the Meriam people. The Act provides:

> An Island Court has jurisdiction to hear and determine –
>
> (b) disputes concerning any matter that –
>
> (i) is a matter accepted by the community resident in its area as a matter rightly governed by the usages and customs of that community; and
>
> (ii) is not a breach of the by-laws applicable within its area or of a law of the Commonwealth or the State or a matter arising under a law of the Commonwealth or the State;

> ...
>
> and shall exercise ... that jurisdiction referred to in provision (b) in accordance with the usages and customs of the community within its area.

Whatever be the precision of Meriam laws and customs with respect to land, there is abundant evidence that land was traditionally occupied by individuals or family groups and that contemporary rights and interests are capable of being established with sufficient precision to attract declaratory or other relief. Although the findings made by Moynihan J do not permit a confident conclusion that, in 1879, there were parcels of land in the Murray Islands owned allodially by individuals or groups, the absence of such a finding is not critical to the final resolution of this case. If the doctrine of *Attorney General v Brown* were applied to the Murray Islands, allodial ownership would have been no bar to the Crown's acquisition of universal and absolute ownership of the land and the extinguishing of all native titles. But, by applying the rule that the communal proprietary interests of the indigenous inhabitants survive the Crown's acquisition of sovereignty, it is possible to determine, according to the laws and customs of the Meriam people, contests among members of the Meriam people relating to rights and interests in particular parcels of land.

VI NATURE OF INTERESTS IN LAND: THE LEGAL-EQUITABLE INTEREST DICHOTOMY

This topic is adequately covered in *Land Law in PNG*.[29] We extract the relevant cases below.

MAIP PTY LTD v AMBRA COFFEE ESTATES PTY LTD [1995] PNGLR 25, National Court of Justice

[The registered proprietor of property mortgaged it to a bank to secure a loan. On default, the bank advertised the property for sale by public tender. The plaintiff was the successful applicant and was required by the bank to act within 14 days in meeting a number of requirements, including payment of deposit, supplying the name in which the purchase was to proceed etc. It was also provided that the mortgagor may redeem up to the date of execution of the contract of sale.

The plaintiff paid the deposit and had arranged the funding of the balance. It went into possession but was, however, subsequently advised that the mortgagor had exercised the right of redemption and the tender offer was withdrawn.]

WOODS J: The plaintiff is claiming certain rights to a property, namely portion 870, Mt Ambra, being an agricultural lease registered vol 62 folio 219 and being a coffee plantation. The plaintiff is claiming rights as the successful tenderer for the property following an advertised mortgage sale, and an implied authority to enter into possession pending completion of the purchase.

There is no evidence that the financial arrangements were confirmed, and it is quite clear that the matters listed in the bank's letter of 14 December were not complied with within 14 days. And there is no evidence yet that the bank was ever advised of the name the purchase

29 *Op cit*, note 12, pp 52–61.

was to be effected in, nor as to who was the solicitor for the purposes of the sale and to whom the bank's lawyers could communicate in the preparation of the contract of sale. It is noted that the letter, supposedly from the plaintiff, paying the deposit was in the name of two different companies.

There were no steps taken to have a contract of sale completed and executed by both parties, and it is trite law that such requires action and information from both parties.

It is also trite law that in dealings with land there can be no rights until a contract embodying the terms has been executed by both parties.

There is no evidence of any separate agreement, either as part of a contract of sale or otherwise, for the occupation of the property pending settlement. The letter of 4 January 1993 from the plaintiff makes no reference to actual occupation of the property pending settlement, merely a reference to taking steps to prevent further deterioration and vandalism.

So in September 1993 there was no contract for sale in existence, there was no agreement for lease or other occupation of the property between the registered proprietor or the bank and the plaintiff, there were no legal rights in the plaintiff to the property. There had merely been a tender and an offer, which had been accepted subject to certain requirements, and those requirements had not been satisfied.

The arrangements between the bank and the mortgagor for continuation of the mortgage are purely matters between the bank and its client. The terms of such arrangement are a private matter between the parties and can be of no concern to this court or any other party who had no legal right to the property. The plaintiff at all times was only a successful tenderer, who had to meet certain requirements and who had yet to sign a contract, and these requirements had never been complied with such that a final contract of sale could be prepared and entered into.

The plaintiff is claiming some equitable right, but to do so the plaintiff must be itself not guilty of delay or other behaviour. In the matter, the plaintiff has clearly delayed and not met the requirements set out in the letter of acceptance from the bank. And it is not as if we are talking of failure to comply within the 14 days noted in the bank's letter of 14 December. There were months of inaction. Why couldn't the bank assume that either the plaintiff was losing interest or could not make appropriate financial arrangements?

The plaintiff claims that it has equitable rights because it entered into occupation of the property and has improved the property. However, there was no agreement for the occupation and no agreement for such improvements to be effected. Of course, the evidence suggests that the plaintiff has itself benefited from its occupation and improvements, analogous to having a farming lease of the property on a seasonal basis. Thus, the plaintiff would be merely a tenant at will, with no right to compensation.

I have been referred to the principle of equitable estoppel, as referred to in a number of Australian cases. As was stated in *Walton Stores v Maher* (1988) 164 CLR 387 at 404 by Mason CJ: '... equity will come to the relief of a plaintiff who has acted to his detriment on the basis of a basic assumption in relation which the other party to the transaction has played such a part in the adoption of the assumption that it would be unfair or unjust if he were left free to ignore it.' In that case, there had been discussions such that a draft lease had been prepared and forwarded for execution, and there was an assumption that the necessary exchange was a formality and the defendant knew that the plaintiff was undergoing costly work on site. This is far removed from the present case, where there had been no draft contract prepared and there had been a failure by the plaintiff to act on the stated requirements. The plaintiff had not even assured the bank that it had the finance for the purchase. A plaintiff seeking equity must not be guilty of laches itself.

In *Austotel Pty Ltd v Franklins Selfserve Pty Ltd* [1989] 16 NSWLR 582, the court emphasised that for equitable estoppel to operate there must be the creation or encouragement by the defendant in the plaintiff of an assumption that a contract will come into existence, or a promise be performed, or an interest granted to the plaintiff by the defendant, and reliance on that by the plaintiff in circumstances where departure from the assumption by the defendant would be unconscionable. Priestly JA in that case at pp 612 and 614 noted that the proposition needs clarification in the light of the facts of each case. In the *Austotel* case as in the *Waltons* case, there had been sufficient negotiations for actual contracts or leases to have been prepared, and even additional action, such as construction. In the present case before me, there had been no indication that there was even finance for the contract, and any occupation, even unauthorised, was no different than a seasonal agricultural license. The facts in the above two examples were much further advanced than in the case before me now.

The plaintiff claims that the defendant would be subject to unjust enrichment. However, it is the plaintiff who has been illegally in occupation of the property, and, anyway, the plaintiff has itself received benefits from his occupation. The cases on unjust enrichment are cases where partners are cohabiting and so conducting themselves that they encouraged the other party to assist in the improvement and development of the asset or property. In this case, there was no encouragement or agreement for the plaintiff to occupy and improve the property.

The plaintiff is challenging the right of the equity of redemption. In this case, this is merely recognising the right of a vendor to withdraw from the offer at any time up until there has been a firm agreement for sale, as evidenced by a contract of sale. The evidence is quite clear that there had never been a final meeting of terms for the proposed contract for sale. There had been inordinate delay in the plaintiff following up from its tender of December 1992. The tender and offer was purely between the bank and the plaintiff, and dealings and relationship between the bank and the defendant were purely matters personal to them.

I have been referred to no authorities that suggest that a party that has merely made an offer and has taken no further steps to finalise the terms and have a contract of sale prepared, let alone executed, can have any rights to the property, whether at law or in equity. The cases of *McCosker v Kuster* [1967–68] PNGLR 182, *Re Luabar Logging Pty Ltd* [1988] PNGLR 124 and *Ningiga v Koavea* [1988–89] PNGLR 312 were situations where the court gave recognition to contracts which, whilst they did not meet legal requirements under the land Act and Stamp Duties Act, gave sufficient facts to establish agreements that could be enforced. And there are a number of cases where squatters have been given some limited rights to government land where the government had not raised objections to their presence and the squatters were found to have interests analogous to a license. However, these facts bear no analogy to the facts in this case before me now.

I find that the plaintiff has no interest in the property which is enforceable at law, and the defendant is entitled to possession and occupation of the property.

I order judgment for the defendant and order the plaintiff to vacate the property forthwith.

CAVE v CAVE (1880) 15 Ch D 639

[A trustee (a solicitor) used trust funds in purchasing an estate which was conveyed to his brother, and afterwards acted as solicitor for his brother, the mortgagee, in raising money on the estate by legal and afterwards, by equitable mortgages. The rule that notice of a trust through his solicitor is not imputed to a mortgagee where the solicitor is a party to a fraud, was discussed:]

Fry J stated the facts, and continued:

[Pages 643–49] The question before me concerns the priority of the liens or charges claimed against the Wandsworth property. The Plaintiff's right to a charge against the original purchaser of the property, Frederick Cave, is not and could not be in dispute. The question, however, arises between persons who claim subsequently to the original purchase by the trustee, or rather by Frederick Cave, who obtained the money from the trustee.

It appears that after the two conveyances were made to Frederick Cave in June and September 1872, Frederick Cave, in February 1873, mortgaged the property to the Defendant Philip Chaplin for the sum of £2,500, and subsequent advances were made by Chaplin which bring the amount in all up to £5,550. With regard to the last of those advances, the sum of £550, it was subsequent to Mr White's advance, and it has not been contended that it can have priority over that. Between the Plaintiff and Chaplin the course of argument has been this: it has been proved that the same solicitor, Mr Charles Cave, who was also surviving trustee, acted in the matter of Chaplin's mortgage both for Chaplin and for the mortgagor, Frederick Cave. The Plaintiffs say: 'You employed the same solicitor as the mortgagor, and you therefore had knowledge of the circumstances affecting Frederick Cave's title against us.' To that Chaplin replies that Charles Cave was a party to a fraud, and that the circumstances are such as to render it impossible to conceive that the facts which were known to Charles Cave were communicated by him to Chaplin.

The question I have to determine is whether the Defendant Chaplin is right or wrong in that contention.

The doctrine applicable to the question has been commonly called that of constructive notice. Lord Chelmsford, in the case of *Espin v Pemberton* 3 De G & J 547, considered that to be an inaccurate description, and thought that the expression 'imputed notice' was the correct one. It is not very material to consider which of the two terms is the more accurate, because there is undoubtedly an exception to the construction or imputation of notice from the agent to the principal, that exception arising in the case of such conduct by the agent as raises a conclusive presumption that he would not communicate the fact in controversy. This exception has been put in two ways. In the very well known case of *Rolland v Hart* Law Rep 6 Ch 678, Lord Hatherley put it substantially in this way, that you must look at the circumstances of the case, and inquire whether the court can see that the solicitor intended a fraud, which would require the suppression of the knowledge of the encumbrance from the person upon whom he was committing the fraud. In *Thompson v Cartwright* 33 Beav 178, the late Master of the Rolls put it rather differently, and it would appear that in his view you must inquire whether there are such circumstances in the case, independently of the fact under inquiry, as to raise an inevitable conclusion that the notice had not been communicated. In the one view notice is not imputed, because the circumstances are such as not to raise the conclusion of law, which does ordinarily arise from the mere existence of notice to the agent; in the other view – that of Lord Chelmsford and Lord Hatherley – the act done by the agent is such as cannot be said to be done by him in his character of agent, but is done by him in the character of a party to an independent fraud on his principal, and that is not to be imputed to the principal as an act done by his agent.

Those being the principles applicable to the decision of this case, I must ask myself what are the circumstances. In the first place the trust moneys had, contrary to the terms of the trust, been invested in the purchase of property at Wandsworth, and that property had been by a gross breach of trust conveyed entirely into the name of Frederick Cave, the husband. That might have been a mere irregularity, but it might have been, and I think in this case it was, something much worse. I find that in October Frederick and Charles Cave proceeded to negotiate a loan from Mr White for £700, and on that occasion Charles Cave, the solicitor, addressed a letter to White, in which, among other things, he said, 'My brother Frederick has lately bought a freehold house and land at Southfields, Wandsworth, close to Wimbledon, for 1,950 pounds; this has compelled him to withdraw some of his capital from the Richmond business'. Those statements are lamentably deficient in accuracy; the intention was to suggest that Frederick was the absolute owner of the house. In my view, in equity he was only owner subject to a lien for the trust money invested in it. It is not true that he had been compelled to withdraw any capital from the Richmond business to purchase the house, for the whole of the money appears to have been derived from the trust fund. Further than that, when the negotiations began with Chaplin for the mortgage that was ultimately completed, Charles Cave stated that the house and property belonged to one of his brothers, which was a statement again intended to induce the belief that the brother was so far the absolute owner as [sic] that he had a right to deal with the property absolutely. Looking at these transactions, I come to the conclusion that there was a design on the part of Frederick and Charles Cave to commit a fraud by obtaining money under false pretences, and that the conveyance of the land into Frederick Cave's name was a step towards that. Having come to that conclusion it is impossible for me to suppose that the loan obtained from Chaplin was not a further step in the same common enterprise, and it seems to me impossible to suppose that Charles Cave would have communicated the real facts to Chaplin.

But the matter does not rest there, for when the transaction is completed by means of the legal mortgage to Chaplin, that document contains absolute covenants for title on the part of Frederick Cave. Frederick Cave thereby covenants with Chaplin 'that he Frederick Cave now hath power to grant all the said premises hereinbefore expressed to be hereby granted to the use of the said Philip Chaplin, his heirs and assigns, and also that if default shall be made in payment of the said sum of £2,500, or any sum which may afterwards be advanced or lent or become owing, or the interest for the same or any part thereof respectively, on the days on which the same is covenanted to be paid, it shall be lawful for the said Philip Chaplin, his heirs and assigns, to enter into and upon all or any of the said premises, and the same thenceforth to hold and enjoy, and to receive the rents and profits thereof without any interruption or disturbance by the said Frederick Cave or any other person, and that free and discharged from or otherwise by the said Frederick Cave, his heirs, executors, or administrators, sufficiently indemnified against all estates, incumbrances, claims, and demands whatsoever'. According to the judgment of the Master of the Rolls in *Thompson v Cartwright* 33 Beav 178; 2 DJ & S 10, to which I have been referred, I am bound to look at the terms of the mortgage in considering whether there was an intention on the part of the solicitors to commit a fraud, and, looking at it, the conclusion I had arrived at independently of them is strongly confirmed.

The conclusion I arrive at is, that Chaplin has sustained the burden cast upon him of proving that the circumstances are such as repel the construction or imputation to the principal of notice to the agent. Therefore I hold that Mr Chaplin's mortgage has a priority over the Plaintiffs.

Questions

1 Has the decision made any clearer the distinction between constructive and imputed notice?

2 Would the theory of agency that an agent's power or authority could be ostensible or apparent have helped the case of the plaintiffs?

As indicated earlier on, sometimes the same legal estate is encumbered with several equitable interests. Such a situation raises questions of priority, ie, which of these should take precedence over the others. The case below deals with that kind of situation.

PILCHER v RAWLINS (1870) 11 LR Eq 53; (1872) 7 Ch App 259 (Lord Hatherley LC, James and Mellish LJJ)

[In April 1851, Pilcher and his co-trustees advanced the trust fund to Rawlins on a legal mortgage of properties X, Y and Z, redeemable five years later. The documents of title were delivered to Pilcher. The mortgage deed recited the trust. Two years later (in 1853) Pilcher was the sole surviving trustee. In April 1856, Pilcher, in consideration of the payment to him by Rawlins of a sum of money (which Pilcher misappropriates), reconveyed to Rawlins, by a deed which noticed the mortgage of 1851, the property X discharged from its burden. Pilcher and Rawlins (who were both solicitors) connived and made out an abstract of title showing the fee simple in Rawlins, which at the same time omitted all reference to the mortgage and reconveyance. With the aid of this abstract, Rawlins created a legal mortgage of property X in favour of Stockwell and Lamb and the title deeds of that property, with the exception of the mortgage deed of 1851 and the deed of reconveyance of 1856, were handed to Stockwell and Lamb. The money advanced by Stockwell and Lamb was shared by Pilcher and Rawlins.

The fraud being discovered, Pilcher's *cestuis que* trust filed this bill claiming priority over Stockwell and Lamb. Rawlins then produced and handed over to Stockwell and Lamb the deed of reconveyance of 1856 (which had hitherto been suppressed). Stockwell and Lamb thus discovered, after the institution of the suit, that they had in fact the legal estate, but not by the documents by which they imagine they had it.

For the plaintiffs it was argued that Stockwell and Lamb either claimed the benefit of the deed of reconveyance of 1856 or else they did not. If they did not, they had merely an equity later in point of time than that of the plaintiffs. If they did, then they had to be treated as having had notice of everything as to which an examination of that deed ought to have led them to inquire, and therefore of the plaintiff's title. On the other hand, Stockwell and Lamb pleaded a *bona fide* purchase for value of the legal estate without notice.]

JAMES LJ (p 269): I entirely concur in the conclusion to which the Lord Chancellor has arrived.

I propose simply to apply myself to the case of a purchaser for valuable consideration, without notice, obtaining upon the occasion of his purchase and by means of his purchase deed some legal estate, some legal right, some legal advantage; and, according to my view of the established law of this court, such a purchaser's plea of a purchase for valuable consideration without notice is an absolute, unqualified, unanswerable defence, and unanswerable plea to the jurisdiction of this court. Such a purchaser, when he has once put in that plea, may be interrogated and tested to any extent as to the valuable consideration which he has given in order to show the *bona fides* or *mala fides* of his purchase, and also the presence or the absence of notice; but when once he has gone through that ordeal, and has satisfied the terms of the plea of purchase for valuable consideration without notice, then, according to my judgment, this court has no jurisdiction whatever to do anything more than to let him depart in possession of that legal estate, that legal right, that legal advantage which he has obtained, whatever it may be. In such a case a purchaser is entitled to hold that which, without breach of duty, he has had conveyed to him.

In the case of *Carter v Carter* (1857) 3 K&J 617, which was decided by the present Lord Chancellor, and which was followed by the Master of the Rolls in this case, and with which I am bound to say I am unable to agree, an exception from that rule was, under the circumstances, supposed to exist.

It is very clearly expressed in a few lines of the judgment in that case: 'But here the purchaser taking the conveyance under one will, supposed by all parties to be really the last will of the testator, finds himself driven to rely upon another and a second will containing on the face of it all the trust which the testator has created'; and that circumstance is supposed to create the exception. To my mind there are to that supposition two short and conclusive answers – the one a matter of principle, and the other a matter of fact. My view of the principle is that when once you have arrived at the conclusion that the purchaser is a purchaser for valuable consideration without notice, the court has no right to ask him, and has no right to put him to contest the question, how he is going to defend himself or what he is going to rely on. He may say, honestly and justly, 'I am not going to tell you. I have got the deeds; I defend them, and you will never be able to make me produce them, and you will never be able to produce secondary evidence of them. I am not obliged to produce them at all; probably before you get half way through your action of ejectment you will find a *jus tertii* which you will not dispose of; the estate is in the hands of a legal tenant to whom I have let it, and no one can determine that tenancy without notice, and no one can give that notice but myself; I will not give that notice, and no court has any power to compel me to give it. I have a right to rely, as every person defending his position has, on the weakness of the title of the person who is seeking to displace me'. That seems to be exactly the position of such a purchaser as this.

The purchaser in *Carter v Carter* 3 K&J 617 did not rely on the will which created the trust; he relied on another title; for the will formed the title of the adverse party. And the answer to that adverse party is, by the good luck which sometimes attends honest men, 'Though you produce an instrument which points out your title, and gives the property to someone else, yet I am prepared with a legal defence in a conveyance which was executed before'. It appears to me that there is no right in this court to prevent the purchaser from setting up that defence to the claim so made against him. If there was ever a case in which, according to my judgment, any court ought to be in favour of a purchaser and against such a title, it is a case in which a testator has, through the grossest negligence, allowed two wills to exist after his death, so that some members of his family produce one will apparently making out a perfectly good title to a mortgagee or purchaser, and then, when a mortgagee or purchaser has been induced unwittingly to pay or advance his money, some other members of the family produce the other will, which has been suppressed or concealed during the whole of that time, and then seek to take the estate away from the mortgagee or purchaser.

It seems to me to be a very ingenious device by which a testator would be able to give his property twice over to his family; but, in my opinion, it is a device which ought not to be encouraged in any way in a court of equity.

I am therefore of opinion that whatever may be the accident by which a purchaser has obtained a good legal title, and in respect of which he has paid his money and is in possession of the property, he is entitled to the benefit of that accident, just as a purchaser would be entitled to avail himself of the possession so acquired, without any reference to the rights of the persons who may be otherwise interested ...

Appeal allowed.

IN RE NISBET AND POTTS' CONTRACT [1905] 1 Ch 391 (Farwell J); affirmed [1906] 1 Ch 386 (CA) (Collins MR, Romer and Cozens-Hardy LJJ)

FARWELL J (p 396): Covenants restricting the enjoyment of land, except of course as between the contracting parties and those privy to the contract, are not enforceable by anything in the nature of action or suit founded on contract. Such actions and suits alike depend on privity of contract, and no possession of the land coupled with notice of the covenants can avail to create such privity: *Cox v Bishop* (1857) 8 DM & G 815. But if the covenant be negative, so as to restrict the mode of use and enjoyment of the land, then there is called into existence an equity attached to the property of such a nature that it is annexed to and runs with it in equity: *Tulk v Moxhay* (1848) 2 Ph 774. This equity, although created by covenant or contract, cannot be sued on as such, but stands on the same footing with and is completely analogous to an equitable charge on real estate created by some predecessor in title of the present owner of the land charged ...

So in *Mander v Falcke* [1891] 2 Ch 554 a mere occupier of land was held to be within the principle. In *London & South Western Railway v Gomm* (1882) 20 Ch D 562, 583, Sir George Jessel states that in his view the doctrine is either an extension in equity of *Spencer's* case (1582) 5 Rep 16a 11th edn, p 55; 15 MLC to another line of cases, or else an extension in equity of the doctrine of negative easements, but that, whatever it was: 'the purchaser took the estate subject to the equitable burden, with the qualification that if he acquired the legal estate for value without notice he was freed from the burden. That qualification, however, did not affect the nature of the burden; the notice was required merely to avoid the effect of the legal estate, and did not create the right, and if the purchaser took only an equitable estate he took subject to the burden, whether he had notice or not.' He says also: 'If it binds the land it creates an *equitable interest* in the land.' These passages are cited as correct in the considered judgment of the Court of Appeal in *Rogers v Hosegood* [1900] 2 Ch 388, 405. It is clear therefore that the person entitled to the benefit of the restrictive negative covenant over Blackacre has an equitable interest in Blackacre, and that such interest has the same nature and qualities as any other equitable interest in land in respect of priority, notice and the like, but that notice forms no part of the cause of action in respect of such equitable interest. The plaintiff's claim depends on the validity and priority of his own charge, not on any notice, unless and until the owner of the land sets up as a defence the plea of purchaser for value without notice and with the legal estate. The fact that the usual contest in such cases is whether the landowner had notice or not has doubtless made it usual to speak of notice as an essential part of the plaintiff's case in order to enable the court to bind the defendant's conscience; but it is quite clear that the equitable charge is created and exists independently of notice, and that no question of binding the defendant's conscience arises until he sets up the legal estate. Then notice became material, because it enabled the court of equity to bind the conscience of the defendant and forbid him to set up the legal estate.

SMITH v JONES [1954] 1 WLR 1089, Chancery Division

[In 1946, the defendant, Jones, purchased a farm at auction. He knew that the farm was in the occupation of a tenant, the plaintiff, Smith. After the purchase, disputes arose between the plaintiff and the defendant as each required repairs to be done but refused to do them himself. Eventually the plaintiff brought this action claiming that his tenancy agreement should be rectified to make the defendant liable for structural repairs. The defendant argued that even if a case for rectification could be made out against the original lessor, he, as a *bona fide* purchaser for value without notice, was not bound by the plaintiff's equity of rectification.

Upjohn J held that the parties to the lease intended it to be in the form commonly used by the lessor (which imposed liability on the tenant for repairs), that they misunderstood the true construction of that form of agreement, and that, in the circumstances, the claim for rectification failed.

His Lordship referred to s 199 of the Law of Property Act 1925, and continued:]

[p 1092] The relevant section which re-enacts exactly, so far as relevant, the provisions of the Conveyancing Act 1882, is to be found in s 199(1) of the Law of Property Act 1925.

The question which I have to answer is this: what inspection and inquiries ought reasonably to have been made by the defendant of the tenant before the sale, so far as relevant to this question? I think the only relevant inquiry that he would have made would have been this: 'May I see your tenancy agreement? I want to see whether it corresponds with the copy agreement I have seen in the auction rooms.' That is the document which governed the rights of the parties.

He ought to have asked whether he had seen a correct copy, but he was under no obligation, in my view, to proceed further and say: 'Does that correctly represent your rights?' In fact, if he had asked that question, the answer honestly but erroneously given would have been 'Yes'. Still less was he bound to take the tenant step by step through the document and ask how the tenant interpreted its provisions. He could not be so bound, and it would be most unwise for any intending purchaser to do so.

In my judgment the defendant is entitled and bound to rely on the terms of the document, and the document speaks for itself. Accordingly, had I come to a contrary conclusion upon the claim for rectification, I should have found that this action was barred by the plea of *bona fide* purchaser for value without notice. In the circumstances, I must dismiss the action.

Equitable estoppel and acquiescence

Since equity aims at achieving fairness, it prevents unjust enrichment and such conduct as gives a party to a transaction an unfair advantage over the other party.

Laches

This is a doctrine of equity designed to end all ligation once and for all times. It precludes the reopening of a matter considered by a court of competent jurisdiction. There are two types:

1 *Res judicata*

2 Acquiescence

Res judicata

The Latin maxim *interest reipublicae ut sit finis litium* sums up the doctrine cogently.

Consider the following case.

THE ADMINISTRATION OF THE TERRITORY OF PAPUA AND NEW GUINEA v GUBA AND DORIGA (1973) 130 CLR 353

BARWICK CJ (pp 639–41): Two submissions have been made in respect of the decision of the Land Board.

First, it is said that the Board was not validly constituted. The reasons given are those which found favour with the learned Chief Justice of Papua and New Guinea. The first step in this reasoning seems to have been that s 9 is but an ancillary provision to s 8 and not an independent provision. It is then said that because all questions as to waste and vacant lands and all cases of disputed ownership of land in which a Papuan native was a claimant could be referred to a Board, the provisions of s 9 cannot literally be applied and that the only questions which could be referred to a Board, even if particular questions could be referred at all, were questions such as had or could have arisen under s 8. Therefore the Board appointed by a proclamation in 1954 could not have been validly constituted to consider the questions submitted to it.

I must say with due respect to the judges of the Supreme Court that I am at a loss to understand why s 9 is not an independent provision or why it is in any case tied to the provisions of s 8. The evident purposes of the two sections are quite disparate. I very much doubt whether the Administrator could refer to a Land Board a claim by a Papuan to land which had already been embraced in an Order in Council made under s 8. That section places the 'allowance' of the claim in the Administrator's hand for decision. Section 9 expressly gives the Board the power to decide the questions referred to it and provides for the decision of the matter by a Court of Appeal. But I need not express a final opinion on this point.

Section 8 provides for the vesting in the Crown of what I might call 'ownerless' land. Ample opportunity is offered for claimants to put forward a claim to its ownership. The provision requires the Administrator to take into consideration any such claim made during the time limited for making such claims and empowers him thereafter at any time to take into consideration a claim that, prior to the making of the Order in Council, the land was owned by the claimant. I phrase the claim in that form because, in my opinion, a successful attack could not be made on an Order in Council on the ground that land embraced in its operation was not ownerless. The appearance of there being no owner is at best the basis for the Order. The period for showing cause, without cause being shown, affords confirmation of that appearance. Thus a claim out of time is in the nature of an appeal for an indulgence.

But in either case the decision upon the claim must be that of the Administrator. The result of his decision is an Order in Council, whether or not the claim is allowed, by the Administrator.

In high contrast to this provision, s 9 gives the Administrator power to appoint a board to decide the question referred: and it provides for an appeal to a court of law from the decision of the Board. It needs no argument that the court does not act as an advisers to the Administrator in the hearing of an appeal on the question of the ownership of land.

It may be, of course, that before the Administrator sets in motion the machinery of s 8, he may set up a Land Board and refer to it for its decision the question whether particular lands are waste and vacant lands, or alleged so to be. Thereafter he may use s 8 according to the way the Board decides, but he will be bound, in my opinion, by the decision of the Board.

The reason why it was thought by the Chief Justice that s 9 could not be read as applying to all disputes was that it was inconceivable that the Ordinance should intend by s 9 to take away the jurisdiction of the court which had cognisance of all such cases where a claim of right to land was made by a Papuan or a question raised as to whether land was waste and vacant. But quite clearly s 9 does not deprive the courts of any jurisdiction they may have. It enables, in my opinion, a binding decision to be made on the matter referred to the Board; by the Board in the first instance and by the court on appeal. That decision will bind the parties before the Board and their privies or those who have had due opportunity to be before it. In appropriate circumstances it will be treated as binding in litigation before the courts. None of these results of s 9 or of action taken under it touch the jurisdiction of the courts.

In my opinion, the meaning of s 9 is that the Administrator may appoint a Board to decide any question as to whether specific land or areas of land are waste and vacant lands and also any dispute as to the ownership of land to which a Papuan is a claimant. Full effect, in my opinion, should be given to the words of the section which need no qualification when it is understood that in the case of waste and vacant lands the question is whether they are in truth such and when it is understood that the claim to ownership is not limited to claims to ownership of lands alleged to be waste and vacant. The section presupposes that the Administrator will in the course of his administration become aware of disputation as to the ownership of land where Papuans are concerned, disputes where the competing views are on the one hand that the land is waste and vacant land not in the ownership of any person and on the other that it is owned by a Papuan who claims it and also disputes where there are competing claims to ownership, one of which is by a Papuan. Of course, the former dispute could be determined by the Administrator after he had made an Order in Council under s 8. The latter could be determined in litigation in the courts of the Territory. But the provision for the appointment of an ad hoc tribunal to determine all these disputes seems eminently suitable to the conditions of the Territory: and, in my opinion, s 9 evidences a clear intention that such a tribunal might be set up with power to decide the disputed questions.

In my opinion, therefore, it is abundantly clear that a Board appointed pursuant to s 9 of the Ordinance was not limited to dealing with waste lands which had been dealt with or fell to be considered under s 8. Power was given to the Board to decide ownership in the case of all disputes on that question. 'All' in this context means 'any' dispute where a Papuan was a claimant. The significant point of s 9 is that the power is to appoint a Board which is to decide. The obligation to act judicially comes from the power to decide the rights of individuals. The Board was in my opinion, quite clearly a tribunal which, having power to decide such rights, was a body to which the prerogative writs would have gone. It was bound to observe the rules of natural justice, even though it might act according to equity and good conscience and not be bound by rules of legal procedure. Though freed of technical rules the Board was bound by legal principles in the decision of such a question as the ownership of land. It was not given power to award land to a person who in its opinion did not own it. Its task, if it was to decide ownership, was to ascertain the existing facts and apply the existing law to those facts in order to decide who did own the land. That, to my mind, is clearly work of a judicial nature and a decision as to the ownership must of necessity, subject to appeal, be final as between the parties before the court or who, being duly notified, could have been before it. I am unable to perceive what relevance questions of judicial power in the constitutional sense have in this connection. What is central to the Board's power is the power to decide. It may well be that in a system where a separation of powers existed that function could be classed as an exercise of judicial power. But it is quite immaterial in the present connection to consider such a question or decided cases which deal with it. In my opinion, the purpose of appointing a Board under s 9 was clearly to resolve a dispute and lay to rest the question of ownership of land to which a Papuan laid claim. It is to be observed that the consequence of the Board's decision was an entry on a register with the intention of giving absolute finality to the matter: see Land Ordinance, s 6. In my opinion, the decision of the Board was binding on the parties to it, their privies and upon those notified of the hearing with opportunity to make their claims and to that extent upon the Land Titles Commission in considering a claim to the same land by one of those parties or a privy of one of those parties or by a person who had the opportunity of claiming or of being heard.

It is said by Daera Guba that he was representing in the instant proceedings the whole Tubumaga clan, that is to say, the Idibana and the Laurina sides of it.

Before the Board in 1954 Daera Guba had appeared as representing the Tubumaga Idibana but the Tubumaga Laurina were also parties before the Board. True, they were not claimants of the present areas of land but they clearly stood by while Daera Guba laid claims to those lands on behalf of one side of the clan; they had opportunity to claim the land.

We have no information as to what would be the consequence of one section of the clan succeeding in a claim to this land. I would suppose that it would really be a decision that the clan owned the land and that the question of the respective rights and interests of both sides of the clan would have to be separately entertained and determined. I have no need to pursue that matter in order to resolve this case. The Tubumaga Laurina were bound by the Board's decision both because, being notified of the hearing and invited to make such claim as it thought fit, it attended the hearing and made no claim; and also, having stood by and allowed the Tubumaga Idibana to claim the land, it cannot now dispute the result. *Nana Ofori Atta II and Another v Nana Abu Bonsra II* [1958] AC 95, lends support to this view of the matter.

In my opinion, the decision of the Board was a final decision. It was a decision which bound Daera Guba, his privies and the Tubumaga Laurina: and it bound the Land Titles Commission. I suppose there could not be a better justification for resort to the principle of estoppel than the present case. The Land Board had witnesses of whose evidence the Land Titles Commissioner did not have the benefit. We are told that every encouragement was given to the Tubumaga people and, indeed, to the Papuans generally to tell all they knew or thought they knew about the title to the ownership of the lands about which the Board was enquiring. No appeal was brought from the Land Board's decision but now, 12 years later, it is sought to agitate the same question again and with lesser information than was available to the Land Board. In developing society, such as the one with which we are concerned, nothing, in my opinion, could be more destructive of confidence in the law than a renewed agitation of a matter fully investigated and decided.

Thus, in my opinion, if contrary to my own opinion it should be thought that the whole of Era Taora was not acquired in 1886, the decision of the Board in 1954 established the ownership of Era Taora by the Administration and precluded the further examination by the Land Titles Commission of that question.

GIBBS J: On behalf of the applicants a number of submissions were urged in support of the contention that even if the Board were validly constituted its decision did not create an estoppel. In the course of these submissions, two misconceptions became manifest. In the first place, some of the applicants' arguments rested on the supposition that the Administration in the present case is endeavouring to set up an issue estoppel. The contention for the Administration is that the Board decided one of the very questions that falls for decision in the present case – whether the Administration is the owner of areas Nos 2, 3 and 4 on plan 'J' – and not that the Board's decision estops the Tubumaga from relitigating issues which were necessarily determined in reaching that decision. In other words, the present case in one of cause of action estoppel, not issue estoppel. Secondly, much attention was directed to authorities that deal with nature of judicial power, for example in relation to Chapter III of the Constitution. In many of the authorities that discuss this form of estoppel, it is said that the estoppel is brought about by a judicial decision, pronounced by a judicial tribunal. Thus in a recent case, *Carl Zeiss Stiftung v Rayner & Keeler Ltd (No 2)* [1967] 1 AC 853, Lord Guest said, at p 933: 'The rule of estoppel by *res judicata*, which is a rule of evidence, is that where a final decision has been pronounced by a judicial tribunal of competent jurisdiction over the parties to and the subject matter of the litigation, any party or privy to such litigation as against any other party or privy is estopped in any subsequent litigation from disputing or questioning such decision on the merits' (*Spencer Bower on Res Judicata*, p 3). The use of the phrase 'judicial tribunal' in this context is convenient as indicating that an estoppel of this kind does not result from a mere administrative decision, but the question whether such an estoppel is raised is not answered by inquiring to what extent the tribunal exercises judicial functions, or whether its status is judicial or administrative: see *Caffoor v Commissioner of Income Tax, Colombo* [1961] AC 584, at pp 597–99, *per* Lord Radcliffe. A fairly obvious example is the case of a court martial, whose sentence might in some circumstances be pleaded as an estoppel (*Hannaford v Hunn* (1825) 2 C & P 148, at p 155; 172 ER 68, at p 71), although not made in the exercise of judicial power (cf *R v Bevan ex p Elias and Gordon* (1942), 66 CLR 452, at pp 66–68; *R v Cox ex p Smith* (1945) 71 CLR 1, at p 23). The doctrine of estoppel extends to the decision of any tribunal which has jurisdiction to decide finally a question arising between parties, even if it is not called a court, and its jurisdiction is derived from statute or from the submission of parties, and it only has temporary authority to decide a matter ad hoc: see *Halsbury's Laws of England*, 3rd edn, Vol 15, pp 212–14; *Spencer Bower & Turner on Res Judicata*, 2nd edn, pp 21–28. It will accordingly not be necessary to canvass the authorities to which we were referred, and which deal either with issue estoppel or with the nature of judicial power.

In *Carl Zeiss Stiftung v Rayner & Keeler Ltd (No 2)* (*supra*), at pp 909–10, Lord Reid said that it 'is clear that the earlier judgment relied on must have been a final judgment, and that there must be identity of parties and of subject matter in the former and in the present litigation'. The Board had power under s 9 of the Land Ordinance 1911–53 to determine finally and conclusively the case of disputed ownership of land that came before it. Under the section, the Board was appointed to 'decide' the case, and to give a 'decision', and these words, *prima facie*, and in the absence of any indication to the contrary, import that the Board was to make a binding determination – see *Spackman v Plumstead District Board of Works* (1885) 10 App Cas 229, at p 235. The fact that an appeal lay from the decision did not make it any the less final – see *Wakefield Corporation v Cooke* [1904] AC 31, at p 36; *Marchioness of Huntly v Gaskell* [1905] 2 Ch 656, at p 667.

There was identity of subject matter in the two proceedings. It is true that the land claimed before the Board included some areas not part of the land claimed before the Commission, and vice versa, but there was some land – areas Nos 2, 3, 4 and 6 on plan 'J' – whose ownership fell to be determined by both tribunals. The Board, however, said that it was not concerned with area No 6, and in the view that I have taken it is unnecessary to consider whether its decision operated to estop the Tubumaga from asserting that they owned that area of land. The native claimants before the Board abandoned their claim to area No 4 and did not press their claim to area No 3, but the decision in relation to both these areas gave rise to an estoppel. The decision in relation to the area the claim to which was abandoned was, at lowest, a decision by default, and such a decision can give rise to an estoppel, although only for what must 'necessarily and with complete precision' have thereby been determined: *New Brunswick Railway Company v British and French Trust Corporation Ltd* [1939] AC 1, at pp 21, 38; *Kok Hoong v Leong Cheong Kweng Mines Ltd* [1964] AC 993, at p 1012. In the present case, the Board necessarily and with complete precision upheld the claim of the Administration to area No 4. If the decision in relation to area No 3 is treated as also going by default, the same result follows: if it is regarded as a decision which was conceded by admission, it none the less can raise an estoppel: *Society of Medical Officers of Health v Hope (Valuation Officer)* [1960] AC 551, at p 566. The Board directly decided the very question that area Nos 2, 3 and 4 were not native land but were owned by the Administration, and (subject to the other questions to be discussed) that decision will operate as an estoppel, notwithstanding that the Board decided other matters as well, and that other matters also arise for decision in the present case.

At this point it is convenient to note a submission of the applicants, which was partly directed to show that the Board was not exercising judicial power, but was also advanced in support of the contention that the Board did not decide the very question that now falls for decision. This was that the provision in s 9 of the Land Ordinance 1911–53 that 'The Board in giving its decision shall be guided by the principles of equity and good conscience and shall not be bound by rules of evidence or legal procedure' exonerated the Board from the duty of deciding the question in accordance with law and allowed it to base its decision in accordance with law and allowed it to base its decision on criteria that were not exclusively legal. Reliance was placed on *Moses v Parker* [1896] AC 245, but there the statute went on to provide that the court should not be 'bound by the strict rules of law and equity in any case', important words which have no counterpart in s 9. It is clear that words in the form of those quoted from s 9 must be regarded as dealing only with procedure, and not as excluding the application of rules of substantive law: see *Peacock v Newtown Marrickville and General Co-operative Building Society No 4 Limited* (1943) 67 CLR 25, at pp 36, 46 and 55, and cases there cited. Moreover, the fact that an appeal lay to the Central Court (then the superior court of the territory) supports the view that the Board was required to make its decision in accordance with legal rules, for otherwise the propriety of its decision could not have been tested on appeal – see *Moses v Parker* (*supra*), at p 248.

Finally, the applicants denied that there was an identity of parties before the Board and the Commission. The native claimants before the Board included the Tubumaga Idibana and the Tubumaga Laurina, but it was the former branch of the iduhu that claimed Era Taora. The application to the Commission was made by Daera Guba on behalf of the descendants of Guba Daera but it emerged at the hearing that Daera Guba was representing both branches of the Tubumaga iduhu. It was submitted that the relevant party before the Board was the Tubumaga Idibana – a communal group – whereas before the Commission the applicants were a number of individuals, represented by Daera Guba, and that if the individuals were members of the group, they were nevertheless proceeding in a differently capacity, and that a decision given against them by the Board in one capacity would not estop them in the other. Of course, neither tribunal had any strict rules of pleading, and before the Commission there was some disconformity between the application, which described the persons represented by Daera Guba as the descendants of Guba Daera, and the statement made by Daera Guba that he was representing the whole clan, but there is not the least doubt, when the evidence is regarded, that his case before the Commission was advanced on the basis that he was representing the whole Tubumaga people – both branches of the iduhu. However, it was then submitted that the decision of the Board could not estop the Tubumaga Laurina, since that branch of the iduhu had laid no claim before the Board to Era Taora. In fact both branches of the iduhu were represented before the Board, and by the same counsel. In my opinion, if there was not an estoppel per *rem judicatam* between the Tubumaga Laurina and the Administration, the former were estopped by their conduct from relitigating the issue of the ownership of the subject land. The Tubumaga Laurina, being a party, and knowing that the Board was required to decide who was the owner of the land in question, stood by, and allowed the Tubumaga Idibana, the other branch of the iduhu, alone to assert its claim against the Administration. In those circumstances, justice and common sense would require the Tubumaga Laurina to be bound by the result: the case is within the general principle on which the decision in *Nana Ofori Atta II v Nana Abu Bonsra II* [1958] AC 95 rests, although not within the precise formulation of that principle in *Wytcherley v Andrews* (1871) LR 2P & D 327, at p 328 which was cited in *Nana Ofori Atta II v Nana Abu Bonsra II* (*supra*), at p 102.

Question

What are the essential requirements for the application of *res judicata*? Did the 'findings' of the Land Board amount to a judicial determination of the issues involved?

PNG READY MIXED CONCRETE PTY LTD v THE INDEPENDENT STATE OF PAPUA NEW GUINEA AND UTULA SAMANA AND SAMPSON KIAMBA [1981] PNGLR 396, National Court of Justice

MILES J (pp 404–05): The claim put forward on behalf of the occupants to defeat the right of the State to possession of the land immediately prior to the granting of the lease is based on the doctrine of equitable estoppel, sometimes called promissory estoppel and in relation to land sometimes called proprietary estoppel. It was discussed at length in the decision of the Court of Appeal in *Crabb v Arun District Council* [1975] 3 All ER 865 at p 868 decided on 23 July 1975, a date about as close to the date of Papua New Guinean Independence as one needs to go for a statement of the English principles applicable under Sched 2.1 of the Constitution. The doctrine is summarised in a long passage from Lord Denning MR at p 871 which cites the old authorities. I will not quote the passage in full. It is summarised in one sentence as follows:

> Short of an actual promise, if he by his words or conduct, so behaves as to lead another to believe that he will not insist on his strict legal rights – knowing or intending that the other will act on that belief – and he does so act, that again will raise an equity in favour

of the other, and it is for a court of equity to say in what way the equity may be satisfied.

In support of the proposition his Lordship referred to recent English authority such as *Inwards v Baker* [1965] 2 QB 29; [1965] 1 All ER 446 and *ER Eves Investment Ltd v High* [1967] 2 QB 379. The decision itself has since been followed twice in the Court of Appeal in *Jones v Jones* [1977] 1 WLR 438 and *Pascoe v Turner* [1979] 1 WLR 431. The pre-Independence Full Court referred to *Inwards v Baker (supra)* in *The Administration v Blasius Tirupia; Re Vunapaladig and Japalik Land* [1971–72] PNGLR 229 at p 243. If I read the judgment correctly their Honours accepted that an equitable defence of the type successfully pleaded in *Inwards v Baker (supra)* would have been available had the facts pleaded supported such a defence. The decision of the court on demurrer was that the allegations did not raise the equitable defence which counsel for the defendant sought to rely on. Further it was held that in the absence of an allegation of fraud s 69 of the Lands Registration Act 1924 protected the registered proprietor from being affected by actual or constructive notice of any claim, right, title or interest other than as appears in the Register Book. No argument was addressed to me in the present case on the Lands Registration Act. It may be observed however that the doctrine of proprietary estoppel imports the notion of equitable fraud: see judgment of Scarman LJ in *Crabb v Arun District Council* [1975] 3 All ER 865 at pp 876–77.

The principles of proprietary estoppel as expounded by Lord Denning MR in *Crabb v Arun District Council (supra)* should be regarded as part of the underlying law of Papua New Guinea. The question is: how far are they applicable to the present case?

The question should be answered in the following way. Once a significant number of persons had taken up residence on the land, built dwelling houses on it, planted trees and the like, it was up to the State if it wished to protect its right to possession of the land to issue some sort of a warning or statement that persons who came on to the land to take up residence and build and plant crops there did so at their own risk. Yet no such warning issued at any time. The result is that those who came took up residence, built houses, planted crops and the like after say 1976 may be regarded as having sufficient interest in the land as to give rise by early 1981 to an equity entitling them to remain on the land despite the State's legal right to possession. Because the State raised no objection to the large influx after 1976, those who had come on to the land prior to 1976 were entitled to accept and did accept that their presence also was tacitly approved and so they should be regarded as having acquired a similar equitable interest by early 1981. The right may be regarded as analogous to a licence and how it might be terminated or revoked will be discussed in a moment.

The inference must be drawn from the evidence that the company through Mr Elliott knew that there were substantial numbers of persons in occupation of the land by the time of the granting of the lease. For two years or thereabouts the company took no steps to encourage the State to obtain vacant possession and despite the latter-hour request to Mr Schweinfurth to issue a notice to quit, Mr Elliott fully expected the occupants to be in possession for some time after the lease was granted. The company was in my view taking a calculated chance that sooner or later, though preferably sooner, the occupants would be ejected. In the meantime it refrained from insisting on vacant possession because such insistence may well have resulted in the State withdrawing its offer to grant the lease to the company.

It was put on behalf of the company that the occupants could not rely on proprietary estoppel unless they satisfied the five *probanda* or tests laid down by Fry J in *Willmott v Barber* (1880) 15 Ch D 96. But the English authorities are clear that by 1975, although the five *probanda* might be used as a 'valuable guide', the ultimate test was whether in the

> circumstances it has become unconscionable for the holder of the legal right to insist on its full enforcement. Even if it is accepted that the occupants must have incurred expenditure in the mistaken belief that they already owned a sufficient interest in the property to justify the expenditure (or that they would obtain such an interest), I think that by 1976 some sort of genuine residential community had been established in the land: those who built thereafter or otherwise took action or incurred expenditure which improved the land did so in the belief that the State would recognise their interest.

Note

This case went on appeal to the Supreme Court which allowed the appeal – on other grounds – *Harman Gawi v PNG Ready Mixed Concrete Pty Ltd* [1984] PNGLR 74. See also *Wine v Giglmai* [1976] PNGLR 34.

Laches is in fact not different from acquiescence for here also the essential ingredient is delay, which defeats the plaintiff's title. Lord Penzance had said in *Emile Erlanger and Others v New Sombrero Phosphate Co* (1878) 3 App Cas 1218 at p 1231 where he tried to draw a difference between acquiescence and laches:

> Delay, as it seems to me, has two aspects. Lapse of time may so change the condition of the thing sold and bring about such a state of affairs that justice cannot be done by rescinding the contract, subject to any amount of allowance or compensations. This is an aspect of delay ... But delay may also imply acquiescence and in this aspect it equally bars a plaintiff's right ...

In laches therefore, the courts will not uphold a claim, the consequences of which would be to deprive defendant of a right acquired under a contract when it is impossible to restore the parties to the positions they held before they entered into the contract.

CHAPTER 4

CO-OWNERSHIP OF LAND

I INTRODUCTION

Co-ownership in Papua New Guinea is still largely regulated by the principles of the underlying law. There is co-ownership where two or more persons are entitled to the simultaneous enjoyment or use of land each co-owner claiming not a separate portion but a mutual right in the whole. There are to main forms of co-ownership: tenancy in common and joint tenancy.

II TYPES OF CO-OWNERSHIP

Tenancy in common

There is a tenancy in common[1] where two or more persons hold land together on terms that each is entitled to a distinct and fixed, but physically undivided, share. The shares need not be equal nor do the interests held need be of the same nature. The only essential feature of a tenancy in common is the 'unity of possession'.[2]

Joint tenancy

There is a joint tenancy where two or more persons together as a group own an estate or interest in land. Joint tenancy has two essential features, which distinguish it from a tenancy in common: (a) the four unities; and (b) the right of survivorship

(a) The four unities

The four unities are: unity of possession; interest; title and time.

There cannot be joint tenancy without the four unities. The following cases deals with this essential feature of joint tenancy.

AG SECURITIES v VAUGHAN AND OTHERS [1988] 3 All ER 1058, House of Lords

[The appellants owned a four bedroom flat. Under separate contracts entered into at different times they granted the right to occupy the flat to four individuals (the 'flat sharers'). The contract entitled each occupant to use the premises in common with other people who might from time to time have a similar right. Rent payable by the occupants

1 The term 'tenancy' in this context has nothing to do with leases. It simply means ownership of an interest.

2 See HA Amankwah and JT Mugambwa (with G Muroa), *Land Law in Papua New Guinea* (Lawbook Co, Sydney, 2001), at p 93.

varied in each contract. The Court of Appeal held that the four 'flat sharers' occupied the flat as joint tenants. On further appeal to the House of Lords.]

LORD TEMPLEMAN: The Court of Appeal ... concluded that the four respondents were jointly entitled to the exclusive occupation of the flat. I am unable to agree. If a landlord who owns a three bedroom flat enters into three separate independent tenancies with three independent tenants each of whom is entitled to one bedroom and to share the common parts, then the three tenants, if they agree, can exclude anyone else from the flat. But they do not enjoy exclusive occupation of the flat jointly under the terms of their tenancies. In the present case, if the four respondents had been jointly entitled to exclusive occupation of the flat then, on the death of one of the respondents, the remaining three would be entitled to joint and exclusive occupation. But, in fact, on the death of one respondent the remaining three would not be entitled to joint and exclusive occupation of the flat. They could not exclude a fourth person nominated by the company. I would allow the appeal.

LORD ACKNER: [E]ach of the respondents commenced his occupation of the flat on different dates, each of their agreements covered different period and each agreement provided for different payments for that occupation. In such circumstances there could not have been a grant of a joint tenancy to all four respondents ...

I would allow the appeal.

LORD JAUNCEY OF TULLICHETTLE: I should be surprised indeed if a joint lease could be created by four separate documents of different dates in favour of four independent persons each paying a different rent and also for different periods of six months. Such an arrangement would, as Sir George Waller [dissenting judge in the Court of Appeals] pointed out be notably deficient in the four unities of interest, title, time and possession ...

Notes

The following is an extract of Sir George Waller's dissenting judgment in the Court of Appeal,[3] which the House of Lords upheld.

SIR GEORGE WALLER: A joint tenancy is one where the tenancy commences on the same day for all, where the term is the same for all, where the rent should not be altered without due notice to all possibly where all are jointly liable for the rent.

Fox LJ has referred to the four unities set out in Megarry and Wade, *The Law of Real Property* (5th edn, 1984), pp 419–22 as the requirements for a joint tenancy and I will consider them.

Unity of interest The extent, nature and duration of each occupant's interest is different. Each one started on a different day and as a result the extent was different because the duration was six months in each case and then monthly. Although each one became monthly after six months, there is no 'act' to create a joint tenancy, as I shall refer to under unity of title.

Unity of title The unity of title for a joint tenancy has to be the same act or document. Megarry and Wade were repeating that which was contained in Blackstone's *Commentaries* (2 Bl Com 180):

> Joint-tenancy cannot arise by decent or act of law; but merely by purchase, or acquisition by the act of the party: and, unless that act be one and the same, the two tenants would have different titles ...

3 *AG Securities v Vaughan* [1988] 2 All ER 173, at p 185.

> Each occupant started with a different document on a different date. Can it be said that it was the same act? In my opinion a new joint tenancy could not arise each time a new person came because the new occupant had six months to run whereas every other occupant was monthly, and it could not arise at the expiration of six months because there was then no 'act' which could create a joint tenancy.
>
> *Unity of time* The interest of each must vest at the same time. If we were considering the first four occupants it would follow that their interest vested at the same time, but as each new occupant arrived the interest of the others had already vested and at the time when the notices to quit were delivered each occupant's interest had vested on different days.
>
> *Unity of possession* This must be possession of the whole. Each occupant was given the right to use the flat and so it could be said that there was unity of right to use the flat. But was that possession of the whole? In *Addiscombe Garden Estates Ltd v Crabbe* [1957] 3 All ER 563 at 568; [1958] 1 QB 513 at 524–25, a case where the 'licence' contained a clause entitling the landlord to enter the land, Jenkins LJ said:
>
> > The importance of that is that it shows that the right to occupy the premises conferred on the grantees was intended as an exclusive right of occupation, in that it was thought necessary to give a special and express power to the grantors to enter. The exclusive character of the occupation granted by a document such as this has always been regarded, if not as a decisive indication, at all events as a very important indication to the effect that a tenancy, as distinct from a licence, is the real subject matter of the document.
>
> The indication is in the opposite direction in this case, but the plaintiff never claimed the right.
>
> I am prepared to accept that there may be an exceptional case where there might be a special arrangement about one of these characteristics, but in my opinion there cannot be a joint tenancy where there are serious doubts about each of the four unities ...

(b) The right of survivorship (jus accrescendi)

Unlike tenants in common, joint tenants, as individuals do not have *distinct* shares in the co-owned land. For this reason upon the death of one joint tenant, his or her interest is extinguished and that of the remaining joint tenants enlarged until eventually the property vests in the last survivor.[4] This is what is known as the 'doctrine of survivorship'. Joint tenants may individually or together nullify the effect of the right of survivorship by severance during their lifetime.[5]

Companies as joint tenants

Under the underlying law, a corporation could not hold in joint tenancy with another corporation or with a human being.[6] The Bodies Corporate (Joint Tenancy) Act (Ch No 143), changed the law. The Act enables corporations to hold property in joint tenancy with humans or with each other. Section 1 of the Act provides:

> (1) Subject to sub-section (2) –

---

4 EH Burn, *Cheshire and Burn's Modern Law of Real Property* (14th edn, Butterworths, London), at 209.

5 See below. For detailed discussion, see *Land Law in Papua New Guinea, op cit*, note 2, at pp 111–18.

6 *Law Guarantee and Trust Society v Bank of England* (1890) 24 QBD 406.

(a) a corporation is capable of acquiring and holding any real or personal property in joint tenancy in the same manner as if it were an individual; and

(b) where a corporation and an individual, or two or more corporations become entitled to any real or personal property under circumstances or by virtue of an instrument which, if the corporation had been an individual, would have created a joint tenancy, they are entitled to the property as joint tenants.

(2) The acquisition and holding of property by a corporation in joint tenancy is subject to the same conditions and restrictions as attach to the acquisition and holding in severalty of property by a corporation.

Section 2 provides:

> Where a corporation is joint tenant of any property, on the dissolution of the corporation the property devolves on the other joint tenant.

Simultaneous deaths

At common law if joint tenants died in circumstances which rendered it impossible to determine who survived the other, the doctrine of survivorship did not apply. Instead their respective next of kin inherited the land as joint tenants.[7] The Simultaneous Deaths Act (Ch No 332), now provides for the devolution of property in the event of simultaneous deaths, or deaths as to which there is a doubt as to the order of death. Section 2 stipulates the scope of the Act:

(1) Subject to section (3), this Act applies to and in relation to –

(a) any property that devolves according to the laws of Papua New Guinea; and

(b) any appointment of a trustee that is to be made according to the laws of Papua New Guinea.

(2) This Act applies whether a death concerned occurred in the country or elsewhere.

(3) This Act does not apply to or in relation to any property the devolution of which is governed by custom.

(4) This Act applies notwithstanding anything in any other law.

Section 3 defines the circumstances in which the Act applies:

(1) This Act applies when two or more persons die or have, after 1 January 1963 (being the date of commencement of the pre-Independence Law Reform (Miscellaneous Provisions) Act 1962), died –

(a) at the same time; or

(b) in circumstances that give rise to doubt as to which of them survived the other or others.

(2) The persons to whom this Act applies in any particular case are the persons concerned whose deaths occurred in the circumstances set out in sub-section (1).

Section 7 prescribes the consequences to the joint property in the event of death of the joint tenants in circumstances describes under the Act:

---

7 *Bradshaw v Toulmin* (1784) Dick 633; 21 ER 417.

> Any property owned jointly and exclusively by two or more of the persons to whom this Act applies, other than property owned by them as trustees, devolves as if it had been owned by them before they died as tenants in common in equal shares.

The effect of these provisions is that the right of survivorship does not apply in the circumstances described; rather the interests of the deceased joint tenants will devolve under their will or as in intestate succession. These provisions, however, do not apply to any property the devolution of which is governed by custom.

Questions

1 The English Law of Property Act 1925, s 184, provides that where all joint tenants died in a common calamity, the younger is deemed to have survived the older. Is this provision fairer (or better) than the PNG provision? Why? Note that under s 11, Simultaneous Deaths Act, the rule that the younger is deemed to have survived the elder applies in all other situations of simultaneous deaths, where the issue is relevant, except as expressly stated in the Act.

2 X and Y are registered as joint proprietors of a house in Port Moresby. They are both killed in a plane crash. In his will X left his interest in the house to his wife. Y died intestate. Discuss how the house will be dealt with.

III CREATION OF JOINT TENANCY AND TENANCY IN COMMON

- Underlying law
- Under the Land Registration Act

(a) Under the underlying law

Words of severance

The common law and equity differed in their approach to the creation of joint tenancy and tenancy in common. The former leaned in favour of joint tenancy whereas the latter favoured tenancy in common.[8] Hence, at common law a grant of land to two or more persons was treated as a joint tenancy unless any one of the four unities was missing or the grant contained 'words of severance'. The latter are words that indicate that the donor intended each grantee to take a separate and distinct share in the land donated. Examples of words of severance include 'share and share alike', 'amongst', 'in equal shares'.[9] Under modern law the courts tend to treat any slightest indication of an intention to divide as creating a tenancy in common. Compare the two cases extracted below.

---

8 See Harpum C, with Grant M and Bridge S, *Megarry and Wade: The Law of Real Property* (6th edn, Sweet & Maxwell, London, 2000), at p 482.

9 For more examples, see *ibid*, at p 483.

MORLEY v BIRD (1798) 3 Ves 629; 30 ER 1192

[A testator devised and bequeathed real and personal property to the defendant on condition that she paid £400 to four persons named in the will. Three of the four named persons pre-deceased the testator. The plaintiff survived him. The issue was whether the legacy was given to the four as joint tenants or tenants in common. If they were joint tenants, the plaintiff as the sole survivor would be entitled to receive the whole £400. On the other hand, if they were tenants in common, the plaintiff would only be entitled to receive his share of £100, the remainder of the gift (which lapsed) reverting to the estate of the testator.]

MASTER OF THE ROLLS [ARDEN]: I wish to give my opinion very explicitly. Great doubts have been entertained by judges both at Law and in Equity as to words creating a joint-tenancy or a tenancy in common ... and it is clear, the ancient law was in favour of a joint-tenancy; and that law still prevails: unless there are some words to sever the interest taken, it is at this moment a joint-tenancy, notwithstanding the leaning of the courts lately in favour of a tenancy in common. A legacy of a specific chattel, a grant of an estate, is a joint-tenancy. It is true, the courts seeing the inconvenience of that have been desirous, wherever they could find any intention of severance, to avail themselves of it; and their successive determinations have laid hold of any words for that purpose. 'Equally to be divided' (*Rigden v Vailler*, 2 Ves sen 252), 'equally, among, between', even in Law I believe, certainly in Equity, create a tenancy in common: but without those words it is a joint-tenancy. But many distinctions have been raised in Equity ... as where persons are in trade, and have joint debts due to them; the courts say, it could not be intended to the prejudice of the family of the deceased partner; therefore not doubting, that it would be a joint-tenancy at Law, in Equity they say, it could not be the agreement. So if two people join in lending money upon a mortgage, Equity says, it could not be the intention, that the interest in that should survive. Though they take a joint security, each means to lend his own and take back his own. But that was never extended to grants. A voluntary bond would survive, if no intention of the party to make a severance appears. Therefore legacies, gifts, grants, etc, are both at Law and in Equity joint; except from the nature of the contract or from the words some intention of severance appears.

This is a legacy to four persons; and there are no words of severance; therefore it is a joint legacy; and the whole interest survives to the survivor, three being dead; and though I agree with those, who think it the least evil, that it should be a tenancy in common, this is one of those cases, in which it is more convenient, that it should remain joint ... The legacy therefore belongs to the Plaintiffs.

ROBERTSON v FRASER (1871) 6 Ch App 696

[A testator bequeathed the residue of his estate to J and F for their absolute use and benefit. By a subsequent codicil he added the name of W so that the will read that the said W 'shall and may participate in the bequest with J and F'. J died in the testator's lifetime while F and W survived him. The issue was whether the bequest to J, F and W was in joint tenancy or tenancy in common. If the former F and W were entitled to the whole gift by right of survivorship; if the latter J's share of the gift lapsed and would pass on intestacy to the testators next of kin.]

LORD HATHERLEY LC: The question to be disposed of on this appeal arises out of the gift of the residue in the will, which constitutes the residuary legatees joint tenants, as varied by the gift in the codicil: [His Lordship then read the clause in the will containing the residuary gift, and also the codicil, and continued:] It is the last clause in the codicil which alone creates the difficulty; and the question has been argued at considerable length, and many cases have been cited on both sides. I should have felt no difficulty in applying the authorities if this clause had occurred in the original will; the only difficulty arises from the fact of its occurring in the codicil. I cannot doubt, having regard to the authorities respecting the effect of such words as 'amongst' and 'respectively', that anything which in the slightest degree indicates an intention to divide the property must be held to abrogate the idea of a joint tenancy, and to create a tenancy in common. Perhaps it would have been well if the courts had held that in bequests, as in partnerships, every community of interest was to be considered a tenancy in common. But that has not been done. However, putting aside such words as 'alike' and 'equally' – for they may be considered more decidedly inconsistent with joint tenancy, inasmuch as the interests of joint tenants are very rarely quite equal, considering the difference that may exist in the ages of the legatees – it does not appear to me that such words as 'amongst' and 'respectively' are at all stronger than 'participate'. I have, therefore, no doubt that the word 'participate' is sufficient to indicate an intention to divide, and to create a tenancy in common. My doubt has been as to the effect of the peculiar form of the codicil; but my doubt is not sufficient to induce me to reverse the decision of the Vice Chancellor.

The testator effects his purpose by way of reference to the original gift in the will. In two places he directs that the will is to be read as if the name of Joseph Warren had been inserted in the original bequest; that alone would have given a joint tenancy to the three. But then he adds the clause: 'So that the said J Warren shall and may participate in such bequest, free of legacy duty, with the said JH Johnson and WJ Fraser.' Some argument has been raised as to the effect of the direction that the bequest is to be free of legacy duty in indicating a tenancy in common; but that argument is sufficiently answered by reference to the Legacy Duty Act (36 Geo 3, c 52), in which the Legislature has specially provided for the payment of legacy duty by joint tenants, although they stand in different degrees of relationship. No difficulty, therefore, arises upon that point. But when we find the testator not contented with inserting the name of the new legatee, but expressing his reason for so doing, we must take the reason as he gives it, and that reason is, that the new legatee may participate with the two other legatees – in other words, that there may be a sharing of the bequest; and all the authorities go to this, that if there is to be a sharing, the shares must be equal; and division being once imported, the true interpretation must be a tenancy in common. There is a fallacy in the argument when it is contended that the testator shews no intention to alter the will because he does not interfere with the form of the bequest. The testator is not altering the will, he is only explaining it. He uses words which the court allows to be explained by very slight indications of intention, and having used them, he goes on, not to alter them, but to explain them by words shewing an intention to create a tenancy in common. On the whole, therefore, far from being clear that the Vice Chancellor was wrong, I am inclined to agree in the conclusion at which he has arrived.

The appeal must be dismissed with costs.

Questions

1 Why did the common law favour joint tenancy over tenancy in common?

2 A testator devised his estate to his children X and Y 'to share alike as joint tenants'. What sort of co-ownership did the testator intend to create? Do you see any

contradiction in the words used by the testator? (See *Re Barbour, deceased* [1967] Qd R 10.)

Presumption of tenancy in common in equity

In equity, as at common law, a grant to two or more persons without words of severance created a joint tenancy.[10] However, in the following cases equity did not follow the law:

- property purchased with funds contributed in unequal shares;
- partnership assets;
- money advanced on mortgage; and
- generally any other circumstances in which equity may infer tenancy in common.

In those situations, in the absence of clear evidence to the contrary, the Court of Equity presumed that the co-owners intended to create a tenancy in common and not joint tenancy. Each of these exceptions is examined below.

(i) Property purchased with funds contributed in unequal shares

Where two or more persons contribute funds in unequal amounts to purchase property, equity presumed that they intended to hold the property in tenancy in common and not in joint tenancy. This rule was stated in Sir W Page Wood's famous exposition in the case of *Robinson v Preston*.[11] He said:

> The law is settled as to the investment of moneys in the names of two or more persons in the purchase of property. If invested in unequal shares, the purchasers remain tenants in common of the purchased property; if in equal shares, and the matter on the face of it purports to be a joint-tenancy, then it is considered by this court to be a joint-tenancy, and no equity is supposed to intervene by which it can be reduced to a tenancy in common.

The presumption could be rebutted by clear evidence to the contrary, for example, where the parties expressly state in their conveyance that they hold as joint tenants.[12] Note in the quotation that if the contribution to the purchase price is equal, joint tenancy is presumed in equity.

Questions

1 Why does equity make a presumption in favour of tenancy in common where contribution to the purchase price is unequal and not where it is equal? Is the distinction logical?

2 Assume that X contributed 75% and Y 25% of the purchase price of a house. The house was conveyed to both of them and they were registered as 'joint owners'. X died recently. Advise his next of kin whether X's estate has any rights over the house.

---

10 *Morley v Bird* (1798) 3 Ves 629; 30 ER 1192.

11 (1858) 4 K & J 505, at 510; 70 ER 211, at 213.

12 See *Goodman v Gallant* [1986] 1 All ER 311 (CA).

(ii) Partnership assets

Property acquired by partners as part of the partnership's assets is presumed to be held by the partners as tenants in common and not as joint tenants. This is irrespective of whether the contribution to the purchase price was equal or unequal. The rule owes its origin to another well known case of *Lake v Craddock*.[13] The rule in *Lake v Craddock* is now incorporated in s 21(2) of the Partnership Act (Ch No 148). The section provides:

> The legal estate or interest in any land that belongs to the partnership devolves according to its nature and tenure and the general rules of law applicable to such land, but in trust, so far as necessary, for the person beneficially interested in the land under this section.

The meaning and effect of this provision is discussed in the following judgment of the National Court.

RE APPLICATION OF HEATHER JOAN HUTCHINSON [1984] PNGLR 71, National Court of Justice

McDERMOTT J: The applicant sought a vesting order over certain real property pursuant to s 29(1)(f) and (h) of the Trustees and Executors Act (Ch No 289). I made the order on 19 April 1984 and now publish my reasons.

The application arises from an assignment for consideration by William Henry Johns of his interest in a business partnership known as South Pacific Beverages (Madang), to his daughter, Heather Joan Hutchinson, on 1 January 1980. In February 1982, a new partnership agreement was entered into by Mrs Hutchinson with the other three partners following Mr Johns' death on 31 January 1982. He died leaving no real or personal estate in this country. It is submitted he was the trustee of his tenant in common partnership interest in real property for the assignee.

The partnership contracted with Rabtrad Madang Pty Ltd in October 1983 to sell all the partnership assets. Completion is conditional upon the partners producing to the purchaser transfers of the various properties in registrable form. As Mr Johns' name still appears on the title deeds, substitution of Mrs Hutchinson's name for that of her father on the title deeds is required.

Pursuant to a vesting order, the Registrar of Titles can give effect to it by altering the title deeds (s 111 of the Land Registration Act 1981). Until probate or administration is granted, the deceased's property vests in the Public Curator (s 44 of the Wills Probate and Administration Act (Ch No 291)) but, he considers, and has stated in affidavit, that he has no interest and, if held to be entitled, would renounce in favour of the legal representative. Mrs Johns is such person and she resides out of the jurisdiction.

Does the legal personal representative have an interest? I have been referred to s 21 of the Partnership Act (Ch No 148) and to *In Re Bourne, Bourne v Bourne* [1906] 2 Ch 427 at 432 and *Re George Livanos, deceased* [1955] St R Qd 362 at 366 where the following from the earlier case was cited as the legal position:

> It is to be borne in mind that the real interest of the partnership in real estate is of a personal character, because wherever the legal estate may be, whether it is in the partners jointly or in one partner or in a stranger it does not matter, the beneficial interest in the real estate belongs to the partnership, with an implied trust for sale for

13 (1732) 3 P Wms 158; 24 ER 1011.

> the purpose of realizing the assets and for the purpose of giving to the two partners their interest when the partnership is wound up and an account taken.

The *Queensland* case is particularly apposite as it is dealing with statutory provisions very similar to our own in the Act to which I have referred. In particular s 21 of the Partnership Act (Ch No 148), which says as follows:

> (1) Partnership property shall be held and applied by the partners exclusively for the purposes of the partnership and in accordance with the partnership agreement.
>
> (2) The legal estate or interest in any land that belongs to the partnership devolves according to its nature and tenure and the general rules of law applicable to such land, but in trust, so far as necessary, for the persons beneficially interested in the land under this section.

As O'Hagan J said (*supra* at 367):

> Section 23 [equivalent to s 21] gives statutory recognition to the trusts of which Romer LJ speaks in *In Re Bourne* (*supra*). Sub-section (2) does not create a new trust. The land is to be held for the persons beneficially entitled who are the surviving partners or the surviving partner. No other person can be said to be beneficially entitled. What passes on the deceased's death to his administrator is not any interest in any asset of the partnership but the deceased's interest in the partnership, which is a different thing.

Section 21 of the Partnership Act (Ch No 148) in providing for the vesting of the legal estate of land held by a deceased partner says that the legal estate is to devolve according to law. The relevant law is found elsewhere and I have already referred to it.

It is clear to me that reliance upon a vesting order will enable the sale of the partnership property to be concluded. The applicant seeks an order to vest the property in the remaining partners. That too appears to be the practical solution.

There is one further consideration – whether the approval of the Minister for certain dealings as required by s 69 of the Land Act (Ch No 185) is necessary. It is submitted that no new interest is created by a vesting order and the section is not applicable to the transaction which will affect the present title deed. I have been referred to *Re Strathblaine Estates Ltd* [1948] 1 All ER 162 where the company was voluntarily wound up but certain real estate owned by it was not transferred to shareholders in accordance with an earlier resolution. A vesting order was sought in respect of the legal interest in the unsold property which was held to be in trust and was not determined by the dissolution. A new legal estate was not created. That case is analogous to what is before me.

I therefore, order that the interest of William Henry Johns as tenant in common of the partnership properties vest in the partners, Madang Lollywater Pty Ltd, Thurston Holdings Pty Ltd, and Thomas William Abberton.

Questions

1 What constitutes partnership property? See ss 21 and 22 of the Partnership Act (Ch No 148).

2 What is a 'partnership'? Does it matter (for the purpose of applying equity presumption in favour of tenancy in common) that the co-owners were not actually engaged in business, but only shared equally the net rent received from leasing the common land?

3 What is the difference between co-ownership and partnership? (See MA Kimuli *et al*, *Introduction to the Law of Business Associations in Papua New Guinea* (2nd edn, Pacific Law Press, Hobart, 1990), at p 136.

(iii) Money advanced on mortgage

Where X and Y in equal shares advance a loan to Z on a mortgage, at law X and Y hold the mortgage as joint tenants but in equity the presumption is that they intended to take the mortgage as tenants in common. Since the rules of equity prevail over the rule of law, upon death of either of them the survivor is deemed in equity to hold the deceased's share in trust for the deceased's estate.[14] The reason for the presumption in favour of tenancy in common is the unlikelihood of the parties intending that whoever happened to die first would forego his or her interest.

Section 80 of the Land Registration Act (Ch No 191) provides:

> (1) Subject to sub-section (2), where a mortgage or charge contains a provision in or to the following effect:
>
> > 'the money to be secured belongs to the mortgagees (*or* chargees, *as the case may be*) on the joint account',
>
> the survivors from time to time of the creditors have the joint right, and the last survivor has the right, both at law and in equity:
>
> (a) to recover and receive and give discharges for the money and interest on the money or the annuity or rent charge secured by the mortgage or charge; and
>
> (b) to exercise and enjoy in respect of the mortgage or charge all the powers and privileges vested in creditors by this Act.
>
> (2) On the death of a creditor the rights referred to in sub-section (1) are not transmitted until a transmission of the mortgage or charge is registered under section 118 or 120 in respect of that creditor.

The purpose of this provision is to protect a mortgagor who deals with the survivor(s) of a joint mortgage by giving power to the survivor to accept repayment of the mortgage loan and to discharge the mortgage. The section does not by itself affect the presumption of a tenancy in common as between the co-mortgagees.[15]

(iv) Other situations where equity presumes a tenancy in common

Traditionally the view was that cases in which joint tenants at law will be presumed to hold as tenants in common in equity was limited to the three specific categories already mentioned above. However, in the following case the Privy Council makes it clear that the class of cases is not so rigidly circumscribed.

MALAYAN CREDIT LTD v JACK CHIA-MPH LTD [1986] AC 549, Privy Council

> [A lease of certain office premises was executed in favour of the plaintiff and the defendant. They took the lease to serve their separate commercial interests. Prior to the execution of the

14 *Re Jackson; Smith v Sibthorpe* (1887) 34 Ch D 732.

15 See *Megarry and Wade: The Law of Real Property*, *op cit*, note 8, 1256.

lease the parties had agreed that the plaintiff should occupy a total of 2,306 square feet of the premises leaving the defendant 3,614 square feet for his use. Rent payments and other service payments were apportioned in proportion to the area they occupied. A dispute arose between the plaintiff and the defendant. The plaintiff sought a judicial order for sale and equal division of the net proceeds; alternatively equal partition of the premises. The High Court of Singapore held that the plaintiff and the defendant were tenants in common holding unequal shares, and dismissed the action. The Singapore Court of Appeal upheld the decision of the High Court. On further appeal to the Privy Council.]

LORD BRIGHTMAN: Their Lordships will deal first with the general principles involved in the case. As the lease itself contains no words of severance, it necessarily takes effect as a grant to the lessees as joint tenants at law. As regards the beneficial interest in the lease in equity, there are three possible situations.

Situation A. The lessees at the inception of the lease hold the beneficial interest therein as joint tenants in equity. This will be the case if there are no circumstances which dictate to the contrary. On subsequent severance, the lessees would hold the beneficial interest in equal shares.

Situation B. The lessees at the inception of the lease hold the beneficial interest as tenants in common in equity in equal shares.

Situation C. The lessees at the inception of the lease hold the beneficial interest as tenants in common in equity in unequal shares.

Situation A is that which is advocated by the plaintiff. The argument is that, in the absence of an express agreement, persons who take as joint tenants at law hold as tenants in common in equity only in three classes of case: first, where they have provided the purchase money in unequal shares; in this case they hold the beneficial interest in similar shares: secondly, where the grant consists of a security for a loan and the grantees were equal or unequal contributors to the loan; again they would hold the beneficial interest in the same shares; and thirdly, where they are partners and the subject matter of the grant is partnership property. See for example, *Snell's Principles of Equity* (28th edn, 1982), pp 37 and 38. The plaintiff contends that the instant case falls into none of these three categories. Therefore it is said that the lessees hold as joint tenants in equity as well as at law, with the result that either party was at liberty to sever the joint tenancy and thus ensure that the beneficial interest was thereafter held in equal shares. Subject to severance, which either party can secure at will, there is no difference between the end result of situation A, and situation B.

Situation C is that which is advocated by the defendant. If situation A applies to the present case, it is not in dispute that there has been a severance.

The matter came before the High Court on affidavit evidence. The trial judge held that as the premises were disproportionately divided between the parties, there was a tenancy in common in unequal shares; in other words, situation C. He said that he was fortified in this view by the fact that the stamp duty was paid in unequal shares, as also the rent. The Court of Appeal reversed the trial judge, holding that there was a joint tenancy which, on later severance, became a tenancy in common in equal shares; in other words, situation A. The Court of Appeal directed a sale.

It seems to their Lordships that where premises are held by two persons as joint tenants at law for their several business purposes, it is improbable that they would intend to hold as joint tenants in equity. Suppose that an accountant and an architect take a lease of premises containing four rooms, that the accountant uses two rooms, and that the architect uses two rooms. It is scarcely to be supposed that they intend that if, for example, the accountant dies first without having gone through the formalities of a severance, the beneficial interest in the entire premises is to survive to the architect. Their Lordships do not accept that the cases in which joint tenants at law will be presumed to hold as tenants in common in equity are as rigidly circumscribed as the plaintiff asserts. Such cases are not necessarily limited to purchasers who contribute unequally, to co-mortgagees and to partners. There are other circumstances in which equity may infer that the beneficial interest is intended to be held by the grantees as tenants in common. In the opinion of their Lordships, one such case is where the grantees hold the premises for their several individual business purposes.

Furthermore, there is no fundamental distinction to be drawn for present purposes between joint tenants who acquire a term of years on payment of a premium and at a token rent, and joint tenants who acquire a term of years on the payment of no premium but at a rack rent. If in the first case the lessees contribute unequally towards the premium, it is plain that they hold the term of years (in the absence of contra-indications) as tenants in common in equity in unequal shares. The premium is the purchase money. In the second case the rent is equivalent to the purchase money. If that is paid in unequal shares, logically the joint tenants should hold the beneficial interest in equity (in the absence of contra-indications) as tenants in common in unequal shares.

There are features in the instant case which appear to their Lordships to point unmistakably towards a tenancy in common in equity, and furthermore towards a tenancy in common in unequal shares: (1) the lease was clearly taken to serve the separate commercial interests of the defendant and the plaintiff. (2) Prior to the grant of the lease the parties had settled between themselves what space they would respectively occupy when the lease came to be granted. This was roughly 62% to the defendant and 38% to the plaintiff. (3) Prior to the grant of the lease, the parties had made meticulous measurements of their respected allotted areas, and divided their liability for the rent and service charge in unequal shares in accordance with the respective areas they would occupy. (4) Prior to the grant of the lease, the plaintiff was invoiced for its due share of the deposit which was to be paid to the landlord as security under the terms of the lease, the apportionment being made in unequal shares in the like manner. This deposit was a sum which was not to be refundable by the landlord until the termination of the lease. The plaintiff did not dispute the principle of this apportionment. (5) After the grant of the lease, the defendant and the plaintiff paid the stamp duty and the survey fees in the same unequal shares. (6) As from the grant of the lease, the rent and service charges were paid in the same unequal shares.

With great respect to the Court of Appeal, their Lordships feel unable to support their conclusion that the parties are beneficially entitled to equal shares. In the opinion of their Lordships, the payment of rent and service charge in unequal shares, the payment of the stamp duty and the survey fee in unequal shares, and the unequal contributions to the deposit payable under the terms of the lease which was to be outstanding for the whole period of the lease, are comparable to the payment of purchase money in unequal shares. All the circumstances point decisively to the inference that the parties took the premises in equity as tenants in common in unequal shares, those shares being (as a result of the meticulous calculations made by the parties) 3,614 shares to the defendant and 2,306 shares to the plaintiff.

Their Lordships are, however, in agreement with the Court of Appeal that a partition of the premises is inappropriate and that they should be sold by order of the court under the Supreme Court of Judicature Act.

(Appeal allowed in part.)

(b) Creation of joint tenancy and tenancy in common under the Land Registration Act

Joint tenancy and tenancy in common are both created by registration of the joint tenants or the tenants in common as such under the Land Registration Act (Ch No 191). Section 34 of the Land Registration Act provides that where two or more persons are registered as 'joint proprietors' of an estate or interest in land, they are 'entitled' to that estate as joint tenants. On the surface this seems to suggest that registration as joint proprietors is conclusive that the co-owners are joint tenants. However, in the case extracted below the Supreme Court of New Zealand interpreted an identical provision as meaning that the co-owners are joint tenants as far as third parties are concerned, but as between the parties registration as joint proprietors is not conclusive of their status.[16]

IN RE FOLEY (DECEASED), PUBLIC TRUSTEE v FOLEY AND OTHERS [1955] NZLR 702, Supreme Court of New Zealand

[The testatrix and her sister, Gertrude, were the joint proprietors of a registered mortgage, which secured a principal sum of £4,000. Gertrude survived the testatrix for a period of slightly over two months. The court was asked to determine whether she became solely entitled both at law and in equity to the mortgage and to the principal and other moneys thereby secured.]

HENRY J: The Land Transfer Act 1952, provides, in s 61, as follows:

> ... any two or more persons named in any Crown grant or in any instrument executed under this Act as transferees, mortgagees, or proprietors of any estate or interest, shall, unless the contrary is expressed be deemed to be entitled as joint tenants with right of survivorship, and every such instrument, when registered shall take effect accordingly.

So far as the legislation is concerned, the testatrix and her sister are 'mortgagees' within the meaning of the word in s 61; and, they were, upon registration of the said mortgage, deemed under s 61 to be entitled as joint tenants with right of survivorship Mr Stephenson argued that s 61 concluded the matter, and, that the court was bound to hold in the absence of a contrary expression in the instrument, that registration caused the instrument to have the effect of creating a joint tenancy in the mortgagees both in law and equity with right of survivorship Mr Adams argued that s 61 is a 'registration' section; and, that the section does not interfere with the jurisdiction of the court in 'trust matters'.

It will be observed that s 61 uses the expression:

> ... shall, unless the contrary is expressed, be *deemed* to be entitled as joint tenants.

Where the Legislature uses the word 'deemed' the court is entitled and bound to ascertain for what purposes and between what persons the statutory fiction is to be resorted to. The

16 See also Whalan, *The Torrens System in Australia* (Lawbook Co, Sydney, 1982), at pp 103–05.

Legislature has not enacted in s 61 that the persons '*shall be entitled* as joint tenants' but that they '*shall be deemed to be entitled* as joint tenants'.

In order to ascertain the effect of s 61 it is necessary to consider ss 61 to 64 (inclusive), which sections are all grouped under the heading 'Registered Proprietors'. Section 62 provides that the estate of the registered proprietor shall, with certain exceptions, be paramount. Section 63 protects the registered proprietor against ejectment except in the cases appearing in paras (a) to (e). Section 64 prevents any person from acquiring by possession or adverse user any title in derogation of the title of the registered proprietor. If s 61 had not been enacted, anyone dealing with the survivor of the persons referred to would be faced with questions as to the exact estate which the survivor took. The section is clearly intended to define the position of a survivor so that the registered instrument may be looked at for the purpose of ascertaining who the person or persons are who are entitled to deal with the estate ...

After considering ss 61–64 (inclusive) in the light of the above, I am of the opinion that the intention of the Legislature is to make registration conclusive so far as concerns parties who act in reliance of the registered instrument. In the case of two or more registered mortgagees appearing in a memorandum of mortgage, they may be treated by the Registrar, and by all persons dealing with them, as joint tenants with right of survivorship, and the registered estates and interests will pass accordingly. But this does not, in my view, exclude the jurisdiction of the court in determining questions between the mortgagees themselves. The purpose of the fiction in s 61 is to make the Register, in so far as the mortgagees are described in the instrument, paramount as between the mortgagees, on the one hand, and any person dealing with the survivor of them, on the other hand. In the result, my conclusion is that s 61 does not preclude the court from entering upon an inquiry as to whether or not a tenancy in common exists between registered mortgagees where the registered instrument is silent on that point ...

[His Honour concluded on the facts of the case that the two sisters intended to hold the mortgage as tenants in common and not as joint tenants.]

Questions

1 Note that s 34 of the Land Registration Act (Ch No 191) states that where two or more people are registered as joint proprietors of an estate or interest, 'they are entitled to that estate or interest as joint tenants'. In contrast, s 61 of the New Zealand Land Transfer Act 1952 says that the joint proprietors '*shall be deemed to be* entitled as joint tenants'. Is this difference in wording a material distinction?

2 Suppose co-owners are registered as joint tenants. Is that conclusive of the nature of their co-ownership? If not, who would bear the burden of proof that they are not joint tenants? Can you think of any circumstances where the parties are registered as joint tenants but in equity are deemed to be tenants in common? See, eg, *Calverley v Green* (1984) 155 CLR 242.

IV RIGHT OF ENJOYMENT AMONGST CO-OWNERS

Co-owners enjoy certain rights and owe certain obligations towards each other. The most important right of a co-owner is the right to possession and enjoyment of the entire co-owned land irrespective of the size of his share. In the eyes of the law the entire land is his to enjoy. For this reason a co-owner who merely occupies or enjoys the land cannot be forced by his co-owners to pay them 'occupational rent' or contribute towards repair expenses or to reimburse them for costs already incurred. Nor can they hold him liable for trespass to land. The following materials illustrate these rules and their exceptions.

(a) No liability for occupation rent

The case extracted below illustrates how this rule operates.

JONES (AE) v JONES (FW) [1977] 1 WLR 438, Court of Appeal

[The defendant's father bought a house for the defendant who left his own house and moved with his family into the house. The defendant contributed one-quarter of the purchase price and understood from his father that the house was his. When the father died the house vested in the plaintiff, the defendant's stepmother. The plaintiff brought proceedings for an order that the house be sold. Alternatively she sought an order for payment in the nature of rent for the defendant's sole occupation of the house. The trial judge ordered the defendant to pay three-quarters of a fair rent for the house to the plaintiff or sale of the house and share the proceeds appropriately. On appeal by the defendant.]

LORD DENNING MR: First the claim for rent. It is quite plain that these two people were in equity tenants in common having a three-quarter and one-quarter share respectively. One was in occupation of the house. The other was not. Now the common law said clearly that one tenant in common is not entitled to rent from another tenant in common, even though that other occupies the whole. That appears from *M'Mahon v Burchell* (1846) 2 Ph 127, 134–35 *per* Lord Cottenham LC, and *Henderson v Eason* (1851) 17 QB 701, 720. Of course if one of the tenants let the premises at a rent to a stranger and received the rent, there would have to be an account, but the mere fact that one tenant was in possession and the other out of possession did not give the one that is out any claim for rent. It did not do so in the old days of legal tenants in common. Nor does it in modern times of equitable tenants in common. In *Bull v Bull* [1955] 1 QB 234, 239, I said:

> ... the son, although he is the legal owner of the house, has no right to turn his mother out. She has an equitable interest which entitles her to remain in the house as tenant in common with him until the house is sold.

As between tenants in common, they are both equally entitled to occupation and one cannot claim rent from the other. Of course, if there was an ouster, that would be another matter: or if there was a letting to a stranger for rent that would be different, but there can be no claim for rent by one tenant in common against the other whether at law or in equity.

Second, the order for sale. Here comes into play the doctrine of proprietary estoppel. It has been considered by this court in *Inwards v Baker* [1965] 2 QB 29 and *Crabb v Arun District Council* [1976] Ch 179. It is quite plain that the principles of those cases apply here.

Old Mr Jones' conduct was such as to lead his son Frederick reasonably to believe that he could stay there and regard Philmona as his home for the rest of his life. On the basis of that reasonable expectation, the son gave up his work at Kingston-upon-Thames and moved to Blundeston. He paid the £1,000 too in the same expectation. He did work on the house as well. It was all because he had been led to believe that his father would never turn him out of the house: it would be his family's home for the rest of his life. He and the rest of the family thought that the father would alter his will or make over the house to the son. The father did not do it, but nevertheless he led the son to believe that he could stay there for the rest of his life. On those two cases it is clear that old Mr Jones would be estopped from turning the son out. After his death, the plaintiff is equally estopped from turning the defendant out.

Similarly, the plaintiff is not entitled to an order for the property to be sold. Nor for any payment to be made by Frederick to her pending sale. Even though there is an implied trust for sale, nevertheless, the courts will not allow it to be used so as to defeat the purposes contemplated by the parties. That appears from *Bedson v Bedson* [1965] 2 QB 666: see what I said at p 679, and *per* Russell LJ, at pp 697 and 698. No order for the sale of this property should be made because that would defeat the very purpose of the acquisition, namely that the son Frederick would be able to be there for his life and remain in it as his home.

The two doctrines go hand in hand to show that no order should be made so as to disturb the son in his possession of the house: nor should he be made to pay anything for staying there.

The ultimate result of the case is that the son has a proprietary interest of a one-quarter share in the house. He is able to stay there for life by virtue of his interest in it, and the plaintiff is estopped from turning him out. Nor can it be sold without his consent. The appeal should be allowed and an order made accordingly.

[Roskill and Lawton LJJ concurred.]

Question

Two sisters were tenants in common of a house, which they occupied. Upon death of one of the sisters, the survivor remained in sole possession for several years. The administrator of the estate of the deceased sister seeks to charge the survivor a proportional amount for occupation rent. Advise the survivor. (See *Luke v Luke* (1936) 36 SR (NSW) 310.)

(b) No compensation for improvements and repair

The ramifications of this rule are clearly brought out in the case extracted below.

LEIGH v DICKESON (1884) 15 QBD 60, Court of Appeal

[The plaintiff and defendant were co-owners of a house. By mutual agreement the house was leased to the defendant for a certain period. The plaintiff brought this action to recover rent due from the defendant. The defendant by way of counter-claim sought to recover from the plaintiff a proportion of the money he spent towards repairs and improvements of the house in proportion to the benefit the plaintiff had received. The trial judge dismissed the counter-claim. On appeal.]

BRETT MR: Does this counter-claim fall within any legal and recognised principle? There was no express request by the tenant in common with him that he should expend the money. What are the legal conditions which enable a man who has expended money to recover it from another? If money has been expended at the express request of another, an action will lie at the suit of the person expending it against the person pursuant to whose request it has been expended. If a person is employed as agent in a business which requires an expenditure in order that it may be carried on, it is equally clear that the principal must indemnify hts agent for the expenditure which he incurs. But the law has gone further; it has been laid down that if one person has requested another to do an act which will cost him money, that is, which will expose him to a legal liability to pay money; the law will imply a promise on the part of the person making the request to indemnify the other for the expenditure to which he has been subjected. But the law has gone even further, and it has been held that if a principal employs an agent in a business, in which, by the usage thereof known to both parties at the time of employment, the agent, although he is under no liability by law, is bound, on pain of suffering an injury or loss in his business, to pay money, the principal is bound to indemnify the agent for the money which the latter may expend in the transaction of the business on his principal's behalf. That, no doubt, is an extreme case, but it has been so decided. But it has been always clear that a purely voluntary payment cannot be recovered back. Voluntary payments may be divided into two classes. Sometimes money has been expended for the benefit of another person under such circumstances that an option is allowed to him to adopt or decline the benefit: in this case, if he exercises his option to adopt the benefit, he will be liable to repay the money expended, but if he declines the benefit he will not be liable. But sometimes the money is expended for the benefit of another person under such circumstances, that he cannot help accepting the benefit, in fact that he is bound to accept it: in this case he has no opportunity of exercising any option, and he will be under no liability. Under which class does this case come? Tenants in common are not partners, and it has been so held: one of them is not an agent for another. The cost of the repairs to the house was a voluntary payment by the defendant partly for the benefit of himself and partly for the benefit of his co-owner; but the co-owner cannot reject the benefit of the repairs, and if she is held to be liable for a proportionate share of the cost, the defendant will get the advantage of the repairs without allowing his co-owner any liberty to decide whether she will refuse or adopt them. The defendant cannot recover at common law; he cannot recover for money paid in equity, for that is a legal remedy: there is no remedy in this case for money paid ... If the law were otherwise, a part-owner might be compelled to incur expense against his will: a house might be situate in a decaying borough, and it might be thought by one co-owner that it would be better not to repair it. The refusal of a tenant in common to bear any part of the cost of proper repair may be unreasonable: nevertheless, the law allows him to refuse and no action will lie against him. [Appeal dismissed.]

COTTON LJ: I think that it must be assumed that the house was in a bad state of repair, and that the repairs executed by the defendant were necessary. As to the claim for improvements, it has been urged that no tenant in common is entitled to execute improvements upon the property held in common, and then to charge his co-tenant in common with the cost. This seems to me the true view, and I need not further discuss the question as to improvements. As to the question of repairs, it is to be observed that when two persons are under a common obligation, one of them can recover from the other the amount expended in discharge or fulfilment of the common obligation; but that is not the position of affairs here: one tenant in common cannot charge another with the cost of repairs without a request, and in the present case it is impossible even to imply a request .... Therefore, no remedy exists for money expended in repairs by one tenant in common, so long as the property is enjoyed in common ... [Appeal dismissed.]

Questions

1 What is the difference between repair and improvement?

2 Do you agree with Brett LJ's rationalisation for not forcing a co-owner to reimburse his companions for repair and or improvements?

3 What advice would you give to a co-owner who wishes to carry out repairs and improvements if the other co-owners are indifferent?

(c) No liability for trespass

The case extracted below explains the working of this rule.

THE PROPRIETOR OF THE CENTRE BUILDING UNITS PLAN NO 343 v BOURNE [1984] 1 Qd R 613, Supreme Court of Queensland

[The plaintiff was the body corporate responsible for the management of a building, which had an arcade of shops. One of these shops was leased to the defendant. The Queensland Building Units Titles Act 1965, provided *inter alia* that the 'common property' of a building shall be held by the proprietors as tenants in common in shares proportionate to their units. A by-law required proprietors to use the common property in such a manner as not unreasonably to interfere with the use of the same by other proprietors or their visitors or customers. In breach of the by-laws, the defendant displayed his merchandise in the common area outside his shop. The management board brought an action in trespass against him.]

DERRINGTON J: The Defendant's case then is that, having at least the rights of a tenant-in-common, although there are certain proscriptions imposed by the statute and by-laws upon his conduct, he cannot be guilty of trespass towards other co-owners except by ouster. Ouster is not suggested here. Conformably with his other arguments, counsel for the plaintiff would argue that the defendant's rights are no more than the residue after deducting from the rights of a tenant-in-common those rights which are lost by virtue of the proscriptions, because the lessor cannot pass any greater rights than he has. Alternatively he would argue that even a tenant-in-common is liable to trespass if he exceeds his rights in relation to his co-owners.

Some support might be suggested for the latter argument in the words of Lord Hatherley LC in *Jacobs v Seward* [(1872) LR 5 HL 464] where he says at p 474:

> So long as a tenant in common is only exercising lawfully the rights he has as tenant in common, no action can lie against him by his co-tenant.

And at p 475:

> As long as the tenant in common is confining his use of that property to its legitimate purpose trover will not lie against him. But the moment he steps from the legitimate use to that which is illegitimate, as the sheriff seems to have done in that case by disposing absolutely of the common property as if the one partner had been the sole owner, trover will lie.
>
> However, those remarks were made in the context of a discussion concerning ouster by destruction of the land by the removal of an essential part of it such as the soil; and

> destruction of the subject matter of the co-ownership and exclusion of the co-owner are the chief forms of ouster.

By way of comparison it is instructive to see the position where a co-owner commits an act which is an interference with the rights of his fellows but which is less than that absolute exclusion or destruction which would amount to ouster. In *Cubitt v Porter* 8 B&C 265 [(sic) 256], Bayley J said:

> One tenant in common has upon that which is the subject matter of the tenancy in common laid bricks and heightened the wall. Yet that be done further than it ought to have been done, what is the remedy of the other party? He may remove it. That is the only remedy he can have. (Cited with approval in *Watson v Gray* (1880) 14 Ch D 192 *per* Fry J at pp 195–96.)

That might be compared with *Stedman v Smith* 8 E&B 1 where, in addition to heightening the wall in which the parties were tenants-in-common, the offending co-owner so acted as to claim exclusive rights, and was thereby guilty of ouster.

Otherwise there is a dearth of authorities discussing the liability in trespass of a co-owner, or someone taking under him, who has some basic restriction upon his conduct and acts in excess of that restriction.

The plaintiff uses as an analogy the line of cases relating to trespass by a licensee who, whilst on land in accordance with his licence, exceeds its terms or remains unlawfully after it has expired ... In the present case, it is argued, the defendant's rights in respect of the common area are similarly limited by reason of the provisions of ... [the Act] and the by-laws; and, to the extent that he transgresses these, he acts outside his rights and is in trespass.

The defendant responds that by virtue of his title he is entitled to possession and that, whilst any transgressions might be the subject of an injunction, they cannot be trespass because of his entitlement to possession. By way of counter-analogy, he refers to the position of a lessee whose lease contains certain covenants restricting his activities upon the demised premises. If he is in breach of such a covenant, the argument runs, he may be in peril of termination of the lease or for an action for breach of covenant, but he cannot be said to be in trespass.

Despite the elegant simplicity of this analogue, it fails because the reason why trespass is not there relevant is that there is no other person in possession who could complain of trespass. Indeed a lessee who holds over after the expiration of his term may be liable in an action of ejectment, but trespass is not available against him because he is lawfully in possession of the land though he wrongly refuses to give it up – *Hey v Moorehouse* (1839) 6 Bing NC 52; *Fleming on Torts* (6th edn), p 39.

However the argument bears the seeds of merit in its reference to the significance of the possession to which the defendant is entitled. Trespass is a remedy for the protection of the possession of one entitled to it against one who is not so entitled, for it consists of an unauthorized intrusion on land in the exclusive possession of another ... But if the entry is authorized, as in this case, then the element of unauthorized entry is missing.

The difference between the defendant's position, where he has the rights of a tenant-in-common subject to certain restrictions, and that of the licensee referred to by the plaintiff's argument is that the defendant has a right to possession but a licensee merely holds a licence to do that which but for the consent would be wrongful. He has no right to possession .... A licence is 'that consent which, without passing any interest in the property to which it relates, merely prevents the acts for which the consent is given from being wrongful'. *Pollock on Torts* (15th edn), p 284; *Winfield and Jolowicz on Tort* (10th edn), p 307. It is for this reason that, whilst conduct in excess of a licence is in general a trespass, the same reasoning is not applicable to one who is in possession and who acts in excess of certain restrictions upon his conduct. It is the distinction as to the right to possession that is decisive.

Consistent with his analysis is the comment in Fleming [*Torts* (6th edn)] p 384 where the author says:

> The gist of private nuisance is interference with an occupier's interest in the beneficial use of his land. The action is thus complementary to trespass which protects his related interest in exclusive possession.

Because the possession of the co-owners of the common property here is not exclusive of that of the defendant, his interference in their rights constitutes a breach of the statute and by-laws or a nuisance, but not trespass.

Questions

1. What is the justification for the rule that co-owners irrespective of the size of their shares are equally entitled to the occupation and use of the property?
2. X and Y are tenants in common of a house in which both reside. X invites his *wantoks* to stay with him. Y objects and threatens to sue X's friends for trespass. Advise Y. (See *Jacobs v Seward* (1872) LR 5 HL 464.)

Exceptions to the 'no liability rule'

As may have been gathered from the foregoing cases, there are exceptions to the rule that a co-owner is not accountable to the others for the use and enjoyment of the common land. Some of these exceptions are considered in the materials below.

(i) Ouster or eviction

Where a co-owner ousts or evicts another co-owner from the common property, the latter might sue in trespass and or claim occupation rent for the period he or she was excluded from exercising his or her right. What constitutes ouster or eviction? The case extracted below throws some light on the issue.

DENNIS v McDONALD [1981] 2 All ER 633, Family Division

[The plaintiff and the defendant cohabited in a *de facto* relationship. Together they bought a dwelling house, which they intended to be their family house. The parties in equal contribution paid part of the purchase price, and they borrowed the rest on security of a mortgage on the house. The house was conveyed to them into their joint names on trust for sale for themselves as tenants in common. After several years of living together the plaintiff left the house because of the defendant's violence or threat of violence towards her. The plaintiff made an application for the sale of the house, alternatively for the defendant to pay her occupation rent. The defendant opposed the application and he submitted that he was not liable to pay occupation rent.]

PURCHAS J: Counsel for the plaintiff submitted, I think correctly, that ... the true position under the old authorities was that the Court of Chancery and Chancery Division would be always ready to inquire into the position as between co-owners being tenants in common either at law or in equity to see whether a tenant in common in occupation of the premises was doing so to the exclusion of one or more of the other tenants in common for whatever purpose or by whatever means. If this was found to be the case, then if in order to do equity between the parties an occupation rent should be paid, this would be declared and the appropriate inquiry ordered. Only in cases where the tenants in common not in occupation were in a position to enjoy their right to occupy but chose not to do so voluntarily, and were not excluded by any relevant factor, would the tenant in common in occupation be entitled to do so free of liability to pay an occupation rent.

In the instant case the plaintiff is clearly not a free agent. She was caused to leave the family home as a result of the violence or threatened violence of the defendant. In the event, whatever might have been the cause of the breakdown of the association, it would be quite unreasonable to expect the plaintiff to exercise her rights as a tenant in common to occupy the property as she had done before the breakdown of the association with the defendant. In my judgment, she falls into exactly the kind of category of person excluded from the property in a way envisaged by Lord Cottenham LC in *M'Mahon v Burchell* [(1846) 2 PH 127]. Therefore, the basic principle that a new tenant in common is not liable to pay an occupation rent by virtue merely of his being in sole occupation of the property does not apply in the case where an association similar to a matrimonial association has broken down and one party, for practical purposes, excluded from the family house ...

[The defendant appealed to the Court of Appeal, but did not contest the judgment in respect of the above matter. See [1982] 1 All ER 590.]

Notes and questions

1 A co-owner is deemed to be evicted not only in those cases of violence or threat of violence, but in all cases where in the circumstances it is unreasonable to expect a co-owner to exercise his or her right to occupy the premises. (See *In Re Thurgood*, unreported judgment of the Supreme Court of Queensland, 8 October 1986, noted Philip Byrnes, 'Occupation rent and statutory trust for sale – a note' (December 1987) Queensland Law Society Journal 441.)

2 Consider the following factual situations and advise the party who is not in occupation whether he or she is entitled to occupation rent:

(i) X and Y were tenants in common of a dwelling house where both resided. X moved out of the house because of constant arguments with Y over X's drinking and smoking habits. Y threatened to call the police if X returned to the house. Is X ousted?

(ii) A and his girlfriend B together bought a flat, which was conveyed to them as tenants in common. Their relationship soured when A returned home one day and found B in bed with C, A's best mate. A, in anger, left the house and now B and C stay together in the flat. A wishes to sue B for occupation rent, advise him of his chances of success.

(ii) Express or implied agreement to pay occupation rent

A co-owner in solo occupation of the land may be liable to pay rent where he or she expressly or impliedly agreed to pay rent to the other co-owner(s). In *Leigh v Dickeson* Cotton LJ observed:[17]

> It has been urged that one tenant in common cannot recover against another for rent, for either of them may enjoy the possession. But in the present case the defendant, although he himself was tenant in common, had possession of the whole of the house by virtue of a lease from his co-tenant in common. A correspondence ensued, as to the terms under which he should remain in occupation of the house. Under these circumstances, I think that the defendant must be considered as holding exclusive possession of the house upon the terms of the lease, and therefore, that he is liable for rent at the same rate as was reserved by the lease.

(iii) Equity

As we shall shortly see, in equity a co-owner who expends money on improvement of the co-owned property may seek, in certain circumstances, contribution from the other co-owners.[18] However, if the improver were in sole occupation of the common property the court, in accordance with the maxim that 'he who seeks equity must do equity', may require him to off-set against his claim an occupation rent.[19]

(iv) Liability to account for profits

In equity, a co-owner is liable to account to his or her co-owner for profits received from a third party's use or occupation of the common property as distinct from income made by the co-owner's investment or use of the common property.[20] As the following case illustrates, it is difficult sometimes to determine whether income received by a co-owner from a third party is the result of that co-owner's investment or is merely the result of the third party's use and occupation of the land.

SQUIRE v ROGERS [1979] 39 FLR 106, Federal Court of Australia

> [The defendant (appellant) and the plaintiff (respondent) were joint lessees of certain land. The lease contained a covenant requiring improvements to be carried out. The plaintiff left the country before any improvements were made and played no further part in the land project. Meanwhile, the defendant spent approximately $100,000 to erect buildings and caused other improvements to be made on the land, and there carried on a business of letting flats and rooms and conducting a caravan site. The plaintiff made an application for the sale of the common leasehold and for an account of the rents and profits. The defendant opposed the application. In the alternative he made a counter application for an adjustment

---

17 (1884) 15 QBD 60, at 66; [1881–85] All ER Rep 1099, 1101–02.

18 *Squire v Rogers* [1979] 39 FLR 106, see extract.

19 *In Re Jones; Farrington v Forrester* [1893] 2 Ch 461, at p 478, *per* North J.

20 *Squire v Rogers* [1979] 39 FLR 106, at 123–24, see extract below. See also *Land Law and Policy in Papua New Guinea, op cit*, note 2, at pp 108–09.

on the sale to the extent of the value the land had increased in value by his investment. The trial judge ordered an account and a sale. On appeal.]

DEANE J [His Honour dismissed the defendant's appeal against the order to sell the property, and continued]: There remains for consideration the defendant's attack on the order for an account ... The cases in which one co-owner can obtain an account of receipts from another co-owner who has had the sole use of the joint property are, except where the sole use has been the result of agreement (whether express, implied or imputed), holding over or actual exclusion, limited to those cases where one co-owner has received more than his share of the rents or other revenues of the common property ... The plaintiff does not allege any relevant agreement between the defendant and herself. The statement of claim did no more than allege that the defendant was, and for some years had been, carrying on the business of permitting persons to occupy cabins and to park caravans on the land for reward to himself. The evidence indicated that 'the business' in question consisted of the business of a caravan and cabin park' and that occupation fees were obtained for the use (to use neutral terms) of furnished flats, single rooms and caravans as well as for the use of parking and associated facilities for caravans. The receipts for which the defendant would be liable to account on the plaintiff's claim are limited to those receipts which can properly be regarded as rents and revenue of the common property itself as distinct from profits which the defendant may have made by his use and occupation of the common property (eg, fees for services and for use of items of equipment). Plainly, the identification of what properly constituted rents and revenue of the common property in that sense required further evidence as to the precise nature of the receipts of the business which the defendant carried on the land and could involve disputed questions of fact and law. In the absence of agreement between the parties, the case should be remitted to the Supreme Court for the ascertainment of the relevant facts and the determination of any such disputed questions. The question of what outgoings should be allowed to the defendant on the taking of the account can only be resolved in the light of whether the appropriate order for an account embraced all or some only (and if so which) of the defendant's receipts from his activities on, and in respect of, the land. The question of outgoings also raises the question of what, if any, allowance should be made to the defendant in respect of expenditure on capital improvements ...

As a general rule, capital expenditure upon permanent improvements to land by one joint owner without the authority of his co-owner creates a passive equity which attaches to the land. The joint owner making the improvements is not entitled to bring proceedings for contribution against his co-owner. In circumstances where his co-owner (or a successor in title of his co-owner other than a purchaser for value without notice) would otherwise unfairly benefit under an order in equity (including partition or sale of the property), he is entitled to an allowance for his expenditure on such improvements to the extent to which they result in the present enhancement of the value (or the price on sale) of the land ...

It appears from the evidence that, with the possible exception of any occupation fees received in respect of the hut erected by the plaintiff and subsequently improved by the defendant and in respect of the use of the site by caravans, any rents and profits received by the defendant in respect of the land were received as a consequence of the use of improvements effected by him. A question arises whether the equitable principles underlying the defendant's entitlement to a limited allowance from the proceeds of sale of his expenditure on improvements (to the extent that they result in an increased price on sale) are, in the circumstances of the case, also applicable to preclude the plaintiff from being entitled, upon accounts upon partition or sale, to receive a one-half share of any rents and profits resulting from the use of the improvements without making a full allowance in favour of the defendant in respect of his expenditure upon those improvements. In my view those principles do so apply. [His Honour referred to *Leigh v Dickeson*, see extract below, and continued.]

In the present case, there is no suggestion that the plaintiff was excluded from the subject land against her will. She voluntarily left it in the occupation of the defendant in the expectation that the defendant would spend money on improvements and, by so spending it, preserve their joint leasehold interest in the land by complying with the covenant requiring the making of improvements. She was aware of the defendant's activities on the land and the fact that he was effecting improvements and made no complaint in that respect. In the circumstances, the plaintiff is not entitled to a one-half share of the rents and profits which the defendant received in respect of the subject land as a result of the use of the improvements which he had effected while denying the defendant's entitlement to an allowance in respect of their cost.

In my view, she is, in the circumstances, only entitled voluntarily to adopt the benefit of the improvements by claiming and receiving one-half of any profit resulting from their use at the price of being liable to contribute to, or make an allowance in respect of, their cost over and above the amount included in the restricted allowance to which the defendant was independently entitled on partition or sale. If she accepts the benefit of the profit earned, she must bear her share of the burden of earning it ...

In the result, the order for an account made by the Supreme Court should be set aside. In the absence of agreement between the parties as to appropriate orders, the matter should be remitted to the Supreme Court for the hearing of further evidence to enable the definition, with some precision, of the receipts and outgoings to be included and allowed on the taking of the account ...

[Forster and Brennan JJ concurred.]

(v) Adjustments and allowance for improvements and repair

Upon termination of co-ownership, by sale or partition, the court may make allowance for expenses incurred by a co-owner for improvement of the land. Cotton LJ's *dictum* in *Leigh v Dickeson*[21] is the authority for this proposition. He said:

> [N]o remedy exists for money expended in repairs by one tenant in common, so long as the property is enjoyed in common; but in a suit for a partition it is usual to have an inquiry as to those expenses of which nothing could be recovered so long as the parties enjoyed their property in common; when it is desired to put an end to that state of things, it is then necessary to consider what has been expended in improvements or repairs: the property held in common has been increased in value by the improvements and repairs; and whether the property is divided or sold by the decree of the court, one party cannot take the increase in value, without making an allowance for what has been expended in order to obtain that increased value; in fact, the execution of the repairs and improvements is adopted and sanctioned by accepting the increased value. There is, therefore, a mode by which money expended by one tenant in common for repairs can be recovered, but the procedure is confined to suits for partition. Tenancy in common is an inconvenient kind of tenure; but if tenants in common disagree, there is always a remedy by a suit for a partition, and in this case it is the only remedy.

21 See extract above.

Notes

A co-owner can only recover if the value of the property actually rises as a result of their act and the amount they can recover is limited to the their actual expenditure. (See *Squire v Rogers, supra,* p 173.)

Questions

1 If a co-owner at his expense erects a house on the land for his own use, he is not obliged to pay occupational rent to the other co-owner(s). If on the other hand he rents the same house to a third party, he must share the profits with the others. Does this make sense? What is the policy explanation for the difference?

2 Suppose a co-owner makes a loss from letting the premises to a third party. Is he or she entitled to demand contribution from the other co-owners? Give reasons.

3 Is the remedy suggested by Cotton LJ in *Leigh v Dickeson* (see extract above) satisfactory?

4 What are the possible policy reasons for limiting the amount of compensation recoverable by the improver to the amount actually spent? What effect is the rule likely to have on a co-owner who is contemplating carrying on improvements on the common land?

V DETERMINATION OF CO-OWNERSHIP

Joint tenancy

A joint tenancy terminates by operation of the rule of *jus accrescendi,* when the survivor becomes the sole owner. Apart from that, joint tenancy may be terminated during the lifetime of the co-owners by (a) severance of tenancy and (b) partition of the land.

(a) Severance

Severance is the process for conversion of joint tenancy into tenancy in common. Sir William Page Wood VC, in his celebrated statement in *Williams v Hensman*[22] described the three ways of severance:

> In the first place, an act of any one of the persons interested operating upon his own share may create a severance as to that share. The right of each joint-tenant is a right by survivorship only in the event of no severance having taken place of the share which is claimed under the *jus accrescendi.* Each one is at liberty to dispose of his own interest in such manner as to sever it from the joint fund – losing, of course, at the same time, his own right of survivorship. Secondly, a joint-tenancy may be severed by mutual agreement. And, in the third place, there may be a severance by any course of dealing sufficient to intimate that the interests of all were mutually treated as constituting a tenancy in common.

22 (1861) 1 J&H 546, at 557; 70 ER 862, at 867.

To the three ways of severance mentioned in the quotation we shall add a fourth one, namely severance by homicide. The operation of these rules of severance is illustrated below.

Severance by act of one joint tenant

(i) Transfer to a third party

A joint tenant may sever by doing an act, which operates upon his or her share. For example, a co-owner severs the joint tenancy if he or she transfers his or her interest to a third party. As the following case illustrates, severance only occurs if the transfer is effective. What constitutes effective transfer of land registered under the Torrens system? See the following case.

CORIN AND ANOTHER v PATTON (1990) 92 ALR 1, High Court of Australia

[The respondent, Ronald Patton, and his late wife were registered as the proprietors of the subject land in joint tenancy, under the Real Property Act 1900 (NSW). Shortly before her death, Mrs Patton sought to sever the joint tenancy with a view to benefit her children. To that end she executed a form of transfer of her estate and interest as joint tenant in the said property to her brother, John Corin, on trust to hold as tenant in common with her husband Ronald Patton. She named herself as the beneficiary of the trust. John Corin signed a deed of trust whereby he acknowledged that he held the interest as a trustee for Mrs Patton. The form of transfer and the deed of trust signed by Mrs Patton and Corin, respectively, were taken away by Smallwood (the solicitor who prepared both documents) to do 'what was necessary' to complete the transaction. The State Bank of New South Wales was in possession of the certificate of title as unregistered mortgagee of the property. Mrs Patton took no action to procure the production of the certificate of title so as to enable the transfer to be registered. At the time of Mrs Patton's death the transfer had not been registered and the certificate of title was still with the Bank. Mrs Patton left a will in which she appointed Mr Corin and the second appellant as executors. The trial judge held that Mrs Patton's unilateral action was not effective to sever the joint tenancy. Accordingly, Mr Patton, as the survivor was the sole owner of the property. The Court of Appeal dismissed the appeal. On further appeal to the High Court.]

MASON CJ AND McHUGH J: [I]t is necessary in this case for the appellants to demonstrate that Mrs Patton effectively alienated the property in equity. Although this may involve questions of whether or not Mrs Patton could have withdrawn from the transactions, the issue is primarily whether or not the property was alienated.

Mr Bennett [QC for the appellants] contended that the rules for determining whether there has been an effective transfer should be relaxed in a case, such as the present, where the purpose of asking the question is to determine whether or not a joint tenancy has been severed. But such an approach cannot be reconciled with principle and would be productive of great uncertainty. Once it is accepted that a transfer is required, it is the general rules relating to transfers of land which must be applied. This particular case involved a voluntary transaction. In this respect we agree with Hope JA that the consent or agreement of Mr Corin to act as trustee did not constitute valuable consideration, and in any event it was not seriously suggested otherwise. Indeed, in the famous case of *Milroy v Lord* (1862) 4 De GF & J 264; 45 ER 1185, in very similar circumstances, the consent or agreement of the transferee to act as trustee was not regarded as constituting valuable consideration.

The long line of earlier authority concerning voluntary conveyances and transfers culminated in the judgments in *Milroy v Lord*. In that case Thomas Medley executed a voluntary deed purporting to assign certain shares to Samuel Lord, to be held by him on trust for Andrew Milroy and his wife. The shares could be transferred only by the making of appropriate entries in the books of the company, but no such action took place. However, Lord held a general power of attorney from Medley authorising him to transfer the shares, and a further power of attorney authorising him to receive the dividends on the shares. The dividends were received by Lord for the following three years, until Medley's death. The issue for decision was whether or not Medley had effected a gift of the shares in equity prior to his death.

The court held that the gift was imperfect. Knight Bruce LJ held that the instrument of transfer was insufficient to constitute Medley a trustee of the shares. Nor did it amount to a specifically enforceable contract. Rather, Medley left imperfect and incomplete that which he might have perfected and completed by making a transfer of the shares so as to confer the legal ownership upon Lord. Turner LJ stated, at 274–75 [1189–90]:

> I take the law of this court to be well settled, that, in order to render a voluntary settlement valid and effectual, the settler [sic] must have done everything which, according to the nature of the property comprised in the settlement, was necessary to be done in order to transfer the property and render the settlement binding upon him. He may of course do this by actually transferring the property to the persons for whom he intends to provide, and the provision will then be effectual, and it will be equally effectual if he transfers the property to a trustee for the purposes of the settlement, or declares that he himself holds it in trust for those purposes ... but, in order to render the settlement binding, one or other of these modes must, as I understand the law of this court, be resorted to, for there is no equity in this court to perfect an imperfect gift. The cases I think go further to this extent, that if the settlement is intended to be effectuated by one of the modes to which I have referred, the court will not give effect by transfer, the court will not hold the intended transfer to operate as a declaration of trust, for then every imperfect instrument would be made effectual by being converted into a perfect trust.

Accordingly, the purported transfer could not be supported as a declaration of trust, and failed as a transfer because the powers of attorney did not suffice to permit Lord to execute a transfer in his favour without express directions from Medley, which Medley had not given.

Two propositions emerged from the observations of Turner LJ. First, the donor must have done everything necessary to be done, according to the nature of the property, in order to transfer the property and render the gift binding. Secondly, if the gift was intended to have been effectuated by one means, the court will not give effect to it by another means. However, as the later cases were to reveal, there was an element of uncertainty in the first proposition. Did it require that the donor must have done himself all that was necessary to be done in order to transfer the property or did he only have to do all that was necessary to be done *by him* in order to achieve that result?

[Their Honours reviewed several Australian cases including *Anning v Anning* (1907) 4 CLR 1049; *Brunker v Perpetual Trustee Co (Ltd)* (1937) 57 CLR 555.]

Accordingly, we conclude it is desirable to state that the principle is that, if an intending donor of property has done everything which it is necessary for him to have done to effect a transfer of legal title, then equity will recognise the gift. So long as the donee has been equipped to achieve the transfer of legal ownership, the gift is complete in equity. 'Necessary' used in this sense means necessary to effect a transfer. From the viewpoint of the intending donor, the question is whether what he has done is sufficient to enable the legal transfer to be effected without further action on his part.

... The question is then whether Mrs Patton did all that it was necessary for her to do in order to effect a transfer. Two obstacles are suggested to completion of the gift. First, the certificate of title remained throughout with the mortgagee and Mrs Patton took no steps to arrange for its production for the purposes of registration. Secondly, it is not clear whether or not Mr Smallwood held the executed transfer on Mrs Patton's instructions or those of Mr Corin.

Whether or not it is correct to say that the production of a certificate of title is 'necessary' to achieve registration on a transfer of Torrens system land, it is apparent that a gift of such land cannot be regarded as complete in equity while the donor retains possession or control of the certificate of title: Dixon J in *Brunker*, at 600–05; *Scoones v Galvin and the Public Trustee* [1934] NZLR 1004. That is because it can scarcely be said that the donor has done everything necessary to be done by him if he has retained the certificate of title, by virtue of the possession of which the gift might well be thwarted.

In the present case Mrs Patton gave no authority for the mortgagee bank to hand the certificate of title to Mr Corin for the purposes of registration. At least, if she authorised Mr Smallwood to obtain the certificate, there is no clear evidence to that effect. [Appeal dismissed.]

BRENNAN J: In the present case, let it be assumed that Mrs Patton delivered to Mr Corin a registrable transfer with the intention of parting with it and the property in it so that Mr Corin might be registered as proprietor of an estate in fee simple as tenant in common with Mr Patton and let it be further assumed that Mr Corin was thereby enabled to require production of the relevant certificate of title to allow registration of the transfer: on those assumptions Mrs Patton had done all that was necessary on her part to make the transfer effective and the transfer was not revocable by her prior to registration. On those assumptions, the elements of an effective gift ... are fulfilled and Mr Corin would have acquired a right under, but subject to, the Real Property Act to have the transfer registered. Yet, at the time of Mrs Patton's death the transfer had not been registered and (in the absence of a certificate of title or a dispensation from production) was not then able to be registered. In those circumstances, it cannot be said that any title to the estate or interest in the land intended to be given by Mrs Patton had passed to Mr Corin. It follows that, prior to her death, Mrs Patton had not divested herself of her estate or interest in the land. She remained a joint tenant; she did not hold her estate or interest as trustee for any person. On her death, Mr Patton took by survivorship and his enlarged estate may be registered under s 101 of the Act. On Mrs Patton's death, Mr Corin's assumed statutory right to registration became valueless for the estate which he was intended to take was then extinguished ... [Appeal dismissed.]

TOOHEY J: The real point is that the transfer to Mr Corin had not been registered at the time of Mrs Patton's death. There was no transaction that equity would enforce; there was a transaction that had not been consummated. There had been no divesting by Mrs Patton of her interest as joint tenant.

The appeal should be dismissed.

(Deane J's judgment is omitted, but see extract of his opinion below, p 185.)

Questions

1 Is *Corin v Patton* a sound decision? Why did the High Court refuse to give effect to Mrs Patton's plain intention to sever her joint tenancy? Are there any policy reasons for the decision?

2 Supposing Mrs Patton had handed Corin a signed memorandum of transfer and the certificate of title, would the joint tenancy have been severed in equity?

(ii) Transfer to each other

Joint tenants may sever their tenancy by making cross-transfer to one another, as the case below illustrates.

WRIGHT AND ANOTHER v GIBBONS (1948) 78 CLR 313, High Court of Australia

[Olinda and Ethel Gibbons were sisters. They together with their sister-in-law, the plaintiff, were registered as joint tenants of certain land. Prior to their death the two sisters executed a memorandum of transfer. By that memorandum Olinda purported to transfer to Ethel her one-third share in the said lands and likewise Ethel purported to transfer her one-third share to Olinda; that is the two made cross-transfers of their interests to each other. This was done in a single document. Their intention was to sever the joint tenancy with one another and with the plaintiff. The memorandum of transfer was registered under the Tasmanian Real Property Act 1862–1935. The plaintiff who survived Olinda and Ethel contended that the joint tenancy had not been severed and consequently as the sole survivor she was entitled to the whole estate. The issue was whether before their deaths the two sisters had severed the joint tenancy in the said land so that the three became tenants in common and the plaintiff took nothing by right of survivorship. On appeal.]

LATHAM CJ: When one joint tenant transfers his interest to another joint tenant the transfer (which at common law was effected by release because each joint tenant is conceived as holding every part and the whole of the land –*'per my et per tout'*) does not operate by way of extinguishment of the estate. A mere extinguishment would enure in favour of B and C, and not only in favour of B in accordance with the intention of the parties. Accordingly such a transfer is said to pass (*mitter*) the estate.

The Real Property Act does not alter the law with respect to joint tenancy. It leaves the incidents of joint tenancy standing a they are determined by the common law and any other relevant statute. But it requires that documents transferring interests in land under the Act should be in a particular form and should be registered: ss 42, 39.

If there are three joint tenants, A, B and C, and one joint tenant A transfer his interest to another joint tenant B, the result is that A then has no interest in the land, B becomes a tenant in common as to one-third interest in the land, and remains a joint tenant with C as to a two-thirds interest. If subsequently B transfers to A the interest which he still has as a joint tenant (A then having become a stranger to the title, his interest having passed to B), there is a further and complete severance. A becomes a tenant in common as to one-third interest with B and C, the transfer working a severance of the joint tenancy between B and

C in the two-thirds interest in the land. The final result is that A, B and C become tenants in common, each having a one-third interest.

If the transfer by B to A were made on a day subsequent to the transfer by A to B, as I have assumed in what has just been said, there would be no doubt as to the result. The difficulty in the present case arises from the fact that there was only one document which came into operation at a particular moment of time, namely upon registration: see Real Property Act 1862, ss 35(2), 39(1). But if the document is construed in accordance with the principle *ut res magis valeat quam pereat,* the transaction can be upheld by regarding the words of transfer by A to B as equivalent to a release and by regarding the words of transfer by B to A as constituting a grant. The transfer by A to B made B a tenant in common with C as to a one-third interest, leaving B and C as joint tenants in respect of a two-thirds interest. That joint tenancy of B and C was severed when B transferred his interest as joint tenant to A. If the document is so interpreted effect is given to the plain intention of the parties so that A, B and C became tenants in common of the land, each owning a one-third interest.

In my opinion the appeals should be allowed and the point of law determined by declaring that the joint tenancy in the land under the Real Property Act was severed by the registration of the transfer dated 6 December 1945.

RICH J: I think that some confusion has occurred by concentrating attention on the principles of common-law conveyancing and not observing the innovation effected by the new or Torrens system. The Torrens system, which is in use in all the States and in New Zealand, originated in two statutes passed in 1858 by the Parliament of South Australia prompted by Sir Robert Torrens whose name the system commemorates. Its basal features are that transactions in land should be carried out by their registration in a government office, thus guaranteeing ownership of an absolute and indefeasible title to realty and that by the exclusive use of a transfer in the statutory form conveyances and assurance which under the old system had become cumbersome and intricate should be simplified.

An examination of the relevant Act – the Real Property Act 1862 (Tas) as originally enacted – shows how the system works. 'Land' includes every estate and interest in land, and 'transfer' means the passing of any estate or interest in land under this Act, whether for valuable consideration or otherwise (s 3). 'Joint tenants', by the statutory fiction 'deemed', are treated as joint proprietors or co-proprietors (ss 87, 88). Registration is provided for in ss 34(3), 37, 42 and Form IV in the first schedule. The scheme of transfer and registration is the only method by which any alienation or disposition of a share or interest in land may be made.

The ownership by two or more persons of real property with the requisites of unity of possession, interest, title and time confers on each such person a share or right severable and capable of alienation. The instrument in question is an adaptation of the form provided in the schedule which is the appropriate and only form by which any share in land registered under the Act can be disposed of. In the instant case the fact that there is only one document and not separate transfers does not, in my opinion, result in a 'futility' but is effective and operates as a severance.

... I would add that, even assuming that the form used by the parties could be regarded as so vitally irregular as to be incapable, upon registration, of producing the result which it was obviously intended to produce – that of vesting the legal estate in Ethel Rose Gibbons and Olinda Gibbons as to one-third each as tenants in common – nevertheless it is clear that it would operate in equity as an agreement for valuable consideration by each to vest in the other a one-third interest as tenant in common, an agreement which would in equity be specifically enforceable by an order directing the execution of whatever might be the proper form of instrument, and would, pending such execution, operate in equity to sever the joint tenancy and create equitable interests as tenants in common ...

For these reasons, I would allow the appeal.

DIXON J: The case can, on this footing, be stated in an abstract way. A, B and C are joint tenants for an estate in fee simple in land under the Real Property Act. By one instrument of transfer A purports to transfer to B his undivided interest in the land and B purports to transfer to A his undivided interest in the land to the intent that they shall all three be tenants in common in equal shares. Upon registration of the transfer is there a severance so that they become tenants in common in equal shares? Clark J answered this question in the negative. The full force of his Honour's reasons for this conclusion can only be understood from a study of the judgment and the learning it contains. The foundation of the decision may, I believe, nevertheless be stated almost in a sentence. It is that in contemplation of law joint tenants are jointly seised for the whole estate they take in land and no one of them has a distinct or separate title, interest or possession. It follows that an attempt on the part of two of three joint tenants mutually to assure each to the other his or her undivided share in the hope that each of their two shares will be taken by a new title and so enure as a several undivided interest, must fail because it can accomplish nothing. An alienation by a joint tenant of an undivided interest to a stranger upon this view, imparts a several interest because such a power is incident to joint tenancy; but that is very different from identifying the respective interests of joint tenants and transposing them.

The principle thus employed is described by *Blackstone*, Vol 2, p 182, as one 'of a thorough and intimate union of interest and possession'.

They [ie, two joint tenants] have not, one of them a seisin of one-half or moiety, and the other of the other moiety; neither can one be exclusively seised of one acre, and his companion of another; but each has an undivided moiety of the whole, and not the whole of an undivided moiety.

... Logical as may seem the deduction that joint tenants have no interests which in contemplation of law are sufficiently distinct to assure mutually one to another, there are many considerations which show that, to say the least, the consequence cannot be called an unqualified truth. The fact is that the principle upon which the deduction is based must itself be very much qualified. It represents only one of two not altogether compatible aspects of joint tenancy, a form of ownership bearing many traces of the scholasticism of the times in which its principles were developed. 'Albeit they are so seised' says *Coke* (186a) ('*scil totum conjunctim, et nihil per se separatim*') 'yet to divers purposes each of them hath but a right to a moitie'. For purposes of alienation each is conceived as entitled to dispose of an aliquot share. The alienation may be partial. One joint tenant for an estate in fee simple may grant a lease of his equal share and during the lease the jointure is suspended and there is a temporary severance and apparently it would not matter that the lease did not commence until after the death of the joint tenant granting it. A joint tenant may grant an estate for life in his share, though in that case it seems that it works a severance of the entire fee simple. If one joint tenant suffered a forfeiture it was not the whole estate but only his aliquot share that was forfeited. If one joint tenant proved to be an alien the Crown, on office found, took only his share. Execution on a judgment for debt against one joint tenant bound his aliquot share and continued to do so in the hands of the survivor if the execution debtor afterwards died ...

But with respect to the alienation of the share of a joint tenant to a companion, special rules applied. Because the alienee was regarded as already in by the infeudation creating the joint tenancy the proper means of assuring the share of the alienor to him was release. The release operated as a discharge of the benefit of the infeudation or feudal contract from one joint tenant to another ...

Take then the present case. A, B and C are joint tenants. A might release or grant (and a grant would be given effect as a release) his aliquot share to B and B would take that share as tenant in common with C. Be would retain his own original aliquot share as joint tenant with C. B's two aliquot shares would be distinguishable by their different incidents. A has become stranger to the jointure. Surely B could by an appropriate assurance impart B's original aliquot share to A. If so he would come in as a tenant in common. He would then 'be in by way of conveyance or title as an assigner'. If the two assurances were made separately and in proper succession it would not matter how short a time elapsed between them. The result would be that A, B and C, having been joint tenants up to the execution of the first assurance, that is up to the release or its equivalent, would upon the execution of the second assurance become tenants in common in equal shares. What is an appropriate assurance for the second transfer or assignment (that of B's original share to A) has of course differed at different times, feoffment, lease and release and grant, but that is immaterial.

Suppose again that A, B and C being joint tenants for an estate in fee simple, A and B joined in an assurance, let us say a grant, of their two aliquot shares to X, as a grantee to uses, to the use of A and B and their respective heirs as tenants in common in equal shares. Would that not have operated to make them tenants in common not only between themselves but also with C? I have not seen a precedent for nor a reference to such an assurance, but I can see no objection to it, unless it be on the alleged ground that, for the purposes of the Statute of Uses, the feoffor, any more than the person seised, cannot be identical with the person entitled to the use. But that has never been the rule where the person entitled to the use takes a different estate or interest or under different limitations or in another right.

While these two instances may show that, independently of the Torrens system, by the use of appropriate assurance, A and B could have severed the jointure between C and themselves as well as between one another, the objection still remains that they could not have done so by mutual releases one to another nor by mutual grants one at least of which must have operated, if at all, as a release. That objection is probably a good one. The strength of the objection will be seen by taking one of the two mutual attempts to transfer the interests. As a release the attempt by A to transfer his share to B cannot operate unless B continues in his position in the jointure. But as a grant it cannot operate unless B has already ceased to occupy his position in the jointure. For him to attempt to change it eo instanti with the operation of the grant or release by himself to A therefore would appear to be inconsistent with both alternatives.

The foregoing shows that under the general law the question depended upon the conveyance or assurance used to effect the mutual transfers of the aliquot shares of the two joint tenants who desired to bring about a severance of the jointure with their companion as well as between themselves. This conclusion, to my mind, reduces the matter to a question of the operation of the Real Property Acts. It does so for two reasons. In the first place the conclusion must mean that not only for the purpose of alienations to strangers but also for the purpose of alienation of a share by one joint tenant to another, the aliquot share of each existed in contemplation of law as a distinct and ascertained proprietary interest.

The second reason is that it shows that the obstacle to concurrent cross-transfers of interests was that, except by employing the Statute of Uses, no assurance existed capable of effecting the transfers simultaneously but only by successive steps.

In approaching the Real Property Acts, it must be borne in mind that the interests of each joint tenant fell within the general statutory principle that all lands and all interests therein lie in grant.

Section 39 of the Real Property Act 1862 provides that upon registration of an instrument the estate or interest specified in the instrument shall pass in the manner set forth and specified in the instrument. Section 42 says that when land is to be transferred (and that must mean an interest therein) the registered proprietor shall execute a memorandum of transfer in the prescribed form containing an accurate statement of the estate or interest intended to be transferred. Section 87 provides that two or more persons who may be registered as joint proprietors of an estate or interest in the land shall be deemed to be entitled to the same as joint tenants. These provisions result in each joint proprietor being entitled as a registered proprietor to transfer his interest by a memorandum of transfer presented for registration (see *Tucker v Coleman* [(1885) 4 NZLR 128]). When this system for the conveyance of distinct legal proprietary interests is applied to the common-law conceptions of the interests of joint tenants it appears to me to follow that an exclusive method of assuring the aliquot share of a joint tenant is provided and that all the consequences ensue which at common law followed the transfer or legal assignment of such a share. Moreover it supplies a method of assurance of general application, that is to say one that will be apt and effective to impart any transferable interest. It is of course subject to the law of capacity or law of persons. But if it is a legal interest, as opposed to equitable, in property and is alienable the system enables the transfer thereof to be made. It is of course true that this train of reasoning still falls short by one step of establishing that the transfer by one joint tenant of his interest may be made to his companion and *e converso* of the companion's share to him. But in my opinion the considerations that have preceded the discussion of the Real Property Acts are enough to make good that step. For those considerations appear to show first that there is no incapacity in one of three joint tenants to take as a tenant in common a transfer of a companion's share; secondly that the companion's share is in contemplation of law a distinct and ascertained proprietary interest; thirdly that by a means of conveyancing that is superseded the result might have been brought about.

The consequence is that if A, B and C are joint tenants, in my opinion cross-transfers may be made at the same time of the respective aliquot interests of A and B to one another and the result is to produce a tenancy in common among A, B and C.

It follows that I think that the appeal should be allowed.

Questions

1 Suppose the instrument of transfer signed by the two sisters was never registered, would there have been severance (a) at law, and (b) in equity? To what extent is the decision influenced by the fact that the transfer was registered?

2 The High Court allowed the appeal even though the alleged severance took place behind the plaintiff's back. Does this mean that severance may be effected without the knowledge, let alone consent, of the others? Is this fair?

3 Quite clearly severance can be effected by a joint tenant transferring his or her interest to a trustee to hold for the benefit of the transferor (see Dixon J's judgment in *Wright and Another v Gibbons, supra*, p 182). Can a joint tenant sever by simply transferring his

or her interest to himself or herself without involving a trustee? See Butt, *Land Law* (4th edn, Lawbook Co, Sydney, 2001), at pp 228–29.

(iii) Unilateral declaration

Can a joint tenant sever by simply announcing to the others that he or she had severed? In *Burgess v Rawnsley*,[23] Lord Denning held that this was possible provided that the notice was in writing and was received by the other co-owners. This view has been rejected in Australia. The reasons for this are contained in the following extract.

CORIN AND ANOTHER v PATTON (1990) 92 ALR 1, High Court of Australia

[For the facts of the case and the rest of the judgment, see above, p 177.]

DEANE J: A joint tenancy should, it was submitted, be treated as 'severed' in equity in any case where, as in the present, one joint tenant has unequivocally signified an intention to bring it to an end. In considering that submission, reference must inevitably be made to the judgment of Lord Denning MR in *Burgess v Rawnsley* [1975] Ch 429. In that case, his Lordship expressed the view (at 439) that it is sufficient for 'severance' of a joint tenancy in equity if 'there is a course of dealing in which one party makes clear to the other that he desires that their shares should no longer be held jointly but be held in common'. Lord Denning's view in that regard was, however, significantly influenced by the provisions of s 36(2) of the Law of Property Act 1925 (UK) which have no Australian counterpart. It is true that there is little to be said from the point of view of logic or common sense for requiring that a joint tenant who desires to convert the joint tenancy into a tenancy in common should go through the charade of assigning his interest to a bare trustee for himself (or, arguably, conveying his interest to himself: cf *Re Murdoch and Barry* (1975) 64 DLR (3d) 222; *Re Sammon* (1979) 94 DLR (3d) 594 at 597; *Freed v Taffel* [1984] 2 NSWLR 322 at 324–25, and Conveyancing Act, s 24). It seems to me, however, that it has long been settled that, where what is involved is unilateral action by but one joint tenant, actual alienation either in law or in equity or at the least something equivalent thereto (eg by operation of estoppel) is necessary for severance of a joint tenancy (see *Partriche v Powlet* (1740) 2 Atk 54 at 55; 26 ER 430 at 431; and, generally, *Nielson-Jones v Feddon* [1975] Ch 222 at 231–34; *Freed v Taffel*, at 324–25). I do not think that it would be appropriate for this court to alter the law in that regard in circumstances where the alteration would have a retrospective effect on conveyancing practice and would be likely to give rise to unintended consequences in other cases. Accordingly, *Burgess v Rawnsley* (and the earlier English cases of *Hawkesley v May* [1956] 1 QB 304 and *Re Drape's Conveyance* [1969] 1 Ch 486) should not be followed in this country.

Burgess v Rawnsley would not, in any event, provide support for the appellants in the present case. To the contrary, Lord Denning MR was at pains to 'emphasise that it [ie, the desire to sever the joint tenancy] must be made clear to the other party' (at 439). Indeed, it was the act of communication of the desire to sever the joint tenancy which was seen as the effective act. In the present case, it has not been suggested that Mrs Patton did anything at all to communicate to Mr Patton at any time before her death the fact that she wished to convert the joint tenancy into a tenancy in common.

23 [1975] 3 All ER 142.

... It follows from what has been said above that there had been no severance, either in law or in equity, of the joint tenancy at the time when Mrs Patton died. That being so, Mr Patton became the owner of the whole by survivorship.

(Appeal dismissed.)

Question

Which view is the National Court likely to follow; that of the English courts or the Australian courts? Why?

(iv) Severance by partial transfer interest

The case below deals with the issue whether the joint tenancy is severed where one joint tenant mortgages his or her interest.

LYONS v LYONS [1967] VR 169, Supreme Court of Victoria

[The applicant, Hazel Lyons, and her late husband, William Patrick Lyons, were registered as proprietors in joint tenancy of certain land. On the death of her husband the applicant claimed sole ownership of the subject land under the doctrine of survivorship One Adelaide Gray (the caveator) lodged a caveat against any dealing in the land in question. She claimed an equitable estate in fee simple as to a half share of the land, as tenant in common. Mrs Gray contended that her interest as tenant in common with the applicant arose by virtue of a severance of the joint tenancy, which she alleged was affected in the lifetime of Patrick Lyons. She argued that the severance occurred, *inter alia*, by the execution and registration of a mortgage granted by the deceased of all his estate and interest in the land to the caveator as security for the repayment of a loan of £25. This is an application by Hazel Lyons for Mrs Gray to show cause why the caveat should not be removed. The issue is whether or not the joint tenancy with her husband was severed by the mortgage executed by the deceased.]

McINERNEY AJ: In the case of land under the general law it is clear that a mortgage by one joint tenant of his interest in the land to a stranger to the tenancy effects a severance of the joint tenancy ... The reason is plain: under the general law the mortgagor conveys his estate in the mortgaged land to the mortgagee. There is thus vested in the mortgagee all the estate and interest formerly vested in the joint tenant mortgagor: but the mortgagee obtains that estate and interest under a different instrument or judicial act than the other joint tenant or tenants, and there is thus no unity of title between the mortgagee and them ...

What, then, is the effect of a mortgage under the Torrens system by one joint tenant to a stranger to the tenancy?

... The industry of counsel and my own research have not discovered any Australian or New Zealand case law on the point I have to decide. There is a respectable body of conveyancing opinion, however, that a mortgage under the Torrens system by one joint tenant does not sever the joint tenancy. Thus in New Zealand a former Registrar General of Land (Mr EC Adams) in his book on the Land Transfer Act, at p 174, para 213, wrote in 1958:

> A mortgage of land under the Land Transfer Act by one or two or more joint tenants, does not break or cause the severance of the joint tenancy. Therefore, if the joint tenant

> who has mortgaged dies before the other joint tenant or joint tenants, the land will vest in the surviving joint tenant or tenants free of the mortgage. It is for this reason that the conveyancer should never advise a mortgage by one joint tenant as an adequate security.
>
> If, however, the joint tenant who has mortgaged is the ultimate survivor, then the mortgage becomes an effective security against the *whole* estate. But where one joint tenant mortgages to a stranger and subsequently transfers his estate or interest in the land to the other joint tenant, the transferee is bound by the mortgage, whether or not he survives the transferor; this is because he claims under the transfer and not by survivorship.

There is some authority in Canada and in the United States of America, which supports the view put forward by Mr Adams. In *Power v Grace* [1932] 2 DLR 793, the Ontario Court of Appeal held that the mere delivery of a writ fi fa to a sheriff directing him to seize the real estate of one of two joint tenants was not sufficient to sever the joint tenancy, so that upon the death of the judgment debtor joint tenant, before any step was taken by the sheriff under the writ, the surviving joint tenant took title free of the claims of the execution creditor. Grant JA, at p 796, quoted with approval the passage in the footnote to p 367 of *Challis on Real Property* (3rd edn), citing *Co Litt*, p 185a, namely: 'In order that a grant by one joint tenant may bind his fellows, it must be the grant of an estate such as rent charge or a right of common.' More directly in point, however, are two American decisions of *Wilken v Young* (1895) 41 NE 68, and *People of California v Nogarr* (1958) 330 P (2nd) 858; 67 Am LR (2nd) 992.

... In essence the facts in *Nogarr's* case were the same as in the present case. The decision of the court was that the mortgage by one joint tenant did not sever the joint tenancy:

> Under the law of this state a mortgage is but a hypothecation of the property mortgaged. It creates but a charge of lien upon the property hypotheticated without the necessity of a change of possession and without any right of possession in the mortgage and does not operate to pass the legal title to the mortgagee.
>
> Inasmuch as the mortgage was but a lien or charge upon Calvert's [the mortgagor joint tenant] interest and as it did not operate to transfer the legal title or any title to the mortgagees or entitle the mortgagees to possession, it did not destroy any of the unities and therefore the estate in joint tenancy was not severed and Elaine and Calvert did not become tenants in common. It necessarily follows that as the mortgage lien attached only to such interest as Calvert had in the real property when his interest ceased to exist, the lien of the mortgage expired with it (*per* Nourse J, 67 Am LR (2nd) 992, at p 996).

This decision was criticized in an article by WA Logan in vol 47 of the Kentucky Law Review, p 565, on the score that though sound in principle, the rule it laid down was of questionable practicability. He favoured the solution of treating the mortgage as merely suspending the joint tenancy until the mortgage was redeemed. But this solution does not commend itself to Dr Mendes Da Costa, in his learned monograph 'Co-ownership under Victorian land law', 3 MULR, at pp 137, 306 and 433. At p 448 he writes: 'But at least three views have been juristically expressed, namely that no severance results (and this is the view generally accepted), that a severance occurs in equity though not at law and a middle view suggesting that the joint tenancy is suspended during the currency of the mortgage but revives upon the mortgage being discharged.' His own preference is, however, for the solution that mortgage by one joint tenant effects a complete severance both at law and in equity (3 MULR, at p 451).

In support of his view he argues that the passage in *Littleton* 286 usually relied on as the basis for the doctrine that a charge upon land does not at common law effect a severance has never been directly upheld, that it was uttered at a time when the law favoured joint tenancy and he adds (*ibid*): 'In any event it is perhaps not easy to discern the merit of extending it automatically to the construction of an Act not passed until some three centuries after Littleton's death'. And at p 452 he asks (rhetorically, so it would appear): 'Why then should the traditional view, uttered in a common law context, mechanically be applied to the construction of a relatively modern statute?'

With respect, this does not seem to me to be the process involved. What is done is first to analyse the juristic nature of the interest conferred on the mortgagee under the statutory form of mortgage: that is seen to be an interest in the land, in the nature of a charge. One must then apply to the situation resulting from the creation of an interest of that nature a very old established doctrine of the common law, namely, that a joint tenancy is severed, *inter alia*, upon the loss of any of the four unities, but it not severed if the four unities remain unaffected. As I understand it, severance by reason of the loss of one or more of the four unities does not depend on the intention of the parties to the transaction – it is a matter to be tested by the result, rather than the intention, of the transaction.

Dr Mendes Da Costa then asks: 'Is it not a more just result, is it not both consistent with the amendment to s 74(2) and more in accordance with the disinclination of the Full Court in *Re Forrest; Trustees Executors Co v Anson, supra*, to draw differences of substance between a mortgage of land under the Act and a mortgage of land under the general law, to hold that a severance does occur' (3 MULR, at p 452).

As to what is the just result in the present case, that must depend on what the legal answer to the problem now before me. Where, as here, the mortgage is to secure the sum of 25 [pounds], I am left with the suspicion that the mortgagee viewed the transaction as one which from the legal point of view was uncertain in its outcome. And what are the merits of the claims of the husband's relatives on the one hand and the widow's on the other, I do not know. But, in any event, I am disposed to agree with the comments of Nourse J, in *People of California v Nogarr* (1958) 67 Am LR (2nd) 992, at p 999: 'There is nothing inequitable in holding that the lien of the respondent's mortgage by foreclosure and sale prior to the death of the mortgagor and thus have severed the joint tenancy. If they chose not to do so but to await the contingency of which joint tenant died first they did so at their own risk. Under the event the lien that they had expired. If the event had been otherwise and the mortgagor had been the survivor the security of their lien would have been doubled.' In the present case the mortgage debt was repayable on 31 December 1961. [His Honour made other observations regarding Dr Mendes Da Costa's views, and continued.]

I do not, therefore, find persuasive Dr Mendes Da Costa's arguments in support of the view that the mortgage effects a severance. Furthermore, it seems to me that if the transaction does not effect a severance (because it does not destroy any of the four unities) there is no real ground for holding that its effect is to suspend the joint tenancy. I therefore accept as correct the reasoning and the conclusion in *People v Nogarr, supra*, according as it does with what I understand to be long-standing conveyancing opinion both in Australia and New Zealand ... It follows that the rights of Mrs Gray, as mortgagee, against the land ceased upon the death of her mortgagor William Patrick Lyons. Consequently, registration of that mortgage after the death of William Patrick Lyons could serve no useful purpose and I think the Registrar of Titles would have been justified in refusing to register it at the date when it was lodged for registration.

Since the mortgage did not sever the joint tenancy the respondents Lyons and O'Connell as executor and executrix respectively of William Patrick Lyons were not entitled to claim any estate in the land as tenants in common with the applicant. They therefore do not show any reason why their caveat No B 988925 should [sic] be removed, and they are not, in my view, entitled to be registered as proprietors of any interest in the land.

Notes

Section 63(a) of the Land Registration Act (Ch No 191) states that the effect of a mortgage created under the Act is to charge the estate or interest specified in the mortgage, but does not operate as a transfer of the secured estate or interest (see Chapter 5). It is thought that, if similar facts were to occur in Papua New Guinea, the National Court would follow the reasoning in *Lyons v Lyons*.

Questions

1 Why does a mortgage created by a joint tenant sever the joint tenancy at common law but not under the Torrens system?

2 'Mortgagees do not and should not accept as viable security, a mortgage by one joint tenant.' Explain why they should not.

3 What precautions should have been taken by Mrs Gray in *Lyons v Lyons* to avoid the loss she suffered?

4 Suppose in *Lyons v Lyons*, the applicant (Mrs Lyons) had pre-deceased her husband, how would the latter's death have affected Mrs Gray's security?

Severance by mutual agreement

An agreement by all the joint tenants to hold as tenants in common is sufficient to sever the joint tenancy.[24] The following case deals with the issue whether an informal agreement could suffice to sever the joint tenancy.[25]

BURGESS v RAWNSLEY [1975] 3 All ER 142, Court of Appeal

[Mrs Rawnsley, the defendant, and Mr Honick, deceased, together bought a flat each contributing half the purchase price. The flat was conveyed to them as joint tenants. The two lived independently in separate parts of the flat. There was evidence that prior to Honick's death he entered into a verbal agreement with Mrs Rawnsley to buy out her interest, but subsequently the latter changed her mind because she wanted more money for her interest. By the time Honick died the sale had not taken place. The plaintiff, administratrix of the deceased's estate, claimed that the tenancy was severed in equity by the oral agreement. The defendant denied the claim arguing that the flat was hers by right of survivorship. The trial judge held in favour of the plaintiff. On appeal.]

BROWNE LJ: Counsel for Mrs Rawnsley conceded, as is clearly right, that if there had been an enforceable agreement by Mrs Rawnsley to sell her share to Mr Honick, that would

24 See *Wright v Gibbons*, see extract above, p 180.

25 See the Frauds and Limitations Act 1988, ss 2–5.

produce a severance of the joint tenancy; but he says that an oral agreement, unenforceable because of s 40 of the Law of Property Act 1925, is not enough. Section 40 merely makes a contract for the disposition of an interest in land unenforceable by action in the absence of writing. It does not make it void. But here Mrs Burgess is not seeking to enforce by action the agreement by Mrs Rawnsley to sell her share to Mr Honick. She relies on it as effecting the severance in equity of the joint tenancy. An agreement to sever can be inferred from a course of dealing ... and there would in such a case *ex hypothesi* be no express agreement but only an inferred, tacit agreement, in respect of which there would seldom if ever be writing sufficient to satisfy s 40. It seems to me that the point is that the agreement establishes that the parties no longer intend the tenancy to operate as a joint tenancy and that automatically effects a severance. I think the reference in Megarry and Wade [*The Law of Real Property*, 3rd edn, 1966, pp 418, 419] to specifically enforceable contracts only applies where the suggestion is that the joint tenancy has been severed by an alienation by one joint tenant to a third party, and does not apply to severance by agreement between joint tenants. I agree with counsel for Mrs Burgess that s 40 ought to have been pleaded, but I should be very reluctant to decide this case on a pleading point.

The result is that I would uphold the county court judge's judgment on his second ground, namely, that the joint tenancy was severed by an agreement between Mrs Rawnsley and Mr Honick that she would sell her share to him for £750. In my view her subsequent repudiation of that agreement makes no difference. I would dismiss the appeal on this ground.

SIR JOHN PENNYCUICK: [I]t is not in dispute that an agreement for severance between joint tenants effects a severance. This is the rule 2 propounded by Page Wood VC in *Williams v Hensman* [(1861) 1 John & H 546 at 557; 70 ER 862 at 867]. The words he uses are contained in one sentence: 'Secondly, a joint-tenancy may be served by mutual agreement.' ... In the present case the judge found as a fact that Mr Honick and Mrs Rawnsley at the beginning of July 1968 agreed on the sale by her to him of her share at the price of £750 ... Once that finding of fact is accepted, the case falls squarely within rule 2 of Page Wood VC. It is not contended that it is material that the parties by mutual consent did not proceed to carry out the agreement. Rule 2 applies equally, I think, whether the agreement between the two joint tenants is expressly to sever or is to deal with the property in a manner which involves severance. Counsel for Mrs Rawnsley contended that in order that rule 2 should apply, the agreement must be specifically enforceable. I do not see any sufficient reason for importing this qualification. The significance of an agreement is not that it binds the parties; but that it serves as an indication of a common intention to sever, something which it was indisputedly within their power to do. It will be observed that Page Wood VC in his rule 2 makes no mention of specific enforceability ... I would dismiss the appeal.

[Lord Denning LJ dismissed the appeal on the ground of severance by 'course of dealing'. See below.]

Questions

1 Is the above decision fair?

2 X and Y are sisters and they are registered as joint tenants of a house in which they both live. Two years ago they verbally agreed to sever the joint tenancy, X seeks your advice as to whether it is possible for her to withdraw from the agreement.

3 A and B are joint tenants. They mutually agree to sever their tenancy. Later they enter into another agreement whereby they declare the former agreement null and void. B survives A. Advise A's next of kin whether she can claim A's share in the property.

Severance by course of dealing

Even in the absence of an actual agreement between the parties, a joint tenancy may be severed by 'any course of dealing sufficient to intimate that the interests of all were mutually treated as constituting a tenancy in common'.[26] What is course of dealing? How does it differ from mutual agreement in rule 2 above? Can a course of dealing be inferred from the conduct of only one of the joint tenants?

BURGESS v RAWNSLEY (1975) 3 All ER 142

[The facts of the case are summarised above.]

LORD DENNING LJ: In ... [*Williams v Hensman*] Page Wood VC distinguished severance 'by mutual agreement' and severance by a 'course of dealing'. That shows that a 'course of dealing' need not amount to an agreement, expressed or implied, for severance. It is sufficient if there is a course of dealing in which one party makes clear to the other that he desires that their shares should no longer be held jointly but be held in common. I emphasise that it must be made clear to the other party. That is implicit in the sentence in which Page Wood VC says –

> ... it will not suffice to rely on an intention, with respect to the particular share, declared only behind the backs of the other persons interested.

Similarly it is sufficient if both parties enter on a course of dealing which evinces an intention by both of them that their shares shall henceforth be held in common and not jointly ...

I come now to the question of notice. Suppose that one party gives a notice in writing to the other saying that he desires to sever the joint tenancy. Is that sufficient to effect a severance? I think it is. It was certainly the view of Sir Benjamin Cherry when he drafted s 36(2) of the Law of Property Act 1925. It says in relation to real estates:

> ... where a legal estate (not being settled land) is vested in joint tenants beneficially, and any tenant desires to sever the joint tenancy in equity, he shall give to the other joint tenants a notice in writing of such desire or do such other acts or things as would, in the case of personal estate, have been effectual to sever the tenancy in equity, and thereupon under the trust for sale affecting the land the net proceeds of sale, and the net rents and profits until sale, shall be held upon the trusts which would have been requisite for giving effect to the beneficial interests if there had been an actual severance.

I have underlined the important words. The word 'other' is most illuminating. It shows quite plainly that, in the case of personal estate, one of the things which is effective in equity to sever a joint tenancy is 'a notice in writing' of a desire to sever. So also in regard to real estate ...

It remains to consider the decision in *Nielson-Jones v Fedden* [1974] 3 All ER 38. In my view it was not correctly decided. The husband and wife entered on a course of dealing sufficient

26 *Per* Page Wood VC in *Williams v Hensman* 1 John & H 546, at 557; 70 ER 862, at 867.

to sever the joint tenancy. They entered into negotiations that the property should be sold. Each received £200 out of the deposit paid by the purchaser. That was sufficient. Furthermore there was disclosed in correspondence a declaration by the husband that he wished to sever the joint tenancy; and this was made clear by the wife. That too was sufficient.

It remains to apply these principles to the present case. I think there was evidence that Mr Honick and Mrs Rawnsley did come to an agreement that he would buy her share for £750. That agreement was not in writing and it was not specifically enforceable. Yet it was sufficient to effect a severance. Even if there was not any firm agreement but only a course of dealing, it clearly evinced an intention by both parties that the property should henceforth be held in common and not jointly.

On these grounds I would dismiss the appeal.

SIR JOHN PENNYCUICK: Counsel for Mrs Burgess advanced an alternative argument to the effect that even if there were no agreement by Mr Honick to purchase Mrs Rawnsley's share, nevertheless the mere proposal by Mr Honick to purchase her share would operate as a severance under rule 3 in *Williams v Hensman* ...

I do not doubt myself that where one tenant negotiates with another for some rearrangement of interest, it may be possible to infer from the particular facts a common intention to sever even though the negotiations break down. Whether such an inference can be drawn must I think depend on the particular facts. In the present case the negotiations between Mr Honick and Mrs Rawnsley, if they can be properly described as negotiations at all, fall, it seems to me, far short of warranting an inference. One could not ascribe to joint tenants an intention to sever merely because one offers to buy out the other for £X and the other makes counter-offer of £Y.

[Browne LJ felt it was unnecessary to express his views on the 'difficult' question of what the effect of negotiations not resulting in an agreement or of a mere declaration would have been. However, he agreed with both Lord Denning and Sir John Pennycuick, that the third rule of severance is separate from the second.]

Questions

1. A and B were joint tenants of a house. They entered into a contract to sell the house to C for K50,000. Under the agreement C was to pay by depositing half of the money into A's bank account and the other half into B's account. Before C paid the purchase price A died. B claims that he is entitled to the whole purchase price by virtue of survivorship Advise A's next of kin. (See *Abela v Public Trustee* [1983] 1 NSWLR 308.)
2. The deceased's husband had executed in favour of the defendant a transfer of his interest in land he held jointly with the plaintiff, who was his estranged wife. He had not delivered the transfer or otherwise parted with possession of it. He had also filed an application in the National Court that the land be sold and the proceeds divided equally between him and the plaintiff. The plaintiff had opposed the application but also had filed documents seeking an order that the land be sold, though with division of the proceeds on a different basis. The deceased died before the National Court had heard his application. The plaintiff claims sole ownership of the land as the survivor. Advise the defendant (see *Patzak v Lytton and The Registrar of Titles* [1984] WAR 353).

3 X and his wife Y were joint tenants of their matrimonial home. Upon separation Y commenced negotiations with X to sell the home and divide the proceeds of sale equally between them. X died after the marriage had been dissolved and the property had been sold though the proceeds of the sale were yet to be divided. In his will X devised to W all his personal and real property. Y seeks a declaration that at the date of X's death the joint tenancy had not been severed. Advise W.

Severance by homicide

It is a rule of public policy of the general law that a person shall not be permitted to profit by his or her own wrong.[27] The following case deals with this rule in relation to the doctrine of *jus accrescendi.*

RE STONE [1989] 1 Qd R 251, Supreme Court of Queensland

[The respondent and his wife were registered as joint tenants of certain property when the respondent strangled his wife. He was found not guilty of murder but guilty of manslaughter on the ground of diminished responsibility and was sentenced to 10 years imprisonment. In her will Mrs Stone left her interest in the said property to various persons. This is an application for a declaration that the joint tenancy subsisting at her death was severed.]

McPHERSON J: Submissions before me concentrated on the question whether the respondent's action in killing Mrs Stone effected a severance of the joint tenancy in the land then subsisting between her and the respondent. The conclusion that it did was in similar circumstances adopted by Napier J in *Re Barrowcliff* [1927] SASR 147, and by Janger J in this court in *Kemp v Public Curator of Queensland* [1969] Qd R 145. An alternative view prevailing in New South Wales at the time of the latter decision was that the slaying of one joint tenant by another did not affect the incidence of survivorship inherent in a joint tenancy, by which the interest of the deceased passes to the surviving joint tenant or tenants, subject however to the imposition of a constructive trust upon the killer to the extent to which his interest is enlarged by his killing of his co-owner: se *Re Thorp* (1961) 80 WN (NSW) 61, 63, *per* Jacobs J, which was followed by Street J in *Rasmanis v Jurewitsch* (1968) 88 WN (Pt 1) (NSW) 59. The rationale of that approach is, as I understand it, that the legal title should follow the course appointed by law, leaving the beneficial interests to be adjusted in light of the fact that a surviving joint tenant has been responsible for the death of his co-tenant.

Several factors persuade me that what I may call the New South Wales approach is the correct one. In the first place, it has, as regards the legal title, the advantage of certainty. The principle that denies to a homicidal joint tenant the benefit of the *jus accrescendi* or right of survivorship is based on a rule of public policy that a person should not benefit from his criminal act, which is traceable to *Cleaver v Mutual Reserve Fund Life Association* [1892] 1 QB 147 and ultimately to *Fauntleroy's* case: *Amicable Society v Bolland* (1830) 2 Dow & Cl 1: 6 ER 630; 4 Bli NS 194; 4 ER 70. See the discussion by Mr Youdan in (1973) 85 LQR 235. Once that is accepted it requires attention to be directed to the circumstances of the killing and the quality of the act, or the state of mind of the actor in doing it. Hence, in *Re Houghton* [1915] 2 Ch 173 and *Re Plaister* (1934) 34 SR (NSW) 547, cited in and evidently adopted by Mack J in *Re Beiers* [1954] QWN 9, it was held that the rule did not apply where the killer was insane.

27 *Rasmanis v Jurewitsch* (1968) 88 WN (Pt 1) (NSW) 59.

Whether or not he was insane at the time he killed is something that may not be apparent or determined unless and until a trial takes place: see, for example, *Re Plaister*. In the meantime, the question whether the title has accrued to the surviving joint tenant or tenants is, on the view taken in *Kemp v Public Curator*, left in a state of uncertainty, which is likely to be productive of great inconvenience. The New South Wales approach has the merit of avoiding such problems leaving it to subsequent proceedings to determine the destination of the ultimate beneficial interests. It also has the merit of explaining how the public policy rule can operate in the face of a statutory provision prescribing the order of distribution on intestacy: cf *Re Pitts* [1931] 1 Ch 546. The murderer may be entitled under the terms of the statute, but what he receives he holds in trust for those who, because of his criminal act, have a better claim to it.

In addition, there is the matter of authority. *Kemp v Public Curator of Queensland* is consistent with *Re Barrowcliff*, but inconsistent with the two New South Wales decisions referred to, the approach in which has since been adopted in Ontario: *Schobelt v Barber* (1967) 60 DLR 519; in New Zealand: *Re Pechar* [1969] NZLR 574; and again more recently in New South Wales in *Public Trustee v Evans* [1985] 2 NSWLR 188. I naturally accord respect to the decision in *Kemp v Public Curator*, but I am not bound by it. I notice that it was decided shortly after the old Supreme Court building was damaged by fire, and that Hanger J said ([1969] Qd R 145, 149) that he was precluded form further investigation of the points involved because of the condition of the Supreme Court Library, the case being one in which, he said, the question appeared to be 'of no substantial importance to the parties to these proceedings'. In the end I am satisfied that I should adopt the reasoning of Street J in *Rasmanis v Jurewitsch* in preference to *Kemp v Public Curator* and *Re Barrowcliff*.

That means in this case that the respondent acquired by survivorship the joint interest at law of Mrs Stone in the subject land, and did so in 1975 when he killed her. What follows depends on the nature and circumstances of the killing. The classification of offences as felonies has been abolished in Queensland, but s 300 of The Criminal Code makes any 'unlawful killing' a crime, which is either murder or manslaughter, according to the circumstances. By s 291 a killing is unlawful unless it is by law authorised, justified or excused. Section 23 is one source of possible excuse for what would otherwise attract criminal responsibility: *R v Mullen* (1938) 59 CLR 124, 128. That section operates by exempting a person from criminal responsibility for an act or omission which occurs independently of the exercise of his will, or for an event which occurs by accident. See, generally, *Kaporonovski v The Queen* (1973) 133 CLR 209, 226–27. Under s 23 of the Code it is possible therefore, for a killing not to amount to a crime at all; and the same is true where s 27 of the Code applies by reason of incapacity arising from mental disease or natural mental infirmity on the part of the killer.

Since the relevant public policy rule is that a person may not benefit from his criminal act, it follows that it would not extend to cases where the killing is excused etc under the Code. But this is not such a case. The respondent here was convicted of manslaughter by unlawfully killing Mrs Stone. I notice that in the article in the *Law Quarterly Review* Mr Youdan suggests that the true rule is, or should be, whether the killing is intentional, thus excluding cases of manslaughter by negligence; but in Queensland such matters are governed by s 23 of the Code, or by provisions like s 289, which has been held to import an element of recklessness or at least 'blameworthiness'; see *Callaghan v The Queen* (1952) 87 CLR 115; *Evigeniou v The Queen* (1964) 38 ALJR 508. The manslaughter of which the respondent was convicted did not, however, result from the application of either of those provisions but from s 304A, which reduces the unlawful killing from murder to manslaughter on account of diminished responsibility. It differs in its operation from the exculpatory effect of s 27 principally in this; that by s 304A only a 'substantial', as distinct from an entire, impairment of capacity is required. If it be relevant at all, there may be cases in which the impairment is so substantial as to deprive the act of killing of much of its criminality, while yet falling short of complete exculpation under s 27. When such a case arises in the present context, it may have to be considered whether the rule of public policy extends to it. Here Mrs Stone was evidently strangled by the respondent, who was sentenced to imprisonment for 10 years, even if with a recommendation for early parole. Reference may be made to *Re Giles* [1972] Ch 544, which was a case of a diminished responsibility killing to which the public policy rule was applied, without necessarily adopting all the reasoning or even the particular conclusion in that case: cf *Public Trustee v Evans* [1985] 2 NSWLR 188, 192–93.

In the later case Young J considered that public policy permitted him to refuse to exclude a woman from taking by survivorship, or from succeeding on intestacy to the estate of her husband, whose death she had caused in the course of a domestic argument in circumstances described as involving 'a very minor degree of criminality'. On the strength of that authority, a submission was advanced on behalf of the respondent here that he should not be obliged to give up the unit. He has lived in it since 1980; it is within walking distance of his business as a hairdresser; he is 71 years of age; and if forced to vacate he says he will suffer severe hardship in finding alternative accommodation. Even if one adopts the approach taken by Young J in *Public Trustee v Evans*, and accepts that there is a discretion to exclude the rule of public policy, the present case is in my view not an appropriate one for doing so. The circumstances of the killing do not appears in any details from the material before me; but, attracting as they did a sentence of 10 years imprisonment, they cannot be regarded as involving criminality in only 'a very minor degree'. If the balance of hardship is relevant, the respondent's two daughters were at a very early age deprived by the respondent's action of the benefits of home and parental affection. Their maternal aunt was, it appears, obliged to take employment in order to help maintain them, and the respondent has not contributed very much to their upkeep since his release from prison. He claims that since 1980 he has paid the expenses and outgoings associated with the property; but, having killed his joint tenant, he has also had the advantage of sole occupation of the unit since 1980. If a trustee for sale is now appointed and the property is sold, there will, in respect of some of these matters, no doubt be adjustments and allowances to be made in the accounts before a final distribution of the proceeds of sale: see Property Law Act, s 43, and *McMahon v Public Curator of Queensland* [1952] St R Qd 197, 201–02. I can see nothing in the respondent's circumstances to raise any equity in his favour, or to prevent the application of the ordinary rule that he should not be permitted to benefit from his criminal act. It may be added that he appears to have been as much as 28 years older than his wife at the time of her death, so that in the natural course of events she might have been expected to survive him and acquire his interest as joint tenant in the land. The benefit accruing to him through her death is therefore not necessarily an insubstantial one.

I accordingly conclude that, by reason of his having killed Mrs Stone in circumstances amounting to manslaughter, the respondent acquired her interest at law as joint tenant; but that he holds it on trust for the persons entitled under her will ...

Notes

In the case of *Public Trustee v Evans* [1985] 2 NSWLR 188, the Supreme Court of New South Wales held that the courts had a discretion to decide in a particular case whether or not to deny a killer the benefit of the right of survivorship. In that case a wife killed her husband during a domestic violence initiated by the husband. Young J held that because her liability involved a very minor degree of criminality, she was not disentitled to the benefit of survivorship. In England, s 2(2) of the Forfeiture Act 1982 (UK) gives the courts discretionary power to apply the public policy rule.

Question

Mr and Mrs X are registered as joint proprietors of their matrimonial home. Mr X is a heavy drinker and he is notorious for domestic violence against his wife. One day Mr X comes home drunk as usual. Mrs X in anger hits him on the head with a heavy object, which subsequently causes his death. Mrs X is convicted of manslaughter but in view of the extenuating circumstances she is only given a three months suspended sentence. Prior to his death Mr X had mortgaged his interest in the house to C as security for a K20,000 loan which is still outstanding. Mrs X claims that the house is hers as sole owner by right of survivorship. C disputes her claim. Advise C.

(b) Partition

Partition is the physical division of the land amongst the co-owners. Partition determines all forms of co-ownership. See below.

Determination of tenancy in common and joint tenancy

Sale or partition

Tenancy in common terminates where the co-owners sell the land and share the proceeds. Instead of sale, the co-owners might terminate their co-ownership by partition of the land. Registration of the former co-owners as sole owners of their respective portions completes the process.[28] Partition can be by voluntary agreement of all the co-owners. It is thought that the National Court Rules (Ch No 38), give the courts power to order a sale in lieu of partition or in event of disputes amongst the co-owners. Rule 33 provides as follows:

> In proceedings relating to land, other than proceedings for possession of land, the court may, at any stage of the proceedings –
>
> (a) order that the whole or any part of the land be sold; and
>
> (b) order that any party in receipt of the rents or profits of the land or otherwise in possession of the land deliver possession to such person as the court may direct.

Rule 34 sets out the manner of sale.

---

28 *Land Law and Policy in Papua New Guinea, op cit*, note 2, at pp 118–19.

CHAPTER 5

MORTGAGES

I INTRODUCTION

A mere undertaking to repay a loan advanced with interest within a specified period is usually not enough. Most financial creditors require in addition security for repayment. Sometimes a creditor might accept a written guarantee by a third party as sufficient security. However, more often, especially where a substantial amount of money is involved, creditors demand security in the form of property, which in the event of default, they may realise and pay themselves out of the proceeds. There are different types of securities, however, the most common and important is a mortgage of land.

II NATURE AND EFFECT OF MORTGAGE

A mortgage may be one at common law or under a statutory provision, ie, one created under the Land Registration Act ('LRA').[1] The difference between the two is that while a mortgage under the common law is a conveyance of a mortgagor's legal title to the mortgagee with the promise to reconvey, under the LRA, a mortgage creates only a charge on the relevant land. Section 2(1) defines a charge as a 'charge on land created for the purpose of securing the payment of an annuity or sum of money other than a debt'. Section 63 states:

> A mortgage or charge –
>
> (a) charges the estate or interest specified in the instrument with the sum of money, interest, annuity or rent charge intended to be secured by the instrument; and
>
> (b) does not operate as a transfer of the secured estate or interest.

Distinction between common law and statutory mortgage

The distinction between the common law mortgage and the statutory mortgage was explained thus by Cockle CJ, in *Trust & Agency Co v Markwell (No 2)*:[2]

> ... I think we must guard ourselves against attributing to the word 'mortgage' in this Act, a meaning identical with its ordinary one. It cannot indeed have such a meaning, for it is the very essence of a mortgage, properly so called, to involve the transfer of an estate from the mortgagor, who loses the legal title, retaining only an equitable one, to the mortgagee, who takes the legal title subject to the rights of the mortgagor against him. But the machinery provided in this Act for carrying out transactions in the nature of loans involve nothing of the kind, and are based upon a conception of an entirely different kind, for it expressly provides that the mortgage under the Act shall not operate or take effect as a transfer of the

1 Ch No 191.

2 (1874) 4 QSCR 50, at 52. Section 60 of the Queensland Real Property Act 1861 is identical with s 62 of the Land Registration Act.

land, estate, or interest intended thereby to be charged. Therefore, we here see something entirely inconsistent with the supposition that the Legislature intended the mortgage created by the Act to be a dealing of the same kind as a mortgage under the old law.

The main legal consequences of the distinction between a mortgage at common law and under the Land Registration Act, are as follows:

(a) A statutory mortgage of itself does not give the mortgagee an immediate right to possession of the mortgaged property or to the reception of the profits of the land.[3] In contrast, at common law in the absence of an express agreement, the mortgagee (because he has the legal title) has the right to immediate possession whether or not the mortgagor is in default.[4]

(b) Since under the Act the mortgagor retains legal title, he or she has a right to exercise all his or her proprietary rights. For example, he or she may sell, lease (or sub-lease) the land[5] or create secondary legal mortgages. Of course, any dealings with the mortgaged land will be subject to the mortgage.[6] On the other hand, at common law the mortgagor can only create equitable interests until the mortgagee reconveys the legal title to him.

(c) At common law where land is held under joint tenancy and one tenant mortgages his or her interest to a stranger the unity of title is destroyed, and, hence, the jointure is severed.[7] The reason is a statutory mortgage, being merely a charge, does not affect unity of title of the joint tenants.[8]

Nature of the mortgagee's interest

Though a statutory mortgage does not operate to transfer the mortgagor's estate to the mortgagee, it creates a distinct interest in land, which may be assigned (s 66 of the LRA) or otherwise dealt with by the mortgagee apart altogether from the estate mortgaged.[9] The following case illustrates this point.

TESSMANN v COSTELLO [1987] 1 Qd R 283, Supreme Court of Queensland

[The plaintiff and his late wife were the registered owners of certain freehold land. In 1984 the plaintiff mortgaged the land to a company ('A Pty Ltd') as security for a loan advanced to the plaintiff's son, the second named defendant. The mortgage was registered. Subsequently, A Pty Ltd assigned the mortgage to the first named defendant who also had the transfer registered in its name. The plaintiff sought to set aside the mortgage alleging that it was procured as a result of undue influence exerted on the plaintiff and his late wife by the second defendant, or on the ground that the second defendant was guilty of 'unconscionable' conduct in making use of his superior position to the detriment of his parents. To overcome the defence of indefeasibility, counsel for the plaintiff argued that the

3 *Partridge v McIntosh & Sons Ltd* (1933) 49 CLR 453.

4 See *Four-Maids Ltd v Dudley Marshall (Properties) Ltd* [1957] Ch 317.

5 Consent of the mortgagee is necessary otherwise the lease will not bind the mortgagee: s 54(2) of the LRA.

6 See s 33(1)(b) of the LRA.

7 *Lyons v Lyons* (1967) VR 169.

8 *Ibid.*

9 *The English Scottish and Australian Bank Ltd v Phillips* (1937) 57 CLR 302, at 321.

indefeasibility provisions did not apply to a statutory mortgage because a statutory mortgage does not create an interest in land; it is simply a chose in action (a right to sue for a debt). Therefore, he submitted that the first defendants being assignees of a chose in action took subject to any equitable interests or obligations affecting that chose in action immediately before the transfer.]

WILLIAMS J: In order to deal with the plaintiff's contention it is necessary to give some further consideration to the nature of a mortgage under the Torrens system legislation. The relevant provision in the Queensland Act is s 60 which provides: 'Every Bill of Mortgage ... shall be construed and have effect only as a security for the sum of money ... intended to be thereby secured and shall not operate or take effect as a transfer of land, estate or interest intended to be thereby charged with the payment of any money.' The provision in the legislation in other States is to similar effect; a Torrens system mortgage is clearly different from what is colloquially called an 'old system mortgage'. In *Partridge v McIntosh & Sons Ltd* (1933) 49 CLR 453 Dixon J (with whom Rich J agreed) said at 466 (dealing with the New South Wales legislation): 'The statutory mortgage does not upon registration effect a transfer to the mortgagee of an estate in the land, or confer on him an immediate right to possession or to perception of the profits of the land. He has, of course, an interest in the land at law, but it is in the nature of a charge.' Dixon, Evatt and McTiernan JJ (who constituted the majority) dealt with the topic in *The English Scottish and Australian Bank Limited v Phillips* (1937) 57 CLR 302, an appeal concerned with the South Australian legislation. The following extracts from their joint judgment taken from pp 321–24 summarise the position as they saw it under that legislation:

> Under the system of registration governing the present case, the statutory charge described as a mortgage is a distinct interest. It involves no ownership of the land the subject of the security. Like a lease, it is a separate interest in land which may be dealt with apart altogether from the fee simple or other estate or interest mortgaged ... In relation to the present case, the most important consideration arising in this plan is the failure to limit the persons who may deal in the interest created by a mortgage or a lease ... A mortgage under the system is the creature of statute and its incidents depend upon the provisions of the statute and so much of the general law as is availed of by or under those provisions ... It appears to us that the plan of the legislation is to treat mortgages as distinct and persisting interests capable of the same ready transfer by registration as estates in fee simple and without any discrimination or concern as to the relation of the transferee or transferor thereof to any other estate or interest in land.

If further support is needed it is provided by the observation of Dixon and Evatt JJ in *Consolidated Trust Company Limited v Naylor* (1936) 55 CLR 423, another decision on the New South Wales legislation. At 434 they said: 'The statute is concerned with dealings in land and it is because a mortgage involves such a dealing that the statute prescribes how mortgages may be transferred and with what consequences.' In each of those cases at some point the members of the court had to consider the equivalent of Queensland s 65 which expressly provides for the transfer of a mortgage; so far as is relevant it provides: 'A registered mortgage ... may be transferred to any person by memorandum of transfer ... and upon such memorandum of transfer ... being registered the estate or interest of the transferor as set forth in such instrument with all rights powers and privileges thereto belonging or appertaining shall pass to the transferee and such transferee shall thereupon become subject to and liable for all and every the same requirements and liabilities to which he would have been subject and liable if named in such instrument originally as mortgagee ...'. The passage from the judgments I have quoted clearly indicate to me that the 'estate or interest' of the transferor of a registered mortgage is an 'interest in land'.

> I have not been able to find any decision which has applied the reasoning of Macnaughton AJ in *Conroy v Knox* (*supra*) in question. Counsel for the plaintiff sought to gain some comfort from the fact that Gibbs J (sitting as a member of the Full Court of this court) referred to the judgment of Macnaughton AJ on two occasions in the course of delivering his reasons in *Friedman v Barrett ex p Friedman* [1962] Qd R 498, but on each occasion the reference was to another part of that judgment; I can find nothing in the reasoning of Gibbs J which would give the least support to the proposition advanced by counsel for the plaintiff.
>
> I have no hesitation in concluding that the statement by Macnaughton AJ that a mortgagee under the Torrens system is not the holder of some estate or interest in land cannot stand in the face of subsequent decisions of the High Court; in my view his statement was wrong and I am not burdened by it as a precedent because, as I have said, it cannot stand against authoritative statements of higher courts.
>
> It follows that ss 44 and 109 of the 1861 Act are relevant to the resolution of the present problem (particularly the former), and if the mortgage was voidable against the original mortgagee, the title of the first defendants acquired by the registration of the transfer of the mortgage to them, is indefeasible, and their title and interest cannot now be challenged by the plaintiff ...

III CREATION OF MORTGAGE

Registered mortgage

Section 62 of the LRA empowers a registered proprietor to create a mortgage in the prescribed form. It provides:

> Creation of mortgage or charge
>
> (1) Where an estate or interest is intended to be made security in favour of a mortgagee the proprietor shall execute a mortgage in the prescribed form.
>
> (2) Where an estate or interest is intended to be made security for the payment of an annuity, rent charge or sum of money in favour of a chargee the proprietor shall execute a charge in the prescribed form.

The prescribed form is Form 8, Sched 1, Land Registration Regulations. Upon registration of the mortgage instrument, the land becomes liable as security (s 26(1)(b) of the LRA). A registered mortgage is sometimes referred to as a 'legal' mortgage and the unregistered an 'equitable' mortgage.

Equitable or unregistered mortgage

An unregistered instrument purporting to create an interest in land is not effective to create an estate or interest in land until it is registered (s 17(1) of the LRA). However, in equity an agreement to create a mortgage is enforceable as an equitable mortgage, if the agreement is evidenced by a written memorandum or is accompanied with sufficient acts of part performance.[10] Section 81 of the LRA specifically recognises the creation of an equitable mortgage by way of deposit of a certificate of title. It reads:

> Equitable mortgages
>
> (1) An equitable mortgage or lien may, by deposit of the instrument of title, be created in respect of –
>
> (a) a security on an estate or interest; or
>
> (b) an instrument affecting an estate or interest.
>
> (2) An equitable mortgagee may lodge a caveat forbidding dealings with the estate, interest or security except dealings subject to the mortgage or lien.
>
> (3) A caveat under sub-section (2) shall state the amount and nature of the charge or lien.

Although the Act only mentions equitable mortgages created by way of deposit of the certificate of title, it does not necessarily mean that it is the only way an equitable mortgage can arise over registered land.[11]

Questions

1 A mortgage creates an interest in land. What does 'interest' in land mean? How does this interest differ from leasehold?

2 What interests in land may be mortgaged? Can customary land be mortgaged? What about converted freehold land?

3 What are the advantages and disadvantages of an unregistered mortgage over a registered mortgage?

4 Ten years ago, X deposited his certificate of title with the ABC Bank for safe-keeping. X's cheque account is overdrawn by K10,000. Recently X entered into a contract to sell his land to Y. The ABC Bank claims that it has an equitable mortgage over the land and has lodged a caveat to prevent any dealings with the land except those subject to its 'equitable mortgage'. Advise Y. (See *Norris v Wilkinson* (1805) 12 Ves 192; 33 ER 73.)

IV RIGHTS AND REMEDIES OF A MORTGAGEE

The remedies of the mortgagee are: action on personal covenant to repay, possession, appointment of a receiver and sale. These remedies are not exclusive; they are cumulative.[12] The relevant cases on these rights are extracted below.

---

10 *Re Leathes ex p Leathes* (1883) 3 Deac & Ch 112.

11 Sykes and Walker, *The Law of Securities* (5th edn, Lawbook Co, Sydney, 1993), at p 316. The National Court retains its jurisdiction to enforce equitable rights, see s 108, LRA.

12 For discussion of these remedies, see HA Amankwah and JT Mugambwa (with G Muroa), *Land Law in Papua New Guinea* (Lawbook Co, Sydney, 2001), at pp 175–99.

Foreclosure

At common law once the mortgagor failed to pay the secured debt by the due date, the property became the mortgagee's absolutely irrespective of any gross difference in value between the balance of money owed and the value of the mortgaged land.[13] Equity, however, regarded a mortgage as a mere security for a debt and the mortgagor as the true owner of the land even though the legal title was with the mortgagee. On this basis, the Court of Equity interfered in the bargain between the mortgagee and the mortgagor and allowed the latter to redeem (pay off the mortgage) even though the date fixed for repayment was long past.[14] Time came when the Court of Equity prevented the mortgagor from recovering his or her loan and declared the mortgagee as absolute owner both at law and in equity. At that stage, it was said that the mortgagee had 'foreclosed' the mortgagor's right to redeem.

Thus, foreclosure may be defined as:

> ... the process whereby the mortgagor's equitable right to redeem was declared by the court to be extinguished and the mortgagee was left owner of the property both at law and in equity. Equity had interfered to prevent the conveyance by way of mortgage from having its full effect; but there had to be some final point at which the mortgagee could enforce his security, and therefore by foreclosure 'the court simply removes the stop it has itself put on'.[15]

The mortgagee's remedy of foreclosure is expressly recognised under the Land Registration Act. Section 74(3) provides:

> A creditor is entitled by action or other proceedings in the court to foreclose the right of the debtor to redeem the mortgage or charged land.

From this provision, it is clear that a mortgagee cannot enforce the foreclosure remedy outside the court. In the case extracted below, Lalor J prescribes the procedure for enforcing a foreclosure in the National Court. Though this case was based on the Land Registration Act (New Guinea) 1924, which was repealed and replaced by the present Act, in the absence of any other local authority, it is submitted that the procedure stipulated by Lalor J is still current.

BOOIJ BROS PTY LTD v BMH CO PTY LTD (1974) unreported judgment N795, Supreme Court of Justice

> **LALOR J**: This is an application made on originating summons on behalf of the Plaintiff, who is also the mortgagee, that an account may be taken of what is due to the mortgagee in respect of principal, interests and costs under a mortgage and for its taxed costs of this summons; and for an order that, in default of the mortgagor paying to the mortgagee the amount so found to be due by a short date to be named for that purpose, the mortgagor shall stand absolutely debarred and foreclosed from his right, interest and equity of redemption of in or to the land tenements and hereditaments comprised in the said mortgage.

13 *G and C Kreglinger v New Patagonia Meat and Cold Storage Co Ltd* [1914] AC 25, at 35.

14 See 32 *Halsbury's Laws of England* (4th edn), para 407. Also *Campbell v Holyland* (1877) 7 Ch D 166.

15 Harpum C, with Grant M and Bridge S, *Megarry and Wade: The Law of Real Property* (6th edn, Sweet & Maxwell, London, 2000), at pp 1187–88.

The foreclosure sought is the statutory foreclosure under s 113(2) of the Lands Registration Act 1924 (New Guinea). Cf Real Property Act 1861, s 60 (Queensland); Real Property Act 1913, s 52 (Papua).

From the affidavit filed it appears that the defendant company is the mortgagor and has since gone into liquidation.

It would appear that the summons has been taken out under Order 19 Rule 1.

There appear to be two difficulties with regard to the present procedure. Firstly, an application for an account under Order 19 Rule 1 presupposes that a writ of summons has been issued and endorsed with a claim for an account and further that either an appearance has been entered or the time for entering an appearance has expired.

Secondly, the order sought is for an order of foreclosure at the same time as taking the account. In *Riggall v Muirhead and Others* (1911) 13 CLR 436, the High Court held that an order could not be made for an account and a foreclosure under similar High Court Rules. Under the Rules of this court Order 19 Rule 4 does give a specific right to obtain an order of foreclosure after account has been taken. Rule 4 provides that in an action in which an account has been taken and in any action in which the writ has been specially endorsed under the provisions of Order 6 Rule 11 the plaintiff may at any time after appearance apply to the court for judgment in a summary way without pleadings and the court shall thereupon proceed to hear and determine the action and to give such judgment as may be just. Order 6 Rule 11 provides for a special endorsement for foreclosure.

It would appear then, that the proper procedure to obtain an account and an order for foreclosure is for a specially endorsed writ to be issued with the mortgagee as plaintiff and the mortgagor as defendant on which a claim for an account and a claim for foreclosure are specially endorsed (Order 6 Rules 9 and 11).

After the time for appearance a summons may then be taken out for an account (Order 19 Rule 1).

Following the taking of the account a summons may then be made under Order 19 Rule 4 for foreclosure (Order 19 Rule 4).

The orders which may be sought on the summons and which will be given on the judgment nisi are set out in (1951) QWN 44. They are:

1 A declaration as to the amount owing under the mortgage the amount being made up of so much principal, interest, fees and costs.

2 An order that the defendant pay to the plaintiff his costs of and incidental to the motion and the action to be taxed.

3 A further order that upon the defendant paying to the plaintiff the amount found to be due under the mortgage and taxed costs as aforesaid the plaintiff shall, at the cost of the defendant, release the said land clear and free from any encumbrances done by the plaintiff or any person claiming by, from or under him.

4 A further order that in default of the defendant paying to the plaintiff the sum of the amount due under the mortgage plus interest to date together with costs the defendant is henceforth absolutely debarred and foreclosed of and from all the right, title interest and equity of redemption of, in or to the said mortgaged property.

5 A further order that the defendant do deliver forthwith to the plaintiff possession of the said land.

6 A further order that the defendant do transfer and convey to the plaintiff his estate and interest in the said land. (See (1952) QWN 13.)

7 A further order that the defendant do forthwith deliver up to the plaintiff possession of the said land.

8 A further order liberty to apply.

As to the time in which the defendant should be limited to pay the amount of money due to the plaintiff two orders can be made. The first, the short period, is for three months, or the ordinary period which is six months. In default of special circumstances the period would be six months. (See Daniell's *Chancery Practice*, 8th edn, Vol II, p 1221 *et seq*.)

I order that this matter be stood over generally.

Effect of foreclosure

A foreclosure order made absolute has the following consequences.

(a) Title vests in the mortgagee

The effect of a foreclosure order is to force the mortgagor to transfer his or her title to the mortgagee in satisfaction of the mortgagee's claims. The transaction is completed by registration of the mortgagee as the proprietor. It should be noted that the foreclosure order does not of itself entitle the mortgagee to be registered as proprietor of the mortgaged land.[16] Registration of the mortgagee can only be effected either by an instrument of transfer appropriately signed by the mortgagor or by registration of a vesting order as provided under s 111 of the Land Registration Act, which reads:

(1) Where the court makes an order to the effect that an estate, interest or security shall vest in a person, the Registrar shall, on being served with an office copy of the order –

(a) register the order; and

(b) issue all certificates of title and other instruments which are necessary to give full effect to the order.

(2) On registration under sub-section (1) –

(a) the order operates to transfer or otherwise vest the estate, interest or security; and

(b) the person named in the order as the person in whom the estate, interest or security is to vest becomes the registered proprietor of that estate, interest or security.

(b) Redeem up, foreclose down

A foreclosure order extinguishes the applicant's mortgage and all other mortgages, if any, which were created subsequent to it, automatically lapse and are removed from the register.[17] For example, if the property is subject to three separate registered mortgages: A, B and C, in that order of priority, and B is granted a foreclosure order, C's security will automatically lapse. For this reason, as a rule of practice, all subsequent mortgagees to the

16 *Stevens v Hoberg* (No 2) [1952] QWN 13.

17 *Fink v Robertson* (1907) 4 CLR 864, at 877 and 880.

applicant joined as parties to the proceedings to give them a chance to contest the application or seek a judicial sale in lieu of foreclosure.[18] On the other hand, A's mortgage, because it is ranked higher in priority than that of B, will not be affected by the foreclosure order and will be endorsed on the certificate of title issued to B.[19] Hence, the maxim 'you redeem up and foreclose down'.

(c) Re-opening the foreclosure

We have seen that once a foreclosure was made absolute the Court of Equity closed its doors to the mortgagor. Nevertheless, the doors were not completely closed because in certain circumstances the court allowed the mortgagor to redeem even after a foreclosure was made absolute. This was called 're-opening a foreclosure'. The following case is a classic illustration of the rule.

CAMPBELL v HOLYLAND (1877) 7 Ch D 166

JESSEL MR: The question in dispute is really whether a mortgagor can be allowed to redeem after an order of foreclosure absolute, and I think, on looking at the authorities, that no Chancellor or Vice Chancellor has ever laid down that any special circumstances are essential to enable a mortgagor to redeem in such a case.

Now what is the principle? The principle in a Court of Equity has always been that, though a mortgage is in form an absolute conveyance when the condition is broken, in equity it is always security; and it must be remembered that the doctrine arose at the time when mortgages were made in the form of conditional conveyance, the condition being that if the money was not paid at the day, the estate should become the estate of the mortgagee; that was the contract between the parties; yet Courts of Equity interfered with actual contract to this extent, by saying there was a paramount intention that the estate should be security, and that the mortgage money should be debt; and they gave relief in the shape of redemption on that principle. Of course that would lead, and did lead, to this inconvenience, that even when the mortgagor was not willing to redeem, the mortgagee would not sell or deal with the estate as his own, and to remedy that inconvenience the practice of bringing a foreclosure suit was adopted, by which a mortgagee was entitled to call on the mortgagor to redeem within a certain time, under penalty of losing the right of redemption. In that foreclosure suit the court made various orders – interim orders fixing a time for payment of the money – and at last there came the final order which was called foreclosure absolute, that is, in form, that the mortgagor should not be allowed to redeem at all; but it was form only, just as the original deed was form only; for the Courts of Equity soon decided that, notwithstanding the form of that order, they would after that order allow the mortgagor to redeem. That is, although the order of foreclosure absolute appeared to be a final order of the court, it was not so, but the mortgagee still remained liable to be treated as mortgagee and the mortgagor still retained a claim to be treated as mortgagor, subject to the discretion of the court. Therefore everybody who took an order for foreclosure absolute knew that there was still a discretion in the court to allow the mortgagor to redeem.

Under what circumstances that discretion should be exercised is quite another matter. The mortgagee had a right to deal with an estate acquired under foreclosure absolute the day

18 *Tylee v Webb* (1843) 6 Beav 552; 49 ER 939. See also PB Fairest, *Mortgages* (2nd edn, Sweet & Maxwell, London, 1980), at p 103.

19 *Fink v Robertson*, *supra*, note 17, at 877.

after he acquired it; but he knew perfectly well that there might be circumstances to entitle the mortgagor to redeem, and everybody buying the estate from a mortgagee who merely acquired a title under such an order was considered to have the same knowledge, namely, that the estate might be taken away from him by the exercise, not of a capricious discretion, but of a judicial discretion by the Court of Equity which had made the order.

That being so, on what terms is that judicial discretion to be exercised? It has been said by the highest authority that it is impossible to say *a priori* what are the terms. They must depend upon the circumstances of each case ... There are certain things laid down which are intelligible to everybody. In the first place the mortgagor must come, as it is said, promptly; that is, within a reasonable time. He is not to let the mortgagee deal with the estate as his own – if it is a landed estate, the mortgagee being in possession of it and using it – and then without any special reason come and say: 'Now I will redeem.' He cannot do that; he must come within a reasonable time. What is a reasonable time? You must have regard to the nature of the property. As has been stated in more than one of the cases, where the estate is an estate in land in possession – where the mortgagee takes it in possession and deals with it and alters the property, and so on – the mortgagor must come much more quickly than where it is an estate in reversion, as to which the mortgagee can do nothing except sell it. So that you must have regard to the nature of the estate in ascertaining what is to be considered reasonable time.

Then, again, was the mortgagee entitled to redeem, but by some accident unable to redeem? Did he expect to get the money from a quarter from which he might reasonably hope to obtain it, and was he disappointed at the last moment? Was it a very large sum, and did he require a considerable time to raise it elsewhere? All those things must be considered in determining what is a reasonable time.

Then an element for consideration has always been the nature of the property as regards value. For instance, if an estate were worth £50,000, and had been foreclosed for a mortgage debt of £5,000, the man who came to redeem that estate would have a longer time than where the estate was worth £5,100, and he was foreclosed for £5,000. But not only is there money value, but there may be other considerations. It may be an old family estate or a chattel, or picture, which possesses a special value for the mortgagor, but which possesses not the same value for other people; or it may be, as has happened in this instance, that the property, though a reversionary interest in the funds, is of special value to both the litigants: it may possess not merely a positive money value, but a peculiar value having regard to the nature of the title and other incidents, so that you cannot set an actual money value upon it. In fact, that is the real history of this contest, for the property does not appear to be of much more money value – though it is of some more – than the original amount of the mortgage. All this must be taken into consideration.

Then it is said you must not interfere against purchasers. As I have already explained, there are purchasers and purchasers. If the purchaser buys a freehold estate in possession after the lapse of a considerable time from the order of foreclosure absolute, with no notice of any extraneous circumstances which would induce the court to interfere, I for one should decline to interfere with such a title as that; but if the purchaser bought the estate within 24 hours after the foreclosure absolute, and with notice of the fact that it was of much greater value than the amount of the mortgage debt, is it to be supposed that a Court of Equity would listen to the contention of such a purchaser that he ought not to be interfered with? He must be taken to know the general law that an order for foreclosure may be opened under proper circumstances and under a proper exercise of discretion by the court; and if the mortgagor in that case came the week after, is it to be supposed a Court of Equity would so stultify itself as to say that a title so acquired would stand in the way? I am of opinion it would not.

Now I come to the circumstances of this case, and I must say they are very strong in favour of opening the foreclosure ... I entirely agree with the various authorities which have been quoted, that reasonable promptness ought always to be shewn. I say reasonable promptness, because what is promptness is, as I have said, not an abstract proposition, but must depend on the circumstances of the case. I think the mortgagor has been sufficiently prompt. I think the purchaser is not in a position to terrorize the court as to the evils that would happen by opening a foreclosure after sale. As I said before, I by no means say that the fact of a sale would not be an important fact; it ought to weigh with the court in opening foreclosure.

I am of opinion, however, that such a sale as this ought to have no weight whatever, and that under the circumstances the mortgagor is entitled to open the foreclosure on the usual terms, that is, on payment of principal, interest, and costs.

(d) Action on a personal covenant

We have seen that after a mortgage sale the mortgagee may sue the mortgagor on a personal covenant for the balance of the money, if any, owed him. Can a similar right be exercised after a foreclosure order is made absolute if the value of the land happens to be less than the mortgaged debt? This was one of the issues raised in *Fink v Robertson*,[20] extracted below.

FINK v ROBERTSON AND ANOTHER (1907) 4 CLR 864, High Court of Australia

[By an instrument of mortgage under the provisions of the Transfer of Land Act 1890 (Victoria), Catherine Fink mortgaged certain land of which she was the registered proprietor, to one James Robertson to secure payment of a sum of £17,000 with interest. The mortgage instrument was duly registered. The mortgagor having defaulted in the payment of the mortgaged debt, the mortgagee, after due compliance with the provisions of the Act, procured an order for foreclosure which was duly entered in the Register Book and a certificate of title to the mortgaged property was issued to him. Subsequently an action was brought by the executors of the mortgagee against Catherine Fink to recover the principle sum of £17,000 together with interest. The defendant contended that by reason of the order of foreclosure procured by James Robertson, and of the registration of him as proprietor of the land under the Transfer of Land Act 1890, the mortgage and any obligations thereunder ceased to be of any operation, and the defendant ceased to be liable in respect of the provisions for payment contained in the mortgage. The Supreme Court of Victoria held in favour of the plaintiffs. The defendant appealed to the High Court.

The judgment of Griffith CJ, Barton and O'Connor JJ, was read by Griffith CJ.]

GRIFFITH CJ: Sections 129 and 130 deal with the right now particularly in question. [Section 129 prescribes a special procedure which must be followed for foreclosure.] Section 130 then proceeds: 'Every such order for foreclosure under the hand of the Registrar when entered in the register book shall have the effect of vesting in the mortgagee or his

20 For discussion of this case, see Sykes and Walker, *Law of Securities*, *op cit*, note 11, at pp 291–92.

transferee the land mentioned in such order, free from all right and equity of redemption on the part of the mortgagor or of any person claiming through or under him subsequently to the mortgage: and such mortgagee or his transferee shall upon such entry being made be deemed a transferee of the mortgaged land, and become the proprietor thereof, and be entitled to receive a certificate of title to the same.'

In our opinion the title of the mortgagee, when so registered as proprietor, is absolute and unimpeachable except on the ground of fraud. This is the plain meaning of the words of ss 74 and 130 when read together. We entirely concur in the reasoning of Faucett J in the case of *Campbell v Bank of New South Wales* [16 NSWLR (Eq) 285], whose judgment, after being reversed by the Full Court of New South Wales, was restored by the Privy Council [11 AC 192], who, however, decided the case on another ground and expressed no opinion on this point. Besides the reasons given by that learned judge there is a further reason: if such an action could be brought, it would, in a case in which there were subsequent incumbrances, involve the re-opening of the register and its restoration to its original condition. Such a proceeding is, we think, wholly inconsistent with the scheme of the Act, and the court has no jurisdiction to order it.

But, except so far as regards the exclusion of the asserted jurisdiction of Courts of Equity to re-open a foreclosure in any case in which it might be just to do so (see *Campbell v Holyland*) [(1877) 7 Ch D 166], there is no necessary inconsistency between the old law and the new, so far as regards the mere effect of the order of foreclosure. If, notwithstanding such an order under the Act, the mortgagee can still sue on his covenant, we have no doubt that the court would not allow him to recover the whole debt by execution unless he is both able and willing to restore the land on payment, nor in any event to issue execution for the whole debt and also retain the land. But this does not dispose of the question whether an action on the covenant will lie after foreclosure. The reasoning on each side involves a fallacy: thus: 'At common law a mortgagee could sue on his covenant after foreclosure, but a Court of Equity would impose conditions upon him: Under the Act, if a mortgagee can sue on his covenant after foreclosure the court will in a proper case impose conditions: therefore there is no reason why he should not sue on the covenant.' Such is the argument on one side. On the other side it is said: 'The court cannot impose the same conditions as before: therefore the action will no longer lie.' The only legitimate conclusion that can be drawn from the premises is that the right to sue on the covenant is not conclusively negatived by the mere circumstance that the mortgagor is no longer entitled to have the foreclosure opened on any other ground than fraud. But this leaves the question whether the continuance of the right to sue is consistent with the provisions of the Act entirely untouched.

We agree that in considering this question regard must be had to the law as it existed before the Act. Now, it was a settled rule that the assignee of an equity of redemption was, in the absence of agreement to the contrary, bound to indemnify the mortgagor against the mortgage debt ... *Dodson v Downey* [[1901] 2 Ch 620]. This obligation was generally regarded as arising from an implied contract. It followed from this doctrine, and also from the doctrine that, when land and a charge upon it are vested in the same person in the same right, the charge is extinguished unless a contrary intention is shown, that if the mortgagor assigned his equity of redemption to the mortgagee simpliciter, the mortgage debt became extinguished so far as it was created by and enforceable under the mortgage deed, for, as Buckley J said: 'A man cannot be the assignee of his own debt and cannot be mortgagee of property of which he is also mortgagor': *Re George Routledge & Sons Ltd; Hummel v George Routledge & Sons Ltd* [[1904] 2 Ch 474]; although, if by other agreement between the parties it appeared that it was intended to keep the charge alive, effect would be given to that intention. (See *per* Cozens-Hardy LJ in *Capital and Counties Bank Ltd v Rhodes* [1903] 1 Ch 631, pp 652–53.)

Bearing this rule of law in mind, and regarding it as still in force except so far as it is inconsistent with the provisions of the Act, we proceed to consider the relevant provisions. It follows from the provisions of s 95 ... that if a mortgagor transfers the mortgaged land to the mortgagee the mortgage is extinguished. The Act does not make express provision to that effect, for it was obviously unnecessary to do so. But the mortgagee would, of course, in such a case be entitled to a certificate of title subject only to incumbrances created by the mortgagor in favour of other persons ... By s 188 provision is made for obtaining a vesting order under the Trustee Act in respect of land subject to the Act, and it is enacted that upon entry in the register book of an order vesting the land in any person, such person 'shall become the transferee and be deemed to be the proprietor thereof' ... Section 230 is as follows: 'Without lessening or prejudicing any of the other rights powers and remedies hereby given and conferred, every proprietor and every transferee when registered of any land lease mortgage or charge shall whilst continuing so registered have the same estates rights powers and remedies and be subject to the same engagements obligations and liabilities and may sue and be sued in his own name at law and in equity in respect thereof or thereupon, in like manner as if he had been the original proprietor of the land by or with whom the engagement obligation or liability sued upon was entered into or incurred, or the original lessee mortgagee or annuitant.'

We are unable to see any reason for limiting the plain meaning of the words 'shall be deemed to be the transferee' (s 188) or the words 'shall have the same estates ... and be subject to the same engagements obligations and liabilities' (s 230), at any rate as between the person from whom the estate is transferred and the person who becomes the transferee or proprietor. We are of opinion that when the Statute says in express terms that a person with respect to whom certain facts can be predicted shall be deemed to be the transferee of land the meaning is that he shall be the transferee to the same intent and with the same consequences as if he had become a transferee by registration of an instrument called an instrument of transfer, and executed by the person whose interest is transferred.

... It is not suggested that a person registered as proprietor upon purchase from a mortgagor is not a transferee in the ordinary sense of the term, and we are unable to see any intelligible distinction between his case and that of a mortgagee becoming transferee by virtue of an order for foreclosure.

Nor is any hardship involved in this construction, for the exercise by the mortgagee of his rights under s 130 is entirely optional on his part. If he desires to escape the obligations of a transferee, and to keep the mortgage alive, he can do so under the other provisions in his favour.

In our opinion the effect of s 230 is that, when a person voluntarily takes advantage of the provisions of the Act to become a transferee of land, he undertakes, upon becoming transferee, all the obligations attached to the ownership of the land in the hands of the person from whom it is transferred, and mortgage is such an obligation, at least as between him and the person from whom the land is transferred.

We think, therefore, that, when a mortgagee becomes transferee of the mortgaged land under an order for foreclosure, the same consequences follow as if he had taken a transfer from the mortgagor under the provisions of s 95. It follows that, as the mortgagor would be entitled to be indemnified by the mortgagee from any claims under the mortgage, the latter cannot enforce it by action against the former. The further rule that when property and the benefit of a charge upon it are vested in the same person the charge is extinguished unless a contrary intention is shown, which may be called a rule of common sense, would also of itself dispose of the question. So far from finding any such contrary intention in the Act, to which alone in the absence of express agreement reference must be made, we find an intention plainly expressed in conformity with the general rule ...

... Suppose, for a moment, that an action on the express or implied covenants in the mortgage is not taken away, and that the court if such an action is brought can impose terms on the mortgagee plaintiff. In such an event what terms would do justice as between the parties? The court could, no doubt, order the plaintiff to transfer the land to the defendant on payment of the mortgage debt and interest. But the defendant may be unwilling to take it or to pay the necessary amount. He has by the mortgagee's election been deprived of the land and of all right to obtain it, and it would be impossible to put him in the same position as if the mortgagee had elected to take advantage of some other provision of the Act in his favour. It is a general rule that when a party is entitled to elect between two inconsistent rights against another, and has done so, he cannot afterwards alter his election without the consent of the other party ...

Again, if the court could require the mortgagor to pay the debt and to accept a transfer of the land, this would not do justice in the case of puisne mortgages which could not be restored to the register. And, if the mortgagor could not pay all the debt, it would be obviously unjust to allow the mortgagee to levy the whole debt by execution without giving credit for an amount equal to the value of that which he has already. Since, then, credit must be given for some sum, how is that sum to be arrived at? If credit is to be given for a sum equal to the value of the land at the date of the foreclosure, the mortgagee might, if the property has risen in value, have a property worth much more than the amount of the debt, and would still be entitled to recover a portion of the debt in addition. If credit is to be given for a sum equal to the value of the land at the date of the action, then, if the property has fallen in value, the mortgagor would be prejudiced by the mortgagee's delay. A third measure of value might indeed, be suggested – the highest value of the land between the date of the foreclosure and the date of the action. Or the court might direct the land to be sold, and the proceeds applied in payment. There is no decided case, and no principle has been cited, which offers a solution of these difficulties, and we see no satisfactory solution ...

If, therefore, there were no more in the Act, than the provisions enabling a mortgagee to obtain an order for foreclosure we should be strongly disposed to hold that, even without the other express provisions on which we rest our judgment, the same consequences would follow.

It was suggested that it would be a strange consequence of a mortgagee obtaining an order of foreclosure in respect of land of comparatively small value were thereby to debar himself from recovering any part of the mortgage debt, which might be much greater than the value of the land. We agree that it would be a very foolish thing for a mortgagee to obtain an order of foreclosure in such a case, unless he was anxious for other reasons to become the owner of the land. But the circumstance that a statutory power may be unwisely used by the donee does not in our opinion afford any reason for cutting down the plain provisions of the Statute.

Appeal allowed.

[The dissenting judgment of Higgins J is omitted.]

Sale in lieu of foreclosure

In England and Australia, the courts have statutory power to order the land to be sold in lieu of foreclosure.[21] There is no such express provision in the Land Registration Act. Nor is there such a power under the underlying law.[22] However, under the National Court Rules 1983, Order 14, the National Court has a general power in proceedings relating to land, at any stage of the proceedings, to order that the subject land or part thereof be sold. Although the rules do not specifically mention foreclosure proceedings, it is thought that the court may use this power to order a sale in lieu of a foreclosure where justice demands. The Rules provide as follows:

> 32 Interpretation (30/1)
>
> In this Division 'land' includes any interest in or right over land.
>
> 33 Power to order sale (30/2)
>
> In proceedings relating to land, other than proceedings for possession of land, the court may, at any stage of the proceedings –
>
> (a) order that the whole or any part of the land be sold; and
>
> (b) order that any party in receipt of the rents or profits of the land or otherwise in possession of the land deliver possession to such person as the court may direct.
>
> 34 Manner of sale (30/3)
>
> (1) This Rule applies where the court has made an order under Rule 33 of this Order that land be sold.
>
> (2) The court may appoint a party or other person to have the conduct of the sale.
>
> (3) The court may permit the person having the conduct of the sale to sell the land in such manner as he thinks fit.
>
> (4) The court may direct any party to join in the sale and conveyance or transfer or in any other matter relating to the sale.
>
> (5) The court may give such further directions as it thinks fit for the purpose of effecting the sale, including directions –
>
> (a) fixing the manner of sale, that is to say, whether the sale is to be by contract conditional on approval of the court, by private treaty, by public auction, by tender, or by some other manner; or
>
> (b) fixing a reserve or minimum price; or
>
> (c) requiring payment of the purchase money into court or to trustees or other persons; or
>
> (d) for settling the particulars and conditions of sale; or
>
> (e) for obtaining evidence of value; or
>
> (f) fixing the remuneration to be allowed to any auctioneer, real estate agent or other person.

---

21 See, eg, s 91, Law of Property Act 1925 (England); s 99(2) Property Law Act 1974–90 (Queensland).

22 32 *Halsbury's Laws of England* (4th edn) para 848.

Questions

1 Under what circumstances would you advise a financial institution to seek a remedy of foreclosure in preference to other remedies? What are the main advantages and disadvantages of a foreclosure remedy?

2 Taka in serious financial difficulties mortgages his State lease to Peta as security for a K10,000 loan. It is agreed that if the money and interest of 30% per annum is not repaid within two years, Peta would immediately become the proprietor of the lease. The mortgage is duly registered. After two years Taka still owes K8,000. Peta declares the lease his as per the mortgage agreement and demands Taka to hand over possession. The land's current value is K20,000. Advise Taka.

3 Y mortgages his house to XZ Bank. When he defaults in payment of his monthly instalments, XZ successfully applies for a foreclosure order, which, subsequently, is made absolute. Y is now in a position to pay the mortgage debt and wants to redeem, but the bank refuses to let him. What are Y's chances of success in a legal action against the bank? Would it make a difference if the bank has already been registered as the proprietor of the subject land?

4 W after successfully applying for a foreclosure absolute discovers that the land's value is far less than the mortgage date. What other remedies, if any, are available to W?

Possession

The power to take possession of the mortgaged property is another remedy available to the mortgagee.[23] Section 74 of the Land Registration Act provides as follows:

> (1) Where default is made in payment of any secured money, a creditor may –
>
> (a) enter into possession of the mortgaged or charged land by receiving the rents and profits of the land; or
>
> (b) distrain on the occupier or tenant of the land under the power to distrain conferred by section 75; or
>
> (c) bring an action of ejectment to obtain possession of the land.
>
> (2) The creditor may bring an action under sub-section (1)(c)
>
> before or after exercising a remedy –
>
> (a) referred to in this section; or
>
> (b) conferred by section 68.
>
> (3) A creditor is entitled by action or other proceedings in the court to foreclose the right of the debtor to redeem the mortgaged or charged land.

23 Under the Torrens system mortgage, the mortgagor retains title and possession of the mortgaged land until he defaults.

Section 75 of the LRA gives the mortgagee in possession power to distrain and sell goods of any occupant of the premises. The limits of these powers as against the occupant should be carefully noted.[24]

Section 75 Power of distraint

(1) Where –

(a) any secured money has been in arrears for 21 days; and

(b) the creditor has made written application to the occupier or tenant of that land for payment of the money,

the creditor may, in addition to his other remedies –

(c) subject to sub-section (2), enter on the land subject to the mortgage or charge and distrain and sell the goods and chattels of the occupier or tenant; and

(d) detain out of the proceeds of that sale the money in arrears and all costs and expenses occasioned by the distress and sale.

(2) An occupier or tenant referred to in sub-section (1) shall not be liable to pay to the creditor a sum greater than the amount of rent which at the time of making the distress is due from him to the debtor or to the person claiming the land under the debtor.

(3) An amount paid by the occupier or tenant to the creditor on written application or realized by distress under this section is, to that extent, a satisfaction of the rent.

Liability of a mortgagee in possession

Assumption of possession entails the imposition of certain statutory and common law duties on the mortgagee. For example, under s 76 of the LRA, a mortgagee who in exercise of his power enters into possession of leased property is liable to the lessor to the same extent as the lessee (mortgagor). The section provides:

A creditor of a leasehold estate (in this section called 'the land') or a person claiming through the creditor becomes, on entering into possession of the land or the rents and profits of the land, liable to the lessor of the land for –

(a) the payment of rent; and

(b) the performance and observance of the covenants contained in the lease or implied under this Act,

to the same extent as the lessee or tenant was liable.

Perhaps, the most onerous obligation of a mortgagee who enters into possession is to account strictly not only for the profits received but also for profits, which he or she ought to have received but for his or her wilful default. The following case deals this principle.

24 In *White v Metcalf* [1903] 2 Ch 567, at 570, Kekewich J said that though for many purposes there is no difference between taking physical possession and possession by collecting rent, they are entirely different things. One of the differences is that a mortgagee who takes possession by collection of rent and profits cannot execute repairs on account of the mortgagor.

WHITE v CITY OF LONDON BREWERY COMPANY (1889) 42 Ch D 237, Court of Appeal

[The plaintiffs owned a public house, and having no money with which to carry on the business, mortgaged the premises to the defendants, a brewing company. When the plaintiffs defaulted the defendants entered into possession. At first the premises were occupied by the defendants' servants (because there were no tenants), but later they were able to let the premises to a tenant who carried on the business of a publican. Under the lease agreement with the defendants the tenant was required to sell only beer brewed by the defendants. For a period of 10 years the defendants kept possession. Subsequently, the defendants exercised their power of sale and sold the premises. Out of the proceeds they paid themselves what was due under the mortgage and the expenses they incurred on account of their being in possession and in selling the premises. The surplus of the money they paid over to a secondary mortgagee. The plaintiff had no complaints against the sale, but alleged that because the lease tied the tenant to take his supplies of beer only from the defendant company, the premises were let for a rent less than that which they might have got if there had been no stipulation to take beer from the defendants. Secondly, he claimed that they made profits on the beer they supplied to the tenant which profits the plaintiff argued were made by and out of the premises. The plaintiff brought these proceedings against the defendant company calling upon them to account for the profits which they had received or ought to have received when they were in possession.]

LORD ESHER MR: [The defendants] are bound to account to him after the sale -for the proceeds of the sale – for any rents which they have received, or but for their wilful neglect or default might have received, from the property while they were in possession – and for any profits which, during that period, they made out of and by the mortgaged property. They have not to account for anything more, and as against that they are entitled to set the expenses which they have fairly incurred in consequence of having been obliged to take possession, and keep possession, and to sell. They have a right to set off against the sale the expenses of the sale. They have a right to set-off against the rents and profits they have received, any rents they have been obliged to pay (inasmuch as this was lease-hold property), and any insurance they were obliged to pay, and anything else which was an expense put upon them by reason of their being obliged to take and keep possession – expenses which they were obliged to incur in order to receive the rents and profits which they are to account for.

But the nominal plaintiff says: 'No, you must account to me for the profits which you have made upon beer which you have supplied to the house, as being part of the rents and profits which you have got out of the mortgaged property.' Can those profits on beer supplied to the house be said to be profits by and out of the premises? Such an idea seems to me simply preposterous, and we cannot entertain it ...

The question as to profits on beer was the real fighting part of the case, and if the learned judge had refused to consider anything else in the matter nobody could have objected. The Plaintiff was playing for high stakes. He did not care about the difference of rent, he wanted £1,990 to be brought in and then his surplus of a little less than £400 would have been nearly £2,400. If a man plays for such high stakes and utterly fails, I feel inclined to say 'you cannot turn around when you have failed on that, and say you are entitled to a trifling advantage on another view of the matter'. But the learned judge took a more indulgent view and said to the mortgagees: 'You took possession of the property, and you let the property; you were bound to the mortgagor to let it for a fair rent, you had no right, for instance, to let those premises for nothing, and then make a profit out of supplying beer to them. If you did not let the property for as good a rent as you could reasonably get, you ought to account for the difference between what you did let it for, and what you ought to have let it for.' The learned judge dealt with the matter upon that footing, and if he was to deal with it at all, that was the right footing. What the fair rent was is a matter of evidence ... Now does the evidence shew that the mortgagees let this house at any time for a less rent than they ought to have got? For the first two years they kept it in their own hands. There is no question but that they had a right to keep it in their own hands, and the evidence is that if they had tried to let it at the time when they took possession they could not have got a tenant. The brewers then put in Moulton as their servant, and the value of the business is carried from nothing at all, by their money and by their servant, to something. After this Moulton takes the house at a rent of £30 for the first year, and £40 for the next, and he was to take his beer from them. He found that he could not make anything of it, and asked them to reduce his rent to £30, and half of that was for furniture which belonged to the company. The evidence is clear that nobody at that time would have given more. In 1873 Hake came at a rent of £60, and the evidence is that nobody would at that time have given more than he gave. The learned judge came to the conclusion that from the year 1874 to the year 1879 the property was let for a less rent than might have been got if there had been no stipulation to take beer from the company, and there being no evidence given on behalf of the plaintiff what amount of rent ought to have been got, the learned judge was obliged to make a guess, and he allowed £20 a year. If he had given only £10, the plaintiff could not have complained. He has got £100, which will go perhaps to assist the second mortgagee to pay the costs for which I have no doubt he is liable, and with that he must be content. The appeal must be dismissed.

[Cotton and Fry LJJ's concurring judgments omitted.]

Note

Because of the heavy responsibilities imposed upon a mortgagee who enters into possession, this remedy is rarely exercised except as a preliminary step towards selling the property. To avoid this responsibly mortgagees in practice appoint receivers to enter into possession of the mortgaged property. Receivers are discussed below.

Questions

1 X mortgages his house to ABC Bank as security for a loan. When X defaults the Bank orders X to vacate the house, which he does. The house remains unoccupied for about three years. Meanwhile thieves break into the house and remove the doors and window panels. The house is in a run-down state. Advise X of any possible remedies against the Bank.

2 A mortgages his house to B. At the time of the mortgage the house is leased to T for five years. When A defaults in payment of his mortgage instalments, B threatens to evict T unless T pays him (B) the outstanding instalments. T has already paid his rent to A in advance. Advise T.

Appointment of a receiver

To avoid the risks involved in taking possession, a mortgagee may appoint a receiver. A receiver is a person appointed to receive the rents and profits of the premises, and use them to reduce the mortgage debt. If there is business to be carried on temporarily the receiver may also be appointed manager (receiver-manager). Curiously there is no express statutory provision which empowers the mortgagee to appoint a receiver. Usually, this power is given to the mortgagee under the mortgage instrument. In the absence of express powers the National Court in exercise of its inherent powers may appoint a receiver at the instance of the mortgagor or the mortgagee in all circumstances where it considers it just to do so. In *White v Metcalf*, Kekewich J explained the notion of a receiver as follows:[25]

> Long before the Legislature intervened to simplify the rights and remedies of mortgagors and mortgagees, it was a very common thing to provide in the mortgage deed that the mortgagee might appoint a receiver, and it was not uncommon, speaking from recollection, to appoint a receiver straightaway by the mortgage deed itself. But in all these cases, according to my recollection, it was always provided that the receiver should be the agent of the mortgagor. He was, of course, appointed for the security of the mortgagee. He was appointed in order that the money should not go to the mortgagor, who might or might not pay the interest to the mortgagee, but should be stopped in the hands of a third person, who would have to pay the rates and taxes and other outgoings affecting the mortgaged property, but subject to that would be directed to pay the interest to the mortgagee, handing the net balance to the mortgagor. That was the notion of the appointment of a receiver by the consent of the parties either by the mortgage deed or under the mortgage deed.

From the point of view of the mortgagee, the main advantage of a receiver is that although the mortgagee appoints the receiver to protect his or her security, normally, the receiver is expressed to be an agent of the mortgagor.[26] This means that the mortgagee is not liable to the mortgagor or secondary mortgagees for the receiver's breaches of duty except where the mortgagee interferes with the receiver's duties.[27] The following National Court decision deals with these principles and the receiver's duty to the mortgagor.

WESTPAK BANK (PNG) LIMITED v HENDERSON AND ANOTHER
[1990] PNGLR 112, National Court of Justice

> [The plaintiffs, Westpak Bank, advanced a loan to a company. The loan was secured by a registered mortgage over the company's leasehold and personally guaranteed by the defendants who were also the directors of the company. Upon default by the company, Westpak Bank demanded payment from the defendants under their guarantee, but payment was not forthcoming. Westpak then exercised its powers under the mortgage and appointed receivers with instructions to take possession and realise the company's assets.

25 [1903] 2 Ch D 567, at 570.

26 *Jefferys v Dickson* (1865–66) 1 Ch App 183, at p 190. A receiver appointed by the court is neither the mortgagor nor the mortgagee's agent. Strictly he is an officer of the court to which he must account for the profits and rents, see Sykes and Walker, *The Law of Securities*, *op cit*, note 11, at pp 129–30.

27 See *Westpak Bank (PNG) Ltd v Maxwell Forbes Henderson and Another* [1990] PNGLR 112, extracted below.

The first receivers were later removed by Westpak and replaced by another firm of receivers. The latter subsequently sold the company's assets and paid the proceeds over to Westpak. The Bank claimed that the proceeds of the sale were not enough to cover all the money owed to it by the company. It commenced these proceedings against the guarantors for the balance of the money. In their defence, they contended that the shortfall was brought about because the receivers negligently sold the company's assets below their true value. The defendants claimed that since Westpak Bank appointed the receivers it was responsible to the company and, ultimately, to them as guarantors, for the receivers' negligence. The defendants made a counter-claim against Westpak for damages for breach of duty.]

SALIKA AJ: The plaintiffs argue that the receivers were appointed for the company and if any duty of care is owed by the receivers to anyone it has to be to the company and not the defendants/cross claimants. However it is argued that, that duty to the company is limited. The plaintiff argues that a receiver only has to act in good faith and under the terms of the mortgage deed.

The plaintiffs further argue that a receiver is usually appointed for the Mortgagee in cases of this nature but the Mortgagee is not responsible for any acts in the receiver. It was submitted that the proposition is enforced by *EXPO International Pty Limited (Receivers and Managers Appointed) (In Liquidation) and Another v Chant and Others* [1979] 2 NSWLR 820 at pp 827g–28a.

It is clear enough to establish that where a receiver and manager is appointed under the terms of a floating charge, and it is expressed to be the agent of the mortgagor, even though the appointment is made by the mortgagee, the latter is not responsible for the action of the receiver and the manager.

The plaintiff went on to argue that the mortgage deed itself puts the issue to rest which provides under Clause (iii) that:

> Provided always that every such Receiver shall be the agent of the mortgagor and that the Mortgagor alone shall be responsible for his acts and defaults.

The plaintiff therefore argues that authorities clearly indicate that in this instant case the receiver was the agent of Agquip Pty Ltd and the Bank was not responsible for the receiver's acts and defaults.

The plaintiff says that it therefore follows then that if a receiver has caused loss it is him who should be sued in his own right as a receiver and not the appointing authority. Furthermore the receiver's duty of care is only to Agquip Pty Ltd who alone can sue the receiver ...

The defendants allege that the receivers failed to exercise reasonable care, skill diligence and competence in carrying out the sale. They allege that the company's assets were sold at an undervalue by the receivers and as such they had suffered damage. The defendants/cross claimants argue that the receivers owed a duty of care to them as guarantors to get the best possible price for the company's assets.

I respectfully do not agree with the submissions of the plaintiff to the extent that the receiver owes no duty of care to the guarantor. I am of the view that a receiver though is the agent of the mortgagor owes a duty of care both to the company and to the guarantor. This is because it is in the interest of both the company and the guarantor. Whatever the receiver does in realising the assets of the company, the guarantor will be affected in so far as determining the liability of the guarantor is concerned. The guarantor is liable to the same extent as the company is. I refer to a judgment of Lord Denning MR in the case of *Standards Chartered Bank Ltd v Walker* [1982] 1 WLR 1410 at pp 1415–16:

> So far as the receiver is concerned, the law is well stated by Rigby LJ in *Gaskell v Gosling* [1896] 1 QB 669, a dissenting judgment which was approved by the House of Lords [1897] AC 575. The receiver is the agent of the company, not of the debenture holder, the bank. He owes a duty to use reasonable care to obtain the best possible price which the circumstances of the case permit. He owes this duty not only to the company, of which he is the agent to clear off as much of its indebtedness to the bank as possible, but he also owes a duty to the guarantor, because the guarantor is liable only to the same extent as the company. The more the overdraft is reduced, the better for the guarantor.

However, I agree with the submission that the bank (mortgagee) is not liable for the acts of the receiver with the exception that the Bank did not interfere with the acts of the receiver, because if the bank interferes with the duties of the receiver it becomes liable.

The receiver was appointed to realise the proceeds of sale of the assets of Agquip Pty Ltd and to pay the net proceeds over the bank so as to satisfy the indebtedness of Agquip Pty Ltd to the bank. When he did that he owed fiduciary duties to the bank, Agquip Pty Ltd and the defendants/cross claimants.

It follows then that in this case the receiver did owe a duty of care to the defendants/cross claimants to secure a good price for the assets of the company and they should have included them in their counter claim. They have not done that. The defendants also did not provide any evidence to suggest that the Bank interfered with the acts or duties of the receivers so as to make the Bank liable but again they have not called evidence in that regard.

I find that the counter-claim has not been substantiated and I accordingly dismiss it and enter judgment in favour of the plaintiff's claim in the sum of K181,648.35 with interest accruing at a daily rate of K38.05 until satisfaction.

Questions

1 The Bank lent K50,000 to Moses on security of his house. The mortgage was duly registered. Though the house was worth K40,000 the Bank thought that it was a safe security as it anticipated the value of the house to appreciate in due course. This never eventuated partly due to a slump in the property market and partly Moses' failure to maintain the house in reasonable repair. The house is currently valued at K30,000. Moses has defaulted in payment of several monthly instalments and still owes the Bank K48,000. Advise the Bank of its best legal remedy.

2 DK borrowed K250,000 from the Bank secured by a registered mortgage over a block of residential flats. The flats are quite popular and are usually fully occupied. DK has defaulted in payment of the interest to his loan. He still owes the Bank K200,000. Assume that the estimated value of the block of flats is about K100,000 and advise the Bank.

3 When Jim defaulted in payment of his mortgage, the Bank appointed Guru to receive the rents and profits of the land. Guru collected the rent and he absconded. Whose loss is it? (See *White v Metcalf* [1903] 2 Ch 567.)

Statutory power of sale

Under the underlying law a mortgagee had no power to sell the mortgaged property free from the mortgagor's equity of redemption[28] unless such power was reserved in the mortgage deed or the sale was sanctioned by a court. The power of sale is now expressly provided by s 68(1)(b) of the Land Registration Act. It arises once the mortgage debt is due[29] subject to compliance with the notice requirements stipulated under ss 67 and 68 of the Act.

> Section 67. Notice of default
>
> 1 Where default is made –
>
> (a) for the period of one month in payment of any secured money the creditor may give to the debtor written notice to pay the money then due or owing; or
>
> (b) in the observance of a covenant binding on the debtor by virtue of a provision expressed or implied in a mortgage or charge the creditor may give to the debtor written notice to observe the covenant.
>
> 2 The notice referred to in sub-section (1) may be given to the debtor –
>
> (a) in person; or
>
> (b) by leaving the notice on the land subject to the mortgage or charge; or
>
> (c) by leaving the notice at the usual or last-known address in the country of the debtor or other person claiming to be entitled to the secured land.
>
> Section 68. Sale of property by mortgagee, etc
>
> 1 Subject to section 72, where the default referred to –
>
> (a) in section 67(1)(a), continues for a further month from the date of the notice referred to in that sub-section; or
>
> (b) in section 67(1)(b), continues for a month from the date of the notice referred to in that sub-section,
>
> the creditor may sell the land the subject of the mortgage or charge or a part of that land.

Section 73(1) gives the parties power in their mortgage agreement to extend or shorten the period of one month specified in s 68(1)(a) or (b), but gives no power to dispense with the whole notice. Subject to s 73(1), the combined effect of ss 67 and 68 is to give the mortgagor a period of grace of at least two months before the mortgagee can proceed with the sale. A sale without a notice served in the prescribed manner is improper and the mortgagee may be held liable in damages for the consequential loss suffered by the mortgagor.[30] A notice is defective if due to the mortgagee's fault it is despatched to the

---

28 Megarry and Wade, *The Law of Real Property* (6th edn, Sweet & Maxwell, London, 2000), at p 1191. The mortgagee could of course assign his interest subject to the equity of redemption.

29 The statutory power is not exercisable if the mortgage debt is not due (*Twentieth Century Banking Co Ltd v Wilkinson* [1976] 3 All ER 361). Note that a default in payment of the interest or even a single instalment may give the mortgagee the right to exercise his power of sale and to use the proceeds to pay off the principle sum even if it is not due (s 70, LRA).

30 *Hoole v Smith* (1881) 17 Ch D 434.

wrong address.[31] Similarly, a notice which does not clearly state the nature of the obligations or which contains substantial errors is defective. For example, in *Clarke v Japan Machines (Australia) Pty Ltd*[32] the mortgagee's notice was held invalid because the amount it stated as owing was enormous and the notice was otherwise equivocal as to the nature of the obligation.

Question

In *Australia and New Zealand Banking Group v Kila Wari*,[33] Salika J held that s 67(1) of the LRA is discretionary in its terms and therefore the mortgagee is not legally obliged to serve a demand notice prior to exercise of his power of sale, except where the contract stipulates for notice. Do you agree with this interpretation of the section? If so how do you reconcile your answer with s 68(1) of the LRA?

Manner of sale

A statutory sale does not need judicial sanction. Therefore, once the conditions of sale are satisfied the mortgagee may immediately proceed to sell. The Act gives the mortgagee extensive incidental powers to determine the manner of sale.

> Section 68. Sale of property by mortgagee, etc
>
> (1) ...
>
> (2) For the purpose of effecting a sale under this section the creditor may execute any document.
>
> (3) The land may be sold in the following ways:
>
> (a) altogether or in lots; or
>
> (b) by public auction or by private contract or partly by public auction and partly by private contract.
>
> (4) The creditor may sell the land subject to any conditions of sale which he thinks fit.
>
> (5) On a sale under this section the creditor may buy in and resell without being liable for loss occasioned by that purchase or resale.

Duties of the seller

The cases extracted below illustrate some of the duties the courts impose on a mortgagee exercising the power of sale.

The sale must be an independent bargain.

---

31 *Australia and New Zealand Banking Group (PNG) Ltd v Kila Wari*, unreported judgment of the National Court of Papua New Guinea, 16 February 1990, N801. See extract below, p 229.

32 [1984] 1 Qd R 404.

33 Unreported judgment of the National Court of Justice, 16 February 1990, N801, see extract below, p 229.

FARRAR v FARRARS LIMITED (1889) 40 Ch D 395, Court of Appeal

[The mortgage being in arrears the three mortgagees sold under the powers of sale to a company, which was specifically formed to purchase the property. The said company was promoted by Farrar, one of the three mortgagees. Farrar had also a substantial shareholding in this company and was its solicitor. The plaintiff's (mortgagors) sought to set the sale aside on the ground that in substance the mortgagees sold to themselves. The trial court held in favour of the mortgagees. On appeal.]

LINDLEY LJ: This action is brought by mortgagors to set aside a sale by their mortgagees ... It was alleged by the Plaintiffs in their statement of claim that the sale was fraudulent and collusive and at an undervalue. Mr Justice Chitty decided that this allegation was not proved, and he gave judgment for the Defendants. The Plaintiffs on appeal did not question the view of the judge that there was no fraudulent sale at an undervalue, but they contended that fraud or no fraud, undervalue or no undervalue, the sale could not stand, inasmuch as it was in substance a sale by a mortgagee to himself and others under the guise of a sale to a limited company.

If this proposition were true the sale could not stand as against the mortgagor. It is perfectly well settled that a mortgagee with a power of sale cannot sell to himself either alone or with others, nor to a trustee for himself ... nor to any one employed by him to conduct the sale ... A sale by a person to himself is no sale at all, and a power of sale does not authorize the donee of the power to take the property subject to it at a price fixed by himself, even although such price be the full value of the property. Such a transaction is not an exercise of the power, and the interposition of a trustee, although it gets over the difficulty so far as form is concerned, does not affect the substance of the transaction.

A sale by a person to a corporation of which he is a member is not, either in form or in substance, a sale by a person to himself. To hold that it is, would be to ignore the principle which lies at the root of the legal idea of a corporate body, and that idea is that the corporate body is distinct from the persons composing it. A sale by a member of a corporation to the corporation itself is in every sense a sale valid in equity as well as at law. There is no authority for saying that such a sale is not warranted by an ordinary power of sale, and in our opinion, such a sale is warranted by such a power, and does not fall within the rule to which we have at present referred. But although this is true, it is obvious that a sale by a person to an incorporated company of which he is a member may be invalid upon various grounds, although it may not be reached by the rule which prevents a man from selling to himself or to a trustee for himself. Such a sale may, for example, be fraudulent and at an undervalue or it may be made under circumstances which throw upon the purchasing company the burden of proving the validity of the transaction, and the company may be unable to prove it. Fraud in the present case is not now alleged; it was alleged in the court below, and was then clearly disproved. But, for reasons which will appear presently, the circumstances attending the sale were such as, in our opinion, throw upon the company the burden of sustaining the transaction. The circumstances alluded to are shortly as follows:

Mr John Riley Farrar was a solicitor, he was one of three mortgagees with a power of sale, he acted for his mortgagees. He sold to a company, more or less promoted by himself, in which he had a substantial interest as a shareholder, and whose solicitor he was. Such a transaction has a suspicious appearance, and at the time of the sale there was apparently such a conflict of interest and duty on the part of Mr Farrar, and such notice to the company of that conflict, as to throw upon the company the burden of upholding the sale. But the sale cannot be set aside on the simple ground that Mr Farrar was a trustee for sale, and was a promoter of and shareholder in the company which purchased from him. It is necessary to see what his duties to his mortgagors were, and what he really did.

A mortgagee with a power of sale, though often called a trustee, is in a very different position from a trustee for sale. A mortgagee is under obligations to the mortgagor, but he has rights of his own which he is entitled to exercise adversely to the mortgagor. A trustee for sale has no business to place himself in such a position as to give rise to a conflict of interest and duty. But every mortgage confers upon the mortgagee the right to realise his security and to find a purchaser if he can, and if in exercise of his power he acts *bona fide* and takes reasonable precautions to obtain a proper price, the mortgagor has no redress, even although more might have been obtained for the property if the sale had been postponed ...

Such being Mr JR Farrar's position and duty as a mortgagee, let us see how he performed it. He and his co-mortgagees were themselves trustees, and he was forced to enter into possession and to work the quarries. He did his best to induce his mortgagors and subsequent incumbrancers to pay him off, failing in this, he advertised the mortgaged property for sale, and part of it, the Birks Royd Quarry, was put up to auction, and there was no bid; he was advised by a very competent person ... that it was useless to persevere in attempting to sell by auction, and no further attempts to sell in that way were made ...

[His Honour considered several other factors and the circumstances which preceded the sale and continued.]

[I]t appears to us that Mr Farrar in no way disregarded his duty to his mortgagors, on the contrary, he was doing the utmost in his power to find a purchaser at the best price that could be got. At this time his interest was to get the best price he could, for his security was by no means ample, he was pursuing that interest, and was discharging his duty at the same time, and he had no conflicting interest in the matter.

This, in our judgment, settles the question. The subsequent agreements and conveyances do no more than give effect to the bargain which was entered into in November, and the real character of which has been already considered.

... The sale here impeached having been made honestly and at a fair value, ought, in our opinion, to be allowed to stand, and there is no hard and fast rule which compels us to hold the contrary.

Appeal dismissed.

Questions

1 What is meant by an 'independent bargain'?

2 Upon default by a mortgagor, XYZ Bank decides to exercise its power of sale. The Bank duly complies with all the legal requirements prior to the exercise of its powers of sale. Advise the Bank whether the Bank can purchase the mortgaged land. (See *ANZ v Bangadilly Pastoral Co Pty Ltd and Others* (1978) 139 CLR 195. Also *Tse Kwong Lam v Wong Chit Sen and Others* [1983] 3 All ER 54 (see extract below, p 233).)

3 At an auction, the seller mortgagee is allowed to 'buy in' (s 68(5) of the LRA). What is meant by 'buy in'? Why would a mortgagee buy in?

The power of sale must be exercised in good faith

The following case expounds the nature of the duty to act in good faith.

LATEC INVESTMENTS LTD v HOTEL TERRIGAL PTY (1964–65) 113 CLR 265, High Court of Australia

[The respondent (mortgagor), Hotel Terrigal Pty Ltd, was the registered proprietor of land under the New South Wales Real Property Act, upon which there was erected the Terrigal Hotel. The land was mortgaged to Latec Investments Ltd, the first named appellant. Upon default by the mortgagor Latec purported to sell the land by public auction, but it bought in because the highest bid was lower than the reserved price. Later it sold the land by private contract to Southern Hotel Pty Ltd, the second named appellant which was also one of Latec's wholly-owned subsidiaries. Southern Hotel was duly registered as the proprietor of the said land free from any incumbrances in favour of Hotel Terrigal. Subsequently Southern Hotel gave an equitable mortgage to another company called MLC Nominees Ltd, the third named appellants, as security for a loan. Five years after the purported sale Hotel Terrigal sought to set aside the sale and transfer of the land to Southern upon the ground that the power of sale had been fraudulently exercised and further sought consequential relief. The Supreme Court of NSW set aside the contract of sale and the memorandum of transfer to Southern on the ground that the mortgagee's power of sale had been exercised in fraud of the mortgagor. On appeal to the High Court, it was common ground that MLC Nominees took its equitable mortgage without notice of the alleged fraudulent sale.]

KITTO J: The mortgagee appointed a receiver ... in June 1958, and on 23 July 1958 the mortgagor went into voluntary liquidation. The mortgagee took no steps to effect a sale until late in September 1958, and not until after its directors had learned that a stranger might be interested in purchasing the property. It made no endeavour to sell to the stranger or to find any other purchaser by private contract. Instead, its board determined at some stage to sell the property to the second appellant, which was one of several subsidiaries of the mortgagee. They had identically composed boards of directors, and the mortgagee held all the shares in the second appellant. Before any sale was made, a firm of estate agents was instructed to put the property up for auction on Friday, 3 October 1958. A Friday was generally recognized as not a good day for such a sale, and the interval of time available for advertisements was significantly less than usual. Nevertheless the auctioneers made efforts to attract potential buyers and some thirty-five people attended the auction. The highest bid received was £58,000. Although the mortgagee's directors knew that an experienced valuer had valued the property six months before at £54,000 for the hotel and £2,500 for the guest house, a reserve of £85,000 had been fixed and the property was accordingly passed in. The auctioneers then advised the mortgagee to accept the offer of £58,000 if a better should not be forthcoming. The mortgagee, however, made no attempt to negotiate with any of the bidders or to obtain any higher offer. Its directors determined – indeed it is a reasonable inference from the unusual features of the submission to auction that for some time they had had it in mind – that to have the Hotel Terrigal owned by one of their group of companies would be better for them than selling it to a stranger. One of the group owned a competing hotel in the same district, and the benefits to be derived from peaceful co-existence had attractions too obvious to be overlooked. The fact that an exercise of the power of sale so as to bring about this result would amount to a virtual foreclosure did not deter them. Without any further attempt having been made to find an outside purchaser, the mortgagee entered into a contract with its subsidiary, the second appellant, to sell the mortgaged property to the latter at the price of £60,000. There was, of course, no bargaining between them. The common board of directors simply fixed the figure and had a contract prepared and executed by both companies. The contract, dated 26 March 1958, provided for payment of £6,000 as a deposit, but fixed no time for payment either of that amount or of the balance of £54,000. The memorandum of transfer, acknowledging receipt by the mortgagee of £19,675, was registered on 25 February 1959. In fact nothing had been paid at that stage. The first mortgage over the property was paid off by the purchaser in the following July, but it was not until a year after the date of the contract that any of the purchase money was paid to the mortgagee. Then the whole outstanding amount was paid in one sum.

The amount owing under the mortgage at the time of the sale was of the order of £86,000. It may be that by no means could a purchaser have been found to buy the property at so high a price, but the course that was followed in respect of the auction was not calculated to test the question. *Vis à vis* the mortgagor, the mortgagee was not bound to use its best endeavour to obtain the highest price procurable; but what it in fact did points pretty clearly to the conclusion that its intention was not really to sell the property but was to ascertain what kind of figure, being put into a contract of sale to the subsidiary, would look like a genuine sale price. As between the mortgagee and the subsidiary it did not matter much what the figure was; but there was an obvious advantage, in case of a possible impeachment of the sale, in selecting a price a little higher than the best bid obtained at an auction. The only danger in holding the auction was that a bid might be obtained which exceeded the amount owing under the mortgage. If that should happen, there could be no excuse for not accepting it, and the hotel would have to pass into a stranger's hands; but, by fixing a short date for the auction and choosing an unpropitious day of the week, as much was done to obviate this unfortunate result as was possible consistently with employing an auctioneer who was no party to the scheme and creating an appearance of a genuine attempt to sell at a proper price.

The onus clearly lay upon the purchaser, being a subsidiary of the mortgagee, to satisfy the court that the power of sale was exercised in good faith, and that reasonable steps were taken to obtain a fair price: *Farrar v Farrars Ltd* [(1889) 40 Ch D 395, p 398]. That onus it signally failed to discharge. The learned trial judge concluded that there was a lack of that kind of good faith which in the eyes of a court of equity is essential to the validity of a mortgagee's sale ... and he also concluded that the collaboration of the mortgagee and the purchaser through their common directors amounted to fraud in the sense of ss 42 and 43 of the Real Property Act 1900 (NSW), so that the mortgagor's claim to have the sale set aside is not defeated by the indefeasibility which those sections accord to a registered title. I have already said enough to show that in the first of these conclusions I agree. As to the second, we were invited to hold that nothing is fraud in the sense which is relevant under the Real Property Act unless it includes a fraudulent misrepresentation. The whole course of authority on this branch of the law is to the contrary. Moral turpitude there must be; but a designed cheating of a registered proprietor out of his rights by means of a collusive and colourable sale by a mortgagee company to a subsidiary is as clearly a fraud, as clearly a defrauding of the mortgagor, as a cheating by any other means ... In the present case it is all very well to say that the directors had reason to think that on a genuine sale they would not have got more than £60,000 for the property. The fact remains – I see no escape from concluding that it is a fact – that the reason why there was only a pretence of attempting to get a better price was simply that the object in view was not really to effect a sale, but was to destroy the mortgagor's interest and get the hotel for the mortgagee's group of companies, without allowing the mortgagor the opportunities to pay off the mortgage which the procedure for foreclosure would have afforded. It is impossible to regard the case as only one of constructive or equitable fraud – there was much more in it than a mere fraud upon the power, as it is sometimes called. There was pretence and collusion in the conscious misuse of a power. It may be that those concerned salved their consciences by telling themselves that the mortgagor company, being already in liquidation, was in so parlous a financial condition that the course they were taking was unlikely in the long run to do anyone any harm. But it was a dishonest course none the less, and the proper name for it is fraud.

If the mortgagor had sought the intervention of the court without delay, the findings of fact with which so far I have dealt would necessarily have led to a decree setting aside the sale as against the mortgagee and the purchaser and granting consequential relief. But nearly five years went by before proceedings were commenced, and it is necessary to consider whether the mortgagor's right to relief is affected by what occurred in that time. First let me be clear about the nature of the right which the mortgagor might have asserted. To say that the court would have set the sale aside as against the mortgagee and its purchaser is not to say that either the contract or the ensuing transfer would or could have been rendered void at law, It means only that the purchaser would (in effect) have been declared compellable to act in relation to the mortgagor as if the mortgagee had sold and transferred not the mortgaged property but only the mortgage and the moneys thereby secured: see *Selwyn v Garfit* [(1888) 38 Ch D 273, p 280] ... The appropriate consequential relief would not have been granted, as in the case of a mortgage of land under common title, on the footing that the sale and transfer had been ineffectual to extinguish an equity of redemption and that the mortgagor was therefore entitled to redeem as against the purchaser ... for the mortgagor had the legal title, not an equity of redemption, and the transfer had operated to deprive him of the legal title by virtue only of special statutory provisions: see ss 58 and 59 of the Real Property Act and ss 109, 110 and 111 of the Conveyancing Act 1919–54 (NSW). The right which the mortgagor had immediately before the sale was a right to have the mortgagee ordered (notwithstanding that the contractual date for payment had passed) to receive what should be found on a taking of accounts to be owing under the mortgage and thereupon to execute a discharge of the mortgage ... After the sale, however, the reasoning which would have led a court of equity, if the land had been under common law title, to refuse to recognize the sale as having destroyed the equity of redemption would have led necessarily to the conclusion that equity would treat the purchaser as if it had taken a transfer of the mortgage only, though with this difference, that since the purchaser, unlike the mortgagee, had acquired the legal estate in the land the mortgagor must be accorded a true equity of redemption. Against the assertion of this equity of redemption, s 112(3)(a) of the Conveyancing Act 1919–61 (NSW) would have afforded no protection, because the purchaser had had the clearest notice of the invalidity of the mortgagee's exercise of its power of sale: see *Bailey v Barnes* ([1894] 1 Ch 25).

But, as I have said, the mortgagor took no step to establish its equity of redemption for nearly five years. One reason was that the voluntary liquidator had no funds available for litigation. But whatever the full tally of the reasons may have been, if there were nothing more to consider than the bare fact of the delay it may be that the mortgagor would not be precluded from asserting its rights even after so long a time ... But an important change in the situation occurred a little more than a year after the sale ...

[The change occurred when Southern acquired an equitable mortgage over the subject land. His Honour discussed at length the issue of priorities between Southern's equitable mortgage and Terrigal's equitable claim to relief to set the sale aside. For reasons stated in the judgment he held that Southern's equitable mortgage prevailed over the latter.] *Appeal allowed.*

[Taylor J concurred with Kitto L's order whilst Menzies J dissented.]

Duty of care

The following case is the leading authority for the proposition that the duty of a selling mortgagee is not only to act in good faith, but must also take reasonable care to obtain the true market value of the property at the date of sale.

CUCKMERE BRICK CO LTD AND ANOTHER v MUTUAL FINANCE LTD [1971] Ch D 949, Court of Appeal

[The plaintiffs were granted planning permission to erect 100 flats and 35 houses on their land. They charged the land to the defendants by way of legal mortgage with payment of £50,000 and other money. Two years later, the mortgage being in arrears and with no development of any kind having started, the defendants' statutory power of sale became exercisable. They went into possession and instructed auctioneers to sell the land. Preparations were made for a sale by public auction. Advertisements remarked on the planning permission for 35 houses but made no mention of the planning permission for flats. The plaintiffs drew that fact to the attention of the defendants and asked that the sale be postponed. The defendants refused, but they undertook to instruct the auctioneers to mention at the sale the existence of the permission for flats. The land was sold for £44,000. The plaintiffs alleged that the land was worth £75,000 and demanded an account on the footing of wilful default, and damages. The trial judge held that the defendants had failed in their duty to the plaintiffs in failing to advertise the planning permission for flats and in refusing to postpone the sale. Both parties asked the judge (in the event of his finding negligence by the defendants) to assess the value of the land on the evidence before him. He found the value to be £65,000 and ordered accounts and inquiries on the basis that the land should have been sold for that figure. The defendants appealed on the ground, *inter alia,* that the judge's finding that the defendants had failed in their duty of care was against the weight of the evidence and they asked for a fresh inquiry as to damages.]

SALMON LJ: It is well settled that a mortgagee is not a trustee of the power of sale for the mortgagor. Once the power has accrued, the mortgagee is entitled to exercise it for his own purposes whenever he chooses to do so. It matters not that the moment may be unpropitious and that by waiting a higher price could be obtained. He has the right to realise his security by turning it into money when he likes. Nor, in my view, is there anything to prevent a mortgagee from accepting the best bid he can get at an auction, even though the auction is badly attended and the bidding exceptionally low. Providing none of those adverse factors is due to any fault of the mortgagee, he can do as he likes. If the mortgagee's interests, as he sees them, conflict with those of the mortgagor, the mortgagee can give preference to his own interests, which of course he could not do were he a trustee of the power of sale for the mortgagor.

Mr Vinelott [Counsel for the appellant/defendants] contends that the mortgagee's sole obligation to the mortgagor in relation to a sale is to act in good faith; there is no duty of care, and accordingly no question of negligence by the mortgagee in the conduct of the sale can arise. If this contention is correct it follows that, even on the facts found by the judge, the defendants should have succeeded.

It is impossible to pretend that the state of the authorities on this branch of the law is entirely satisfactory. There are some *dicta* which suggest that unless a mortgagee acts in bad faith he is safe. His only obligation to the mortgagor is not to cheat him. There are other *dicta* which suggest that in addition to the duty of acting in good faith, the mortgagee is under a duty to take reasonable care to obtain whatever is the true market value of the mortgaged property at the moment he chooses to sell it: compare, for example, *Kennedy v de Trafford* [1896] 1 Ch 762; [1897] AC 180 with *Tomlin v Luce* (1889) 43 Ch D 191, 194.

The proposition that the mortgagee owes both duties, in my judgment, represents the true view of the law. Approaching the matter first of all on principle, it is to be observed that if the sale yields a surplus over the amount owed under the mortgage, the mortgagee holds this surplus in trust for the mortgagor. If the sale shows a deficiency, the mortgagor has to make it good out of his own pocket. The mortgagor is vitally affected by the result of the sale but its preparation and conduct is left entirely in the hands of the mortgagee. The proximity between them could scarcely be closer. Surely they are 'neighbours'. Given that the power of sale is for the benefit of the mortgagee and that he is entitled to choose the moment to sell which suits him, it would be strange indeed if he were under no legal obligation to take reasonable care to obtain what I call the true market value at the date of the sale. Some of the textbooks refer to the 'proper price', others to the 'best price'. Vaisey J in *Reliance Permanent Building Society v Harwood-Stamper* [1944] Ch 362, 347, 365, seems to have attached great importance to the difference between these two descriptions of 'price'. My difficulty is that I cannot see any real difference between them. 'Proper price' is perhaps a little nebulous, and 'the best price' may suggest an exceptionally high price. That is why I prefer to call it 'the true market value'.

In *Tomlin v Luce* (1889) 41 Ch D 573; (1889) 43 Ch D 191, the first mortgagees by mistake misdescribed the property being offered for sale. It was knocked down for £20,000. When the buyers discovered the mistake they refused to complete unless they were allowed £895 off the purchase price. This allowance was made and the price accordingly reduced to £19,105. The second mortgagees, who can be treated as in the same position as mortgagors, brought an action against the first mortgagees claiming that those mortgagees were responsible for the mistake of their auctioneer, that as a result of this mistake £895 had been deducted from the purchase price, and that this deduction ought not to be allowed in taking the account between the first and second mortgagees. The trial judge found in favour of the plaintiff and disallowed the whole of the £895. This was obviously wrong because the first mortgagees could only be answerable for any loss occasioned by the misdescription. The question should have been: but for the misdescription, would the land have sold for anything and if so how much more than £19,105? The judge's order was accordingly varied in the Court of Appeal. Cotton LJ, after pointing out the judge's mistake, said at p 194:

> The defence seems really to have been ... directed to this, that the first mortgagees, selling under their power, employed a competent auctioneer, and were not answerable for any blunder which the auctioneer committed. There they were wrong, and that point was not, I think argued before us ... What we think is this – that the first mortgagees are answerable for any loss which was occasioned by the blunder made by their auctioneer at the sale.

Bowen and Fry LJJ concurred. Although the point was not argued in the Court of Appeal, the passage in Cotton LJ's judgment which I have read must be treated with the greatest respect. He was a master in this branch of the law, and he and the other members of the court as well as counsel treated the point as too plain for argument. Indeed it had long been so regarded by the courts: see *Wolff v Vanderzee* (1869) 20 LT 353 and *National Bank of Australasia v United Hand-in-Hand and Band of Hope Co* (1879) 4 App Cas 391 in which the Privy Council expressed the clear view that a mortgagee is chargeable with the full value of the mortgaged property sold if, from want of due care and diligence, it has been sold at an undervalue. It would seem, therefore, that many years before the modern development of the law of negligence, the courts of equity had laid down a doctrine in relation to mortgages which is entirely consonant with the general principles later evolved by the common law.

Then came *Kennedy v de Trafford* [1896] 1 Ch 762; [1897] AC 180 (with which I will presently deal) in which none of the authorities to which I have referred were cited. After that case came *McHugh v Union Bank of Canada* [1913] AC 299, in which *Kennedy v de Trafford* was not cited. In the *McHugh case*, Lord Moulton, in giving the opinion of an exceptionally strong Board, said, at p 311:

> It is well settled law that it is the duty of a mortgagee when realising the mortgaged property by sale to behave in conducting such realisation as a reasonable man would behave in the realisation of his own property, so that the mortgagor may receive credit for the fair value of the property sold.

In that case the plaintiffs recovered damages because of a depreciated price having been realised for mortgaged horses on account of the negligent manner in which the mortgagees had had them driven to market. Mr Vinelott argues that this case was concerned only with the duty of a mortgagee to take care to preserve the mortgaged property when he goes into possession so as not to preclude the equity of redemption and has nothing to do with the mortgagee's duty upon a sale. I am afraid that I cannot accept that the case is susceptible of being explained away in the manner which Mr Vinelott suggests.

I now come to *Kennedy v de Trafford* [1896] 1 Ch 762; [1897] AC 180 which is the linchpin of the defendants' case on the law. Carswell and Dodson were tenants in common in fee simple of certain freehold property and in 1877 they mortgaged it to Sir Humphrey de Trafford for £60,000 with a provision for redemption and re-conveyance to the mortgagors as tenants in common with the usual power of sale after six months' notice. In 1886 Carswell was adjudicated bankrupt and Kennedy was appointed his trustee. Sir Humphrey de Trafford having died, his executors gave notice to pay off the mortgage. Kennedy having refused to redeem, the mortgagees gave him and Dodson notice of their intention to sell if they could obtain the principal interest and costs outstanding. Having advertised for tenders without result, the mortgagees in 1889 sold to Dodson for a sum equal to the principal interest and costs, £54,000 being left on mortgage and the residue paid off. Before the sale Kennedy was informed of all particulars except the name of the purchaser. In 1891 he discovered that the purchaser was Dodson. He did nothing until 1895, when he brought proceedings against the mortgagee, Dodson being joined as a defendant, to set aside the sale as invalid, alternatively for damages for negligence. Kennedy won at first instance but lost in the Court of Appeal. From that decision he appealed to the House of Lords. The House did not take time for consideration but dismissed the appeal out of hand, Lord Herschell and Lord Macnaghten observing that it was as hopeless an appeal as they had ever heard. There was no allegation of bad faith against the mortgagees and the Court of Appeal and the House of Lords concluded that there was no evidence of negligence, nor that any better price could have been obtained than the price paid by Dodson. Mr Vinelott strongly relies, however, upon certain observations made in that case by Lindley LJ in the Court of Appeal [1896] 1 Ch 762, 772 and by Lord Herschell in the House of Lords [1897] AC 180, 183. The passage in Lindley LJ's judgment appears to me to be rather equivocal. In that passage he seems perhaps to be resiling from what he had said in *Farrar v Farrars Ltd* (1889) 40 Ch D 395, 411, namely, that the duty of a mortgagee is to take reasonable precautions to obtain a proper price. I agree with Mr Vinelott that the word 'recklessly' in the context of those passages connotes something akin to bad faith and more than gross carelessness. It means not caring whether or not the interests of the mortgagors are sacrificed. I do not regard these passages, however, as overruling *Tomlin v Luce* (1889) 43 Ch D 191 and the earlier authorities to which I have referred. Indeed they were never cited in *Kennedy v de Trafford*. Lord Herschell, in the first part of the passage relied on by Mr Vinelott, certainly expresses grave doubt as to whether a mortgagee in exercising a power of sale is under any duty except to act in good faith. I think, however, that in the second part of that passage he expressly refrains from deciding whether or not in such circumstances a mortgagee owes a duty to take reasonable precautions as well as a duty to act in good faith. It was certainly unnecessary for him to decide that question for the purpose of the case he was considering because, as he points out, the mortgagees in that case had taken all reasonable precautions in exercising their powers of sale and no allegation of bad faith was made. In my view, therefore, *Kennedy v de Trafford* does not weaken the effect of the other cases to which I have referred. I accordingly conclude, both on principle and authority, that a mortgagee in exercising his power of sale does owe a duty to take reasonable precautions to obtain the true market value of the mortgaged property at the date on which he decides to sell it. No doubt in deciding whether he has fallen short of that duty the facts must be looked at broadly, and he will not be adjudged to be in default unless he is plainly on the wrong side of the line.

The only other matter that remains to be considered is Mr Vinelott's submission that even if the defendants were under a duty to take reasonable precautions, they discharged that duty by going to reputable auctioneers and estate agents and leaving the sale in their hands. Mr Vinelott submits that the defendants are not responsible for any blunder which their agents may have committed. That submission certainly cannot be squared with Cotton LJ's judgment in *Tomlin v Luce* (1889) 43 Ch D 191. I do not think, however, that it is necessary for me to express any concluded view upon it. The point was not taken below. Indeed the judge expressly states that the defendants did not seek to suggest that they were not responsible for any blunder committed by their agents ...

Since, for the reasons I have indicated, I am against the defendants on the law and consider the judge's findings of fact and assessment of value to be altogether unassailable, I would dismiss the appeal.

[Cairns LJ agreed, Cross LJ dissented on the facts.]

In the case below the National Court applied the duty of care rule to the mortgagee.

AUSTRALIA AND NEW ZEALAND GROUP (PNG) LTD v KILA WARI, unreported, 16 February 1990, N801 National Court of Papua New Guinea

[The plaintiff, ANZ Bank, advanced a loan of K153,000 to the defendant upon security of a registered mortgage over certain leasehold property. The defendant defaulted in repayment of the loan whereupon the plaintiff allegedly served on him a written default notice and a demand for payment. A further notice was allegedly sent to the defendant, but to no avail. Subsequently the plaintiff invited tenders in the *Post Courier* (a local daily) for a mortgage sale of the subject property. The property was sold for K130,000 which was insufficient to cover all the money owed to the plaintiff by the defendant. These proceedings were commenced to recover the balance of the money. The defendant made a counter-claim for damages on two main grounds. Firstly, that the sale was improper because the plaintiff did not send him default notices as required under ss 67 and 68 of the Land Registration Act. Secondly, that the plaintiff did not exercise reasonable care to obtain a fair market price for the property.]

SALIKA AJ: The next argument by the defendant was that the plaintiff improperly exercised its power of sale under ss 67 and 68 of the Land Registration Act.

Section 67 is in these terms:

67 Notice of Default.

(1) where default is made:

(a) for a period of one month in payment of any secured money the creditor may give notice to the debt or written notice to pay money then due or owing; or

(b) in the observance of a covenant binding on the debtor by virtue of a provision expressed or implied in a mortgage or charge the creditor may give to the debtor written notice to observe the covenant.

(2) The notice referred to in sub-section (1) may be given to the debtor:

(a) in person; or

(b) by leaving the notice on the land subject to the mortgage or charge; or

(c) by leaving the notice at the usual or last-known address in the country of the debtor or other person claiming to be entitled to the secured land.

Sub-section (1)(a) means that if the debtor defaults in the payment of any secured money for a period of one month then the creditor may give to the debtor written notice to pay the money then due or owing.

The plaintiff argues that the requirement for the notice under sub-section (1)(a) is not obligatory but merely discretionary. In other words it argues that it need not give the debtor any notice under that provision. In this case the Bank did endeavour to give the defendant the notice ... That notice is dated the 19 January 1987. That notice was however addressed to PO Box 5149, Boroko, whereas the box number on the mortgage document is PO Box 1549, Boroko. Furthermore there is uncontested evidence of Mr Wari that he had in early 1986 advised the Bank of his change of address to PO Box 911, Hohola. Mr Wari also gave evidence that he did receive correspondence from the Bank at the Hohola address and that the Bank was aware of his change of address. The plaintiff did not call evidence to the contrary. I must therefore accept Mr Wari's evidence on that aspect. In any case the notice that was posted by registered mail was returned unclaimed to the Bank. Mr Kona, an employee of the Bank, in his affidavit admits that fact. The Bank therefore was aware that Mr Wari had not been given or served the notice.

The plaintiff argues that the notice under s 67(1)(a) is not obligatory. It is also my view that the terms of s 67(1)(a) is discretionary in itself, however in most cases mortgage documents will themselves govern whether a written notice is obligatory or not. In this case clause 1 of the mortgage clearly required the demand notice to be in writing and the Bank did choose and in fact sent a written notice addressed to a wrong address and returned unserved.

The question of service then comes in. Section 5 of the Interpretation Act Chapter No 3 provides that:

5 Meaning of Service by post etc

(1) where a statutory provision authorises or requires a document to be served by post, (whether the expression served or the expression 'gives' or 'send' or any other expression is used), then unless the contrary intention appears the service shall be deemed to be effected by properly addressing, prepaying (except where under a law the document may be sent by post free of charge) then posting the document as a letter.

It is undisputed evidence that the notice was not properly addressed and was returned to the Bank. Clause 30 of the mortgage document provides for the mode of giving demand or notice and one of them is registered mail. The simple fact that the notice was wrongly addressed and then after posting it returned unclaimed to the sender is clear evidence that the notice was not served. I accordingly find that the notice dated 19 January 1987 under s 67(1)(a) of the Land Registration Act and Clause 1 of the Mortgage document was not served and I find that the Bank was ware of that fact.

Mr Kassman sought to rely on the fact that Mr Wari knew through the receipt of Bank statement that he was in arrears. The Bank statement is not a notice of demand. It is merely information from the bank how much you spend and how much you receive and the balance. In other words it shows you the state of your account. The fact that Mr Wari knew of his arrears in not a demand in writing required under clause 1 of the Mortgage. The bank had that duty to demand in writing from Mr Wari to pay up in accordance with clause 1 of the mortgage. It attempted to but did not serve it. I reject that argument by Mr Kassman.

The plaintiff also sought to rely on letters sent by the bank to the defendant dated 26 November 1986 and 5 January 1987, however those letters were also wrongly addressed. In all circumstances I find that there was no written notice consistent with s 67(1)(a) of the Land Registration Act and clause 1 of the mortgage document.

It would follow then that all transactions that the Bank entered into were irregular after that. The Bank was in breach of the mortgage document. It therefore could not proceed to exercise its powers of sale.

The final matter was that the property was sold at an undervalue. In 1987, four days before the Bank accepted a tender a valuation was done of the property at the request of the Bank. Mr Veraga is a registered valuer of 13 years' experience who practises on his own account as Veraga Valuation Centre Pty Ltd valued the property at K160,000. That valuation did not include a full inspection of the property. He would not agree on cross examination that the value of the property was below K160,000 as at May 1987.

The Bank records tendered to the court as evidence indicated that the property was valued by the Bank at K182,000 in November of 1986. On 14 May 1987 (five months later) it was valued by Mr Veraga at K160,000. That was not a full valuation. On 18 May 1987 (four days later) the bank accepted the offer of K130,000.

The English case of *Cuckmere Brick Company Limited and Another v Mutual Finance Limited* [1971] 2 All ER 633 which is applicable in Papua New Guinea sets out that:

> In exercising the power of sale, however, the mortgagee was not merely under a duty to act in good faith, ie, honestly and without disregard for the mortgagors interest, but also to take reasonable care to obtain whatever was the true market value of the mortgaged property at the moment he chose to sell it.

In this case there is no direct evidence that the mortgagee did not act in good faith, however can it be said that the mortgagee took into account the mortgagors interest when he chose to sell the property at an under value? Can it also be said that the mortgagee took reasonable care to obtain the true market value of the property at the time it sold it? The evidence is that the property was valued at K160,000 at the minimum and may have been K182,000. The Bank sold it for K130,000, some K30,000 less through the tender process. Mr Wari gave evidence that when he saw the advertisement in the newspaper he rang the manager of the Bank and complained about it and made certain proposals. The Bank did not consider his proposals and went ahead to put the property on tender and sold it. The Bank did not call any oral evidence so Mr Wari's oral and tested evidence stands alone on that aspect. Applying the principles of the English case here I think the Bank disregarded the mortgagees' interest in view of the evidence before the court. I think the Bank should have at least taken note of the mortgagors proposals and considered them instead of turning a blind eye to them and going ahead and selling the property at an undervalue. That kind of approach would have been appropriate to the circumstances of Papua New Guinea in so far as solving disputes by consensus is concerned.

The tender received for the property ranged from K71,000 to K102,000. The property was valued at K160,000. Mr Wari gave evidence that he rang the relieving manager of the Bank and pointed out to him that mortgage sales did not get good market prices. However his efforts to dissuade the Bank from selling the property did not eventuate and as a result the property was sold undervalue.

I find from this evidence that the Bank failed in its duty to take reasonable care in obtaining the true market value of the property. I take into account the fact that several bids were received; however clearly there were other options open under clause 15 of the Mortgage. The Bank could have rescinded the offers and withdrawn the tender and arranged something else. Whilst I am mindful of the fact that the Bank is not obliged to listen to the defendant, I think there was still room to get the defendant involved to get a good price which he was also agreeable to.

In summarising the plaintiffs claim for damages it must fail because of the fact that it breached clause 1 of the Mortgage Document in not giving a demand notice in writing to the defendant. The defendant never received the demand notice. The letters and the Bank statement did not constitute a demand notice, therefore the Bank whilst it has power of sale under the Mortgage wrongly exercised it. I also find that the Bank exercised little care to obtain a fair market price for the property. I accordingly dismiss its claim.

The defendant on the other hand has filed a cross claim against the plaintiff for damages for loss of the property and for loss of reputation and for the mental anguish and nervous shock he suffered. As I have found that the notice of 19 January 1987 was not served on the defendant the Bank's actions after that were irregular and illegal. It has now deprived Mr Wari of the property. It follows then that Mr Wari has suffered damages and should be compensated for the wrongful acts of the Bank, in not only selling the property but selling it at an under value.

It is submitted that the value of the property by the Bank itself was over K180,000 whilst the private valuer Mr Veraga put the price at K160,000 with the qualification that his valuation at the time was not a formal one which meant that a full inspection of the property was not carried out. He further gave evidence that had he done a full inspection the value would have been higher. I am prepared to find that the value may have been more than K160,000 because Mr Wari gave evidence that he engaged a company to do improvements on the house – and the driveway. Improvements cost him K20,000, that is probably why the Bank's valuation is higher than Mr Veraga's because Mr Dooley from the Bank may have done a full inspection of the property. Mr Veraga would not agree with Mr Kassman that the value of the property was under K160,000. Instead he said the value would be higher because of the improvements and refurnishings done to the property. I am, on that evidence prepared to put a price tag on the property at K180,000. This would mean the property was sold under value to the tune of K50,000. Of that K50,000, K30,000 would have offset the loan and K20,000 would have been surplus to be paid to Mr Wari.

In relation to the claim for damages for loss of reputation and mental anguish I find that there really is no evidence of loss of reputation. There is no evidence that because of the incident he lost the Chairmanship of PTC Board or lost business or lost his job or did not get loans from other banks.

There is also no evidence that because of the incident his friends shunned him or avoided him. No independent evidence was called on that aspect.

... For loss of the property I award him K20,000 taking into account the fact that the property was valued at K160,000 without full inspection. The property was worth about K180,000 because Mr Wari spent about K20,000 to improve the place. Had the Bank sold the property at its true market value of K180,000 the Bank would have got its money of K160,000 owing back and the remainder of K20,000 would have been Mr Wari's.

In relation to the mental distress I award him a sum of K500 because whilst he was psychologically affected he did not break down. He did not lose his reputation. I think the K500 is a reasonable sum in view of the fact that this has worried him for about two years.

Notes and questions

1 Acting Justice Salika said, in his judgment, that while he was mindful of the fact that the Bank was not obliged to listen to the defendant in exercising its powers of sale, he thought that there was still room to involve him so as to secure a price which was also agreeable to him. Also he observed that the involvement of the defendant would have been appropriate to the circumstances of Papua New Guinea in so far as resolving disputes by consensus was concerned. Does this mean that the seller mortgagee has to consult the mortgagor when preparing to exercise the power of sale? If not, what has the mortgagee got to do to satisfy the requirements expressed by the learned Acting Judge?

2 If the property is valued at a certain price but in the market it actually fetches a lower price (as indeed happened in this case), is the mortgagee obliged to withdraw the property from the market? See *Cuckmere Brick Company Ltd v Mutual Finance Ltd*, extracted above, p 226.

3 Salika AJ purports to rely upon the principle of duty of care espoused in *Cuckmere Brick Company Ltd v Mutual Finance Ltd* (see extract above). Was its principle properly applied? Would you say that in purporting to apply its principle his Honour imposed a greater duty of care upon the seller mortgagee than the principle of that case actually warranted? See J Mugambwa, 'The mortgagee's duty on sale: *Australia and New Zealand Banking Group (PNG) Ltd v Kila Wari*' (1990) (20) Melanesian Law Journal 155.

TSE KWONG LAM v WONG CHIT SEN AND OTHERS
[1983] 3 All ER 54, Privy Council

[In 1963 the appellant (mortgagor) arranged for the construction of a 15 storey building, containing 90 shop, office and flat units, on land leased by him in Hong Kong. He financed the construction partly by advance sales and partly by borrowing a sum of $1.4m on the security of a legal mortgage over the remainder of the building. By 28 February 1966, 54 of the units remained unsold despite a considerable reduction in price. Meanwhile, arrears of interest under the mortgage amounted to some $76,500. On 28 April the mortgagee required payment of all principal and interest due under the mortgage and gave notice of his intention to exercise his power of sale if payment was not made by 29 May. When the appellant failed to make payment the mortgagee arranged for the mortgaged property to be sold at a public auction on 24 June and placed advertisements in three newspapers on three separate days giving notice of the auction and a minimum description of the property. The particulars and conditions of sale contained only the bare legal requirements and disclosed that there would be a reserve price and that the vendor reserved to himself the right to bid generally or withdraw the property at any time. The prospective purchaser was required to pay 20% of the purchase price on the date of the auction and the balance on or before 23 July 1966, time being of the essence. The mortgagee, without consulting the auctioneer or other estate agents about the sate or the reserve, fixed the reserve at $1.2m. On 20 June 1966 at a board meeting of a company (this company was entirely financed by the mortgagee and its directors were the mortgagee, his wife and his son) it was resolved that the mortgagee's wife should bid up to $1.2m for the property at the auction on behalf of the company. At the auction the auctioneer introduced the property, announced the reserve price (which he had been given shortly before the auction) and invited bids. The only bid came from the mortgagee's wife who bid the reserve price of $1.2m. The property was knocked down to her. Subsequently the mortgagee advanced $1.2m to the company by way of an interest-free loan and the company paid that sum to the mortgagee in return for an assignment of the property. The mortgagee then claimed some $400,000 from the appellant, being the amount alleged to be still outstanding in respect of principal and interest under the mortgage after payment of the $1.2m for the property. The appellant disputed the sum claimed and also counterclaimed to set aside the sale to the company on the ground that the sale to the company had been improper and at an undervalue. The mortgagee's claim was referred to an arbitrator, who found that the amount owed by the appellant was some $239,000. Judgment was given for that amount in favour of the mortgagee but execution was suspended pending determination of the appellant's counterclaim. In May 1979 judgment was given for the appellant on the counterclaim, the judge finding that the price paid by the company was not a proper price. However, the judge refused to set aside the sale to the company because of the lapse of time and instead awarded the appellant damages. Both parties appealed to the Hong Kong Court of Appeal which set aside the judgment. The appellant appealed to the Privy Council.]

LORD TEMPLEMAN: Counsel for the borrower submitted that the sale to the company should be set aside because the mortgagee who sold the property was interested in the company which bought the property. There was a conflict between the interest of the mortgagee as vendor in obtaining the highest price and the interest of the mortgagee in the company as purchaser to pay the lowest price. A sale by a mortgagee to a company in which he was interested would only be upheld if the sale was at arm's length and the mortgagee played no part in the decision of the company to buy or in the implementation of that decision.

Counsel for the mortgagee submitted that a mortgagee may exercise his power of sale in favour of a company in which the mortgagee is interested but must satisfy the mortgagor or the court that the mortgagee took reasonable steps to obtain the true market value. In the present case the mortgaged property was purchased by the company at an auction which the courts below described as 'unimpeachable' or 'impeccable'. The price bid by the company and accepted by the auctioneer represented the true market value because no higher bid was received. Both counsel relied on authority for their submissions ...

Counsel for the borrower submitted that a mortgagee, his solicitor or agent cannot be allowed to purchase because they cannot resolve the conflict between their interest to buy for the lowest price with their duties to sell for the highest price. Therefore, he said, whenever there is such a conflict, the sale will not be upheld. In the present case there was clearly a conflict between the interest of the mortgagee in securing that the company secured the mortgaged property at the lowest price and the duty of the mortgagee to sell for the highest price. Counsel for the borrower admits that there can be no general rule that a company in which a mortgagee is interested cannot purchase the mortgaged property. He submits that the company can only do so where the sale is negotiated at arm's length and where it is clear that the mortgagee had no influence on the decision of the company to purchase or on the implementation of that decision ...

In the view of this Board on authority and on principle there is no hard and fast rule that a mortgagee may not sell to a company in which he is interested. The mortgagee and the company seeking to uphold the transaction must show that the sale was in good faith and that the mortgagee took reasonable precautions to obtain the best price reasonably obtainable at the time. The mortgagee is not however bound to postpone the sale in the hope of obtaining a better price or to adopt a piecemeal method of sale which could only be carried out over a substantial period or at some risk of loss. This view of the matter is consistent with the decision of the House of Lords in the *York Buildings Co v MacKenzie* (1795) 3 Cr S & P 378. In that case an agent for creditors purchased an estate of the insolvent at auction. The sale was set aside although 11 years elapsed before the sale was impugned. Lord Loughborough LC referred to two extreme arguments (at 398), first that 'the quality of common agent, barred his exercising any right as a purchaser', and second, that

> ... if he was not disabled absolutely in point of law from purchasing, he must stand in the position of all the rest of mankind, and might purchase as advantageously as he could, provided there was no gross practice or direct fraud.

The Lord Chancellor rejected both extremes and held that agents were entitled to purchase but:

> The bargain must be perfectly fair and equal, at the best price, because they are placed in a situation which they are bound, in the first instance, to act against their own advantage, and for the advantage of their employers; and if they sacrifice that interest and advantage, with view of profiting and taking the interest of it to themselves, the purchase will be liable to be set aside, the advantage will not come to themselves, and the breach of confidence will not avail them.[34]

In the present case in which the mortgagee held a large beneficial interest in the shares of the purchasing company, was a director of the company and was entirely responsible for financing the company, the other shareholders being his wife and children, the sale must be closely examined and a heavy onus lies on the mortgagee to show that in all respects he acted fairly to the borrower and used his best endeavours to obtain the best price reasonably obtainable for the mortgaged property.

34 See 3 Cr & P 378, at 398–99.

Sale by auction does not necessarily prove the validity of a transaction. In *Hodson v Deans* [1903] 2 Ch 647, at a sale by auction by a friendly society in exercise of their power of sale as mortgagees, the secretary of the committee which fixed the reserve and instructed the auctioneer bought the property for himself having 'conceived the idea of buying ... and making a profit for himself out of the transaction' (see *per* Joyce J at 651). The judge found (at 653) that:

> ... the property was sold at an undervalue, not of itself so great as to invalidate the sale, but still at an undervalue. The investment committee could not have sold privately to themselves either as representing the society or as individuals at a price fixed by themselves, nor could they, I think, have so sold to one or more of their number. It is said that any such objection is cured by the fact that the sale was by auction. I do not think so. At all events ... the onus is on the defendant to show that everything was done fairly and *bona fide*.

... In *Cuckmere Brick Co Ltd v Mutual Finance Ltd* [1971] 2 All ER 633 at 646 ... Salmon LJ, after considering all the relevant authorities ... concluded, with the subsequent agreement of Cross and Cairns LJJ that:

> ... both on principle and authority, that the mortgagee in exercising his power of sale does owe a duty to take reasonable precautions to obtain the true market value of the mortgaged property at the date on which he decides to sell it.

In the result their Lordships consider that in the present case the company was not debarred from purchasing the mortgaged property but, in view of the close relationship between the company and the mortgagee and in view in particular of the conflict of duty and interest to which the mortgagee was subject, the sale to the company for \$1.2m can only be supported if the mortgagee proves that he took reasonable precautions to obtain the best price reasonably obtainable at the time of sale.

On behalf of the mortgagee it was submitted that all reasonable steps were taken when the mortgagee, with adequate advertisement, sold the property at a properly conducted auction to the highest bidder. The submission assumes that such an auction must produce the best price reasonably obtainable or, as Salmon LJ expressed the test, the true market value. But the price obtained at any particular auction may be less than the price obtainable by private treaty and may depend on the steps taken to encourage bidders to attend. An auction which only produces one bid is not necessarily an indication that the true market value has been achieved.

In the present case, the mortgagee threatened on 28 February 1966 to sell the property if certain arrears of interest was not paid; it was then obvious that the borrower was in difficulties. On 28 April the mortgagee canned in the principal and gave notice of his intention to sell the property if the principal and interest, which the mortgagee alleged to amount to \$1.6m, were not paid by 29 May 1966. The mortgagee had ample opportunity to consult and instruct estate agents. The property could have been offered for sale by auction or by private treaty or by announcing that the property would be sold by public auction if not previously sold by private treaty. The property could have been sold as a whole or in units. The mortgagee might have been advised that, as happened, a sale by auction might not produce any independent bidders; that the number of potential purchasers able and willing in 1966 to pay over \$1m for this building was limited ... [etc] The mortgagee was advised by his solicitor's managing clerk that a sale by auction was 'fairer' but the mortgagee does not appear to have considered the possibility that a higher price could be obtained by a sale by private treaty to an independent third party at a price recommended by an estate agent as being the best obtainable after the agent had had an opportunity to explore the market. Moreover, the mortgagee does not appear to have taken any step to secure any interest in the auction. The mortgagee's solicitors prepared particulars and conditions of sale which were dated 9 June. On the same day the sale was advertised in three newspapers. There is no evidence that the advertisement did more than give notice of the bare fact of the auction coupled with a minimum description of the property. The particulars and conditions of sale contained only the legal requirements. There was no evidence that anyone requested a copy of the particulars and conditions or asked to inspect the property. The conditions of sale disclosed that there was a reserve price, that the vendor reserved the right to bid, that 20% of the purchase price was payable after the auction and that the balance was payable one month thereafter, time being of the essence. A reader of the first advertisement had just 15 days in which to make detailed inquiries and investigations and to organise his finances so that he was prepared to engage in competitive bidding possibly with a vendor and with a borrower who knew all about the property and might be puffing the sale. There was no evidence that anyone took the elementary precautions which a purchaser of a building for a sum in excess of $1m would expect to take before venturing to bid at an auction ...

This confirms the impression that the auctioneers were not instructed to do more than put the property under the hammer, a procedure which may be appropriate to the sale of second hand furniture but is not necessarily conducive to the attainment of the best price for freehold or leasehold property. It was not of course in the interests of the company that enthusiasm for the sale should be stimulated or that the reserve should be settled by anyone other than the mortgagee.

The reserve of $1.2m was fixed by the mortgagee and was the price at which he advised and intended that the company should purchase. The mortgagee was a property investor and speculator. The company was his family company and he held shares in and financed the company. The mortgagee would not have advised the company to bid $1.2m for the property unless he thought that was an advantageous price for the company to pay.

The company, unlike an independent bidder, knew all about the property through the mortgagee and knew the amount of the reserve in advance. The company and the mortgagee did not have to arrange finance. The company bought the property for $1.2m provided by the mortgagee who received back that sum in reduction of his mortgage debt. The sale transferred from the borrower to the mortgagee's family company at a price advised by the mortgagee the chance of making a profit which the mortgagee could not acquire for himself. The borrower was exposed to an action for $200,000 being the difference between $1.2m, the price paid by the company and $1.4m the amount of the mortgage debt. That left the mortgagee with a hold over the borrower which he exercised when the borrower complained about the sale. If, as appeared probable, the borrower could not pay $200,000 the mortgagee would suffer a loss which he could have prevented by advising the company to bid $1.4m for the property. No doubt the mortgagee did what was best for himself and the company.

The only indication that $1.2m represented the market value of the property was the fact that no one at the auction bid more than $1.2m. But the fact that no one bid more than $1.2m at this auction does not necessarily mean that the property could not have been sold for more than $1.2m if the mortgagee had consulted estate agents about the method of sale and the amount of the reserve and had instructed them to try to interest the investing public in the property. There was no competitive bidding and the company purchased the property at a price fixed by the mortgagee. There is no sufficient evidence that this particular auction produced the true market value ...

Where a mortgagee fails to satisfy the court that he took all reasonable steps to obtain the best price reasonably obtainable and that his company bought at the best price, the court will, as a general rule, set aside the sale and restore to the borrower the equity of redemption of which he has been unjustly deprived. But the borrower will be left to his remedy in damages against the mortgagee for the failure of the mortgagee to secure the best price if it will be inequitable as between the borrower and the purchaser for the sale to be set aside. In the present case it is submitted on behalf of the mortgagee and the company that the borrower is debarred by the terms of his mortgage from any remedy save damages. Alternatively, the mortgagee and the company submit that the delay on the part of the borrower in pursuing his counterclaim has rendered it unjust for the building to be restored to the borrower.

... [I]n the view of the Board, there is nothing in the legal charge that enables or could enable the mortgagee to uphold a sale which is defective because the mortgagee failed to fulfil the duty imposed on him by the law to take all reasonable steps to obtain the best price reasonably obtainable. The borrower is not therefore debarred by the terms of the legal charge from seeking to set aside the sale to the company.

The borrower has however been guilty of inexcusable delay in prosecuting his counterclaim ... The borrower contends that these delays have not been prejudicial to the mortgagee who will receive principal and interest. But the borrower also seeks an account from the mortgagee on the basis of wilful default. Moreover, either the mortgagee or the company must have been put to expense in maintenance and repairs of the building and may have laid out moneys on other matters which could have been better employed elsewhere. The borrower by his delay achieved a favourable position; if the property decreased in value he could either abandon his action or seek damages in setting aside the sale. If the property increased in value he could persist with his claim to set aside the sale. In the circumstances the Board consider that the borrower is not entitled to have the sale set aside but is entitled to the alternative remedy of damages. That was the view of the trial judge.

The measure of damages must be the difference between the best price reasonably obtainable on 24 June 1966 and the price of $1.2m paid by the company ... In ... the circumstances the Board consider that the action must be remitted to the Court of Appeal of Hong Kong for that court to make such directions as may be considered necessary for the assessment of damages.

Appeal allowed.

Questions

1 Moresby Mortgage Bank (MMB) lent Cholai K100,000 on security of his house in Boroko. The mortgage was duly registered. When Cholai defaulted in the payment of his monthly instalments, MMB served on him a notice under s 67 of the LRA, demanding payment of the money due, but Cholai was unable to pay. After 30 days MMB took possession of Cholai's house with the object of selling it to recover K90,000 which Cholai still owed the bank. MMB had the house valued by Smarts, a property valuer, who estimated its current value at K90,000. However, Smarts advised against immediate sale because, in his opinion, according to economic indications, property prices were likely to appreciate in the very near future. He thought that if the sale was delayed for at least six months the property might fetch up to K100,000. MMB ignored Smart's advice and instructed a firm of auctioneers to proceed with the sale

immediately. A month later the house was sold at an auction for K85,000. Two months after the auction sale, the purchaser sold the house for K105,000.

Advise Cholai of his possible course of action, if any, against MMB.

2 X defaulted in payment of K50,000 which was secured by a mortgage to the Bank. After serving on him the requisite statutory notices and otherwise satisfying all the requirements prior to a mortgage sale, the Bank instructed Oceana, a reputable real estate agent firm, to proceed with the sale either by private contract or by auction. Oceana placed one advertisement in a local newspaper, which disclosed that the property was going to be sold by public auction under power of sale within two weeks from the date of the notice. A week before the auction TP offered to buy the property for K55,000, but Oceana advised the Bank not to accept the offer because they were likely to get a higher offer at the auction. Only two people attended the auction and the highest bid was K50,000. The property was sold for K50,000.

X seeks your advice of his possible remedies against the Bank.

'Harsh' and 'oppressive' acts under s 41 of the Constitution (Ch No 1)

Section 41 of the Constitution, declares unlawful any 'harsh' or 'oppressive' acts done under a valid law. The section reads as follows:

> (1) Notwithstanding anything to the contrary in any other provision of any law, any act that is done under a valid law but in the particular case
>
> (a) is harsh or oppressive; or
>
> (b) is not warranted by, or is disproportionate to, the requirements of the particular circumstances or of the particular case; or
>
> (c) is otherwise not, in the particular circumstances, reasonably justifiable in a democratic society having a proper regard for the rights and dignity of mankind,
>
> is an unlawful act.
>
> (2) The burden of showing that sub-section (1)(a), (b) or (c) applies in respect of an act is on the party alleging it, and may be discharged on the balance of probabilities.
>
> (3) Nothing in this section affects the operation of any other law under which an act may be held to be unlawful or invalid.

The interpretation of this section is fraught with controversy. A wide interpretation holds that s 41 is a controlling mechanism, which applies to the exercise of any statutory power notwithstanding any other law. A narrow interpretation limits its application to the exercise of qualified and basic rights set out in the Constitution.[35] The two following cases illustrate unsuccessful attempts to invoke the section against the exercise of a mortgagee's remedies deriving from the Land Registration Act. It should, however, be stressed that though the applicants were unsuccessful in both cases, the issue whether s 41 applies to the exercise of a mortgagee's statutory powers, remains unanswered until the Supreme Court decides definitively.

35 See cases cited *In the Matter of an Application by Rose Tarere et al v Australia and New Zealand Banking Group (PNG) Ltd* [1988] PNGLR 201, see extract below.

IN THE MATTER OF AN APPLICATION BY ROSE TARERE AND OTHERS v AUSTRALIA AND NEW ZEALAND BANKING GROUP (PNG) LTD AND IN THE MATTER OF SECTION 41 OF THE CONSTITUTION OF THE INDEPENDENT STATE OF PNG
[1988] PNGLR 201, National Court of Justice

[The co-plaintiffs defaulted in the payment of their mortgage debts to the defendant bank. The bank pursuant to its powers under the mortgage sold the properties. The co-plaintiffs sought declarations pursuant to s 41(1) of the Constitution that the actions of the bank in selling the properties were harsh and oppressive and/or not warranted by or were disproportionate to the requirements of the particular case.]

HINCHCLIFFE J: The co-plaintiffs seek declarations pursuant to s 41 of the Constitution of Papua New Guinea. The matter arises out of the mortgagee sale by the defendant of eight properties at Rabaul. The co-plaintiffs claim that the circumstances in which the defendant proceeded with such action was unlawful and an example of the type of declaration sought is as follows:

A declaration that the actions of the defendant in selling the property at Lot 1 Section 58, Rabaul is harsh and oppressive and/or is not warranted by or is disproportionate to the requirements of the particular case to Rose Tarere and by virtue of s 41(1) of the National Constitution is an unlawful act.

Section 41 in so far as is relevant provides:

Proscribed Acts

(1) Notwithstanding anything to the contrary in any other provision of any law, any act that is done under a valid law but in the particular case
   (a) is harsh or oppressive, or
   (b) is not warranted by, or is disproportionate to, the requirements of the particular case ...

is an unlawful act.

The burden of showing that sub-section (1)(a),(b) or (c) applies in respect of an act is on the party alleging it, and may be discharged on the balance of probabilities.

At the commencement of the hearing Mr Pato, who appeared for the co-plaintiffs conceded that the defendant was the mortgagee in possession of the various State Leases pursuant to its mortgages and had authority to foreclose under the terms of the subject mortgages under the relevant provisions of the Land Registration Act (Ch No 191) of the Revised Laws of Papua New Guinea.

That matter was not taken any further by the defendant which did surprise me to a certain extent because it seemed to me that it could be argued that if such a concession was made then the implication is that it is also conceded that s 41 of the Constitution did not apply. Needless to say the point was not raised and I do not propose to mention it again.

Mr O'Regan QC, who, together with Mr Coady, appeared for the defendant, submitted that s 41 of the Constitution did not apply to this case. If that submission was successful then of course that would be the end of the matter and the co-plaintiffs would fail from the outset in their bid to seek declaration.

Mr Pato submitted that the issue is now settled since *SCR No 1 of 1984; Re Minimum Penalties Legislation* [1984] PNGLR 314. He said:

> There can be no question as to the application of s 41 to the instant case. Hence, the defendant's submission that s 41 does not apply is with respect misconceived.

It is clear that s 41 applies to the provisions of 'any law' notwithstanding anything to the contrary in any other law. The contextual applicability argument developed by Bredmeyer and McDermott JJ in *SCR No 1 of 1984; Re Minimum Penalties Legislation* [1984] PNGLR 314 and advanced by counsel has already been rejected by the majority of the judges in that court, namely Kidu CJ, Kapi Dep CJ and Kaputin J. It is argued that Kaputin J cannot be said to have clearly supported the views of the Chief Justice and Deputy Chief Justice. We submit he did, when his Honour states at p 351 of his judgment –

> ... Section 41 provides a *controlling mechanism* and whatever way we look at it, no statutory laws can avoid it. [Emphasis own.]

And his Honour goes on to state (at 352):

> It is unfortunate that the power was slotted in between the qualified rights provisions. It could have been placed somewhere else in the Constitution as it is not limited to qualified rights only. It is submitted that it is implicit form [sic] these words that his Honour was speaking in the same vein as the Chief Justice and the Deputy Chief Justice that the application of s 41 is not limited to qualified and basic rights.

Mr Pato went on to say that:

> Indeed, support for this interpretation of the analysis of s 41 in that case may be found in the judgment of McDermott AJ as he then was in *Raz v Matane* [1986] PNGLR 38. His Honour, when commenting on the views of the Supreme Court in *SCR No 5 of 1985; Re Raz v Matane* [1985] PNGLR 329 stated at p 30 of his judgment as follows:
>
>> However, Amet J favoured a more limited role for s 41 and whilst I have differed on his view of the nature of this 'right', I too, in agreement with Bredmeyer J in *SCR No 1 of 1984; Re Default Penalties* [1984] PNGLR 418, limited an action under s 41 to rights set out in the Constitution. But on this issue we were in the minority; Kidu CJ, Kapi DCJ and Kaputin J favoured a wide interpretation for the section, and that is the present state of the law and how this case has thus come to pass.

Sometime after final submissions from counsel, Mr Pato, by letter, referred me to *Independent State of Papua New Guinea v Lohia Sisia* [1987] PNGLR 102 at 111 of that judgment, where Bredmeyer J said:

> ... the ambit of s 41 was considered by the Supreme Court in *SCR No 1 of 1984; Re Minimum Penalties Legislation* [1984] PNGLR 314. The majority, Kidu CJ, Kapi Dep CJ and Kaputin J, decided that the section applies to any act done under a valid law and is not limited to an act done under law which restricts one of the constitutional rights.

In that appeal Cory and Barnett JJ concurred with Bredmeyer J but they did not give any reasons.

The submission made by Mr O'Regan QC has caused me considerable concern because it seems to me that what Kaputin J said in *SCR No 1 of 1984; Re Minimum Penalties Legislation* may well not be supporting the views of the Chief Justice and the Deputy Chief Justice. If that is so then the situation now is that the s 41 argument is still undecided or the majority view is in fact that of Bredmeyer and McDermott JJ in *SCR No 1 of 1984*.

In his submissions, Mr Pato did not refer to what Kaputin J said (at 350) of *SCR No 1 of 1984*, which I believe is of importance. It reads:

> After a close look at the purpose of s 41 I have now come to the view that such power does apply to protection of qualified rights as well as to basic and fundamental rights.

What I glean from that is that his Honour was making it clear that s 41 applied to all of Pt III, Div 3 – Basic Rights, of our Constitution, and not only the qualified rights Sub-division C in which s 41 is situated. To my mind that makes sense when read together with the passages referred to by Mr Pato (at 351 and 352). Clearly the passage (at 351) is referring to statutory laws connected with Constitutional basic rights. The passage (at 352) is in effect confirming what his Honour said (at 351), that the power relates to all basic rights and not just qualified rights.

From my reading of Kaputin J's judgment I am of the view that he did not take the matter any further and did not adopt the wider view of the Chief Justice and Deputy Chief Justice. I am prepared to say that the judgment of Kaputin J is equivocal. I certainly could not say that he clearly supports the Chief Justice and the Deputy Chief Justice.

It seems that after *SCR No 1 of 1984* it was taken for granted that Kaputin J was in the majority. Even the headnote (at 351) reads as follows:

> (*Per* Kapi Dep CJ and Kaputin J.) The provisions of s 41 of the Constitution apply to all acts done under any valid law including constitutional laws and may apply to the non-discretionary judicial act of imposing a minimum penalty to the extent that such an act may in a particular case be declared invalid or unlawful by the Supreme Court.

I am of the view that that part of the headnote is misleading as far as the judgment of Kaputin J is concerned.

As has already been referred to, McDermott AJ in *Raz v Matane* referred to the majority view in *SCR No 1 of 1984* but did not analyse Kaputin J's judgment and I am of the view that he erred in saying that Kaputin J was in the majority. It is clear that McDermott AJ took a different course to the one he took in *SCR No 1 of 1984* because he thought Kaputin J was in the majority in *SCR No 1 of 1984*.

Likewise Bredmeyer J in *Independent State of Papua New Guinea v Lohia Sisia* took a different course to the one he took in *SCR No 1 of 1984* because he thought that Kaputin J was in the majority. Bredmeyer J did not analyse the judgment of Kaputin J either and as previously stated Cory J and Barnett J, although concurring with Bredmeyer J, gave no reasons.

I am of the view that I am not bound to follow the conclusions reached by Bredmeyer J and McDermott AJ in the said cases when they stated that Kaputin J was in the majority in *SCR No 1 of 1984*. In the event that they had analysed Kaputin J's judgment and then commented as to how it became part of the majority then that would be a different matter. But they did not and I cannot agree with them.

Therefore I am of the view that at its highest the judgment of Kaputin J in *SCR No 1 of 1984* is equivocal and on that basis it would seem that the s 41 argument is still undecided. Returning to *SCR No 1 of 1984*. I concur fully with the judgment of Bredmeyer J and there is nothing I wish to add to it. It becomes clear that the submission of Mr O'Regan QC must succeed and that the co-plaintiffs must fail in this action.

Perhaps I should also refer to that part of Mr Pato's submission where he stated as follows:

> Besides the contextual interpretation urged if correct on the basis on which it is put forward, should be rejected as in a developing country such as Papua New Guinea, such a construction of the Constitution is reflective of a literalist approach and this should be rejected as being inappropriate to the circumstances of Papua New Guinea

> and for the reasons given in *PLAR No 1 of 1980* [1980] PNGLR 326 and 336 *per* Wilson J and 347 *per* Andrew J.

I do not agree with that submission. I am of the view that the wider interpretation of s 41 could create confusion and uncertainty which is not good for stability. Stability is important in a developing country such as Papua New Guinea. A situation would arise, and probably by now has arisen, where acts have been done which are authorised by law (and having nothing to do with basic rights) only to discover that the acts could be declared unlawful. I agree with Mr O'Regan QC when he said:

> Planning commercial and indeed other activities on the basis that there was an ascertainable and settled legal order would be impossible.

The wider interpretation could create an abuse of the court process and encourage people to take action under s 41 purely as a delaying tactic ...

Application dismissed.

BANK OF PAPUA NEW GUINEA v MUTENG BASA [1992] PNGLR 271, National Court of Justice

[The defendant defaulted in the repayment of a mortgage debt to the plaintiff bank. The bank demanded vacant possession of the mortgaged property. The defendant in his defence pleaded that the plaintiff bank in the exercise of its remedies under the terms of the mortgage acted unreasonably and without due regard to his livelihood, therefore, its act was 'harsh and oppressive' within the meaning of s 41(1) of the Constitution.]

BROWN J: The defence cannot stand. It is not available as Mr Kua [for the plaintiff] says, under s 41 of the Constitution since the contractual relationships of the parties do not impinge on a constitutional right. I agree with Mr Kua where he says the reasoning of Hinchcliffe J in *Tarere v ANZ Bank Group (PNG) Ltd* [1988] PNGLR 201 is applicable in this case. The judge held that the provisions of s 41 of the Constitution relating to harsh or oppressive acts done under a valid law cannot be invoked in relation to the valid exercise of a mortgagee's power of sale deriving from the Land Registration Act, Ch 191. I find that the plaintiff is entitled to an order for ejectment under s 74(1)(c) of the Land Registration Act, having pleaded the right in the mortgage and proved to my satisfaction the default in payment giving rise to the circumstances envisaged by that section. On the fact of the ledger in evidence, no credits have been made (apart from a reversal entry) to the staff housing account of the defendant since his cessation of employment on 16 August 1990, and in his own evidence he concedes this.

Dr Marat for the defendant has failed to address the effect of the loan and mortgage documents, but clearly they are contractual, binding both parties according to their tenor. I see no reason to depart from that basic premise.

Clause 6 of the mortgage reads:

> If default be made by the mortgagor in repayment of any instalments of principal and/or interest at any time or in the performance or observance of any covenant herein expressed or implied then immediately thereupon or at any time thereafter all monies hereby secured or any instalment there or costs charges and expenses as aforesaid shall be at the option of the mortgagee forthwith due and payable.

The evidence of default is in the ledger. That is the best evidence. I find that the plaintiff has the right to possession on default and is, accordingly, entitled to an order in terms of the statute. Clause 7 of the mortgage provides:

> The powers of sale, entry, possession, distress and ejectment and all other powers conferred by the Land Registration Act, Ch 191 or by any further amendment thereof may be exercised by the mortgagee at any time after the default in payment of the monies hereby secured ...

While Dr Marat has attempted to mount an argument on the basis of the unfortunate effect his cessation of employment had on his client, his subsequent employment and more recent unemployment had adversely affected the defendant's ability to both service the loan and seek refinance, and thus unilaterally he seeks to avoid the existing agreement with the bank in this fashion. This argument is not available to the defendant. He continues to be bound by the terms of the mortgage agreement notwithstanding a change in his personal circumstances. There is no suggestion that the agreement was harsh and unconscionable at the time it was entered into, and so there is no need for me to speculate on the effect of such a state of affairs on this contract. The evidence is certainly to the contrary. The interest rate is 3%, clearly a preferred rate at the time the loan was taken out, and repayments were made by way of salary deductions from at least July 1987 until August 1990 without complaint. To say, after the money in the loan had passed to the defendant for the purchase of his house property, that his impecunious state now gives rise to a defence to the bank's claim under contract in the absence of some contractual or tortuous basis, is demurrable. Mr Kua has taken the point, there is no defence apparent on the face of the pleadings ...

[Judgment for the plaintiff.]

Question

In the case of *Tarere v ANZ Bank*, Hinchcliffe J said that a wide interpretation of s 41 (which would enable the court to intervene in the exercise of a mortgagee's remedies derived from the Land Registration Act) would create 'confusion and uncertainty'. Do you agree?

Protection of the purchaser

So far, we have considered judicial protection of a mortgagor where the mortgagee realizes his or her security. It should be remembered, however, that in a sale there is a third person, namely the purchaser. To a certain extent, a purchaser at a mortgage sale is protected in event of impropriety in the conduct of the sale. This is provided for under s 69 of the Land Registration Act and reads as follows:

> **Protection of purchaser**
>
> (1) All sales, contracts, matters and things authorized by section 68 are as valid and effectual as if made, done or executed by the debtor, and in particular the written receipt of the creditor is a sufficient discharge to a purchaser for the amount of the purchase money specified in the receipt.

(2) No purchaser under a sale authorized by section 68 –

  (a) is answerable for the loss, misapplication or non-application of the purchase money paid by him; or

  (b) is obliged to see to the application of the purchase money paid by him; or

  (c) is concerned to enquire as to the fact of any default or notice under section 67 or 68.

The following judgment of the High Court of Australia discusses the limits of the purchaser's protection under a corresponding provision.

FORSYTH v BLUNDELL (1973) 129 CLR 477, High Court of Australia

[The plaintiffs (Mr and Mrs Blundell) mortgaged their land to Associated Securities Ltd (ASL) as security for a loan. Upon default, ASL, purporting to exercise their statutory powers of sale, arranged to sell the property by public auction. They fixed the reserve price at $120,000 which amount was equal to what the mortgagor owed them under the mortgage. Prior to the auction date ASL held discussions with another company referred to here as XL, which expressed an interest to pay out the mortgage or bid up to $150,000. Despite these discussions, ASL sold the property by private contract to Shell Ltd (the purchaser) for $120,000. ASL did not mention to Shell Ltd XL's expressed interest to pay $150,000 for the same property. Nor did ASL inform XL of Shell's offer. Before completion of the transfer to Shell Ltd, the plaintiffs brought proceedings for a declaration that the sale to Shell Ltd was not *bona fide* and for an injunction against ASL to restrain it from completing the transfer to Shell Ltd. The trial judge, Fox J, found that ASL did not only act negligently, but it 'recklessly' 'sacrificed' the interests of the mortgagor. On this finding, he declared that the sale had not been a *bona fide* exercise of ASL's (the mortgagee's) power of sale, and granted an injunction restraining ASL from completing the transfer. ASL, Shell and Forsyth (Shell's agent), separately, appealed. It was contended for Shell and Forsyth that a mortgage sale can only be set aside or its completion restrained where the purchaser has been guilty of corruption or collusion or where the sale price was so low as to be evidence of fraud. It was submitted that where all that is established is a failure to take reasonable precautions to obtain a proper price, a sale cannot be set aside. The mortgagor's remedy in the latter situation is in damages or an account against the seller mortgagee.]

WALSH J: In my opinion, the decision that there was a breach of duty on the part of ASL should not be set aside by this court.

The next question is whether or not the plaintiffs were entitled, in consequence of that breach of duty, to obtain an injunction to restrain the completion of the contract between ASL and Shell.

In the Supreme Court Fox J was not satisfied that at the time of the contract Shell had notice of the breach of duty or of facts from which an inference of conclusion of breach of duty should have been drawn. It has been urged for the plaintiffs that this court should interfere with that finding. But I do not think that we should do so. In my opinion, the reasons stated by his Honour for his conclusion have not been shown to have been based upon a misunderstanding of the evidence or otherwise affected by error which would warrant us in refusing to accept it. I do not propose to examine all the evidence relating to this question. The breach of duty that was found to have occurred depended mainly upon the facts and circumstances consisting of or disclosed by the discussions between Blundell and

Owen and between Sykes and Owen which took place before the making of the contract. The officers of Shell were not parties to those discussions and were not given any full account of them ...

I proceed to consider whether the plaintiffs were entitled, having regard to the findings made at the trial, to injunctive relief. I stated earlier that I did not think it was necessary to decide whether or not a breach of duty for which a mortgagee can be held liable is made out if all that is found is that he has acted negligently, although in good faith, in carrying out a sale. That statement needs some elaboration. If a mortgagee has acted in breach of his duty, it may become necessary to decide whether the available relief is limited to making him liable to make good to the mortgagor such loss as has been caused by that breach of duty or includes the obtaining of an order to set aside a conveyance or transfer by which a sale had been carried into effect or, in cases in which the contract of sale has not been completed, an injunction to restrain the mortgagee from completing it. On behalf of Shell it was argued that if a mortgagor has any remedy in respect of negligence in carrying out a sale, this must be limited in all cases to holding the mortgagee liable to account for the loss suffered. In this case there is a question whether or not in the circumstances it was proper for the Supreme Court to grant an injunction to restrain ASL from completing the agreement made with Shell. But, in my opinion, the answer to that question does not depend upon the acceptance or rejection of the distinction made in the submissions to which I have just referred. This is not a case in which the only relevant finding against ASL was a finding of negligence. In effect, there was also a finding that in making the contract there was a reckless disregard of the interests of the mortgagor. I am of opinion that in such circumstances the completion of the contract may be restrained.

It has been argued that a passage in the judgment of Kay J in *Warner v Jacob* [(1882) 20 Ch D 220, at p 224] which has often been quoted in subsequent cases, is an exhaustive and correct statement of the circumstances in which a sale will be set aside or an injunction granted and it is said, therefore, that if a mortgagor has any remedy in respect of a sale not shown to have been affected by 'corruption or collusion with the purchaser' or to have been at a price so low as in itself to be evidence of fraud, his only remedy can be in damages. In my opinion, this submission should not be accepted. There may be an improper exercise of a power of sale (that is one which constitutes a breach of the duty owed to the mortgagor) where although there is not any actual fraud (in the ordinary sense of that term) or any collusion between the mortgagee and the purchaser, there is improper conduct which goes beyond mere negligence in carrying out the sale. There may be impropriety of various kinds. What has sometimes been described as a fraud on the power and sometimes as a wilful or reckless disregard of the interests of the mortgagor and sometimes as a sacrificing of the interests of the mortgagor does not necessarily involve, in my opinion, the commission of actual fraud ... I think it is in accordance with authority and that it should be affirmed that there may be conduct which amounts to a reckless sacrificing of the interests of a mortgagor, although it is not shown that there is an actual intention to defraud him or that there is corruption or collusion with the purchaser. It is concerning conduct of that kind that inquiry must be made in this case whether or not it warranted the granting of an injunction.

I do not doubt that as between himself and his mortgagee who has conducted himself in that way in entering into a contract of sale, a mortgagor is entitled to invoke the aid of the court to prevent the completion of the contract. As between those parties, the proprietary right of the mortgagor will be protected against such a wrongful alienation by the mortgagee. But the critical question is whether the purchaser under the contract acquires a right which entitles him to have the contract completed and therefore precludes the grant of any injunction to restrain its completion. In dealing with that problem I leave aside for the present the statutory provisions which are said to have a bearing upon it.

It has been submitted that a person who has entered into a contract as purchaser cannot be affected in any case by impropriety on the part of the mortgagee, not involving collusion with the purchaser. It has been put as an alternative argument that, if a purchaser may be affected by notice of the facts which constitute the impropriety (not involving collusion), he can be affected only if he has such notice at the time when he enters into the contract. In my opinion, if the mortgagee does not exercise the power of sale 'in good faith' (in the sense explained above) and the purchaser had knowledge of the facts which show the lack of good faith, the purchaser cannot obtain a right superior to the right of the mortgagor. Even when a contract made in such circumstances is carried to completion, in many cases the transaction may be set aside, or alternatively, the conveyance or transfer treated as operating only as a transfer of the mortgage and of the debt secured by it, and not as a transfer of the mortgagor's interest: see *Latec Investments Ltd v Hotel Terrigal Pty Ltd (In Liquidation)* [(1965) 113 CLR 265, pp 274–75]. But if the person who agrees to purchase has no notice of any impropriety at the date of contract and continues to have no notice at the time when it is completed, he will obtain a title which cannot be challenged by the mortgagor. (It is here assumed that all statutory and contractual conditions essential to the exercise of the power of sale have been fulfilled.)

If the purchaser is without notice of the relevant facts at the date of the contract, but the mortgagor takes action to challenge its propriety before completion and proves that on the part of the mortgagee it was improper, the question is whether the purchaser has a right which prevails over the right which the mortgagor would have, as between himself and the mortgagee, to restrain the completion of the contract. That is the question in this case.

The mortgagor's interest was, of course, prior in time to any interest acquired by the purchaser. The right of the mortgagor was not merely an equity of redemption. The mortgages did not operate as transfers of his title to the land: see the Ordinance, s 93(1). His title could be divested by a transfer in pursuance of a contract of sale made by the mortgagee in the exercise of the power of sale. But until that occurred, he retained a legal interest in the land.

Even if the contest between these parties should be resolved on the basis that there is a competition between equitable interests, in my opinion the position of the purchaser, so far as the applicable general principles are concerned, would not be any better. In my opinion, the situation was not one in which it was open to the purchaser to claim that, although it had not acquired a legal estate, it could maintain, against a claim by the mortgagor to prevent the completion of the sale, a defence that it was a purchaser for value without notice. After a consideration of the decision and of the judgments in *Latec Investments Ltd v Hotel Terrigal Pty Ltd (In Liquidation)* ... I am of opinion that the circumstances in which the interest of the trustee for the debenture holders in that case was held to prevail over the claim of the mortgagor were so different from those upon which the contest here depends that the case is not an authority upon which Shell can rely.

I am of opinion, also, that the contest cannot be resolved in favour of Shell by the application of the principles upon which in *Abigail v Lapin* [[1934] AC 491] and *Breskvar v Wall* [(1971) 126 CLR 376] the claims of the parties whose interests were first in time were postponed to the claims of the other parties. This is not merely for the reason that in the present case Blundell had more than an equitable interest. If his interest is considered as being for present purposes no more than an equitable interest, his conduct did not contribute, in my opinion, to any false assumption or belief upon which Shell acted in entering into the transaction (see *Breskvar v Wall*) ... nor did it affect Shell in any other way which would make it inequitable to assert against Shell the interest of Blundell.

By executing the mortgages and defaulting in payments under them, Blundell did bring about a situation in which ASL was empowered to sell the property. But if the mortgagee did not act *bona fide* in the exercise of the power of sale, and the purchaser, being unaware of this, assumed that the mortgagee was acting *bona fide*, that assumption was not one which any conduct of Blundell caused the purchaser to make.

If a contract of sale had been made which was not affected by any impropriety, it would not have been open to the mortgagor to claim that until the contract had been completed his right to redeem the mortgage continued notwithstanding the contract and was superior to the right of the purchaser. Although he retained his title to the land this was subject to the power of sale as defined in the Ordinance and as incorporated into the mortgage instruments. In my opinion, a contract of sale properly made in the course of the exercise of that power is binding upon the mortgagor, not because the mortgagee contracts as agent for the mortgagor, but because by entering into a mortgage to which the Ordinance applies the mortgagor makes his own rights subject to its provisions, including those which confer and regulate the power of sale, and, therefore, subject to any action which is properly taken in good faith by the mortgagee. In this question, I regard as applicable and as correct the decision in *Waring (Lord) v London and Manchester Assurance Co Ltd* [[1935] 1 Ch 310], approved in *Property & Bloodstock Ltd v Emerton* [[1968] 1 Ch 94], that a contract by the mortgagee to sell the property is binding, before completion, upon the mortgagor unless it be proved that the mortgagee exercised his power of sale in bad faith. But here it is contended that as a matter of general principle and independently of the meaning and effect of the provisions of ss 94(2), 94(3) and 94(5) of the Ordinance, such a contract is binding *before completion* upon the mortgagor, even if the mortgagee acted in bad faith, unless he acted in collusion with the purchaser, or alternatively, unless the purchaser had knowledge *at the date of the contract* of the facts which affected the propriety of the sale. In my opinion, this proposition should not be accepted. If the matter is to be determined in accordance with the general principles by which disputes as to priority between competing claims are resolved, there is no principle which operates to postpone the right of the mortgagor to that of the purchaser. In my opinion, the authorities to which we were referred do not support the foregoing submission. As Fox J said, many of the cases dealing with the matter were cases in which there had been a conveyance or transfer ...

It was argued that the position of a purchaser from a mortgagee is analogous to that of a purchaser who makes a contract with an agent acting within his ostensible authority but in breach (unknown to the purchaser) of his duty to his principal. In my opinion, the analogy is not acceptable. The mortgagee in making a sale is acting on his own behalf and primarily in his own interests. The sale is not one by which the mortgagor, through the medium of an agent, is disposing of his own property. It is one by which his property is being divested from him. If the power vested in the mortgagee is properly exercised the mortgagor is bound. But if it is not exercised in good faith there is, in my opinion, no reason that can be derived from any general principle for holding that before completion the purchaser gets a good title as against the mortgagor.

It is necessary now to refer to some provisions of the Ordinance. In the Supreme Court it was argued that Shell had a title which was made unimpeachable by s 94(5) of the Ordinance which is in these terms:

> Where a transfer is made in professed exercise of the power of sale conferred by this Ordinance, the title of the transferee shall not be impeachable on the ground that no

> case has arisen to authorize the sale or that due notice was not given or that the power was otherwise improperly or irregularly exercised, but any person damnified by an unauthorized or improper or irregular exercise of the power shall have his remedy in damages against the person exercising the power.

In my opinion, his Honour was correct in rejecting that submission, which was not pressed at the hearing of these appeals. The provision applies where a transfer is made and is not applicable in this case. But counsel for Shell relied on s 94(2) which is in these terms:

> All sales, contracts, matters and things made, done or executed in pursuance of the last preceding sub-section shall be as valid and effectual as if the mortgagor or encumbrancer had made, done or executed them, and the receipt or receipts in writing of the mortgagee or encumbrancee shall be a sufficient discharge to the purchaser of the land, estate or interest, or of any portion thereof, for so much of his purchase money as is thereby expressed to be received.

In the Supreme Court Fox J said that counsel for Shell mentioned that provision but without making any submission thereon. His Honour then expressed the view that the first part of the provision, which derives from the earliest Real Property Acts, was introduced to ensure that a mortgagee could give title and could contract to do so, although he himself had not title. His Honour said that the purpose was not to give more protection to a purchaser than he had under the general law. I agree with respect with that view. The second part of s 94(2) does give protection to a purchaser in relation to his payment of the purchase money and its subsequent application by the mortgagee. But the first part of the provision should be regarded as supplementary to the powers conferred upon the mortgagee by s 94(1) to sell the estate and interest of the mortgagor and to make and execute all such instruments and documents as are necessary for effecting the sale thereof.

A literal reading of the words of s 94(2) might lead to the result that no challenge could be made by a mortgagor to a contract of sale made by a mortgagee after default had occurred for the period mentioned in s 94(1) upon any ground at all relating to the improper conduct of the mortgagee, regardless of whether or not the impropriety was at all times known to the purchaser. Thus, if a contract provided for a sale at such an undervalue as would be regarded, according to the authorities, as being itself evidence of fraud, it could not be said that if an owner had himself entered into such a contract he could have it set aside as fraudulent merely because of the inadequate contract price, without any proof that he was induced by the fraud of the purchaser to enter into it. If s 94(2) is read as rendering such a contract immune from challenge when made by a mortgagee, it goes further in protecting the contract of a purchaser prior to completion than does s 94(5) in protecting a purchaser to whom a transfer has been made. In my opinion, it should not be so read.

The protection given by s 94(5) extends, when a transfer has been made, not only to a case where the sale is unauthorized or made without due notice, but also to a case in which the power is being 'otherwise improperly or irregularly exercised' ... In s 94(3) of the Ordinance a purchaser is given a limited protection against failure to make inquiries. He is not concerned to inquire as to the fact of any default or notice having been made or given as provided in s 93. But he is not expressly relieved from inquiry as to whether the power is otherwise being properly and regularly exercised. That circumstance has no direct bearing on the present case, where the question is not whether the purchaser has lost, by failure to inquire, a protection to which otherwise it would have been entitled. But the inclusion in s 94 of sub-s (3), together with the inclusion of sub-s (5), indicates, in my opinion, that one ought not to give to sub-s (2) an effect which would give a purchaser, before completion, a complete immunity from the intervention of the court to restrain the completion of a contract made by him with a mortgagee who did not exercise the power of sale in good faith ...

It was submitted that the immunity of the purchaser (before as well as after completion) afforded by s 94(2) is no greater than the purchaser would have under the general law without its aid. It was said that the sub-section is directed only to cases in which the occasion for the exercise of the power of sale has in fact arisen and the formalities for its exercise have been duly carried out, whereas s 94(5) applies if the power of sale has not become exercisable, because some condition upon which the power depends has not been fulfilled. In the former class of case, it was submitted, the purchaser may rely on the contract, against a challenge to its propriety made before completion, except where he has himself been guilty of collusion or fraud. I have already given reasons for rejecting the view that the right of a mortgagor to impugn a contract of sale made by his mortgagee is confined in that way ... In my opinion, if the submission on behalf of Shell as to the effect of s 94(2) were accepted, it would extend greatly the protection to which a purchaser from a mortgagee has been regarded as being entitled, according to general principles and according to the interpretation which has been placed judicially on various protection clauses commonly contained in mortgage instruments or in legislation regulating the exercise by mortgagees of their powers of sale. In particular, the provisions in similar terms, contained in various Acts, which have been in force since the establishment of the Torrens system, have not been interpreted as having the effect which the submission seeks to put upon s 94(2). In my opinion, the submission should not be accepted.

In the Supreme Court the question was raised whether an injunction should be granted against Shell and Mr Forsyth, as well as against ASL. But counsel for the plaintiffs did not then press for this and the injunction against ASL. In this court it has been submitted that there should be an injunction against Shell. I think that that is correct and that the order of the Supreme Court should be varied by adding an order restraining Shell its servants and agents from completing the contract of sale. It is not necessary, in my opinion, to make a similar order directed personally to Mr Forsyth ...

[Mason J concurred; Menzies J dissented.]

Questions

1. Was this case (*Forsyth v Blundell*) decided on the basis of s 94 of the Real Property Ordinance 1925–61 (ACT), or on the basis of the general law or both? Note that there is no provision under the Land Registration Act, which corresponds with s 94, of the Australian Capital Territory Real Property Ordinance. Is this a strong ground for distinguishing the case in PNG?
2. Is *Forsyth v Blundell* authority for the view that a sale by a mortgagee in breach of his duty to the mortgagor may be set aside as against the purchaser? If not, under what circumstances would such a sale be set aside?
3. Would the court have set aside the sale if the transfer to the purchaser (Shell Ltd) had been registered? See also *McKean v Maloney* (1988) 1 Qd R 628; and *Latec Investments Ltd v Hotel Terrigal Pty*.

Application of proceeds of sale

Although the mortgagee in exercise of his or her power of sale is not a trustee, he or she holds the proceeds of sale as a trustee.[36] Section 68(6) stipulates how the proceeds of sale must be applied:

(6) The purchase money arising from a sale under this section shall be applied –

- (a) firstly, in payment of the expenses occasioned by the sale; and
- (b) secondly, to the extent that money remains after the payment specified in Paragraph (a) – in payment of a registered mortgage or charge taking precedence to the mortgage or charge to which the power of sale was exercised and to which the sale was not subject; and
- (c) thirdly, to the extent that money remains after the payment specified in Paragraph (b) – in payment of the creditor: and
- (d) fourthly, to the extent that money remains after the payment specified in Paragraph (c) – in payment in order of priority, of registered mortgages or charges that are subsequent to the mortgage or charge in relation to which the power of sale was exercised; and
- (e) finally, to the extent that money remains after the payment specified in Paragraph (d) – in payment to the debtor.

The following case deals with the liability of the seller mortgagee to secondary mortgagees with regard to the proceeds of sale.

WEST LONDON COMMERCIAL BANK v RELIANCE PERMANENT BUILDING SOCIETY (1885) 29 Ch D 954, Court of Appeal

[A legal mortgage was created in favour of the defendant building society. Later the mortgagor created an equitable mortgage in favour of the plaintiff bank. With the subsequent concurrence of the defendant, the mortgagor sold the mortgaged property. He used the proceeds to pay off the defendant's debt and he retained the remainder of the proceeds of the sale. The second equitable mortgagee brought these proceedings against the mortgagor (who did not appear) and the defendant. The trial judge made a finding of fact that the defendant mortgagee had notice of the second mortgage although at the time of sale it had forgotten about it.]

COTTON LJ: It is established by the cases that where there are first, second and third mortgagees, the first mortgagee, even though he has notice of the second mortgage, can transfer the legal estate to the third mortgagee, if he had no notice when he took his security of the second mortgage, so as to give the third mortgagee priority over the second: that is to say, the first mortgagee can transfer his security to the third mortgagee, though the result may be to oust a person who would otherwise have had priority over the third mortgagee. Whether this is right, or whether we should so decide if such a case came before us, or whether the third mortgagee should, under such circumstances, be held liable to the second mortgagee, I give no opinion, for in the present case we have no transfer of the *Reliance's* mortgage subject to redemption by the person entitled to redeem – which would be, in fact, an ordinary transfer of mortgage – but a conveyance of the land by the first mortgagees free

36 *In Re Thomson Mortgage Trusts* [1920] 1 Ch 508.

from the mortgage debt, so as to give the purchaser an absolute interest in the land. That is what the society did. They turned the land into money, and they executed this deed with the intention that their debt alone should be paid, and they disregarded the second mortgage and allowed the mortgagor to put the remainder of the money into his own pocket. In my opinion, that places the case in a different position from that of a transfer of a mortgage by the first mortgagee, for that he has authority to do when he is paid his money; but when the first mortgagee, as owner of the property and having the control over it, turns the land into money – for the owner of the equity of redemption cannot, without the concurrence of the first mortgagee, himself turn the land into money – if he, the first mortgagee, does so with knowledge that the money is not going to be applied in a proper manner, he is, in my opinion, as liable for the money as if he had received it under an express obligation to give it to the person properly entitled to it. It is conceded that if he exercises his power of sale as mortgagee, whether under the terms of the mortgage deed or by statute, he is answerable for the money he receives if he pays it to the wrong person, that is to say, if he passes over the second mortgagee and pays it to the mortgagor who has no right to receive it. Ought we, then, to make any distinction between such a case and the present? Here the first mortgagees, though they did not concur with the mortgagor in putting up the property for sale, did concur with him in the conveyance. Having done so with the knowledge that part of the purchase money was going to be applied in violation of a right of which they had had notice, they are, in my opinion, just as liable as if they had received the whole of the money. Not being able to give a good receipt for the whole of the money, they must be held liable for that portion of it for which they could not give a good receipt, for it was in their power to refuse to concur in the sale unless the whole of the purchase money was properly applied. I am, therefore, of opinion that the decision appealed from is right ... and that the Plaintiffs have established their right to make the Defendants, the Reliance Society, as well as Pike, answerable for the money received. I should add that I do not wish to suggest that the officers of the society were actually aware of the existence of the Plaintiff's charge at the time of the sale: it seems to have been forgotten.

LINDLEY LJ: I am also of opinion that the judgment of the court below is right. There are various ways of looking at this matter, and I should like to look at it as if the Reliance Society had present to their minds at the time of the sale the fact that the bank were second mortgagees. Would it not then be a clear case, both in law and in morality, against the society? They, with full knowledge of the facts, would then have paid the money or allowed it to be paid to the mortgagor. It is perfectly true that I have assumed a fact which did not exist, for the society had not present to their minds the existence of the second mortgage, since, although they had received the notice, they had mislaid or forgotten it. They acted perfectly honestly; but if we are to treat them, as we must treat them for legal purposes, as having notice, it follows that they are still liable. What is the answer made to that? It is this, that Messrs Shaen and Roscoe, who received the money, were acting for the mortgagor and the first mortgagees under separate authorities. I was struck with that argument, but it does not appear to me to cover the ground stated by Lord Justice Cotton, because, even if Messrs Shaen and Roscoe had no authority to receive for the first mortgagees more than the amount of their debt, still they, as agents for the first mortgagees, facilitated the payment of the balance of the money to the mortgagor and allowed it to go in the wrong direction: consequently, as regards this balance, the first mortgagees are liable for the act of their agents ... In my opinion the appeal fails.

[Bowen LJ concurred.]

Effect of a mortgage sale

If the sale is conducted in a manner which complies with ss 67 and 68 of the LRA, and otherwise complies with all the legal requirements, the purchaser acquires title to the land. The transaction is completed by registration of the purchaser as provided in s 71:

> On registration of a transfer executed by a creditor for the purpose of a sale under s 68 the estate or interest of the debtor specified in the transfer passes to and vests the purchaser freed and discharged from all liability on account of all registered mortgages or charge to which the sale was not subject.

The title of the purchaser would be subject to any mortgage registered before that of the seller mortgagee. For example, if the land was subject to three registered mortgages, namely, A, B and C, registered in that order, if B exercised the power of sale the land would be sold free of mortgage C but will remain subject to mortgage A. C would have to look to B for payment out of the proceeds in accordance with s 68(6) of the LRA, while A need not do anything as his security remains intact. Indeed it would be in the purchaser's interest to pay off A because if the mortgagor defaults in paying A, the latter could cause the property to be sold (or exercise any other rights available to a mortgagor) free of the purchaser's title.

Equitable mortgagee's power of sale

An unregistered mortgagee cannot exercise the statutory power of sale. The reason is that since the mortgage is not endorsed on the certificate title of the mortgaged property, the mortgagee cannot sign the memorandum of transfer to confer a legal title to the purchaser. Hence, an equitable mortgagee wishes to realise the security by way of sale, he or she must either have the mortgage registered or seek a judicial order for sale of the property.[37]

Discharge of the mortgage by payment

We have so far considered situations where the mortgagor defaults in payment of the mortgaged debt. In practice, most mortgages are discharged by payment. The following provisions stipulate the procedure for discharge of a mortgage registered under the Land Registration Act:

> Section 77
>
> (1) On production to the Registrar of an instrument in the prescribed form purporting to discharge mortgaged or charged land –
>
> (a) in respect of all or part of the estate or interest secured; or
>
> (b) in respect of part of the land, the Registrar shall register the discharge.
>
> (2) On registration under sub-section (1) –
>
> (a) the estate or interest in whole or part; or

37 *Ryan v O'Sullivan* [1956] VLR 99, at p 100, *per* Deane J.

(b) the part of the land, as the case may be, ceases to be subject to or liable for the money secured by the mortgage or charge.

(3) This section does not apply to a charge to which section 78 applies.[38]

Section 79

(1) Where –

(a) a mortgagee of land is absent from the country; and

(b) there is no person in the country authorized to give a receipt to the mortgagor for the mortgage money at or after the date appointed for the redemption of the mortgage.

the Head of the Department responsible for financial matters –

(c) may receive the mortgage money, with any arrears of interest then due, in trust for the mortgagee or other person entitled to the money; and

(d) shall give a receipt for the money received by him.

(2) On receipt of the mortgage money under sub-section (1) interest payable under the mortgage ceases to run or accrue.

(3) On production of a receipt under this section the Registrar shall register and discharge.

(4) The registration under sub-section (3) is a valid discharge of the mortgage, and has the same force and effect as the corresponding entry made under section 77.

V RIGHTS OF THE MORTGAGOR

We have seen the various duties imposed upon the mortgagee under the Land Registration Act and the underlying law. These duties obviously constitute some of the mortgagor's rights as well. In addition, there are several principles of equity, which seek to protect the mortgagor against the mortgagee. Equity's protection of the mortgagor is summed up in the maxim 'once a mortgage always a mortgage'. This maxim applies in two ways: (i) the test for a mortgage is substance and not form; and (ii) no clogs on the equity of redemption.[39]

(i) Substance not form

Whether a transaction is a mortgage or some other transaction is a question of substance and not form. Thus, if the parties intend to create a mortgage but refer to their transaction as a sale or lease or some other transaction, once the court is satisfied that they intended to create a mortgage, in equity the transaction is considered a mortgage and all the consequences of a mortgage will follow.[40]

38 Section 78 deals with a registered charge which secures an annuity or sum of money contingently on the occurrence of an event.

39 See Megarry and Wade, *The Law of Real Property, op cit*, note 28, at p 1228.

40 See, eg, *Grangeside Properties Ltd v Collingwood Securities Ltd and Others* [1964] 1 All ER 143.

(ii) No clogs on the equity of redemption

This means that the court will not permit any attempt by the mortgagee to exclude the mortgagor's right to redeem his property. This principle will be illustrated under the following sub-headings: irredeemableness; option to purchase; postponement of redemption; and collateral advantage.

Irredeemableness

A provision in a mortgage agreement that totally excludes the mortgagor's right to redeem has no effect in the eyes of a court of equity.[41] Nor is a provision that the mortgagor must redeem within a specified period or forfeit his or her estate to the mortgagee, have a legal effect. Irrespective of the clause the mortgagor can always redeem until foreclosure by order of court.

Option to purchase

A clause in the mortgage deed that gives the mortgagee an option to purchase the mortgaged property is a clog because it deprives the mortgagor of his or her right to redeem.

The following case deals with both irredeemableness and option to purchase.

SAMUEL v JARRAH TIMBER & WOOD PAVING CORPORATION LIMITED [1904] AC 323, House of Lords

[J Ltd mortgaged their shares to S under terms which gave S an option to buy the shares at 40% of their face value any time within 12 months of the date of the mortgage. When S attempted to exercise his option to purchase J Ltd refused to sell. J Ltd sought a declaration that the option was invalid and that they were entitled to redeem their shares. The trial judge and the Court of Appeal granted the order sought. On appeal to the House of Lords.]

EARL OF HALSBURY LC (read by Lord Macnaghten): My Lords, I regret that the state of the authorities leaves me no alternative other than to affirm the judgment ... A perfectly fair bargain made between two parties to it, each of whom was quite sensible of what they were doing, is not to be performed because at the same time a mortgage arrangement was made between them. If a day had intervened between the two parts of the arrangement, the part of the bargain which the appellant claims to be performed would have been perfectly good and capable of being enforced; but a line of authorities going back for more than a century has decided that such an arrangement as that which was here arrived at is contrary to a principle of equity, the sense or reason of which I am not able to appreciate, and very reluctantly I am compelled to acquiesce in the judgments appealed from.

LORD MACNAGHTEN: I take it to be an established rule that a mortgagee can never provide at the time of making the loan for any event or condition on which the equity of redemption shall be discharged and the conveyance absolute. And there is great reason and justice in this rule, for necessitous men are not, truly speaking, free men, but to answer a present exigency will submit to any terms that the crafty may impose upon them.

41 *Re Wells* [1933] 1 Ch 29, at p 52, *per* Lawrence LJ.

This doctrine, described by Lord Henley as an established rule nearly 150 years ago, has never, so far as I can discover, been departed from since or questioned in any reported case. It is, I believe, universally accepted by text-writers of authority. Speaking for myself, I should not be sorry if your Lordships could see your way to modify it so as to prevent its being used as a means of evading a fair bargain come to between persons dealing at arm's length and negotiating on equal terms. The directors of a trading company in search of financial assistance are certainly in a very different position from that of an impecunious landowner in the toils of a crafty money-lender. At the same time I quite feel the difficulty of interfering with any rule that has prevailed so long, and I am not prepared to differ from the conclusion at which the Court of Appeal has arrived.

LORD LINDLEY: The first question is, What is the true nature of this agreement? Is it a mortgage with an option to purchase, or is it a conditional sale? Or is it an agreement giving Samuel an option to hold the debenture stock as a mortgage or a purchase? It appears to me to be clearly a mortgage with an option to purchase. A loan of 5,000l. on security was what the company wanted, and what Samuel agreed to let the company have on terms. They were not bargaining for anything else. As soon as the 5,000l. was advanced and the debenture stock was placed at Samuel's disposal he was in the position of mortgagee of that stock. He had the rights of a mortgagee, and the company had the rights of a mortgagor. There was that reciprocity and mutuality of remedies which distinguish a mortgage transaction from a conditional sale and from other transactions more or less resembling a mortgage, but not really constituting a mortgage. The transaction was in my opinion a mortgage, plus, amongst other things, an option to purchase, which if exercised by the mortgagee would put an end to the mortgagor's right to redeem – ie, would prevent him from getting back his mortgaged property. This was the view taken by Kekewich J and by all the members of the Court of Appeal, and I am unable myself to view the transaction differently.

In *Lisle v Reeve* [[1902] 1 Ch 53, p 68] Buckley J suggested some instances in which he considered a mortgagee might validly stipulate for an option to buy the equity of redemption; but although his decision was affirmed first by the Court of Appeal and afterwards by this House (*Reeve v Lisle*) ... [[1902] AC 461] the affirmance proceeded entirely on the fact that the agreement to buy the equity of redemption was no part of the original mortgage transaction, but was entered into subsequently, and was an entirely separate transaction to which no objection could be taken. It is plain that the decision would not have been affirmed if the agreement to buy the equity of redemption had been one of the terms of the original mortgage ...

I cannot help thinking that both parties intended that the two options to purchase the 30,000l debenture stock and to underwrite further capital or debenture stock if issued were to be exercisable even after payment off of the 5000l. But the decisions of this House in *Noakes & Co Limited v Rice* ... [[1902] AC 24] and *Bradley v Carritt* ...[[1903] AC 253] conclusively shew that, whatever might have been intended, Samuel could not have been entitled to exercise either option after repayment of his loan. But these decisions ... emphatically recognise the old doctrine, 'Once a mortgage always a mortgage', which is too well settled to be open to controversy. Lord Hardwicke said in *Toomes v Conset* ... [3 Atk 261]: 'This court will not suffer in a deed of mortgage any agreement in it to prevail that the estate become an absolute purchase in the mortgagee upon any event whatsoever.' But the doctrine is not confined to deeds creating legal mortgages. It applies to all mortgage transactions. The doctrine 'Once a mortgage always a mortgage' means that no contract between a mortgagor and a mortgagee made at the time of the mortgage and as part of the mortgage transaction, or, in other words, as one of the terms of the loan, can be valid if it

> prevents the mortgagor from getting back his property on paying off what is due on his security. Any bargain which has that effect is invalid, and is inconsistent with the transaction being a mortgage. This principle is fatal to the appellant's contention if the transaction under consideration is a mortgage transaction, as I am of opinion it clearly is ...
>
> *Appeal dismissed.*

Notes

In *Reeve v Lisle and Others*,[42] the House of Lords held that if, subsequent to the mortgage, the parties entered into a separate and independent contract to grant the mortgagee an option to purchase the mortgaged property, such a contract is not invalid even though its effect is to deprive the mortgagor of his right to redeem. In that case the defendant mortgaged his property to the plaintiff under terms to pay within a period of two years. When the defendant defaulted, the parties entered into another contract to extend the period of payment to five years, in consideration that the defendant gave the plaintiff an option to join the defendant as a partner in his business. In an action for breach of contract the trial judge held that the mortgage and the agreement formed really one transaction, but that the agreement was valid as a conditional sale, and that the rule against clogging an equity of redemption had no application. This decision was affirmed on appeal.

Questions

1. X owed TP K20,000 secured by a mortgage. Upon default TP threatened to exercise his power of sale. X hastily arranged to borrow K20,000 from his friend Y to pay off the debt. The transaction was carried out by a transfer of the existing mortgage to Y for K20,000 and by a contemporaneous written agreement between X and Y giving Y the option to buy the mortgaged property upon condition that he did not demand payment of the principle sum secured by the mortgage for two years. X seeks your advice whether the option is a clog. (See *Lewis v Frank Love Ltd* [1961] 1 All ER 446.)
2. How would a mortgagee go about entering into a mortgage agreement which gives him an option to purchase or lease the mortgaged property without risking or infringing the rules of equity? Would it be enough if the option to purchase was granted under a separate document?
3. What is the rationale for protecting the mortgagor? Is this protection justifiable in all cases?

Postponement of the redemption date

Mortgages sometimes provide that the mortgagor shall not redeem earlier than a specified date. The advantage, of course, from the mortgagee's viewpoint is that the longer it takes to pay the debt the more interest he receives, plus other collateral advantages under the mortgage.[43] The question is whether a provision which precludes

---

42 [1902] AC 461.

43 See below, 'collateral' advantages.

early redemption (where the mortgagor is in a position to pay) is a clog on redemption and, therefore, void. Compare the following two cases.

'Illusory' right to redeem

JAMES FAIRCLOUGH v SWAN BREWERY COMPANY LTD
[1912] AC 565, Privy Council

[The defendant had a lease for 17 years over a hotel, which he mortgaged to the plaintiff brewing company as security for a loan. The terms of the mortgage were, *inter alia*, as follows. Firstly, that the defendant must not redeem earlier than six weeks before his leasehold expired. Secondly, that during the continuance of the mortgage the defendant must not purchase beer from any other person other than the mortgagee. The defendant sought an early redemption so that he could be released from the obligation under the second clause. The issue was whether the clause was a 'clog' on the equity of redemption.]

LORD MACNAGHTEN: [I]t is now firmly established by the House of Lords that ... equity will not permit any device or contrivance being part of the mortgage transaction or contemporaneous with it to prevent or impede redemption. The learned counsel on behalf of the respondents admitted, as he was bound to admit, that a mortgage cannot be made irredeemable. That is plainly forbidden. Is there any difference between forbidding redemption and permitting it, if the permission be a mere pretence? Here the provision for redemption is nugatory. The incumbrance on the lease the subject of the mortgage according to the letter of the bargain falls to be discharged before the lease terminates, but at a time when it is on the very point of expiring, when redemption can be of no advantage to the mortgagor even if he should be so fortunate as to get his deeds back before the actual termination of the lease. For all practical purposes this mortgage is irredeemable. It was obviously meant to be irredeemable. It was made irredeemable in and by the mortgage itself.

Appeal allowed.

Question

Why did Lord Macnaghten hold that the right to redeem was 'illusory'?

KNIGHTSBRIDGE ESTATES TRUST LIMITED v BYRNE AND OTHERS
[1939] Ch 441, Court of Appeal

[The appellants (Knightsbridge) mortgaged their freehold estate to the respondents (Byrne) to secure a loan. By deed the appellants covenanted to repay the debt over a period of 40 years paying half-yearly equal instalments. A few years later, the appellants, wishing to take advantage of falling interest rates, sought to repay and discharge the mortgage before the date for payment so that they could get a loan elsewhere on better terms. The appellants instituted proceedings for a declaration that the clause postponing redemption for 40 years was a clog on the equity of redemption and, therefore, void. The trial judge dismissed the application. On appeal.]

GREENE MR: It was not contended that a provision in a mortgage deed making the mortgage irredeemable for a period of years is necessarily void. The argument was that such a period must be a 'reasonable' one, and it was said that the period in the present case was an unreasonable one by reason merely of its length ...

Now an argument such as this requires the closest scrutiny, for, if it is correct, it means that an agreement made between two competent parties, acting under expert advice and presumably knowing their own business best, is one which the law forbids them to make upon the ground that it is not 'reasonable'. If we were satisfied that the rule of equity was what it is said to be, we should be bound to give effect to it. But in the absence of compelling authority we are not prepared to say that such an agreement cannot lawfully be made. A decision to that effect would, in our view, involve an unjustified interference with the freedom of business men to enter into agreements best suited to their interests and would impose upon them a test of 'reasonableness' laid down by the courts without reference to the business realities of the case ...

Assuming ... without in any way deciding, that the period during which the contractual right of redemption is postponed must be a 'reasonable' one (a question which we will now proceed to examine), we are of opinion that the respondents have failed to establish (and the burden is on them) that there is anything unreasonable in the mere extension of the period for 40 years in the circumstances of the present case.

But in our opinion the proposition that a postponement of the contractual right of redemption is only permissible for a 'reasonable' time is not well-founded. Such a postponement is not properly described as a clog on the equity of redemption, since it is concerned with the contractual right to redeem. It is indisputable that any provision which hampers redemption after the contractual date for redemption was passed will not be permitted. Further, it is undoubtedly true to say that a right of redemption is a necessary element in a mortgage transaction, and consequently that, where the contractual right of redemption is illusory, equity will grant relief by allowing redemption. This was the point in the case of *Fairclough v Swan Brewery Co* [[1912] AC 565] ...

Moreover, equity may give relief against contractual terms in a mortgage transaction if they are oppressive or unconscionable, and in deciding whether or not a particular transaction falls within this category the length of time for which the contractual right to redeem is postponed may well be an important consideration. In the present case no question of this kind was or could have been raised.

But equity does not reform mortgage transactions because they are unreasonable. It is concerned to see two things – one that the essential requirements of a mortgage transaction are observed, and the other that oppressive or unconscionable terms are not enforced. Subject to this, it does not, in our opinion, interfere. The question therefore arises whether, in a case where the right of redemption is real and not illusory and there is nothing oppressive or unconscionable in the transaction, there is something in a postponement of the contractual right to redeem, such as we have in the present case, that is inconsistent with the essential requirements of a mortgage transaction? Apart from authority the answer to this question would, in our opinion, be clearly in the negative. Any other answer would place an unfortunate restriction on the liberty of contract of competent parties who are at arm's length – in the present case it would have operated to prevent the respondents obtaining financial terms which for obvious reasons they themselves considered to be most desirable. It would, moreover, lead to highly inequitable results. The remedy sought by the respondents and the only remedy which is said to be open to them is the establishment of a right to redeem at any time on the ground that the postponement of the contractual right to redeem is void. They do not and could not suggest that the contract as a contract is affected, and the result would accordingly be that whereas the respondents would have had from the first the right to redeem at any time, the appellants would have had no right to require payment otherwise than by the specified instalments. Such an outcome to a bargain entered into by business people negotiating at arm's length would indeed be unfortunate, and we should require clear authority before coming to such a conclusion ...

[The trial judge] ... does not express the opinion that the postponement in the present case is to be regarded as void by reason merely of its length. He holds that the period is 'having regard to all the provisions of the deed, unreasonable'... We find ourselves unable to take the view that the court is entitled in such a case as the present to treat as unreasonable provisions in a mortgage deed entered into by two parties such as we have here with the assistance of competent advisers for all the court can know, provisions which may appear to it to be disadvantageous to the mortgagor may have been regarded by him, and correctly regarded, as of no practical consequence from a business point of view ...

Appeal allowed.

Note: A further appeal to the House of Lords was dismissed, but on different grounds ([1940] AC 613).

Collateral advantages

Sometimes, terms are inserted in a mortgage agreement to give the mortgagee other advantages in addition to the repayment of the principal sum and interest. The additional advantages are commonly referred to as 'collateral advantages'. These could take any number of forms. A simple example is a provision (usually inserted where the mortgagee is a manufacturer and the mortgagor a dealer in his products), which precludes the mortgagor from selling products other than those bought from or manufactured by the mortgagee. Before the 19th century the traditional view of the Court of Equity in England was that the essence of a mortgage was a security for money lent, therefore, any other advantage foreign to this basic object was considered void.[44] This strict approach was partly influenced by the prevailing public policy and the laws enacted in the form of 'usury' laws, which placed restriction on the interest which could legally be exacted by money lenders.[45] Gradually this policy was relaxed in line with the social economic and political changes in the 19th century.[46] As the cases extracted below show, the courts have relented in their hostility towards collateral advantages over the years and this trend will probably continue.

Collateral advantages expiring with the mortgage

BIGGS v HODDINOTT [1895–99] All ER 625, Court of Appeal

[A covenant contained in a mortgage of a hotel to a brewer provided that during the continuance of the mortgage (which was expressed to be irredeemable for five years) the

44 See *Jennings v Ward* (1705) 2 Vern 520; 23 ER 923.

45 See *G and C Kreglinger v New Patagonia Meat and Cold Storage Company Ltd* [1914] AC 25, at 36–38 *per* Haldane LC (see extract below, p 264).

46 The last of the usury laws was repealed in 1854, *ibid*, *per* Parker LJ, p 55.

mortgagor would only sell on the premises beer brewed by the mortgagee. The mortgagor sought an earlier redemption and a release from the trade agreement. His application was unsuccessful. On appeal.]

SIR NATHANIEL LINDLEY MR: We have listened to a very ingenious and learned argument with a view to induce us to lay down a proposition of law which would be very unfortunate for business men. The proposition is, that while two people are engaged in a mortgage transaction they cannot enter into any other transaction with each other, and that any such transaction must be entered into before or after the mortgage, so that it cannot be said that the mortgagee gets any collateral advantage out of the mortgage.

Counsel for the defendants did not attempt to uphold this on any rational principle, but relied on authority. Of course we must follow the authorities whether we like them or not, but do they support that proposition? *Jennings v Ward* [(1705) 2 Vern 520; 23 ER 935] ... was the first case relied on. That was a redemption suit, and the stipulation which was in question seriously interfered with the right of redemption of the mortgaged property on payment of principal, interest, and costs, and Sir John Trevor MR ordered redemption without regard to that stipulation. He said (2 Vern at p 520):

> A man shall not have interest for his money and a collateral advantage besides for the loan of it, or clog the redemption with any by-agreement.

That language has found its way into the books, and it has been understood as if he meant exactly what he said without regard to the circumstances of that case, and it has been said that a mortgagee cannot have principal, interest, and costs, and also some collateral advantage. But when the authorities are considered, it is found that the general proposition has been departed from again and again ... The proposition as stated in *Jennings v Ward* is too wide. If properly limited it is good law and good sense, and when one looks at the cases where it has been applied and those where it has not, one sees what it means.

The principle is this: a mortgage is regarded in equity as a security for the money advanced, and a mortgagor may always redeem on payment of principal, interest, and costs; and no bargain which prevents such redemption is valid. There is another principle which is not peculiar to mortgages, and that is that an unconscionable bargain will not be enforced; and there is no case of any bargain being set aside which does not come under one of these two heads.

I think the decision of Romer J was right; and to say, as we are asked to do, that a covenant like this one is a collateral advantage and must be disregarded as unconscionable would be to lay down a proposition which would shock any business man, and we are not driven to do it by authority and are not going to say that ... Appeal dismissed.

CHITTY LJ: This is a mortgage for a term of years effected in the usual way, and it contains a covenant by the mortgagors during the continuance of the security to take all their beer from the mortgagee, and a covenant by the mortgagee to supply it. It is contended that the covenant by the mortgagors is void in equity.

The first observation I desire to make is that it in no way affects the equity of redemption, as redemption can take place just as if the covenant was not in the deed. There is no stipulation that damages for breach of the covenant shall be covered by the security, so this is not a case where the equity of redemption is affected. In equity a mortgage has always been looked upon as only a security for money, and here the right of the mortgagors to redeem on payment of principal, interest, and costs is maintained. It is said that a general principle has been established that a mortgagee shall not stipulate for any collateral advantage to himself, and that there are authorities which show that. That has not been made out. I think the real principle is that the mortgagee shall not impose on the mortgagor any unconscionable or oppressive bargain. There is nothing of that kind in this case. The arrangement is for the common benefit of both parties. Though the mortgagee does by the operation of the covenant get an opportunity for the sale of his beer, the mortgagors get presumably good beer supplied upon the usual terms. It would be contrary to good sense to say that this trade contract entered into by two business men with their eyes open, should be set aside on the ground of its being contrary to some fanciful doctrine of equity.

... In this case the covenant does not fall within any such supposed rule of equity as the defendants have contended for.

[Henn Collins LJ concurred.]

Note

The editor of the *All England Replacement Report* notes (at 625), that Lindley MR's *dictum* that 'a mortgagor may always redeem on payment of principal, interest, and costs and no bargain which prevents such redemption is valid' must be read subject to the qualification that the right to redeem may be postponed, so long as this will not be unreasonable or oppressive. See also *G and C Kreglinger v New Patagonia Meat Cold Storage Co Ltd* [1914] AC 25, extracted below.

A collateral advantage continuing after redemption

NOAKES & Co LIMITED v RICE [1902] AC 24, House of Lords

[The respondent mortgaged his leasehold public house to the appellant brewing company as security for a loan. Under the mortgage agreement the respondent covenanted that during the continuance of the term, and whether any money should or should not be owing on the security of the mortgage, he will not use or sell any liquors except such as should be purchased of the appellant (mortgagee). The respondent wanted to pay off the debt before the term expired. They sought a judicial declaration to the effect that upon payment to the appellant of all moneys due the appellant should reconvey the property together with a release of all covenants contained in the mortgage; and that the appellant was not entitled thereafter to the benefit of the covenant in question. The lower courts granted the order. The mortgagee appealed to the House of Lords.]

LORD DAVEY: My Lords, there are three doctrines of the Courts of Equity in this country which have been referred to in the course of the argument in this case. The first doctrine to which I refer is expressed in the maxim: 'Once a mortgage always a mortgage.' The second is that the mortgagee shall not reserve to himself any collateral advantage outside the mortgage contract; and the third is that a provision or stipulation which will have the effect of clogging or fettering the equity of redemption is void.

My Lords, the first maxim presents no difficulty: it is only another way of saying that a mortgage cannot be made irredeemable, and that a provision to that effect is void ...

My Lords, the second doctrine to which I refer, namely, that the mortgagee shall not reserve to himself any collateral advantage outside the mortgage contract, was established long ago when the usury laws were in force. The Court of Equity went beyond the usury laws, and set its face against every transaction which tended to usury. It therefore declared void every stipulation by a mortgagee for a collateral advantage which made his total remuneration for the loan indirectly exceed the legal interest. I think it will be found that every case under this head of equity was decided either on this ground, or on the ground that the bargain was oppressive and unconscionable. The abolition of the usury laws has made an alteration in the view the court should take on this subject, and I agree that a collateral advantage may now be stipulated for by a mortgagee, provided that no unfair advantage be taken by the mortgagee which would render it void or voidable, according to the general principles of equity, and provided that it does not offend against the third doctrine. On these grounds I think the case of *Biggs v Hoddinott* [[1898] 2 Ch 307] ... in the Court of Appeal was rightly decided.

The third doctrine to which I have referred is really a corollary from the first, and might be expressed in this form: once a mortgage always a mortgage and nothing but a mortgage. The meaning of that is that the mortgage shall not make any stipulation which will prevent a mortgagor, who has paid principal, interest, and costs, from getting back his mortgaged property in the condition in which he parted with it. I do not dissent from the opinion expressed by my noble and learned friend opposite (Lord Lindley), when Master of the Rolls, in the case of *Santley v Wilde* [[1899] 2 Ch 474] ... He says: 'A clog or fetter is something which is inconsistent with the idea of security; a clog or fetter is in the nature of a repugnant condition.' But I ask, 'security' for what? I think it must be security for the principal, interest, and costs, and, I will add, for any advantages in the nature of increased interest or remuneration for the loan which the mortgagee has validly stipulated for during the continuance of the mortgage. There are two elements in the conception of a mortgage: first, security for the money advanced; and, secondly, remuneration for the use of the money. When the mortgage is paid off the security is at an end, and, as the mortgagee is no longer kept out of his money, the remuneration to him for the use of his money is also at an end. I confess I should have decided the case of *Santley v Wilde* ... differently from the way in which it was dealt with in the Court of Appeal. After the payment of principal and interest, and everything which had become payable up to the date of redemption, the property in that case remained charged with the payment to the mortgagee of one-third share of the profits, and the stipulation to that effect should, I think, have been held to be a clog or fetter on the right to redeem. The principle is this – that a mortgage must not be converted into something else; and when once you come to the conclusion that a stipulation for the benefit of the mortgagee is part of the mortgage transaction, it is but part of his security, and necessarily comes to an end on the payment off of the loan. In my opinion, every yearly or other recurring payment stipulated for by the mortgagee should be held to be in the nature of interest, and no more payable after the principal is paid off than interest would be. I apprehend a man could not stipulate for the continuance of payment of interest after the principal is paid, and I do not think he can stipulate for any other recurring payment such as a share of profits. Any stipulation to that effect would, in my opinion, be void as a clog or fetter on the equity of redemption ...

Now, applying what I have said to the present case, the decision becomes easy. In the first place, I do not think that the respondent's covenant to deal exclusively with the brewers continued after the payment off of the loan and the redemption; and secondly, if it did, it was an attempt to charge it on the property, and that constituted a clog or fetter which, according to well-established principles, was void.

Appeal dismissed.

HALSBURY LC: [M]y Lords, taking this case, it appears to me that undoubtedly this was a mortgage, and that the equity of redemption is clogged and fettered here by the continuance of an obligation which would render this house less available in the hands of its owner during the whole period and beyond the whole period of the term, apart from the realization of the security. Under those circumstances, as a matter of the merest and simplest reasoning, I am wholly unable to come to any other conclusion than that there is a clog and fetter here which the law will not permit.

That seems to me, my Lords, to be the whole of this case ...

LORD MACNAGHTEN LJ: Redemption is of the very nature and essence of a mortgage, as mortgages are regarded in equity. It is inherent in the thing itself. And it is, I think, as firmly settled now as it ever was in former times that equity will not permit any device or contrivance designed or calculated to prevent or impede redemption. It follows as a necessary consequence that, when the money secured by a mortgage of land is paid off, the land itself and the owner of the land in the use and enjoyment of it must be as free and unfettered to all intents and purposes as if the land had never been made the subject of the security.

In the present case it is hardly necessary to appeal to this principle. The mortgage deed under consideration expressly and in terms provides that on repayment of the money advanced the mortgagees are to reconvey the mortgaged premises to the mortgagor, or as he shall direct. That, of course, means that the land is to be reconveyed freed and discharged from all burden and liability in respect of or arising out of the contract under which the advance was made ...

Appeal dismissed.

[Lindley and Shand LJJ concurred.]

G AND C KREGLINGER v NEW PATAGONIA MEAT COLD STORAGE CO LTD [1914] AC 25, House of Lords

[The respondents (New Patagonia) were a company carrying on the business of preserving and canning meat. In the course of this business they had at their disposal a large number of sheepskins. The appellants (Kreglinger) were a firm of woolbrokers. By an agreement dated 24 August 1910, the appellants lent the respondents a sum of money secured by a floating charge over all the respondents' property. In their agreement the appellants promised that provided the respondents punctually paid the interest due they would not demand repayment of the principal sum until 30 September 1915. However, the respondents were free at any time to pay off the loan subject to giving one calendar month's notice. The agreement further provided that for a period of five years from the date thereof the respondents should not sell sheepskins to any person other than the appellants so long as the latter were willing to buy at the best price offered by any other person and that the respondents should pay to the appellants a commission on all sheepskins sold by them to any other person. The respondents paid off the loan in a space of only two and a half years (as they were entitled to do under the agreement), but the appellants claimed that their right to purchase the sheepskin continued for the full five years regardless. It was submitted for the respondents that the right claimed by the appellants restricted their freedom of trade and was therefore in the nature of a clog. Moreover, that whether this right clogged the right to redeem or was in the nature of a collateral advantage, it was not intended and it could not endure after redemption. The trial judge agreed that the right to purchase the sheepskin was a clog on the equity of redemption and void. The Court of Appeal affirmed the decision. On further appeal.]

VISCOUNT HALDANE LC: My Lords, before I refer to the decisions of this House which the courts below have considered to cover the case, I will state what I conceive to be the broad principles which must govern it.

The reason for which a Court of Equity will set aside the legal title of a mortgagee and compel him to reconvey the land on being paid principal, interest, and costs is a very old one. It appears to owe its origin to the influence of the Church in the courts of the early Chancellors.

As early as the Council of Lateran in 1179, we find, according to Matthew Paris (*Historia Major*, 1684 edn at pp 114–15), that famous assembly of ecclesiastics condemning usurers and laying down that when a creditor had been paid his debt he should restore his pledge ... It was therefore not surprising that the Court of Chancery should at an early date have begun to exercise jurisdiction *in personam* over mortgagees. This jurisdiction was merely a special application of a more general power to relieve against penalties and to mould them into mere securities. The case of the common law mortgage of land was indeed a gross one. The land was conveyed to the creditor upon the condition that if the money he had advanced to the feoffor was repaid on a date and at a place named, the fee simple should revest in the latter, but that if the condition was not strictly and literally fulfilled he should lose the land for ever. What made the hardship on the debtor a glaring one was that the debt still remained unpaid and could be recovered from the feoffor notwithstanding that he had actually forfeited the land to his mortgagee. Equity, therefore, at an early date began to relieve against what was virtually a penalty by compelling the creditor to use his legal title as a mere security.

My Lords, this was the origin of the jurisdiction which we are now considering, and it is important to bear that origin in mind. For the end to accomplish which the jurisdiction has been evolved ought to govern and limit its exercise by equity judges. That end has always been to ascertain, by parol evidence if need be, the real nature and substance of the transaction, and if it turned out to be in truth one of mortgage simply, to place it on that footing. It was, in ordinary cases, only where there was conduct which the Court of Chancery regarded as unconscientious that it interfered with freedom of contract. The lending of money, on mortgage or otherwise, was looked on with suspicion, and the court was on the alert to discover want of conscience in terms imposed by lenders. But whatever else may have been the intention of those judges who laid the foundations of the modern doctrines with which we are concerned in this appeal, they certainly do not appear to have contemplated that their principle should develop consequences which would go far beyond the necessities of the case with which they were dealing and interfere with transactions which were not really of the nature of a mortgage, and which were free from objection on moral grounds. Moreover, the principle on which the Court of Chancery interfered with contracts of the class under consideration was not a rigid one. The equity judges looked, not at what was technically the form, but at what was really the substance of transactions, and confined the application of their rules to cases in which they thought that in its substance the transaction was oppressive ...

The principle was thus in early days limited in its application to the accomplishment of the end which was held to justify interference of equity with freedom of contract. It did not go further. As established it was expressed in three ways. The most general of these was that if the transaction was once found to be a mortgage, it must be treated as always remaining a mortgage and nothing but a mortgage. That the substance of the transaction must be looked to in applying this doctrine and that it did not apply to cases which were only apparently or technically within it but were in reality something more than cases of mortgage, *Howard v Harris* [(1681) 1 Vern 33; 2 Ch Cas 147] and other authorities show. It was only a different application of the paramount doctrine to lay it down in the form of a second rule that a mortgagee should not stipulate for a collateral advantage which would make his remuneration for the loan exceed a proper rate of interest. The Legislature during a long period placed restrictions on the rate of interest which could legally be exacted. But equity went beyond the limits of the statutes which limited the interest, and was ready to interfere with any usurious stipulation in a mortgage. In so doing it was influenced by the public policy of the time. That policy was now changed, and the Acts which limited the rate of interest have been repealed. The result is that a collateral advantage may now be stipulated for by the mortgagee provided that he has not acted unfairly or oppressively, and provided that the bargain does not conflict with the third form of the principle. This is that a mortgage (subject to the apparent exception in the case of family arrangements to which I have already alluded) cannot be made irredeemable, and that any stipulation which restricts or clogs the equity of redemption is void. It is obvious that the reason for the doctrine in this form is the same as that which gave rise to the other forms. It is simply an assertion in a different way of the principle that once a mortgage always a mortgage and nothing else.

My Lords, the rules I have stated have now been applied by Courts of Equity for nearly three centuries, and the books are full of illustrations of their application. But what I have pointed out shows that it is inconsistent with the objects for which they were established that these rules should crystallize into technical language so rigid that the letter can defeat the underlying spirit and purpose. Their application must correspond with the practical necessities of the time. The rule as to collateral advantages, for example, has been much modified by the repeal of the usury laws and by the recognition of modern varieties of commercial bargaining. In *Biggs v Hoddinott* [[1898] 2 Ch 307] ... it was held that a brewer might stipulate in a mortgage made to him of a hotel that during the five years for which the loan was to continue the mortgagors would deal with him exclusively for malt liquor. In the 17th and 18th centuries a Court of Equity could hardly have so decided, and the judgment illustrates the elastic character of equity jurisdiction and the power of equity judges to mould the rules which they apply in accordance with the exigencies of the time. The decision proceeded on the ground that a mortgagee may stipulate for a collateral advantage at the time and as a term of the advance, provided, first, that no unfairness is shown, and secondly, that the right to redeem is not thereby clogged. It is no longer true that, as was said in *Jennings v Ward* [(1705) 2 Vern 520] 'a man shall not have interest for his money and a collateral advantage besides for the loan of it'. Unless such a bargain is unconscionable it is now good. But none the less the other and wider principle remains unshaken, that it is the essence of a mortgage that in the eye of a Court of Equity it should be a mere security for money, and that no bargain can be validly made which will prevent the mortgagor from redeeming on payment of what is due, including principal, interest, and costs. He may stipulate that he will not pay off his debt, and so redeem the mortgage, for a fixed period. But whenever a right to redeem arises out of the doctrine of equity, he is precluded from fettering it. This principle has become an integral part of our system of jurisprudence and must be faithfully adhered to.

My Lords, the question in the present case is whether the right to redeem has been interfered with. And this must, for the reasons to which I have adverted in considering the history of the doctrine of equity, depend on the answer to a question which is primarily one of fact. What was the true character of the transaction? Did the appellants make a bargain such that the right to redeem was cut down, or did they simply stipulate for a collateral undertaking, outside and clear of the mortgage, which would give them an exclusive option of purchase of the sheepskins of the respondents? The question is in my opinion not whether the two contracts were made at the same moment and evidenced by the same instrument, but whether they were in substance a single and undivided contract or two distinct contracts ... The question is one not of form but of substance, and it can be answered in each case only by looking at all the circumstances, and not by mere reliance on some abstract principle, or upon the *dicta* which have fallen obiter from judges in other and different cases. Some, at least, of the authorities on the subject disclose an embarrassment which has, in my opinion, arisen from neglect to bear this in mind. In applying a principle the ambit and validity of which depend on confining it steadily to the end for which it was established, the analogies of previous instances where it has been applied are apt to be misleading. For each case forms a real precedent only in so far as it affirms a principle, the relevancy of which in other cases turns on the true character of the particular transaction, and to that extent on circumstances.

My Lords, if in the case before the House your Lordships arrive at the conclusion that the agreement for an option to purchase the respondents' sheepskins was not in substance a fetter on the exercise of their right to redeem, but was in the nature of a collateral bargain the entering into which was a preliminary and separable condition of the loan, the decided cases cease to present any great difficulty. In questions of this kind the binding force of previous decisions, unless the facts are indistinguishable, depends on whether they establish a principle ... What is vital in the appeal now under consideration is to classify accurately the transaction between the parties. What we have to do is to ascertain from scrutiny of the circumstances whether there has really been an attempt to effect a mortgage with a provision preventing redemption of what was pledged merely as security for payment of the amount of the debt and any charges besides that may legitimately be added. It is not, in my opinion, conclusive in favour of the appellants that the security assumed the form of a floating charge. A floating charge is not the less a pledge because of its floating character, and a contract which fetters the right to redeem on which equity insists as regards all contracts of loan and security ought on principle to be set aside as readily in the case of a floating security as in any other case. But it is material that such a floating charge, in the absence of bargain to the contrary effect, permits the assets to be dealt with freely by the mortgagor until the charge becomes enforceable. If it be said that the undertaking of the respondents which was charged extended to their entire business, including the right to dispose of the skins of which they might from time to time become possessed, the comment is that at least they were to be free, so long as the security remained a floating one, to make contracts in the ordinary course of business in regard to these skins. If there had been no mortgage such a contract as the one in question would have been an ordinary incident in such a business. We are considering the simple question of what is the effect on the right to redeem of having inserted into the formal instrument signed when the money was borrowed an ordinary commercial contract for the sale of skins extending over a period. It appears that it was the intention of the parties that the grant of the security should not affect the power to enter into such a contract, either with strangers or with the appellants, and if so I am unable to see how the equity of redemption is affected. No doubt it is the fact that on redemption the respondents will not get back their business as free from obligation as it was before the date of the security. But that may well be because outside the security and consistently with its terms there was a contemporaneous but collateral contract, contained in the same document as constituted the security, but in substance independent of it. If it was the intention of the parties, as I think it was, to enter into this contract as a condition of the respondents getting their advance, I know no reason either in morals or in equity which ought to prevent this intention from being left to have its effect. What was to be capable of redemption was an undertaking which was deliberately left to be freely changed in its details by ordinary business transactions with which the mortgage was not to interfere. Had the charge not been a floating one, it might have been more difficult to give effect to this intention. In *Noakes & Co v Rice* [[1902] AC 24] this difficulty is illustrated, for the House held that what had been inserted in the shape of a covenant by the mortgagor to buy the beer of the mortgagee after redemption of the public-house mortgaged was really a term of the mortgage and was inoperative as being, not merely a collateral agreement, but in truth a restriction on the right to get back the security free from the terms of the mortgage. That was the case of the mortgage of a specific property. The decision that the transaction was what it was held to be is at all events readily intelligible. In *Bradley v Carritt* [[1903] AC 253] it was decided that the mortgagor of shares in a tea company who had covenanted that he would use his best endeavours to secure that always thereafter the mortgagee should have the sale of the company's tea had permanently fettered himself in the free disposition and enjoyment of the shares. It was held that though the covenant did not operate *in rem* on the shares it amounted to a device or contrivance designed to impede redemption. The decision was a striking one. It was not unanimous, for Lord Lindley dissented from the conclusions of Lord Macnaghten and Lord Davey ... And it certainly cannot, in my opinion, be taken as authoritatively laying down that the mere circumstance that after redemption the property redeemed may not, as the result of some bargain made at the time of the mortgage, be in the same condition as it was before that time, is conclusive against the validity of that bargain.

To render it invalid the bargain must, when its substance is examined, turn out to have formed part of the terms of the mortgage and to have really cut down a true right of redemption. I think that the tendency of recent decisions has been to lay undue stress on the letter of the principle which limits the jurisdiction of equity in setting aside contracts. The origin and reason of the principle ought, as I have already said, to be kept steadily in view in applying it to fresh cases. There appears to me to have grown up a tendency to look to the letter rather than to the spirit of the doctrine. The true view is, I think, that judges ought in this kind of jurisdiction to proceed cautiously, and to bear in mind the real reasons which have led Courts of Equity to insist on the free right to redeem and the limits within which the purpose of the rule ought to confine its scope. I cannot but think that the validity of the bargain in such cases as *Bradley v Carritt* ... and *Santley v Wilde* [[1899] 2 Ch 474] ... might have been made free from various questions if the parties had chosen to seek what would have been substantially the same result in a different form. For form may be very important when the question is one of the construction of ambiguous words in which people have expressed their intentions. I will add that, if I am right in the view which I take of the authorities, there is no reason for thinking that they establish another rule suggested by the learned counsel for the respondents, that even a mere collateral advantage stipulated for in the same instrument as constitutes the mortgage cannot endure after redemption ...

The result of the consideration I have given to this appeal is that I think the contention of the appellants is right.

LORD MERSEY: My Lords, I agree, and I desire to add only a few words. The transaction out of which this dispute arises ... [t]hough embodied in one document it is an agreement made up of two parts. The first part consists of a promise by the appellants, who are merchants, to lend to the respondents, who are a trading company, money at interest on the security of a floating charge over the company's undertaking; the second part consists of an agreement by the company to give to the lenders the option of purchasing for a time their periodical production of sheepskins. The whole transaction is of a most ordinary commercial kind.

It is contended that the contract is a mortgage to which the equitable doctrine prohibiting the imposition of a clog on a mortgagor's right to redeem applies, and that, therefore, on payment off of the loan the borrowers are entitled to have back their undertaking freed from any further obligation to sell or deliver sheepskins. Now, whether a transaction is or is not such a mortgage is a question of intention; and it seems that it has always been the practice of the Courts of Chancery to admit oral evidence to assist in solving the question. No evidence is adduced on this point on the part of the respondents, so that your Lordships are left by them to determine the intention merely from the words which the parties have used in drawing up their agreement. These words are, in my opinion, too plain and simple to leave any doubt as to their meaning. The obligation to sell sheepskins created by clause 8 of the agreement was to endure in any event until August 1915. That was the plain intention of both parties to the agreement, and the only effect of applying to the contract the equitable doctrine against clogging the right to redeem would be to defeat that intention and to enable one of the parties to inflict an injustice on the other.

I have nothing to say about the doctrine itself. It seems to me to be like an unruly dog, which, if not securely chained to its own kennel, is prone to wander into places where it ought not to be. Its introduction into the present case would give effect to no equity and would defeat justice.

LORD PARKER OF WADDINGTON: My Lords, the defendants in this case are appealing to the equitable jurisdiction of the court for relief from a contract which they admit to be fair and reasonable and of which they have already enjoyed the full advantage. Their title to relief is based on some equity which they say is inherent in all transactions in the nature of a mortgage. They can state no intelligible principle underlying this alleged equity, but contend that your Lordships are bound by authority. That the court should be asked in the exercise of its equitable jurisdiction to assist in so inequitable a proceeding as the repudiation of a fair and reasonable bargain is somewhat startling, and makes it necessary to examine the point of view from which Courts of Equity have always regarded mortgage transactions. For this purpose I have referred to most, if not all, of the reported cases on the subject, and propose to state shortly the conclusions at which I have arrived.

[His Honour reviewed several cases, including *Noakes & Co v Rice; Samuel v Jarrah Timber and Wood Paving Corporation* (see extracts above, pp 262 and 255), and continued.]

My Lords, after the most careful consideration of the authorities I think it is open to the House to hold, and I invite your Lordships to hold, that there is now no rule in equity which precludes a mortgagee, whether the mortgage be made upon the occasion of a loan or otherwise, from stipulating for any collateral advantage, provided such collateral advantage is not either: (1) unfair and unconscionable; or (2) in the nature of a penalty clogging the equity of redemption; or (3) inconsistent with or repugnant to the contractual and equitable right to redeem.

[After outlining the terms of the parties' agreement Parker LJ continued:]

I doubt whether, even before the repeal of the usury laws, this perfectly fair and businesslike transaction would have been considered a mortgage within any equitable rule or maxim relating to mortgages. The only possible way of deciding whether a transaction is a mortgage within any such rule or maxim is by reference to the intention of the parties. It never was intended by the parties that if the defendant company exercised their right to pay off the loan they should get rid of the option. The option was not in the nature of a penalty, nor was it nor could it ever become inconsistent with or repugnant to any other part of the real bargain within any such rule or maxim. The same is true of the commission payable on the sale of skins as to which the option was not exercised. Under these circumstances it seems to me that the bargain must stand and that the plaintiffs are entitled to the relief they claim.

[Halsbury and Atkinson LJJ agreed.]

Appeal allowed.

Notes and questions

1 Was *Kreglinger* decided on the ground that the mortgage and the collateral advantage though in the same document were really separate transactions; or on the ground that a collateral advantage, even if stipulated to continue after repayment, provided it is not unconscionable, is not a clog?

2 Several writers have commented upon this case. For example, Sykes and Walker, *The Law of Securities, op cit*, note 11, at pp 75–76, notes that *Kreglinger* is:

> ... explainable only on the ground that in some cases one really has two transactions, a contract for a loan and mortgage which is the mortgage transaction, and a contract embodying the collateral stipulation, even though for convenience they are embodied in the same document. When this position is reached, then the separate transaction involving the collateral stipulation will stand even though it contemplates existence during the period after redemption and affects the mortgaged property before and after redemption. To determine, however, the limits of the mortgage transaction and to decide whether there is but one transaction or two is almost a metaphysical problem and one that bristles with difficulties. One wonders whether this test would ever have come into existence as an accepted one had there not existed the necessity of harmonizing *Bradley v Carritt* with the case of *Kreglinger*. In practice each case will turn on its own facts, the judge selecting such facts as will give an indication of the true nature of the collateral stipulation and the degree of connection between it and the mortgage contract. It is probably today too rash to say that the general rule is that of invalidity, that *Noakes v Rice* represents the general rule and that the *Kreglinger* case instances a comparatively rare exception. Such may once have been the position but the trend of judicial attitudes has changed. Such conceptualistic analyses as that involved in *Kreglinger* may indeed be deplored, but it cannot be said that the *Kreglinger* case arrived at anything like a simple proposition that collateral covenants should stand unless unreasonable, notwithstanding Goff L's rather optimistic interpretation in *Cityland and Property (Holdings) Ltd v Dabrah* [[1968] Ch 166].

Cheshire and Burn's Modern Law of Real Property (14th edn, Butterworths, London) at p 646, comments that Lord Chancellor Haldane's approach in *Kreglinger* of treating the agreement as constituting two contracts provides the court with a much needed flexibility in the area of collateral advantages and enables it to adapt the earlier strict rules to modern circumstances. The learned authors continue:

> *Bradley v Carritt* ... [[1903] AC 253] thus represents the high-water mark of the conception of a mortgage as an onerous obligation imposed upon a necessitous borrower, in whose favour the court should therefore intervene.[47] The *Kreglinger* case, on the other hand, reveals a judicial appreciation of a mortgage as a transaction freely concluded by businessmen without colour of oppression, which should therefore form no exception to the

47 Waldock, *Law of Mortgages* (2nd edn), Chapter VIII.

maxim *pacta sunt servanda*. This is a more realistic and reasonable approach, and one more compatible with the business conditions of the 20th century.

3 Gawi, the registered owner of certain factory premises, borrows K100,000 from Wantok Pty Ltd, one of his principal suppliers of parts in his manufacturing process. The loan is secured by a registered mortgage over the factory. One of the clauses in the mortgage stipulates that the mortgagor shall purchase a certain quantity of parts each year from the mortgagee for use in his business during the continuance of the mortgage and for the period of two years thereafter in the event of his continuing to engage in his manufacturing process. Discounting the restraint of trade doctrine, advise Gawi whether the clause is enforceable.

Mortgagee's rights under special statutory provisions

The rights and remedies of a mortgagee under the Land Registration Act are in certain situations varied under special statutory provisions. Examples of such provisions are extracted below.

(a) Land acquired by compulsory process

Where the State by compulsory process[48] acquires land that is encumbered with a mortgage, the Land Act regulates the rights of the mortgagee. In this regard the relevant provisions are: ss 98, 100–03, and are reproduced below:

Section 98

(1) Where land acquired by compulsory process under this Act was, at the date of acquisition, subject to a mortgage, the mortgagee may either:

(a) claim compensation under Division 2; or

(b) by notice to the Minister, waive his rights to compensation.

(2) If the mortgagee makes a claim for compensation, he shall state in his claim:

(a) the amount of principal due under the mortgage at the date of acquisition; and

(b) the amount of interest, costs and charges due under the mortgage at that date.

(3) The Minister may, by written notice served on a person who is or may be a mortgagee, require him, at his option:

(a) to make a claim under this Act for compensation as mortgagee; or

(b) to waive his rights to compensation.

(4) If the person referred to in sub-section (3) fails to make a claim for compensation in accordance with this Act within two months, or such further period as the Minister in Writing allows, after the service of the notice under that sub-section, he shall be deemed to have waived his rights to compensation as mortgagee.

(5) Where a mortgagee claims compensation under this Act, the acquisition of the land has, to the extent to which the compensation payable to the mortgagee under section 103(1) is sufficient to satisfy the mortgage debt and interest, costs and charges due to the

48 See s 12 of the Land Act 1996; s 7 of the Land Acquisition (Development Purposes) Act (Ch No 192); and s 9 of the Land (Underdeveloped Freeholds) Act (Ch No 193).

mortgagee under the mortgage as at the date of acquisition, the effect of extinguishing the liability of the mortgagor under the mortgage as from the date of acquisition.

(6) A mortgagee who waives his rights to compensation is debarred from claiming or recovering as mortgagee any compensation or other amount from the State.

(7) Waiver of his rights to compensation by a mortgagee, or failure by a mortgagee to claim compensation, does not affect his rights and remedies against the mortgagor or in respect of land included in the mortgage other than the land acquired.

Section 100

(1) Where an amount has been paid to or recovered by a mortgagee under a mortgage in respect of a liability that, on the making of a claim by the mortgagee, is deemed to have been extinguished as from the date of acquisition by virtue of section 98(5):

(a) the mortgagee is liable to repay the amount to the person who paid it; and

(b) the Minister may deduct from the compensation payable to the mortgagee, and pay to the person who paid that amount, so much of the amount as has not been so repaid.

(2) A payment made by the Minister in accordance with sub-section (1)(b) shall be deemed to have been made in discharge of the obligation of the mortgagee under sub-section (1)(a).

Section 101

(1) In this section, 'proceedings' means any action to enforce the rights of a mortgagee under a mortgage, whether or not the proceedings are in a court, including action with a view to taking possession of or selling land, or to foreclosing.

(2) Where –

(a) any land acquired by compulsory process under this Act was, at the date of acquisition, subject to a mortgage; and

(b) proceedings by the mortgagee in relation to the mortgage.

(i) were pending at the date of acquisition; or

(ii) are commenced or proposed to be commenced after that date and before compensation had been paid in full to the mortgagor in respect of the acquisition,

the National Court may

(c) on the application of the mortgagor and subject to such conditions as the court thinks fit order a stay of the proceedings or enjoin the mortgagee against commencing or continuing the proceedings; and

(d) make such other orders as it thinks necessary.

Section 103

(1) The compensation payable to a mortgagee is an amount equal to the sum of

(a) the principal secured by the mortgage at the date of acquisition; and

(b) any interest, costs or charges due to the mortgagee under the mortgage at that date,

but not exceeding the compensation payable to the mortgagor in respect of the land.

(2) For the purposes of sub-section (1), the compensation payable to the mortgagor shall be deemed to be:

   (a) if there was only one mortgage over the land – the compensation that would have been payable to the mortgagor if there had been no mortgage over the land; or

   (b) if there were more mortgages than one over the land – the compensation that would have been payable to the mortgagor if there had been no mortgage over the land, less the amount, or the sum of the amounts, of principal, interest, costs and charges due at the date of acquisition to a mortgagee or mortgagees in respect of a mortgage or mortgages having priority over the mortgage in respect of which the compensation is to be determined.

(3) In addition to the compensation referred to in sub-section (1), the mortgagee is entitled to payment by the State:

   (a) of interest on the amount of principal included in the compensation at the lowest rate (whether for prompt payment or otherwise) provided by the mortgage, from the date of acquisition to

      (i) the date of payment of compensation; or

      (ii) where payment is delayed through a default of the mortgagee, the date when payment would have been made but for the default; and

   (b) if the principal was not repayable (with or without notice) at the date when interest ceased to be payable under Paragraph (a):

      (i) of the costs of the mortgagee of re-investing the principal included in the compensation; and

      (ii) if a loss of interest is reasonably to be expected, regard being had to the rate of interest secured by the mortgage and the rate of interest obtained or likely to be obtained on the re-investment – of a reasonable allowance for loss of interest until the date on which the principal would have been repayable (with or without notice).

Section 104

The compensation payable to a mortgagee under section 103(1) shall be deducted from the compensation that would have been payable to the mortgagor if the mortgage did not exist, and interest under section 111 is payable to the mortgagor on the reduced amount only.

Section 105. Execution of discharge of mortgage debt

On payment or tender of the compensation to the mortgagee, he shall, if so required by the mortgagor and at the expense of the mortgagor, execute a discharge of the mortgage debt to the extent to which the liability of the mortgagor under the mortgage is extinguished by virtue of section 98(5).

Section 106. Rights of mortgagor where mortgagee does not claim

Where a mortgagee does not claim compensation, the mortgagor is entitled to the same compensation as if the mortgage did not exist, and, in addition, to such amount (if any) as he should justly receive as compensation in respect of:

(a) interest on the mortgage debt accruing after the date of acquisition; and

(b) any other liability to the mortgagee.

Section 107

Where land that is subject to a mortgage is acquired by compulsory process under this Act and the whole or part of the mortgage debt is not discharged by virtue of this Act, the mortgagee retains, in respect of the whole or the part of the mortgage debt, as the case may be, his rights and remedies against the mortgagor (other than rights and remedies in relation to the land acquired) and in relation to any other land that is subject to the mortgage.

(b) Land (Tenure Conversion) Act 1963–83 (No 15 of 1964)

The registered proprietor of customary land, which was converted into freeholds under the Land (Tenure Conversion) Act, has the power to mortgage or charge his or her land in the same way, and to the same extent as any other registered proprietor (s 26(a)). However, in the event of default in payment of the mortgage debt, the remedies of the mortgagee against the land are drastically limited by s 26(b)(ii) and (iii) of the Land (Tenure Conversion) Act.

Section 26

(b) The Registrar of Titles shall register against the proprietorship a limitation that –

(ii) the land may be mortgaged or charged but, notwithstanding anything in any law in force in the Territory or a part of the Territory to the contrary contained, the mortgagee or chargee is not entitled to remain in possession for longer than three years or to foreclose the right of the mortgagor or charger to redeem the mortgaged or charged land; and

(iii) the land shall not be taken under a writ of execution or under or in consequence of a bankruptcy or insolvency, or in any similar or analogous manner; and

subject to section 26A of this Ordinance, the Administrator shall not approve under Part VII of the Land Ordinance 1962 of, and the Registrar of Titles shall not register, a transfer or dealing contrary to a limitation registered under the last preceding paragraph.

The Minister may, however, direct the Registrar of Titles to cancel the limitations imposed under s 26(b) if he is satisfied that the proposed dealing will not adversely affect the interests of the registered proprietor (s 26A).

Questions

1 What are the policy reasons for limiting the mortgagee's remedies against the mortgagor under the above Act? Do you agree with this policy?

2 John Kwe is the registered proprietor of certain land in Madang. He applies for a loan from ABC Bank on security of his land. The bank has never granted a loan on security of converted freehold land. Advise the bank of the various legal and other factors it should consider is deciding whether to accept the security.

CHAPTER 6

LEASES

I LEASES AND LICENCES DISTINGUISHED

There is no statutory definition of a 'lease'. Under the underlying law, a lease is an estate or interest in land for a fixed period of certain duration usually, but not necessarily,[1] in consideration of the payment of rent. A licence, on the other hand is permission to the licensee to enter the licensor's land for some specified purpose or purposes which otherwise would be a trespass.[2] The main distinguishing feature of a lease and a licence is that a licence does not create an interest in the land.[3] For this reason a licence, unlike a lease, does not bind a third party who purchases the land, even though he has notice of the licence. However, as the following case illustrates, in certain circumstances the court in exercise of its equitable powers may intervene and restrain a third party from ejecting a licensee.

PNG READY MIXED CONCRETE PTY LTD v THE INDEPENDENT STATE OF PAPUA NEW GUINEA AND OTHERS [1981] PNGLR 396, National Court of Justice

[Between 1969 and 1987, a group of people ('second respondents') occupied certain government land without the consent or dissent of the relevant government officials. They erected dwellings on the land and planted trees and gardens on it. According to the evidence, they entertained some expectation that the government would let them stay on the land indefinitely. In 1981, the government granted the applicant, PNG Ready Mixed Concrete, a lease of 99 years over the subject land. The applicant and the government were both aware of the existence and extent of the occupation by the second respondents but neither took any action against them. PNG Ready Mixed Concrete Company (the Company) instituted these proceedings for declaratory orders of its rights over the suit property. At the time of its application the company's lease had not been executed nor registered under the Land Registration Act (Ch No 191).]

MILES J: I shall consider the case on the basis that the company has acquired a legal leasehold estate but without making a positive decision to that effect, and without consideration of what implications, if any, arise from the facts first, that no lease has been executed and secondly, that the company's interest has not been registered under the Lands Registration Act.

The questions for determination then are first, what was the nature of the interest, if any, vested in the occupants at the time of the company being granted the lease and secondly, did the company have notice of such interest so that it took subject to that interest?

1 See Amankwah, Mugambwa and Muroa, *Land Law in Papua New Guinea* (Lawbook Co, Sydney, 2001), pp 120–21.

2 *Radaich v Smith and Another* (1959) 101 CLR 209, at 222, *per* Windeyer J.

3 *Thomas v Sorrell* (1673) Vaugh 330 at 351; 124 ER 1098, at 1109.

[His Honour found that at the time of the agreement to lease the land the government and the company were both aware of the presence of the squatters on the land. He continued:]

The claim put forward on behalf of the occupants to defeat the right of the state to possession of the land immediately prior to the granting of the lease is based on the doctrine of equitable estoppel, sometimes called promissory estoppel and in relation to land sometimes called proprietary estoppel. It was discussed at length in the decision of the Court of Appeal in *Crabb v Arun District Council* [[1975] 3 All ER 865 at 868] decided on 23 July 1975, a date about as close to the date of Papua New Guinean Independence as one needs to go for a statement of the English principles applicable under Sched 2.1 of the Constitution. The doctrine is summarised in a long passage from Lord Denning MR at 871 which cites the old authorities. I will not quote the passage in full. It is summarised in one sentence as follows:

> Short of an actual promise, if he by his words or conduct, so behaves as to lead another to believe that he will not insist on his strict legal rights – knowing or intending that the other will act on that belief – and he does so act, that again will raise an equity in favour of the other, and it is for a court of equity to say in what way the equity may be satisfied.

... The principles of proprietary estoppel as expounded by Lord Denning MR in *Crabb v Arun District Council* (*supra*) should be regarded as part of the underlying law of Papua New Guinea. The question is: how far are they applicable to the present case.

The question should be answered in the following way. Once a significant number of persons had taken up residence on the land, built dwelling houses on it, planted trees and the like, it was up to the state if it wished to protect its right to possession of the land to issue some sort of a warning or statement that persons who came on to the land to take up residence and build and plant crops there did so at their own risk. Yet no such warning issued at any time. The result is that those who came took up residence, built houses, planted crops and the like after say 1976 may be regarded as having sufficient interest in the land as to give rise by early 1981 to an equity entitling them to remain on the land despite the state's legal right to possession. Because the state raised no objection to the large influx after 1976, those who had come on to the land prior to 1976 were entitled to accept and did accept that their presence also was tacitly approved and so they should be regarded as having acquired a similar equitable interest by early 1981. The right may be regarded as analogous to a licence and how it might be terminated or revoked will be discussed in a moment ...

It was put on behalf of the company that the occupants could not rely on proprietary estoppel unless they satisfied the five *probanda* or tests laid down by Fry J in *Willmott v Barber* [(1880) 15 Ch D 96]. But the English authorities are clear that by 1975, although the five *probanda* might be used as a 'valuable guide', the ultimate test was whether in the circumstances it has become unconscionable for the holder of the legal right to insist on its full enforcement. Even if it is accepted that the occupants must have incurred expenditure in the mistaken belief that they already owned a sufficient interest in the property to justify the expenditure (or that they would obtain such an interest), I think that by 1976 some sort of genuine residential community had been established in the land: those who built thereafter or otherwise took action or incurred expenditure which improved the land did so in the belief that the state would recognise their interest.

In these circumstances ... I propose to make a declaratory order which recognises the company's right to possession subject to the equitable right of the occupants to remain in possession for a period of time appropriate to the circumstances. [The period ordered varied from six to 12 months.]

Notes

The applicants in *PNG Ready Mixed Concrete Pty Ltd* did not appeal against Miles J's decision. In a subsequent case involving the same land, *Harman Gawi v PNG Ready Mixed Concrete Pty Ltd* [1984] PNGLR 74, Kapi Dep CJ, in the Supreme Court, observed (at 77) that since Miles J's decision was never appealed against 'the declaration of the equitable right of the occupants and the extent of this right is settled and cannot be questioned now'. In the same case, McDermott J noted without comment (at 79) Miles J's decision that the squatter's right was analogous to a licence and enforceable against the company. Arguably, Miles J's decision in *PNG Ready Mixed Concrete Pty Ltd* is authority for the view that a licence in certain situations may confer some form of equitable interest, which is enforceable against third parties with notice. However, the court did not directly address this particular issue.

II ESSENTIAL FEATURES OF A LEASE

Leases have two essential features, which distinguish them from licences:

- certainty of duration; and
- exclusive possession.

Certainty of duration

This means that both the beginning and ending of a lease must be certainly known or ascertainable before the lease takes effect. A right of occupation for an uncertain duration is not a lease. The following cases illustrates this principle.

LACE v CHANTLER [1944] 1 All ER 305, Court of Appeal

[The plaintiff sub-let a dwelling house to the defendant for the 'duration of the war'. The issue raised was whether letting 'for the duration of the war' creates a valid lease.]

LORD GREENE MR: The question immediately arises whether a tenancy for the duration of the war creates a good leasehold interest. In my opinion, it does not. A term created by a leasehold tenancy agreement must be expressed either with certainty and specifically or by reference to something which can, at the time when the lease takes effect, be looked to as a certain ascertainment of what the term is meant to be. In the present case, when this tenancy agreement took effect, the term was completely uncertain. It was impossible to say how long the tenancy would last. Mr Sturge in his argument has maintained that such a lease would be valid, and that, even if the term is uncertain at its beginning when the lease takes effect, the fact that at some future time it will be rendered certain is sufficient to make it a good lease. In my opinion, that argument is not to be sustained.

I do not propose to go into the authorities on the matter, but in Foa's *Landlord and Tenant*, 6th edn, p 115, the law is stated in this way, and, in my view, correctly: 'The *habendum* in a lease must point out the period during which the enjoyment of the premises is to be had; so that the duration, as well as the commencement of the term, must be stated. The certainty of a lease as to its continuance must be ascertainable either by the express limitation of the parties at the time the lease is made, or by reference to some collateral act which may, with equal certainty, measure the continuance of it, otherwise it is void. If the term be fixed by reference to some collateral matter, such matter must either be itself certain (eg, a demise to hold for 'as many years as A has in the manor of B') or capable before the lease takes effect of being rendered so (eg, for 'as many years as C shall name'). The important words to observe in that last phrase are the words 'before the lease takes effect'. Then it goes on: 'Consequently, a lease to endure for 'as many years as A shall live,' or 'as the coverture between B and C shall continue' would not be good a lease for years, although the same results may be achieved in another way by making the demise for a fixed number (99 for instance) of years 'determinable upon A's death, or the dissolution of the coverture between B and C'. In the present case, in my opinion, this agreement cannot take effect as a good tenancy for the duration of the war.

[Mackinnon and Luxmoore LJJ agreed.]

Appeal dismissed.

In the following case, the House of Lords reaffirmed that certainty of duration is an essential feature of all leases, including periodic tenancies (ie, weekly, fortnightly, monthly, and yearly tenancies).

PRUDENTIAL ASSURANCE CO LTD v LONDON RESIDUARY AND OTHERS [1992] 3 All ER 504, House of Lords

[Before 1930, the plaintiffs' predecessor in title owned land with a street frontage on which there were shop premises. In 1930 the London Country Council the (LCC) purchased a strip of the land along the street frontage for future road widening and purported to lease it back to the plaintiffs' predecessor in title under an agreement which provided by clause 6 that the tenancy would continue until the land was required for road widening by the LCC. Over 60 years later, the road had not been widened. Subsequently, the LCC's freehold title over the strip vested in the defendants who are private companies with no power to widen the road. The defendants purported to terminate the lease by serving on the plaintiffs six months' notice to quit. The plaintiffs sought declarations that the notice to quit was null and void because the tenancy could only be determined if the land was required for road-widening purposes in accordance with clause 6 of the agreement. The defendants argued that clause 6 was void because it purported to create a lease for uncertain duration. The trial judge agreed. The Court of Appeal reversed the decision holding that the principle of certainty of duration expressed in *Lace v Chantler* [1944] 1 All ER 305, did not apply to periodic tenancies. On appeal to the House of Lords.]

LORD TEMPLEMAN: [His Honour after discussing several authorities concluded]: These authorities indicate plainly enough that the agreement in the present case did not create a lease and that the tenancy from year to year enjoyed by the tenant as a result of entering into possession and paying a yearly rent can be determined by six months' notice by either landlord or tenant. The landlord has admittedly served such a notice. The Court of Appeal has however concluded that the notice was ineffective and that the landlord cannot give a valid notice until the land is required 'for the purposes of the widening of Walworth Road' in conformity with clause 6 of the agreement.

The notion of a tenancy from year to year, the landlord binding himself not to give notice to quit which was once rejected by Lord Mansfield and exploded long before 1807 according to Lawrence J in *Doe d Warner v Browne* (1807) 8 East 165 at 167, 103 ER 305 at 306 was however revived and applied by the Court of Appeal in *Charles Clay & Sons Ltd v British Railways Board* [1971] 1 All ER 1007; [1971] Ch 725. In that case a lease for a period of six months from June 1920 was expressed to continue from half year to half year until determined. The agreement provided for the determination of the agreement by three months' written notice given by either party to the other subject to a proviso that the landlords should not exercise that right unless they required the premises for their undertaking. The successors to the landlords served a six months' written notice to quit under the Landlord and Tenant Act 1954 although they did not require the premises for their undertaking. The Court of Appeal, upholding Foster J, declared that the notice to quit was invalid and of no effect because the landlords did not require the premises for their undertaking. The Court of Appeal held that the decision in *Lace v Chantler* [1944] 1 All ER 305 ... did not apply to a periodic tenancy and declined to follow *Doe d Warner v Browne* (1807) 8 East 165; 103 ER 305 or *Cheshire Lines Committee v Lewis & Co* (1880) 50 LJQB 121. Russell LJ, delivering the judgment of the court, held that the decision in *Lace v Chantler* did not apply to a tenancy from year to year and said [1971] 1 All ER 1007 at 1010:

> ... we are persuaded that, there being no authority to prevent us, it is preferable as a matter of justice to hold parties to their clearly expressed bargain rather than to introduce for the first time in 1971 an extension of a doctrine of land law so as to deny the efficacy of that bargain.

My Lords, I consider that the principle in *Lace v Chantler* ... reaffirming 500 years of judicial acceptance of the requirement that a term must be certain applies to all leases and tenancy agreements. A tenancy from year to year is saved from being uncertain because each party has power by notice to determine at the end of any year. The term continues until determined as if both parties made a new agreement at the end of each year for a new term for the ensuing year. A power for nobody to determine or for one party only to be able to determine is inconsistent with the concept of a term from year to year: see *Doe d Warner v Browne* (1807) 8 East 165; 103 ER 305 and *Cheshire Lines Committee v Lewis & Co* (1880) 50 LJQB 121. In *Charles Clay & Sons Ltd v British Railways Board* [1971] 1 All ER 1007 ... there was no 'clearly expressed bargain' that the term should continue until the crack of doom if the demised land was not required for the landlord's undertaking or if the undertaking ceased to exist. In the present case there was no 'clearly expressed bargain' that the tenant shall be entitled to enjoy his 'temporary structures' in perpetuity if Walworth Road is never widened. In any event principle and precedent dictate that it is beyond the power of the landlord and the tenant to create a term which is uncertain.

A lease can be made for five years subject to the tenant's right to determine if the war ends before the expiry of five years. A lease can be made from year to year subject to a fetter on the right of the landlord to determine the lease before the expiry of five years unless the war ends. Both leases are valid because they create a determinable certain term of five years. A lease might purport to be made for the duration of the war subject to the tenant's right to determine before the end of the war. A lease might be made from year to year subject to a fetter on the right of the landlord to determine the lease before the war ends. Both leases would be invalid because each purported to create an uncertain term. A term must either be certain or uncertain. It cannot be partly certain because the tenant can determine it at any time and partly uncertain because the landlord cannot determine it for an uncertain period. If the landlord does not grant and the tenant does not take a certain term the grant does not create a lease.

The decision of the Court of Appeal *Charles Clay & Sons Ltd v British Railways Board* [*supra*] was taken a little further in *Ashburn Anstalt v Arnold* [1988] 2 All ER 147 ... That case, if it was correct, would make it unnecessary for a lease to be of a certain duration. In an agreement for the sale of land the vendor reserved the right to remain at the property after completion as licensee and to trade therefrom without payment of rent:

> ... save that it can be required by Matlodge Ltd [the purchaser] to give possession on not less than one quarter's notice in writing upon Matlodge certifying that it is ready at the expiration of such notice forthwith to proceed with the development of the property and the neighbouring property involving *inter alia* the demolition of the property.

The Court of Appeal held that this reservation created a tenancy. The tenancy was not from year to year but for a term which would continue until Matlodge Ltd certified that it was ready to proceed with the development of the property. The Court of Appeal held that the term was not uncertain because the vendor could either give a quarter's notice or vacate the property without giving notice. But of course the same could be said of the situation in *Lace v Chantler* ... The cumulative effect of the two Court of Appeal authorities, *Charles Clay & Sons Ltd v British Railways Board* ... and the *Ashburn* case, would therefore destroy the need for any term to be certain.

In the present case the Court of Appeal was bound by the decisions in *Charles Clay & Sons Ltd v British Railways Board* and the *Ashburn* case. In my opinion both those cases were wrongly decided. A grant for an uncertain term does not create a lease. A grant for an uncertain term which takes the form of a yearly tenancy which cannot be determined by the landlord does not create a lease. I would allow the appeal. The trial judge, Millett J, reached the conclusion that the six months' notice was a good notice. He was of course bound by the Court of Appeal decision but managed to construe the memorandum of agreement so as to render cl 6 ineffective in fettering the right of the landlord to serve a notice to quit after that landlord had ceased to be a road widening authority. In the circumstances this question of construction need not be considered. For the reasons which I have given the order made by Millett J must be restored. The respondent must pay the costs of the appellants before the House and in the courts below.

[Griffiths, Goff of Chievelley, Browne-Wilkinson and Mustill LJJ concurred.]

Appeal allowed.

Questions

1 Discuss the validity of the following arrangements:

  (a) To X a lease of an office suite on the ground floor of a building under construction at Lot 20, University Way, Waigani, for a term of 10 years from the date of completion of the building.

  (b) To W a lease until she dies (see s 49(1) of the Land Registration Act (Ch No 191)).

  (c) 'To T a lease of my house, provided she pays rent of K50 per week I will not terminate the lease until I complete my University studies.'

  (d) 'To T a lease of my house for three years, but if I complete my studies earlier than three years I may terminate the lease.'

2 What are the policy reasons, if any, for the requirement that duration of a lease must be certain?

Exclusive possession and intention to create a lease

Exclusive possession is the right to use premises to the exclusion of others including the landlord. In *Street v Mountford*, Lord Templeman explained the right of exclusive possession as follows:[4]

> The tenant possessing exclusive possession is able to exercise the rights of an owner of land, which is in the real sense his land albeit temporarily and subject to certain restrictions. A tenant armed with exclusive possession can keep out strangers and keep out the landlord unless the landlord is exercising limited rights reserved to him by the tenancy agreement to enter and view and repair.

Controversy abounds whether a grant of exclusive possession of land for a period certain is conclusive evidence that the grantee is a lessee and not a mere licensee. The 'traditional' view was that a person granted exclusive possession in return for payment of rent, was necessarily a lessee or a tenant.[5] However, some English cases departed from this viewpoint and held that in addition to exclusive possession (and certainty of duration) the courts had to determine whether the parties had the intention to create a lease.[6] The leading authority in this regard is Lord Denning's judgment in *Errington v Errington and Woods*.[7] In *Radaich v Smith*,[8] the High Court of Australia declined to follow the 'new' trend and reasserted the view that a grant of exclusive possession is conclusive of a lease irrespective of the intention of the parties. In *Street v Mountford*, the English House of Lords followed the High Court of Australia judgment in *Radaich*. Both judgments are extracted below.

RADAICH v SMITH AND ANOTHER (1959) 101 CLR 209, High Court of Australia

> [By a deed termed a 'licence' the respondents (Mr and Mrs Smith) granted to the appellant (Radaich) for a term of five years 'the sole and exclusive licence': to supply refreshments to the public 'admitted to' a certain lock-up shop 'and to carry on the business of a milk bar therein'. Throughout the deed, the parties referred to each other as licensor and licensee and avoided any reference to a lease. The issue was whether the appellant occupied the shop as a licensee or as a tenant.]
>
> **WINDEYER J**: The distinction between a lease and a licence is clear. 'A dispensation or licence properly passeth no interest, nor alters or transfers property in anything but only makes an action lawful which without it had been unlawful': *Thomas v Sorrell* [(1673) Vaugh 330]. Whether when one man is allowed to enter upon the land of another pursuant to a contract he does so as licensee or as tenant must, it has been said, 'be in the last resort a question of intention', *per* Lord Green MR in *Booker v Palmer* [[1942] 2 All ER 674, at 676]. But intention to do what? – Not to give the transaction one label rather than another. Not to escape the legal consequences of one relationship by professing that it is another. Whether the transaction creates a lease or a licence depends upon intention, only in the sense that it

4 *Street v Mountford* [1985] 2 All ER 289, at 292, see extract below, p 290.

5 *Ibid*, at 292.

6 See for example, *Errington v Errington and Woods* [1952] 1 KB 290.

7 [1952] 1 KB 290, see extracts below. Also see *Halsbury's Laws of England*, 4th edn; Vol 27(1), paras 6–7, and the cases there referred to.

8 (1959) 101 CLR 209, see extract below.

depends upon the nature of the right which the parties intend the person entering upon the land shall have in relation to the land. When they have put their transaction in writing this intention is to be ascertained by seeing what, in accordance with ordinary principles of interpretation, are the rights that the instrument creates. If those rights be the rights of a tenant, it does not avail either party to say that a tenancy was not intended. And conversely if a man be given only the rights of a licensee, it does not matter that he be called a tenant; he is a licensee. What then is the fundamental right which a tenant has that distinguishes his position from that of a licensee? It is an interest in land as distinct from a personal permission to enter the land and use it for some stipulated purpose or purposes. And how is it to be ascertained whether such an interest in land has been given? By seeing whether the grantee was given a legal right of exclusive possession of the land for a term or from year to year or for a life or lives. If he was, he is a tenant. And he cannot be other than a tenant, because a legal right of exclusive possession is a tenancy and the creation of such a right is a demise. To say that a man who has, by agreement with a landlord, a right of exclusive possession of land for a term is not a tenant is simply to contradict the first proposition by the second. A right of exclusive possession is secured by the right of a lessee to maintain ejectment and, after his entry, trespass. A reservation to the landlord, either by contract or statute, of a limited right of entry, as for example to view or repair, is, of course, not inconsistent with a grant of exclusive possession. Subject to such reservations, a tenant for a term or from year to year or for a life or lives can exclude his landlord as well as strangers from the demised premises. All this is long established law: see *Cole on Ejectment* (1857), pp 72, 73, 287, 458.

Recently some transactions from which in the past tenancies at will would have been inferred have been somewhat readily treated as creating only licences. And it has been said – especially in connection with family relationships, charity or hospitality – that allowing a person to have the exclusive possession of premises does not necessarily indicate a tenancy as distinct from a licence. These decisions are largely a by-product of rent restriction statutes and other legislation here and in England. They are all explicable if they mean, as I think they all do, that persons who are allowed to enjoy sole occupation in fact are not necessarily to be taken to have been given a right of exclusive possession in law. If there be any decision which goes further and states positively that a person legally entitled to exclusive possession for a term is a licensee and not a tenant, it should be disregarded, for it is self-contradictory and meaningless. We are not here concerned with the way in which a court of equity would control the parties in the exercise of legal rights, but with the simple question whether at law this document created a lease or a licence. And the proper touchstone still is: did it give the so called licensee a legal right to the exclusive possession of the premises during the term? The question must of course, be resolved by considering the terms of the deed. But they are to be read in relation to the relevant surrounding circumstances, in particular the nature of the premises; for this deed, like any other instrument, is to be interpreted having regard to its subject matter. Here the subject premises are in fact a lock-up shop at The Spit, Mosman. It was said that the stated case does not expressly state this to be so. This is true, and the learned judge who heard the appeal in the Supreme Court may have been somewhat hampered because the case stated by the magistrate did not fully describe the subject premises. But it is stated that they are No 83 Parriwi Road, Mosman; and from the deed itself it appears that this is a separate part of a larger holding held by the respondents the so called licensors – under a special lease from the Crown, a form of tenure under the Crown Lands Acts of New South Wales. From the deed itself it is also a reasonable inference that the subject premises are a lock-up shop used as a refreshment room and milk bar and adjacent to another shop where fish foods are sold ... Turning then to its terms: its opening operative clause is expressed to be a grant for a five-year term of 'the sole and exclusive licence and privilege to supply refreshment to the public admitted to premises situate at 81–83 Parriwi Road, The Spit, Mosman, and to carry on the business of a milk bar therein in such rooms as are shown in the sketch contained in Sched one annexed hereto and the right to use of toilet at rear and passage thereto'. These words, standing by themselves, would create only an exclusive licence to supply refreshments, which is essentially different from an exclusive right to possession. But these opening words are not at all appropriate to the actual circumstances – and they do not stand by themselves. To describe the lock-up shop as 'such rooms as are shown in sketch' is inapt, for one room, the shop, is what is shown by the sketch. And it is inapt to speak of a right to supply refreshments 'to the public admitted to premises 82–83'. And several of the later provisions are not only not appropriate to a mere licence to sell refreshments on the landlord's premises, but clearly suppose a grant of possession of specific premises to the appellant so that she can carry on a business there. It was argued that the deed follows an accepted precedent for the grant of a licence, having been taken from the form given in *Evatt and Beckenham's Conveyancing Precedents*, 2nd edn (1938) p 542, which in turn is taken from a form in The Conveyancer vol 10, p 485. We have to decide what is the result of the words used by the parties, not what is the result which the draftsman of a form thought they would have. But what has happened is simply that the form has been used in circumstances for which it was never intended. In The Conveyancer it is described as a 'Licence for the Exclusive Right of Supplying Refreshments within a Railway Station or Building'; and in *Evatt and Beckenham's Precedents* as 'Licence for the Exclusive Right of Supplying Refreshments within a Building'. Whether all its clauses are really appropriate to a licence to sell refreshments at a stall on a railway station or in the foyer of a theatre to persons admitted to such premises need not be considered. It is inapt to create a licence of a lock-up milk bar at The Spit. References in the deed to the licensee 'giving up possession of the said building occupied by her', and to 'that part of the premises occupied by her' are consistent with a tenancy, and in their setting are not really consistent with the supposed licence. The appellant is required to keep her business open during business hours. Clearly she could shut it at other times. I imagine all concerned would have been astounded if they had been told that the appellant had no right to exclude persons from her shop; that the respondent might, if he wished, license other people to carry on any activity there other than the sale of refreshments, provided their presence did not prevent her selling refreshments or conducting the milk bar; and that, although she might lock the shop up at night and on holidays, the respondents could not only enter it themselves whenever they wished but could admit as many persons as they chose, provide them with keys and license them to use the premises in the absence of the appellant for any purpose of pleasure or business they liked, provided only that they did not sell refreshments. If the matter is to be tested by the apparent intention of the parties arising from the circumstances, that clearly was not their intention. If it is to be tested, as I consider it is, by their intention as reflected in the words of their deed with knowledge of the nature of the subject premises, then, in the words of Blackburn J (as he then was) in *Roads v Overseers of Trumpington* [(1870) LR 6 QB 56] the whole nature of the agreement shows that the appellant was intended to have exclusive possession of the land: [(1870) LR 6 QB, at 63]. The use in what purports to be the principal provision of the deed of words taken from a precedent designed for another purpose cannot outweigh its total effect ...

The magistrate was right. The deed created a lease of the part of the building shown in the sketch annexed to it, that is the shop, and a licence in relation to the part described as 'the toilet at rear and passage thereto'. The question in the stated case should be answered accordingly.

[McTiernan, Taylor, Menzies JJ and Dixon CJ agreed that the test of exclusive possession is decisive.]

Appeal allowed.

The following case is a good illustration of the application of the *Radaich v Smith* principle. The case also discusses some of the factors, which the courts take into account to determine whether an occupier has exclusive possession.

LEWIS v BELL (1985) 1 NSWLR 731, Court of Appeal of New South Wales

MAHONEY JA: Near the Randwick Racecourse in Sydney, there is a complex of stables and associated facilities described as 'Connaught Lodge'. The stable complex is delineated in a plan copy of which is before the court. It consists of a number of horseboxes, other facilities, and certain living quarters, all built along the edges of a rectangular area of land. The inner portion of the rectangle is comprised, as to a substantial part, of an exercise ring and other facilities. That in respect of which rights were granted to the defendant Mr Lewis comprises a number of horse boxes along one side of and in one corner of the rectangle, together with certain other facilities at other places in the area and staff accommodation situated at a third place in the rectangle.

The Australian Jockey Club, through the chairman of its committee Mr Bell, granted to the defendant certain rights in relation to part of the complex. The rights were granted by a document made on 1 October 1983, which, on the face of it, purports to be a complete statement of the transaction recorded in it ...

The document in question commences with the words 'This Licence Agreement'. It recites that 'the AJC controls the premises described in the First Schedule hereto' and that 'the AJC has agreed to allow the trainer to use the said premises on the terms and conditions hereinafter contained'. The following clauses of the document set forth those terms and conditions.

Clause 1 is in the following terms:

> The AJC and the trainer agree that this agreement shall operate for a term of one month from 1 October 1983, and thereafter from month to month providing however and it is hereby agreed that it may be determined at any time by either party giving to the other party one month's notice of such determination in writing save that it shall be automatically determined without the necessity for notice if the trainer is disqualified or suspended provided that the committee in its absolute discretion may permit the trainer the use of the premises on such terms and conditions as may be laid down by the committee.

Clause 2 provides that:

> The monthly fee payable in advance by the trainer to the AJC on the first working day of each month for the use of the premises shall be the amount specified in the Second Schedule hereto ...

Clause 3 obliges the trainer 'to pay interest on any unpaid rent' at the rate specified.

The agreement obliges the trainer to repair damage done to the premises and to keep them and surrounding areas in good and sanitary order and condition: cl 4; to control all horses kept on the premises; cl 5; and to give up the premises in good order and condition upon termination of the agreement: cl 6. Provision is also made in respect of the care of the horses on the premises: cl 7; acts apt to avoid any insurance policy of the AJC: cl 10; payment of charges for services on the premises: cl 11; and the compliance by the trainer with certain statutory notices: cl 15.

It is stipulated that the trainer 'shall only use the premises for the stabling of horses which are being prepared for racing under the rules of racing and shall not without the written consent of the Australian Jockey Club first had and obtained stable any horse of which he is not the trainer': cl 12; and he must use the stables 'solely for the purpose of training racehorses': cl 17.

Clause 14 provides:

> The trainer shall permit the AJC and its authorised officials to enter and inspect the premises provided twenty-four (24) hours notice is given except in special circumstances.

Clauses 8 and 9 are in the following terms:

> 8 Nothing contained in this agreement shall be construed as granting or shall be deemed to grant to the trainer any estate or interest in the licensed premises and save as to the rights hereby conferred on the trainer the licensed premises remain in the possession and control of the AJC.
>
> 9 The rights given to the trainer by this agreement are personal to the trainer and are not assignable or transferable nor may they be held on trust for any person.

On 13 November 1984, the AJC gave notice to Mr Lewis terminating the rights he held under the document. On 24 December 1984, it took proceedings in this court to recover possession of the premises. On 4 April 1985, Miles J found in favour of the plaintiff and held that the AJC was entitled to judgment for possession. The defendant Mr Lewis has appealed to this court against that judgment.

Mr McQuillan, for the defendant, has submitted that his Honour's judgment was wrong for two main reasons: first, because the document constitutes a lease and that lease was not effectively terminated by what the plaintiff did; and, second, that (if the document be only a licence) that licence was not effectively terminated and consequently Mr Lewis is entitled to remain in occupation of the premises.

The first submission: whether a lease –

As I have said, the document is described as a 'licence agreement'. However, Mr McQuillan has submitted that the rights granted are of a leasehold nature. He relies for this submission upon, in the main, two things: the claim that the terms of the document show that it was the parties' intention that the defendant be a lessee; and the claim that that which was granted to Mr Lewis could not have been effective without, and therefore must be held to include, the right to a leasehold interest in the premises. In these submissions reliance was placed upon the decision of the High Court of Australia in *Radaich v Smith* (1959) 101 CLR 209.

In determining whether the relationship created by a document is one of lessor and lessee, it is necessary to decide what is the test, or tests, of the existence of such a relationship. The conventional view was that there was one test and that it was whether the grantee was given the rights to exclusive possession of the premises: see *Glenwood Lumber Co Ltd v Phillips* [1904] AC 405 at 408 ... However, in England there was (at least in some of the decisions) a departure from this. Exclusive possession was seen as relevant but not decisive; or, alternatively, was seen as being one of the several tests of the existence of the relationship of lessor and lessee: see *Halsbury's Laws of England*, 4th edn, vol 27, parts 6–7 at 13–15, and the cases there referred to.

In the present case, it was accepted, or at least assumed, that the test is that of exclusive possession. That, in my opinion, is correct. It is the test which was adopted by at least the majority of their Honours in *Radaich v Smith* (see at pp 214, 217–20, 223) ...

It is not necessary to analyse the precise nature of the right to exclusive possession which is here in question. It is, for present purposes, sufficient to say that it involves that the lessee have the general right to exclude others, including the lessor, from the premises, subject at least to such specific provisions for entry as may be particularly provided for in the document ...

Whether a particular document grants such a right to the grantee depends, of course, upon the construction of the document. Regard is to be had, in the normal process of construction, to all of the terms of the document considered in their context. But, with this rule in mind, certain things may be said as to the process of determining whether the rights granted are those of a lessee.

First, if the right to exclusive possession is the test, then, in determining whether the grantee has been given the right of exclusive possession, the court must go initially to the terms of the grant: see *Radaich v Smith* (at 223) *per* Windeyer J. The grant of a right to exclusive possession, in terms, is of course *prima facie* sufficient. But the use, in the operative part of the document, of words such as 'lease' or 'devise' will ordinarily be understood to involve the grant of such a right. Conversely, if what is granted is not in terms exclusive possession or if the words used in the grant are not words understood to convey the right of exclusive possession, then (subject to what I shall say) the transaction is *prima facie* not one of lease. Thus, if that which is granted is not of its nature the right to possession or exclusive possession but, eg, the right to use the premises only for a defined and particular purpose, there will *prima facie* be no lease.

But there are cases in which it is not clear from the terms of the grant, construed in the light of the whole agreement and its context, what it is that is being granted by them. In such cases, it is necessary to determine what is granted by looking at other aspects of the transaction. Thus, a grant may not be in terms of 'possession' but of something else. It may be the grant of a right to occupy premises: cf *O'Keefe v Malone* [1903] AC 365 at 377; *Landale v Menzies* (1909) 9 CLR 89 at 91, 100, 101; the right to 'carry on a business on' the premises: cf *Radaich v Smith* (at 210); or, as in the present case, the right 'to use' the premises either generally or in a particular way. In such cases, the court must, by the process of construction, determine whether what is granted is mere occupation or use, or is possession in the relevant sense. And where what is granted is possession, it still, in principle, may remain to be decided whether what is granted is exclusive possession. But it is not necessary to consider, in this case, whether there can be a distinction between possession and exclusive possession and (if there can) what distinctions there may be between possession and exclusive possession in this context.

In deciding, in such cases, whether what has been granted is the right to exclusive possession, the court, in the process of construction, has in practice looked, *inter alia*, to two things: the nature of the rights which, in terms, have been granted; and the intention of the parties.

The nature of the rights which have been granted has been seen of significance for this purpose because, as the argument is put, if the grantee has been granted such rights, it is to be inferred that he was (or was not) granted the right to exclusive possession. And that inference has been put on at least two bases. First, it has been held proper to infer that the right granted do not carry by implication the grant of exclusive possession because the rights granted are inconsistent with the right to exclusive possession. Thus, a leasehold interest is an interest in land and, as such, is of its nature transferable: *Richardson v Landecker* (1950) 50 SR (NSW) 250 at 255; 67 WN 149 at 151. If the right granted is, of its nature, not transferable or is otherwise personal to the grantee it will, as such, not be a leasehold interest: cf *Abbeyfield (Harpenden) Society Ltd v Woods* [1968] 1 WLR 374 at 376; [1968] 1 All ER 352(n) at 353. In principle, where the rights are of their nature inconsistent with there being a lease, there will be no implication of a grant of exclusive possession.

Second, it has been held necessary to infer the grant of exclusive possession because the rights which have in terms been granted can be enjoyed only by one who has been granted exclusive possession. The grant of exclusive possession has been inferred from the nature of what has been expressly granted. This was the basis of the decision of their Honours in *Radaich v Smith* (see at pp 215, 217, 221, 223–25).

Where the argument for the existence of a lease is of this kind, it is, I think, important to have in mind that the argument depends upon the process of implication. Such an implication is, in my opinion, of the same nature as that involved in, for example, the implication of a term in the construction of transactions generally: at least, the principles upon which the implication is to be made are the same. These principles have been discussed in eg, *Liverpool City Council v Irwin* [1977] AC 239 at 255; and were referred to in *Codelfa Construction Pty Ltd v State Rail Authority of New South Wales* (1982) 149 CLR 337: see, eg (at 345 *et seq*) *per* Mason J (at 400 *et seq*); *per* Brennan J. As was there indicated, there are several and distinct bases upon which terms may be implied. In a case such as the present, the basis of implication is normally that it is necessary in order to give business efficacy to the rights which otherwise have been granted. Such being its basis, the implication will not be made merely because it is reasonable or convenient to do so; it must be necessary that the implication be made. And it will not be made if the parties have directed their attention to the subject matter of the suggested implication and have otherwise provided or have stipulated in terms that no such implication is to be made.

And that leads to the significance of intention in deciding whether the rights granted are of the nature of a lease. There is a difference between the Australian and the English cases as to the significance in this regard of the parties' intention: at least, there is a difference in the way in which that significance is stated. In the Australian cases, it is the nature of the rights which are granted which determines the matter: see *Radaich v Smith*, in England, 'the decisive consideration is the intention of the parties': *Halsbury*, para 6 at 13.

But, in my opinion, part at least of the difference lies in the different meanings given to 'intention'. It is necessary, I think, to consider the significance of the parties' intention at two stages in the court's reasoning: that in which it decides what is the nature of the rights which are granted by the transaction; and that in which, the nature of the rights having been determined, it decides whether the relationship is to be classified as one of lease or licence.

At the first stage, that of construction of the document, intention has the functions which ordinarily it has in accordance with the accepted rules of interpretation and construction. In the process of construction, the court's purpose is to determine, from the words used in their context, what was the intention of the parties as to what should be the rights granted. That intention is, of course, to be taken from the words used. But, once the intention has been ascertained, words which, eg, would in isolation convey a more limited right may be construed as granting exclusive possession, and vice versa. And, in the process of construction, an express statement of the parties' intentions as to, eg, the nature of the relationship to be created, will be of substantial, though not necessarily conclusive, importance: it will, in accordance with the rules of construction, yield to the intention to be derived from the document as a whole.

Similarly, intention will be relevant in the construction of the document for the purpose of deciding what terms are to be implied. Thus, if the grant of the right to exclusive possession depends, in the instant case, upon whether, eg, the business efficacy test requires its implication, an express statement by the parties of their intention may, in accordance with the established rules governing the implication of terms, operate to prevent such an implication.

At the second stage, that of classification, the significance of intention will, in Australia, be less. Once the nature of the rights granted is finally determined, the classification of the transaction, as lease or licence, will depend upon whether the rights are or are not those of exclusive possession. It is in this sense that, as it has been said, expressions of intention are irrelevant: the parties cannot 'escape the legal consequences of one relationship by professing that it is another': *Radaich v Smith* (at 222) *per* Windeyer J.

One further thing may be said as to the significance of intention. It is, in my opinion, important in determining the nature of a transaction, to have in mind that, in the end, it is for the parties to determine what rights they will grant and accordingly what is the nature of their transaction. The parties (or the party who effectively determines the form of the transaction) may desire, eg, that the transaction does not produce the incidents of a lease and they may, to achieve that result, grant or reserve rights which are inconsistent with the grant of exclusive possession. For example, in circumstances in which it would ordinarily be expected that the rights granted would carry, by implication, the right to exclusive possession, the transaction may reserve to the grantor the right to possession or to do such things in relation to the premises as are inconsistent with the grantee having exclusive possession. And that may be done in order that the transaction be one of licence rather than of lease. If, upon its proper construction, that be the transaction into which the parties have entered, effect should, in my opinion, be given to it according to its terms.

There are, of course, cases in which rights purport to be granted or reserved which are intended never to be operative. Instances of this have been found in, eg, the context of legislative restrictions on eviction or control of rents. The court may treat such rights as not having operation and construe the transaction accordingly. But, if on its proper construction the relevant rights were intended to be granted then, in my opinion, the transaction is to be construed and classified accordingly.

I come now to apply these principles to the present case. In my opinion, Miles J was correct in his construction and classification of the transaction. That which is the subject of the agreement is 'the use of the premises': the document does not purport to grant possession or exclusive possession. I do not think that, as a matter of construction, that which is granted should be read as possession or exclusive possession or that, by implication, a right to exclusive possession is to be seen as granted.

The property over which the rights of user are granted is, in substance, a series of separate boxes or rooms, situated at different parts of the general stable complex. Areas adjacent are obviously to be used by or in common with others. The use which is granted is, in terms, for a limited purpose only, viz, for the stabling of horses 'which are being prepared for racing under the rules of racing' and of which the grantee is trainer: cll 12 and 17. The rights are in terms stated to be 'personal to the trainer' and therefore not assignable: cl 9; and the stables may not be used for 'any horse of which he is not the trainer': cl 12. And the intention of the parties, as expressed in the document, is that the transaction be one of licence rather than lease. It is so described; and cl 8 states, in terms, that that which is granted is not an estate or interest and that the property shall 'remain in the possession and control of the AJC'.

The main submission of the defendant was, in my opinion, that, because what is granted is the right to use premises to stable racehorses, it is to be implied, as a matter of construction, that that right is exclusive and that, upon reasoning similar to that adopted in *Radaich v Smith*, there is by implication a grant of exclusive possession. And, it may be added, that argument was seen, in *Radaich v Smith*, as being of such force that the implication was drawn notwithstanding that the parties had used a form which the established precedent books had put forward as creating a licence rather than a lease.

There is, of course, force in this argument: it follows from the rights granted to the defendant that some term must be implied. But the question is whether the implication is that the defendant have exclusive possession.

The grant of a right to use premises as stables for horses or as accommodation for employees will carry certain rights by implication. The grant of such a right, whether in the context of a lease or licence, will ordinarily require by implication that the grantor will not, for example, grant to a third party the right to stable horses or to accommodate employees in the same areas. But an exclusive licence to stable a horse in a horse box is not, as such, a right to exclusive possession of that box. A licensor may covenant not to grant a concurrent licence to another and yet not be held to have given the licensee a right to exclusive possession of the box. In the present context, I do not think that the implication is that what was intended to be granted was possession or exclusive possession.

Reference was made in argument to the provisions of cl 14. The argument was that, if possession was retained to the AJC and the trainer had merely a licence exclusive of third parties, it would not have been necessary to provide specifically for entry and inspection by 'the AJC and its authorised officials'. The force of this argument depends upon the assumption that the clauses of the document are self consistent and do not overlap I do not think that the drafting of the document warrants such an assumption. Clause 8 stipulates for the retention of possession and control by the AJC and it may be that cl 14 was added by way of preventing disputes or, perhaps, because of the obligations imposed upon a trainer as to the security of stables under the rules of racing.

There are in the document terms which, standing alone, would support an inference of exclusive possession: terms such as 'rent' and 'sub-let' are arguably such. However, such terms are not inconsistent with a relationship of licensor and licensee and, in the context of the document, I do not think that they warrant an inference that the rights intended to be created were those of possession or of exclusive possession. In my opinion, the defendant was not the lessee of the AJC ...

[Appeal dismissed. Other members of the court agreed.]

Question

Do you understand *Lewis v Bell* to decide that exclusive possession is 'decisive' or is just of 'first importance' in determining whether the intention of the parties was to create a lease or a licence?

STREET v MOUNTFORD [1985] 2 All ER 289, House of Lords

LORD TEMPLEMAN: My Lords, by an agreement dated 7 March 1983 the respondent Mr Street granted the appellant Mrs Mountford the right to occupy the furnished rooms Nos 5 and 6 at 5 St Clements Gardens, Boscombe from 7 March 1983 for £37 per week, subject to termination by 14 days' written notice and subject to the conditions set forth in the agreement. The question raised by this appeal is whether the agreement created a tenancy or a licence.

A tenancy is a term of years absolute. This expression, by s 205(I)(xxvii) of the Law of Property Act 1925, reproducing the common law, includes a term from week to week in possession at a rent and liable to determination by notice or re-entry. Originally, a term of years was not an estate in land, the lessee having merely a personal action against his lessor. But a legal estate in leaseholds was created by the *Statute of Gloucester* (6 Edw I (1278) and the Act 21 Hen 8 C 15 (Recoveries (1529)). Now by s 1 of the Law of Property Act 1925 a term of years absolute is an estate in land capable of subsisting as a legal estate. In the present case, if the agreement dated 7 March 1983 created a tenancy, Mrs Mountford having entered into possession and made weekly payments acquired a legal estate in land. If the agreement is a tenancy, the occupation of Mrs Mountford is protected by the Rent Acts.

A licence in connection with land while entitling the licensee to use the land for the purposes authorised by the licence does not create an estate in the land. If the agreement dated 7 March 1983 created a licence for Mrs Mountford to occupy the premises, she did not acquire any estate in the land. If the agreement is a licence then Mrs Mountford's right of occupation is not protected by the Rent Acts. Hence the practical importance of distinguishing between a tenancy and a licence ...

Counsel for Mrs Mountford seeks to reaffirm and re-establish the traditional view that an occupier of land for a term at a rent is a tenant providing the occupier is granted exclusive possession. It is conceded on behalf of Mr Street that the agreement dated 7 March 1983 granted exclusive possession to Mrs Mountford. The traditional view that the grant of exclusive possession for a term at a rent creates a tenancy is consistent with the elevation of a tenancy into an estate in land. The tenant possessing exclusive possession is able to exercise the rights of an owner of land, which is in the real sense his land albeit temporarily and subject to certain restrictions. A tenant armed with exclusive possession can keep out strangers and keep out the landlord unless the landlord is exercising limited rights reserved to him by the tenancy agreement to enter and view and repair. A licensee lacking exclusive possession can in no sense call the land his own and cannot be said to own any estate in the land. The licence does not create an estate in the land to which it relates but only makes an act lawful which would otherwise be unlawful.

Counsel for Mr Street relies on recent authorities which, he submits, demonstrate that an occupier granted exclusive possession for a term at a rent may nevertheless be a licensee if, in the words of Slade LJ in the present case, 'there is manifested the clear intentions of both parties that the rights granted are to be merely those of a personal right of occupation and not those of a tenant'. In the present case, it is submitted, the provisions of the agreement ... manifest the clear intention of both parties that the rights granted are to be those of a personal nature and not those of a tenant.

My Lords, there is no doubt that the traditional distinction between a tenancy and a licence of land lay in the grant of land for a term at a rent with exclusive possession. In some cases it was not clear at first sight whether exclusive possession was in fact granted. For example, an owner of land could grant a licence to cut and remove standing timber. Alternatively, the owner could grant a tenancy of the land with the right to cut and remove standing timber during the term of the tenancy. The grant of rights relating to standing timber therefore required careful consideration in order to decide whether the grant conferred exclusive possession of the land for a term at a rent and was therefore a tenancy or whether it merely conferred a bare licence to remove the timber ...

In the case of residential accommodation there is no difficulty in deciding whether the grant confers exclusive possession. An occupier of residential accommodation at a rent for a term is either a lodger or a tenant. The occupier is a lodger if the landlord provides attendance or services which require the landlord or his servants to exercise unrestricted access to an use of the premises. A lodger is entitled to live in the premises but cannot call the place his own. In *Allan v Liverpool Overseers* (1874) LR 9 QB 180 at 191–92 Blackburn J said:

> A lodger in a house, although he has the exclusive use of rooms in the house, in the sense that nobody else is to be there, and though his goods are stored there, yet he is not in exclusive possession in that sense, because the landlord is there for the purpose of being able, as landlords commonly do in case of lodgings, to have his own servants to look after the house and the furniture, and has retained to himself the occupation, though he has agreed to give the exclusive enjoyment of the occupation to the lodger.

If on the other hand residential accommodation is granted for a term at a rent with exclusive possession, the landlord providing neither attendance nor services, the grant is a tenancy; any express reservation to the landlord of limited rights to enter and view the state of the premises and to repair and maintain the premises only serves to emphasise the fact that the grantee is entitled to exclusive possession and is a tenant. In the present case it is conceded that Mrs Mountford is entitled to exclusive possession and is not a lodger. Mr Street provided neither attendance nor services and only reserved the limited rights of inspection and maintenance and the like set forth in cl 3 of the agreement. On the traditional view of the matter, Mrs Mountford not being a lodger must be a tenant.

There can be no tenancy unless the occupier enjoys exclusive possession; but an occupier who enjoys exclusive possession is not necessarily a tenant. He may be owner in fee simple, a trespasser, a mortgagee in possession, an object of charity or a service occupier. To constitute a tenancy the occupier must be granted exclusive possession for a fixed or periodic term certain in consideration of a premium or periodical payments. The grant may be express, or may be inferred where the owner accepts weekly or other periodic payments from the occupier.

Occupation by service occupier may be eliminated. A service occupier is a servant who occupies his master's premises in order to perform his duties as a servant. In those circumstances the possession and occupation of the servant is treated as the possession and occupation of the master and the relationship of landlord and tenant is not created: see *Mayhew v Suttle* (1854) 4 E & B 347; 119 ER 137. The test is whether the servant requires the premises he occupies in order the better to perform his duties as a servant:

> Where the occupation is necessary for the performance of services, and the occupier is required to reside in the house in order to perform those services, the occupation being strictly ancillary to the performance of the duties which the occupier has to perform, the occupation is that of a servant.

(See *per* Mellor J in *Smith v Seghill Overseers* (1875) LR 10 QB 422 at 428; cf [1874–80] All ER Rep 373 at 375.)

The cases on which counsel for Mr Street relies begin with *Booker v Palmer* [1942] 2 All ER 674. The owner of a cottage agreed to allow a friend to install an evacuee in the cottage rent free for the duration of the war. The Court of Appeal held that there was no intention on the part of the owner to enter into legal relationships with the evacuee. Lord Greene MR said (at 677):

> To suggest there is an intention there to create a relationship of landlord and tenant appears to me to be quite impossible. There is one golden rule which is of very general application, namely, that the law does not impute intention to enter into legal relationships where the circumstances and the conduct of the parties negative any intention of the kind. It seems to me that this is a clear example of the application of that rule.

The observations of Lord Greene MR were not directed to the distinction between a contractual tenancy and a contractual licence. The conduct of the parties (not their professed intentions) indicated that they did not intend to contract at all.

In the present case the agreement dated 7 March 1983 professed an intention by both parties to create a licence and their belief that they had in fact created a licence. It was submitted on behalf of Mr Street that the court cannot in these circumstances decide that the agreement created a tenancy without interfering with the freedom of contract enjoyed by both parties. My Lords, Mr Street enjoyed freedom to offer Mrs Mountford the right to occupy the rooms comprised in the agreement on such lawful terms as Mr Street pleased. Mrs Mountford enjoyed freedom to negotiate with Mr Street to obtain different terms. Both parties enjoyed freedom to contract or not to contract and both parties exercised that freedom by contracting on the terms set forth in the written agreement and on no other terms. But the consequences in law of the agreement, once concluded, can only be determined by consideration of the effect of the agreement. If the agreement satisfied all the requirements of a tenancy, then the agreement produced a tenancy and the parties cannot alter the effect of the agreement by insisting that they only created a licence. The manufacture of a five-pronged implement for manual digging results in a fork even if the manufacturer, unfamiliar with the English language, insists that he intended to make and has made a spade.

It was also submitted that, in deciding whether the agreement created a tenancy or a licence, the court should ignore the Rent Acts. If Mr Street has succeeded, where owners have failed these past 70 years, in driving a coach and horses through the Rent Acts, he must be left to enjoy the benefit of his ingenuity unless and until Parliament intervenes. I accept that the Rent Acts are irrelevant to the problem of determining the legal effect of the rights granted by the agreement. Like the professed intention of the parties, the Rent Acts cannot alter the effect of the agreement.

In *Marcroft Wagons Ltd v Smith* [1951] 2 All ER 271; [1951] 2 KB 496 the daughter of a deceased tenant who lived with the mother claimed to be a statutory tenant by succession and the landlords asserted that the daughter had no rights under the Rent Acts and was a trespasser. The landlords expressly refused to accept the daughter's claims but accepted rent from her while they were considering the position. If the landlords had decided not to apply to the court for possession but to accept the daughter as a tenant, the moneys paid by the daughter would have been treated as rent. If the landlords decided, as they did decide, to apply for possession and to prove, as they did prove, that the daughter was not a statutory tenant, the moneys paid by the daughter were treated as mesne profits. The Court of Appeal held with some hesitation that the landlords never accepted the daughter as tenant and never intended to contract with her although the landlords delayed for some six months before applying to the court for possession. Roxburgh J said ([1951] 2 All ER 271 at 277; [1951] 2 KB 496 at 507):

> Generally speaking, when a person, having a sufficient estate in land, lets another into exclusive possession, a tenancy results, and there is no question of a licence. But the inference of a tenancy is not necessarily to be drawn where a person succeeds on a death to occupation of rent-controlled premises and a landlord accepts some rent while he or the occupant, or both of them is or are considering his or their position. If this is all that happened in this case, then no tenancy would result.

In that case, as in *Booker v Palmer*, the court deduced from the conduct of the parties that they did not intend to contract at all.

Errington v Errington [1952] 1 All ER 149; [1952] 1 KB 290 concerned a contract by a father to allow his son to buy the father's house on payment of the instalments of the father's building society loan. Denning LJ referred (see [1952] 1 All ER 149 at 154; [1952] 1 KB 290 at 297) to the judgment of Lord Greene MR in *Booker v Palmer* where, however, the circumstances and the conduct of the parties negatived any intention to enter into legal relationships. Denning LJ continued ([1952] All ER 149 at 154–55; [1952] 1 KB 290 at 297–98):

> We have had many instances lately of occupiers in exclusive possession who have been held to be not tenants, but only licensees – when a requisitioning authority allowed people into possession at a weekly rent ... when a landlord told a tenant on his retirement that he could live in a cottage rent free for the rest of his days ... when a landlord, on the death of the widow of a statutory tenant, allowed her daughter to remain in possession, paying rent for six months: *Marcroft Wagons Ltd v Smith*; when the owner of a shop allowed the manager to live in a flat above the shop, but did not require him to do so, and the value of the flat was taken into account at £1 a week in fixing his wages ... In each of those cases the occupier was held to be a licensee and not a tenant ... The result of all these cases is that, although a person who is let into exclusive possession is, *prima facie*, to be considered a tenant, nevertheless he will not be held to be so if the circumstances negative any intention to create a tenancy. Words alone may not suffice. Parties cannot turn a tenancy into a licence merely by calling it one. But if the circumstances and the conduct of the parties show that all that was intended was that the occupier should be granted a personal privilege with no interest in the land, he will be held only to be a licensee.

In *Errington v Errington* and in the cases cited by Denning LJ there were exceptional circumstances which negatived the *prima facie* intention to create a tenancy, notwithstanding that the occupier enjoyed exclusive occupation. The intention to create a tenancy was negatived if the parties did not intend to enter into legal relationships at all, or where the relationship between the parties was that of vendor and purchaser, master and service occupier, or where the owner, a requisitioning authority, had no power to grant a tenancy. These exceptional circumstances are not to be found in the present case, where there has been the lawful, independent and voluntary grant of exclusive possession for a term at a rent.

If the observations of Denning LJ are applied to the facts of the present case it may fairly be said that the circumstances negative any intention to create a mere licence. Words alone do not suffice. Parties cannot turn a tenancy into a licence merely by calling it one. The circumstances and the conduct of the parties show that what was intended was that the occupier should be granted exclusive possession at a rent for a term with a corresponding interest in the land which created a tenancy ...

In *Facchini v Bryson* [1952] 1 TLR 1386, an employer and his assistant entered into an agreement which, *inter alia*, allowed the assistant to occupy a house for a weekly payment on terms which conferred exclusive possession. The assistant did not occupy the house for the better performance of his duty and was not therefore a service occupier. The agreement stipulated that 'nothing in this agreement shall be construed to create a tenancy between the employer and the assistant'. Somervell LJ said (at 1389):

> If, looking at the operative clauses in the agreement, one comes to the conclusion that the rights of the occupier, to use a neutral words, are those of a lessee, the parties cannot turn it into a licence by saying at the end 'this is deemed to be a licence'; nor can they, if the operative paragraphs show that it is merely a licence, say that it should be deemed to be a lease.

Denning LJ referred to several cases including *Errington v Errington* and *Cobb v Lane* and said (at 1389–90):

> In all the cases where an occupier has been held to be a licensee there has been something in the circumstances, such as a family arrangement, an act of friendship or generosity, or such like, to negative any intention to create a tenancy ... In the present case, however, there are no special circumstances. It is a simple case where the employer let a man into occupation of a house in consequence of his employment at a weekly sum payable by him. The occupation has all the features of a service tenancy, and the parties cannot by the mere words of their contract turn it into something else. Their relationship is determined by the law and not by the label which they choose to put on it.

The decision, which was thereafter binding on the Court of Appeal and on all lower courts, referred to the special circumstances which are capable of negativing an intention to create a tenancy and reaffirmed the principle that the professed intentions of the parties are irrelevant. The decision also indicated that in a simple case a grant of exclusive possession of residential accommodation for a weekly sum creates a tenancy ...

In the *Addiscombe* case [1957] 3 All ER 563 at 571; [1958] 1 QB 513 at 528 Jenkins LJ referred to the observations of Denning LJ in *Errington v Errington* [1952] 1 All ER 149 at 154; [1952] 1 KB 290 at 297 to the effect that 'The test of exclusive possession is by no means decisive'. Jenkins LJ continued:

> I think that wide statement must be treated as qualified by his observations in *Facchini v Bryson* ((1952) 1 TLR 1386 at 1389); and it seems to me that, save in exceptional cases of the kind mentioned by Denning LJ, in that case, the law remains that the fact of exclusive possession, if not decisive against the view that there is a mere licence, as distinct from a tenancy, is at all events a consideration of the first importance.

Exclusive possession is of first importance in considering whether an occupier is a tenant; exclusive possession is not decisive because an occupier who enjoys exclusive possession is not necessarily a tenant. The occupier may be a lodger or service occupier or fall within the other exceptional categories mentioned by Denning LJ in *Errington v Errington*.

In *Isaac v Hotel de Paris Ltd* [1960] 1 All ER 348; [1960] 1 WLR 239 an employee who managed a night bar in a hotel for his employer company which held a lease of the hotel negotiated 'subject to contract' to complete the purchase of shares in the company and to be allowed to run the nightclub for his own benefit if he paid the head rent payable by the company for the hotel. In the expectation that the negotiations 'subject to contract' would ripen into a binding agreement, the employee was allowed to run the nightclub and he paid the company's rent. When negotiations broke down the employee claimed unsuccessfully to be a tenant of the hotel company. The circumstances in which the employee was allowed to occupy the premises showed that the hotel company never intended to accept him as a tenant and that he was fully aware of that fact. This was a case, consistent with the authorities cited by Lord Denning in giving the advice of the Judicial Committee of the

Privy Council, in which the parties did not intend to enter into contractual relationships unless and until the negotiations 'subject to contract' were replaced by a binding contract ...

In the present case the Court of Appeal held that the agreement dated 7 March 1983 only created a licence. Slade LJ accepted that the agreement and in particular cl 3 of the agreement:

> ... shows that the right to occupy the premises conferred on [Mrs Mountford] was intended as an exclusive right of occupation, in that it was thought necessary to give a special and express power to [Mr Street] to enter ...

Before your Lordships it was conceded that the agreement conferred the right of exclusive possession on Mrs Mountford. Even without cl 3 the result would have been the same. By the agreement Mrs Mountford was granted the right to occupy residential accommodation. Mr Street did not provide any services or attendance. It was plain that Mrs Mountford was not a lodger. Slade LJ proceeded to analyse all the provisions of the agreement, not for the purpose of deciding whether his finding of exclusive possession was correct, but for the purpose of assigning some of the provisions of the agreement to the category of terms which he thought are usually to be found in a tenancy agreement and of assigning other provisions to the category of terms which he thought are usually to be found in a licence. Slade LJ may or may not have been right that in a letting of a furnished room it was 'most unusual to find a provision in a tenancy agreement obliging the tenant to keep his rooms in a 'tidy condition'. If he was right about this and other provisions there is still no logical method of evaluating the results of his survey. Slade LJ reached the conclusion that 'the agreement bears all the hallmarks of a licence, rather than a tenancy, save for the one important feature of exclusive occupation'. But in addition to the hallmark of exclusive occupation of residential accommodation there were the hallmarks of weekly payments for a periodical term. Unless these three hallmarks are decisive, it really becomes impossible to distinguish a contractual tenancy from a contractual licence save by reference to the professed intention of the parties or by the judge awarding marks for drafting. Slade LJ was finally impressed by the statement at the foot of the agreement by Mrs Mountford 'I understand and accept that a licence in the above form does not and is not intended to give me a tenancy protected under the Rent Acts'. Slade LJ said:

> ... it seems to me that if [Mrs Mountford] is to displace the express statement of intention embodied in the declaration, she must show that the declaration was either a deliberate sham or at least an inaccurate statement of what was the true substance of the real transaction agreed between the parties ...

My Lords, the only intention which is relevant is the intention demonstrated by the agreement to grant exclusive possession for a term at a rent. Sometimes it may be difficult to discover whether, on the true construction of an agreement, exclusive possession is conferred. Sometimes it may appear from the surrounding circumstances that there was no intention to create legal relationships. Sometimes it may appear from the surrounding circumstances that the right to exclusive possession is referable to a legal relationship other than a tenancy. Legal relationships to which the grant of exclusive possession might be referable and which would or might negative the grant of an estate or interest in the land include occupancy under a contract for the sale of the land, occupancy pursuant to a contract of employment or occupancy referable to the holding of an office. But where as in the present case the only circumstances are that residential accommodation is offered and accepted with exclusive possession for a term at a rent, the result is a tenancy ...

My Lords, I gratefully adopt the logic and the language of Windeyer J [in *Radaich v Smith*]. Henceforth the courts which deal with these problems will, save in exceptional circumstances, only be concerned to inquire whether as a result of an agreement relating to residential accommodation the occupier is a lodger or a tenant. In the present case I am satisfied that Mrs Mountford is a tenant, that the appeal should be allowed, that the order of the Court of Appeal should be set aside and that Mr Street should be ordered to pay the costs of Mrs Mountford here and below.

[The other Law Lords agreed with Lord Templeman's reasoning.]

Appeal allowed.

Notes

In England, in spite of *Street v Mountford*, the issue whether exclusive possession is decisive of a lease is still troublesome (see K Gray, *Elements of Land Law* (2nd edn, Butterworths, London, 1993), pp 708–28). The English position is peculiar because of the ongoing controversy surrounding rent control regulations. The PNG courts are yet to resolve the legal position (see Amankwah, Mugambwa and Muroa, *Land Law in Papua New Guinea* (Lawbook Co, Sydney, 2001), pp 122–23).

Questions

1 What significance, if any, does Lord Templeman attach to the *subjective* intention of the parties in determining whether their arrangement was a lease or licence?

2 What is the legal significance in Papua New Guinea of the distinction between a lease and a licence?

3 The Highland Darts Club (HDC) is a lessee of a large room, which houses the club's bar. The HDC management verbally allows Charlie to manage the club on its behalf. Charlie obtains a liquor licence in his own name and, at first, accounts to the HDC for receipts and expenditure. Later, Charlie and HDC verbally agree for Charlie to pay all the bars' expenses and keep all profits. Under their agreement, Charlie promises to pay HDC K500 per month, which happens to be the exact amount HDC pays for leasing the room. Advise HDC whether its relationship with Charlie is that of a landlord and tenant or licensor and licensee.

III CREATION OF LEASES

A lease constitutes an interest in land. The Frauds and Limitation Act 1988 (No 3), prescribes formalities for the creation of interests in land. The following provisions of the Act are especially relevant to the creation of leases:

2 CREATION, ETC, OF INTEREST IN LAND

(1) Subject to sub-section (2) and section 5 –

(a) no interest in land can be created or disposed of except –

(i) by writing signed –

(A) by the person creating or disposing of the interest; or

(b) by that person's agent lawfully authorised in writing for the purpose; or

(ii) by operation of law; or

(iii) by will ...

(2) Nothing contained in sub-section (1) shall be construed as affecting the creation or operation of resulting, implied or constructive trusts, and that sub-section shall be read and construed accordingly.

3 EFFECT WHERE INTEREST IN LAND CREATED BY PAROL

(1) Subject to sub-section (2) and section 5, where –

(a) an interest in land created by parol; and

(b) the creation of that interest is not in accordance with section 2(1)(a)(i),

that interest shall, notwithstanding any consideration having been given in respect of it, have the force and effect of an interest at will only.

(2) Nothing contained in sub-section (1) shall be construed as affecting the creation, by parol, of a lease that –

(a) takes effect in possession for a term not exceeding three years; and

(b) is at the best rent that can reasonably be obtained without taking a fine,

and that sub-section shall be read and construed accordingly.

5 SAVINGS IN RESPECT OF SECTIONS 2 AND 3

Nothing contained in section 2 or 3 shall –

(a) ...

(b) affect the operation of the law relating to part performance.

Registration requirement for creation of a lease exceeding three years

Under the Land Registration Act, a lease in excess of three years must be registered. Section 49 of the Act relevantly provides as follows:

(1) Where a proprietor intends to lease land for a life or lives or for a term of years exceeding three years he shall execute a lease in the prescribed form, and the lease shall be registered.

(2) Where a lease for a term of three years or less is executed in the prescribed form the lease may be registered.[9]

Also s 54(1) provides as follows:

(1) Where the proprietor of a lease under this Act sub-lets for a term of three years or more he may do so by executing a sub-lease in the prescribed form.

The prescribed form for creation of a lease is Form 5 of the Land Registration Regulations.[10] An instrument purporting to create a lease, which does not comply with

9 See also s 17(1) and 17(2), LRA. See Chapter 9 with respect to the status of unregistered instruments of transfer.

10 Regulation 11, Schedule 1.

this form is not registrable.[11] Note that though there is not requirement to register a lease, which does not exceed three years, it is registrable if in the prescribed form.[12]

Effect of failure to register a lease

What is the effect of failure to register a lease that exceeds a period of three years? Under the underlying law, which is the applicable law in such a case, the effect of failure to comply with the legal requirements for the creation of a lease differs at law and in equity. Generally speaking, a registered lease is equated with a legal lease under the underlying law, whereas an unregistered lease corresponds with an 'equitable lease'.[13]

At law

At common law, although an informal instrument by itself creates no common law term in the land, entry into possession pursuant to the instrument will constitute a common law tenancy at will *inter partes* upon such terms of the unregistered lease as are applicable to a tenancy at will. The tenancy at will is terminable at any time by either party, but if the tenant at will begins to pay rent calculated on a regular periodic basis, a yearly, monthly or other periodical tenancy will be created. The following case illustrates these common law principles.

MOORE v DIAMOND [1929–30] 43 CLR 105, High Court of Australia

[The appellant leased to the respondent certain premises for a term of five years at a weekly rental of £10. The respondent immediately entered into possession even though the lease was not registered. Before the five years had expired the parties by written agreement extended the lease by another five years at a weekly rental of £16.10s. When the first term expired the respondent remained in possession of the premises, paying rent of £16.10s weekly in advance. The new lease was not registered. In the meantime disputes having occurred with reference to the new lease, the respondent went out of possession of the premises after giving one week's notice of termination. The appellant claimed rent due on the basis that the unregistered lease created a yearly tenancy, which could only be determined by six months notice. The respondent argued that the lease created a weekly tenancy, which he properly terminated by a week's notice and, therefore, at law no rent was thereafter payable. The Supreme Court held that the tenancy was one from week to week and not from year to year. Appeal to the High Court.]

KNOX CJ, RICH AND DIXON JJ: The conclusion which sufficiently appears is that the respondent remained, and the appellant permitted him to remain, in occupation of the premises after 30 November 1927 in intended performance of the agreement and that the appellant, as lessor, accepted, and the respondent, as lessee, paid the weekly sum of £16.10s from 1 December 1927 to 17 November 1928, as the rent stipulated for in the agreement. An

11 See s 18(1), LRA.

12 Section 49(2). See also s 17(2), LRA.

13 See *Harman Gawi v PNG Ready Mixed Concrete Pty Ltd* [1984] PNGLR 74, at 77–78, *per* Kapi Dep CJ. His Honour held that an unregistered State lease does not create a legal estate until registered, at 77.

examination of the correspondence shows that it does support the conclusion that a complete agreement was made. As the agreement for a lease was not a demise, but an executory contract to grant a lease, it could not operate to create an *interesse termini* and, immediately upon the effluxion of the prior term, the respondent became at law (although of course not in equity) a tenant at will only. Upon the first payment of rent he became entitled at law to a term, but the question is whether the term was from week to week or from year to year. In *Hamerton v Stead* [(1824) 3B & C 478, at 483; 107 ER 811, at 813] Littledale J said: 'Where parties enter under a mere agreement for a future lease they are tenants at will; and if rent is paid under the agreement, they become tenants from year to year, determinable on the execution of the lease contracted for, that being the primary contract'... It was well settled at law that the terms and conditions of the agreement, save in so far as they are inconsistent with a tenancy from year to year, apply to the tenancy. It was further settled that the tenancy from year to year continued only during the term contracted for, and expired at the end of that term by effluxion of time without notice to quit, being in the meantime liable to a sooner determination by notice to quit ... These principles applied whenever the tenant held under an agreement for a lease whether the agreement was expressed as an executory contract or consisted of an intended demise for more than three years void, because not under seal. In such cases the contractual intention of the parties is completely expressed in a binding manner, but is formally inefficacious to create a legal interest of the intended duration.

There is little resemblance between such a case and the very many instances in which a person has been let into, or has retained, possession of land without any express contract, and the question is whether he is a tenant, and if so, for a term of what duration. Such cases occur when a tenant overholds; when a tenant for life has granted a lease in excess of his power and dies before its determination, and the remainderman allows the lessee to retain possession; when a mortgagor has granted a lease without statutory or other power; and when the terms of entry are too vague or uncertain to be ascertainable. In such cases payment or acknowledgment of rent constitutes evidence of the establishment of a tenancy, and the fact that the rent is paid by reference to a year, or aliquot part of a year, affords evidence of a tenancy from year to year. The existence and duration of the tenancy in such a case were, however, questions of fact. On the other hand, in *Doe d Thomson v Amey* [(1840) 12 A & E 476; 113 ER 892], in deciding that a proviso for re-entry formed a condition of a tenancy from year to year, implied from entry and payment of rent pursuant to an agreement for a lease containing such a condition, Patterson J said [(1840) 12 A & E, at 480; 113 ER, at 893–94]: 'The terms upon which the tenant holds are in truth a conclusion of law from the facts of the case, and the terms of the articles of agreement.'

In the one case the question is what common intention should be attributed to the parties, in the other the question is what duration of tenancy replaces that upon which they have expressly agreed? In the latter case it is difficult to see why the period in respect of which rent is paid should afford a criterion of or determine the term ...

In the many cases at law in which it was decided that a tenant entering or holding under an agreement for a lease became on payment of rent a tenant from year to year, the rent or the tender has been annual; and apparently no case has before come for decision in which the rent was not calculated by reference to a year or a part of a year. At an early stage of the history of tenancies from year to year a presumption arose in favour of that tenure. In his *History of English Law*, vol VII, p 245, Sir WS Holdsworth says that the ruling of Hold CJ that the tenancy could only be terminated at the end of each year 'shows that opinion was beginning to lean in favour of construing a tenancy, when no certain term was mentioned, as a tenancy from year to year'. In the latter part of the 18th century this leaning became so pronounced that, on one occasion, Lord Mansfield even went so far as to say that, 'in the country, leases at will ... being found extremely inconvenient exist only notionally; and were succeeded by another species of contract which was less inconvenient'. This, of course, was an exaggeration. Tenancies at will still exist; and the presumption of the existence of a tenancy from year to year, arising from the payment of rent, can always be rebutted. But the presumption had undoubtedly come to be very strong in the 18th century – so strong that it was held that, though the *Statute of Frauds* had enacted that a parol lease should operate only as a lease at will, such a parol lease will operate as a lease from year to year 'if rent has been paid thereunder'. This presumption has continued and still prevails. In principle there appears to be no reason why the circumstance that the rent paid under an agreement for a term of five years is weekly should displace this presumption in favour of the yearly tenancy. The doctrine which justifies reference to the period of the rent in order to ascertain the term no doubt is that the rent is a compensation for the land, and the parties have so understood it. A quarterly payment thus implies a yearly tenancy because it is part of the compensation for a year's holding. When the parties agree for a five years' holding with weekly payments of the compensatory rent, their intention is not that each week's rent shall represent a distinct and therefore terminable holding of a week. The weekly rent is part of the compensation for the entire period. Where the intention of the parties is to hold for a greater duration than a yearly tenancy would give them, and this intention fails because of its want of appropriate expression or of formal demise, the presumption or assumption that a general holding is from year to year supplies the term.

It follows that at law, whatever may be the position in equity, the respondent should be considered a tenant from year to year.

[The judgments of Isaacs and Starke JJ omitted.]

Appeal allowed.

Questions

1 What is your understanding of the above judgment? Was a yearly tenancy implied because of the manner in which rent was paid (ie, by reference to a year) or was it implied as soon as the respondent began payment of rent (ie, reference to a period rent was considered paid being irrelevant)? See Butt, *Land Law* (4th edn, Lawbook Co, Sydney, 2001), at p 228.

2 What terms are applicable to the implied periodic tenancy? See also *Dockrill v Cavanagh* (1944) 45 SR (NSW) 78.

3 A lease which does not exceed three years need not be registered, but may be registered if it is in a registrable form (see s 49(2) of the LRA). What are the advantages of registering a short term lease? See s 28(3) of the LRA. Also see, eg, *Mercantile Credits Ltd v Shell Co of Australia Ltd* (1976) 136 CLR 326.

Notes

Although a purported lease, which does not comply with the legal formalities may be terminated at the will of either party (see *Moore v Diamond, supra*), whoever terminates the agreement may be liable for breach of contract. A good illustration is the case of *Leitz Lee Holme Stud Pty v Robinson* [1977] 2 NSWLR 544. In that case, the defendant went into possession of premises and paid rent under an unregistered six years lease. Three years later, the defendant terminated the lease by giving one month's notice. The plaintiff accepted the defendant's repudiation of the contract and brought proceedings for damages for breach of contract. The defendant contended that since the lease was not registered it was a tenancy at will, which he was entitled to terminate and he could not be sued for doing something which he was lawfully entitled to do. Glass JA dismissed the argument as a misconception of the law. His Honour observed (at 547):

> The agreement and the tenancy at will are independent sources of rights. At no stage do they merge, so that the termination of the estate automatically extinguishes the agreement. The relevant principles are, in my view, as follows. A lease of land under the Real Property Act [corresponds with the Land Registration Act] for a term exceeding three years creates no legal term unless it is both registrable and registered. But the informal instrument may be treated as evidencing an agreement for a formal lease ... The unregistered memorandum of lease operates merely as an agreement specifically enforceable in equity, but not itself creating a legal term in the land ... Entry into possession and payment of rent bring into existence a common law tenancy upon such terms of the unregistered memorandum as are applicable to the tenancy at will. But, in so far as the memorandum operates as an agreement, it retains a separate identity as the repository of the substantial rights of the parties. The doctrine relevant for present purposes had been previously worked out in relation to demises which were void at law, not having been made by deed as required by the statute. The purported lease, nevertheless, took effect as an executory agreement for a lease enforceable in equity, and there entitling the lessee to a formal lease ... The existence or otherwise of a contract is determined exclusively by common law principle ... Accordingly, when ... [authorities] allude to an informal lease operating as an agreement for a lease enforceable in equity, they affirm, not only the availability of equitable relief, but also the existence of a contract at law. If the innocent party deems damages to be adequate, there is no reason why the contract may not be enforced at law.

The court held that the plaintiff was entitled to sue for damages for loss of bargain for the remaining three years of the lease agreement. See also *Wine v Giglmai* [1990] PNGLR 462, at 467–68, extract below, p 306.

In equity

In equity, failure to follow legal formalities to create a lease did not necessarily render the purported lease void. The doctrine of part performance[14] enabled the Court of Equity, in certain cases, to decree the execution of a formal lease in cases where no lease had been made and where the agreement for a lease was oral only. Consequently, in equity the parties' rights and obligations were enforceable as if a legal lease had been obtained. The leading authority is *Walsh v Lonsdale*, extracted below.[15]

WALSH v LONSDALE (1882) 21 Ch D 9

> [The defendant under a written contract which was not under seal agreed to lease a mill to the plaintiff for a term of seven years at an annual rental payable in advance. The plaintiff entered into possession and for one and half years paid rent quarterly, and not in advance

14 For a classical statement of the principle of part performance see Lord Justice Selborne's judgment in *Maddison v Alderson* [1881–85] All ER Rep 742, at 747–48.

15 See also discussion in *Wine v Giglmai* [1990] PNGLR 462, extracted below.

as agreed. The defendant demanded that the rent be paid in advance but the plaintiff did not comply. Thereupon the defendant distrained upon the plaintiff's goods. The plaintiff commenced these proceedings claiming illegal distress. The plaintiff argued that since the lease was not executed by deed as was required by law, there was only a tenancy at will which by virtue of possession and payment of rent became a legal tenancy from year to year. And since payment of rent in advance is inconsistent with a yearly tenancy, it followed that the distress was unlawful.]

JESSEL MR: There is an agreement for a lease under which possession has been given. Now since the Judicature Act the possession is held under the agreement. There are not two estates as there were formerly, one estate at common law by reason of the payment of the rent from year to year, and an estate in equity under the agreement. There is only one court, and the equity rules prevail in it. The tenant holds under an agreement for a lease. He holds, therefore, under the same terms in equity as if a lease had been granted, it being a case in which both parties admit that relief is capable of being given by specific performance. That being so, he cannot complain of the exercise by the landlord of the same rights as the landlord would have had if a lease had been granted. On the other hand, he is protected in the same way as if a lease had been granted; he cannot be turned out by six months' notice as a tenant from year to year. He has a right to say, 'I have a lease in equity, and you can only re-enter if I have committed such a breach of covenant as would if a lease had been granted have entitled you to re-enter according to the terms of a proper proviso for re-entry'. That being so, it appears to me that being a lessee in equity he cannot complain of the exercise of the right of distress merely because the actual parchment has not been signed and sealed ...

[Cotton and Lindley LJJ in separate judgments concurred.]

Appeal upheld.

Notes

1 The principle of *Walsh v Lonsdale* applies under the Torrens system. Thus, if a lease which exceeds three years is not registered as required by s 17(1) of the LRA, it takes effect as an equitable lease (see *Ahern v LA Wilkinson (Northern) Ltd* [1929] St R Qd 66). See also *Wine v Giglmai* [1990] PNGLR 462, see extract below.

2 Specific performance is a discretionary remedy, which the court may refuse to grant. For example, the court may refuse to make the order of specific performance if the applicant is in breach of some provision of the agreement he is seeking to enforce. Thus, in *Coatsworth v Johnson* (1886) 55 LJQB 220 (CA), the court refused to decree specific performance of a lease where the tenant seeking the order was in arrears in paying rent and was also in breach of other terms of the agreement. See also *Warmington and Another v Miller* [1973] 2 All ER 372.

3 In equity, a tenancy may also arise by estoppel. Estoppel is a principle of equity, which precludes a person who has induced another to rely upon his representation from denying the truth of the facts represented. In the context of the relationship of landlord and tenant a landowner who has allowed a tenant to enter into possession cannot question the validity of his grant (see Harpum C, with Grant M and Bridge S, *Megarry and Wade: The Law of Real Property* (6th edn, Sweet & Maxwell, London, 2000), at pp 799–801). Nor can a tenant who has entered into possession, for example, refuse

to pay rent on the ground that the lease is void. The cases of *Wine v Giglmai*, and *In the Matter of Luabar Logging Pty Ltd and in the Matter of the Companies Act* (Ch No 145) [1988] PNGLR 124, both extracted below, illustrate this point. In *Wine*'s case, Brunton J held that the principle of *Walsh v Lonsdale* applies to a tenancy, which arises by estoppel.

Questions

1 'The effect of *Walsh v Lonsdale* was often summed up in the words "a contract for a lease is as good as a lease". For many purposes this is true, but as a generalisation it is misleading for it ignores the vital differences between legal and equitable interests' (*Megarry and Wade: The Law of Real Property, op cit*, note 3 above, at 773–75). Discuss. (See, eg, s 33 of the LRA, and cases in note 2, above. See also *Harman Gawi v PNG Ready Mixed Concrete Pty Ltd* [1984] PNGLR 74.

2 Under a written agreement, L promised to grant T a lease for a term of six years. Both parties executed the agreement and they obtained the Minister's approval. But the lease was not registered since it was not in a registrable form. T nonetheless entered into possession and for a while paid rent on a regular basis. Later T fell in arrears in the payment of his rent. When L demanded rent in arrears T terminated the lease by giving six months notice. Advise L of *all* possible remedies available to him at law and in equity (see, eg, *Ahern v LA Wilkinson (Northern) Ltd* [1929] St R Qd 66; and *Leitz Lee Holme Stud Pty Ltd v Robinson* [1977] 2 NSWLR 544).

3 L orally agrees to lease his house to T for two years effective at some time in the future. Before T takes possession, L changes his mind. T sues for specific performance alternatively for damages for breach of contact. What result?

Approval of the Minister

Under Part XVII of the Land Act 1996, the Minister must approve certain dealings in land, including leases, before they take effect.[16] The object is to protect a national interest in land.[17]

SECTION 128. APPROVAL OF CONTROLLED DEALINGS AND PERMITTED DEALINGS

(1) In this section –

'controlled dealing' means a disposition of a contract or agreement to dispose of a leasehold estate but does not include a transmission or a permitted dealing;

'instrument' means a document giving effect, or intended to give effect to a controlled dealing;

'leasehold estate' means –

1 an urban development lease; or

2 a lease or sub-lease the term or remaining term of which exceeds five years; or

16 This Part does not apply to or in relation to customary land (s 127, Land Act 1996).

17 See James, *Land Law and Policy in Papua New Guinea*, PNG Law Reform Commission, Monograph No 5 (1985), p 167. Although James' comment was with reference to s 69 of the former Land Act, the underlying policy is still the same.

3 a lease or sub-lease for a term of five years or less which contains an option to renew for a further term which, together with the original term exceed five years;

'permitted dealing' means a disposition of or a contract or agreement to dispose of a leasehold estate which has been prescribed as a dealing in respect of which Ministerial approval is not necessary to make it valid and effective;

'transmission' means the acquisition of title to or an interest in a leasehold estate consequent on the death or insolvency of the owner.

(2) A controlled dealing is void and of no effect unless approved by the Minister.

(3) Where the Minister refuses to approve a controlled dealing, he shall notify the reasons for his refusal to the person seeking the approval.

(4) The grantee or transferee or intended grantee or transferee of a controlled dealing shall, within 28 days of the execution of the relevant instrument –

1 present the instrument to the Department for endorsement with a certificate of approval; and

2 lodge a duplicate copy of that instrument with the Department.

(5) A person referred to in sub-section (4), who refuses or fails to comply with sub-section (4), is guilty of an offence.

Penalty: A fine not exceeding K5,000.00.

Default penalty: A fine not exceeding K500.00.

(6) A duplicate or certified copy prepared solely for the purposes of sub-section (4)(b) is not liable to stamp duty.

(7) For the avoidance of doubt, it is hereby declared that a transfer, transmission or dealing with an estate or interest arising under or subject to –

1 the Forestry Act 1991; or

2 the Mining Act 1992; or

3 the Petroleum Act (Chapter 198)

is not a controlled dealing for the purposes of this Act.

The two cases extracted below deal with the issue whether, in situation where a tenant enters into possession before the Minister's approval of the lease, the lease agreement binds both parties. Readers should note that these cases deal with approval requirements under s 69 of the former Land Act (cap 185).

IN THE MATTER OF LUABAR LOGGING PTY LTD AND IN THE MATTER OF THE COMPANIES ACT (Ch No 145) [1988] PNGLR 124, National Court of Justice

[This is a creditor's petition for the winding up of a company on the ground of inability to pay its debts; namely K5,400 for rent for nine months under a lease which is stamped but not approved under s 69 of the Land Act.]

BREDMEYER J: Mr Konecny [for the Company] ... says that the lease is void and thus a debt created under it cannot be recovered because of s 69 of the Land Act (Ch No 185) and because the parties by their express words in cl 9 declared that the lease should have no force or effect until it was approved ...

A little history is in order here. The forerunner to this section in New Guinea was s 3 of the Transfer of Land Control Ordinance 1951 which is quoted in *McCosker and King v Kuster* which is a 1954 case but is published in [1967–68] P&NGLR 182. Note that it uses the word 'and' between (a) and (b) of sub-s (4). To paraphrase, the section is deemed not to be contravened if the transaction (a) is expressed to be subject to the approval of the Administrator, *and* (b), provides that, unless and until that approval is given, the contract or agreement shall have no force or effect.

The section continued in that form in the first amalgamated Land Ordinance for the two territories, in s 75 of the Land Ordinance 1962. By an amendment No 5 of 1966 the section was repealed and replaced by a new version, the most important change being that the word 'or' was substituted for 'and' in the two legs of what became sub-s (3). That section is now s 69 of the Land Act (Ch No 185) with the Minister substituted for the Administrator.

That change from 'and' to 'or' is an important one and one which is, I believe, overlooked by many conveyancers. Section 69 is not breached if the document creating an interest in land is expressed to 'be subject to the approval of the Minister'. There is no need to go on and also declare that the document is of no force and effect until that approval is given.

Despite the fact that this lease was not approved and the parties expressly stated in cl 9 that until such approval was obtained the lease was to be of no force and effect, neither side acted on that clause. The tenant went into possession and paid the rent and, on the landlord's part, she allowed the tenant into possession and collected the rent. I consider that it is just that the tenant is now estopped from saying that the lease is of no force and effect. Although cl 9 is clearly worded and there is a strong logical argument for saying that the lease is void because unapproved and by the express agreement of the parties, *McCosker and King v Kuster*, already cited, is to the contrary. The document there contained a clause in the same form as cl 9. Yet despite that, Ollerenshaw AJ, citing much Australian authority, said that the parties were not without legal obligations to each other (at 189) and granted specific performance to the transferee. That decision has been widely followed, as far as I know, in Papua New Guinea. I know of no reported case to the contrary.

Mr Konecny cited to me two Australian cases. *Gaudron v Mackay* (1936) 60 (NSW) WN 11, which is indeed to the contrary but is in my view, overwhelmed by the authorities cited in *McCosker*. The second case he cited, *Marks v Jolly* (1938) 38 SR (NW) 351, I consider supports my view. In that case the defendant granted a lease to the plaintiff without the consent of the Water Conservation and Irrigation Commission as required by a section of an Act, which provided that any dealing should not be valid for any purpose whatsoever unless the consent of the Commission had been obtained. The plaintiff went into possession, paid the rent for the first three months, of 200 pounds, and no consent was obtained. After the expiration of three months, he was evicted and he sued for the recovery of the rent paid. He failed in the District Court and his appeal to the Full Court of the Supreme Court was dismissed. I rationalise the decision this way. The parties intended a tenancy, they agreed on a rent, the tenant went into possession, he enjoyed the benefit of the tenancy and he paid the rent: therefore he could not later recover the rent. The same would apply in this case. If, for example, Luabar Logging sued for recovery of rent after having enjoyed possession, it would fail. A party cannot be allowed to blow hot and cold, to have the benefit of a contract and then escape the obligation which is the consideration for the benefit. It is like eating one's cake and then having it too.

In this case, I propose to follow *McCosker*'s case. I have read the affidavits carefully. I accept the petitioner's affidavit evidence and Luabar Logging had the lease, did not terminate it or quit it in any way, that it put Mr Alex Subramanium in as tenant, and that he was not put there by the petitioning creditor or her agent.

I make the winding up order and I award costs to the petitioning creditor against the company.

(Order accordingly.)

WINE v GIGLMAI [1990] PNGLR 462, National Court of Justice

[Giglmai, the respondent/plaintiff, entered into an agreement to lease certain commercial premises to Wine, the appellant/defendant. The agreement was expressed to be subject to the Minister's approval 'and unless and until such approval is given those presents shall have no force and effect'. Wine went into possession. When he defaulted in the payment of rent Giglmai brought these proceedings in the District Court, Kundiawa. In the court it transpired that Giglmai did not have a State lease in the first place, and apparently the lease was never approved by the Minister. The court found in favour of Giglmai and Wine appealed to the National Court. Justice Brunton quashed the decision of the District Court on grounds that there were no facts on the face of the record upon which a decision could have been made. His Honour referred the case to the District Court for re-hearing before a Senior Resident Magistrate.]

BRUNTON J: For the guidance of the District Court I make the following observations.

There would appear to be a lease or lease agreement between the parties, evidenced by the written lease that during the period 15 November 1988 to 15 November 1989, Wal Wine would rent from Bill Giglmai the buildings and improvements at allotment 4, section 8, Kerowagi, and that in consideration for an annual rental of K4,200, to be paid in accordance with the terms of the second schedule of the lease, Wal Wine should have the undisturbed and unhindered occupancy of the premises.

If Wal Wine did in fact occupy the premises at allotment 4, section 8, Kerowagi, during the period 15 November 1988 to 15 November 1989; if he conducted a business on those premises, then he is bound by the terms of his agreement with Bill Giglmai, and he should pay the rent he promised to pay.

Bill Giglmai appears to have had possession of lot 4, section 8, Kerowagi, under the belief that he was the successor to the Simbu Cattlemen's Association. Bill Giglmai may have thought he was the leaseholder from the State. His exact status at law is unclear, although he ended up being given a licence to occupy the land by the State, pending the issue of a State lease – see the letter from the Department of Lands and Physical Planning, Waigani, JE/008/004 of 6 March, 1989, to Mr Giglmai.

What is clear is that Wal Wine entered into a lease with Mr Bill Giglmai to rent the premises of which Mr Giglmai was the apparent owner/occupier. If Mr Giglmai moved out, and Mr Wine moved into these premises – in accordance with the terms of an agreement – evidenced in the so called 'Lease' – then Mr Wine is bound by the agreement.

... [S]ection [69], as it applies to leases, deals with two things:

1 a lease (s 69(1)(c));

2 a contract or agreement made for the purpose of entering into a transaction referred to in sub-section (1)' (namely a lease).

It distinguishes between a lease and a contract or agreement for a lease.

A lease which has not been approved is of no effect (s 69(1)).

But a *contract or agreement for a lease* is effective if it is expressed to be subject to the approval of the Minister, or if it provides that until the Minister approves it the contract has no force or effect.

Now, the agreement for the lease in this case was subject to the approval of the Minister AND was of no force and effect until such approval was given.

However, both parties appeared to proceed on the basis that approval had been given. The words 'and unless and until such approval is given these present shall have no force and effect' were ignored by mutual consent, which is evidenced by Wal Wine acting as if he was a lessee, and by Bill Giglmai acting as if he was a landlord.

The words 'subject to any approval which may be required under the provisions of the Land Act 1962' have not been affected by the conduct of the parties. Their conduct is consistent with them believing approval had been granted, or would be granted.

There is then compliance in the contract or agreement for the lease with s 69(3)(a) of the Land Act – and it is not affected by s 69(2) of that Act.

Section 69, Land Act is restricted in its application.

Section 69 of the Land Act is not unlike s 41 of the Real Property Act 1900 (NSW). EA Francis in his text *The Law and Practice Relating to Torrens Title in Australia*, Vol I, Butterworths, Sydney, 1982 at 229 says:

> It is, of course abundantly clear (and it has been so held by the courts on numerous occasions), that notwithstanding the generality of the words of these provisions [ie, s 69 of the Land Act], they are restricted in their application to the passing or creation of an estate or interest at law, and that, in equity, an instrument which is unregistered is by no means devoid of all effect. As was said by Harvey J in *Tietyens v Cox* (1916) 17 SR (NSW) 48 at 54: '... the whole course of judicial interpretation of the Real Property Act has recognised the old law and practice of conveyancing as still applicable to equitable interests in land under the Act.'

This view has been followed in at least three reported decisions in Papua New Guinea *McCosker and King v Kuster* [1967–68] P&NGLR 182; *Re Luabar Logging Pty Ltd* [1988] PNGLR 124 at 126, *per* Bredmeyer J; and *Ningiga v Koavea* [1988–89] PNGLR 312.

Leases and agreements for a lease

Because the lease was for a period of one year (see second schedule to the lease) the form of the lease was not subject to either the Land Registration Act 1981, s 49(1), or the Frauds and Limitations Act, s 3(2). Nevertheless the lease was in writing. As a lease it had no effect because Ministerial approval was lacking in accordance with s 69(1) of the Land Act. That section only affects the lease in law; it does not affect the lease in equity.

The law in Papua New Guinea, before Independence, was summarised by JA Griffin QC in *Land Law: Notes and Materials*, Faculty of Law, University of Papua New Guinea, 1970, at 75–76, in the following terms:

> Equitable Leases:
>
> An agreement to let land may operate as an immediate demise and give to the lessee or tenant a legal estate in Land (see *Doe d Phillip and Walters v Benjamin* (1839) 9 Ad & E

> 644; 112 ER 1356 (KB) but if the agreement is intended to be merely an agreement for a lease, ie, an agreement that the proposed lessor will lease and the proposed lessee will take the land, it creates at common law only contractual and not property rights; and for failure by either party to carry out the agreement the other party has at common law only an action for damages. Again if the transaction between the parties is intended to operate as an actual lease, but it does not comply with formalities required by law, it can operate only as an agreement for a lease, with the consequences just indicated ...
>
> In equity, however, an agreement for a lease, or an informal lease treated as an agreement for a lease, has a greater effect than at common law. In earlier times the Chancellor in his Court of Chancery, would give the remedy of damages for breach of specific performance, whereas the common law would give only the remedy of damages for breach of agreement ... Furthermore, a court of equity, applying the maxim that equity treats as done that which ought to be done, treats a party as having acquired the estate or rights which he ought to have acquired. Thus if L has agreed to lease land to T for five years, equity treats T as having acquired the five year estate in the land which he is entitled to obtain (by action for specific performance), and not as having merely a right of action for damages.

The leading case is *Walsh v Lonsdale* (1882) 21 Ch D 9 (CA) in which Jessel MR said (at 14):

> There is an agreement for a lease under which possession has been given. Now since the Judicature Act 1873 (UK) the possession is held under the agreement. There are not two estates as there were formerly, one estate at common law by reason of the payment of the rent from year to year, and an estate in equity under the agreement. There is only one court, and the equity rules prevail in it. The tenant holds under an agreement for a lease. He holds, therefore, under the same terms in equity as if a lease had been granted, it being a case in which both parties admit that relief is capable of being given by specific performance.

In short, a court which has powers to hear actions in law and equity will treat the parties to an agreement for a lease as having the rights and obligations which they would have had if one of the parties had pursued the available remedies and obtained the legal lease.

Halsbury confirms this view, citing *Walsh v Lonsdale* (*supra*) in *Halsbury's Laws of England* (4th edn), Vol 1, para 1306:

> Equity looks upon that as done which ought to be done or which is agreed to be done, but this maxim does not extend to things which might have been done; nor will equity apply it in favour of everybody, but only those who had a right to pray that the thing should be done.

And at para 1307:

> Where, for example, possession is held under an agreement for a lease, of which specific performance would be ordered, the parties are treated in equity as being in the same position with regard to their respective rights as if a lease had been granted. Similarly, money which would have been payable under a contract if the defendant had not wrongfully prevented anything from becoming due will be treated as a debt in equity, although it is not a debt at law.

Estoppel: tenants estopped from disputing landlords title

But the matter does not end there. The common law has a well established principle of estoppel that where tenants enter onto land, as tenants to a landlord, and have continued to enjoy the land, they are estopped from asserting that they have enjoyed or held the land otherwise than as tenants: see *Hatfield v Alford* (1846) 1 Legge 330; 23 Aust Digest (2nd edn), 110. This seems to me to be an eminently suitable rule of law for the conditions which exist in this country.

In this case, if Mr Wine has entered onto the land he would have appeared to have entered onto the land as a tenant. The lease agreement bears witness to that. The lease agreement shows that both parties recognised their relationships to be that of landlord and tenant. The tenant is estopped from now saying that he held the land otherwise than as a tenant. The effect of this is that as far as a claim for rent is concerned the tenant cannot dispute his landlord's title.

The effect of the estoppel when it does apply is that the tenant cannot set up lack of title in the landlord to grant the lease as a defence to an action for breach of covenant or for rent due: see *Monroe v Kerry* (1710) 1 Bro Parl Cas 67 cited in HA Hill and JH Redman, *Law of Landlord and Tenant* (15th edn) at 13.

However it has been said that an estoppel applies only while the tenant is in possession. Once the tenancy has ended and the tenant is out of possession he is no longer estopped from establishing that the lessor has no right to grant the lease: see *Harrison v Wells* [1966] 3 All ER 524 at 527–28, *per* Harman LJ.

Salmon LJ in *Harrison v Wells* was most uneasy with this proposition of law. His Lordship said (at 530):

> The whole point, and the only point, which enables this defendant to succeed turns on the fact that he actually surrendered and went out of possession. It is perhaps difficult to see for this purpose what is the material difference between a tenant who remains over as a tenant on sufferance, and a tenant who goes out of possession. The first one has taken all the advantages under the lease; he has had all the consideration that the lease purported to confer on him. So has the second in respect of the period during which he enjoyed the tenancy. The first man would clearly be estopped from denying his apparent landlord's title. Why not the second?
>
> This rule of estoppel is founded, I think, on the well known principle that one cannot approbate and reprobate. It is founded also on this consideration, that it would be unjust to allow the man who has taken full advantage of a lease to come forward and seek to evade his obligations under the lease by denying that the purported landlord was the landlord. I ask myself why should it make any difference that the tenant has gone out of possession if (as in this case) he has taken the whole of the consideration under the lease during the period in which he chose to remain in possession under the lease? I confess that I find it very difficult to discover any sensible answer to this question.
>
> The rule relating to estoppel, although founded on broad principle, is nevertheless highly artificial and dependent entirely on precedent.

So, the English Court of Appeal declared this rule of common law to be law despite the fact that it was 'highly artificial and dependent entirely on precedent'. It allowed a tenant who had done £740 worth of damage to his landlord's property to escape scot-free, despite the fact that Salmon LJ could find no 'sensible' basis for the rule.

In my view, such a rule of law is inappropriate (Constitution, Sched 2.2) to the circumstances of this country because it is not uncommon for people in Papua New Guinea to make promises in relation to registered land on the basis that their application to the Minister for Lands for approval of the lease will be granted. The administrative process within the Department of Lands, in the past has been notoriously slow, and in the context of the granting of State leases the concept of the 'granted application' arose, for those applicants for leases who had their applications for a State lease approved, but who were never actually issued a document called a 'State lease'.

In the case of leases between private parties which are carved out of a State lease, the parties need to be assured that their mutual promises will be respected by the courts, until the administrative process within the Department of Lands and Physical Planning has functioned in accordance with the terms of the Land Act. The need for certainty should not be disturbed by importing 'highly artificial' rules of English common law, which even the Court of Appeal have difficulty in regarding as 'sensible'.

It is comforting to note that after Independence, in 1977, the English Court of Appeal reversed its own decision in *Harrison v Wells* in the case of *Industrial Properties (Barton Hill) Ltd v Associated Electrical Industries Ltd* [1977] 2 All ER 293. The Court of Appeal, in *Industrial Properties* held that *Harrison v Wells* was wrongly decided *per incuriam*. Lord Denning MR in *Industrial Properties* corrected the law in the following terms (at 301):

> If a landlord lets a tenant into possession under a lease, then, so long as the tenant remains in possession *undisturbed by any adverse claim* – then the tenant cannot dispute the landlord's title. Suppose the tenant (not having been disturbed) goes out of possession and the landlord sues the tenant on the covenant for rent [as Mr Giglmai did with Mr Wine] or for breach of covenant to repair or to yield up in repair. The tenant cannot say to the landlord: 'You are not the true owner of the property.'

This, in my view, correctly states the law in Papua New Guinea.

The need to develop the law of equity in Papua New Guinea

In the introduction of this judgment I raised the issue of the transactional costs of the Land Act on rural development in Papua New Guinea. Although the Land Act was adopted by Parliament at Independence, and there have been some alterations to it, as a legislative model it is Australian and bureaucratically centralist in its form.

All State leases are issued from Waigani. All the ministerial approvals under s 69 of the Act have to come from Waigani. This is the law, and of course, as a matter of law the courts are bound by it. But this does not mean that the courts are powerless. 'In interpreting the law the courts shall give paramount consideration to the dispensation of justice': Constitution, s 158(2). The word 'law' in that provision includes the Underlying Law, which in turn includes those rules of the law of equity that have been received into law under the appropriate schedule to the Constitution.

The law of equity was always used by the courts to ameliorate the injustices of the harshness of common law or statute. It is therefore available to develop the Underlying Law and to ease those pressures on litigants that arise from the inefficiencies of centralist and unreformed statute law.

In the case of land administration there are good legal grounds for developing the law of equity to ensure that justice is done in particular cases. The Organic Law on Provincial Government (Ch No 1) says that land and land development is a concurrent legislative power shared, in accordance with the provisions of the Organic Law, between the National and Provincial governments. Now, 15 years after Independence, there has been no substantial amendment to the Land Act which would move the nature of its power away from a centralist model, towards the decentralised goal which is envisaged in the Constitution, Pt VIA – 'Provincial government and Local government', and in the Organic

Law on Provincial Government. Neither does there appear to have been any substantial delegation of power to provinces in land matters under Pt VIII of the Organic Law.

Whether or not Parliament amends a statute is a matter for Parliament. Whether or not the executive delegates its statutory powers to the provinces is a matter for the executive. But if omissions by other parts of government, in particular cases before the courts, result in injustices, then the issue may fall within the jurisdiction of the courts. In these circumstances where unreformed statutes not only produce injustices, but tend to go against the spirit of the Constitution, then the courts should not be slow in providing appropriate remedies to do justice between the parties.

In this case a statute would appear to have invalidated an agreement between two businessmen. The agreement involved only a small sum of money: K4,200, but it still was subject to ministerial approval. The landlord appears to have thought he held a State lease, under the Land Act, when it appears he did not hold a lease, but may have been no more than an applicant to have a lease transferred into his name. These irregularities are not surprising when the land is in Kerowagi and the necessary approvals have to come from Port Moresby.

At law the relationship between Mr Giglmai and the State was irregular. It appears he was taking steps, or took steps to regularise it. The relationship between Mr Giglmai and Mr Wine was a private matter – it was only affected by public law to the extent of its non-compliance with the Land Act. In these circumstances, it is proper that the courts enforce the private agreements of the parties, to the extent that they do not conflict with public law (the Land Act). The courts can recognise the lease (otherwise unenforceable) as an equitable lease. Here the claim is liquidated – it is for rent only. That does not go to the legal title of the land. It does not affect the State's title. If the State is aggrieved over any irregularity about the title it has separate remedies against Mr Giglmai, although on the papers before the District Court it appears that the State was prepared to grant a licence to Mr Giglmai, while his application for the transfer of the State lease from the Simbu Cattlemen's Association was under consideration by the Land Board.

[Appeal upheld; case remitted to District Court for rehearing.]

Questions

1 Discuss the difference between s 127 of the Land Act 1996, and s 69 of the Land Act (cap 185).

2 What difference if any, would it make if the above cases were dealt with under s 127 of the current Land Act?

3 What is the difference between a lease and an agreement for a lease?

IV RIGHTS AND DUTIES OF LANDLORD AND TENANT

Covenants and conditions

Technically, a covenant is a promise in a deed. However, in practice the expression denotes an express or implied term in any lease agreement. A condition is a term so important that any breach of it gives a right to terminate the agreement, whereas breach of a covenant does not entitle termination except where the agreement expressly says so.

In most written lease agreements, landlords reserve themselves a right to terminate for breach of any covenant.

Express covenants

Parties to a lease are free to incorporate any terms in a lease provided of course the terms are not contrary to the law. For convenience Sched 3 of the Land Registration Act sets out terms commonly expressed in leases. The parties are free to adopt all or any of these terms. The terms are expressed in a short form as well as a detailed form. Section 52 states:

> A covenant in a lease expressed in a short form of words specified in Column 2 of Schedule 3 implies against the lessee the covenant that is set out in Column 3 of that Schedule opposite the short form of words as fully and effectively as if the covenant was set out fully in the lease.

For example, it suffices to state in the lease that the lessee shall insure the premises. The meaning and extent of the lessee's obligation to insure is determined by reference to Column 3 opposite the term 'insurance'. The object of the provision is to avoid prolixity in the drafting of leases.

Implied covenants

At common law, certain covenants are implied in all leases unless excluded by the parties. Some covenants are implied against the landlord others are implied against the tenant. The following materials illustrate some of the most common implied covenants.

Covenants implied against the landlord

(i) Covenant for quiet enjoyment

KENNY v PREEN [1963] 1 QB 499, English Court of Appeal

> [The plaintiff/respondent, an elderly widow, leased two rooms from the defendant/appellant on a weekly basis. Disputes arose between the two whereupon the defendant served on the plaintiff a notice purporting to terminate the lease. When she refused to quit the defendant sent her a series of letters threatening to evict her from the rooms and to put her property on the street. On several occasions, the defendant made calls at the plaintiff's rooms knocking on her door demanding to have the rooms and shouting threats at her. The defendant ignored letters from the plaintiff's solicitor disputing the purported notice to quit. The plaintiff brought an action against the defendant claiming breach of the covenant of quiet enjoyment implied by law. The trial judge found in favour of the plaintiff. The defendant appealed.]

PEARSON LJ: Mr Lester has contended on behalf of the landlord that the evidence does not reveal any breach of the covenant, because the landlord only made communications to the tenant and did nothing amounting to physical interference with the tenant's possession and enjoyment of the premises. He relied on passages in the judgment in *Owen v Gadd*, [[1956] 2 QB 99] and on judgments in previous cases there cited, as showing that some direct physical interference is necessary to constitute a breach of the covenant.

Mr Sheridan has contended on behalf of the tenant, first, that a mere challenge by the landlord to the tenant's title, a denial by him of her title, would be sufficient to constitute a breach of covenant; secondly, that in this case there was in fact some physical interference with the tenant's possession and enjoyment of the premises; and thirdly, more generally, that on the facts of this case, taken as a whole, there was a breach of the covenant. He cited *Edge v Boileau* [(1885) 16 QBD 117, 119] as showing that physical interference is not necessarily required to constitute a breach of the covenant. That was a case in which the landlord was held to have committed a breach of the covenant by telling the subtenants to pay their rent to him instead of to the tenant. It is easy to see that that was an interference by the landlord with the tenant's enjoyment of his rights as tenant.

The judge accepted Mr Sheridan's first contention that a mere challenge by the landlord to the tenant's title, a denial by him of her title, would be sufficient to constitute a breach of the covenant. I am not able to adopt the judge's view on that point. We are not concerned in this case with a denial of the tenant's initial title by virtue of the letting, and I am not considering whether or not that could be a breach of the covenant. In this case the landlord was asserting that the tenant's title, her right to possession of the premises, although initially valid, had been wholly determined by a notice to quit. In my judgment, a landlord by merely making that assertion, however wrong he may be, does not commit a breach of covenant. He is entitled to make that assertion, at any rate if he believes it to be true, frequently, emphatically and even rudely. He is entitled also to threaten proceedings in the courts for possession and damages.

In the present case, however, there was much more than that. The landlord evaded answering the solicitors' letters raising the tenant's defences to his claim. He concentrated his attention on the tenant herself and tried, by a series of threatening communications, to drive her out of her possession of the premises. The threats were not merely of legal proceedings: there were threats of physical eviction of the tenant and removal of her belongings. Moreover, there was an element of direct physical interference by repeatedly knocking on the door and shouting the threats to her. That element of direct physical interference was not trivial but substantial in this case, because it was persisted in and because it has to be seen against the background of the threatening letters.

The implied covenant for quiet enjoyment is not an absolute covenant protecting a tenant against eviction or interference by anybody, but is a qualified covenant protecting the tenant against interference with the tenant's quiet and peaceful possession and enjoyment of the premises by the landlord or persons claiming through or under the landlord. The basis of it is that the landlord, by letting the premises, confers on the tenant the right of possession during the term and impliedly promises not to interfere with the tenant's exercise and use of the right of possession during the term. I think the word 'enjoy' used in this connection is a translation of the Latin word *'fruor'* and refers to the exercise and use of the right and having the full benefit of it, rather than to deriving pleasure from it.

The nature of the implied covenant was explained in *Budd-Scott v Daniell* [[1902] 2 KB 351, 355–56], in judgments of a Divisional Court. Lord Alverstone CJ said: 'Apart from authority it would certainly seem, on principle and in common sense, that when one person agrees to give possession of his house for a time to another, that ought to carry with it an agreement that he, the landlord, and those claiming through him, will not dispossess the tenant during that time.' Therefore, unless there is some special meaning attached to the word 'demise', the good sense of the thing would seem to be that, upon an agreement to let, a covenant or contract was to be implied that the landlord and those claiming under him would not disturb the possession of the tenant. Unless driven to do so by authority, I should hesitate a long time before drawing any distinction in that respect between the words 'agree to let' and 'demise'.

I would decide on two grounds in favour of the tenant's contention that there was, in this case, a breach of the covenant for quiet enjoyment. First, there was a deliberate and persistent attempt by the landlord to drive the tenant out of her possession of the premises by persecution and intimidation, and intimidation included threats of physical eviction of the tenant and removal of her belongings. In my view that course of conduct by the landlord seriously interfered with the tenant's proper freedom of action in exercising her right of possession, and tended to deprive her of the full benefit of it, and was an invasion of her rights as tenant to remain in possession undisturbed, and so would in itself constitute a breach of covenant, even if there was no direct physical interference with the tenant's possession and enjoyment. No case of this kind has ever been considered by the courts before, and I do not think the *dicta* in the previous cases should be read as excluding a case of this kind where a landlord seeks, by a course of intimidation, to 'annul his own deed', to contradict his own demise, by ousting the tenant from the possession which the landlord has conferred upon her.

Secondly, if direct physical interference is a necessary element in the breach of covenant that element can be found in this case to a substantial extent, as I have already stated ...

Appeal dismissed. [Ormerod and Donovan LJJ agreed.]

Notes

1 The case indicates that where a landlord uses physical force to evict a tenant, the tenant may sue him for breach of covenant of quiet enjoyment. See also *Lavender v Betts* [1942] 2 All ER 72.

2 The landlord is not liable for breach of covenant for quiet enjoyment where the interference is due to unlawful activities of other persons, unless the landlord authorised their activities or their interference is an inevitable consequence of a purpose the landlord authorised (see *Malzy v Eichholz* [1916] 2 KB 308).

Questions

1 What does quiet enjoyment mean?

2 Suppose the landlord threatens to bring a legal action against his tenant for alleged breach of the tenancy agreement. Is the threat of legal action a breach of covenant of quiet enjoyment? See *McCall v Abelesz and Another* [1976] QB 585 (CA).

3 L leases a building to T for purposes of retail trade. A month later L's contractors erect scaffolding in front of the windows and door of the shop in order to carry out repairs to the upper part of the building, which were occupied by L. The poles interfere with access to T's shop, which result in loss of business. Advise T whether he has a cause of

action against L for breach of covenant for quiet enjoyment. (See *Owen v Gadd and Others* [1956] 2 QB 99 (CA).)

(ii) Covenant not to derogate from grant

The underlying law implies a term against the landlord that he will not frustrate the use of the land for the purpose, which in contemplation of *both* parties, it was intended.

ALDIN v LATIMER CLARK MUIRHEAD & CO LTD [1894] 2 Ch 437

[In 1878, one Munro leased part of his land to the defendant for a term of 21 years for carrying on timber trade. At the date of the lease the greater part of the adjacent land retained by Munro was open space. After Munro's death in 1892, the defendants purchased both portions of land. The latter proceeded to erect buildings on the adjacent land in such a manner that they affected the free flow of air to the plaintiff's timber drying sheds. The plaintiff contended that the defendant's acts either constituted derogation from the grant or breach of covenant of quiet enjoyment.]

STIRLING J: The legal principle invoked on behalf of the plaintiff appears to be recognised in several modern cases ...

The result of these judgments appears to me to be that where a landlord demises part of his property for carrying on a particular business, he is bound to abstain from doing anything on the remaining portion which would render the demised premises unfit for carrying on such business in the way in which it is ordinarily carried on, but that this obligation does not extend to special branches of the business which call for extraordinary protection ...

In the present case, the lease of 1 July 1878, was not merely granted for the purpose that the land demised might be used by the plaintiff for the purpose of carrying on his business as a timber merchant, but it contains an express covenant binding him to carry on that business. In my opinion, Munro became subject to the obligation to abstain from doing anything on his adjoining property which would substantially interfere with the carrying on of that business in the ordinary course; and that obligations binds the present defendants, as assigns from him, subject to the existing lease. By the instrument of 7 May 1888, which is under seal, and for which valuable consideration was given by the plaintiff, a like obligation became imposed on Munro, and to it the defendants are subject ...

I think that the plaintiff is entitled to an inquiry what sum of money will compensate him for the damage done to him by reason of the defendants' buildings rendering the sheds of the plaintiff less fit for use by him in the ordinary course of his business as a timber merchant ...

Note

The covenant not to derogate from the grant does not apply where the tenant uses the land for a 'special purpose' or a purpose which was not in the contemplation of both parties at the time of the lease (see, eg, *Robinson v Kilvert* [1888] 41 Ch D 88 (CA)).

Questions

1 What is the difference between a covenant not to derogate from grant and a covenant of quiet enjoyment? Can you think of a factual situation where (a) both covenants overlap and (b) where one but not the other is breached? (See *Telex (Australasia) Pty Ltd v Thomas Cook & Son (Australasian) Pty Ltd* [1970] 2 NSWR 257.)

2 T is a dealer in highly sensitive scientific equipment. He leases part of L's premises for his business. Later L installs an air conditioner in the building complex. The noise of the air conditioner interferes with T's equipment. T wishes to sue L for breach of covenant not to derogate from the grant and the covenant of quiet enjoyment. Advise L. (See *Telex (Australasia) Pty Ltd v Thomas Cook and Son (Australasia) Pty Ltd* [1970] 2 NSWR 257.)

3 L leases part of his land to T for purposes of carrying on a business of storing highly inflammable liquids. Later L leases the adjoining land to TP for the purpose of a welding business. Because of TP's business, the Minister cancels T's inflammable liquids storage licence. T sues L for breach of covenant for quiet enjoyment and the covenant not to derogate from grant. What are his chances of success? (See *Harmer v Jumbi (Nigeria) Tin Areas Ltd* [1921] 1 Ch 200.)

(iii) Covenant of fitness for human habitation

The landlord does not normally undertake that the premises leased are or will be fit for human habitation. Nor is he liable to repair them.[18] However, where premises are rented ready furnished, the common law implies against the landlord that they are fit for human habitation. The following case deals with the scope of this implied covenant.

CRUSE v MOUNT [1932] All ER Rep 781, Chancery Division

[The defendant, the landlord, leased an unfurnished flat to the plaintiff. Subsequently, the plaintiff was forced to vacate the flat because it had serious structural defects which rendered it unfit for human habitation. It was not in dispute that the landlord was unaware of the defects. The tenant sued the landlord for breach of covenant while the landlord counter-claimed for rent due.]

MAUGHAM J: I now turn to the consideration of the question whether, in regard to the letting of a flat for immediate occupation, there is an implied condition that the premises are fit for human habitation. The leading case on the subject of furnished lodgings is *Smith v Marrable* (1843) 11 M&W 5; 152 ER 697. That is the well known case where Lady Marrable took a house in Brighton for five or six weeks, and found after she entered into possession that it was so infested with bugs that it was impossible for her to remain in it. The case was before Parke B, Lord Abinger CB, Alderson and Gurney BB. I should add that the agreement was in writing, so that it was not a case of a merely oral agreement. The learned judges held that a man who let a ready furnished house did so under the implied condition or obligation that the house was in a fit state to be inhabited, and that, if the demised premises were encumbered with a nuisance of so serious a nature that no person could reasonably be expected to live in them, the tenant was at liberty to throw the lease up ...

18 See *Cheshire and Burn's Modern Law of Real Property* (14th edn, Butterworths, London), p 373.

Since then, *Smith v Marrable* ... has, on one ground or another, constantly been followed, and I, at any rate, do not intend to cast any doubt on its being a correct decision. Accordingly, the matter stands thus, that, in regard to the letting of furnished premises, there is an implied condition that the premises shall be fit for human habitation at the date when the tenancy begins, and that, if they are not so fit, the lessee can throw up the tenancy. In regard to an unfurnished house, for the reasons given in *Hart v Windsor* [(1844) 12 M&W 68; 152 ER 1114] which, I think, will readily occur to anyone who knows that unfurnished houses are constantly let in a very bad state (that condition being one which is reflected in the rent) – it has been held that there is no such condition or warranty ...

Accordingly, it seems to me that ... I must hold that a landlord is entitled to let a flat in a building without being held to be giving such an implied warranty. The tenant is not, therefore, entitled to maintain an action for damages for breach of warranty, nor is he entitled, by treating the warranty as a condition, to put an end to the lease.

Notes

1 In *Summers v Salford Corporation* [1943] AC 283, at 289, Lord Atkin observed that: 'If the state of repair of a house is such that by ordinary user damage may naturally be caused to the occupier, either in respect of personal injury to life or limb or injury to health, then the house is not in all respects reasonably fit for human habitation.' Each case depends on its own facts, but examples of a house which is unfit for human habitation would include a house with exposed live electricity wires; a house with a blocked toilet system and so on.

2 The obligation of the landlord to provide a house which is fit for reasonable habitation is only implied at the beginning of the lease and does not continue throughout the lease period (see *Sarson v Roberts* [1895] 2 QB 395).

Questions

1 Do you agree with the reasoning in *Cruse* that the reason the common law does not imply a covenant of fitness for human habitation in a lease of unfurnished houses was that such houses are constantly let in 'a very bad state'? Is this reasoning justifiable in the circumstances of PNG?

2 In some States in Australia, if premises are rented for residential purposes the landlord is deemed to undertake that the premises are fit for residential purposes and that they will remain fit during the currency of the tenancy (see, eg, s 7(a)(ii) of the Residential Tenancies Act 1975 (Queensland)). Would you recommend enactment of similar legislation in PNG? Do you envisage any problems of a practical nature in implementing that sort of legislation?

3 UPNG provides accommodation for its members of staff. The Uni allocates John, a new lecturer, a house on 3rd Street on the campus. The house is dirty, the paint is peeling off on some of the walls and the grass needs cutting. John wishes to sue the University for breach of covenant of fitness for human habitation. Advise John. (If more facts are needed to answer this question state them and why.)

'Usual' covenants

In addition to implied covenants under the underlying law, 'usual' covenants may be implied where the lease makes reference to 'usual' covenants. 'Usual' is a technical term. It refers to those terms of a lease, which are usual or common according to the prevailing commercial and conveyancing practice in the locality.[19]

Covenants implied by Statute

The Land Registration Act implies in a lease certain powers and covenants in favour of the lessor:

> **50 Powers of lessor**
>
> The following powers are, by virtue of this Act, implied in a lease, in favour of the lessor:
>
> (a) that he may by himself or his agents at all reasonable times enter on the demised property and view the state of repair of the demised property, and may serve on the lessee or leave at his last or usual place of abode in the country or on the demised property a written notice of any defect, requiring him within a reasonable time, specified in the notice, to repair the property; and
>
> (b) that in case the rent or part of the rent is in arrear for a period of six calendar months, or in case default is made in the fulfilment of a covenant whether expressed or implied in the lease on the part of the lessee and is continued for a period of six calendar months, or in case the repairs required by the notice are not completed within the time specified in the notice, the lessor may re-enter and take possession of the demised property.
>
> **51 Covenants implied against lessee**
>
> (1) Subject to sub-section (2), the following covenants are, by virtue of this Act, implied in a lease against the lessee:
>
> (a) that he will pay the rent reserved by the lease at the times specified in the lease and will pay all rates and taxes which are payable in respect of the demised property during the continuance of the lease; and
>
> (b) that he will keep and yield up the demised property in good and tenantable repair.
>
> (2) Where a building erected on demised property under this Act is destroyed by fire, storm, flood or tempest, or otherwise by the act of God and without default on the part of the lessee, then, unless the lease stipulates otherwise, the covenants implied by virtue of sub-section (1) are suspended until the lessor has reinstated the building in good and tenantable repair.

Notes

1 Under s 100 of the Land Registration Act, the parties may by express agreement modify or exclude any implied covenant.

---

19 *Flexman v Corbett* [1930] 1 Ch 672.

2 The LRA does not imply any covenants against a lessor. Can you think of possible reasons why this is so?

Meaning of 'good and tenantable repairs'

The clause 'keep and yield up possession in good and tenantable repair' is quite common in lease agreements. Its meaning and effect is discussed in the following case.

PROUDFOOT v HART (1890) 25 QBD 42, Court of Appeal

[The plaintiff/appellant under a written agreement let certain premises to the defendant/respondent, for a term of three years subject to a covenant that during the said term the defendant shall 'keep the premises in good and tenantable repair, and so leave the same at the expiration thereof'. The issue was whether the tenant was in breach of covenant.]

LORD ESHER MR: What is the true construction of a tenant's contract to keep and deliver up premises in 'tenantable repair'? Now, it is not an express term of that contract that the premises should be *put* into tenantable repair, and it may therefore be argued that, where it is conceded, as it is in this case, that the premises were out of tenantable repair when the tenancy began, the tenant is not bound to put them into tenantable repair, but is only bound to keep them in the same repair as they were in when he became the tenant of them. But it has been decided – and, I think, rightly decided – that, where the premises are not in repair when the tenant takes them, he must put them into repair in order to discharge his obligation under a contract to keep and deliver them up in repair. If the premises are out of repair at any time during the tenancy the landlord is entitled to say to the tenant, 'you have now broken your contract to keep them in repair'; and if they were out of repair at the end of the tenancy he is entitled to say, 'you have broken your contract to deliver them up in repair'. I am of opinion that under a contract to keep the premises in tenantable repair and leave them in tenantable repair, the obligation of the tenant, if the premises are not in tenantable repair when the tenancy begins, is to put them into, keep them in, and deliver them up in tenantable repair. Now, what is 'tenantable repair'? Definitions have been given at different times by the courts ... The result of the cases seems to be this: the question whether the house was, or was not, in tenantable repair when the tenancy began is immaterial; but the age of the house is very material with respect to the obligation both to keep and to leave it in tenantable repair. It is obvious that the obligation is very different when the house is 50 years older than it was when the tenancy began. Lopes LJ has drawn up a definition of the term 'tenantable repair' with which I entirely agree. It is this: 'Good tenantable repair is such repair as, having regard to the age, character, and locality of the house, would make it reasonably fit for the occupation of a reasonably-minded tenant of the class who would be likely to take it.' The age of the house must be taken into account because nobody could reasonably expect that a house 200 years old should be in the same condition of repair as a house lately built; the character of the house must be taken into account, because the same class of repairs as would be necessary to a palace would be wholly unnecessary to a cottage; and the locality of the house must be taken into account, because the state of repair necessary for a house in Grosvenor Square would be wholly different from the state of repair necessary for a house in Spitalfields. The house need not be put into the same condition as when the tenant took it; it need not be put into perfect repair; it need only be put into such a state of repair as renders it reasonably fit for the occupation of a reasonably-minded tenant of the class who would be likely to take it. I think our definition is an expansion of the definitions given in the earlier cases, or rather it is a collocation of all the different parts of the definition to be collected from those cases ...

I will add a few words as to the way in which the definition should be worked out in the present case. The official referee appears to have said that in his view 'tenantable repair' included painting, papering, and decorating. If he meant, as I think he must have meant, that it included *all* papering, painting, and decorating, I have no hesitation in saying that his construction of the term 'tenantable repair' was wrong. Again, he has said that the tenant's obligation is to 'repaper with similar paper to that which was on the walls before, and repaint with similar paint to that which was on the painted portion of the premises before'. I think that view was wrong also. With regard to the papering, Cave J in the court below, said: 'I cannot see how in any case a man can be bound to put new paper on the walls simply because the old paper which was on at the time when he took the house, or which he has subsequently put on the walls, has become worn out'. I agree that he is not bound to repaper simply because the old paper has become worn out, but I do not agree with the view that under a covenant to keep a house in tenantable repair the tenant can never be required to put up new paper. Take a house in Grosvenor Square. If when the tenancy ends, the paper on the walls is merely in a worse condition than when the tenant went in, I think the mere fact of its being in a worse condition does not impose upon the tenant any obligation to repaper under the covenant, if it is such a condition that a reasonably-minded tenant of the class who take houses in Grosvenor Square would not think the house unfit for his occupation. But suppose that the damp has caused the paper to peel off the walls, and it is lying upon the floor, so that such a tenant would think it a disgrace, I should say then that the tenant was bound, under his covenant to leave the premises in tenantable repair, to put up new paper. He need not put up paper of a similar kind – which I take to mean of equal value – to the paper which was on the walls when his tenancy began. He need not put up a paper of a richer character than would satisfy a reasonable man within the definition.

The same view applies as to painting. If the paint is in such a state that the woodwork will decay unless it is repainted, it is obvious that the tenant must repaint. But I think that his obligation goes further than that. A house in Spitalfields is never painted in the same way as one in Grosvenor Square. If the tenant leaves a house in Grosvenor Square with painting only good enough for a house in Spitalfields, he has not discharged his obligation. He must paint it in such a way as would satisfy a reasonable tenant taking a house in Grosvenor Square. As to whitewashing, one knows it is impossible to keep ceilings in the same condition as when they have just been whitewashed. But if, though the ceilings have become blacker, they are still in such a condition that a reasonable man would not say, 'I will not take this house because of the state of the ceilings', then I think that the tenant is not bound, under this covenant to leave the house in tenantable repair, to whitewash them ...

[Case sent back to the official referee. Lopes LJ agreed.]

Questions

1 Why is a different test of 'tenantable repair' applied to a house in 'Spitalfields' and a house in 'Grosvenor Square'? (Compare a house in Koki suburb with a house in Boroko East.)

2 L owns several high covenant houses in downtown Port Moresby. Under a written agreement, she leases one of her houses to X for a term of three years. At the time of the lease, the house is very dirty and needs repainting. Several windows and doors

are broken and the garden unattended. X, desperate for accommodation, accepts possession of the house. He puts cardboard in place of broken windows. When the lease expires X leaves the house more or less as he found it: dirty and still unpainted. L sues X for breach of covenant to maintain and deliver up the house in good and tenantable repair. Advise X. (See *David Lambu v The Independent State of PNG* [1988] PNGLR 121, extracted below.)

The following case deals with a clause similar to that in *Proudfoot v Hart* (extracted above), except in the instant case the landlord assumed the obligation to keep the premises 'in good and tenantable repair'.

DAVID LAMBU v THE INDEPENDENT STATE OF PAPUA NEW GUINEA
[1988] PNGLR 121, National Court of Justice

BREDMEYER J: This is a claim for damages of K6,500 for breach of a covenant to repair in a lease. David Lambu signed a tenancy agreement for the lease of a high covenant house at Gerehu on 6 September 1984. The agreement let the land, residence, and improvements, 'together with the furniture, fittings and household effects now or hereinafter [sic] issued to the tenant' at a rent of K23 per fortnight. By clause 3(a) the landlord agreed with the tenant:

> To keep in good and tenantable repair the said premises and the furniture, fittings and household effects of the Landlord therein in respect of all damage caused by accidental fire or fair wear and tear.

What does that clause mean? Where the premises are dilapidated at the start of the lease, does it mean that the government has to put them in good repair and then keep them in good repair, or does it mean keep the premises in the same state of repair as they were in at the commencement of the lease? I have come to the view that the latter view is correct for three reasons. First, the covenant is not 'to put and keep in repair' but simply to keep in good and tenantable repair. The former clause, 'to put and keep in repair' is quite common in leases. Secondly, *Halsbury's Laws of England* (4th edn, 1981), para 298 at 231, says that the liability of a landlord to repair must be construed with reference to the state of the premises at the commencement of the lease, and the landlord is not bound to give to the tenant during the term a different thing from that which the tenant took at the commencement of the tenancy. Cases are cited for that proposition a leading one being *Pembery v Lamdin* [1940] 2 All ER 434.

Thirdly, the interpretation is reasonable; it accords with commercial reality. If premises are very dilapidated, the would-be tenant offers a low rent. Or, if the tenant wants K5,000 or K6,000 worth of repairs done at the outset he bargains with the landlord. He says 'I would like the house to be painted' etc, and the landlord says 'I am willing to do that if you agree to a rent of K150 per week'. In other words the rent is fixed by agreement to reflect the lack of repair, or the state of good repair, or the cost of putting the premises in a state of good repair. In this case, a rent of K23 per fortnight is a nominal rent for a high covenant house at Gerehu. I take judicial notice of that. I consider that the government was only obliged under this clause to keep the premises in the same state of repair as they were in at the outset of the lease.

Certain furniture was in the house when it was leased but no schedule of furniture was annexed to the lease, thus the plaintiff has no claim for furniture which was not there.

I accept Mr Lambu as a truthful witness. He said that as he and his family began using the furniture it deteriorated. For example, as they used the dining table, the bottom began to rot away. The backs of the dining chairs came off and the seats of most of them came off. The frames of the lounge chairs came apart.

He said that in one bedroom the roof was leaking as he saw seepage marks on the ceiling. He said the verandah boards were not a problem when they entered the house but became a problem one or two years later as termites ate them and nails came loose.

Mr Lambu reported this lack of repair to the government, as he was required to do under cl 2(r) of the lease, but got no response. This lack of repair is a breach of the lease and sounds in damages.

Mr Lambu also gave evidence on leaking pipes. There is a separate clause in the lease requiring the landlord to repair leaking pipes but these were repaired so there is no breach there.

What is the measure of damages flowing from the breach? Mr Lambu claimed in the writ K6,500 damages. In evidence he said he borrowed K3,000 from the bank in January 1988. He spent K1,600 of the loan on replacing floor and wall tiles in the kitchen, bathroom and toilet, replacing flywire and verandah floor boards. He spent K750 on electrical work as follows:

- replacing all existing fluorescent lights;
- replacing faulty general power outlets;
- replacing elements on the stove;
- replacing drive belt for washing machine;
- installing additional security lights.
  (This is not a repair.)

According to *Halsbury, op cit*, para 307, p 238, where there has been a breach by the landlord of his covenant to repair, *prima facie* the measure of damages for such a breach is the difference in value to the tenant of the premises, from the date he gave notice of the disrepair down to the date of the assessment, between the premises in their condition at the time of assessment and their value if the landlord, on receipt of the notice, had fulfilled the obligations of his covenant. In this case it would be from the date of notice until the date he ceased to be a tenant. I agree that this is a fair measure of the damages. It would be most unfair to award say K3,000 damages to Mr Lambu for the cost of putting the premises in the state of repair which the landlord should have maintained, because since cessation of the lease, Mr Lambu has become the purchaser. On 30 July 1987 he agreed to purchase the house for K23,301.04 in its unrepaired state. If the government had just spent say K3,000 on repairs, the purchase price may well have been K3,000 more. To award K3,000 now would be to give the plaintiff a double benefit, K3,000 plus a diminished purchase price.

Applying the principle quoted in *Halsbury,* I assess the damages due to the lack of repair as a diminution of rent from K23 to K19 per fortnight over the period of the lease. That is K4 per fortnight from 6.9.84 to 3.7.87 equals 75 fortnights x K4 = K300. I award damages of K300. I see no reason why I should not apply O 22, r 25 of the National Court Rules and I order costs to the plaintiff on the District Court Scale.

Question

What is the difference between a covenant 'to keep the premises in good and tenantable repair' and 'to put and keep the premises in good and tenantable repair'? Which of these two covenants is implied under s 51 of the LRA?

Notes

1 In *Warren v Keen* [1954] 1 QB 15 at 20, Lord Denning said that apart from express contract, a tenant does not owe a duty to the landlord to keep the premises in repair. His Lordship added that the only duty of the tenant is to use the premises in a 'husbandlike, or what is the same thing, a tenantlike manner'. Denning LJ explained that the expression 'tenantlike manner' meant that:

> The tenant must take proper care of the place. He must, if he is going away for the winter, turn off the water and empty the boiler. He must clean the chimneys, when necessary, and also the windows. He must mend the electric light when it fuses. He must unstop the sink when it is blocked by his waste. In short, he must do the little jobs about the place which a reasonable tenant would do. In addition, he must, of course, not damage the house, wilfully or negligently; and he must see that his family and guests do not damage it; and if they do, he must repair it. But apart from such things, if the house falls into disrepair through fair wear and tear or lapse of time, or for any reason not caused by him, then the tenant is not liable to repair it.

2 The obligation to keep premises in a 'tenantlike manner' is less onerous than the obligation implied under s 51(1)(b) of the LRA, *supra*, p 318. It is not clear whether s 51(1)(b) is implied only in long term leases registered under the Act, or in all leases, including yearly, monthly and other periodic tenancies not registered under the Act. As a matter of common sense one is inclined to argue that the covenant is only implied in registered leases because it would be unfair to imply the onerous statutory covenant to repair in a weekly tenancy agreement or other unregistered leases. The counter argument is that there is nothing in the section or the Act as a whole to exclude the application of the section to short term unregistered leases.

Covenants and conditions implied in State leases

The grant of State leases is subject to certain covenants and conditions stipulated in the Land Act 1996. See Chapter 7.

Sub-lease and assignment

A sub-lease arises where a lessee creates a lease, which is less than the term which the lessee has.[20] An assignment on the other hand is an absolute transfer of the remainder of the lease to a third party. In *Milmo v Carreras*[21] Lord Greene MR observed:

> [I]n accordance with a very ancient and established rule, where a lessee, by a document in the form of a sub-lease, divests himself of everything that he has got (which he must

20 The sub-lease must expire at least one day before the expiration date of the headlease.
21 [1946] KB 306, at 310.

> necessarily do if he is transferring to his so called sub-lessee an estate as great as, or purporting to be greater than, his own) he from that moment is a stranger to the land, in the sense that the relationship of landlord and tenant, in respect of tenure, cannot any longer exist between him and the so called sub-lessee. The relationship must depend on privity of estate. I myself find it impossible to conceive of a relationship of landlord and tenant which has not got that essential element of tenure in it, and that implies that the tenant holds of his landlord, and he can only do that if the landlord has a reversion. You cannot have a purely contractual tenure. Tenure exists by reason of privity of estate.

Under the underlying law the power to sub-lease or assign is incidental to every leasehold, including a periodic lease, unless the power is expressly excluded in the lease document.[22] In practice, the power to assign or sub-lease is usually excluded or granted subject to the landlord's consent.[23] Where the power is excluded, the landlord at his discretion may waive this right with or without any conditions for his consent. But if he refuses to waive his right he cannot be compelled however unreasonable are the grounds for his refusal.[24] Total exclusion of the lessee's power to sub-lease or assign is uncommon because it reduces the value of the lease. Instead, most leases restrict the power to assign or sub-lease subject to the consent of the lessor. Where the power to sub-lease or assign is qualified it is implied that the lessor shall not unreasonably withhold his consent.[25] The test for reasonableness is discussed in the case which follows.

IN RE GIBBS AND HOULDER BROTHERS & CO LTD'S LEASE
HOULDER BROTHERS & CO LTD v GIBBS
[1925] Ch 198, Chancery Division

> [Under a 21-year lease, the plaintiffs covenanted not to assign the premises, or any part thereof, without written consent of the defendants, such consent not to be unreasonably withheld. The plaintiffs sought to assign the residue of the lease to Roneo Ltd. The latter were already leasing the defendants' other premises. The defendants withheld their consent because if Roneo Ltd terminated their existing lease the defendants would find it extremely difficult to get other tenants to occupy the vacated premises. The plaintiffs brought action for a declaration that the ground for refusal was unreasonable.]
>
> **TOMLIN J**: Where a lease contains a provision of this kind under which a consent is not to be withheld unreasonably, 'unreasonably' must be a word having a meaning with reference to some particular conditions, and the withholding must be unreasonable in reference to some particular considerations. The real question on such a clause is this: what are the considerations which the court is entitled to regard in determining whether or not a particular reason for refusal is justified within the meaning of the clause?
>
> It is said by Mr Simonds on behalf of the lessor that a clause such as this must be read in such a way that, for the purpose of determining reason or unreason, the court is entitled to have regard to all the circumstances which may affect the interest of the lessor, however extrinsic they may be to the fact of the lease, or the user of the premises in the lease, or the personality of the lessee or assignee; in other words, that wherever a lessor finds that an

---

22 *Keeves v Dean* [1924] 1 KB 685, at 695, *per* Scrutton LJ.

23 See for example, Land Registration Act (Ch No 191), Sched 3, item no 8, where it is implied that the lessee 'will not without leave assign or sub-let'.

24 *Viscount Tredegar v Harwood and Others* [1929] AC 72.

25 See *In Re Gibbs & Houlder Brothers & Co Ltd* [1925] Ch 198, see extract below.

assignment to a particular individual may result in something which will be detrimental to him wholly without regard to the character of the assignee, or the user which the assignee may make of the premises, the lessor may assert that as a reason for refusing his assent. On the other hand it is said: no, the considerations with reference to which reason or unreason is tested must necessarily be much narrower than that; they must be reasons which have some relation to, and arise in some way out of, the personality of the lessee or the proposed user or occupation of the premises, and the mere fact that some indirect detriment may follow to the lessor by reason of the assignment does not of itself afford the lessor a ground for refusing his assent to the assignment.

A great number of cases have been cited to me ... The question is what I am to make of all that. I come to the conclusion that the principle as stated – and I hope I am not disrespectful in putting it this way – by AL Smith LJ in *Bates v Donaldson* [[1896] 2 QB 241] is accurately stated, and when he said what he did say, he meant what he said, and that it is by reference to the personality of the lessee or the nature of the user or occupation of the premises, that the court has to judge of the reasonableness of the lessor's refusal. It is quite true that the injury threatened or apprehended to the lessor may be in respect of something which has nothing to do with the lease of the demised premises; it may be in relation to other property of which he is the owner, but the danger must come from the nature of the user or occupation or from the personality of the assignee. In the present case what is the real reason of the refusal? The real reason is not one which had anything to do with the personality of the lessee, or with the user or occupation of the premises; the real reason is that the lessor wants to prevent the assignee from giving up other premises of which he is also lessor; in other words, his real purpose in refusing an assignment is not in relation to the demised premises at all, but in relation to other property, and to bring pressure to bear on the assignee not to give up a tenancy of different premises belonging to him.

In my view, therefore, the necessary conclusion is that the refusal in this case was unreasonable, and that being so the lessee is free to assign.

Questions

1 In view of the landlord's business interests, were the grounds for withholding of consent necessarily unreasonable?

2 Why do landlords restrict the tenants' right to sub-lease or assign leases?

Notes

1 In most factual situations it is not easy to determine whether or not the grounds for the landlord's refusal to give consent to the tenant to assign or sub-lease are unreasonable or not. Obviously each case depends on its own facts. The courts have suggested various tests and principles to be applied. In the case of *International Drilling Fluids Ltd v Louisville Investments (Uxbridge) Ltd* [1986] 1 All ER 321, at 325–26, Lord Justice Balcombe after considering several authorities summarised the relevant propositions as follows:

(1) The purpose of a covenant against assignment without the consent of the landlord, such consent not to be unreasonably withheld, is to protect the lessor from having his premises used or occupied in an undesirable way, or by an undesirable tenant or assignee: see *per* AL Smith LJ in *Bates v Donaldson* [1896] 2

QB 241 at 247; [1895–99] All ER Rep 170 at 174; approved by all the members of the Court of Appeal in *Re Gibbs & Houlder Bros & Co Ltd's Lease* [1925] Ch 575; [1925] All ER Rep 128.

(2) As a corollary to the first proposition, a landlord is not entitled to refuse his consent to an assignment on grounds which have nothing whatever to do with the relationship of landlord and tenant in regard to the subject matter of the lease: see *Re Gibbs & Houlder Bros & Co Ltd's Lease*, a decision which (despite some criticism) is binding on this court: see *Bickel v Duke of Westminster* [1976] 3 All ER 801; [1977] QB 517.

A recent example of a case where the landlord's consent was unreasonably withheld because the refusal was designed to achieve a collateral purpose unconnected with the terms of the lease is *Bromley Park Garden Estates Ltd v Moss* [1982] 2 All ER 890; [1982] 1 WLR 1019.

(3) The onus of proving that consent has been unreasonably withheld is on the tenant; see *Shanley v Ward* (1913) 29 TLR 714 and *Pimms Ltd v Tallow Chandlers in the City of London* [1964] 2 All ER 145 at 147; [1964] 2 QB 547 at 564.

(4) It is not necessary for the landlord to prove that the conclusions which led him to consent were justified, if they were conclusions which might be reached by a reasonable man in the circumstances: see *Pimms Ltd v Tallow Chandlers in the City of London* [1964] 2 All ER 145 at 147; [1964] 2 QB 547 at 564.

(5) It may be reasonable for the landlord to refuse his consent to an assignment on the ground of the purpose for which the proposed assignee intends to use the premises, even though that purpose is not forbidden by the lease: see *Bates v Donaldson* (1896) 2 QB 241 at 244; [1895–99] All ER Rep 170 at 173.

(6) There is a divergence of authority on the question, in considering whether the landlord's refusal of consent is reasonable, whether it is permissible to have regard to the consequences to the tenant if consent to the proposed assignment is withheld. In an early case at first instance, *Sheppard v Hong Kong and Shanghae Banking Corp* [1872] 20 WR 459 at 460 Malins VC said that by withholding their consent the lessors threw a very heavy burden on the lessees, and they therefore ought to show good grounds for refusing it. In *Re Gibbs v Houlder Bros & Co Ltd's Lease* [1925] Ch 575 at 584; [1925] All ER Rep 128 at 133 Warrington LJ said:

> An act must be regarded as reasonable or unreasonable in reference to the circumstances under which it is committed, and when the question arises on the construction of a contract, the outstanding circumstances to be considered are the nature of the contract to be construed and the relations between the parties resulting from it.

In a recent decision of this court, *Leeward Securities Ltd v Lilyheath Properties Ltd* (1984) 271 EG 279, a case concerning a sub-letting which would attract the protection of the Rent Act, both Oliver and O'Connor LJJ made it clear in their judgments that they could envisage circumstances in which it might be unreasonable to refuse consent to an underletting, if the result would be that there was no way in which the tenant (the sub-landlord) could reasonably exploit the premises except by creating a tenancy to which the Rent Act protection would apply, and which inevitably would affect the value of the landlord's reversion. O'Connor LJ said (at 283):

> It must not be thought that, because the introduction of a Rent Act tenant inevitably has an adverse effect upon the value of the reversion, that that is sufficient ground for the landlords to say that they can withhold consent and that the court will hold that that is reasonable.

To the opposite effect are the *dicta, obiter* but nevertheless weighty, of Viscount Dunedin and Lord Phillimore in *Viscount Tredegar v Harwood* [1929] AC 72 at 78, 82; [1928] All ER Rep 11 at 14, 16. There are numerous other *dicta* to the effect that a landlord need consider only his own interests: see, for example, *West Layton Ltd v Ford* [1979] 2 All ER 657 at 663; [1979] QB 593 at 605 and *Bromley Park Garden Estates Ltd v Moss* [1982] 2 All ER 890 at 896; [1982] 1 WLR 1019 at 1027. These *dicta* must be qualified, since a landlord's interests, collateral to the purposes of the lease, are in any event ineligible for consideration: see para (2) above.

But in my judgment a proper reconciliation of those two streams of authority can be achieved by saying that while a landlord need usually only consider his own relevant interests, there may be cases where there is such a disproportion between the benefit to the landlord and the detriment to the tenant if the landlord withholds his consent to an assignment, that it is unreasonable of the landlord to refuse consent.

(7) Subject to the propositions set out above, it is, in each case, a question of fact, depending on all the circumstances, whether the landlord's consent to an assignment is being unreasonably withheld: see *Bickel v Duke of Westminster* [1976] 3 All ER 801 at 805; [1977] QB 517 at 524, and *West Layton Ltd v Ford* [1979] 2 All ER 657 at 663, 664; [1979] QB 593 at 604, 606.

2 Failure to seek prior consent before leasing or assigning is a breach of covenant even if the landlord would not have had any reasonable excuse to refuse or that the failure to seek consent was an oversight (*Barrow v Isaacs & Son* [1891] 1 QB 417 (CA)). However, an assignment or sub-lease made without consent of the lessor is not void, but is voidable at the discretion of the lessor (*Massart v Blight and Another* (1951) 82 CLR 423).

3 Where the lessee feels that the lessor's grounds for withholding consent to an assignment or sub-lease are unreasonable, the lessee may either seek a judicial declaration to that effect, or may take a chance and proceed to sub-lease or assign regardless of consent. If the lessee chose the latter course of action, it would be up to the lessor to challenge the lessee's action. If the lessor succeeds the lessee would be in breach of covenant, which might be a ground for forfeiture, but if the lessor fails the lessee would not incur any liability (*Yared v Spier and Others* [1979] 2 NSWLR 291).

Enforcement of covenants in leases

The right to sue for breach of a covenant in a lease is dependent upon the legal relationship of the parties to a lease. The general rules under the underlying law are as follows.

Privity of contract

Where there is privity of contract between the parties then all the terms of the lease are enforceable as between the parties on normal contractual principles. Thus, as between the original parties to the lease all the terms of the lease are enforceable for the duration of the lease. Even if one party transfers his interest to another person, he (the transferor) continues to be liable under the original contract unless the other party agrees to release him from the contract.[26]

Privity of estate

Where there is no privity of contract between the parties but there is, privity of estate (ie, a relationship of landlord and tenant) only covenants which touch and concern the land are enforceable.[27] This will be the situation where one of the original parties to the lease assigns his interest to a third party. Suppose L leases his land to T1. Later T1 assigns the lease to T2. There is no privity of contract between L and T2 but there is privity of estate, since T2 steps into the shoes of T1. Covenants that do not touch and concern the land are known as personal covenants because they only bind those privy to the covenants. The following case lays down some guidelines for determining whether or not a covenant does touch and concern the land.

P & A SWIFT INVESTMENTS (A FIRM) v COMBINED ENGLISH STORES GROUP PLC [1988] 3 WLR 313, House of Lords

[L leased its premises to a limited liability company. The defendant/appellant acted as a surety to the tenant and guaranteed the performance of the lessee's obligations under the lease. Subsequently, the original landlord assigned the reversion to the respondent/plaintiff. There was no express assignment of the benefit of the tenant's covenant or of the benefit of the surety's covenant. The tenant defaulted in the payment of rent, the respondent failing to recover the rent from the tenant brought these proceedings against the surety to recover the amount of the unpaid rent. The issue is whether a surety's covenant touches and concern the land.]

LORD OLIVER OF AYLMERTON: In my opinion the question of whether a surety's covenant in a lease touches and concerns the lease falls to be determined by the same test as that applicable to the tenant's covenant. That test was formulated by Bayler J in *Congleton Corporation v Pattison* (1808) 10 East 130 and adopted by Farwell J in *Rogers v Hosegood* [1900] 2 Ch 388, 395:

> ... the covenant must either affect the land as regards mode of occupation or it must be such as *per se*, and not merely from collateral circumstances, affects the value of the land.

The meaning of those words '*per se*, and not merely from collateral circumstances' has been the subject matter of a certain amount of judicial consideration and the judgment of Sir Nicolas Browne-Wilkinson VC in *Kumar v Dunning* [1987] 3 WLR 1167 (where the problem was identical to that in the instant case save that the covenant was given on an assignment and not on the grant of the lease), contains a careful and helpful review of the authorities.

26 *Thursby and Others v Plant* (1670) 1 Wms Saund 230; 85 ER 254. See illustration in 'Notes' below.

27 See *Rogers v Hosegood* [1900] 2 Ch 388 (CA).

No useful purpose would be served by repeating this here and I am both grateful for and content to accept both his analysis and his conclusion that the correct principle was that pronounced by Best J in *Vyvyan v Arthur* (1823) 1 B & C 410, 417, and approved by this House in *Dyson v Forster* [1909] AC 98:

> The general principle is, that if the performance of the covenant be beneficial to the reversioner, in respect of the lessor's demand, and to no other person, his assignee may sue upon it; but if it be beneficial to the lessor, without regard to his continuing owner of the estate, it is a mere collateral covenant, upon which the assignee cannot sue.

The Vice Chancellor stated his conclusion, at 1177:

> From these authorities I collect two things. First, that the acid test whether or not a benefit is collateral is that laid down by Best J, namely, is the covenant beneficial to the owner for the time being of the covenantee's land, and to no one else? Secondly, a covenant simply to pay a sum of money, whether by way of insurance premium, compensation or damages, is a covenant capable of touching and concerning the land provided that the existence of the covenant, and the right to payment thereunder, affects the value of the land in whomsoever it is vested for the time being.

It is objected that this states the matter too broadly because, for example, it is said that it would involve the conclusion that a simple covenant to pay an annuity of £x per annum to the owner for the time being of Blackacre would then be treated as a covenant touching and concerning the land because it would enhance the value of the land. This is, I think, to read the Vice Chancellor's words too literally, for it is, as it seems to me, implicit in them that he is referring to a monetary obligation related to something which issues out of or is to be done on or to the land. His approach to the problem (which, again, I respectfully adopt), emerges from the following passage from his judgment, at p 1174:

> The surety covenant is given as a support or buttress to covenants given by a tenant to a landlord. The covenants by the tenant relate not only to the payment of rent, but also to repair, insurance and use of the premises. All such covenants by a tenant in favour of the landlord touch and concern the land, ie, the reversion of the landlord. The performance of some covenants by tenants relates to things done on the land itself (eg, repair and user covenants). Other tenants' covenants (eg, payment of rent and insurance) require nothing to be done on the land itself. They are mere covenants for the payment of money. The covenant to pay rent is the major cause of the landlord's reversion having any value during the continuance of the term. Where there is privity of estate, the tenants' covenant to pay rent touches and concerns the land: *Parker v Webb* (1822) 3 Salk 4. As it seems to me, in principle a covenant by a third party guaranteeing the performance by the tenant of his obligations should touch and concern the reversion as much as do the tenants' covenants themselves. This view accords with what, to my mind, is the commercial common sense and justice of the case. When, as in the present case, the lease has been assigned on the terms that the sureties will guarantee performance by the assignee of the lease, justice and common sense ought to require the sureties, not the original tenant, to be primarily liable in the event of default by the assignee. So long as the reversion is not assigned, that will be the position. Why should the position between the original tenant and the sureties be rendered completely different just because the reversion has been assigned, a transaction wholly outside the control of the original tenant and the sureties?

I entirely agree and would add only this. It has been said that the surety's obligation is simply that of paying money and, of course, in a sense that its true if one looks only at the remedy which the landlord has against him in the event of default by the tenant. But for my part I do not think that this is a complete analysis. The tenant covenants that he will do or refrain from doing certain things which undoubtedly touch and concern the land. A surety covenants that those things shall be done or not done as the case may be. Now it is true that the remedy for breach will sound in damages only, but the primary obligation is the same, namely that which is covenanted to be done will be done. Take for instance the tenant's covenant to repair. There is nothing here requiring personal performance by the tenant. The effect of the covenant is that the tenant must procure the premises to be kept in repair. Equally, a guarantee by the surety of the repairing covenant is no more than a covenant or warranty that the guarantor will procure that the tenant, in turn, procures the premises to be kept in repair. The content of the primary obligation is, as it seems to me, exactly the same and if that of the tenant touches and concerns the land that of the surety must, as it seems to me, equally do so.

Formulations of definitive tests are always dangerous, but it seems to me that, without claiming to expound an exhaustive guide, the following provides a satisfactory working test for whether, in any given case, a covenant touches and concerns the land: (1) the covenant benefits only the reversioner for the time being, and if separated from the reversion ceases to be of benefit to the covenantee; (2) the covenant affects the nature, quality, mode of user or value of the land of the reversioner; (3) the covenant is not expressed to be personal (that is to say neither being given only to a specific reversioner nor in respect of the obligations only of a specific tenant); (4) the fact that a covenant is to pay a sum of money will not prevent it from touching and concerning the land so long as the three foregoing conditions are satisfied and the covenant is connected with something to be done on, to or in relation to the land.

For my part, I am entirely satisfied that the decision of the Court of Appeal in *Kumar v Dunning* [1987] 3 WLR 1167 was correct and was reached for the correct reasons. The instant case is indistinguishable in any material respect. Nothing I think turns upon the precise terms of the covenant in either case. It follows that I would dismiss this appeal.

[Templeman and Ackner LJJ agreed.]

Questions

1 Using the formula proposed by Oliver LJ, discuss which of the following covenants touches and concerns the land:

(i) covenant by a tenant to pay rent, rates and taxes;

(ii) covenant by a landlord to repair the premises;

(iii) covenant to renew a lease (see *Muller v Trafford* [1901] 1 Ch 54);

(iv) covenant to purchase the reversion (see *Woodall v Clifton* [1905] 2 Ch 257; cf *Griffiths v Pelton* [1958] Ch 205);

(v) covenant by a landlord to refund a security deposit paid by a tenant if upon expiration of the lease there was no breach (see *Hua Chiao Commercial Bank Ltd v Chiaphua Industries Ltd* [1987] AC 99).

Notes

1 Under general contract law, a benefit (but not a burden) of a contract, unless where otherwise expressly provided, may be assigned to a third party. The assignee is then

entitled to enforce the contract in his own right. On this basis a benefit of a covenant which does not touch and concern the land (personal covenant) if expressly assigned may be enforced by the assignee against the original party to the lease. For example, an option to purchase is a personal covenant. Such a covenant cannot be enforced by the assignee of the lease unless the covenant was expressly assigned with the lease (see *Esther Investments Pty Ltd v Cherrywood Pty Ltd* [1986] WAR 279). It should be pointed out that an option to renew the lease, unlike option to purchase, runs with the land, hence the assignee of the lease may take advantage of it even though the option was not specifically assigned with the lease (see *Weg Motors Ltd v Hales and Others* [1962] Ch 49).

2 Notwithstanding the assignment, the original parties remain liable under the principle of privity of contract (see *Moule v Garrett and Others* (1872) LR 7 Ex 101).

Assignment of the reversion

At common law, covenants touching and concerning the land run with the lease, but not with the reversion.[28] Thus, if L leases to T and before the lease expires L sells the freehold to L2, the latter cannot sue T for breach of any covenant except the covenant to pay rent. Section 3 of the Landlord and Tenant (Miscellaneous Provisions) Act (Ch No 189) replaced the common law:[29] It provides:

> (1) Rent reserved by a lease, and the benefit of a covenant or provision in a lease having reference to the subject matter of the lease and to be observed and performed by the lessee, and every condition of re-entry and other condition contained in a lease –
>
> (a) are annexed and incident to, and go with, the reversionary estate in the land or in any part of it immediately expectant on the term granted by the lease, notwithstanding severance of the reversionary estate; and
>
> (b) are capable of being recovered, received, enforced and taken advantage of by the person entitled, subject to the term, to the income of the whole or any part, as the case requires, of the land leased.
>
> (2) Sub-section (1) extends to a covenant to do an act relating to the land even if the subject matter was not in existence when the covenant was made.
>
> (3) The benefit of a condition of re-entry or forfeiture for a breach of a covenant or condition in a lease is capable of being enforced and taken advantage of by the person entitled, subject to the term, to the income of the whole or any part, as the case requires, of the land leased, even if he became, by conveyance or otherwise so entitled after the condition of re-entry or forfeiture had become enforceable.
>
> (4) This section does not make enforceable a condition of re-entry or other condition that was waived or released before the person concerned became entitled.
>
> (5) This section applies to –
>
> (a) leases made before 15 September 1975 (being the date of commencement of the pre-Independence Imperial Laws Replacement Act 1975), but with respect only to –
>
> (i) rent accruing due after that date; and

28 *Megarry and Wade: The Law of Real Property*, (6th edn, Sweet & Maxwell, London, 2000), p 905.

29 This section can be traced to the English Grantees of Reversions Act 1540 (32 Hen 8, c 34).

(ii) the benefit of a condition of re-entry or forfeiture for a breach committed after that date of a covenant, condition or provision contained in the lease; and

(b) leases made after that date.

By virtue of this section, breach of a covenant to pay rent or any other covenant 'having reference to the subject matter'[30] is enforceable by the grantee or assignee of the reversion. Section 4 of the Act imposes upon the assignee of the reversion the *obligation* of a covenant entered into by the original lessor 'with reference to the subject matter of the lease'.

4 Obligation of lessors' covenants

(1) If and as far as the lessor has power to bind the reversionary estate immediately expectant on the term granted by the lease, the obligation of a covenant entered into by a lessor with reference to the subject matter of the lease –

(a) is annexed and incident to, and goes with, the reversionary estate, or the several parts of it, notwithstanding severance of the reversionary estate; and

(b) may be taken advantage of and enforced by the person in whom the term is from time to time vested by conveyance, devolution in law or otherwise.

(2) If and as far as the lessor has power to bind the person from time to time entitled to the reversionary estate, the obligation may be taken advantage of and enforced against any person so entitled.

(3) This section applies to –

(a) leases made before 15 September 1975 (being the date of commencement of the pre-Independence Imperial Laws Replacement Act 1975), but so far only as relates to breaches of covenant committed after that date; and

(b) leases made after that date.

The following example may illustrate the above provision. Suppose L leases *Greenacre* to T for five years. L covenants, *inter alia,* to supply clean water to the premises for the duration of the lease. Before the lease expires, L sells *Greenacre* to L2. Under s 4 of the above Act, the covenant entered into by L binds L2 to supply water to the premises and T can accordingly enforce the covenant against him.

Neither privity of contract nor of estate

Where there is neither privity of contract nor privity of estate between the parties, the covenants in the lease are not enforceable by either party. Suppose L (original landlord) leases to T1 (original tenant) who then sub-leases to T2 (sub-lessee). There is no privity of contract between L and T2. Nor is there privity of estate between them since L is not T2's landlord. In this scenario, there is both privity of contract and privity of estate between L and T1. Likewise, by virtue of the sub-lease there is privity of contract and estate between T1 and T2. Thus, if T2 (tenant in possession) defaults in payment of his rent or breaches other covenants in the lease, L cannot sue him directly. L will have to sue T1 who will

30 This phrase means the same thing as 'touch and concern the land', see *Megarry and Wade: The Law of Real Property, op cit,* note 28, pp 972–73.

then sue T2 for breach of contract. There are, however, some exceptions to this rule. First, as we have seen, in case of express assignment of a benefit of a covenant the assignee is entitled to enforce the covenant in his own right.[31] Secondly, in equity, the burden of a covenant is enforceable if it is a *restrictive* covenant.[32] Thirdly, action may be possible where authorised by statute.[33]

Enforcement of covenants under the Land Registration Act

(i) Upon assignment of lease

A lease registered under the Land Registration Act may be transferred by an instrument in the prescribed form. Section 55 relevantly provides that:

> (4) On registration of a transfer of a lease –
>
> (a) the estate of the transferor, as specified in the transfer, with all rights, powers and privileges belonging to that estate passes to and vests in the transferee; and
>
> (b) the transferee becomes subject to and liable for the same requirements and liabilities to which he would have been subject and liable if he had been named originally in the lease as the lessee.
>
> (5) The rights, powers and privileges passing to the transferee by virtue of sub-section (4) include –
>
> (a) the right to sue on the lease the subject of the transfer; and
>
> (b) all interest in and right to recover a debt, sum of money or damages under the lease.
>
> (6) The operation of sub-section (5)(b) is not affected by reason only that the right of recovery is a chose in action.
>
> (7) This section does not prevent a court of competent jurisdiction giving effect to a trust affecting the debt, sum of money or damages referred to in sub-section (5)(b) where the transferee is a trustee for any other person.

On a literal reading, s 55(4)(a) and (b) seem to say that upon registration of a transfer of a lease *all* covenants, irrespective of whether or not they touch and concern the land, bind the transferee and that the latter can enforce any covenant in the original lease against the original lessor. However, there is no direct authority to support this proposition.

(ii) Upon sub-lease

As we have seen, where L leases to T and T sub-leases to ST, there is neither privity of contract nor privity of estate between L and ST. Where a sub-lease is created and registered under the Land Registration Act, s 54 provides:

31 See 'Notes' above.

32 See *Tulk v Moxhay* (1848) 2 Ph 774; 41 ER 1143. Restrictive covenants are discussed below in Chapter 8.

33 Section 3, Landlord and Tenant (Miscellaneous Provisions) Act (c 189) deems all covenants to run with the reversion (see *Arlesford Trading Co Ltd v Servansingh* [1971] 1 WLR 1080).

(4) In addition to the covenants declared by this Act to be implied in every lease, there shall be implied in every sub-lease the following covenant by the sub-lessor with the sub-lessee and his transferees:

that he will during the term hereby granted pay the rent reserved by and perform and observe the covenants and agreements contained in the original lease, and on his part to be paid performed and observed.

(5) The covenant implied by sub-section (4) is binding on the sub-lessor, his executors, administrators and trustees.

The effect of s 54(4) is that if T sub-leases to ST, all the terms of the headlease (ie, L and T's original lease) are implied in the sub-lease in addition to any other terms T and ST may have agreed upon. A literal reading of the section may suggest that the section gives L the power to enforce directly against ST all covenants in the headlease even though there is neither privity of estate nor privity of contract between L and ST. However, it is doubtful whether the court would give the section such a wide interpretation, which radically differs from the common law unless satisfied that that was the legislative intention. It is thought that the appropriate procedure would be for L to sue T because, under s 54(5) of the LRA, T is accountable if ST breaches any covenant in the headlease. Moreover, T is liable to L based on their original contract. Alternatively, L may terminate the headlease, which would effectively terminate the sub-lease (see s 54(6)(a) of the LRA). T may of course sue ST for breach of contract and for reimbursement.[34]

V REMEDIES FOR BREACH OF COVENANTS

Tenant's remedies

Where the landlord defaults in the performance of any covenant in the lease, the tenant may sue him for breach of contract and seek appropriate remedies under the ordinary principles of the law of contract. For example, if the landlord is in breach of covenant of quiet enjoyment, the tenant may sue him for damages and or seek an injunction to restrain the landlord from breaching the covenant.[35] The tenant may also terminate the lease, but only if the breach constitutes a repudiation of the lease agreement. The case below deals with the rights of a tenant to terminate a lease.

LAURINDA PTY LTD AND OTHERS v CAPALABA PARK SHOPPING CENTRE PTY LTD (1989) 85 ALR 183, High Court of Australia

[Capalaba, the defendant, was erecting a shopping arcade. It entered into an agreement (in the form of a deed) to lease shop 79 to Laurinda, the plaintiff, for a term of six years. Laurinda entered into possession and commenced paying rent though the lease was unregistered. In spite of constant reminders, Capalaba delayed for a period of 10 months to execute the appropriate forms to have the lease registered. Subsequently, Laurinda

34 *Moule v Garrett* (1872) LR 7 Ex 101.
35 *Lavender v Betts* [1942] 2 All ER 72.

terminated the lease citing Capalaba's conduct in failing to sign the forms as constituting a repudiation of its obligation under the lease. Laurinda sued for a declaration that it lawfully terminated the lease and for damages for breach of contract.]

BRENNAN J: Two questions arise: (1) was Capalaba's failure a breach of a term of the agreement for lease? If so, (2) was it a breach which entitled Laurinda to rescind? ... [His Honour answered the first question in the affirmative and continued.]

A right in one party to rescind a contract will arise when the other party repudiates a contract generally, but it may also arise when the other party repudiates a term of the contract. A right to rescind depends on the importance of the term repudiated. Here, the subject of the agreement was the granting of a legal lease for a term of six years. The implied promise by Capalaba to procure registration of an appropriate instrument was thus at the heart of the agreement. It was a promise of such importance to the promisee that it would not have entered into the contract unless it had been assured of substantial performance and this ought to have been apparent to the promisor. It answered the criterion of an essential promise in the sense that an outright repudiation of the promise would have entitled Laurinda to rescind. The criterion of an essential promise which I have stated in terms relevant to the present case is derived from the criterion expressed by Jordan CJ in *Tramways Advertising Pty Ltd v Luna Park* (NSW) Ltd (1938) 38 SR (NSW) 632 (at 641–42) and frequently adopted in this court, most recently in *Ankar Pty Ltd v National Westminster Finance (Australia) Ltd* (1987) 162 CLR 549 at 556; 70 ALR 641, but I have modified it by using the term 'substantial performance' rather than the usual formula of 'a strict or a substantial performance'. The modification is necessary when, no day for performance being stipulated and the subject matter of the promise not being such as to require strictly timeous performance, time is not of the essence of the promise either in law or in equity: *Canning v Temby* (1905) 3 CLR 419 at 425; *Louinder v Leis* [(1982) 149 CLR 509, at 533]. When time is not of the essence, the promisee must have been willing to enter into the contract without an assurance that the promise would be performed strictly, albeit with an assurance that the promise would be performed substantially. Thus, Laurinda would not have been entitled either at law or in equity to rescind the contract as soon as a reasonable time for procuring registration had elapsed. As Griffith CJ said in *Canning v Temby*, at 426:

> In one sense, of course, time is always of the essence of a contract to be performed within a reasonable time. But that is not the sense in which the term 'of the essence' is used.

Where an essential term – in the sense defined – is to be performed within a reasonable time, there being no stipulated day for performance, and that time passes without performance, the innocent party does not acquire a right to rescind unless the defaulting party repudiates or has repudiated his obligation to perform. Barwick CJ and Jacobs J observed in *Neeta (Epping) Pty Ltd v Phillips* (1974) 131 CLR 286 at 306; 3 ALR 151 at 167:

> Contracts for the sale of land, creating as they do equitable interests in the land, do not easily go off except pursuant to an express condition of the contract or pursuant to an express repudiation nor a repudiation clearly to be inferred.

The same observation may be applied to agreements for lease. More than a mere failure in timeous performance is necessary to warrant an inference of repudiation, but delay may be so serious as to amount to a refusal to perform and in such a case an innocent party has a right to rescind: see *De Soysa v De Pless Pol* [1912] AC 194 at 202–03; *Holland v Wiltshire* (1954) 90 CLR 409 at 420.

The difference between a contract which contains a stipulated day for performance of an essential term and a contract which, expressly or impliedly, requires performance within a reasonable time is important when the question is whether, on failure to perform within the time limited by the contract, the innocent party is entitled to rescind. In the former case, a right to rescind arises at law when the stipulated day passes; in the latter, that right does not necessarily arise when the reasonable time expires but only when repudiation is clearly to be inferred from the circumstances in which the delay occurs. Delay will amount to repudiation if the defaulting party 'evinces an intention no longer to be bound by the contract ... or shows that he intends to fulfil the contract only in a manner substantially inconsistent with his obligations and not in any other way': *Shevill v Builders Licensing Board* (1982) 149 CLR 620 at 625–26; 42 ALR 305; *Progressive Mailing House Pty Ltd v Tabali Pty Ltd* (1985) 157 CLR 17 at 33, 40; 57 ALR 609. If the inference to be drawn from the circumstances is that the defaulting party intends to perform an essential promise after some minor delay, repudiation cannot be inferred; but if the inference is that the defaulting party intends so to delay performance that the promisee will be substantially deprived of the benefit of the promise, repudiation can be inferred. The inference is not lightly drawn: *Progressive Mailing House Pty Ltd v Tabali Pty Ltd* (CLR at 32) ...

A right to rescind is one thing; fairness in the exercise of that right is another. In some circumstances, equity asserts a jurisdiction to restrain the exercise of a right to rescind. As I attempted to explain in *Louinder v Leis* (CLR at 532–36), a notice to complete does not make time of the essence of the contract when the contract itself does not do so, but it is a step towards lifting an equitable restraint on the exercise of a right to rescind which arises *aliunde*. Therefore, when a contract requires performance of an essential promise within a reasonable time and a valid notice to complete on or before a specified day is given by the innocent party, the significance of the notice is twofold: primarily, it fixes a day when, if the default is not remedied, the party in default will be held to have repudiated the promise; and, secondly, it will show that, for equity's purposes, it is fair for the innocent party to exercise that right: see *per* Fry J in *Green v Sevin* (1879) 13 Ch D 589 at 599, and *per* Isaacs J in *Maynard v Goode* (1926) 37 CLR 529 at 538. Where a contract contains a promise to be performed within a reasonable time, a notice to complete does not insert the time it prescribes into the contract and make that time of the essence, but the notice is evidence which may support the inference of repudiation, from which the innocent party's right to rescind arises and it clears the way for the exercise of that right.

When a reasonable time is prescribed for performance of an essential term of a contract, a notice to complete requiring performance of that term by a specified day can be given only if the party to whom it is given is already in breach of his contractual obligation: *Neeta (Epping) Pty Ltd v Phillips* (CLR at 299). But it would be futile to give a notice if, in the event of the default complained of persisting beyond the time limited by the notice, repudiation were not to be inferred from the circumstances then existing. Therefore, in considering whether the time limited by a notice is reasonable in such a case, it is necessary to consider whether an inference of repudiation would be drawn from non-performance if that were to persist beyond that time ... [His Honour discussed the facts of the case and continued.]

The onus to establish that the time was reasonable rested on Laurinda. The only evidence was that of Capalaba's solicitor who said that 'it would be unlikely to expect that you could get a shopping centre lease stamped and registered within 14 days' although application for expedited stamping and expedited registration could be made to the relevant authorities. Having regard to this fact and the factors earlier mentioned, I should think that the 13 days effectively allowed for registration was unreasonably short. I would not draw an inference merely from Capalaba's non-performance in registering the lease, which continued until the time limited by the letter had expired, that Capalaba had repudiated the contract.

However, his Honour found that Capalaba simply declined to perform its obligation 'until it suited it' and that Laurinda 'was entitled to regard the conduct of [Capalaba] as repudiatory in a relevant sense and to treat the contract as discharged'. The finding was based in part upon facts which emerged at the trial, showing that Capalaba had deliberately delayed in executing the lease, securing the mortgagee's consent, stamping and registering the lease (or tendering a registrable lease) because Capalaba's commercial interests were better served by delay.

Repudiation is not ascertained by an inquiry into the subjective state of mind of the party in default; it is to be found in the conduct, whether verbal or other, of the party in default which conveys to the other party the defaulting party's inability to perform the contract or promise or his intention not to perform it or to fulfil it only in a manner substantially inconsistent with his obligations and not in any other way. In *Freeth v Burr* (1874) LR 9 CP 208 at 213, Lord Coleridge CJ spoke of acts or conduct which 'do or do not amount to an intimation of an intention to abandon and altogether to refuse performance of the contract' or of acts and conduct which 'evince an intention no longer to be bound by the contract'. This was followed by the Earl of Selborne LC in *Mersey Steel and Iron Co (Ltd) v Naylor, Benzon & Co* (1884) 9 App Cas 434 at 438–39:

> I am content to take the rule as stated by Lord Coleridge in *Freeth v Burr* ... which is in substance, as I understand it, that you must look at the actual circumstances of the case in order to see whether the one party to the contract is relieved from its future performance by the conduct of the other; you must examine what that conduct is, so as to see whether it amounts to a renunciation, to an absolute refusal to perform the contract, such as would amount to a rescission if he had the power to rescind, and whether the other party may accept it as a reason for not performing its part ...

The question whether an inference of repudiation should be drawn merely from continued failure to perform requires an evaluation of the delay from the standpoint of the innocent party. Would a reasonable person in the shoes of the innocent party clearly infer that the other party would not be bound by the contract or would fulfil it only in a manner substantially inconsistent with that party's obligations and in no other way? Different minds may easily arrive at different answers. If one looks merely at Capalaba's conduct in the circumstances known to Laurinda when the letter of 21 August 1986 was written, Capalaba's failure to register the lease did not amount to repudiation. The shortness of the time for registration limited by that letter and the absence of an intimation in the letter that that time would be regarded as of the essence deprive the letter of 21 August of the effect which a valid notice to complete would have had. Looking solely at Capalaba's delay in registering the lease, the position was analogous to that which Dixon J found to exist in *Diamond v Moore* (1931) 45 CLR 159 where, in a dissent which turned on the facts, he said (at 179–80):

> But if they wished to rely upon the lessor's failure to perform her contract within a period of time as distinguished from some refusal by her to observe the obligations imposed upon her, it was necessary for the lessee to name some time by which performance was demanded, and in doing so to fix a period sufficient to enable her solicitors to receive her instructions.

I would not infer repudiation merely from non-registration within the time limited by the letter. However, I am unable to agree with the Full Court who, accepting that the notice was ineffectual, held that 'until an effectual notice was given the delay continued but that alone was insufficient to make evident any intention on the part of [Capalaba] that it would not be bound by the contract'. Repudiation may be established without proof of an effective notice to complete. The absence of an effective notice means that the other evidence must be examined to determine whether a clear inference of repudiation should be drawn, but it does not preclude the drawing of that inference.

If the evidence showed no more than 14 days of continued non-registration of the lease after 21 August 1986, I would not draw the inference of repudiation. But the letter of 21 August was followed by Capalaba's solicitors' letter of 3 September 1986. After assurances that the lease had been executed and the costs of stamping and registration had been paid, advice was given in March 1986 that the lessee's stamped parts of the lease would be provided as soon as the lease was available after its return from Melbourne expected 'in the not too distant future', but there was no further communication from Capalaba or its solicitors. Then, stimulated by Laurinda's letter of 21 August 1986, Capalaba's solicitors, on the eve of the expiration of the time limited, advise merely that they have referred the letter to their client 'for its response', undertaking to advise their 'client's instructions'. The long and unexplained delay from March to September 1986 ending with a letter stating that the solicitors required further instructions with respect to completing what had been promised over five months earlier is sufficient foundation for the drawing of an inference of repudiation. It is the inference which Laurinda drew and although it cannot be said that no other reasonable inference is open, it is a reasonable inference which can be clearly drawn. I have vacillated in arriving at this conclusion but, having arrived at it, I would allow the appeal and restore the judgment of Connolly J.

[Mason CJ, Deane, Dawson and Gaudron JJ in separate judgments agreed.]

Notes

1 Though the case deals mainly with delay in performing a term of a contract in a lease, the principles expounded are of general application to breaches of any term of a lease. Essentially, a mere breach of a covenant in a lease does not give rise to the right to terminate the lease.

2 In practice, ordinary tenants are probably unlikely to sue the landlord for breach of covenant because they cannot afford the cost or fear that the landlord might evict them if they did. Sometimes tenants withhold rent in order to force the landlord, for example, to repair the leased premises. Can you envisage any legal difficulties with this 'remedy'?

3 Where the landlord is in breach of covenant to repair the premises, the tenant, subject to service of notice of disrepair on the landlord, may carry out the repairs and deduct the cost from outstanding rent. If the landlord sues the tenant for the shortfall, the tenant can make a cross-claim or set-off for the expenses incurred in carrying out the repairs (see *British Anzani (Felixstow) Ltd v International Marine Management (UK) Ltd* [1980] QB 137). In equity, there is a wider scope for a set-off plea (see *Knockholt Pty Ltd v Graff* [1975] Qd R 88).

Question

Would you advocate statutory intervention to protect tenants against landlords? Discuss the sort of intervention you would like to see and the advantages and disadvantages of any such intervention.

Landlord's remedies

The landlord can sue the tenant for breach of contract and seek appropriate remedies under the law of contract. In addition, the landlord has the following remedies, which are unique to the law of leases.

Distress

This is an ancient remedy of self-help. If rent was in arrears, the landlord could enter the leased premises and take possession of goods on the premises to the value of rent owing. At common law, the landlord had no right to sell the goods without a court order.[36] It would seem that the common law rule is still applicable in 'New Guinea'. In 'Papua', the Distress Replevin and Ejectment Act 1867 (Queensland, adopted),[37] gives the landlord power to sell the distrained goods, without resort to the courts, if the rent due is not paid after five days (s 58).

Forfeiture

Forfeiture is the termination of a lease by the lessor before the term has expired. Under the underlying law the lessor is only entitled to enforce forfeiture for breach of a condition and not breach of a covenant unless the right of forfeiture is expressly reserved in the lease. In practice, the distinction between a condition and a covenant is probably not significant. This is due partly to the fact that most formal leases reserve to the landlord the power of re-entry in the event of breach of any term. In addition, s 50(b) of the Land Registration Act implies a term that the lessor has the power of re-entry for breach of any express or implied condition or covenant in a registered lease.[38] Section 50(b) relevantly reads:

> ... in case the rent or part of the rent is in arrear for a period of six calendar months, or in case default is made in the fulfilment of a covenant whether expressed or implied in the lease on the part of the lessee and is continued for a period of six calendar months, or in case the repairs required by the notice are not completed within the time specified in the notice, the lessor may re-enter and take possession of the demised property.

Readers should note that the breach must continue for a period of six months before the landlord can exercise the power of re-entry. However, the parties may agree for a shorter or longer period than six months (s 100 of the LRA). Also, note that except in case of breach of covenant to repair,[39] there is no statutory requirements for the lessor to give notice of breach of covenant before forfeiture.

Landlord may enforce forfeiture by 'self-help' or judicial proceedings.

---

36 See generally *Megarry and Wade: The Law of Real Property, op cit*, note 28, pp 891–94.

37 See James, *Land Law and Policy in Papua New Guinea, op cit*, note 17, p 108, n 68.

38 See also ss 4 and 5, Summary Ejectment Act (Ch No 202).

39 Compare with breach of covenants implied in a State lease, see Chapter 7.

(i) Self-help

Where the lessee is in breach and the right of re-entry accrues, the lessor is entitled to enter physically and take possession without resort to the courts. If the lessee resists the lessor may use reasonable force to eject him.[40] Provided no more than reasonable force is used the lessor is not civilly or criminally liable for his action.[41] Self-help is a fast and cheap remedy but is inadvisable where there is a risk of breach of the peace.

(ii) Judicial proceedings – summary ejectment

Where the lessee is in breach and the lessor is entitled to re-enter, the lessor may commence proceedings for possession. Proceedings to regain possession are usually instituted under the Summary Ejectment Act (Ch No 202). Section 3 thereof stipulates the procedure for re-entry upon termination of a lease by effluxion or for breach of covenant other than covenant to pay rent.[42]

Section 3 Proceedings for possession on determination of lease

(1) Where –

(a) the term or interest of a lessee of premises held by him has ended or has been duly determined; and

(b) the lessee, or (if the lessee does not actually occupy the premises or occupies only a part of the premises) a person by whom the whole or part of the premises is then actually occupied, neglects or refuses to quit and deliver up possession of the premises or of the part of the premises, as the case may be,

the lessor of the premises may make a complaint to a magistrate of a District Court against the person for the recovery of the premises, or of the part of the premises, and the magistrate may issue a summons in the prescribed form to that person.

(2) Where the person to whom the summons is directed under sub-section (1) –

(a) does not appear before a District Court at the time named in the summons; or

(b) appears and does not satisfy the court that there is reasonable cause why he should not give possession of the premises or of the part of the premises of which he is then in possession,

and still neglects or refuses to deliver up possession of the premises or of the part of the premises of which he is then in possession, then on proof of the matter of the complaint the court may order him to deliver up possession of the premises or of the part of the premises to the complainant, either immediately or on or before a day named in the order.

(3) Where an order made under sub-section (2) is not obeyed, a magistrate of a District Court may, at the request of the complainant, issue a warrant in the prescribed form directed to a member of the Police Force requiring him, within a period specified in the warrant, not being more than 30 clear days from the date of the warrant –

---

40 *Hemmings and Wife v The Stoke Poges Golf Club and Another* [1920] 1 KB 720, cited with approval in *Jivetuo and Another v The Independent State of Papua New Guinea* [1984] PNGLR 174, at 176.

41 *Jivetuo and Another v The Independent State of PNG*. See also s 275 of the Criminal Code (Ch No 262).

42 The procedure to enforce forfeiture for breach of covenant to pay rent is governed by ss 4 and 5, see below.

(a) to enter into the premises by force and with assistants if necessary; and

(b) to give possession of the premises or of the part of the premises to the complainant.

(4) In a complaint under this section against a lessee or occupier the complainant may add a claim not exceeding K500.00 for rent or mesne profits (or both) down to the day appointed for the hearing or to any preceding day named in the complaint, and any misdescription in the nature of the claim may be amended at the hearing.

(5) If the lessor does not appear at the time named in the summons, the court shall dismiss the complaint.

The following case is an illustration of proceedings brought under the Summary Ejectment Act.

REGIONE v PALMS TAVERN PTY LTD [1988–89] PNGLR 150, National Court of Justice

BREDMEYER J: This is an appeal against an order of the Port Moresby District Court dated 4 October 1988 striking out two complaints. The first complaint relates to Lot 5 on Deposited Plan 34, a block of land situated at Badili. It states that the plaintiff is the owner of Lot 5 and leased the Lot to the defendant for 35 years. The defendant was required to pay all rates and taxes. The complaint states that the defendant has breached the lease in that it has failed to pay rates and taxes since 1982 to date and that it has sub-divided the land into three allotments and sub-leased it without the consent of the plaintiff. The complainant claims: (a) possession of the premises; (b) damages for breach of the agreement; and (c) mesne profits from the date of the service of the notice to quit until delivery of possession. The second complaint is between the same parties and for some curious reason also has the same District Court number – No 12 of 1988. It relates to the adjoining Lot 6 and recites that the plaintiff leased this land to the defendant for 15 years and that the defendant has breached the lease in the following ways:

(a) a rental instalment of K256 for the month of September 1987 was not paid on time and when it was later paid that payment was rejected;

(b) the defendant failed to pay rates to the National Capital District Interim Commission from 1982 to date;

(c) the defendant failed to 'replace, repair and keep and maintain in a clean and good condition' the interior of the building and the fixed improvements.

The plaintiff claims: (a) possession of the premises; (b) damages for breach of the said agreement; and (c) mesne profits from the date of serving the notice to quit until delivery of possession.

The defendant requested particulars of the claim for damages and for mesne profits and, although these were not formally supplied, the defendant tendered an affidavit setting out the arrears of rates owed to the National Capital District Interim Commission. The arrears to May 1988 on Lot 5 were K18,724.85 and on Lot 6 were K16,392.28. After numerous adjournments and preliminary objections in the District Court, the magistrate, on 4 October 1988, struck out the complaints, said the case was to be referred to the National Court, and ordered each party to pay its own costs. The reasons for the striking out were twofold. The first was that, although the Summary Ejectment Act (Ch No 202) was not pleaded in either complaint, the appellant was seeking to rely on it. The magistrate ruled that this case did not come within ss 3, 4, 5 or 6 of the Act and hence the District Court had no jurisdiction to hear the case for ejectment. Secondly, the learned magistrate considered that the damages claimed exceeded K10,000 and thus exceeded the jurisdiction of the District Court.

I consider that the complaints were correctly dismissed by the magistrate although I differ with him slightly on the reasons. The Summary Ejectment Act (Ch No 202) confers power on the District Court to give ejectment orders in the circumstances set out in ss 3, 4, 5 and 6 of the Act. I consider that s 3 properly applies to the facts of these two complaints. Section 3 reads:

Proceedings for possession on determination of lease

(1) Where –

(a) the term or interest of a lessee of premises held by him has ended or has been duly determined; and

(b) ...

the lessor of premises may make a complaint to the Magistrate of a District Court against the person for the recovery of the premises ...

Each lease has a clause allowing the landlord to re-enter on breach of a covenant. The complaints do not recite that the landlord has re-entered, indeed it is clear that he has not re-entered and the defendant lessee is still in possession of each Lot. Re-entry is also known as forfeiture, see *Halsbury's Laws of England* (3rd edn), Vol 23, para 1389. At para 1395, it states:

> Actual entry is not necessary in order to take advantage of the forfeiture. Where the cause of forfeiture is complete, the landlord can bring an action to recover possession, and the bringing of the action is equivalent to actual entry.

So this action, if proved, amounts to a due determination of the lease and thus brings it within the scope of s 3.

Section 3(4) of the Summary Ejectment Act provides:

> (4) in a complaint under this section against a lessee or occupier the complainant may add a claim not exceeding K500 for rent or mesne profits (or both) down to the day appointed for hearing or to any preceding day named in the complaint ...

It is clear to me that the plaintiff is claiming much more than K500 on each complaint. In a situation like this, the plaintiff can state in the complaint that he claims K10,000 which is the limit of the District Court's jurisdiction, and abandon the excess above K10,000, or he could say the same thing to the magistrate at a hearing. It would have been appropriate for the plaintiff to have said that, as the defendant was applying to have the case struck out as exceeding the jurisdiction of the District Court under s 21 of the District Courts Act (Ch No 40). As there was not such application I consider that the magistrate was entitled to regard the claim as being outside his jurisdiction.

A minor reason for dismissing the complaint in relation to Lot 6 relates to the claim that one instalment of rent for K256 was outstanding for the month of September 1987. The complaint alleged that that was a breach of covenant and was one of the breaches which justified an order for recovery of possession. Under s 4 of the Summary Ejectment Act, recovery of premises when the rent is in arrears is only possible when the lease is held on a weekly, monthly or quarterly tenancy or for a term not exceeding three years. The lease of Lot 6 is a lease for 15 years.

I consider the learned magistrate was right in dismissing these complaints and thereby paving the way for the plaintiff to bring the same action if he wants to in the National

Court. If he does do so, he should combine the two complaints in the one action. I also consider that it is in the plaintiff's best interests to do so because the National Capital District Interim Commission can sue him for the K35,000 land rates which are outstanding. Even though under the leases Palms Tavern Pty Ltd is required to pay those rates, the plaintiff is primarily responsible to pay them. If the plaintiff were to proceed in the District Court, the only way he could do so would be by abandoning the excess. By so doing he is not able to sue Palms Tavern Pty Ltd for the excess, yet he remains liable to the Interim Commission for the whole sum.

The appeal is dismissed with costs granted to the respondent.

Appeal dismissed.

Notes

In *Harman Gawi v PNG Ready Mixed Concrete Pty Ltd* [1984] PNGLR 74, the Supreme Court held that proceedings for recovery of possession of land under the Summary Ejectment Act are intended to provide a quick remedy to people who have a clear title to land. Accordingly, the Act does not apply where the title to land is in dispute or unclear (*per* Kapi Dep CJ, at 77, and McDermott J at 79).

Breach by non-payment of rent

Special provision apply under ss 4 and 5 of the Summary Ejectment Act (Ch No 202) for recovery of possession where the tenant defaults in the payment of rent:

Section 4 Recovery of premises when rent is in arrears

(1) Subject to this section where the rent payable by a lessee holding premises by the week, month, or quarter, or a longer term not exceeding three years, is in arrear for –

- (a) 10 days in the case of a weekly tenancy; or
- (b) 21 days in the case of a monthly tenancy; or
- (c) 30 days in the case of a quarterly tenancy; or
- (d) 42 days in the case of a tenancy for a longer term,

the lessor may, without formal demand or re-entry, make a complaint to a magistrate of a District Court who may issue a summons in the prescribed form directed to the lessee, and the service of the summons stands in place of a demand or re-entry.

(2) The power conferred on a lessor by sub-section (1) maybe exercised only –

- (a) if a right of re-entry for the non-payment of rent has not been expressly conferred on the lessor by agreement with the lessee, on the expiration of the relevant period referred to in sub-section (1)(a), (b), (c) or (d); or
- (b) if a right of re-entry has been conferred on the lessor by agreement with the lessee –
  - (i) on the accrual of the right of re-entry in accordance with the terms of the agreement; or
  - (ii) at the expiration of the relevant period referred to in Paragraph (a),

  whichever first occurs.

(3) Where there is a tenancy and no agreement as to its duration, the lessee shall, for the purposes of this section, be deemed to hold the premises by the month.

(4) If the lessee pays into a District Court all the rent in arrear and the costs at least five clear days before the day appointed for the hearing of the complaint, the complaint shall be deemed to be withdrawn.

(5) If –

(a) the lessee does not make the payments specified in sub-section (4); and

(b) does not appear at the time named in the summons, or, if appearing, does not show reasonable cause why the premises should not be recovered,

the District Court may, on proof of the matter of the complaint, order the lessee to deliver up possession of the premises to the complainant, immediately or on or before a day named in the order.

(6) Where an order under sub-section (5) is not obeyed, a magistrate of a District Court may, at the request of the complainant issue a warrant in the prescribed form directed to a member of the Police Force requiring him, within a period specified in the warrant, not being more than 30 clear days from the date of the warrant –

(a) to enter by force and with assistants if necessary, into the premises; and

(b) to give possession of the premises to the complainant.

(7) From the time of the execution of the warrant issued under sub-section (6) –

(a) the complainant holds the premises discharged of the lease; and

(b) the lessee and all persons claiming by, through or under him are barred from all relief so long as the order under sub-section (5) is not reversed.

Section 5 Recovery of possession by lessor

(1) Where –

(a) a lessee holding premises at a rent under a demise or agreement, written or oral, who is in arrear for two months, deserts the premises and leaves them uncultivated or unoccupied so that no sufficient distress can be had to countervail the arrears of rent; and

(b) no right or power of re-entry in case of the non-payment of rent is given or reserved by the demise or agreement, to the lessor, a District Court may, at the request of the lessor, his lawyer or agent and on proof of the matters specified in Paragraphs (a) and (b), issue a warrant directed to a member of the Police Force requiring him –

(c) to enter and inspect the premises; and

(d) to affix or cause to be affixed on some conspicuous part of the premises a notice in writing specifying the day (not sooner than 14 days from the affixing of the notice) on which he will return to inspect the premises a second time.

(2) If the lessee or some person on his behalf pays the rent in arrear into the District Court that issued the warrant at least two clear days before the day specified in the notice affixed under sub-section (1)(d), the warrant shall be deemed to have been withdrawn.

(3) Where on the second inspection referred to in sub-section (1)(d) –

(a) the lessee or some person on his behalf does not appear and pay to the member of the Police Force the rent in arrear; or

(b) there is not a sufficient distress on the premises,

the District Court may issue a warrant directed to a member of the Police Force requiring him, on or before a day to be named in the warrant, to enter into the premises and put the lessor into possession of the premises.

(4) On the execution of a warrant under sub-section (3), the lease of the premises to the lessee as to any demise contained in the lease becomes void.

Questions

1 Compare and contrast the conditions and procedure for the recovery of possession under ss 4 and 5. Discuss possible reasons for the difference.

2 Your client, LL, the landlord, informs you that T, his tenant, is in arrears with his rent. LL wants you to institute legal proceedings to evict T. Assume that you want to proceed under the Summary Ejectment Act. Which provision would be the most appropriate? If you need further facts to answer the question, state them and the reasons why you want more information.

Waiver of right to enforce forfeiture

When a breach occurs which entitles the lessor to re-enter, the lessor may waive his right of forfeiture. Waiver may be express or implied from the lessor's conduct.

SEGAL SECURITIES LTD v THOSEBY [1963] 1 QB 887, Queen's Bench Division

[The tenant was in breach of the covenant to use the premises for the purpose of a private residence. The landlord sent her a statutory notice to remedy the breach within 28 days. Before the notice had expired, by a letter headed 'without prejudice', the landlord demanded the rent payable in advance for the ensuing quarter. The letter stated that the 'demand and receipt for rent is made or given without prejudice to the service of the notice ... and to any breaches of covenant in respect of user'. The tenant sent a cheque for the rent but the landlord sent it back. Shortly thereafter, the landlord commenced these proceedings claiming, *inter alia*, forfeiture for breach of covenant of use. The tenant denied breach of covenant and, alternatively, relied on the demand for rent as constituting waiver.]

SACHS J [His Honour found that the tenant was in breach of the covenant as alleged, he turned to consider whether there had been a waiver]: When one approaches the law relating to waiver of forfeiture, one comes upon a field – one might say a minefield – in which it is necessary to tread with diffidence and warily.

In this field of law, one point, however, is plain and was conceded by counsel for the landlord. The law as to the effect of the acceptance of rent 'without prejudice' must be taken as that stated in a classic passage in the judgment of Parker J in *Matthews v Smallwood* [[1910] 1 Ch 777, 786] ... This well known exposition of the common law rule that acceptance of rent without prejudice is in law a waiver, reads: 'It is also, I think, reasonably clear upon the cases that whether the act, coupled with the knowledge, constitutes a waiver is a question which the law decides, and therefore it is not open to a lessor who has knowledge of the breach to say "I will treat the tenancy as existing, and I will receive the rent, or I will take advantage of my power as landlord to distrain; but I tell you that all I shall do will be without prejudice to my right to re-enter, which I intend to reserve"'. That is a position which he is not entitled to take up. If, knowing of the breach, he does distrain, or does receive the rent, then by law he waives the breach, and nothing which he can say by way of protest against the law will avail him anything.

It is thus a matter of law that once rent is accepted a waiver results. The question of *quo animo* it is accepted in forfeiture cases is irrelevant in relation to such acceptance. (I would mention that of course that is not so where the acceptance of rent has to be considered after the expiry of a lease by effluxion of time or notice – a distinction which has been adverted to in more than one authority.) Where forfeiture is involved, in essence once the landlord has knowledge of a past breach, the law thus treats the rent as a piece of cake equivalent to the land out of which it derives: its nutritional qualities in the landlord's hands being unaffected by attaching to it the label 'without prejudice', the law treats that attachment as having no effect.

Whether a demand for rent made without prejudice similarly operates as a waiver has, apparently, not been specifically decided. When one looks at the authorities, it is, however, clear that a demand can operate as a waiver in the same way as an acceptance: an instance of this view is to be found in the opinion of Bramwell B in *Croft v Lumley* [(1858) 6 HLC 672, 705]. That demand is often stated in textbooks and authorities to need to be 'unqualified' or 'unequivocal' – words that seem to have originated before Parker J's view of the law became fully accepted, and at a time when the position of a receipt of rent 'without prejudice' was still in doubt. Nowadays, however, a word such as 'unqualified' seems redundant where the demand itself speaks specifically of 'rent' ...

At this stage it is right to mention that there was for a long time much able argument before me, and much discussion of authorities on the question whether the continued breach of covenant in the present case was a series of continuing breaches within the meaning of those words as they apply to breaches of covenants to repair, or whether, on the other hand, once it was discovered and known to the landlord that the tenant was in breach the landlord only had a single election. It was urged by counsel for the tenant that once the landlord had thus accepted rent he could not in future play cat and mouse with the tenant and bide the time for enforcing a forfeiture ... I think, however, *Doe d Ambler v Woodbridge* (1829) 9 B & C 376, although the covenant was in quite different terms, binds me to hold that whatever may be the position in relation to user for other types of business, yet, when it is user by lodgers, the breach is a continuing one within the meaning of the phrase as I have used it.

One thus has to consider the position on the basis that this is a case where, according to the rule in *Penton v Barnett* [1898] 1 QB 276 there were a fresh series of breaches after 6 July of which the landlord is entitled, subject to any waiver, to take advantage without serving a further notice under s 146 of the Law of Property Act 1925.

With that rule in mind, I now turn to the important and decisive question as to the circumstances in which a demand for or acceptance of rent payable in advance constitutes a waiver of breaches during the period covered by the rent demanded. Clearly it cannot be a waiver of future breaches of which the landlord has no advance knowledge ... Equally clearly, an acceptance of rent in advance does waive a once and for all – that is to say, a non-continuing – breach in the past: such a waiver applies both to the past and to the period covered by the rent.

As regards continuing breaches, it seems to me that, in the absence of express agreement, the acceptance of rent in advance can at highest only waive those breaches that are at the time of demand known to be continuing, and to waive them for such period as it is definitely known they will continue. When it is a question of estimating the chances as to whether the tenant's breach will continue, the position is, in my view, different, irrespective of whether those chances are high or low. The object of a covenant by which rent has to be paid in advance is to obtain a certain security for that payment ... A landlord cannot, to my mind, lightly be deprived of the benefit of such rights: he cannot be put in the position of having to wait until the end of the period covered by the rent before demanding or accepting it merely because there are chances that the tenant may so break or continue in breach of covenant as to render himself liable to forfeiture.

Taking seriatim the breaches which are relevant and the submissions made by counsel for the tenant in relation to them, one turns first, of course, to the pre-8 June breaches. The payment of rent due on 24 March clearly waived all breaches before that date, and it may just be arguable that the landlord's knowledge in the particular circumstances of this case, was such that the landlord knew definitely that the breach would continue throughout the ensuing quarter: if so, there would have been a waiver as regards also the breaches up to 8 June. But anyway those breaches were waived by the demand for rent made on 25 June. That demand of 25 June, as already indicated, waived all breaches up to the time that the 8 June notice under s 146 of the Law of Property Act 1925, was issued and, therefore, the landlord cannot rely in this action on those breaches as constituting a foundation for bringing this action.

What, however, is the position as regards those breaches which occurred between 6 July and the date of the issue of the writ? Counsel for the tenant argued persuasively that at the time of the 25 June demand the landlord had such knowledge of the state of affairs that the landlord must have known definitely that the tenant would remain in breach after the notice had expired. Counsel also advanced other arguments as to why the knowledge of what he termed 'the state of affairs generally' was such that the demand operated as a waiver. These arguments were attractive, even though not supported by any questions on the subject of such knowledge put to, or answers given by, Mrs Segal. I do not, however, think that the tenant, even in the present case, can say that the landlord must be taken to have had definite knowledge that the breaches would continue after the expiration of the notice. Incidentally, in that respect, one observes that the tenant has in fact now told the ladies in question to go, and they have gone.

Nor do I think that any argument favourable to the tenant's case can be founded on the breaches during the period of 25 June to 6 July.

It follows that in the upshot I feel bound to hold that the plea of waiver does not succeed.

Question

LL leases his high covenant house in Boroko to T for a period of five years. LL reserves a right of re-entry in the event of breach of any term expressed or implied in the lease. T is in breach of the agreement to maintain the house in a tenantable repair and rent is in arrears for three months. Assume that LL is your client. She wants you to terminate the lease and to commence proceedings for re-entry. Before you proceed as instructed, T (having heard from a third party of the impending proceedings) sends LL a cheque of K2,000 by way of part payment of arrears of rent. LL asks you whether she can keep the money but proceed with her legal action to eject T. Discuss the practical and legal factors you would consider in advising LL.

Relief against forfeiture

Where the lessee is in breach of the tenancy agreement and the lessor, rightfully, determines the lease, the lessee may seek judicial relief against forfeiture. The effect of relief is that in spite of the breach, which entitles forfeiture the lease is restored to its original position.[43] The judicial power to grant relief against forfeiture is both inherent and statutory.

Equity

The enforcement of forfeiture entails loss to the lessee of proprietary interest in land. Under the underlying law the Court of Equity,[44] being a court of justice, always regarded the proviso for re-entry for non-payment of rent as merely security for the rent. Hence, if the landlord could be restored to his position by payment of arrears of rent and other moneys due, including costs and expenses to which the landlord had been put, the court could grant the tenant relief against forfeiture of his tenancy.[45] The following case discusses these principles.

GILL AND ANOTHER v LEWIS AND ANOTHER [1956] 2 QB 1, Court of Appeal

[The defendants, Lewis and Wright, held in joint tenancy a lease of two houses owned by the plaintiffs. They proved to be bad payers of rent, always falling in arrears. The landlord instituted proceedings for possession and recovery of rent in arrears. At the time of the action, Wright was in prison serving a sentence for indecent assault on boys committed on the premises. Though writs were served upon both men, neither appeared and a default judgment was given in favour of the plaintiff. However, before the judge signed the judgment, the defendants paid all arrears of rent and the costs. The court thereupon granted relief against forfeiture. The plaintiff appealed.]

JENKINS JJ: On the part of the plaintiff landlords it is urged that the court's jurisdiction in this matter is a discretionary jurisdiction; and, while it is conceded that in the ordinary way the court will make the order as a matter of course when satisfied that the landlord has received, or has been tendered, all that is due to him for rent and for costs, that is not a wholly inflexible rule, for the conduct of the tenant may be looked into, and if upon looking into his conduct it may appear that it would be inequitable or unfair to grant relief, the court ought, in the exercise of its discretion, to refuse relief.

As ground on which, in his submission, relief should have been refused by the judge in the present case, Mr Grundy relied, in effect, on three matters. The first was the previous history of the difficulties which the landlords had experienced in extracting the rent from the defendants; the second was the elusive habits of the defendants, which led to difficulties of service; and the third was the defendant Lewis's conviction of the two acts of indecent

---

43 *Gill and Another v Lewis and Another* [1956] 2 QB 1, see extract below.

44 The National and Supreme Courts have jurisdiction to grant equitable relief under their general powers to apply the principles of the Court of Equity, see *Adoption of Common Law*, Schedule 2.2, Constitution of Papua New Guinea (Ch No 1). The District Courts may also give equitable remedies where a case is within their monetary jurisdiction, see *Wine v Giglmai* [1990] PNGLR 462, at 468–69, see extract above, p 306.

45 *Howard v Fanshawe* [1895] 2 Ch 581, at 588, *per* Sterling J. See also *Shiloh Spinners Ltd v Harding* [1973] AC 691, at 722, *per* Lord Wilberforce.

assault, committed actually upon a part of the demised premises. Taking all those matters into consideration the judge (says Mr Grundy) ought to have come to the conclusion that the defendants here were so wholly unmeritorious that it would be inequitable to grant them relief so as to saddle the landlords for a further period with such undesirable tenants.

On the other hand, Mr Rochford, for the defendants, says that, although there may be exceptions, a case must be an exceptional one indeed for the court to refuse relief on other grounds when all the rent and costs have been paid up. He does not go so far, I think, as to say that the court would never refuse relief, but he says that the court would only do so in very exceptional circumstances, such as do not exist in this case ...

As to the conclusion of the whole matter, in my view, save in exceptional circumstances, the function of the court in exercising this equitable jurisdiction is to grant relief when all that is due for rent and costs has been paid up, and (in general) to disregard any other causes of complaint that the landlord may have against the tenant. The question is whether, provided all is paid up, the landlord will not have been fully compensated; and the view taken by the court is that if he gets the whole of his rent and costs, then he has got all he is entitled to so far as rent is concerned, and extraneous matters of breach of covenant, and so forth, are, generally speaking, irrelevant.

But there may be very exceptional cases in which the conduct of the tenants has been such as, in effect, to disqualify them from coming to the court and claiming any relief or assistance whatever. The kind of case I have in mind is that of a tenant falling into arrear with the rent of premises which he was notoriously using as a disorderly house: it seems to me that in a case of that sort if the landlord brought an action for possession for non-payment of rent and the tenant applied to the court for relief, the court, on being apprised that the premises were being consistently used for immoral purposes, would decline to give the tenant any relief or assistance which would in any way further his use or allow the continuance of his use or the house for those immoral purposes. In a case of that sort it seems to me that it might well be going too far to say that the court must disregard the immoral user of the premises and assist the guilty tenant by granting him relief.

I cannot, however, find any facts in the present case approaching the exceptional state of affairs I have in mind. Here we have the previous actions for rent, but, in my view, those are not material; and it will be remembered that Rigby LJ said in *Newbolt v Bingham* (1895) 72 LT 852 that he knew of no case where a court of equity had refused relief because actions had had to be brought on previous occasions to recover rent. Nor, in my view, can anything really be made of the difficulty experienced in finding the two defendants for the purpose of bringing proceedings against them to recover the rent. Other breaches of covenant are hinted at, but none of them is clearly dealt with in the evidence, and I do not think it can affect the result so far as the present case is concerned. If there are indeed other breaches of covenant, then a landlord objecting to them has his remedy in bringing an action for breach of the covenants in questions after all proper notices have been given.

We are left as the sole reason for refusing relief the fact of the two acts of indecent assault committed by the defendant Lewis at No 92, Ifield Road, against two boys. Mr Grundy urged that that matter was enough in itself to justify the court in refusing relief. This is the aspect of the case which has occasioned me most difficulty, but, in my view, that matter is not in itself enough to justify the court in refusing relief. So far as the evidence goes, although there are some rather vague hints in an affidavit file on the plaintiffs' side, this was apparently one isolated instance. We have no evidence at all beyond the bare fact of the conviction; we know nothing of the circumstances. I should add that it is a charge made against one only of the two joint tenants, and the acts were done at one only of these two houses, which are comprised in two separate and distinct leases.

I am therefore of opinion that no such exceptional case is here made out as to justify the court in refusing relief on payment or tender of the whole of the amount due. Accordingly, if the matter depends on the equitable jurisdiction to give relief, I think that the defendants are entitled to succeed in this appeal ...

[Appeal dismissed. Hodson and Singleton LJJ agreed.]

Questions

1 Discuss possible circumstances in which the court may refuse to grant relief against forfeiture.

2 L leased certain office premises to T Ltd. When T Ltd defaulted in paying a portion of the rent, L lawfully re-entered and took possession. Shortly thereafter, T Ltd managed to pay the unpaid rental but was in financial difficulties and unable to meet its debts to its other creditors. T Ltd seeks relief against forfeiture. Discuss T Ltd's chances of success. (See *Direct Food Supplies (Vic) Pty Ltd v DLV Pty Ltd* [1975] VR 358.)

Notes

1 A tenant could apply for relief against forfeiture even when the landlord re-entered peacefully and without the assistance of a court (see *Howard v Fanshawe* [1895] 2 Ch 581).

2 The traditional view was that relief against forfeiture could not be granted for breach of any other covenant other than non-payment of rent (see *Wadman v Calcroft* (1804) 10 Ves Jun 67; 32 ER 768). In the case of *Shiloh Spinners Ltd v Harding* [1973] AC 691, at 723–24, Lord Wilberforce cast doubt upon this view. He observed:

> I would fully endorse this: it remains true today that equity expects men to carry out their bargains and will not let them buy their way out by uncovenanted payment. But it is consistent with these principles that we should reaffirm the right of courts of equity in appropriate and limited cases to relieve against forfeiture for breach of covenant or condition where the primary object of the bargain is to secure a stated result which can effectively be attained when the matter comes before the court, and where the forfeiture provision is added by way of security for the production of that result. The word 'appropriate' involves consideration of the conduct of the applicant for relief, in particular whether his default was wilful, of the gravity of the breaches, and of the disparity between the value of the property of which forfeiture is claimed as compared with the damage caused by the breach.

(See also *Pioneer Gravels (Qld) Pty Ltd v T & T Mining Corporation Pty Ltd* [1975] Qd R 151.)

Statutory relief against forfeiture

Summary Ejectment Act

Section 4(4) of the Summary Ejectment Act (Ch No 202) provides that in an action for ejectment for non payment of rent:[46]

> If the lessee pays into a District Court all the rent in arrear and the costs at least five clear days before the day appointed for the hearing of the complaint, the complaint shall be deemed to be withdrawn.

It would seem that the provision applies irrespective of the agreement of the parties. In addition, it would seem that the District Court has no discretion in the matter once the requirements of the section are complied with by the lessee.[47] It is thought that this section does not oust the courts' general equitable jurisdiction to grant relief against forfeiture.[48] Hence, a lessee can pursue the statutory remedy subject to strict compliance with s 4(4) of the Summary Ejectment Act, or the equitable remedy which is discretionary and not subject to any strict rules. For example, if a lessee fails to pay all the rent in arrears as provided in s 4(4), he cannot seek relief against forfeiture under the Act. However, the tenant may seek equitable relief from forfeiture if he pays the outstanding rent. Likewise, a lessee who peacefully gives up possession on ground of breach of covenant to pay rent, does not qualify for relief under s 4(4), but, presumably, he could still seek equitable relief from forfeiture.[49]

Distress Replevin and Ejectment Act 1867 (adopted Queensland)[50]

Sections 118 and 119 provide for relief against forfeiture for breach of covenant to pay rent or to insure premises against loss or damage by fire. They read:

> **Section 118**
>
> In case of any ejectment for a forfeiture brought for non-payment of rent the court or a judge shall have power upon a rule or summons to give relief in a summary manner but subject to appeal as hereinafter mentioned up to and within the like time after execution and subject to the same terms and conditions in all respects as to payment of rent costs and otherwise as in a court of equity and if the lessee his executors, administrators or assigns

46 See *supra*, on power of the lessor to recover possession under the Act for non-payment of rent.

47 See also s 5(2), Summary Ejectment Act, *supra*, p 344.

48 In *Shiloh Spinners Ltd v Harding* [1973] AC 691, at 724–25, Lord Wilberforce dismissed counsel's argument that a statutory provision (eg, under the English Law of Property Act 1925) for specific machinery for granting relief against forfeiture of leases negatived an intention that corresponding jurisdiction should exist outside the case of leases. His Honour opined that, 'where the courts have established a general principle of law or equity, and the legislature steps in with particular legislation in a particular area, it must, unless showing a contrary intention, be taken to have left cases outside that area where they were under the influence of the general law. To suppose otherwise involves the conclusion that an existing jurisdiction has been cut down by implication, or by an enactment moreover which is positive in character (for it amplifies the jurisdiction in case of leases) rather than negative'.

49 *Howard v Fanshawe* [1895] Ch 581.

50 This Act only applies in 'Papua'. There is no comparable legislation in 'New Guinea'. See James, *Land Law and Policy in PNG, op cit*, note 17, p 103.

> shall upon such proceeding be relieved he and they shall hold the demised lands according to the lease thereof made without any new lease.
>
> **Section 119**
>
> In the case of any ejectment for a forfeiture for breach of covenant or condition to insure against loss or damage by fire the court or a judge shall have power upon a rule or summons to give relief in a summary manner but subject to appeal as hereinafter mentioned in all cases in which such relief may now be obtained in a court of equity under the provisions of 'The Equity Act of 1867' and upon such terms as would be imposed in such court.

Section 118 seems to provide statutory sanction for the application of the equitable relief against forfeiture. Nonetheless, it is thought that s 118 does not oust the inherent equity jurisdiction of the courts.[51]

VI TERMINATION OF LEASES

A lease may terminate by effluxion of time; notice; surrender; merger and forfeiture. We will consider each one separately.

Effluxion of time

Under the underlying law, a lease for a fixed term automatically terminates when the fixed period expires. No notice is required to terminate the lease. If the tenant remains in possession, with the landlord's consent, he becomes a tenant at will.[52] On the other hand, if a tenant remains in possession, without consent or objection of the landlord, he becomes a tenant at sufferance.[53] Both tenancies at will and at sufferance become periodic tenancies once the tenant pays rent and the landlord accepts it on a regular basis.

Notice to quit

A lease for a fixed period cannot be terminated by notice by either party unless the right to terminate is expressly reserved in the agreement or in the event of a breach which entitles the innocent party to terminate the lease prematurely.[54] Periodic tenancies on the other hand are by nature terminable by either party by giving an appropriate notice commensurate with the length of the tenancy: a weekly tenancy is terminable by one week's notice, a monthly tenancy by a month's notice, and a yearly tenancy by six months' notice.[55] As the following case illustrates, a notice to terminate a periodic tenancy is ineffective unless it expires at the end of a full period (week, month, year etc).

---

51 See *Shiloh Spinners v Harding, supra,* p 350.

52 *Meye v Electric Transmission Ltd* [1942] Ch 290.

53 *Remon v City of London Real Property Co Ltd* [1921] 1 KB 49.

54 *Cheshire and Burn's Modern Law of Real Property, op cit,* note 18, p 435.

55 See Amankwah, Mugambwa and Muroa, *Land Law in Papua New Guinea, op cit,* note 1, p 137.

QUEEN'S CLUB GARDENS ESTATES LTD v BIGNELL [1924] 1 KB 117, King's Bench Division

[The defendant was a weekly tenant and had been a weekly tenant for a very long time. The week ran from Saturday each week to the same day in the next week. On a Friday the plaintiffs served on the defendant a notice to quit 'a week from Monday next'. The notice purported to be 'the requisite week's notice for the termination' of the tenancy. In an action for possession, the defendant challenged the validity of the notice.]

LUSH J: In order to ascertain [the necessary requisites of a notice to quit a weekly tenancy] ... there are two points to be considered – namely: first, what length of notice to quit must a landlord or tenant give to determine a weekly tenancy; second, whether the notice to quit must expire at the end of the weekly term or may expire during the currency of that term?

With regard to the first point – namely, what ought the length of the notice to quit be – several possible answers have been suggested. It has been said for instance that it would be a week's notice, or as was once said by a very learned judge, half a week's notice, or more than a week's notice, or a reasonable notice. Cases are to be found in the books, some of which lay down one of these proposition and some another. Several cases have decided that a reasonable notice is all that is necessary. I cannot bring myself to accept that view. A notice to quit which was expressed to be to quit at the end of a reasonable time would clearly not be a good notice because it would not be definite or certain. Again, if a landlord or tenant gave a notice to quit on such and such a date, no one would know whether it was a valid notice until some jury or other tribunal had found that it was in fact reasonable, because in the absence of such a finding even reasonable people might take different views as to whether it was in the circumstances a reasonable notice to quit. The tendency of modern decisions, however, has been to define a reasonable notice to quit as being a week's notice. That in my opinion is the proper view. I think that the law is that in the case of a weekly tenancy a week's notice to quit is that which should be given ... In the present case the notice to quit ... was a week's notice, and I think that, so far as its duration was concerned, it was sufficient.

The second point – namely, whether the notice to quit must expire at the end of a current week, or may be made to expire on any day the landlord or tenant chooses to fix – is of a more serious character. The conflict of the authorities on that question is a little surprising ... I think the true view is that in any periodic tenancy, whether it be yearly, quarterly, monthly, or weekly, the notice to quit must expire at the end of the current period. It has been clearly settled, as is admitted, that in the cases of a yearly tenancy and a quarterly tenancy the notice to quit must expire at the end of the current period, and that in either of those cases it would be bad if it were made to expire in the middle of that period. The question is whether the same rule applies to a weekly tenancy, and, I may add, to a monthly tenancy, for they both stand on the same footing ... It seems to me to follow from the nature of a weekly tenancy – and the same principle will apply in the case of any other periodic tenancy – that the notice to quit must expire at the end of a particular week. A weekly tenancy is a tenancy by the week, just as a quarterly tenancy is a tenancy by the quarter. If the week's notice to quit is not given so as to expire at the end of a particular week, but at some other time, then another week begins before the notice expires, and this must mean that another complete week has begun. The tenancy being by the week, I do not see how it is possible for either party to give a notice to quit to expire during the currency of a week. When a fresh week begins the tenancy continues for another week, just as, in the case of a quarterly tenancy, when a fresh quarter begins, the tenancy continues for another quarter. In my view, apart from authority, when a new week is entered upon it is for the complete week, and the tenant can only leave or the landlord turn him out when a complete week expires. On any other view I find the greatest difficulty in knowing what is to become of the rent. The rent is only due at the end of the week. Supposing that in a weekly tenancy which commenced on a Saturday the landlord or the tenant gives notice to quit on a Wednesday, is the tenant to pay rent from the Saturday to the Wednesday or not? The rent would not be apportionable ... I do not see what is to happen to the rent in the case of a weekly tenancy if the landlord or the tenant can determine the tenancy in the middle of a week. Apart from authority, my own view, therefore, is that all these periodic tenancies stand on the same footing, and that, in the case of a weekly tenancy, if either party wishes to give notice to quit he must take care that it is a notice which expires at the end of a week, unless of course the parties have agreed otherwise. If the party who desires to give notice is doubtful as to the day on which the period expires, he can make sure that the notice will be valid by adding the words that are given in the common form of notice to quit to the effect that if the date mentioned is not the real date on which the period expires, then the notice to quit is to expire on the proper day of expiry next after the expiration of the current period.

[After discussing several authorities his Honour concluded:] For these reasons I think the notice to quit which was given in the present case is bad. It was not a notice to quit which was to expire at the end of a week. The rule that a notice to quit is bad which does not comply with the condition prescribed by law that it must expire at the proper time, may seem to be somewhat technical to persons who are not acquainted with the law relating to these matters, but one cannot on that account depart from the rule and abstain from applying it. I am therefore of opinion that the judgment of the learned county court judge was wrong and this appeal should be allowed.

[Salter J agreed.]

Questions

1. Why should a notice to quit expire at the end of a current period? Do you agree with the reasoning of Lush J that any other rule would lead to a problem of apportionment of rent? Would you agree that this requirement for a valid notice is too stringent? What reforms, if any, would you like to see in this area?
2. Assume that your landlord client has instructed you to issue a notice on one of his tenants to terminate his monthly tenancy, but your client is not sure of the exact day of the week or month the tenancy commenced. How would you word the termination notice? See *Sidebottom v Holland* [1895] 1 QBD 378.
3. A yearly tenancy commenced on 1 March of a given year, what is the latest date for giving a valid termination notice for the tenancy to end in the year immediately following?

Note

A tenancy at will is determinable by either party at any time. In *Martinali v Ramuz and Others* [1953] 1 WLR 1196, at 1199, Lord Denning said: 'It is elementary that a tenancy at will is determined by a demand for possession, not by a notice to quit.' The tenant must be given reasonable time to leave (*Crane v Morris* [1965] 1 WLR 1104, at 1108).

Surrender

If before a lease expires the lessee gives up possession of the land to the lessor and the lessor accepts possession, the lease merges in the landlord's reversion. In the event, the lease is terminated by surrender.[56] Under the Insolvency Act (Ch No 253), the trustee in bankruptcy may surrender a lease by disclaiming it.[57]

Questions

1 Under what circumstances may a lessee wish to surrender a lease?

2 If a lessee surrenders the lease, is he liable for rent which: (a) accrued before the surrender; (b) after the surrender? See *Buchanan v Byrnes* (1906) 3 CLR 704.

Merger

Merger is the exact opposite of surrender. If the lessee buys out the landlord's reversionary interest, this extinguishes the lease.

Forfeiture

See above for discussion of termination of a lease by forfeiture.

Compensation for improvements

Under the underlying law, upon termination of the lease the lessee has no right to compensation for the improvement, which he carried on the land. His right is limited to the removal of 'tenant's fixtures'.[58] The underlying law only applies to leases of private freehold land. With reference to State leases, the Land Act 1996 makes provision for payment of compensation to the outgoing tenant for the value of the improvement effected by him during the currency of the lease.[59]

Land Registration Act

Under s 148 of the Land Registration Act, compensation for improvements on the land may be claimed in certain circumstances. The section provides:

Improvements

(1) Subject to sub-section (2), where the defendant in an action of ejectment or a person through whom he claims has made improvements on the land since obtaining a certificate of title for the land he may, whether he admits or denies the plaintiff's title –

56 *Ibid*, at p 138.

57 The Registrar is required to register a disclaimer upon proof that the trustee has disclaimed the lease: s 57 of the Land Registration Act (Ch No 191).

58 See materials in Chapter 3.

59 See materials in Chapter 7. See also James, *Land Law and Policy in Papua New Guinea*, *op cit*, note 17, pp 30–31.

(a) give notice to the plaintiff of the fact of the improvements being made; and

(b) set a value on those improvements and also on the land as distinct from those improvements; and

(c) give evidence relating to those improvements at the trial.

(2) Sub-section (1) does not apply in the case of an action of ejectment against a fraudulent proprietor.

(3) Subject to sub-section (4), where –

(a) a defendant gives notice in accordance with sub-section (1); and

(b) a verdict is found for the plaintiff, or his title is admitted,

the court shall assess the value of the improvements, and shall also separately assess the value which the land would have had if the improvements had not been made.

(4) Where the court assesses the value of improvements under sub-section (3), a writ of possession shall not issue unless the plaintiff first pays into court for the use of the defendant the value of the improvements so assessed, deducting only the costs (if any) to which he is entitled in the action.

(5) Where the plaintiff fails to make the payment referred to in sub-section (4) within three months after verdict –

(a) the plaintiff is entitled to have judgment to recover only the sum separately assessed as the value of the land together with costs of suit; and

(b) the defendant is entitled, on satisfaction of that judgment, to retain the land and improvements.

Note

Note that the provision applies whether the registered proprietor against whom the ejectment proceedings are brought is a lessee or holder in fee simple. The section is capable of two interpretations. A wide interpretation of the section suggests, for example, that if a registered lease is terminated and the lessor brings an action of ejectment against the lessee,[60] the latter is entitled to claim compensation from the lessor for the improvements he made on the land. If this interpretation is correct, it means, with reference to registered private leases, that the section overrides the underlying law insofar as it makes provision for compensation for the improvements, which the lessee cannot remove.[61] Also, arguably, a lessee of a registered State lease which is forfeited who is not entitled to compensation under Land Act, in an action to eject him from the land, may claim compensation from the Minister under s 148 of the Land Registration Act.[62] A narrow interpretation of s 148 is that its scope is limited to ejectment in the context of the Act. For example, where a *bona fide* purchaser for value is registered through fraud of a third party in circumstances where he is not protected by the exceptions to indefeasibility,

60 See s 146(2)(c) of the LRA.

61 A strict reading of the section means that compensation can only be claimed in ejectment proceedings. Thus, if the lessee voluntarily vacates the premises at the termination of the lease, he cannot claim compensation under the section!

62 However, this interpretation may mean that s 148 of the LRA is inconsistent with the provisions of the Land Act, if so the latter would prevail; see James, *Land Law and Policy in Papua New Guinea, op cit*, note 17, p 30.

he may be ejected.[63] The effect of the section is that if such a person is ejected from the land, he may claim for compensation from the plaintiff for the improvements he made on the land.

63 See s 146(2) of the Land Registration Act.

CHAPTER 7

STATE LEASES

I CLASSIFICATION OF LEASES

Leases in Papua New Guinea are classified into two groups: private and State lease. A 'private lease' is a lease of private freehold land. A 'State lease' is a lease from the State granted under or continued in force by the Land Act 1996.[1] Most State leases are granted over government-owned land. However, the Minister may grant a State lease over customary land leased by the government from the traditional owners.[2] Where a State lease is granted over customary land the terms in the lease must not conflict with the terms under which the government originally leased the land from the customary owners (s 67 of the LA).

Most alienated land in Papua New Guinea is held under State lease. This is the result of the past deliberate colonial policy not to grant freehold estates. The independent governments have maintained the policy.[3]

Significance of the classification

State and private leases generally share all the common law features of leases. Moreover, subject to certain variations, the provisions of the Land Registration Act (Ch No 191), apply to both State and private leases.[4] Section 36 of the Land Registration Act provides as follows:

> **36 Application of Act to State leases**
>
> (1) Except where the contrary intention appears, this Act applies to the Register of State Leases and to State leases as if –
>
> (a) the Register of State Leases were the Register Book; and
>
> (b) a State lease were a certificate of title.
>
> (2) In particular, a State lease, on registration, is subject to the provisions of this Act, and may be dealt with for the same purposes and in the same manner, subject to the Land Act, as if it had been granted by a registered proprietor and registered in the Register Book.
>
> (3) Notwithstanding sub-section (1)(b), a State lease may be dealt with in any manner applicable to any other form of lease.

---

1 See s 2(1) of the Land Act 1996, and s 2(1) of the Land Registration Act (Ch No 191).

2 Section 10(4) of the Land Act empowers the Minister to lease, rather than purchase, customary land from the traditional owners subject to conditions stated in the sections. The term 'government land' includes both land owned by the government and customary land leased to the government, see s 2(1) of the LA.

3 James, *Land Law and Policy in Papua New Guinea*, PNG Law Reform Commission, Monograph No 5 (1985), p 119, argues that quite apart from policy, which was against freehold grants, there was no power to grant freeholds in Papua after the Land Ordinance 1911 (Papua), and in New Guinea after the enactment of the Land Ordinance 1962.

4 Section 99(7) of the Land Act provides that the Land Registration Act does not apply to State leases of government-owned buildings.

The main difference between State leases and private leases is that State leases are granted subject to the provisions of the Land Act. The Act stipulates the terms and conditions under which State leases shall be granted.[5] Thus, as a general guide with reference to any matter dealing with State leases the primary source of the law applicable is the Land Act. Other laws may of course apply, but subject to the provisions of this Act.[6]

II GRANT OF STATE LEASE

Procedure

Section 64(1) of the Land Act prohibits alienation of government land except in accordance with the provisions of the Act or another law. By s 65 the Minister has the power to grant a State lease in the manner provided by the Land Act. One of the requirements of the Act is that the Minister makes a grants of State leases upon recommendation of the Land Board established under the Act.[7] The provisions of the Act extracted below deal with the role of the Board and prescribed general procedure for the grant of a State lease.[8]

> **55 Establishment of the Land Board**
>
> (1) A Land Board is hereby established.
>
> (2) The Land Board shall consist of –
>
> (a) a Chairman; and
>
> (b) such other members, as the Minister thinks proper,
>
> appointed by the Minister by notice in the *National Gazette.*
>
> **57 Functions of the Land Board**
>
> (1) In addition to such other functions as are conferred on it by this Act, the Land Board shall consider and make a recommendation on any matter referred to it by the Minister or by the Department.
>
> (2) Except where the Minister is empowered by this or any other Act to make a direct grant of a State lease, the Land Board shall consider all applications for grant of leases which have been investigated and referred to it by the Department and all other matters that are remitted to it by the Minister for its consideration.

---

5 See s 29(1) of the Land Act, also generally Part VI.

6 For illustration of this point, see, eg, *Steamship Trading Company Limited v Minister of Lands and Physical Planning and Others* (unreported, N1959, OS 552 of 1999; and *Hi Lift Company Pty Ltd v Secretary For Agriculture and The State of Papua New Guinea* (unreported, N2004, OS 329 of 2000). See extracts of both cases in Chapter 9, at pp 440 and 443.

7 For judicial observation on the role of the Land Board, see Wood J in *Application of Moge Enga and Kuipi Group in the Matter of the Decision of the Minister for Lands Concerning Section 30 Allotment 7 Mount Hagen* [1995] PNGLR 31 at 35–36 (see extract below, p 373).

8 For discussion of the procedure, see Amankwah, Mugambwa and Muroa, *Land Law in Papua New Guinea* (Lawbook Co, Sydney, 2001), pp 148–49.

58 Meetings of the Land Board, reports, etc

(1) At least seven days before a meeting of the Land Board, the Chairman shall publish in the *National Gazette* a list of –

(a) the applications and other matters to be considered; and

(b) lands to be dealt with,

by the Board at the meeting.

(2) The Chairman shall notify by post every person who, in his opinion, is interested in an application or matter, of the date on which it will be considered by the Land Board.

(3) The meeting of the Land Board shall be held not less than seven days nor more than 42 days after the publication of the list referred to in sub-section (1), and the Board shall deal with applications and matters, hear any objections and report on the applications or matters within 14 days to the Minister.

(4) The Chairman shall cause meetings of the Land Board to be held as he thinks necessary.

(5) Subject to section 106, for the conduct of business at a meeting of the Land Board –

(a) three members, of whom one is the Chairman or a Deputy Chairman nominated for the purpose under section 55(5), are a quorum; and

(b) the Chairman or the Deputy Chairman nominated for the purpose, shall preside; and

(c) all matters shall be decided by the majority of votes of the members present; and

(d) the person presiding has a deliberative and, in the event of an equality of votes on a matter, also a casting vote.

(6) The person presiding at a meeting of the Land Board shall –

(a) where he thinks it necessary to do so; or

(b) where he is directed by the Chairman to do so,

exclude any or all members of the public from the meeting.

(7) The Departmental Head or his delegate –

(a) may attend any meeting of the Board; and

(b) shall, where so requested by the Chairman, attend a meeting of the Board,

in the capacity of adviser to the Board.

(8) Where the Land Board –

(a) takes evidence at a meeting from which members of the public have been excluded; or

(b) is directed by the Minister that the recommendation of the Board is not to be made available to members of the public; or

(c) deals with an application or matter that has been specified in the notice in the *National Gazette* under sub-section (1) to be the subject of a confidential report,

it shall report on it within 14 days to the Minister.

(9) In respect of each application the Land Board shall recommend –

(a) the applicant to whom, in the opinion of the Land Board, the State lease should be granted; and

(b) the applicant who, in the opinion of the Land Board, is the second-choice successful applicant; and

(c) the applicant who, in the opinion of the Land Board, is the third-choice successful applicant,

and where the Land Board, in making a recommendation in any case, considers that two or more applicants are of equal merit, it may decide the matter by ballot and shall report on the ballot to the Minister within 14 days.

(10) The Chairman shall forward notice of the Land Board's recommendations, other than a recommendation to which sub-section (8) applies, to every person who, in his opinion, is interested in an application or matter dealt with by the Board.

(11) A member of the Land Board shall not sit on any matter in which he is directly or indirectly interested.

68 Advertisement of lands available for leasing

(1) Except where land has been exempted from advertisement under section 69, the Departmental Head shall give notice, by advertisement in the *National Gazette*, of all lands available for leasing under this Act.

(2) An advertisement under sub-section (1) shall contain the following information:

(a) the type of lease available to be granted;

(b) the purpose of the lease;

(c) the length of the lease;

(d) a description of the land to be leased;

(e) the amount of rent (if any) payable for the first period of the lease;

(f) in the case of a special purposes lease – any royalties that are payable;

(g) the terms and conditions of the lease;

(h) the reserve price;

(i) such other information as the Departmental Head thinks fit or the Minister directs.

(3) A statement contained in an advertisement under this section does not in any way bind the State in the granting of a lease over land the subject of the advertisement or constitute an offer to lease land.

69 Duty to advertise State leases

(1) A State lease shall not be granted without first being advertised in accordance with section 68 unless the land has been exempted from advertisement under sub-section (2).

(2) The Minister may exempt land from advertisement for application or tender –

(a) where the lease is granted to a governmental body for a public purpose; or

(b) where it is necessary to relocate persons displaced as a result of a disaster as defined in the Disaster Management Act (Chapter 403); or

(c) where a lessee applies for a further lease; or

(d) where the State has agreed to provide land for the establishment or expansion of a business, project, or other undertaking; or

(e) where the land applied for adjoins land owned by the applicant and is required to bring the holding up to a more workable unit, providing that the claims of other neighbouring landowners are considered and their views taken into account in deciding whether to exempt the land from advertisement in favour of the applicant; or

(f) where the Department responsible for foreign affairs recommends that land be made available to the applicant for consular premises; or

(g) where the land is required for the resettlement of refugees; or

(h) where the applicant has funded the acquisition of the land from customary landowners in order to acquire a State lease over it; or

(i) where a lease is to be granted under section 99 or 102; or

(j) where a new lease is granted under section 110, 130 or section 131.

70 How applications for State leases to be made

An application for a State lease shall –

(a) be made in the approved form; and

(b) be accompanied by the prescribed fee for the registration of the application.

71 As a general rule, the Land Board shall consider all applications for State leases

Subject to section 72, the Land Board –

(a) shall hear all applications for State leases; and

(b) shall recommend to the Minister the persons (if any) to whom leases should be granted; and

(c) may make such other recommendations to the Minister in connection with an application as the Board considers proper.

72 Power of Minister to grant State lease direct

The Minister may grant, on application or otherwise –

(a) a lease over any land acquired under the Lands Acquisition (Development Purposes) Act (Chapter 192) (Repealed); and

(b) a lease over land which has been the subject of a declaration under section 111; and

(c) a lease granted under section 102; and

(d) a lease granted under section 99,

without referring the matter to the Land Board.

73 Dealing with Tenders

(1) Where the land is required to be offered for lease by tender, a tender notice shall –

(a) contain the particulars specified in section 68; and

(b) specify the reserve price for the land.

(2) A tender for an amount less than the reserve price specified under sub-section (1)(b) is invalid and shall not be considered.

(3) Land that has been offered for lease in accordance with sub-section (1) may –

(a) if unleased, be re-offered for lease by tender; or

(b) after the first or any subsequent unsuccessful offer for lease by tender, be granted on application under this Act.

(4) The successful tenderer shall pay to the State the amount of his tender.

(5) The successful tenderer is entitled to a State lease of the land the subject of the tender, in accordance with the tender notice.

74 Publication of names of successful applicants, etc, in the *National Gazette*

The Departmental Head shall publish in the *National Gazette* –

(a) the name of the successful applicant for each State lease, together with particulars of the lands to be leased to him; and

(b) in respect of that State lease and those lands –

(i) the name of the applicant considered the second-choice successful applicant; and

(ii) the name of the applicant considered the third-choice successful applicant,

to whom a Letter of Grant may be forwarded on accordance with sections 75 and 79.

75 Notice to successful applicants

As soon as practicable after the publication of the notice under section 74, the Departmental Head shall forward a Letter of Grant to each successful applicant (as specified in section 74(a)) notifying him of –

(a) the date of the publication of the notice in the *National Gazette*; and

(b) the terms and conditions of the proposed lease; and

(c) details of all fees due, outstanding tender moneys and any other amounts payable in respect of the proposed lease; and

(d) the need to sign and return an accompanying Lease Acceptance Form to reach the Departmental Head within 28 days of the publication of the notice in the *National Gazette*, or such later date as is stated in the Letter of Grant, in order to accept the grant of the lease.

76 Acceptance of terms and conditions of proposed leases and execution of State leases

(1) The Minister, on behalf of the Independent State of Papua New Guinea, shall execute three copies of a State lease and forward the original and a duplicate to the Registrar of Titles for registration.

(2) A successful applicant, who forwards a duly signed Lease Acceptance Form to the Departmental Head in accordance with section 75, thereby accepts the terms and conditions of the proposed lease as set out in the Letter of Grant and shall be deemed to have executed the lease on the date on which the Minister executes the lease.

Note

Sections 68–76, inclusive, do not apply to grant of a lease for a special agricultural and business purpose (see s 102(6)). Readers should also note that there are additional procedural requirements for the grant of business and residence purpose lease (s 95), special purpose lease (s 101), and urban development lease (see generally Division 10, Part XII). Some of these provisions are extracted below.

Question

Who decides whether or not to make a grant of a State lease: is it the Minister or the Land Board? See *Application of Moge Enga and Kuipi Group* [1995] PNGLR 31, and *Wandaki v Minister for Lands and Another* [1996] PNGLR 116. See extracts of both cases below, at pp 373 and 375 respectively.

Right of appeal

The Land Act makes provision for aggrieved persons to appeal against grant of a State lease in certain circumstances. The relevant provisions of the Act are extracted below.

PART VIII – Appeals and Reports

62 Appeals

(1) A person aggrieved by a decision of the Land Board may, not later than 28 days after notice is forwarded under section 58(10), forward a notice of appeal to the Minister.

(2) An appeal shall be accompanied by a deposit of K500.00, which shall, subject to sub-section (3), be refunded when the appeal has been decided.

(3) If the Head of State, acting on advice, thinks that the appeal has been made on frivolous grounds, the Head of State, acting on advice, may reject the appeal and direct that the whole or any portion of the deposit shall be forfeited to the State.

(4) Subject to sub-section (5), the Head of State, acting on advice, shall determine an appeal under this section, and his decision is final.

(5) Where an appeal under this section is upheld, the Head of State, acting on advice, may refer the matter back to the Land Board for re-hearing.

63 Reference or reports to Minister

(1) A report or recommendation of the Land Board shall –

(a) if no appeal is made under section 62, at the expiration of the period referred to in sub-section (1) of that section; or

(b) if any such appeal is made, after the appeal is determined,

be referred to the Minister.

(2) In addition to any other powers conferred by or under this Act, the Minister shall, if he disagrees with a report or recommendation of the Land Board, and may for any other reason –

(a) refer any matter back to the Board for re-hearing, the taking of fresh evidence, the furnishing of a further or additional report, or otherwise; or

(b) refer any matter to the National Executive Council.

(3) The decision of the Head of State, acting on advice, on a matter referred to the National Executive Council under sub-section (2)(b), is final.

Notes

There is no right of appeal to the courts against the Minister's decision to grant or not grant a State lease. However, any aggrieved person may seek a judicial review.[9] The case below illustrates an action for judicial review on the ground, *inter alia*, that the Minister did not follow the prescribed procedure under the Land Act 1996.

STEAMSHIP TRADING COMPANY LTD v MINISTER OF LANDS AND PHYSICAL PLANNING, GARAMUT ENTERPRISES LTD AND GUISE AND OTHER MEMBERS OF THE NATIONAL LAND BOARD
unreported, N1959 PNG National Court of Justice, OS 552 of 1999

[For detailed facts of this case, see Chapter 9. Suffice to say certain government land was gazetted for public tender pursuant to s 68 of the Land Act. Before the tenders closed the Minister, purporting to act under s 69(2) of the Land Act, exempted the land from public tender. Subsequently, the Minister granted the second respondent (Garamut) a State lease, and the latter registered the lease in its name under the Land Registration Act. The plaintiffs sought a judicial order to nullify the lease on the ground that the Minister did not follow the prescribed procedure under the Land Act.]

SHEEHAN J [His Honour outlined the facts of the case in a chronological order, and continued:]

Plaintiff's case

The challenge to the issue the State lease is made on the basis of failure to observe the procedures laid down by the Land Act. Although the property was originally gazetted for tender, it was subsequently withdrawn from public tender (before closure of tenders) on the basis that the Minister had granted an exemption from advertising. Since none of the reasons the Minister gave for allowing the exemption from public tender fell within the exemptions allowed by s 69 of the Act, then the withdrawal from tender was invalid. There was no reissue of the tender, therefore the property was not tendered pursuant to s 68 of the Land Act and a major breach of the Act occurred.

Further error is shown, it was argued because the State lease is purported to have been granted to Garamut at meeting No 2004 of the Land Board held over 29 and 30 September 1999. If that was so, then the requirement under s 58 of the Land Act that all applications to be considered at any meeting of the Land Board shall be Gazetted at least seven days prior to a meeting, was not complied with. There was no publication in the *Gazette* of 11 September 1998 that preceded meeting 2004 (and which listed the applications for consideration) that the second Defendant's application was on that agenda and would be considered.

There is a further challenge in that the commercial land supposedly granted to Garamut at Land Board meeting 2004 at the end of September 1998 was in fact then not Gazetted as land available for commercial purposes; that is, it was not gazetted as being rezoned commercial until 15 October 1998. Accordingly, it was not possible to grant a commercial lease in respect of that land at that time.

9 See *Burns Philip (PNG) Ltd v The State and Others* (1989) unreported, N769, discussed in Amankwah, Mugambwa and Muroa, *Land Law in Papua New Guinea*, *ibid*, pp 146–47.

Finally the Plaintiff points out that the Land Board meeting 2004 took place both before the land was advertised for tender, that is on 5 November 1998, before it was exempted from an advertisement by the Minister on 8 October 1998, and before the exemption from advertisement was gazetted on 15 of December 1998. Therefore, the Plaintiff contends any application for the Land could not have validly been considered at Land Board Meeting No 2004.

Defence

Opposing the application Counsel for Garamut Enterprises Limited the second Defendant (Garamut) contended that the application must fail because essentially the process by which Garamut had been granted title to the Land substantially complied with the provisions of the relevant Acts ...

Decision

The Plaintiff's complaint is that the rezoning of the land and the issue of lease to Garamut occurred through breaches of the governing statutes committed by both first and third Defendants. That is, the decision granting rezoning and the issue of the lease are illegal, unreasonable and void. When are decisions void for illegality and or unreasonableness?

In *Judicial Review of Administrative Action*, the learned authors state at p 295:

> an administrative decision is flawed if it is illegal. A decision is illegal if:
>
> (1) it contravenes or exceeds the terms of the power which authorises the making of the decision; or
>
> (2) it pursues an objective other than that for which the power to make the decision was conferred.

A statute may prescribe the manner that an authority shall conduct its duties. Those requirements may be such as to impose procedures that amount to conditions precedent to the exercise of power conferred. Examples are an obligation to consult or the need to follow specified procedural steps. Where the wording of a statute prescribes that those requirements 'shall' be met, then the inference is that the provision is mandatory and any failure to carry out that duty must result in the decisions being held in breach and therefore unlawful.

But failure to meet all statutory requirements precisely will not invariably result in decisions taken, being held illegal. The court under its powers of review may in its discretion decline to find decisions illegal where a breach is not seen as violating the interest intention or objects of a statute. This is clearly summarised in *Judicial Review of Administrative Action* at para 5-060 where it states:

> All statutory requirements are *prima facie* mandatory. However, in some situations the violation of a provision will, in the context of the statute as a whole and the circumstances of the particular decision, not violate the objects and purpose of the statute. Condoning such a breach does not, however, render the statutory provision directory or discretionary. The breach of the particular provision is treated in the circumstances as not involving a breach of the statute taken as a whole. Furthermore, logically, a provision cannot be mandatory if a court has discretion not to enforce it.

Again, very often an Act provides for determination in the discretion of the statutory authority.

The task of the court in evaluating whether a decision is a illegal is essentially one of construing the content and the scope of the instrument conferring the power in order to determine whether the decision fall within its 'four corners'. In so doing the courts enforce the rule of law, requiring administrative bodies to act within the bounds of the powers there have been given. They also act as guardians of Parliament's will – seeking to ensure that the exercise of power is what Parliament intended. (*Op cit.*)

Therefore, where a statutory discretion is given under a law, that discretion can only be used to promote the policy and objects of the Act. This may be found by the examination of the Act and this is a matter of interpretation for the court. If as a result of such examination, it is found the decision of a tribunal or authority would frustrate the policy of the Act, the court is entitled to intervene *Padfield v Minister of Agriculture, Fisheries and Food* [1968] AC 997; see also *Darvell v Auckland Legal Services* [1993] NZLR 111; *R v Sec for State ex p Fire Brigades Union* [1995] 2 All ER 244. These decisions follow the principle that where the exercise of a statutory discretion has the object or leads to a result which denies or fails to achieve the object and purpose of the Act the courts may set such determination aside not only as illegal but also as unreasonable.

In the *Wednesbury* case (*Associated Provincial Pictures Houses Limited v Wednesbury Co* [1948] 1 KB 223) Lord Greene stated that a decision can be set aside if it: 'is so unreasonable that no reasonable authority could ever come to it.' He went on to expand on matters constituting unreasonableness. These include bad faith, fraud, dishonesty, disregard of public policy, and failure to take into account matters which are bound to be considered. Some of these of course overlap and may result in a decision being set aside for illegality as much as for unreasonableness. Fraud clearly is both illegal and unreasonable.

Fraud generally implies a notion of dishonesty but that is not exclusively so. Fraud also encompasses situations where there need not be dishonesty, that is moral fraud. *Beaman v ARTS Limited* [1948] 1 All ER 465. The court in its equitable jurisdiction may find equitable or constructive fraud where there is no 'deceit or circumvention'. The unconscionable abuse of lawful authority or *prima facie* valid contractual power can be such as to raise a presumption of fraud ...

The courts therefore will reject an interpretation of a statute that would allow what Parliament has clearly indicated by the Act should not occur, or allows an authority to refrain from doing what Parliament has indicated should be done ...

Where fraud is relied on as a cause of action then there must be actual fraud pleaded and strictly proved. But in equity that is not necessary so ...

The essential duty for an authority entrusted with the implementation of statutory duties for the benefit of the public (particularly when such duties include the exercise of discretionary powers) is to act only within and according to the objects and purposes of the statute. It cannot evade this duty. Thus where the Land Act clearly has the purpose, as a matter of National interest to provide a transparent procedure for the alienation of State, land, the authorities entrusted with the supervision of those procedures may be said to be acting fraudulently – and it is fraud whether there is dishonesty or otherwise – when it acts with the intention of achieving an object directly opposed to the purposes of the statute.

The prime consideration for a court in a challenge to the validity of a statutory authority's decision must be the decision itself and reasons, if any, given to support it. There may be no duty to give reasons at all and a duty is not always expressed in a statute. Some do (eg, Commissions of Enquiries Act (s 15)) while in others it may be implied from the nature of the processes required by the Act and or the consequences a determination might have on citizens' rights.

Again failure to give any reasons can lead to conclusions of maladministration. Judicial Review empowers a court to find error of law, for example, for failure to act within jurisdiction or for failure to consider relevant matters. When a decision is challenged and no reasons are given, the court is obliged either to itself consider the evidence backgrounding the decision or to conclude from the lack of reasons, that valid reasons do not exist.

In *Re Gegeyo v Minister for Lands and Physical Planning* [1987] PNGLR 331 Amet J as he then was, said that:

> ... if a decision making authority gives no reasons in a case when it might reasonably be expected to do so, the courts may infer it had no good reason for reaching its conclusions and act accordingly.

The learned judge in a case that followed that decision, the *Application of the National Capital District Interim Commission* [1987] PNGLR 339 at 343 went on to say:

> furthermore it leaves wide open for allegations and inferences that such decisions were made with ulterior motives and for reasons other than in the public interest. It seems to me that is even more imperative to consult and give reasons when public authorities, administrative tribunals and executive government are dealing with matters of public interest which will affect the welfare and interest of the public at large, such as public reserves where large sums of public funds are expended by public trustee to improve such reserves for benefit and enjoyment of the whole public, of a city or town such as in these two cases and it behoves the relevant departmental officers concerned and the decision making tribunal to be diligent and to act with integrity and fairness and above approach in the conduct of its business so that no aspersions can be cast on their motives.

That decision was followed by Brunton J in *National Capital District Interim Commission v Crusoe Pty Limited* 1989 N836 where the court held failure to follow the mandatory procedures of the Town Planning Act (the forerunner of the Physical Planning Act) were fatal to a rezoning arbitrarily made by the Minister ...

It is under these principles of law that the challenges of breach of the relevant statutes must be considered.

Rezoning

The preamble to the Physical Planning Act 1989 says that it is:

> ... an Act to establish a comprehensive mechanism for Physical Planning at National and Provincial levels of government and to provide powers for the planning and regulation of physical development ... and for related purposes ...
>
> ...
>
> Section 4 of the Act specifies that particular matters are primarily of National (as opposed to Provincial) interest for the purposes of this Act ... Section 5 of the Act spells out the considerations a Physical Planning authority must take into account in respect of any particular application ... There then follow 22 matters which the authorities faced with a planning application must determine.
>
> ...

7 Duties of Minister Responsible for Physical Planning

(1) it shall be the duty of the Minister to ensure in the public interest that the land is used in accordance with sound Physical Planning principles and that there is consistency and continuity in the preparation and execution of development plan

throughout Papua New Guinea and in the general exercise of general Physical Planning control in Papua New Guinea.

Section 77(3)(e) says that applications for rezoning shall be made by the owner of the land the subject to the application or the agent of that owner. Section 97 details the matters which shall be taken into account on consideration of appeals. Essentially these are a reconsideration in terms of those matters arising under s 5 ... Sched 1 of the Regulations under the Act provides that land zoned open space includes *'public open space, public parks and recreation areas and other public reserves'*.

Clearly therefore the development and zoning of land are not simply matters affecting only a particular piece of land and its owner. The Act designates these matters as being of National importance and prescribes a code of practice to ensure transparency and public participation in the development of land. The authorities empowered including appeal authorities are directed to the manner and matters of consideration of application and on appeal. The Minister is directed to ensure the objectives of the Act.

...

Garamut's application for rezoning was declined by the NCD Physical Planning Board for declared reasons and the National Physical Planning Board likewise recommended to the Minister the appeal be rejected for reasons notified to him. The Minister nonetheless granted the appeal. He notified the National Tribunal that he had considered all the matters raised but granted the appeal. He gave no reasons.

There is no doubt that the Minister has the authority and discretion to decide an appeal. But equally there can be no doubt that such a discretion does not give the Minister the right to decide an appeal on personal preference or whim. By law such a discretion can only be exercised within the scope and authority of the Act itself. The courts are empowered by Judicial Review to set aside as an excess of jurisdiction, as unreasonable ... and as illegal, any purported exercise of discretion that fails to consider relevant matters or does not follow the legitimate purposes and scope of the Act.

Applying the principles cited in the *Gegeyo* and *Lonrbo* cases, the known facts and circumstances in this case appear to point overwhelmingly in favour of the decisions of both Physical Planning Authorities which considered that open space was more appropriate for public use than for commercial exploitation. There being no sense or explanation for the Ministers decision that those views were wrong and that there was good reason for changing the public open space to commercial for the benefit of a single applicant, the court can only draw the conclusion that he had no valid reason for his decision. Accordingly, it cannot stand and the rezoning must be quashed as invalid.

Land Act 1996 – issue of lease

This Act is also described as an Act giving effect to National Interest and for of public purposes ...

Under Part IX which deals with the alienation of government land, s 64 states:

> ... government land shall not be alienated otherwise than under this Act or another law ...

Part X of the Act which follows, provides for State leases: s 65 says:

> The Minister may grant State leases of government land as provided by this Act.

While there is a power granted by s 72 for the minister to grant leases directly (not relevant in these proceedings) the general rule is that the Land Board shall consider all application for State leases (section 71) ... The manner in which the Board is directed to conduct its procedures is set out in ss 57, 58 ...

The Board is of course bound as well by the other provisions of the Land Act regarding the issue of State leases, particularly s 67 that no lease shall be granted in contravention of zoning requirements of the Physical Planning Act and it must abide by ss 68 and 95 which requires that unless exempted by the Minister the Departmental Head, that is the Secretary for Lands, shall give notice by advertisement in the *National Gazette* of all land available for leasing under the Act. That section also spells out the detailed information that must be supplied to the Public.

The scope of exemption from tender is limited to specific situation: [s 69] ...

The content and directives of the Act plainly demonstrate that the intention and purpose of the Act is provide an open transparent system of access to State lands, and an orderly and fair process of disposition of those lands by the Minister on behalf of the State. Citizens, given due and adequate notice as to the availability of State land, are able to compete on an equal footing with one another by public open tender for a State lease.

Substantial compliance

It is argued for Garamut that notwithstanding breaches of statutes as may have occurred through the actions of the Minister or the Land Board, the Company acted appropriately throughout. It had simply applied for rezoning of land. When refused that rezoning it had appealed, the appeal was upheld. Similarly when it had applied for a lease an exemption to tender had been granted. The Minister had cited reasons under s 69(2) and though not specified, it might be taken that he acted under s 69(2)(d), an agreement to provide land for establishment of a business. The Minister had approved and processed the State lease now registered. Accordingly it was argued that there had been substantial compliance with the procedures prescribed by the statutes.

I am satisfied that this is not so. While Garamut's application for rezoning and the procedures before the Planning Board and Tribunals may be said to be unexceptional, they resulted in the refusal of the application by the authorised tribunals. The critical non compliance occurred with the Minister failing to give any reasons why the Tribunals determinations should be set aside. However reasonable Garamut's application or appeal they cannot mend a fundamental breach of the law.

The facts ... clearly show outstanding breaches of the provisions and terms of both Acts. The rezoning of the land from public open space to commercial was done without reasons being offered and even had it been valid, was not gazetted till after the grant of lease by the Land Board in September 1998. The Land Board gave no notice of its intention to consider an application from Garamut as required by s 58 nor was any tender of the property gazetted till after the September meeting in fact had taken place. The tender was withdrawn on a decision of the Minister unlawfully exercised and notified to the public as withdrawn, after the meeting had taken place. Parties who had in fact tendered in response to the advertisement plainly were adversely affected.

Finally there is substantial reason to doubt whether the application of Garamut was ever considered at the September meeting of the Land Board at all, because the members purporting to have approved the lease were not minuted as being present at the meeting and thus in terms of s 58(5)(c) present to determine the grant. Given that there is no contradiction of this particular evidence and taking all the other anomalies into account I am certainly not able to conclude on the balance of probabilities that the Land Board ever considered Garamut's application at meeting 2004. The balance is towards that it did not.

Of all the anomalies the Minister's grant of an exemption from the tender of the lease was a critical breach of the statute. He had no authority or power to introduce exemptions that were not contemplated by the Act and to that extent his decision was illegal.

It was made in face of his own earlier determination that there were no grounds for withdrawing the land from public tender. It was granted for 'special reasons' which do not comply with the provisions of s 69(2) of the Act and even as considered as special reasons fail to achieve that status. To say that an applicant needs the land and was willing to carry out and pay for the survey simply does not amount to special reasons.

More significantly the use of the phrase 'special reasons' indicates that the Minister was not even aware of the provisions of the Act under which he was obliged to consider such a matter. Under s 57 of the old Land Act the Minister was granted wide discretion on this issue. He was able to act on 'special reasons'. But that Act was repealed by the 1996 Act. Section 69(2) is specific on the grounds of grant of such exemption. There is no provision of unspecified 'special reasons'. Claiming to act under s 69(2) without specifying a listed exemption is not enough and gives no credence or validity to such a decision. As for the suggestion the Minister was referring to s 69(2)(d) there is simply no evidence of such an agreement and even Garamut does not assert one.

The prescribed procedures under the Land Act simply did not occur. From the time Garamut's application was lodged the processing of the application failed totally to follow the requirements of the Land Act. The breaches were gross, a travesty, to the extent that it can be said the Act was not followed at all. But further, to the extent that the Minister made a disposition of State land which was not open to scrutiny but removed from the public without the sanction of the Act, granted private access to State land, conferring an advantage, particularly a commercial advantage on a single applicant without reason, the grant clearly is not only outside the scope and purposes of the Act, unreasonable and unlawful, it is a fraud on the Act itself. The grant in fact was a nullity and no lease, no interest in land, no title was issued in accordance with the Act.

[Order for nullification of grant.]

Notes

1 The defendants sought to challenge Steamship's standing to sue as 'aggrieved' person since Steamship was not a losing applicant. However, Sheehan J held that as a corporate citizen, the plaintiff was entitled to complain of breaches of procedures and duties imposed by statute. Further, as a business competitor of Garamut the plaintiff was entitled complain against what it saw as a grant of an unlawful commercial advantage.

2 The court also dismissed the defendants' argument that since the lease was registered under the Land Registration Act, it was indefeasible except on ground that the second respondent was a party to the alleged fraud. For detailed discussion of this issue, see materials in Chapter 9.

Distinction between 'review' and 'appeal'

The *Steamship* case, above, mainly deals with a situation where the Minister did not follow the statutory procedure for the grant of a State lease. The following cases deal with other possible avenues for judicial review of the Minister's decision. Although these cases were decided under s 11 of the previous Land Act (Ch 185), they are still current as that provision is identical with s 62 of the Land Act 1996.

APPLICATION OF MOGE ENGA AND KUIPI GROUP IN THE MATTER OF THE DECISION OF THE MINISTER FOR LANDS CONCERNING SECTION 30 ALLOTMENT 7 MOUNT HAGEN
[1995] PNGLR 31, National Court of Papua New Guinea

[The Land Board recommended to the Minister to grant to the applicants (plaintiffs) a State lease over the subject land. Other persons who had applied for grant of the same lease appealed to the Minister pursuant to s 11 of the Land Act (cap 185),[10] to refer the matter back to the Board for reconsideration, and the Minister agreed. The Minister did not give reasons for his decision. The plaintiffs seek a judicial review of the Minister's decision on the ground that it was unreasonable and unfair.]

WOODS J: The lawyer for the State has submitted that once losing applicants have appealed, it is open to the Minister to reject the recommendation the Land Board merely because the applicants have exercised their right of appeal, that there is no requirement in the provisions of the Land Act for appeals to state the reasons, and that the Minister has an absolute discretion. The lawyer states that the applicant still has avenues open it to reapply before the Land Board at the new sitting.

The lawyers for the other appellants against the Land Board recommendation reiterate these submissions. They assert that the Land Act imposes no criteria for the right of appeal, and this court can insist on any criteria where none is laid down. They say the Minister only has to have a belief that the Land Board may have acted unfairly. They say that, even if the Minister may have appear to have acted unfairly, that is not enough for this court to intervene by way of judicial review. The court can only intervene if the Minister has acted unlawfully, and he clearly has not acted unlawfully here, as the Act specifically gives him the power to consider the recommendation of the departmental secretary and act on it.

It is submitted that the applicant has the onus to satisfy the court that the Minister has acted unlawfully, and the applicant has not satisfied that onus. The furtherest the applicant may have gone is to show that the Minister has acted unfairly against the applicant, who was the person originally recommended for the grant of the lease.

The simplest statement of the principles to be applied in considering whether an administrative action is subject to control by judicial review has been stated in the case *Council of Civil Service Unions v Minister for the Civil Service* [1984] 3 All ER 935 under three heads:

(b) Illegality, where the decision-making authority has been guilty of error of law.

(c) Irrationality, where the decision-making authority has acted so unreasonably that no reasonable authority would have made a decision.

10 This provision corresponds with s 62 of the Land Act 1996.

(d) Procedural impropriety, where the decision-making authority has failed in its duty to act fairly.

It must be reiterated that this court is not concerned with the actual decision made by the relevant administrative bodies, namely the Land Board or the Minister. This court is not considering the respective merits of the different applicant's applications. This court is considering the decision-making process, whether that process has miscarried in some fashion so as to justify interference.

So what is this procedure under the Land Act? It is a procedure for the fair and impartial granting of State leases over State land. This is done by setting up a specialist board whose duty it is to consider applications and decide between the merits of different applicants and make an appropriate recommendation to the appropriate functionary, whose duty it is to sign the actual lease on behalf of the State. The Board does all this by advertising that the respective parcel of land is available for applicants to apply for and then, in due course, holding a hearing, when applicants can present their evidence and other material to attest to their suitability. There is no suggestion here that any special preference was to be given to any particular class of person, whether by way of original landowning rights or prior dealing with the State. All this was done, and at the end of the day the applicant was the so called successful applicant, being the person whose name was presented to the Minister in the recommendation. To this point there is no suggestion of any irregularity, apart from some unsupported allegation in letters of appeal. So what is the status of the appeals? What do they mean?

The State and some parties submit that the mere fact of an appeal is grounds for the Minister to, in his discretion, reject the recommendation and, thereby, reject the detailed work and consideration of his expert committee or board. This does not make sense in any terms. Why was a specialist board set up to do this work of considering the most suitable applicant for a grant of State land if this means nothing to the Minister? Can the Minister reject a recommendation on any or no ground or because of his own personal predilections or preferences? I cannot find under any rationale that this is our system of government. That suggests a government by ministerial decree, or dictatorship. The Land Act is an act which gives every citizen or organisation an equal chance to apply for land, and it sets up a specialist body to consider these matters. The merits of this specialist body must mean something, fairness and impartiality. There is then an appeal. An appeal is a procedure of law which presupposes principles of justice. The person who considers an appeal must act judicially, not arbitrarily. This means he must act on good reasons. There must be good reasons presented to support an appeal, and a person considering an appeal must indicate to the parties interested why he has acted the way he has, and not secretly. His reasons should not be secret.

So what was the nature of these appeals? They were by losing applicants, but they did not present any coherent reasons. They made allegations, but presented no basis of evidence to support allegations. The submission by the Secretary for Lands itself does not present any support for the allegations, support which it would have had from its own records if there was any merit in the allegations. The Secretary merely repeats the allegations but gives no departmental decision which suggests that one of the appellants was supposed to be given preferred treatment. The Secretary seems to support the suggestion that the Minister's discretion is an arbitrary one. To take these suggestions to their logical conclusion, any losing applicant, by the mere fact of lodging an appeal, could force rehearings forever and, thereby, hold up all development of land in the country.

The Lands Department and the granting of leases for State land is not an exclusive fiefdom of the Minister for Lands. The system of government in PNG is a democratic form of government, where all persons have equal rights. These equal right are subject to regulations and control. For example, to allow every person an equal right and chance to acquire State leases, there is a specialist body called Board set up to consider the merits of applicants. Thus, the granting of State leases is not the sole prerogative of the Minister. He is merely the functionary who, at the end of the day, signs the grant of the lease after the specialist body has considered the best applicant. Whilst he is also the functionary who can reconsider the recommendation of the Board if there are real suggestions of maladministration, he cannot interfere if all has been done properly. If he interferes, he can only do it judicially, that is why the word appeal is used, or if there is some special reason of good government. As Amet J said in *Gegeyo v Minister for Lands* [1987] PNGLR 331 at 338, the Minister does have discretion to act for good cause; however, 'In this whole area of administrative decision making involving the legislature, the executive government and other tribunals there is no room for arbitrary decision-making'. In this case before me now, there have been no reasons or evidence presented to the Minister suggesting wrong-doing by the Land Board or that all applicants did not get a fair hearing before the Land Board. The Minister therefore had acted unreasonably and outside the boundary of his discretion in rejecting the recommendation of the Land Board, and is subject to review by this court.

I declare that the decision of the Minister for lands to reject the Land Board recommendation is harsh and oppressive, that he has not exercised his discretion according to principles of natural justice and fairness, and his ruling is, therefore, invalid. I order that the applicant is the successful applicant for the grant of a State lease over the land described as section 30 allotment 7, Mount Hagen, and I order that the Secretary for Lands take all appropriate steps to issue the subject lease.

Question

Assume that in the above case there was no appeal. However, the Minister purporting to Act under s 63(2) of the Land Act 1996, referred back to the Board its recommendation for re-hearing on the grounds that he disagreed with its recommendation, would the decision of the court be the same? Give reasons for your answer. See the following case.

WANDAKI v MINISTER FOR LANDS AND ANOTHER
[1996] PNGLR 116, National Court of Justice

[The National Land Board recommended a grant of a State lease to the second respondent. The applicant (plaintiff) successfully appealed to the Minister (first respondent) and the latter referred the matter back to the Board for re-hearing. The Board in its Meeting No 1879, recommended the grant of a State lease to the applicant. However, the Minister purporting to act under s 12(2) of the Land Act (Ch 185)[11] rejected the Board's recommendation and he referred the matter to the Western Highland Land Board (WHP) for re-hearing. The latter, in its Meeting No 1900, recommended to the Minister to grant a State lease to the second respondent. The applicant appealed to the Minister, pending the Minister's decision he instituted these proceedings for a judicial review of the Minister's decision to refer Board's

11 This provision corresponds with s 63(2) of the Land Act 1996.

recommendation (Meeting No 1879) to the WHP Land Board, and a second order for the Minister to grant a State lease to the applicant as per that recommendation.]

INJIA J: In this review, whilst the applicant challenges the decision of the Minister as to the relevance, appropriateness or reasonableness of the reason given by the Minister to refer the matter back to the WHP Land Board for re-hearing, he does not take issue with the WHP Land Board decision No 1900. The applicant relies on principles enunciated by Woods J in the *Re Moge Enga & Kuipi Group* [1995] PNGLR 31.

Mr Tamutal of Counsel for the second respondent submits that the application is an abuse of the process of the court because applicant did not challenge the decision of the Minister but instead accepted the decision of the Minister and appeared before the Land Board and when the WHP Land Board made a decision against him, he took issue in these proceedings not with the Board decision but the Minister's decision. Mr Tamutal submits that because the applicant's appeal to the Minister against the Provincial Land Board decision is still pending determination, it is an abuse of process of the court for the applicant to seek judicial review of the Minister's initial decision to refer the matter to the Provincial Land Board. He relies on the principles enunciated by the Supreme Court in the *Independent State of Papua New Guinea v Kapal* [1987] PNGLR 417 which were adopted and expounded upon by the Supreme Court in *Kekedo v Burns Philip (PNG) and Others* [1988–89] PNGLR 122.

It is necessary to first set out the relevant provisions of the Land Act I will consider or apply namely, s 8(1), (2); s 9, (a); s 11(1); 12(1), (2) and s 33 ... [See corresponding provisions of the Land Act 1996: ss 57, 58, 62, and 63.]

...

In this case, the decision appealed against and the decision for which judicial review is sought are different but, the end sought under both options is the same – that the Minister grant a State lease to the applicant. At the outset, I do not think the applicant is wrong in law in pursuing both options at the same time: *Kekedo v Burns Philip (PNG) Ltd, ante*, p 123. But, there is a problem with the appeal option. There is no evidence to show when the Board notified the applicant of its decision in Meeting No 1900 as required by, s 9(9) but, assuming that he was so notified on the date the decision was made (30/7/93), his appeal was late by three (3) weeks. Therefore, the appeal was incompetent and it is a nullity. Was the Minister under a legal duty to entertain the incompetent appeal? Clearly, he has no statutory power to consider an incompetent appeal or to validate an incompetent appeal. Therefore, the WHP Land Board decision remains valid and effective unless it is quashed by this court in the exercise of its judicial review jurisdiction.

The question to be asked in this review is whether the Minister acted *ultra vires* the Land Act, committed an error of law, committed a breach of natural Justice, reached a decision which no reasonable Minister for Lands could have reached or abused his powers: *Kekedo v Burns Philip (PNG) Ltd, ante*, p 123.

In this review, the applicant does not challenge the decision of the WHP Land Board, whereas he challenges the Minister's decision to reject the National Land Board's recommendation made in favour of the applicant and to refer the matter to the WHP Board for a re-hearing under s 12(2)(a).

A recommendation to the Minister by the Land Board for a Lease is made under s 33 of the Act. The word 'recommend' used in s 33(b) and the phrase 'if he disagrees with the recommendation of the Land Board, and may for any other reason' used in s 12(2)(a) implies that the Minister has the unfettered discretion to decide whether to accept or reject the recommendation of the Land Board. Is the Minister under a statutory duty to give reason(s) for his decision made under s 12(2)(a)? On the face of s 12(2)(a), he is under a duty to give a reason for his decision to refer the matter back to the Land Board for re-hearing, the reason being either that he disagrees with the Land Board's recommendation or for 'any other reason'. The categories of 'reasons' for referring the matter back for re-hearing are unlimited. Is the Minister under a statutory duty to give good, appropriate or relevant reasons for his disagreement, etc? On the face of s 12(2)(a), clearly he is under no such duty, the rationale, it seems, being that the power the Minister exercises at this stage is an executive power which is permeated by a wide range of prevailing socio-political and economic government policy considerations. It is not for this court or any other courts to question the soundness or otherwise of his reasons based on public considerations.

The power or discretion the Minister exercises at this stage is exercised on his own volition as distinct from an appeal under s 11. In an appeal, a party aggrieved by the decision of the Land Board seeks to invoke the exercise of the Minister's statutory power in his favour. There are competing interests involved which the Minister has to determine. I agree with Woods J in *Re Moge Enga & Kuipi Group, ante,* that (at p 5):

> An appeal is a procedure of law which presupposes principles of justice, the person who considers an appeal must act judicially, not arbitrarily, this means he must act on good reasons, there must be good reasons presented to support an appeal and a person considering an appeal must indicate to the parties interested why he has acted the way he has and not secretly, his reasons should not be secret.

I do not accept the applicant's submission that the Minister is under a duty to act judicially or not arbitrarily and that he must act on good reasons whilst exercising his power under s 12(2)(a). In the present case, the Minister gave a reason for disagreeing with the recommendation of the National Land Board and referring the matter to the WHP Land Board for a re-hearing. He acted in compliance with s 12(2)(a) by giving reasons for his decision. Whether the decision he gave was good, appropriate or sound is not a matter for review by this court.

It cannot be said that the Minister acted arbitrarily or in breach of natural Justice because he was under no statutory duty to afford an opportunity to the applicant to be heard before he made his decision. He acted in accordance with his powers under s 12(2)(a). He reached a decision which he was entitled to reach in the circumstances. He did not abuse his powers in that, he did not make a decision which determined the rights of parties but merely referred the matter to the WHP Land Board to re-hear the matter and make its own decision. He did not give any directions as to how the WHP Land Board should conduct the re-hearing – such directions which were calculated to favour the second respondent. The applicant did not take issue with the Minister's decision either before the WHP Land Board or by way of judicial review. The applicant must be taken to have accepted the Minister's decision and the reasons as being good and proper. The applicant was not impeded in any way by the WHP Land Board or the Minister in the presentation of his case before the WHP Land Board. The applicant stood at equal par with the other applicants before the WHP Land Board. And when the WHP Land Board's decision did not favour him he took issue with its decision.

In this review he has challenged the Minister's decision giving jurisdiction to the WHP Land Board to re-hear the matter, which Jurisdiction the applicant accepted in the first place by appearing before the Board. The court cannot conduct a review of the decision of the Minister which the applicant has by his conduct accepted.

For these reasons, I am not satisfied that the grounds for review have been made out by the applicant and I dismiss the application with costs to the second respondent.

[Application dismissed.]

III PURPOSES FOR WHICH A STATE LEASE MAY BE GRANTED

As may be recalled, under s 65 of the Land Act the Minister may grant State leases of government land only as provided by this Act. Section 67 prohibits the Minister to grant a State lease for a purpose that would be in contravention of zoning requirements under the Physical Planning Act 1989, or any other law relating to physical planning. The following provisions indicate the terms implied in a State lease and the purposes for which the Minister may grant such a lease.

82 Reservations, conditions, etc, in leases

(1) In this section, 'petroleum' means naturally occurring hydrocarbons in a free state, whether gaseous, liquid or solid, other than coal, shale or a substance that may be extracted from coal, shale or other rock by the application of heat or by a chemical process.

(2) In addition to such reservations, covenants and improvement and other conditions as are prescribed, a State lease shall contain such other reservations, covenants and conditions as the Minister considers proper.

(3) There is implied in a State lease –

(a) a reservation to the State of all minerals and mineral substances in or on the land the subject of the lease (including gold, silver, copper, tin, metals, ores and substances containing metals), gems, precious stones, coal, shale, mineral oils and valuable earths or substances, together with the right, subject to any law relating to mining, to authorize a person to enter on the land to search for, mine, work or win, recover and remove them or any of them and to do all things necessary or convenient for those purposes; and

(b) a reservation to the State of all petroleum on or below the surface of the land the subject of the lease, together with all rights necessary for the purpose of searching for and obtaining petroleum in any part of the land and all rights of way and easements for pipelines and for other purposes required for searching for, obtaining or conveying petroleum; and

(c) a reservation to the State of all helium found in association with petroleum on or below the surface of the land the subject of the lease, together with all rights necessary for the purpose of searching for, obtaining or conveying helium similar to the rights served by Paragraph (b) in respect of petroleum; and

(d) a condition that the lessee will, subject to section 119, use the land *bona fide* for the purpose only for which it is granted, or for a purpose ancillary to that purpose.

83 Rent

(1) The rent on a State lease is as is prescribed.

(2) Notwithstanding sub-section (1), the Minister may, not earlier than 10 years after the commencement of the term of a State lease as calculated in accordance with section 81,

where in any particular case he thinks fit and after considering a report of the Land Board, impose such lower rental as he thinks proper and as is specified in the notice (if any) given under section 68 in relation to the lease.

(3) The unimproved value of the land comprised in a State lease shall be re-assessed every 10 years, calculated from the commencement of the term of the lease, except where the Minister for some special reason, fixes an earlier date from which the periods of 10 years shall be calculated.

(4) A re-assessment takes effect, as from 1 January next following the giving by the Departmental Head to the lessee of notice of the re-assessment.

(5) Subject to section 116, where for any special reason he thinks fit, the Minister may, on the application of the lessee and after considering a report of the Land Board, remit or postpone in whole or in part, for such period and on such terms as he thinks proper, payment of rent on a State lease.

(6) Rent up to the next 1 January is payable on the granting of an application for a State lease or on the termination of any period of remission of rent granted, and afterwards annually in advance on 1 January in each year.

(7) The Departmental Head shall, as soon as practicable after 31 December in each year –

(a) prepare a list with the names of lessees from whom rent is due; and

(b) publish a notice in the *National Gazette* that the list has been prepared and may be inspected.

(8) Once the list referred to in sub-section (7) has been notified in the *National Gazette*, it shall be received in any court as *prima facie* evidence in each case that the rent is due and unpaid and that payment of the rent, where necessary, has been lawfully demanded.

Division 2 Improvements on land to be leased

84 Improvements on land to be leased

(1) Subject to sections 120 and 100 and 102, if there are improvements on land to be leased under this Act, the lessee may be required to pay an amount in respect of the improvements fixed by the Minister, after considering a report of the Land Board.

(2) Where a lessee is required to pay an amount in respect of improvements on the land the subject of his lease, the Minister may permit him to pay for them by annual instalments.

(3) The rate of payment in respect of improvements and the rate of interest payable are as prescribed.

85 Insurance on improvements not paid for

(1) While an amount payable in respect of improvements (including interest) under section 84 remains unpaid, the lessee shall insure the improvements and keep them insured with an insurer approved by the Departmental Head in the joint names of the State and the lessee according to their respective rights and interests, for their full insurable value, against loss or damage by fire or any other risk against which the Departmental Head requires him to insure.

(2) The lessee shall punctually pay all premiums and other sums necessary for effecting and keeping up insurance required under sub-section (1), and shall immediately hand to the Departmental Head every policy and receipt relating to the insurance.

(3) Notwithstanding anything in any law, all moneys received or recoverable under or by virtue of any insurance required under this section shall, at the option of the Departmental Head, be applied in or towards –

(a) substantially re-building or repairing the improvements lost or damaged; or

(b) paying or satisfying the amount (including interest) remaining unpaid in respect of those improvements,

and the surplus (if any) shall in either case be paid to the lessee.

(4) If a lessee fails to comply with this section, the Departmental Head may –

(a) insure the property or keep it insured in accordance with this section; and

(b) recover the cost of doing so from the lessee as a debt.

86 Maintenance of improvement

(1) A lessee shall –

(a) maintain all improvement referred to in section 85 in good order and condition; and

(b) carry out any requirement in that regard of the Departmental Head or of a person authorized for the purpose by the Departmental Head.

(2) If the improvements suffer loss or damage, the lessee shall –

(a) immediately make good the loss or damage to the satisfaction of the Departmental Head; and

(b) carry out any requirement in that regard of the Departmental Head or of a person authorized for the purpose by the Departmental Head.

(3) If a lessee fails to comply with this section the Departmental Head may take or cause to be taken such action as he, in his discretion, thinks desirable to maintain the property in or to restore the improvements to good order and condition, or to make good the loss or damage, and may recover the cost of doing so from the lessee as a debt.

Division 3 Agricultural Leases

87 Grant of Agricultural lease

Subject to this Act, the Minister may grant a lease for agricultural purposes for such term not exceeding 99 years, and for such area of government land, as seem to him proper.

88 Improvement conditions

An agricultural lease shall contain conditions prescribing the minimum improvements to be carried out by the lessee.

Division 4 Pastoral Leases

89 Grant of Pastoral lease

Subject to this Act, the Minister may grant a lease for pastoral purposes for such term, not exceeding 99 years, and for such area of government land, as seem to him proper.

90 Stocking conditions

A pastoral lease shall contain conditions as to the minimum stocking required of the lessee.

91 Inquiry into depasturing of stock

(1) The Minister may at any time direct the Departmental Head to inquire into the number of stock depastured on the land comprised in a pastoral lease.

(2) When directed to do so under sub-section (1), the Departmental Head shall inquire into, and report to the Minister on, the number of stock depastured on the land comprised in the lease.

(3) If the Minister is satisfied that the land is likely to be permanently injured on account of the number of stock being depastured on the land, and after considering a report of the Land Board, he may cause notice to be served on the lessee requiring him –

- (a) within a time specified in the notice to reduce the number of stock depastured on the land to not more than such number; and
- (b) to comply with such other conditions and restrictions as to the depasturing of stock,

as the Minister thinks proper and as are specified in the notice.

(4) Section 63 does not apply to or in relation to a report of the Land Board under sub-section (3).

Division 5 Business and Residence Leases

92 Grant of Business and Residence Leases

Subject to this Act, the Minister may grant leases of government land for business or residence purposes, or for both business and residence purposes.

93 Terms of Leases

A residence lease, business lease or lease for both business and residence purposes may be granted for such term, not exceeding 99 years, as to the Minister seems proper.

94 Specification of classes of business

A business lease or lease for both business and residence purposes may specify the class or classes of business for which the land may be used.

95 Land in physical planning areas

Subject to sections 69 and 73, before a lease under this Division of land in a physical planning area is granted, the land shall, in the first instance, be offered for lease by tender.

Division 6 Mission Leases

96 Grant of Mission Lease

(1) The Minister may grant a lease of government land to –

- (a) a corporation having for its object the establishment or conduct, in the country, of a Christian mission; or
- (b) a person in trust for an institution or body having any such object.

(2) A lease under sub-section (1) may be granted for such term, not exceeding 99 years, as to the Minister seems proper.

97 Purpose of Mission Lease

A mission lease may be granted for –

(a) the purpose of –
   (i) a church; or
   (ii) a dwelling-house or houses for members or persons employed by or working in connection with the mission; or
   (iii) a school; or
   (iv) a hospital; or
   (v) a building for any other charitable, educational or religious purpose; or
   (vi) gardens or pastures for purposes ancillary to any of the purposes specified in Sub-paragraphs (i) to (v) inclusive; and

(b) the construction or operation, for the purposes of the establishment or conduct in the country of a Christian mission, of an aerodrome, and the erection or maintenance of hangars and other buildings required for the operation of an aerodrome.

98 Rent

Rent is not payable for a mission lease.

Division 7 Leases of government-owned Buildings

99 Leases of land on which there are government-owned buildings

(1) The Minister may, by written agreement grant a lease of government land on which there is a building the property of the State.

(2) Sections 49, 68 to 76 inclusive, 82, 83 and 122 do not apply to or in relation to a grant of a lease of government-owned buildings.

(3) A lease may be granted under this section for business or residence purposes, or for both business and residence purposes.

(4) A lease may be granted under this section on a weekly, fortnightly, monthly or quarterly tenancy.

(5) A lease under this section shall –
   (a) contain such reservations, covenants, conditions and provisions as are prescribed to be included in a lease under this section, and such additional reservations, covenants, conditions and provisions as the Minister determines; and
   (b) take effect according to its tenor.

(6) This Act, other than this section and section 145, does not apply to or in relation to a lease granted under this section, but the law that would apply to and in relation to a lease of land held for an estate in fee simple applies to and in relation to a lease granted under this section as if the land leased were held by the State for an estate in fee simple.

(7) The Land Registration Act (Chapter 191) does not apply to leases granted under this section.

Division 8 Special Purposes Leases

100 Grant of special purposes leases

(1) Subject to section 69 and to sub-section (2), where the Minister thinks that the grant of a lease under any other Division of this Part would not be appropriate or would not be possible, he may grant a special purposes lease of government land.

(2) A special purposes lease shall not be granted for private residence purposes within a physical planning area.

(3) A special purposes lease may be granted for such term, not exceeding 99 years, and for such area of government land, as seem to the Minister proper.

(4) Subject to sub-sections (5) and (6), the rent for a special purposes lease is such (if any) as seems to the Minister proper and as is specified in the lease.

(5) In addition to, or in place of, rent, the Minister may make a special purposes lease subject to the payment of such royalties on any substance or thing to be recovered from or taken off the land the subject of the lease as he thinks proper and as are specified in the lease.

(6) At such times, in such manner, and on such basis as are specified in a special purposes lease, the Minister may –

(a) re-appraise the rent payable; or

(b) where in the lease no rent is specified, impose rent; or

(c) vary or impose royalty on any substance or thing referred to in sub-section (5).

(7) Sections 83 and 84 do not apply to or in relation to a special purposes lease.

101 Special purposes lease of land in physical planning area

Subject to section 69, before a lease under this Division of land within a physical planning area is granted the land shall, in the first instance, be offered for lease by tender.

Division 9 Special Agricultural and Business Leases

102 Grant of special agricultural and business leases

(1) The Minister may grant a lease for special agricultural and business purposes of land acquired under section 11.

(2) A special agricultural and business lease shall be granted –

(a) to a person or persons; or

(b) to a land group, business group or other incorporated body,

to whom the customary landowners have agreed that such a lease should be granted.

(3) A statement in the instrument of lease in the approved form referred to in section 11(2) concerning the person, land group, business group or other incorporated body to whom a special agricultural or business lease over the land shall be granted, is conclusive evidence of the identity of the person (whether natural or corporate) to whom the customary landowners agreed that the special agricultural and business lease should be granted.

(4) A special agricultural and business lease may be granted for such period, not exceeding 99 years, as to the Minister seems proper.

(5) Rent is not payable for a special agricultural and business lease.

(6) Sections 49, 68 to 76 inclusive, 82, 83, 84 and 122 do not apply to or in relation to a grant of a special agricultural and business lease.

(7) Notwithstanding anything in this Act, a special agricultural and business lease shall be effective from the date on which it is executed by the Minister and shall be deemed to

commence on the date on which the land subject to the lease was leased by the customary landowners to the State under section 11.

Division 10 Urban Development Leases

103 Interpretation

In this Division –

'Physical Planning Board' means a Physical Planning Board established under the Physical Planning Act 1989 which has jurisdiction in respect of the land over which an urban development lease is to be granted;

'Chief Physical Planner' means the Chief Physical Planner appointed under section 6 of the Physical Planning Act 1989.

104 Urban Development Leases to be granted over land in physical planning areas suitable for Sub-division

(1) Subject to section 69, where there is government land within a physical planning area that is suitable for sub-division in accordance with this Division, the land shall, in the first instance, be offered for lease by tender.

(2) A tender document shall contain the following:

(a) the particulars specified in section 68;

(b) the information provided by the Chief Physical Planner or his delegate under

(c) section 105;

(c) such other information as the Departmental head thinks fit or the Minister directs;

(d) the reserve price for the land.

(3) Land that has been offered for lease in accordance with sub-section (1) may –

(a) if unleased, be re-offered for lease by tender; or

(b) after the first or any subsequent unsuccessful offer for lease by tender, be granted on application under this Act.

105 Conditions precedent to land being advertised for sub-division

Before land is offered for lease under this Division, the Chief Physical Planner or his delegate, shall –

(a) certify –

(i) that the land is –

(A) within a physical planning area; and

(B) properly zoned; and

(C) suitable for sub-division; and

(D) suitable for release; and

(ii) after consultation with the relevant authorities, that the State will not incur undue expense in the provision of electricity, water and other services to the proposed sub-division; and

(b) provide –

(i) a plan showing the location of the land; and

(ii) an assessment of the sub-division potential of the land; and

(c) specify –
   (i) the development conditions that will apply to the lease; and
   (ii) the conditions that will apply in respect of the infrastructure and zoning when part or the whole of the land subject to the lease is subsequently surrendered.

106 Grant of Urban Development Lease of government Land

(1) A tender shall –
   (a) specify the amount offered; and
   (b) be accompanied by –
      (i) a preliminary proposal for the sub-division; and
      (ii) a preliminary sketch plan of the proposed sub-division; and
      (iii) a preliminary proposal for the infrastructure; and
      (iv) evidence of the financial and other resources of the tenderer available for the sub-division.

(2) When considering tenders or applications for the grant of an urban development lease, the Land Board shall consist of five persons including –
   (a) the Chairman or a Deputy Chairman; and
   (b) the Surveyor General or his delegate; and
   (c) the Chief Physical Planner or his delegate.

(3) A tender of an amount less than the reserve price is invalid and shall not be considered.

(4) The successful tenderer shall pay to the State the amount of his tender.

(5) The successful tenderer is entitled to an urban development lease of the land the subject of the tender, in accordance with the tender notice.

(6) The Minister is not bound to accept the highest or any tender.

(7) The grant of an urban development lease does not imply an approval of the preliminary proposals for the sub-division and infrastructure of the preliminary sketch plan of the proposed sub-division which are lodged with the tender in accordance with sub-section (1).

107 Urban sub-division by lessee of a State lease

(1) The lessee of a State lease of land within a physical planning area that is zoned as suitable for urban sub-division may apply to the Minister to surrender the lease or part of the lease in exchange for an urban development lease over the whole or part of the land comprised in the first-mentioned lease.

(2) An application under this section shall be accompanied by –
   (a) a preliminary proposal for the sub-division; and
   (b) a preliminary sketch plan of the proposed sub-division; and
   (c) a preliminary proposal for the infrastructure; and
   (d) evidence of the financial and other resources of the applicant available for the sub-division; and
   (e) evidence that the land is zoned as suitable for urban sub-division.

(3) If the Minister, on the advice of the Land Board as constituted in accordance with section 106(2), is satisfied that –

 (a) the preliminary proposal –

  (i) appears suitable; and

  (ii) is consistent with a general plan for development within the physical planning area; and

 (b) the State will not incur undue expense in the provision of electricity, water and other services to the proposed sub-division,

 he may grant a lease under this section conditional on the surrender of the whole, or such part as the Minister determines, of the lease in respect of which the application was made.

108 Terms and conditions of Urban Development Leases

An urban development lease –

(a) shall –

 (i) be for a term not exceeding five years; and

 (ii) contain –

  (A) a covenant that, within one year or such further time as the Minister in any particular case allows after the granting of the lease, the lessee will submit for the approval of the Physical Planning Board an application for full planning permission or sub-division and zoning, and a final proposal for sub-division, together with survey plans; and

  (B) a covenant that the lessee will conform with a determination of the Physical Planning Board under section 108(3);

  (C) a covenant that after the Physical Planning Board has given its approval under Clause (a)(ii)(A), the lessee will submit a cadastral survey plan of the sub-division to the Surveyor General or his delegate for registration; and

  (D) such other covenants and conditions, including the restrictions on disposal prescribed by section 70, as the Land Board thinks proper or as are prescribed; and

(b) may contain a requirement for the surrender, on such terms and conditions as are specified in the lease or as are agreed on between the Physical Planning Board and the lessee, of areas of the land the subject of the lease that are not and will not, under the final proposal for sub-division, be required for business or residence purposes; and

(c) may contain covenants that are to be inserted in new leases granted on the surrender of developed parts of the sub-division.

Note

In addition to the above implied terms, s 82 of the Land Act implies a term that any minerals found on or in land the subject of a State lease belongs to the government and that the lessee shall endeavour to use the land *bona fide* only for the purpose for which it is granted or ancillary purpose. The Minister has also the power to impose other reservations, covenants and conditions, as he considers proper (s 82(2)). Since the Land Registration Act (Ch No 191) applies to State leases, the covenants implied therein against the lessee are also implied in a State lease except where the covenants are inconsistent with the provisions of the Land Act or the terms expressed in a State lease.[12]

IV TERMINATION OF A STATE LEASE

Forfeiture of State lease

Forfeiture is the ultimate penalty for breach of covenants in a State lease. The power to terminate a State lease by forfeiture is subject to special statutory provisions under the Land Act 1996.[13]

122 Forfeiture of State lease

(1) The Minister may, by notice in the *National Gazette*, forfeit a State lease –

(a) if rent on the lease remains due and unpaid for a period of six months; or

(b) if fees are not paid in accordance with this Act; or

(c) if the amount payable in respect of improvements is not paid in accordance with this Act; or

(d) if –

(i) a covenant or condition of the lease; or

(ii) a provision of this Act relating to the lease; or

(iii) a requirement of a notice under section 91 relating to the lease,

is not complied with; or

(e) if the granting of the lease has been obtained, in the opinion of the Minister, wholly or partly as a result of statements that were, to the knowledge of the lessee, false or misleading.

(2) Before forfeiting a State lease under sub-section (1), the Minister –

(a) shall serve notice on the lessee calling on him to show cause, within a period specified in the notice, why the lease should not be forfeited on the ground or grounds specified in the notice; and

(b) may, whether or not cause has been shown in accordance with a notice under Paragraph (a), serve on the lessee a notice requiring him, within a period specified in the notice, to comply with the covenants or conditions of the lease or the provisions of this Act.

(3) The Minister shall not forfeit a lease under this section unless –

(a) the lessee has failed to comply with a notice under sub-section (2)(a) or (b); or

(b) the lessee has failed to show good cause why the lease should not be forfeited.

(4) Copies of a notice of forfeiture and a notice under sub-section (2)(a) or (b) shall be served on all persons who, to the knowledge of the Departmental Head, have or claim

12 See James, *Land Law and Policy in PNG*, *op cit*, note 3, p 91.

13 For discussion see Amankwah, Mugambwa and Muroa, *Land Law in Papua New Guinea*, *op cit*, note 8, pp 159–64; James, *Land Law and Policy in PNG*, *op cit*, note 3, pp 99–105.

to have a right, title, estate or interest in, to or in relation to the land, or such of them as can with reasonable diligence be ascertained and found.

(5) No acceptance of rent by the State waives a right to forfeit a lease under this Act.

(6) For the purposes of this section the grant of an application for a State lease shall be deemed to be the grant of the lease.

123 Revocation of Forfeiture

(1) Where a State lease (hereafter called 'the revoked lease') has been forfeited under section 122 by mistake, and provided that a notice under section 75 has not been published in the *National Gazette* in respect of another applicant, the Departmental Head may, by notice published in the *National Gazette*, revoke the notice of forfeiture.

(2) Where the Departmental Head publishes a notice under sub-section (1), the revoked lease shall be treated as valid and as effectual as if the forfeiture had not occurred.

Forfeiture is completed by publication of the notice of forfeiture in the *National Gazette*,[14] and entry in the appropriate Register of State leases.[15] A tenant whose lease is forfeited is not entitled to compensation for the value of the improvements he carried out on the land.[16]

Judicial review of forfeiture

The procedural requirements for enforcing forfeiture in s 122(2) of the Land Act 1996, mirror the rules of natural justice. A person aggrieved by the Minister's decision to forfeit a lease may either apply to the National Court for a judicial review of the decision (s 155(2)(b), Constitution) or appeal against the decision.[17] The following case discusses s 46(2) of the former Land Act (which is identical with s 122(2) of the 1996 Act) and the court's powers to review forfeiture of a lease.

Notice to show cause – Minister must act fairly and reasonably

HIGHLANDS PRODUCE BUYERS LTD v MINISTER FOR LANDS [1988] PNGLR 39, National Court of Justice

[In 1953, the government granted the applicant a State lease for agricultural purposes subject to a covenant for improvement of the land. At the time of these proceedings, the land had over 15,000 coffee trees, which were still producing coffee. On 26 June 1987 the Minister gave the applicant notice to show cause why the lease should not be forfeited on ground of failure to pay rent for more than six months. The notice was served on the applicant on 9 July 1987. There was no dispute that the PNG Banking Corporation, which had a mortgage over the land, did not receive copy of the notice. On 1 October 1987 a notice of forfeiture of the lease was published in the *National Gazette*. The applicant brought these proceedings for a judicial review of the decision.]

---

14 If the lessee appeals the notification has no effect until the court determines the appeal: s 142(3) of the Land Act, see below, p 392.

15 Section 39 of the Land Registration Act.

16 Section 119(8) of the Land Act 1996.

17 Section 142 of the Land Act 1996, see extract below, p 392.

WOODS J: The background of this is as deposed by the manager of the applicant as follows:

> In 1984 a confrontation developed between the Applicant and its employees and persons who describe themselves as 'traditional land owners' of this land. The Applicant and its employees were systematically harassed [sic] by these people and it became unsafe for the Applicant's sub-manager to work at the plantation. Because of the physical danger to the Applicant's employees, since 1984 the Applicant has not maintained the plantation to the same standard as previously. As well, much of the fencing has been stolen.
>
> In 1984, negotiations for the purchase of the land were entered into with the Applicant and 'traditional land owners' but it seems that this group has now fragmented into a number of sub groups and these negotiations have broken down. More recently, some of these persons have come forward to purchase the property and the applicant believes that it is possible for a sale to be negotiated with them. Annexed and marked with the letter 'H' is a copy of a letter of 9 November 1987 sent by people from the Korepa and Yamiufa villages to the Minister for Lands.

The next thing the applicant knew was a notice of forfeiture dated 8 September 1987 which was gazetted on 1 October 1987. The applicant immediately took these proceedings.

There is an inherent jurisdiction in the National Court to review administrative decisions and ensure that decision making bodies act fairly and in accordance with the law.

The question is therefore, has the Minister acted properly in accordance with the provisions in the Land Act?

There is no argument that the State has the power to forfeit a lease if the conditions in a lease are not complied with. But at all times it is expected that people will act reasonably and responsibly. A person shall not be dispossessed of his land without proper procedures according to law. Were the discretion and powers of the Minister exercised according to the provisions of the Act and according to provisions of natural justice and fairness?

I do not see any real basis for the forfeiture for non-payment of rent. That was paid each year. The State seems to be basing its ground on the maintenance of the plantation in a good husbandlike manner – there is no argument that the original improvement covenant has been complied with.

Without going into what is meant by properly maintaining the property once the improvement covenant has been complied with the Act specifically provides for notice to be given to show cause. If the law provides an opportunity for the person to explain then the law must mean that any explanation will be given proper consideration. This does not seem to have been done. The officers who advise the Minister for Land appeared to have given no consideration to the explanation or made any attempt to investigate the explanation. Instead the Minister just rushed with rather inordinate haste to forfeit. In the circumstances of this explanation it would be incumbent on the State as lessor to investigate carefully this explanation to ensure that a situation is not created whereby people are able, by an unlawful act (the occupation of land contrary to s 113 of the Land Act) to take the law into their own hands and in due course gain a claim to land by that unlawful act. This would create a dangerous precedent. Whilst one can ask why the applicant did not press the State as lessor to help it resolve the problem, it does appear that the applicant was trying to resolve the problem with so called descendants of the original traditional owners of the land.

Whilst I am satisfied that the Minister has acted harshly and contrary to the reasonable requirements of the Land Act in his consideration or lack of consideration of the explanation given following the notice to show cause, it is quite clear that the Minister has not complied with a fundamental provision of proper notice, namely notice to a mortgagee who has his interest clearly noted on the lease.

I am therefore satisfied that this is a matter in which the National Court should review the action of the Minister for Lands and I find that the provisions of the Land Act have not been complied with.

I therefore order that the notice of forfeiture dated 8 October 1987 be set aside and I order that the Registrar of Titles remove any reference to the notice of forfeiture from the State lease volume 43 folio 31.

(Orders accordingly.)

Application for judicial review based on failure to follow the prescribed procedure for forfeiture of a State lease. The case also considers the effect of delay in applying for judicial review.

DAVIS v PITZZ (SECRETARY FOR LANDS AND PHYSICAL PLANNING) AND THE INDEPENDENT STATE OF PAPUA NEW GUINEA [1988–89] PNGLR 147, National Court of Justice

[The applicant was the holder of a 99 year State lease subject to an improvement covenant which required the lessee at all times to maintain improvements on the land to the value of K600. In 1980 the applicant proposed to construct 12 units on the land. The plans were submitted to the relevant authorities for approval. In anticipation of approval, the applicant demolished a building on the land with a view to replace it with the units. In August 1983, a government valuer found the land vacant and unimproved. A show cause notice under s 46(2) of the Land Act, Ch 185 (which is identical with s 122(2) of the Land Act 1996) was sent to the applicant. Correspondence ensued between the applicant and government officials. Following a meeting of the Land Board, of which the applicant was advised but did not attend because she received the notice late, the Board recommended to the Minister to forfeit the lease for failure to comply with the improvement covenant and failure to pay rent. On 11 April 1984, the applicant was advised of the forfeiture. Between 1984 and 1986, the applicant made several representations to the Board and the Minister to reverse the decision, but to no avail. Subsequently the applicant brought those proceedings for judicial review of the Minister's decision.]

BREDMEYER J: It is clear that a number of legal errors were made in the forfeiting of this lease. It is not every breach of a statute which will result in a remedy for the person affected by that breach. Some breaches are minor and can be overlooked. Other breaches which affect a person's rights, cannot be overlooked. The subject is discussed in more detail in *Sylvanus Goria v National Parks Board* [1982] PNGLR 364 at 367–68. In this case I consider that I can ignore one minor breach but that the other breaches are important. The minor breach was that the notice to show cause under s 46(2) of the Act which was sent to Mrs Irene Davis was unsigned and undated. In the circumstances I consider that a minor technical breach only because Mr Dogo Olewale, a delegate of the Minister, did sign and date the same notice to show cause which was sent to the co-lessee, Mrs Schubert. Thus Mr Olewale did decide to serve a notice to show cause on the co-owners of the block and it is only a minor mistake that he failed to sign and date one of those notices. The position would have been different if the only notice sent out was undated and unsigned as that would indicate it was not sent by a person with authority to do so.

I consider that the officials made four major mistakes which go to the question of natural justice and Mrs Davis' rights as a lessee. The first is that five clear days notice of the hearing of the Land Board was given in the *Gazette* instead of seven. That is an important breach as obviously Parliament thought at least seven days notice in the *Gazette* was necessary in case the tenant did not get the notice by mail as was the case here. Secondly, the Land Board was not told that the rent was paid and was not outstanding at its meeting held in February 1984; and thirdly, it was not told of Mrs Davis' explanation as to why the land was unimproved. Clearly Mrs Davis could have left the domestic quarters or a carport or something on the block to the value of K600 or more and avoided forfeiture. Nevertheless, natural justice requires that her explanation which I find as a fact was sent in her letter of 11 October 1983 be put before the Land Board. I consider that letter was received by the Secretary for Lands but for some reason was missing from the file and hence not put to the Land Board.

The fourth failure, which I regard as very serious indeed, is that Mrs Davis was misled as to her appeal rights. As I said, she was given an official letter dated 11 April 1984 advising her of her right to appeal to the Governor General within 28 days on payment of a K10 deposit. A person is entitled to rely on an official letter from a government department setting out appeal rights and it is grossly unfair later to tell that person that the letter was incorrect, that the law had been amended and that the appeal was invalid. I regard those breaches of natural justice as very serious and am very sympathetic to the application for judicial review.

Delay

I need to consider the question of delay. The lease was forfeited by a notice published in the *Gazette* on 17 April 1986. This action was brought on 5 July 1988. Under s 112 of the Land Act, a person can appeal against forfeiture of a lease 'within 28 days ... or such further time as the National Court shall allow'. In *Placer Holdings Pty Ltd and the Land Act* [1982] PNGLR 326, the applicant knew of the forfeiture but chose not to appeal within the time limit. The applicant's lawyer thought that he could persuade the Land Board to regrant the lease. That course of action was unsuccessful and the trial judge held that the applicant's lawyer had not been lulled into any sense of false security by the Lands Department. The applicant applied to extend the time in which to appeal seven months later and the application was refused as being out of time.

A tenant who has had his lease forfeited can sidestep the 28-day appeal time limit by applying for a review of the decision by way of a declaration, see *Dent v Kavali* [1981] PNGLR 488, or by applying for judicial review, as had been done in this case. However, both of those remedies can be refused if there is undue delay. Order 16, r 4(1) and (2), of the National Court Rules requires an application for judicial review to be brought within four months of the decision made. Where there has been undue delay, whether within the four-month period or outside it, that can be a reason for refusing the relief sought if the court considers the granting of the relief sought would be likely to cause substantial hardship to any person or substantially prejudice the rights of any person or would be detrimental to good administration. In *NTN Pty Ltd v Post and Telecommunication Corporation* [1987] PNGLR 70, a 16-month delay was rejected as unreasonable. In *Papua New Guinea v Lohia Sisia* [1987] PNGLR 102, which was an application for a declaration, a delay of five-and-a-half years was rejected as unreasonable. In this case the delay is nearly two years three months but I propose to overlook the delay and grant the relief sought for the following reasons. First, the land has not been leased to anyone else. This distinguishes it from the situation in the NTN case where the TV licensee spent large sums of money on its broadcast operation in the 16 months after the grant of the licence. Secondly, Mrs Davis was given some hope that her alternative method of redress, namely lobbying with the Minister to have the land regranted to her, was likely to be successful as per the Minister's minute of 18 July 1986 which I have already quoted. Thirdly, although delay of over two years in challenging an administrative decision is likely to be detrimental to good administration, in this case the State chose not to argue the question of delay.

I quash the Minister's decision declaring the lease forfeited and I grant costs of this case to the plaintiff against the second defendant. I also dissolve the interim injunction granted herein on 22 February 1989 and successively extended to date, as is now no longer necessary.

[Ministerial decision to forfeit lease quashed.]

Appeal against forfeiture

Section 142 of the Land Act 1996 gives any interested person a right of appeal against a decision of forfeiture of a State lease. The section provides as follows:

142 Appeal to National Court

(1) An interested person may appeal to the National Court on –

...

(b) the forfeiture of a lease.

(2) An appeal under sub-section (1) shall be made within 28 days after the matter complained of, or within such further time as the National Court for any special reason allows.

(3) Where an appeal is made under sub-section (1), the matter complained of has no effect until –

(a) the National Court has decided the appeal; or

(b) where no further appeal is made to the Supreme Court – the period prescribed for making an appeal has expired; or

(c) where a further appeal is made to the Supreme Court – the Supreme Court has decided the appeal,

and, subject to sub-section (4), a lessee may in the meantime continue lawfully to occupy the land the subject of the appeal and to exercise his rights, and shall fulfil his obligations, under the lease.

There is no definition in the Act of the expression 'interested person' for the purpose of appeal. Undoubtedly, the term would include the lessee whose lease is forfeited, a sub-lessee, mortgagee,[18] and any other person prejudiced by the decision to forfeit.

In the absence of special reasons, the courts will not entertain an appeal against forfeiture made outside the 28-day prescribed period.

18 See *Highlands Produce Buyer Ltd v Minister for Lands*, extracted above, p 388.

PLACER HOLDINGS PTY LTD AND THE LAND ACT (CH 185) [1982] PNGLR 326, National Court of Justice

KAPI DEPUTY CJ: This is an application for extension of time within which to appeal under the Land Act (Chapter 185), s 112(2).

Placer Development Ltd was granted a government lease (Vol 50, Folio 59) under the Land Act. The lease was forfeited by the government on 1 May 1980. The applicant and its lawyers became aware of this forfeiture on 16 May 1980. Under the Land Act (s 112(2)) an interested person may appeal to the National Court on a forfeiture of a lease within 28 days or within such further time as the court may allow. The applicant did not appeal against the forfeiture within 28 days. The application to extend time was not filed until 23 December 1980. This application came before Miles J on 27 February 1981. The State was not represented. The application was granted and time extended to 23 December 1980. The applicant filed a notice of appeal on that day.

Subsequently, the State made an application to Miles J to set aside his order of extension of time. A number of new matters were raised which were not brought to his Honour's attention during the hearing of the earlier application. The most important matter was a decision of Williams J in *In Re Proposed Appeal by Constantinou* [1977] PNGLR 1. This case stands for the proposition that an application for extension of time within which to appeal under s 112(2) of the Land Act, cannot be made outside the time limited for appeal (ie, 28 days). His Honour felt bound by this decision and he came to the conclusion that had this authority been brought to his attention earlier, he would not have made the order he made. He set aside his earlier order on this basis.

The applicant appealed to the Supreme Court on the basis that the *Constantinou* case was wrongly decided and that an applicant could make an application outside the 28 days period and it was a matter for the National Court in the exercise of its discretion whether to grant the application or not. The Supreme Court upheld the appeal and sent the matter back for rehearing on the merits. See *Placer Holdings Pty Ltd v PNG* [1982] PNGLR 16.

I am required to consider the merits of this application under s 112(2) of the Land Act which provides:

> An appeal under sub-s 1 shall be made within 28 days after the matter complained of, or within such further time as the National Court for any special reason allows.

What are the proper principles which should guide the court in considering applications under this provision?

In construing the provision I do not intend to define the meaning of 'special reason'. What is or may not be a 'special reason' on the particular facts of a case should be left to the discretion of the court in the particular case. However, some assistance can be obtained from cases dealing with general statutory provisions on extension of time. Section 34(2) of the then Supreme Court (Full Court) Ordinance 1968 provided as follows:

> The time within which notice of appeal, or notice of an application for leave to appeal, may be given, may be extended at any time by the Full Court of a judge.

In construing this provision, the then Full Court said:

> From authorities cited before us we take the proper construction of s 34(2) to be that an extension of time will not be granted as a matter of course but that the court will in

every case require *substantial reasons* to be advanced before granting such a concession. (Emphasis mine.)

It appears to me from the foregoing cases [omitted] that the words 'special reason' in s 112(2) of the Land Act specify the type of reason which the courts have implied into more general provisions. I consider the principles set out in the above cases applicable in this case:

1 leave will not be granted as a matter of course;

2 there must be special reason, or substantial reason, or satisfactory reason, or cogent and convincing reasons or exceptional circumstances shown for the delay;

3 there must be some merit in the grounds of appeal;

4 whether leave is granted is in the discretion of the court;

5 the onus is on the applicant to satisfy the court.

The applicant was made aware of the forfeiture on 16 May 1980. The applicant's lawyers were advised immediately on the same day. The applicant and its lawyers had 12 days in which to lodge an appeal against the forfeiture. I consider that they had enough time in which to lodge the appeal. The applicant does not allege that its lawyers did not have enough time to lodge the appeal. They allowed the 28 days period to lapse.

The only reason which it puts forward as a special reason is that its lawyers were given to understand by the Department of Lands that the same land would come up for tender and that it would submit a new tender. The lawyer for the applicant apparently determined that it had good prospect of success and advised not to appeal and wait for the new tender. The applicant's submission is that its lawyers were lulled into a false security and therefore determined not to appeal.

[His Honour considered the evidence and concluded:]

I have come to the following conclusions:

(a) That there is no evidence to show that the applicant's lawyer was lulled into a false security by the Department of Lands that its application in the new tender would be successful.

(b) The choice not to appeal within time was made by the applicant upon advice by its own lawyer. The lawyer's advice was based on his own independent opinion of the success of the new tender. The prospect of success in the new tender was very remote at the time the decision was made not to appeal. The applicant and its lawyer took this course out of their own accord.

(c) When the applicant was made aware that it ran the risk of not having this land approved by the town planner in July 1980, it took no action to secure the right of appeal by applying for extension of time at an earlier date.

(d) Upon receipt of advice by the town planner that the land would not be up for tender on 12 November 1980, the applicant took no action until 34 days later. No explanation has been given for this delay.

I am not satisfied that any special reason has been shown by the applicant.

The applicant further relied on the provision of s 155(4) of the Constitution. This argument was not fully developed.

This provision has been fully considered in *Avia Aihi v The State* [1981] PNGLR 81, and *SCR No 2 of 1981; Re s 19(1)(f) of the Criminal Code* [1982] PNGLR 150. These cases have established that power given under this provision is remedial in nature and cannot be used to create primary rights. There must be an existing right. This power can be used to protect or enforce existing rights. In principle, I consider that the right to apply for an extension of time in which to appeal under s 112(2) of the Land Act could equally be enforced under the second leg of s 155(4) of the Constitution. However, I do not consider that the provision takes the matter any further than the Land Act. Under s 155(4) of the Constitution, the court may make orders which 'are necessary to do justice in the circumstances of a particular case'. What is justice in the circumstances means justice according to law. The court cannot apply its own action of justice. The law to be applied on an extension of time in the context of this case is in s 112(2) of the Land Act. That is to say, the exercise of the court's discretion can only be exercised in favour of extension of time for a special reason. I have already concluded that the applicant has failed to show any special reason.

Application refused.

Question

What is the difference between judicial review and an appeal?

Fine in lieu of forfeiture

Section 124 the Land Act 1996, empowers the Minister, at his discretion, to impose a fine instead of forfeiture.

124 Fee instead of forfeiture

(1) If a term, covenant or condition of a State lease is not complied with, the Minister may, in his discretion, instead of taking action under section 122, serve notice on the lessee calling on him to show cause, within a period specified in the notice, why a non-compliance fee should not be imposed under this section.

(2) If the lessee fails, within the period specified in the notice under sub-section (1), to show good cause why the non-compliance fee should not be imposed, the Minister may, by written notice served on the lessee, impose a non-compliance fee not exceeding K100.00 per month for each month for which the non-compliance has continued or continues.

(3) If a non-compliance fee imposed under this section is not paid within the time limited for the purpose in the notice under sub-section (2), the Minister may, by notice in the *National Gazette*, forfeit the lease without regard to any formalities or requirements of this Act preliminary to the forfeiture of a State lease, or otherwise.

(4) No acceptance of rent by the State waives a right to impose a non-compliance fee or forfeit a lease under this section.

(5) For the purposes of this section a grant of an application for a State lease shall be deemed to be the grant of the lease.

A lessee aggrieved by the Minister's decision to impose a fine may apply to the court for review. It is noteworthy that the section does not give a right of appeal against the fine. However, presumably, the lessee could appeal if default in payment of the fine results in forfeiture.

Relief from forfeiture

It is possible that in addition to the statutory remedies, a State lessee could seek judicial equitable relief against forfeiture.[19]

Surrender of State lease

A lessee of a State lease may terminate the lease by surrender.

110 Surrender of land in the Sub-division and Grant of new leases

(1) On the completion, to the satisfaction of the Chief Physical Planner or his delegate of development of all or any part of the land the subject of an urban development lease, the lessee may surrender all or part of the land and a new lease or new leases shall be granted over the developed portions of the land –

(a) in the name of the lessee; or

(b) at the direction of the lessee.

(2) The new lease or new leases shall contain the covenants and conditions specified under sections 107(c) and 109(3).

(3) On the partial surrender of a lease in accordance with sub-section (1), the rent, covenants and conditions of the lease may be varied to such extent as the Minister, on the recommendation of the Departmental Head, thinks proper.

Question

Under what circumstances may a lessee wish to surrender a State lease?

Compensation for improvements

The Land Act 1996 makes provision for the compensation payment to the outgoing tenant for the value of the improvement effected by him during the currency of the lease.[20]

119 Payment for improvements on expiration of lease

(1) In this section –

'improvements' means improvements made, or in respect of which a payment has been made, by the outgoing lessee, that are suitable to the land and add to its leasing value, other than improvements in respect of which the lessee has received payment under this section;

'value' means the value on the day after the date of expiration of the lease.

(2) Where, after the expiration of the term of a State lease of land on which there are improvements, the lessee is granted –

(a) a further lease of the land; or

(b) a lease of part only, or that includes part only, of the land,

---

19 See Chapter 6. See also James, *Land Law and Policy in Papua New Guinea*, *op cit*, note 3, p 103.

20 For discussion, see James, *Land Law and Policy in Papua New Guinea*, *op cit*, note 3, pp 30–31.

the provisions of section 84 do not apply in respect of the improvements in relation to the further lease, unless he has received payment for the improvements under this section.

(3) Subject to this section, where on the expiration of the term of a State lease of land on which there are improvements the lessee applies for and is not granted a further lease of the land, or is granted a further lease of part only, or that includes part only, of the land, the Minister shall, within six months after the expiration, pay to the outgoing lessee the value of the improvements on the land, or on the part of the land not included in the further lease, as the case may be.

(4) Where, within the period of six months referred to in sub-section (3), a State lease of the land or part of the land the subject of the expired lease is granted to a person other than the outgoing lessee, the Minister shall pay to the outgoing lessee, on or before the date of grant of the new lease, the value of the improvements on the land or that part of the land, as the case may be.

(5) Subject to sub-sections (6) and (13), this section does not entitle a lessee who does not apply for a further lease of the land the subject of his lease to payment for improvements on the land at the expiration of the lease, but he may remove such of the improvements as are severable on or before the expiration, doing as little damage as may reasonably be to the land.

(6) Where a lease is surrendered under this Act, the lessee may remove such of the improvements as are severable on or before the surrender, doing as little damage as may reasonably be to the land.

(7) If the outgoing lessee and the incoming lessee (if any) –

(a) agree as to –

(i) the amount to be paid for improvements for which the outgoing lessee is entitled to receive payment by the State or that he is entitled to remove under this section; and

(ii) the time and manner of payment; and

(b) notify the Minister in writing of their agreement before the date on which a lease is granted to the incoming lessee,

then –

(c) the amount payable in respect of the improvements under section 84 is payable by the incoming lessee to the outgoing lessee; and

(d) the Minister ceases to be liable under this section to pay the value of the improvements to the outgoing lessee; and

(e) section 84 does not apply in respect of those improvements in relation to the new lease.

(8) This section does not apply to or in relation to a lease that is forfeited under this Act.

(9) Where, between –

(a) the date of the expiration of the term of a State lease of land on which there are improvements for which the outgoing lessee is entitled to receive payment or which he is entitled to remove under this section; and

(b) the date of the grant of a State lease of the land or a part of the land to the outgoing lessee or another person, the State derives revenue, part or all of which is directly attributed to those improvements on the land or that part of the land, the Minister shall pay to the lessee, from time to time as the Minister determines, the revenue or such part of the revenue as is directly attributable to the improvements, less the amount of any expenditure incurred by the State in maintenance and other costs in respect of the improvements.

(10) Without prejudice to any other remedies that are available, the Minister may deduct from moneys payable by him under this section –

(a) moneys due during the term of the lease and outstanding to the State in respect of the term, or in respect of the land the subject of the lease; and

(b) if the outgoing lessee has continued to occupy the land after the expiration of the term of the lease – any occupation fee outstanding.

(11) The lessee of a special purposes lease or mission lease may remove, on or before the expiration of the lease, such of the improvements on the land the subject of the lease as are severable, doing as little damage as may reasonably be to the land, but otherwise is not entitled to payment under this section in respect of the improvements.

(12) The amount to be paid under this section shall be determined, and is recoverable, as nearly as may be in the same manner as compensation under Part IV.

(13) For the purposes of this section, where a lease expires and a further lease cannot be granted because the land the subject of the lease is reserved from lease or further lease under this Act –

(a) the lessee shall be deemed to have applied for and not to have been granted a further lease over that land; and

(b) the period of six months specified in sub-section (3) shall be deemed to expire at the end of the period of one month after the date of expiration of the lease.

Notes

Readers should note the following. Firstly, compensation is only payable: (i) where a lessee applies for an extension of his lease and the government refuses to grant the extension; or (ii) grants extension over only part of the land (s 119(3)); or (iii) where an extension of the lease cannot be granted because the land the subject of the lease is reserved from further lease (s 119(13)). Secondly, an outgoing tenant who does not seek a renewal of the lease (s 119(5)), or who surrenders the lease (s 119(6)), or a lessee of a special purpose lease or mission lease (s 119(11)), is not entitled to compensation for the improvements. However, the lessee may remove any severable improvements, which he erected on the land doing as little damage to the land as possible. Thirdly, where a State lease is forfeited, the tenant is not entitled to compensation for the improvements (s 119(8)). The section does not say whether or not a tenant whose lease is forfeited has the right to remove severable improvements. Finally, compensation for improvements is payable by the Minister within six months of expiration of the lease (s 119(3)), but if within those six months the land is leased to another person compensation must be paid on or before the date of grant of a new lease (s 119(4)).

CHAPTER 8

EASEMENTS AND RESTRICTIVE COVENANTS

I INTRODUCTION

Two landowners may agree among themselves to give each other certain rights over the other's land. The rights include easements and restrictive covenants.[1] Though these rights do not constitute estates in the land, they are interests in land and as such may be enforced against whoever is the landowner irrespective of privity of contract.

II EASEMENTS

An easement is a right which attaches to a particular piece of land and which allows the owner of that land either to use the land of another person in a particular manner or restrict its use by that other person to a certain extent.[2] A right of way over another's land is a common example of an easement.

Essential features[3]

A right over another person's land is not an easement unless it satisfies certain legal requirements of an easement:

(a) there must be in existence a dominant and servient tenement;

(b) the right must accommodate the dominant tenement;

(c) the dominant and the servient tenements must not be owned and occupied by the same person; and

(d) the right must be capable of forming the subject matter of a grant.

The case of *In Re Ellenborough Park*, extracted below, is the classical illustration of these features.

IN RE ELLENBOROUGH PARK [1955] 3 All ER 667, Court of Appeal

> [A developer sub-divided a large block of land into small plots, which were sold to various persons. They left out an inner portion of the block, known as Ellenborough Park, to be maintained as a pleasure ground for the enjoyment at all times by the owners of the surrounding plots in common with each other, subject to contribution of a proportionate amount to the cost of the upkeep of the park. During the war years, the government requisitioned the Park, and the surrounding owners could not use it. The government paid a yearly compensation rent, and an amount for dilapidation. The respective owners of the

1 Other rights include profits *à prendre* and licenses. Licences are discussed in Chapter 6.

2 *Cheshire and Burn's Modern Law of Real Property* (14th edn, Butterworths, London), p 490.

3 For discussion see Amankwah, Mugambwa and Muroa, *Land Law in Papua New Guinea* (Lawbook Co, Sydney, 2001), pp 213–15.

plots (ownership of the plots had changed hands many times so that none of the current owners was an original purchaser) claimed a share of the compensation on the basis that they had an easement over the Park. Danckwerts J found in their favour. Appeal to the Court of Appeal.]

SIR EVERSHED MR (Reading the judgment of the court): The substantial question raised in this appeal is whether the respondent ... being the owners of certain houses fronting on, or, in some few cases, adjacent to, the garden or park known as Ellenborough Park ... have any right known to the law, and now enforceable by them against the owners of the park, to the use and enjoyment of the park ...

The substantial question in the case ... is one of considerable interest and importance ... [I]f the owners of the houses are now entitled to an enforceable right in respect of the use and enjoyment of Ellenborough Park, that right must have the character and quality of an easement as understood by, and known to, our law. It has, therefore, been necessary for us to consider carefully the qualities and characteristics of easements ...

For the purposes of the argument before us counsel were content to adopt, as correct, the four characteristics formulated in Dr Cheshire's *Modern Real Property* (7th edn), p 456 *et seq*. They are: (i) there must be a dominant and a servient tenement; (ii) an easement must accommodate the dominant tenement; (iii) dominant and servient owners must be different persons; and (iv) a right over land cannot amount to an easement unless it is capable of forming the subject matter of a grant.

The four characteristics stated by Dr Cheshire correspond with the qualities discussed by Gale in his second chapter, sections 2, 5, 3, and 6 and 8 respectively. Two of the four may be disregarded for present purposes, viz, the first and the third. If the garden or park is, as it is alleged to be, the servient tenement in the present case, then it is undoubtedly distinct from the alleged dominant tenements, viz, the freeholds of the several houses whose owners claim to exercise the rights. It is equally clear that if these land respectively constitute the servient and dominant tenements, then they are owned by different persons. The argument in the case is found accordingly to turn on the meaning and application to the circumstances of the present case of the second and fourth conditions, ie, first, whether the alleged easement can be said in truth to 'accommodate' the dominant tenement, in other words, whether there exists the required 'connection' between the one and the other; and, second, whether the right alleged is 'capable of forming the subject matter of a grant'. The exact significance of this fourth and last condition is, at first sight perhaps, not entirely clear. As between the original parties to the 'grant' it is not in doubt that rights of this kind would be capable of taking effect by way of contract or licence. But for the purposes of the present case, as the arguments made clear, the cognate questions involved under this condition are: whether the rights purported to be given are expressed in terms of too wide and vague a character; whether, if and so far as effective, such rights would amount to rights of joint occupation or would substantially deprive the owners of the park of proprietorship or legal possession; whether, if and so far as effective, such rights constitute mere rights of recreation, possessing no quality of utility or benefit; and on such grounds cannot qualify as easements.

[His Honour stated the terms of the conveyance and continued:]

... [I]t is clear from the deed from which we have quoted, and from the other deeds in like form made (as must be assumed) in respect of the remaining premises in Ellenborough Crescent, that the original common vendors were engaged on a scheme of development of this part of the White Cross Estate designed to produce a result of common experience; namely, a row of uniform houses facing inwards on a park or garden which was intended to form, and formed in fact, an essential characteristic belonging, and properly speaking 'appurtenant', to all and each of them. In substance, instead of each house being confined to its own small or moderate garden, each was to enjoy in common, but in common exclusively with the other houses in the crescent, a single large 'private' garden. In our judgment, the substance of the matter is not in this respect affected by the fact that some few houses in the immediate proximity of, but not actually fronting on, the park were also entitled to share the privilege. This extension of the privilege may no doubt be unusual and (at first sight at any rate) out of line with the conception of the square and its surrounding houses as a symmetrical unit. It has, therefore, a bearing on the question of the 'connection' between the right enjoyed and the premises of the relevant house owners; and must be discussed under the head of Dr Cheshire's first condition. In our judgment, the language of the deed of 1864 is clear to the effect that the right of enjoyment of the garden was intended to be annexed to the premises sold, rather than given as a privilege personal to their purchaser. The enjoyment was not exclusive to those premises alone; it was to be held in common with the like rights annexed to the other houses in (and in some few cases in close proximity to) the square or crescent. But it was not contemplated that like rights should be otherwise extended so as to belong in any sense to premises not forming part of (or at least closely connected with) the square or their owners. The position of the grant in the deed and its language show that, in the respects we have mentioned, the right granted was intended and treated as in *pari materia* with the rights of way and drainage similarly conferred. The relevant part of the deed opens with the general formula 'Together with all ways ... easements rights and appurtenances to the said plot of land ... appertaining'. The rights of way (admittedly easements properly so called) follow immediately the general formula, being linked to it by the words 'and particularly'. The next two words are 'And also', which, in turn, introduce the garden rights now in question in language which repeats the phrase used in relation to the rights of way – 'in common with the other persons to whom such easements may be granted'. In our judgment, if the construction of this part of the deed does not tend to the conclusion that the garden rights, like the rights of way, were particular examples of the general grant of easements and rights appurtenant to the plot conveyed, it is at least made clear that the garden rights were (so far of course as they properly could be) of the same character quoad the land conveyed as the rights of way and drainage. It was conceded that the rights, if effectual and enforceable, were conditional, that is, on the house owners making their appropriate contributions to the cost of upkeep In this respect, again, they were analogous, by the terms of the deed, to the rights of way over Crescent and Walliscote Roads. As a complement to the rights of enjoyment of the garden, subject to the condition of contribution, was the covenant by the vendors against building on the park and to the effect that the park should at all times remain as an ornamental garden. Counsel for the owners of the park did not seriously challenge the contentions of counsel for the owners of the houses that in their context the words of the covenant to which we have last referred could fairly be construed as implying a negative covenant on the vendors' part against any user by them of the park otherwise than as a garden. There is clear authority that, if such be the substantial effect of the covenant, its benefit and burden will run with the land. The last consideration appreciably reinforces the view which we take of the meaning and intention of the deed to attach the garden rights in all respects like the rights of way and drainage to the land conveyed.

It remains to interpret the actual terms of the grant itself – 'the full enjoyment of the pleasure ground set out and made ...'. Counsel for the owners of the park fastened on the presence of the word 'full', and the absence of any indication of the way in which the pleasure ground was to be used – or of any limitations on its use – and contended that the right or privilege given was a *jus spatiandi* in its strict sense, that is, a right to go or wander on the park and every part of it and enjoy its amenities (and even its produce) without stint.

We do not so construe the words in their context. Although we are now anticipating to some extent the question which arises under the fourth of Dr Cheshire's conditions, it seems to us, as a matter of construction, that the use contemplated and granted was the use of the park as a garden, the proprietorship of which (and of the produce of which) remained vested in the vendors and their successors. The enjoyment contemplated was the enjoyment of the vendors' ornamental garden in its physical state as such – the right, that is to say, of walking on or over those parts provided for such purpose, that is, pathways and (subject to restrictions in the ordinary course in the interest of the grass) the lawns; to rest in or on the seats or other places provided; and, if certain parts were set apart for particular recreations such as tennis or bowls, to use those parts for those purposes, subject again, in the ordinary course to the provisions made for their regulation; but not to trample at will all over the park, to cut or pluck the flowers or shrubs, or to interfere in the laying out or upkeep of the park. Such use or enjoyment is, we think, a common and clearly understood conception, analogous to the use and enjoyment conferred on members of the public, when they are open to the public, of parks or gardens ...

We pass accordingly to a consideration of the first of Dr Cheshire's conditions – that of the accommodation of the alleged dominant tenements by the rights as we have interpreted them. For it was one of the main submissions by counsel for the owners of the park that the right of full enjoyment of the park granted to the purchaser by the conveyance of 23 Dec 1864, was insufficiently connected with the enjoyment of the property conveyed in that it did not subserve some use which was to be made of that property; and that such a right accordingly could not exist in law as an easement. In this part of his argument, counsel was invoking a principle which is, in our judgment, of unchallengeable authority, expounded, in somewhat varying language, in many judicial utterances. We think it unnecessary to review the authorities in which the principle has been applied; for the effect of the decisions is stated with accuracy in Dr Cheshire's book at p 457. After pointing out that:

> ... one of the fundamental principles concerning easements is that they must be not only appurtenant to a dominant tenement, but also connected with the normal enjoyment of the dominant tenement ...

and referring to certain citations in support of that proposition the learned author proceeded:

> We may expand the statement of the principle thus: a right enjoyed by one over the land of another does not possess the status of an easement unless it accommodates and serves the dominant tenement, and is reasonably necessary for the better enjoyment of that tenement, for if it has no necessary connection therewith, although it confers an advantage upon the owner and renders his ownership of the land more valuable, it is not an easement at all, but a mere contractual right personal to and only enforceable between the two contracting parties.

Can it be said, then, of the right of full enjoyment of the park in question which was granted by the conveyance of 23 Dec 1864, and which, for reasons already given was, in our view, intended to be annexed to the property conveyed to ... [the respondent], that it accommodated and served that property? It is clear that the right did, in some degree, enhance the value of the property and this consideration cannot be dismissed as wholly irrelevant. It is, of course, a point to be noted; but we agree with the submission of counsel for the owners of the park that it is in no way decisive of the problem; it is not sufficient to show that the right increased the value of the property conveyed unless it is also shown that it was connected with the normal enjoyment of that property. It appears to us that the question whether or not this connection exists, is primarily one of fact, and depends largely on the nature of the alleged dominant tenement and the nature of the right granted. As to the former, it was in the contemplation of the parties to the conveyance of 1864 that the property conveyed should be used for residential and not commercial purposes. That appears from the conveyance itself, and the covenant by the purchaser already quoted, that the dwelling-house, etc, which he bound himself to build should not:

> ... be occupied or used as an open or exposed shop or for any purpose of trade or commerce other than a lodging house or private school or seminary ...

without the vendor's written consent. Since it is stated in para 4 of Mr Rendell's affidavit in support of the summons and has been conceded that all the conveyances of plots for building purposes fronting or near Ellenborough Park were as regards (*inter alia*) user substantially the same as the conveyance of 1864, the inevitable inference is that the houses which were to be built on the plots were to constitute a residential estate. As appears from the map which is exhibit 'G' to Mr Rendell's further affidavit of 13 Oct 1955, the houses which were built on the plot around and near to Ellenborough Park varied in size, some being large detached houses and others smaller and either semi-detached or in a row. We have already stated that the purchasers of all the plots which actually abutted on the park were granted the right to enjoy the use of it as were also the purchasers of some of the plots which, although not fronting on the park, were only a short distance away from it. As to the nature of the right granted, the conveyance of 1864 shows that the park was to be kept and maintained as a pleasure ground or ornamental garden, and that it was contemplated that it should at all times be kept in good order and condition and well stocked with plants and shrubs; and the vendors covenanted that they would not at any time thereafter erect or permit to be erected any dwelling-house or other building (except a grotto, bower, summer-house, flower-stand, fountain, music-stand or other ornamental erection) within or on any part of the pleasure ground. On these facts counsel for the owners of the park submitted that the requisite connection between the right to use the park and the normal enjoyment of the houses which were built around it or near it had not been established. He likened the position to a right granted to the purchaser of a house to use the zoological gardens free of charge or to attend Lord's cricket ground without payment. Such a right would undoubtedly, he said, increase the value of the property conveyed, but could not run with it at law as an easement, because there was no sufficient nexus between the enjoyment of the right and the use of the house. It is probably true, we think, that in neither of counsel's illustration would the supposed right constitute an easement, for it would be wholly extraneous to, and independent of, the use of a house as a house, ie, as a place in which the householder and his family live and make their home; and it is for this reason that the analogy which counsel sought to establish between his illustrations and the present case cannot, in our opinion, be supported. A much closer analogy, as it seems to us, is the case of a man selling the freehold of part of his house and granting to the purchaser, his heirs and assigns, the right appurtenant to such part, to use the garden in common with the vendor and his assigns. In such a case the test of connection, or accommodation, would be amply satisfied; for just as the use of a garden undoubtedly enhances, and is connected with, the normal enjoyment of the house to which it belongs, so also would the right granted, in the case supposed, be closely connected with the use and enjoyment of the part of the premises sold. Such, we think, is in substance the position in the present case. The park became a communal garden for the benefit and enjoyment of those whose houses adjoined it or were in its close proximity. Its flower beds, lawns and walks were calculated to afford all the amenities which it is the purpose of the garden of a house to provide; and apart from the fact that these amenities extended to a number of householders instead of being confined to one (which on this aspect of the case is immaterial) we can see no difference in principle between Ellenborough Park and a garden in the ordinary signification of that word. It is the collective garden of the neighbouring houses to whose use it was dedicated by the owners of the estate and as such amply satisfied, in our judgment, the requirement of connection with the dominant tenements to which it is appurtenant. The result is not affected by the circumstance that the right to the park is in this case enjoyed by some few houses which are not immediately fronting on the park. The test for present purposes, no doubt, is that the park should constitute in a real and intelligible sense the garden (albeit the communal garden) of the houses to which the enjoyment is annexed. But we think that the test is satisfied as regards these few neighbouring, though not adjacent, houses. We think that the extension of the right of enjoyment to these few houses does not negative the presence of the necessary 'nexus' between the subject matter enjoyed and the premises to which the enjoyment is expressed to belong.

Counsel for the owners of the park referred us to, and to some extent relied on, *Hill v Tupper* (10) (1863) (2 H&C 121), but in our opinion there is nothing in that case contrary to the view which we have expressed. In that case the owner of land adjoining a canal was granted the exclusive right to let boats out for hire on the canal. He did so and then sought to restrain a similar activity by a neighbouring landowner. He sought to establish that his grant constituted an easement but failed. As Pollock CB said in his judgment (2 H&C at p 126):

> ... it is not competent to create rights unconnected with the use and enjoyment of land, and annex them to it so as to constitute a property in the grantee.

It is clear that what the plaintiff was trying to do was to set up, under the guise of an easement, a monopoly which had no normal connection with the ordinary use of his land, but which was merely an independent business enterprise. So far from the right claimed sub-serving or accommodating the land, the land was but a convenient incident to the exercise of the right. For the reasons which we have stated we are unable to accept the contention that the right to the full enjoyment of Ellenborough Park fails *in limine* to qualify as a legal easement for want of the necessary connection between its enjoyment and the use of the properties comprised in the conveyance of 1864 and in the other relevant conveyances.

We turn next to Dr Cheshire's fourth condition for an easement – that the right must be capable of forming the subject matter of a grant. As we have earlier stated, satisfaction of the condition in the present case depends on a consideration of the questions, whether the right conferred is too wide and vague, whether it is inconsistent with the proprietorship or possession of the alleged servient owners, and whether it is a mere right of recreation without utility or benefit.

To the first of these questions the interpretation which we have given to the typical deed provides, in our judgment, the answer; for we have construed the right conferred as being both well defined and commonly understood. In these essential respects the right may be said to be distinct from the indefinite and unregulated privilege which, we think, would ordinarily be understood by the Latin term *'jus spatiandi'*, a privilege of wandering at will over all and every part of another's field or park, and which, though easily intelligible as the subject matter of the grant in question, viz, the provision for a limited number of houses in a uniform crescent of one single large but private garden. Our interpretation of the deed also provides, we think, the answer to the second question; for the right conferred no more amounts to a joint occupation of the park with its owners, no more excludes the proprietorship or possession of the latter, than a right of way granted through a passage or than the use by the public of the gardens of Lincoln's Inn Fields (to take one of our former examples) amount to joint occupation of that garden with the London County Council, or involve an inconsistency with the possession or proprietorship of the council as lessees. It is conceded that in any event the owners of the park are entitled to cut the timber growing on the park and to retain its proceeds. We have said that in our judgment, under the deed, the flowers and shrubs grown in the garden are equally the property of the owners of the park. We see nothing repugnant to a man's proprietorship or possession of a piece of land that he should decide to make of it and maintain it as an ornamental garden, and should grant rights to a limited number of other person to come into it for the enjoyment of its amenities.

The third of the questions embraced in Dr Cheshire's fourth condition rests primarily on a proposition stated in Theobald's *The Law of Land* (1929), at p 263, where it is said that an easement 'must be a right of utility and benefit and not one of mere recreation and amusement'. It does not appear that a proposition in similar terms is stated by Gale ... In any case if the proposition be well founded, we do not think that the right to use a garden of the character with which we are concerned in this case can be called one of mere recreation and amusement ... No doubt a garden is a pleasure, and on high authority it is the purest of pleasures; but, in our judgment, it is not a right having no quality either of utility or benefit as those words should be understood. The right here in suit is, for reasons already given, one appurtenant to the surrounding houses as such, and constitutes a beneficial attribute of residence in a house as ordinarily understood. Its use for the purposes, not only of exercise and rest but also for such normal domestic purposes as were suggested in argument – for example, for taking out small children in perambulators or otherwise – is not fairly to be described as one of mere recreation or amusement, and is clearly beneficial to the premises to which it is attached ...

For the reasons which we have stated, Danckwerts J came in our judgment, to a right conclusion in this case and accordingly the appeal must be dismissed.

Appeal dismissed.

Questions

1 Why was the right to enjoy the Ellenborough Park not an easement as regards houses that were not immediately fronting the park?

2 What are the legal consequences of the distinction between an easement and a licence?

3 Ela is the registered proprietor of two adjacent lots (A and B) situated in Port Moresby. Lot A has a house built on it whilst lot B is vacant land. Ela leases a small room in the house to Papua Car Dealers Pty Ltd (PCD), one of the largest car dealers in the country. PCD is actually not interested in the tiny room. Rather PCD's interest is in lot B, which it wants to use for purposes of displaying its new cars. As part of the deal, ELA agrees to grant PCD the sole and exclusive right to display its cars for sale on lot B for as long as it continues to lease the room on lot A. PCD pays K20 per month as rent for the room and K1000 for the right to display its cars on lot B. Mosbi Japan Motors (MJM), a rival car dealer, without authority displays its cars on lot B. Advise PCD whether it has a cause of action against MJM. (See *Hill v Tupper* (1866) 2 H&C 121; 159 ER 51.)

Creation of easements

There are various ways of creating easements: by statute;[4] express grant; express reservation or grant in a transfer; implied reservation or grant; necessity; and intended easements. An easement is by express grant if the owner of the servient land expressly dedicates an easement over his land for the benefit of the dominant land. In contrast, an easement is by express reservation where the owner of the dominant land sells part of his land and expressly reserves an easement over that land in favour of the land he retains. An easement by implied grant or reservation is created by implication. Generally, the courts are reluctant to imply an easement in favour of the grantor, except an easement of way of necessity and an intended easement.

Easements created by implied grant

WHEELDON v BURROWS [1874–80] All ER Rep 669, Court of Appeal

[T was the owner of certain real property which included a plot of vacant land and an adjoining plot on part of which was erected a workshop whose windows overlooked the vacant land. In January 1876, T sold the vacant plot to the plaintiff. The conveyance contained no reservation in express terms of any right to the grantor in respect of the land he retained. A month later T sold the rest of the land to the defendant. Following a dispute between the plaintiff and the defendant, the plaintiff erected hoardings near the edge of her land facing the windows of the defendant's workshop, thereby obstructing the light entering through the workshop windows. The defendant knocked down these hoardings asserting a right to an easement of light in respect of the windows. The plaintiff brought an action in trespass.]

THESIGER LJ: This action arises from a claim on the part of the defendant to have as of right the light enter into those windows, or, to put it in another way, to prevent the plaintiff from obstructing these windows by building on her land. Upon the matter coming before the Vice Chancellor, he held that no right in respect of the windows was reserved, either impliedly or expressly, under the conveyance of January 1876; and consequently that the defendant, as privy in estate with the grantor of the land which was the subject of the conveyance, was entitled to no right of light through those windows. In other words, he decided that the plaintiff was entitled to build upon her land, although the result of that building might be to obstruct these lights.

I am of opinion, both upon principle and upon authority, that the Vice Chancellor decided rightly. We have had a considerable number of cases cited to us, and out of them I think that two propositions may be stated as what I may call the general rules governing cases of this kind. The first of these rules is that on the grant by the owner of a tenement of part of that tenement as it is then used and enjoyed, there will pass to the grantee all those continuous and apparent easements and quasi easements which are necessary to the reasonable enjoyment of the property granted, and have been and are at the time of the grant used by the owner of the entirety for the benefit of the part granted. The second proposition is that, if the grantor intends to reserve any right over the tenement granted, it is his duty to reserve it expressly in the grant. Those are the general rules governing cases of this kind, but the

4 Statutory easements are usually created in favour of government bodies, see for example, s 30(3) of the Electricity Commission Act (Ch No 78).

second of those rules is subject to certain exceptions. One of those exceptions is the well known exception which attaches to cases of what are called ways of necessity; and I do not dispute for a moment that there may be, and probably are, certain other exceptions ...

Both of the general rules which I have mentioned are founded upon a maxim which is as well established by authority as it is consonant to reason and common sense – namely, that a grantor shall not derogate from his grant. It has been argued before us that there is no distinction between what has been called an implied grant and what is attempted to be established under the name of an implied reservation; and that such a distinction between the implied grant and the implied reservation is a mere modern invention and one which runs contrary, not only to the general practice upon which land has been bought and sold for a considerable time, but also to authorities which are said to be clear and distinct upon the matter. So far, however, from that distinction being one which was laid down for the first time by, and which is to be attributed to, Lord Westbury in *Suffield v Brown* [(1864) 4 De GJ & SM 185; 46 ER 888], it appears to me that it has existed almost as far back as we can trace the law upon the subject. [His Lordship discussed several authorities and continued.]

These cases in no way support the proposition for which the defendant in this case contends; but, on the contrary, support the proposition that in the case of a grant you may imply a grant of such continuous and apparent easements or such easements as are necessary to the reasonable enjoyment of the property conveyed, and have in fact been enjoyed during the unity of ownership, but that, with the exception to which I have referred of easements of necessity, you cannot imply a similar reservation in favour of the grantor of land ...

For these reasons, therefore, the appeal must be dismissed.

[James and Baggallay JJ agreed.]

Questions

1 Why are the courts more inclined to find an easement by implied grant?

2 Do you understand Thesiger LJ to be saying that 'continuous and apparent' on one hand, and 'reasonably necessary to the enjoyment of land' on the other, are distinct or are alternative requirements for implying that a quasi-easement was intended to pass with the land conveyed? (See *Megarry and Wade: The Law of Real Property* (6th edn, Sweet & Maxwell, London, 2000), pp 1108–10.)

Easement of way of necessity

BARRY v HASSELDINE [1952] Ch 835

[In 1947 the plaintiffs' predecessor in title bought from the defendant a parcel of land which was enclosed on all sides either by land retained by the grantor or land belonging to strangers. At the date of conveyance, the plaintiffs' predecessor had access to the highway via a disused airfield abutting the highway. The use of the airfield was with the permission of the owners. Subsequently, the latter withdrew their permission. The plaintiffs claim a right of way over the defendants land to and from the highway.]

DANCKWERTS J: In those circumstances, in my opinion, if nothing else had occurred, the law would clearly have implied in favour of the grantee of the triangular piece of land a way of necessity – that is to say, a right of way to enable the grantee to obtain access over the grantor's land in some line to be chosen by the grantor; so that the triangular piece of land would be of some use to the grantee instead of being useless, as it would be if no right of way existed. I am satisfied that the law would have implied such a right notwithstanding that the piece of land granted by the conveyance of 1947 was not completely surrounded by the grantor's land, but on three sides abutted on to land which belonged to other persons.

The matter is not entirely clear on the authorities ... In my opinion, however, if the grantee has no access to the property which is sold and conveyed to him except over the grantor's land or over the land of some other person or persons whom he cannot compel to give him any legal right of way, common sense demands that a way of necessity should be implied, so as to confer on the grantee a right of way, for the purposes for which the land is conveyed, over the land of the grantor; and it is no answer to say that a permissive method of approach was in fact enjoyed, at the time of the grant, over the land of some person other than the grantor because that permissive method of approach may be determined on the following day, thereby leaving the grantee with no lawful method of approaching the land which he has purchased.

Accordingly, I have come to the conclusion that, if there were nothing else in this case, this would be a case in which the law would imply a way of necessity in favour of the grantee ... which would inure to the benefit of the plaintiff as the ultimate grantee of the land.

Judgment for the plaintiff.

Questions

1 X sub-divided her land into two parcels. She sold one parcel to Y and retained the other. At the time of conveyance the land sold had access to the highway. However, following a landslide the highway was permanently closed. There is another highway but it can only be reached via X's land. X refuses to grant Y permission to go over her land. Can Y claim a right of way of necessity over X's land? (See *Midland Railway Company v Miles* (1886) 33 Ch D 632.)

2 Peter sold to Kibi certain land, which had access to a public road. Kibi claims that the public road is not properly laid – it has several pot-holes and whenever it rains, the road is impassable except for four-wheel drive trucks. There is another public road, which is suitable for traffic but it can only be reached via Peta's land. Advise Kibi whether he is entitled to an easement of way of necessity over Peta's land

Intended easement

WONG v BEAUMONT PROPERTY TRUST LTD
[1965] 1 QB 173, Court of Appeal

[The defendant's predecessor in title leased the basement of a building to the plaintiff's predecessor in title for the purposes of carrying on a business of a restaurant, the lessee covenanting, *inter alia*, to keep the premises open as a popular restaurant, to control and eliminate all smells and odours caused by such a use of the premises and to comply with the health regulations. At the time the lease was entered into the covenants as to ventilation could not be complied with unless a ventilation system was installed on the premises with a duct fixed to the outside back of the part of the landlord's building not leased to the tenant.

The plaintiff, current tenant, in order to comply with the health ventilation regulations sought to construct a ventilation system with an external duct installed on the landlord's building. However, the defendant, the current landlord, refused to give permission for the erection of a duct on the back of its building. The plaintiff claimed that he was entitled to put up a duct outside the building without the landlord's consent. The trial judge granted the declaration. The defendant appealed.]

LORD DENNING MR: The question is: has the plaintiff a right to put up this duct without the landlord's consent? If he is to have any right at all, it must be by way of easement and not merely by way of implied contract. He is not the original lessee, nor are the defendants the original lessors. Each is a successor in title. As between them, a right of this kind, if it exists at all, must be by way of an easement. In particular, an easement of necessity. The law on the matter was stated by Lord Parker of Waddington in *Pullback Colliery Co Ltd v Woodman* [1915] AC 634, where he said, [at 646] omitting immaterial words, 'The law will readily imply the grant or reservation of such easements as may be necessary to give effect to the common intention of the parties to a grant of real property, with reference to the manner or purposes in and for which the land granted ... is to be used. But it is essential for this purpose that the parties should intend that the subject of the grant ... should be used in some definite and particular manner. It is not enough that the subject of the grant ... should be intended to be used in a manner which may or may not involve this definite and particular use'. That is the principle which underlies all easements of necessity. If you go back to Rolle's *Abridgment* you will find it stated in this way: 'If I have a field inclosed by my own land on all sides, and I alien this close to another, he shall have a way to this close over my land, as incident to the grant; for otherwise he cannot have any benefit by the grant.'

I would apply those principles here. Here was the grant of a lease to the lessee for the very purpose of carrying on a restaurant business. It was to be a popular restaurant, and it was to be developed and extended. There was a covenant not to cause any nuisance; and to control and eliminate all smells; and to comply with the Food Hygiene Regulations. That was 'a definite and particular manner' in which the business had to be conducted. It could not be carried on in that manner at all unless a ventilation system was installed by a duct of this kind. In these circumstances it seems to me that, if the business is to be carried on at all ... the lessee is to 'have any benefit by the grant' at all – he must of necessity be able to put a ventilation duct up the wall. It may be that in Blackaby's [the plaintiff's predecessor in title] time it would not have needed such a large duct as is now needed in the plaintiff's time. But nevertheless a duct of some kind would have had to be put up the wall. The plaintiff may need a bigger one. But that does not matter. A man who has a right to an easement can use it in any proper way so long as he does not substantially increase the burden on the servient tenement. In this case a bigger duct will not substantially increase the burden.

There is one point in which this case goes further than the earlier cases which have been cited. It is this. It was not realised by the parties, at the time of the lease, that this duct would be necessary. But it was in fact necessary from the very beginning. That seems to me sufficient to bring the principle into play. In order to use this place as a restaurant, there must be implied an easement, by the necessity of the case, to carry a duct up this wall. The county court judge so held. He granted a declaration. I agree with him ...

[Pearson and Salmon LJJ agreed. Appeal dismissed.]

Easements under the Land Registration Act (Ch No 191)

The Land Registration Act makes provision for the registration of easements created over land registered under the Act. The relevant provisions are as follows:

Section 95 Registration of easements

(1) Where an easement affecting land (in this section called 'the servient land') is created for the purpose of being annexed to or used and enjoyed together with other land (in this section called the 'dominant land') the Registrar shall –

(a) in relation to the dominant land – enter a memorial of the instrument creating the easement on the folio of the Register Book constituted by the certificate of title for that land; and

(b) in relation to the servient land – register the easement.

(2) Sub-section (1)(b) does not affect the operation of section 33(1)(d).

96 Certificate of title evidence as to easements

Where a certificate of title contains the words 'together with a right of carriage-way over the road delineated and coloured brown on the said map' or words to a similar effect, those words have the same effect as if the words contained in Part 1 of Sched 2 were set out fully in the certificate of title.

Extinguishment of easements

Easements may be lost or extinguished by any of the ways discussed below.

Express extinguishment

An easement may be extinguished by agreement of the parties. Usually this is by release or surrender.[5]

Merger

Where the dominant and servient land come into a common ownership, all the easements affecting the land are merged and extinguished.[6]

Abandonment

If the beneficiary of an easement abandons an easement, the easement is extinguished forever.[7] As the following case illustrates, the courts do not lightly infer abandonment.

TREWEEKE v 36 WOLSELEY ROAD PTY LTD (1972) 128 CLR 274, High Court of Australia

[In 1927 a block of land was divided into two lots: A and B. Lot A had a frontage to the beach whilst lot B did not. An easement of way was granted to the transferee of lot B and his successors in title to pass and repass over and along a strip of land three feet wide along and within the north western boundary of lot A to the beach. The easement was noted on each certificate of title. Ownership of both lots changed hands. At the time of the action, Mrs

5 *Waterlow v Bacon* (1866) LR 2 Eq 514.

6 *Buckby v Coles and Price* (1814) 5 Taunt 311; 128 ER 709.

7 *James v Stevenson and Others* [1893] AC 162 (PC).

Treweeke was the registered proprietor of lot A. 36 Wolseley Road Pty Ltd was the registered proprietor of lot B. At all times the right of way had been impassable due to vertical rock faces, and since 1928, because of an impenetrable bamboo plantation. In 1950, the then owner of lot A installed a swimming pool across the right of way and an iron fence was erected across the way. At no time did the owners of lot B use the entire way. There was evidence that occupants of lot B used a footpath over adjoining land to get to the beach. In 1967, the owner of the adjacent land blocked off the said path. Thereupon, 36 Wolseley Road Pty Ltd asserted their easement of way over lot A. Mrs Treweeke, owner of lot A, applied for judicial declarations, *inter alia*, under s 89(1)(b) of the Conveyancing Act 1919 (NSW), that the said easement had been abandoned. The Supreme Court of New South Wales dismissed the application. Appeal to the High Court.]

McTIERNAN J: As regards the request for an order under s 89(1)(b), there is no proof of extinguishment of the right of way by agreement, that is by express release. Mrs Treweeke's case is that extinguishment was effected by acts and omissions amounting to abandonment of the right of way. 'As a general rule a release, whether express or implied, must be made by a party whose estate or interest in the dominant tenement is, as regards duration, either greater than or at least co-extensive with the period for which the easement exists': *Halsbury's Laws of England*, 3rd edn, Vol 12, p 562, para 1222. On the subject of 'Duration' this principle is enunciated at p 530, para 1151: 'An easement may be created by express grant for interests analogous in their duration to an estate in fee simple, an estate for life, an estate for years, or even a smaller interest.' It is clear from the express grant of the right of way that its duration is intended to be co-extensive with the duration of the estate in fee simple. The relevant 'acts of omissions' would need to be things done or omitted by a dominant owner holding an estate in fee simple in the dominant tenement which would amount to abandonment of the right of way or from which abandonment could be reasonably presumed. 'Extinguishment by release may be effected either by express release or by circumstances occurring from which a release must be presumed (*Crossley & Sons Ltd v Lightowler* [(1867) 2 Ch App 478]. In all cases of release the competency of the releasing part is of the utmost importance ...': *Halsbury's Laws of England*, 3rd edn, Vol 12, p 563, para 1221. 'The extinguishment of an easement by implied release must be based upon the presumed intention of the dominant owner (*Crossley & Sons Ltd v Lightowler* ... It is a question of fact whether an act amounts to an abandonment or was intended as such': *Halsbury's Laws of England*, 3rd edn, Vol 12, p 564, para 1226. There is no proof of any act or omission on the part of the respondent which has the character of abandonment in relation to the right of way. The same is true as regards previous dominant owners. Mrs Treweeke's evidence in her affidavit is tendered presumably to prove lack of use of the right of way by the occupants of the premises on the dominant tenement, which, as already stated, are home units. It is not shown that any occupant was competent to extinguish the right of way by express or implied release. It is said in *Gale on Easements*, 14th edn (1972), at p 317: '... as an easement, when once created, is perpetual in its nature, being attached to the inheritance and passing with it, some acquiescence on the part of the absolute owner of the dominant tenement is necessary to give effect to any act of abandonment.' There is no evidence of such acquiescence on the part of the respondent. It cannot reasonably be presumed that the intention of any occupant of the home units was to abandon the right of way. Residents of the home units gave evidence that they were informed by the agent of the respondent of the existence of the right of way. The evidence, which the learned judge acted upon to make his finding of some use of part of the right of way, presents an inference from Mrs Treweeke's evidence that no person from the home units ever went along any part of the strip of land in respect of which the right of way was granted. Mrs Treweeke relied upon an incident as evidence of abandonment as to which the learned judge made this finding: In 1933, following an incident in which an occupant of No 36 Wolseley Road fell down the steep incline near the boundary between the two allotments and damaged a tree on the applicant's land, a fence was built between the two allotments, although it would appear that probably this fence stands on the respondent's land. This fence was a wire fence, and some of the wire in the fence was replaced in August or September 1967. Half the cost of the original construction of the fence was paid by the owners for the time being of the respondent's land.' Assuming the competency of the occupant to release the right of way, I do not think that it is a reasonable conclusion that the building of the fence amounted to an abandonment of the right of way or was intended as such. The evidence shows that it was not expensive; it is movable; and it is within the dominant tenement. A gate could be inserted in the fence to admit of egress from and access to the servient tenement. The evidence of this incident is not, in my opinion, so cogent that it is reasonable to find that the erection of the fence amounted to a renunciation or disclaimer of the right of way. In any case the last-mentioned finding as to user appears to relate to after 1933.

The important element in the case is non-user of the total length of the strip of land as a way. Part of it was frequently used as far as an opening in the boundary fence to which the strip of land is adjacent. Residents of the home units went through that opening and proceeded from there over the neighbouring allotment to the beach. Their reason for turning aside from the boundary would appear to be that the strip of land was not passable further on. The grant by which the right of way was created imposes no obligation on either the servient owner or the dominant owner to make the strip of land passable. An obligation to do so does not arise at law or in equity. The case is one of mere non-user. It is established that a right will not be extinguished by non-user alone: *Seaman v Vawdrey* [(1810) 16 Ves 390; 33 ER 1032]. In *Ward v Ward* [(1852) 7 Ex 838; 155 ER 1189] a right of way was held not to have been lost by mere non-user for a period of much longer than 20 years, it being shown that the way was not used because the owner had a more convenient mode of access through his own land. (I quote the summary of the facts of the case in *Gale on Easements*, 14th edn (1982), at p 340.) In that case Alderson B said: '... The presumption of abandonment cannot be made from the mere fact of non-user. There must be other circumstances in the case to raise that presumption ... the non-user, therefore, must be the consequence of something which is adverse to the user.' There is no proof of user of the right of way along the total length of the strip of land since the creation of the right of way, a period longer than 40 years. 'The duration of the period of non-user is only material as one element from which the dominant owner's intention to retain or abandon his easement may be inferred; and what period may be sufficient in any particular case must depend on the strength of the other indication of intention and all other accompanying circumstances. If, however, the period of suspension of user is of very long duration, it appears that the suspension alone may raise a *prima facie* presumption of abandonment to the extent of throwing upon the person seeking to uphold the right the burden of showing that some indication of his intention to preserve the right was manifested during the period of suspension': *Halsbury's Laws of England*, 3rd edn, Vol 12, p 564, para 1228. (For a review of cases, see *Gale on Easements*, 14th edn (1972), pp 339–43.) The non-user of the total length of the way can reasonably be put down to its precipitous condition at places. It is not reasonable to attribute non-user to renunciation of such a pleasant amenity as a path to the beach at Double Bay. There is ample evidence of the utilization of passable parts of the *locus in quo* of the right of way as the first stage of daily journeys to the beach by residents of No 36 Wolseley Road, the dominant tenement. There is evidence of a survey being procured by the owner of one of the home units to determine the precise course of the right of way along the north western boundary of the servient tenement. There is evidence that the respondent's agent informed some of the people residing at No 36 Wolseley Road about the existence of the right of way when purchasing their home units. The correspondence which is in evidence proves that the respondent complained to Mrs Treweeke about the swimming pool when the survey established that it obstructed the right of way. In my opinion, upon the whole of the evidence there is clear proof of the intention of the respondent to retain the right of way. I do not think it can be presumed that release of the right of way occurred at any time before or since the respondent acquired the property, No 36 Wolseley Road.

In my opinion the appeal should be dismissed.

[Mason J agreed, Walsh J dissented.]

Notes

The courts in Papua New Guinea have no statutory powers to extinguish or modify easements.

III RESTRICTIVE COVENANTS

Technically a covenant is a promise contained in a deed, though in practice the term is used to include contractual promises not made under deed. Covenants between immediate parties are enforceable in accordance with the ordinary principles of the law of contract. For example, assume that A is the registered proprietor of Blackacre and his neighbour, B, is the registered proprietor of Whiteacre. Under a written contract with B, A undertakes:

(a) that he will keep under repair a road used by A and B to get to the public road;

(b) that he will contribute K100 per year towards the salary of the local priest;

(c) that he will only use Whiteacre for residential purposes.

If A threatens to breach any of these promises B can sue him for breach of contract.

Suppose B sells Blackacre (the dominant land) to C, there would be no privity of contract between C and A. Hence, in the event of A's failure to perform his obligations C cannot sue A for breach of contract. However, at common law an assignee of the dominant land (C) may enforce against the original covenantor (A) any covenant which touches and concerns the land. In the case of *Smith and Snipes Hall Farm Ltd v River Douglas Catchment Board*,[8] Lord Justice Tucker said that a covenant which touches and concerns the land must 'either affect the land as regards mode of occupation, or must be such as *per se*, and not merely from collateral circumstances, affects the value of the land, and it must then be shown that it was the intention of the parties that the benefit thereof should run with the land'. Thus, in our example, C may enforce against A covenants 'a' and 'c', but not covenant 'b' which appears to be a mere personal covenant.

If A transfers Whiteacre (the servient land) to P, at common law P would not be bound by the covenants entered into by A. This is because at common law a burden of a

8 [1949] 2 All ER 179, at 183.

covenant does not run with the land.[9] In other words at common law an assignee of the servient land is not bound by covenants entered into by his predecessor in title.[10] However, in equity certain covenants may be enforced against the assignee of the servient land, provided that they are 'restrictive covenants'.

A restrictive covenant is a covenant which restricts the use of the covenantor's land (servient land) for the benefit of the covenantee's land (dominant land). The classical illustration of restrictive covenants is the case of *Tulk v Moxhay* extracted below.

TULK v MOXHAY [1843–60] 3 All ER Rep 9, House of Lords

[Tulk owned a block of vacant land in the middle of Leicester Square, London, as well as several houses adjoining the square. He sold the vacant block to E who entered into a covenant with Tulk that he would keep the square as a garden and not build on it. The piece of land so conveyed passed by diverse conveyances until it was subsequently sold to Moxhay. Moxhay did not make any undertaking regarding the land though he had notice of his predecessors' undertakings. Moxhay was preparing to construct buildings on the subject land when Tulk sought an injunction to stop him. The Court of Appeal granted the injunction. Moxhay appealed to the House of Lords.]

LORD COTTENHAM LC: That this court has jurisdiction to enforce a contract between the owner of land and his neighbour purchasing a part of it that the purchaser shall either use or abstain from using the land purchased in a particular way is what I never knew disputed. Here there is no question about the contract. The owner of certain houses in the square sells the land adjoining, with a covenant from the purchaser not to use it for any other purpose than as a square garden. It is now contended, not that the vendee could violate that contract, but that he might sell the piece of land, and that the purchaser from him may violate it without this court having any power to interfere. If that were so, it would be impossible for an owner of land to sell part of it without incurring the risk of rendering what he retains worthless. It is said that, the covenant being one which does not run with the land, this court cannot enforce it, but the question is not whether the covenant runs with the land, but whether a party shall be permitted to use the land in a manner inconsistent with the contract entered into by his vendor, with notice of which he purchased. Of course, the price would be affected by the covenant, and nothing could be more inequitable than that the original purchaser should be able to sell the property the next day for a greater price, in consideration of the assignee being allowed to escape from the liability which he had himself undertaken.

That the question does not depend upon whether the covenant runs with the land is evident from this, that, if there was a mere agreement and no covenant, this court would enforce it against a party purchasing with notice of it, for if an equity is attached to property by the owner, no one purchasing with notice of that equity can stand in a different situation from that of the party from whom he purchased ...

Appeal dismissed.

9 The rule is different where there is privity of estate, see Chapter 6.

10 *Austerberry v Corporation of Oldham* (1885) 29 Ch D 750.

Questions

1 What is the possible policy justification for enforcing restrictive covenants against an assignee of the servient land?

2 In our earlier example above which of the covenants are restrictive covenants?

3 X covenants with Y not to let the fence which separates their land fall into disrepair. X sells his land to W. Is W bound by the covenant?

4 M Ltd owned land in Lae on which a horse racing circuit had been constructed. Five years later M Ltd bought land in Sogeri on which it constructed another horse racing circuit. Thereafter all horse race meetings were held on the Sogeri circuit. Subsequently, M Ltd sold the Lae land to P Ltd. In the conveyance P Ltd covenanted not to use the Lae land for horse race meetings. A year later P Ltd sold the land to X Ltd. The latter bought with notice of the restriction though it did not make any specific undertaking regarding use of the land. X Ltd wants to revive the popular horse race meetings on the Lae circuit, but M Ltd has threatened it with legal action. Advise X Ltd. (See *Clem Smith Nominees Pty Ltd v Farrelly and Farrelly; Adelaide International Raceway Pty Ltd and Mallala Motor Racing Co Pty Ltd* (1978) 20 SASR 227.)

5 Give examples of situations where restrictive covenants could be of practical importance.

Notes

1 A covenant is not a restrictive covenant unless it complies with the following requirements:

(i) The covenant must be negative in nature and substance. In other words the covenant must restrict the servient land owner from doing something and not impose a positive duty to do something.[11] Generally a covenant which requires the covenantor to expend money in order to comply with the covenant is not a restrictive covenant.[12]

(ii) The covenant must be made for the benefit of the land retained by the covenantee. This means that there must be dominant and servient land. If at the time the covenant is entered into the covenantee has no land to be benefited, the covenant is a personal covenant which only binds the immediate parties.[13] This rule does not apply where there is a scheme of development, discussed below.

(iii) The original covenantor and covenantee must have intended that the burden and the benefit of the covenant runs with the servient and the dominant land, respectively.[14] Usually the intention is expressed in the agreement.

It has effect only in equity.

2 Restrictive covenants have effect only in equity.[15]

---

11 *Haywood v The Brunswick Permanent Benefit Building Society* (1881) 8 QBD 403.

12 *Megarry and Wade: The Law of Real Property* (6th edn, Sweet & Maxwell, London, 2000), p 1116.

13 *London City Council v Allen and Another* [1914–15] All ER Rep 1008.

14 *Federated Homes Ltd v Mill Lodge Properties Ltd* [1980] 1 WLR 594.

15 See Amankwah, Mugambwa and Muroa, *Land Law in Papua New Guinea, op cit*, note 3, p 225.

Scheme of development

Assume that D Ltd, a construction and land development company, purchases a large block of land overlooking Ela beach. D Ltd sub-divides the block into several lots which are numbered 1–10. D Ltd wishes the land to develop in an orderly fashion. For example, it wants only high covenant houses to be built on the lots and the houses not to exceed a particular height so that all houses would have a view of the sea. D Ltd sells each lot subject to these covenants. Because of privity of contract, D Ltd could of course enforce the covenants against each original purchaser. However, once it has sold the last lot it is unlikely that it will be interested in policing the covenants.[16] For the scheme to be effective the owners of the lots themselves should be able to enforce the covenants against each other. This may not be possible under the rules of enforcement of restrictive covenants discussed above. As it has been seen, a restrictive covenant does not run with the land unless at the time the covenant was entered into the covenantee owned the land to be benefited.[17] For example, assume that D Ltd sells lots 1–10 in that order. When it sells lot 1 it can enter into covenants for the benefit of lots 2–10 because it owns those lots. When it sells lot 2 it can only enter into covenants for the benefit of lots 3–10, but not lot 1 because the latter is not its land. Consequently, the owner of lot 1 cannot enforce the covenants against other lot owners, even though the covenants were purportedly intended to benefit all the ten lots. For the same reason the owner of lot 2 could enforce the covenants against the owner of lot 1 but not against the owners of lots 3–10. In other words the right to enforce the covenants would depend on the order of purchase from D Ltd. The purchaser of lot 1 would be in the worst position because he cannot enforce the covenants against the other lot owners, though they can enforce the covenants against him. In contrast, the owner of lot 10 could enforce the covenants against everyone else though none (apart from D Ltd) could enforce the covenants against him. However, where the lots are part of a scheme of development, each purchaser has a right to enforce the covenants against the other irrespective of the date of purchase. The case of *Elliston v Reacher* illustrates the requirements for the existence of a scheme of development and is extracted below.

ELLISTON v REACHER [1908] 2 Ch 374

[In 1860 a building society acquired title to a large estate. It sub-divided the estate in numbered lots for sale. The lots were sold using identical conveyances and imposing identical restrictions upon each purchaser. One of the restrictions was that no hotel, tavern, or beer-house should be built on any lot, or any house used as such without the vendor's consent. In this case the plaintiff's and the defendant's predecessors in title, respectively, bought their lots subject to the aforementioned restrictions. The plaintiff sought an injunction to prevent the defendants from using their (defendants') lot for the purpose of a hotel.]

> **PARKER J** [His Honour held that the defendants' land was subject to the aforementioned restrictive covenants, and continued]: In my judgment, in order to bring the principles [of a building scheme] ... into operation it must be proved: (1) that both the plaintiffs and

16 D Ltd only devised the scheme to make the land more attractive to maximise its profits.

17 See *London City Council v Allen*, *supra*, note 13.

defendants derive title under a common vendor; (2) that previously to selling the lands to which the plaintiffs and defendants are respectively entitled the vendor laid out his estate, or a defined portion thereof (including the lands purchased by the plaintiffs and defendants respectively), for sale in lots subject to restrictions intended to be imposed on all the lots, and which, though varying in details as to particular lots, are consistent and consistent only with some general scheme of development; (3) that these restrictions were intended by the common vendor to be and were for the benefit of all the lots intended to be sold, whether or not they were also intended to be and were for the benefit of other land retained by the vendor; and (4) that both the plaintiffs and the defendants, or their predecessors in title, purchased their lots from the common vendor upon the footing that the restrictions subject to which the purchases were made were to enure for the benefit of the other lots included in the general scheme whether or not they were also to enure for the benefit of other lands retained by the vendors. If these four points be established, I think that the plaintiffs would in equity be entitled to enforce the restrictive covenants entered into by the defendants or their predecessors with the common vendor irrespective of the dates of the respective purchases. I may observe, with reference to the third point, that the vendor's object in imposing the restrictions must in general be gathered from all the circumstances of the case, including in particular the nature of the restrictions. If a general observance of the restrictions is in fact calculated to enhance the values of the several lots offered for sale, it is an easy inference that the vendor intended the restrictions to be for the benefit of all the lots, even though he might retain other land the value of which might be similarly enhanced for a vendor may naturally be expected to aim at obtaining the highest possible price for his land. Further, if the first three points be established, the fourth point may readily be inferred, provided the purchasers have notice of the facts involved in the three first points; but if the purchaser purchases in ignorance of any material part of those facts, it would be difficult, if not impossible, to establish the fourth point. It is also observable that the equity arising out of the establishment of the four points I have mentioned has been sometimes explained by the implication of mutual contracts between the various purchasers, and sometimes by the implication of a contract between each purchaser and the common vendor, that each purchaser is to have the benefit of all the covenants by the other purchasers, so that each purchase is in equity an assign of the benefit of these covenants. In my opinion the implication of mutual contract is not always a perfectly satisfactory explanation. It may be satisfactory where all the lots are sold by auction at the same time, but when ... there is no sale by auction, but all the various sales are by private treaty and at various intervals of time, the circumstances may, at the date of one or more other sales, be such as to preclude the possibility of any actual contract. For example, a prior purchaser may be dead or incapable of contracting at the time of a subsequent purchase, and in any event it is unlikely that the prior and subsequent purchasers are ever brought into personal relationship, and yet the equity may exist between them. It is, I think, enough to say ... that where the four points I have mentioned are established, the community of interest imports in equity the reciprocity of obligation which is in fact contemplated by each at the time of his own purchase.

[His Honour discussed the facts of the case and concluded:]

Under all the circumstances of the case it is in my opinion sufficiently established not only that the predecessors of the plaintiffs and the defendants respectively had notice of the intention of their common vendors that the restrictions in question should enure for the benefit of all the lots offered for sale, but that they made their respective purchases on that footing ... I hold, therefore, that the plaintiffs are ... entitled in equity to enforce the covenants in question.

Questions

1 What are the conditions for the existence of a scheme of development?

2 In the case what reasons does Parker J give for the enforcement of restrictive covenants under a building scheme?

3 Suppose a purchaser buys a lot without notice of the existence of a building scheme, is the purchaser bound by the restrictive covenants? Can he enforce the restrictive covenants against other lot owners?

Note

It has been held in subsequent cases that the four points specified in *Elliston v Reacher* for the existence of a building scheme are just guidelines. The crucial requirement is the existence of a common interest and a common intention that the covenants be enforceable by each purchaser against the others.[18]

Discharge of restrictive covenants

A restrictive covenant may be discharged in any of the following ways:

(i) By operation of law, where, for example, both the dominant and the servient properties fall into the same hands.[19]

(ii) When a court of equity exercises its discretion not to enforce it at the suit of the covenantee or his successor.[20]

(iii) By agreement between the parties.

It should be noted that there is no express statutory power given to the courts to extinguish restrictive covenants.[21]

Restrictive covenants and the Torrens system

The Land Registration Act (Ch No 191) makes no provision for the registration of restrictive covenants. This is probably because restrictive covenants are equitable interests and the Torrens system generally discouraged registration of equitable interests.[22] In some jurisdictions in Australia the Registrars assumed the liberty to make notations of restrictive covenants on the certificate of title of the land with which they are burdened. The legal efficacy of such notation (which has no statutory sanction) against a subsequent

---

18 See *In Re Dolphin's Conveyance* [1970] 1 Ch 654.

19 *In Re Tiltwood, Sussex* [1978] Ch 269.

20 *Shaw and Another v Applegate* [1978] 1 All ER 123.

21 In some jurisdictions in Australia, the courts have statutory power to modify or extinguish easements and restrictive covenants. See for example, s 129C of the Western Australia Transfer of Land Act 1893.

22 See, eg, trusts, s 104, LRA.

registered proprietor of the burdened land is questionable.[23] The better view seems to be that restrictive covenants are not enforceable against subsequent registered proprietors.[24]

23 Whalan, *The Torrens System in Australia* (Lawbook Co, Sydney, 1982), p 110. In some of the jurisdictions, there is provision for registration of restrictive covenants. See for example, s 129A of the Transfer of Land Act of Western Australia.

24 *Norton v Kilduff* [1974] Qd R 47.

CHAPTER 9

REGISTRATION OF TITLES

I INTRODUCTION

The Land Registration Act (Ch No 191) provides for a system of conveyance and registration of title to land. The Act reflects a system of conveyance commonly known as the Torrens system of land registration, which originated from Australia.[1] All dealing in alienated land, including State leases upon registration,[2] are subject to the provisions of the Act. Customary land converted into freeholds under the Land (Tenure Conversion) Act)[3] may be registered under the Land Registration Act.

II ESSENTIAL CHARACTERISTICS

The Torrens system has two main characteristics:

A Title by registration

B Indefeasibility of title

These two features are inter-dependent and they are both central to the Torrens system. We examine and illustrate the two features.

A Title by registration

Under the Torrens system of conveyance, interests in land are created or transferred by registration of the transaction in the manner prescribed by the Act. Section 17(1) of the Land Registration Act, provides that, except for a lease for a term which does not exceed three years, 'an instrument is not effective to pass or create an estate or interest until the instrument is registered in accordance with this Act' Section 26 indicates the effect of registration. It reads:

> (1) On registration of an instrument –
>
> (a) the estate or interest specified in the instrument passes or ceases; or
>
> (b) the land becomes liable as security; or
>
> (c) the land is encumbered,
>
> in the manner and subject to the covenants and conditions set out in the instrument or declared by this Act to be implied in instruments of that nature.

1 For background information, see Whalan, *The Torrens System in Australia* (Lawbook Co, Sydney, 1982), pp 5–12. See also Amankwah, Mugambwa and Muroa, *Land Law in Papua New Guinea* (Lawbook Co, Sydney, 2001), p 195.

2 See s 36(2), LRA. There is no provision for registration of government-owned land.

3 Section 11(1)(a) and (b), c 15.

(2) As soon as a memorial of an instrument has been entered on the appropriate folio of the Register Book, the instrument shall be deemed to be embodied in the Register Book.

Registration gives the registered proprietor title, which is conclusive except as limited by the Land Registration Act.[4] In an oft-quoted statement, Chief Justice Barwick observed in *Breskvar and Another v Wall and Others:*[5]

> The Torrens system of registered title ... is not a system of registration of title but a system of title by registration. That which the certificate of title describes is not the title which the registered proprietor formerly had, or which but for registration would have had. It is the title which registration itself has vested in the proprietor. Consequently, a registration which results from a void instrument is effective according to the terms of the registration. It matters not what the cause or reasons for which the instrument is void.

However, the certificate of title and the Register Book constitute mere *evidence of title* created by registration; they do not constitute the title conferred by the Land Registration Act.[6] The following case illustrates the significance of this distinction.

THE CUSTODIAN OF EXPROPRIATED PROPERTY AND ANOTHER v TEDEP AND OTHERS (1964) 113 CLR 318, High Court of Australia

[The Custodian of Expropriated Property (the appellant) was the registered proprietor in fee simple of 466 hectares of land situated in the Gazelle Peninsula. The registration was effected pursuant to the Land Registration Ordinance 1924 (PNG). In terms of s 68 of the Ordinance the appellant held its estate absolutely free from all prior estates, interests, rights, claims and demands which could or might have been, had, made or set up in, to upon or in respect of the subject land. This was the state of the Register book when in 1942 it was destroyed during the Japanese occupation. Also destroyed was the duplicate certificate of title held by the appellant. In 1960, a fresh certificate of title was issued to the appellant under the Land Titles Restoration Ordinance 1951. Two years later, the respondents, acting on behalf of the original traditional landowners (the Tolai), instituted an appeal to the Supreme Court for a declaration that they and their ancestors had never legally alienated the disputed land and, accordingly it was still their land. The trial judge, Mann CJ, upheld their claim on the ground (*inter alia*) that since the Register book and the appellants' certificate of title were destroyed the appellant had no title to the land. The Custodian appealed to the High Court of Australia.]

BARWICK CJ, McTIERNAN, KITTO, TAYLOR and MENZIES JJ: [T]he learned Chief Justice considered that the destruction of the registers and the provisions of the Land Titles Restoration Ordinance produced a result which left him free to give effect to the claim that the subject land, or part of it, was owned by the native community or communities represented by the native respondents. His Honour seems to have arrived at this conclusion by, first of all, holding that upon the destruction of the registers the title of the appellant as the registered proprietor of the land was destroyed. He took the view that registration under provisions such as those contained in the Ordinance dealt with the subject of ownership only 'at an evidentiary and procedural level'. 'It arms the registered proprietor' he said 'with conclusive evidence that he has a clear title, and production of this evidence

4 Sections 11(1) and 33, LRA.

5 (1971) 126 CLR 376, at 385–86, see extract below, p 427.

6 See Whalan, *Torrens System in Australia, op cit*, note 1, p 83.

excludes the possibility of a contrary case being made out by anybody'. And 'on the assumption that the titles will forever remain on the register, this has the practical effect of conferring a permanent paramount title, but it does not otherwise expressly destroy competing interests; it merely renders them harmless'. Further, he added 'the whole foundation of the statutory concept of title is destroyed by the destruction of the register itself' and he observed that the legislature had 'acted upon the view that the statutory legal title is itself destroyed, and that the process of restoration of titles is no mere matter calling for secondary evidence of what was recorded on that piece of statutory paper, but was regarded as recreating a new statutory right to replace the former right and to owe its validity to the Restoration Ordinance'. 'On no other view' he said 'could the machinery provisions of the New Guinea Land Titles Restoration Ordinance be explained'.

In our view these conceptions are plainly erroneous. The indefeasibility of the title of a registered proprietor under systems of title such as that erected by the Land Registration Ordinance does not depend upon ability to produce the register or duplicate certificate of titles; it depends, in the present case, upon the provisions of the Ordinance itself, and particularly upon s 68, which, at all relevant times, has remained in force and, by virtue of which, at the moment of and by the act of registration, the estate of the registered proprietor became absolutely free from any prior asserted legal interest not noted on the register. Accordingly the destruction or loss of a register book, accidentally or otherwise, does not destroy the title thus accorded to the registered proprietor ...

It may, and should at this stage be observed, that his Honour's conclusions cannot be supported by any reference to any supposed 'policy of protection of native land interests' for if those conclusions are correct one consequence would be the destruction of native rights created by registration since, in any case where native rights had been the subject of registration pursuant either to s 26(3) or ss 38 or 39, upon the destruction of the register it would be necessary to re-assert and re-establish, independently, the existence of native rights in the land. Again, if those conclusions be correct, all titles to land subject to the provisions of the Ordinance would be thrown open leaving every individual, native or not, free to assert a claim not founded on registration or upon a right to registration.

Appeal allowed.

B Indefeasibility of title

The second essential feature of the Torrens system is the principle of indefeasibility of title. This means that once a person is registered as the proprietor, his or her title cannot be divested or attacked by rival claims to the land or interest in which he or she is registered except as prescribed under the Land Registration Act. The principle of indefeasibility is not defined in the Act, but its meaning is extracted from the following provisions:

Section 11 Certificate of title to be evidence

(1) The Registrar's duplicate of a certificate of title, when registered –

(a) is evidence of the particulars it specifies; and

(b) is conclusive evidence, in relation to the land it describes, that the person named in the certificate of title –

(i) as seised of an estate in land; or

(ii) as taking or otherwise entitled to an estate or interest in the land, is seised of, possessed or entitled to that estate or interest, as the case may be; and

(c) is conclusive evidence that the property comprised in the certificate of title is under this Act.

(2) The other duplicate of a certificate of title, when registered, is evidence of the particulars it specifies and of those particulars being entered in the Register Book.

Section 33 Protection of registered proprietor

(1) The registered proprietor of an estate or interest holds it absolutely free from all encumbrances except [as prescribed in this section].[7]

Section 45 Transferee not affected by notice

(1) Subject to section 28 notwithstanding any rule of law or equity to the contrary, a transferee, whether voluntary or not, of land is not, except in case of fraud, affected by actual or constructive notice of a registrable claim, right, title or interest other than those which have been notified or protected by entry in the Register Book according to this Act.

(2) Sub-section (1) does not deprive creditors or rights or remedies given or provided by the Mercantile Act.

Section 146 Ejectment against registered proprietor

(1) Subject to sub-section (2), a certificate of title is an absolute bar and estoppel to an action of ejectment against the person named in the certificate of title as seised of or entitled to the land.

(2) ...[8]

(3) This Act does not subject to an action for ejectment a purchaser or a mortgagee, acting in good faith and for valuable consideration.

(4) The operation of sub-section (3) is not affected by the fact that the vendor or mortgagor, as the case may be –

(a) was registered through fraud or error; or

(b) derives from or through a person registered as proprietor through fraud or error, whether by wrong description of land or of its boundaries or otherwise.

(5) For the purpose of bringing an action of ejectment against a person registered as proprietor, the registration of that person is equivalent to possession by him of the land in respect of which the action is brought.

The following cases illustrate the operation of the principle of indefeasibility. Please note that the principle of indefeasibility is subject to several exceptions, some of which are mentioned in the cases below, but they will be dealt with later.

Claims of traditional land-owners against registered proprietors

The compatibility of customary interests and Torrens system title is problematic, as the case below illustrates.

7 The exceptions are discussed below.

8 Exceptions to sub-section (1) are discussed below.

THE ADMINISTRATION OF THE TERRITORY OF PAPUA AND NEW GUINEA v BLASIUS TIRUPIA AND OTHERS IN RE VUNAPALADIG AND JAPALIK LAND [1971–72] PNGLR 229, Supreme Court of P&NG

[The plaintiff, the Administration, claimed to be entitled as registered proprietor to possession of two parcels of land in East New Britain. It sought injunctions and orders for possession against the defendants who it alleged were wrongfully in occupation of the said land. German nationals allegedly 'bought' the land from the defendants' ancestors during Germany's administration of the Territory. In 1928 and 1934 respectively, the Custodian of Expropriated Property was registered as proprietor of the land under the Lands Registration Ordinance 1924. In 1968–69 the plaintiff, purchased the land from the then registered proprietor.]

MINOGUE CJ, CLARKSON AND KELLY JJ: The substance of the plaintiff's case is that the subject lands were lands brought under the Lands Registration Ordinance, that final orders were made under the restoration legislation and certificates of title issued; that the plaintiff was a purchaser who became a registered proprietor by transfer; that it was a *bona fide* purchaser for value without notice of any other right title or interest and that consequently it was entitled to the relief sought, either an injunction on the footing that it was in possession of the lands or, alternatively, to what in effect was an order of ejectment if the plaintiff was not in possession.

As we understand the defendants' case they rely on a legal interest flowing directly from their uninterrupted possession from 'time immemorial' and from the laws of the Territory and an equitable interest from their long and notorious possession which amounts to notice and an interest of such a nature that notwithstanding registration under the Torrens system it calls for recognition by the court. The claim is of having acquired a right of ownership or some right of possession which detracts from or perhaps wholly extinguishes the plaintiff's right. It was submitted that the registration of the plaintiff's predecessors in title was effected in breach of a fiduciary duty owed by the plaintiff to the native owners of the lands. The plaintiff Administration had through its negligence, error or neglect brought about a situation where registration took place and it could not now assert any rights thought to be flowing from its registration in derogation of the rights possessed by the defendants and the other members of their kinship groups which in effect amounted to rights of absolute ownership Mr Enderby for the defence sought to show that by a combination of the Mandate granted to the Commonwealth of Australia over the Territory of New Guinea in 1920, of the terms of the New Guinea Act of that year and of the provisions of the Laws Repeal and Adopting Ordinance of 1921, of the Land Ordinance of 1922 and of the Lands Registration Ordinance of 1924, there was a duty cast on the Administration of the Territory of New Guinea to protect native land rights which were in effect to be regarded as inalienable. More specifically he argued that assuming the truth of the facts asserted in the defence (which of course we must do on this demurrer) it was clear that the Director of District Services and Native Affairs had not carried out the duties imposed upon him by the Lands Registration Ordinance. Those duties were to refer the question of possible native rights in relation to any land to the Central Court for enquiry and determination in every case where he was of opinion that there were natives or native communities having rights of any description over any land owned occupied or used by or for any person other than a native, and where he had been served with a notice that it was proposed to bring land under the Ordinance to cause careful enquiries to be made as to the existence of native rights to that land and to refer the question of native rights in relation to land to the Central Court for determination. (See ss 22 and 24.) If he had carried out these duties, so it was said, registration could not have been effected in the face of the obvious native rights which existed in and over the lands. He further went on to argue that the Administration was responsible for the neglect errors and omissions of the Director and consequently was in breach of a fiduciary duty. True it is that the Director had a number of statutory duties imposed upon him and it is clear that those duties were aimed at the protection of native rights to land. However, even if it be the case that in the performance of those duties the Director was acting as the agent of the Administration it would not follow that the Ordinance which imposed those duties on him thereby imposed on the Administration a fiduciary duty towards persons who might possess native land rights, nor that the failure of the Director to carry out his statutory duties would amount to a breach of fiduciary duty on the part of the Administration. In any event whatever breach of duty there may have been by the Director or vicariously by the Administration cannot avail the defendants against the clear and conclusive provisions of ss 57 and 68 of the Lands Registration Ordinance, the effect of which is to confer an indefeasible legal title to land on the registered proprietor: *The Custodian of Expropriated Property v Tedep* [(1964) 113 CLR 318] makes this proposition clear beyond doubt. As was said in the case, at pp 331–32: 'The indefeasibility of the title of a registered proprietor under systems of title such as that erected by the Lands Registration Ordinance ... depends ... upon the provisions of the Ordinance itself, and particularly upon s 68 ... by virtue of which, at the moment of and by the act of registration, the estate of the registered proprietor became absolutely free from any prior asserted legal interest not noted on the register.' And see also at pp 336–37.

The conclusiveness of a title under the Lands Registration Ordinance receives further support if any is needed from s 16 of the Land Titles Commission Ordinance 1962 which provides that where a decision of the Land Titles Commission in is conflict with a title previously registered under the Lands Registration Ordinance that registered title shall to the extent of the conflict prevail. We note of course that there is no allegation of fraud in these cases and in our view the submission of Mr Jeffrey is correct that, whatever the events preceding the issue of the Certificate of Title, upon registration native land rights survive against the registered proprietor only to the extent that they are recognized on the title. In the circumstances we do not find it necessary to determine the legal relationship between the Administration and the Director in this context as whatever that relationship may be the position of the Administration as registered proprietor is not affected ...

Note

The principle that a registered certificate of title is inviolable against native land rights was employed in several cases to frustrate the traditional land owners' attempts to reclaim alienated land, which they felt (and still do) was unfairly acquired from them. For example, in *Blasius Tirupia and Others v The Administration of The Territory of Papua and New Guinea* [1973] PNGLR 34, at 40, the Full Court reiterated that a registered title could not be disputed by reference to unregistered native land rights. See also *The Custodian of Expropriated Property and Another v Tedep and Others* (1964) 113 CLR 318, extracted above, at p 422. The frustration of the traditional landowners is expressed by William Kaputin, then a young University of Papua New Guinea law graduate, in his article: 'Indefeasibility and justice', in Sack (ed), *Problem of Choice – Land Law in Papua New Guinea's Future* (ANU, Canberra, 1974), pp 158–63. Kaputin made a scathing attack against the use of the principle of indefeasibility against indigenous land claims. He asserted that the Australian colonial administration introduced the principle of indefeasibility to protect foreigners' land titles, which both the administration and the courts knew were dubious.

Questions

1 What are the possible policy justifications for a registered title to prevail over claims by the indigenous land-owners? Would you say that in these cases registration should not be paramount? Why?

2 '[O]nce registered the interest is as stated and if it is not recorded, then it does not exist' (*per* RTJ Stein and MA Stone, *Torrens Title* (Butterworths, Sydney, 1991), at 31). Discuss with illustrations from decided cases and practical examples.

Title registered under a void instrument of transfer

BRESKVAR AND ANOTHER v WALL AND OTHERS
(1971) 126 CLR 376, High Court of Australia

[The Breskvars (plaintiffs/appellants) borrowed money from one Petrie on security of their land. They handed Petrie their certificate of title and a memorandum of transfer of the property signed in blank (space for the name of the transferee was left blank). Under the Queensland Stamp Act 1894, a blank instrument of transfer was 'absolutely void and inoperative' both at law and in equity. Petrie without authority of the appellants inserted in the memorandum of transfer the name of Wall, first respondent, as the transferee and had the transfer registered in Wall's name. Wall then sold to A Pty Ltd, which bought in good faith and without notice of earlier transactions. Before A Pty Ltd could register its transfer in pursuance of the contract with Wall, the Breskvars lodged a caveat to prevent registration and they commenced these proceedings to have Wall's registration cancelled and the Register rectified to restore their names as proprietors. Their application was based on two main arguments. Firstly, that since the memorandum of transfer was executed by way of security only it was ineffective to transfer the fee simple estate to Wall. Secondly, that in any event the memorandum of transfer was void because of the Stamp Act. Though the Supreme Court found that both Wall and Petrie acted fraudulently, it dismissed the application. On appeal to the High Court.]

BARWICK CJ: [E]xcept in and for the purposes of such excepted proceedings the conclusiveness of the certificate of title is definitive of the title of the registered proprietor. That is to say, in the jargon which has had currency, there is immediate indefeasibility of title by the registration of the proprietor named in the register. The stated exceptions to the prohibition on actions for recovery of land against a registered proprietor do not mean that 'indefeasibility' is not effective. It is really no impairment of the conclusiveness of the register that the proprietor remains liable to one of the excepted actions any more than his liability for 'personal equities' derogates from that conclusiveness. So long as the certificate is unamended it is conclusive and of course when amended it is conclusive of the new particulars it contains.

The Torrens system of registered title of which the Act is a form is not a system of registration of title but a system of title by registration. That which the certificate of title describes is not the title which the registered proprietor formerly had, or which but for registration would have had. The title it certifies is not historical or derivative. It is the title which registration itself has vested in the proprietor. Consequently, a registration which results from a void instrument is effective according to the terms of the registration. It matters not what the cause or reason for which the instrument is void. The affirmation by the Privy Council in *Frazer v Walker* [1967] 1 AC 569 of the decision of the Supreme Court of New Zealand in *Boyd v Mayor & C of Wellington* [1924] NZLR 1174 at 1123 now places that conclusion beyond question. Thus, the effect of the Stamp Act upon the memorandum of transfer in this case is irrelevant to the question whether the certificate of title is conclusive of its particulars.

[Other members of the court expressed similar views.]

Appeal dismissed.

Question

'The Torrens system of registered title ... is not a system of registration of title but a system of title by registration' (*per* Barwick CJ in *Breskvar v Wall* (1971) 126 CLR 376, at 385). Discuss.

Forged instrument of transfer

FRAZER v WALKER AND OTHERS [1967] 1 AC 569, Privy Council

[Mr Frazer, the appellant, and his wife were the registered proprietors as joint tenants of the subject land. Mrs Frazer purporting to act on behalf of herself and that of the appellant arranged to borrow $3,000 from the second respondent which sum was to be secured by a mortgage over the said land. She signed a bill of mortgage in favour of the second respondent and forged the appellant's signature thereon. The mortgage was then registered. When she defaulted in her repayment of the loan, the second respondent caused the land to be sold to the first respondent. The latter had the transfer registered. It was common ground that all the respondents at all material times acted in good faith without knowledge of the forgery. In an action for possession against the appellant, it was contended on his behalf that since his signature to the bill of mortgage was a forgery, the mortgage and the subsequent sale of the property were null and void. The appellant counter-claimed for a declaration that he was the beneficial owner of an undivided half-interest in the subject land; and for an order directing the Registrar to cancel all entries or memorials in favour of all the respondents and to restore his name and that of his wife as the joint owners of the disputed land. The New Zealand Supreme Court and the Court of Appeal held in favour of the respondents on ground of indefeasibility of title. On further appeal to the Privy Council.]

LORD WILBERFORCE: Their Lordships will deal first with the appellant's claim against the second respondents. This raises the question whether it was open to the appellant to bring proceedings affecting the validity of the mortgage against the second respondents, whose interest as mortgagees was entered in the register, and claiming cancellation of this entry. This question must be considered by reference to the provisions of the Land Transfer Act, 1952. The relevant sections may be considered under five main headings.

I Those sections which deal with the procuring of registration, the principal of which are ss 42, 157 and 164.

Section 42 contains a prohibition against registration of any instrument except in the manner provided in the Act and unless the instrument is in accordance with the provisions of the Act. Section 157 requires every instrument, including such as charge any estate, to be signed by the registered proprietor and attested. Section 164 prohibits the registrar from receiving any instrument such as a charge unless there is indorsed thereon a certificate that it is correct for the purposes of the Act signed by the applicant or party claiming under the instrument, a licensed land-broker or a solicitor employed by the applicant or party. The appellant invoked these sections, and reg 24 of the Land Transfer Regulations 1948, in support of an argument that the forged mortgage could not be received for registration or validly registered and consequently that the mortgage never became entitled to the benefit of registration. Their Lordships cannot accept this argument, which would be destructive of the whole system of registration. Even if non-compliance with the Act's requirements as to registration may involve the possibility of cancellation or correction of the entry – the provisions as to this will be referred to later – registration once effected must attract the consequences which the Act attaches to registration whether that was regular or otherwise. As will appear from the following paragraphs, the inhibiting effect of certain sections (eg, ss 62 and 63) and the probative effect of others (eg, s 75) in no way depend on any fact other than actual registration as proprietor. It is in fact the registration and not its antecedents which vests and divests title.

II Those sections which provide protection to the registered proprietor against claims and proceedings. These are ss 62 and 63. Without attempting any comprehensive or exhaustive description of what these sections achieve, it may be said that while s 62 secures that a registered proprietor, and consequently anyone who deals with him, shall hold his estate or interest absolutely free from encumbrances, with three specified exceptions, s 63 protects him against any action for possession or recovery of land, with five specified exceptions. Sub-section (2) of s 63 is a particularly strong provision in his favour: it provides that the register is, in every court of law or equity, to be an absolute bar to any such action against the registered proprietor, any rule of law or equity to the contrary notwithstanding. It is to be noticed that each of these sections excepts the case of fraud, s 62 employing the words 'except in case of fraud', and s 63 using the words 'as against the person registered as proprietor of that land through fraud'. The uncertain ambit of these expressions has been limited by judicial decision to actual fraud by the registered proprietor of his agent: *Assets Co Ltd v Mere Roihi* [1905] AC 176, 210, PC.

It is these sections which, together with those next referred to, confer upon the registered proprietor what has come to be called 'indefeasibility of title'. The expression, not used in the Act itself, is a convenient description of the immunity from attack by adverse claim to the land or interest in respect of which he is registered, which a registered proprietor enjoys. This conception is central in the system of registration. It does not involve that the registered proprietor is protected against any claim whatsoever; as will be seen later, there are provisions by which the entry on which he relies may be cancelled or corrected, or he may be exposed to claims *in personam*. These are matters not to be overlooked when a total description of his rights is required. But as registered proprietor, and while he remains such, no adverse claim (except as specifically admitted) may be brought against him.

III Those sections which state the effect of the certificate of title. The principal section on this subject is s 75. The certificate, unless the register shows otherwise, is to be conclusive evidence that the person named in it is seised of or as taking estate or interest [sic] in the land therein described as seised or possessed of that land for the estate or interest therein specified and that the property comprised in the certificate has been duly brought under the Act. This section is of a similar character to those last discussed; it creates another – a probative – aspect of 'indefeasibility', nonetheless effective, though, as later provisions show, there are means by which the certificate may be cancelled or its owner compelled to hold it upon trust or to deliver it up through an action *in personam.*

IV Those sections which deal with correction or calling in of the certificate. The principal sections are ss 80 and 81 and s 85 ...

V Those sections which relate to the position of third parties dealing with a registered proprietor: these are, in effect, ss 182 and 183. Section 182 deals with notice. In all systems of registration of land it is usual and necessary to modify and indeed largely to negative the normal rules as to notice, constructive notice, or inquiry as to matters possibly affecting the title of the owner of the land.

The effect of these provisions upon the claim of the appellant against the second respondents must now be considered. It does not in their Lordships view admit of any doubt. Although a mortgage of a fee simple does not take effect as a transfer of the fee simple (see s 100) it does create a charge on the land which the Act treats as an estate or interest in the land (see s 2, definitions of 'estate or interest' and 'proprietor'). It is therefore apparent that the appellant's counter-claim against the second respondents, in so far as it sought a declaration that the appellant's interest in land was not affected by the purported mortgage and a declaration that the mortgage was a nullity, was an action for recovery of land within the terms of s 63. Insofar as it sought cancellation by the court of the entry of the mortgage on the register, it could only be based on s 85. The proceeding does not fall within either the exception of fraud or within any of the other exceptions allowed by s 63. The power of cancellation by the court is also excluded by the express terms of s 85, because the proceeding (for the recovery of land) is itself barred. No question of the invocation of the registrar's powers under ss 80 and 81 arises in the case. The conclusion must follow that the appellant's claim against the second respondents was correctly dismissed by Richmond J, and their Lordships find that his judgment on this point is supported by the authorities.

The leading case as to the rights of a person whose name has been entered upon the register without fraud in respect of an estate or interest is the decision of this board in *Assets Co Ltd v Mere Roihi*. The board there was concerned with three consolidated appeals from the Court of Appeal in New Zealand, which had decided in each case in favour of certain aboriginal natives as against the registered proprietors. In each appeal their Lordships decided that registration was conclusive to confer upon the appellants a title unimpeachable by the respondents. The facts involved in each of the appeals were complicated and not identical one with another, a circumstance which has given rise to some difference of opinion as to the precise *ratio decidendi* – the main relevant difference being whether the decision established the indefeasibility of title of a registered proprietor who acquired his interest under a void instrument, or whether it is only a *bona fide* purchaser from such a proprietor whose title is indefeasible. In *Boyd v Mayor etc of Wellington* [1924] NZLR 1174, the majority of the Court of Appeal in New Zealand held in favour of the former view, and treated the *Assets Co* case as a decision to that effect. The decision in *Boyd v Mayor etc of Wellington* related to a very special situation, namely, that of a registered proprietor who acquired his title under a void proclamation, but with certain reservations as to the case of forgery it has been generally accepted and followed in New Zealand as establishing, with the supporting authority of the *Assets Co* case, the indefeasibility of the title of registered proprietors derived from void instruments generally.

Their Lordships are of opinion that this conclusion is in accordance with the interpretation to be placed on those sections of the Land Transfer Act 1952, which they have examined. They consider that *Boyd*'s case was rightly decided and that the ratio of the decision applies as regards titles derived from registration of void instruments generally. As regards all such instruments it established that registration is effective to vest and to divest title and to protect the registered proprietor against adverse claims.

The failure of the appeal against the second respondents entails (and it was not contended otherwise) that it must equally fail against the first respondent. But their Lordships would add that the action against that respondent was an action for the recovery of land within the meaning of s 63 and that it would be directly barred by that section, quite apart from the fact that it could not be maintained against the other respondents. The appellant could not bring his case against the first respondent within any of the exceptions to that section.

Questions

1 Levana entrusts her certificate of title with her lawyer for safe custody. Meri, a cleaner at the lawyer's office, steals the certificate of title and using forged instruments of transfer sells the land to Simon, who buys in good faith without notice of the forgery. Simon is subsequently registered as the proprietor of the subject land. Levana and Simon assert rival claims over the land. Advise Levana.

2 Assume that Jones, an expatriate, enters into negotiations to purchase certain land from members of a certain clan. X forges the clan leaders' signatures on a document offering to sell the land to the government. The government buys the land and pays the money to X. Subsequently the government grants Jones a State lease over the subject land, which he registers. Jones had no knowledge of X's fraud until registration of the transfer. X absconds with the money and his whereabouts are unknown. The clan leaders seek your legal advice as to their claim over the subject land.

State lease issued in breach of prescribed statutory procedure

The Land Act 1996 prescribes the procedure and conditions for grant of a State lease. The following cases deal with the issue whether the principle of indefeasibility avails a registered proprietor of a State lease granted in breach of the Act.

MUDGE AND MUDGE v SECRETARY FOR LANDS AND OTHERS
[1985] PNGLR 387, Supreme Court of Justice

[The Mudges (plaintiffs/appellants) had expressed interest in acquiring a piece of land adjoining their property in Boroko and had been in touch with the relevant authorities to have the land rezoned. They had left the matters to take their normal course. In the meantime, unknown to them, D Pty Ltd (the third respondents) took their own independent action to acquire the same land and were granted a lease of the land. The following day they had the lease registered under the Land Registration Act. The appellants unsuccessfully applied to the National Court for a declaration that the lease was void. Their counsel argued that the lease was granted in breach of ss 9(2) and 29(3) of the Land Act (Chapter No 185). The former provision requires the Chairman of the Land Board to inform all interested parties of the date of the hearing of any application before him. The latter provision prohibits grant of a State lease for a purpose which is in contravention of the Town Planning Act (Chapter No 204). Counsel submitted that since the lease was illegally granted by the Board it was null and void and that the indefeasibility provisions of the Land Registration Act could not be relied upon because there had been a failure at the outset. Bredmeyer J held that there had been a breach of the Act as alleged by the appellants but refused to make an order nullifying the lease because of the principle of indefeasibility. On appeal to the Supreme Court.]

KIDU CJ: [T]he real question for determination by this court is whether, apart from exceptions enumerated in the Land Registration Act, s 33, land once registered attracts the principle of indefeasibility of title. This Act and its forerunners – the Real Property Ordinance (Papua) and the Land Registration Ordinance (NG) – are based on Australian Acts. They all reflect what is commonly known as the Torrens system of land registration. Under legislations based on this system (in Australia and New Zealand) it is now settled law that, apart from exceptions mentioned in the relevant legislations, once land is registered under the Torrens system the owner acquires indefeasibility of title. The relevant judicial authority in respect of New Zealand is the Privy Council decision in *Frazer v Walker* [1967] 1 AC 569 and in Australia it is the decision of the High Court in *Breskvar v Wall* (1971) 126 CLR 376. Counsel for the appellants ignored these authorities. The thrust of his main submission was that as the Land Registration Act had to be read subject to the Land Act any breach or non-compliance of the latter Act rendered registration of any estate or interest in land invalid. The Land Act does not say this. But Mr Donigi relied on ss 36(2), 37, 38(1)(c) and 39 of the Land Registration Act. However, I consider that these provisions in no way affect the indefeasibility of title of a State lease once it is registered. Section 33 is too clear to have its effect eroded by the provisions relied upon by the appellants' counsel.

PRATT J: I agree with Bredmeyer J that had the appellant taken proceedings even after the issue of the lease but before registration, he may well have obtained a declaration and associated order of the court requiring the Land Board to carry out its functions in a proper manner, and more particularly to determine the issue only after requirements of the Land Act, s 9(9) and s 29(3), had been observed. But that was not the factual position that was placed before his Honour. The course which appellant's counsel has therefore been forced to pursue in this case is really a frontal attack on the principle of indefeasibility of title under the Torrens system in our Land Registration Act, s 33.

The sections dealing with State leases are contained in Pt IV of the Land Registration Act. By s 36(1) the provisions of the Act apply to a 'Register of State Leases' and the section equates such Register with that of the ordinary register book and a State lease with an ordinary certificate of title. By s 36(2) a State lease is 'subject to the provisions of this Act ... as if it had been granted by a registered proprietor and registered in the register book'. The part of the sub-section which I have omitted is not relevant to the present problem in my view, as we are not concerned here with any question of particular requirements under the Land Act regarding methods of dealing with the lease or restrictions placed thereon by the Act. In short, a State lease when registered is in the same position as an ordinary certificate of title under the Torrens system and is therefore subject to the indefeasibility provisions set out in s 33 of the Act.

Section 33 of the Land Registration Act has many counterparts in other jurisdictions. An excellent collection of these counterparts may be found in the work by Francis, *The Law and Practice Relating to Torrens Title in Australia*, Vol 1, at p 573ff, wherein he deals with all the Australian States and New Zealand.

A divergence of views developed between Australia and New Zealand as to whether there was immediate indefeasibility on registration or whether such indefeasibility was deferred. The latter view was certainly the one followed for at least three decades in Australia after the decision of the High Court in *Clements v Ellis* (1934) 51 CLR 217 which, although an equally divided decision, led to an adoption of the principle enunciated by Dixon J that first registration pursuant to a void instrument need not carry the protection granted by the indefeasibility provisions under the Torrens Acts. The New Zealand approach resulted in an eventual appeal to the Privy Council in the celebrated case of *Frazer v Walker* [1967] 1 AC 569 and although their Lordships were not obliged by the facts before them to resolve the dispute between the Australian and New Zealand courts, they did go out of their way to support the principle that registration of a void instrument was, in the absence of fraud, effective to vest and divest title and to protect the registered proprietor against adverse claims': *Frazer v Walker* at 584 (see also the most helpful article of Professor Sackville in (1973) 47 ALJ 526).

Faced with the conflict between the Privy Council and the High Court of Australia, Street J, as he then was, resolved the question in the New South Wales Supreme Court in the matter of *Mayer v Coe* [1968] 2 NSWR 747. With respect I believe that his Honour's conclusions are quite compelling as to why the view of the Privy Council in *Frazer v Walker* should be preferred. At p 754 of his judgment, Street J says as follows:

> The Privy Council has gone out of its way to dismiss the appeal on a broader ground than was necessary, a ground more far-reaching than [sic] that which sufficed for the New Zealand Court of Appeal. It seems inescapable that their Lordships have done this deliberately to set at rest the doubts that have for many years plagued this particular branch of real property law in Australia and New Zealand. The Privy Council's decision is direct and binding authority laying down that a registered proprietor who acquires his interest *under an instrument void for any reason whatever* obtains on registration as indefeasible title. This will avail him against all, unless:
>
> (a) there is a specific basis under the statute rendering him open to challenge; an example of such a specific basis of challenge is actual fraud on his part or on the part of his agent ...

This is in fact what the learned trial judge said in the present matter at p 16 of his judgment:

> Mr Donigi has been unable to satisfy me that his client comes under any of the nine exceptions stated there [s 33 and s 36] or that s 160 and s 161 which give the Registrar a limited power to correct instruments and titles, has any application to the facts of this case. I have not been cited any authorities on Torrens Acts elsewhere to show that when a Crown lease has been granted in breach of several statutory provisions, its registration can be upset in the absence of fraud or one of the other stated exceptions.

With that view, I would respectfully agree.

[Wood J gave a concurring judgment.]

Appeal dismissed.

Questions

1 What are the possible policy reasons for allowing a registered proprietor to succeed even though the lease was issued in breach of the Land Act? Would you say that this decision would encourage grants of land in contravention of express statutory provisions? (However, see note 3, below.)

2 Why did the plaintiff's counsel seek to argue that indefeasibility under the LRA was 'deferred' and not immediate? See note 1, below.

Notes

1 Platt J refers to the controversy in Australian and New Zealand judicial decisions as to whether indefeasibility is immediate or is deferred. 'Immediate indefeasibility' means that upon registration title is forthwith immune from attack subject to exceptions in the Act. 'Deferred indefeasibility' on the other hand, means that registration does not protect a registered title that immediately derived from a void or an illegal transaction but one, which is a step away from it. The difference can be illustrated as follows. Assume that X is the registered proprietor of a State lease. Y forges X's signature and transfers the lease to BP1 who is a *bona fide* purchaser for value. Under immediate indefeasibility, BP1's title is immune from attack by X once the transfer is registered. In contrast, with deferred indefeasibility, regardless of registration, BP1's title remains defeasible at the suit of X. However, if before BP1 is divested of the lease he transfers it to BP2, a *bona fide* purchaser for value, on registration BP2 would acquire an indefeasible title (because he is a step away from the fraudulent transfer) as well as subsequent purchasers from BP2. In the *Mudge* case, Platt J (at pp 395–96) held that under the Land Registration Act indefeasibility is immediate and not deferred as argued by counsel for the Mudges. Kidu CJ and Wood J did not expressly reject the deferred indefeasibility concept.

2 In *Mamun Investments v Ponda* [1995] PNGLR 1, the Supreme Court cited *Mudge* with approval. Kapi DCJ and Injia J (at p 9) said, 'As the Supreme Court held in *Mudge* ... even when a State lease issued under the Land Act have been issued irregularly and in breach of the provisions of the that Act, registration under the Land Registration Act will confer an indefeasible title'. See also *Keindip v The State of Papua New Guinea* [1993] PNGLR 28; *Timano v Timano* [1993] PNGLR 334; *Maki v Minister For Land and Others*, unreported, N1568, PNG National Court of Justice, OS No 149 of 1995.

3 The Supreme Court in *Emas Estate Development Pty Ltd v John Mea and Another* [1993] PNGLR 215, cast in doubt the authority of *Mudge*'s case. See the extract below.

EMAS ESTATE DEVELOPMENT PTY LTD v JOHN MEA AND ANOTHER
[1993] PNGLR 215, Supreme Court of Justice

AMET J: The appellant appeals from the whole of the judgment of Los J in the National Court given on 31 July 1992 at Waigani in proceedings OS No 273 of 1991. Upon a judicial review of the decision of the second respondent, Minister for Lands, to forfeit the State lease over the portion of land, allotment 11, section 2, Boroko, held by the first respondent, John Mea, and its subsequent allocation or grant to the appellant, the trial judge ordered that the land be reallocated to the first respondent. I set out, hereunder, the factual history of this matter.

The first respondent, John Mea, was the owner of the State lease over this parcel of land, having been given it by EE Kriewaldts and Company Limited in 1976 for long service to the company. On the land was a fully furnished three bedroom house in which John Mea lived, plus domestic quarters in the back. An update inspection was conducted on various run-down and unimproved blocks in Boroko and Korobosea on 7 and 8 December 1988. The report on this property showed that rent was paid to date. The comments in respect of the property were that the house was run-down, with parts of walls, door, and windows broken, that it was completely run-down, and the lessee had to demolish the house and rebuild. The lessee was to be asked to explain his lack of maintenance on existing improvements. Subsequently, on 16 February 1989, a letter of demand for outstanding rent of K20.00, being K10.00 for arrears and K10.00 for the current annual rent, was forwarded to the first respondent. The first respondent paid the outstanding rent on 10 April 1989. On 24 October 1989, the Lands Department issued a notice to show cause pursuant to s 46(2) of the Land Act Ch 185, addressed to the first respondent at c/o PO Box 1219, Boroko. The notice required the first respondent 'to show cause why that lease should not be forfeited on the grounds that you have refused or neglected to comply with the improvement covenant or condition in that lease and you have failed to pay the rent for a period of more than six months. If sufficient cause is not shown within one month of the date of this notice, the lease may be declared forfeited'. Subsequently, on 2 March 1990, a forfeiture notice was issued by the second respondent. Minister for Lands, pursuant to s 46(1) of the Act forfeiting the lease on the grounds that:

(a) the improvement conditions imposed by the Land Act have not been fulfilled in respect of the land;

(b) the rent remains due and unpaid for a period of more than six months.

The forfeiture notice was gazetted on 26 April 1990. Subsequently, the Minister was advised by the department and, pursuant to s 57(5), the Minister issued an exemption from public advertisement and tender notice in respect of the forfeited land. There were subsequently two applicants for the allocation of the land, the appellant Emas Estate and an employee of the Lands Department, one Leo Minjan. The Lands Board subsequently granted the lease to the appellant. Mr Minjan, aggrieved by that decision, appealed to the Minister pursuant to s 11 of the Land Act on 29 October 1990. Whilst that appeal was still pending, the lease was issued to the appellant on 28 March 1991 and registered on 29 July 1991. I note that the lease was not actually signed by the Minister in person but by one Otta Karo as a delegate of the Minister.

The first respondent contended before the National Court that he had not received any notice to show cause under s 46(2) of the Land Act, nor was he aware of the subsequent forfeiture and the reallocation of land to the appellant. In September 1990, he had torn down the house to build the new one at the cost of K70,000.00. He deposed to an affidavit in the National Court that he only became aware of the forfeiture and the subsequent re-leasing of the land in October 1990, when he made enquiries at the Lands Department. He deposed that he immediately instructed Mr GO Emilio, a lawyer, who wrote to the Assistant Secretary, Southern Region, of the Lands Department on 4 October 1990, which letter was exhibited in the court below in relation to the forfeiture and the first respondent's lack of notice of the second respondent Minister's intention to forfeit his land. There was no reply to this letter of the 4 October 1990. On 2 July 1991, the first respondent again instructed Karingu and Sitapai Lawyers, who wrote to the Secretary for the Department of Lands again in a similar vein that the first respondent had not been served Notice to Show Cause, pursuant to s 46(2) of the Act. Again, there was no reply to this letter up until this date.

It was in these circumstances that the first respondent obtained leave and sought judicial review of the second respondent's decisions to forfeit his land for the reasons stipulated above, and to subsequently re-lease it to the appellant.

The trial judge found on the basis of evidence before him that the first respondent did not received [sic] the notice to show cause, as was a necessary requisite to the Minister exercising his discretion to forfeit the lease.

Secondly, the learned trial judge found, as a matter of fact, that when the notice to show cause was issued on 24 October 1989, which was forwarded by mail to the address PO Box 1219, Boroko, and which the trial judge found was not received by the first respondent, the first respondent was not in arrears of rent, nor was there any rent outstanding because, as evidenced by the official receipt issued on 10 April 1989, the first respondent had already paid the outstanding amount of K20.00. Consequently, the second ground for forfeiture, that is that there was outstanding rent in excess of six months, could not be sustained, and the department and the Minister had in fact erred in this conclusion. The learned trial judge found, therefore, that the Minister had no power to issue such a notice in respect of this ground.

In relation to the allegation of the breach of improvement condition, the first respondent contended that he had been in occupation of the house at all times until September of 1990, when he demolished the house in order to rebuild a K70,000.00 house in its place. The learned trial judge concluded that, if the Minister and the department were prepared to issue notice for alleged failure to pay rent to-date, then the allegation of the breach of the improvement condition was suspect.

I, too, agree with the factual conclusion of the learned trial judge. First, I agree that the notice to show cause pursuant to s 46(2) was forwarded by mail instead of being personally served on the first respondent and, consequently, there is no proof that the first respondent in fact received it. His evidence in the National Court, evidenced by letters written by his lawyers on two occasions to the department, clearly raised the issue at the earliest opportunity of his contention that he had not been properly served notice to show cause. Consequently, there is just not sufficient evidence that, in fact, the first respondent received and, thus, was properly served the notice to show cause. Secondly, I agree with the learned trial judge that the allegation in the notice to show cause that the first respondent had rent outstanding just could not be sustained on the evidence before the court. The documentary receipts and the records of inspection clearly revealed that, at the time of the issuing of the notice to show cause on 24 October 1989, the first respondent was, in fact, up-to-date with his rental payments. I, therefore, agree with the finding of the learned trial judge that this ground for the forfeiture could not be upheld. In any event, the amount alleged to be in arrears, K20.00, is so relatively insignificant an amount that it could not justify the exercise of a discretion to forfeit a substantial property.

These, in my view, are the primary reasons why the forfeiture in the first instance was invalid. And, in my view, it was quite properly set aside by the learned trial judge. Furthermore, in my view, the subsequent transactions in respect of this property leave much to be desired. Firstly, on 8 March 1990, within but six days of the forfeiture notice by the Minister, he was persuaded by interested officers of the Lands Department to exempt the land from public advertisement for applications and tender. Secondly, there being two applicants only, the unsuccessful applicant, Leo Minjan, lodged an appeal to the Minister pursuant to s 11 of the Act. This appeal remains undetermined to this time. The lease was subsequently issued on 28 March 1991, and signed not by the Minister but by one Otta Karo as delegate of the Minister, and subsequently registered on 29 July 1991.

The issue at the end of the day is whether, in these circumstances, the registration of the lease vests in the appellant indefeasibility of title as against the first respondent. My view is that the circumstances are so irregular and unlawful at the very outset to the subsequent transactions that it ought not to prevail. I consider that the learned trial judge properly set aside the forfeiture of the lease by the Minister and ordered its reallocation to its rightful owner, the first respondent. The manner in which the matter was handled subsequent to the forfeiture – the land exempted from public advertisement within a very short time of less than a week, a new lease issued whilst a legitimate aggrieved applicant had lodged an appeal which is still outstanding, and the new lease signed not by the Minister but by a departmental officer as delegate – are all, to my mind, less than satisfactory, highly irregular, and tantamount to fraud, such that the registration of the title should not be allowed to stand.

The issues in this case raise for consideration the principle of indefeasibility of title under the Torrens land registration system that hitherto has been applied in this jurisdiction. I do not believe that the system is necessarily appropriate in circumstances such as this, where an individual land owner is deprived of his title to land by irregular procedure on the part of officials and a department of the State, to the advantage of a private corporation. I do not accept that quite clear irregularities and breaches of the statutory provision should remain indefeasible. I believe that, although those irregularities and illegalities might not amount strictly to fraud, they should, nevertheless, still be good grounds for invalidating subsequent registration, which should not be allowed to stand. To not do so would be harsh and oppressive against the innocent individual leaseholder, such as the first respondent.

I disagree with the further contention on the part of the appellant that damages are adequate remedy for the aggrieved first respondent. I do not believe this is a satisfactory remedy for the wrong done to the first respondent. It is not an easy task to pursue a claim for damages against the State which is quite costly. Similarly, I do not necessarily accept that, quite simply because the appellant, a private corporation, has incurred expenses and mortgaged the property, it would suffer greater prejudice and damage which a remedy of damages could not rectify, as against the first respondent doing the same.

For these reasons in the end result, I do not believe that the errors, irregularities, and illegalities and possible fraud on the part of the officers and the Department of Lands ought to prevail to deprive the first respondent. In the end result, on balance, my conclusions are that the land, the property of the first respondent, was wrongly and unlawfully forfeited by the second respondent, when he had, in fact, not breached any condition of his lease. He had lost his property. The Minister and the department erred in law and, in my view, there is no reason at all, in principle, why the first respondent should not be entitled to the reallocation of his property to him. The balance of convenience, equity, justice, and fairness, in my conclusion, between the individual wronged, the first respondent, and the appellant corporation compels me to the view that the first respondent's interest should prevail. I consider that damages would be adequate remedy for the appellant corporation against the second and third respondents. I have concluded also that the doctrine of indefeasibility of title under the Torrens system of land registration is one that does not necessarily apply, nor is it necessarily appropriate in the circumstances such as this that will continue to be experienced by ordinary papua New Guinean landowners against the might of the State and private corporations. For this fundamental reason, I am of the view that this doctrine, which has hitherto been applied without any examination as to its appropriateness and applicability in the development of the underlying law for this country, should not be applied to this case.

I would dismiss the appeal with costs.

BROWN J (dissenting): Mr Karingu, for the first respondent, argued that the Supreme Court should not interfere with the trial judge's findings, for the notice of appeal was silent as to the requirements of s 14(1) of the Supreme Court Act to specify errors in law or fact made by the trial judge on the factual situation before the trial judge. Rather, as Mr Molloy states, the judge's reasons are misconceived, for the true facts have not been disclosed. It is not right to say, as Mr Karingu has argued, that 'there was no *bona fide* third party involved'. The company was clearly the registered proprietor of a leasehold interest in the subject land following a grant by the Department of Lands and Physical Planning. The fact has been glossed over by Mr Karingu. Mr Karingu further argued that fraud was apparent on the evidence of Leo Minjan, whose affidavit, sworn on 5 November 1992, was admitted into evidence on the hearing of this appeal. In those circumstances, Mr Karingu says the company does not have an indefeasible title in terms of s 33(1)(a) of the Land Registration Act, and he relied on the trial judge's reasoning, which has been quoted above. We consider, however, that the reference by the trial judge to there being 'not any *bona fide* party involved', cannot be support for Mr Karingu's assertion that there is fraud in the company. The *bona fides* of the company were not the subject of investigation in the judicial review proceedings. The trial judge was unaware of the fact that the company was the present registered proprietor of the State lease. The use of the affidavit of Leo Minjan in these circumstances does not evidence any fraud on the part of the successful tenderer for the fresh State lease, Emas Estate Development Pty Ltd, although it may be evidence of some procedural irregularities in the Department of Lands. There is confirmatory evidence of advertisement in relation to the subject land, and public tenders were called for, but there is no suggestion that Emas has perpetrated a fraud in the tender process. In the circumstances of this case, I find that there is little reason to depart from the reasoning of this court in *Mudge v Secretary for Lands* [1985] PNGLR 387, where the court had reason to consider the principle of indefeasibility of title. Notwithstanding that a state lease issued under the Land Act may have been issued irregularly and in breach of the provisions of that act, registration under the Land Registration Act will confer an indefeasible title. Whilst no argument was mounted in relation to s 41 of the Constitution, it is interesting to note that Pratt J dealt with that issue at p 398:

> The final ground of appeal to which I intend to refer is the claim by the appellant that the outcome of the court's application of the law in this matter will bring about a result which is harsh and oppressive on the appellants and thus by the Constitution, s 41, any such act, be it done under a valid law or otherwise, is unlawful. Again I am unable to appreciate how the issue of a registered lease with indefeasibility under the Land Registration Act, s 33, and thereby ensures the continuance in this jurisdiction of such principle and the paramountcy of the Torrens system generally, can be said to be harsh and oppressive and thereby unlawful when the person making such claim does not even have a legal or equitable interest in the matter.

Once an indefeasible title to the subject land has been found, (and here there can be no question about that in the face of the State lease vol 1 folio 138 in the name of the company), John Mea has no legal or equitable interest in the land. This court has already said that registration of leases is effective to vest an indefeasible title in the registered proprietor, subject to exceptions enumerated in s 33 of the Land Registration Act. [His Honour cited with approval the judgments of Kidu CJ in *Mudge v Secretary for Lands*; of Barwick CJ in *Breskvar v Wall* (1971) 126 CLR 376.]

I am sure that had the trial judge been made aware of the true situation in relation to the grant and registration of the fresh lease affecting the subject land, he would not have made the orders that he did, for the company had then an indefeasible title upon registration on 29 July 1991.

The order of the judicial review should be quashed as a nullity, based as it was on facts shown to be patently wrong ...

SALIKA J: I have read the judgment of my brothers, and I say the following on my own behalf. I agree with the factual information that both my brothers have included in their respective judgments. I agree, in principle, that where a title has been registered under one's name, it is not capable of being annulled, except whether title has been acquired through fraud. I think other exceptions suitable for Papua New Guinea circumstances should be included such as:

1 where title has been registered fraudulently;

2 where title has been registered while a court or tribunal is deliberating on the subject land;

3 where title has been registered under influence of position of power or money;

4 where title has been registered under circumstances giving rise to possible breach of principles of natural justice.

I lay out these conditions because land is a very important commodity in this country. government land is very scarce in this country, and people or corporations applying for lease of government land must be seen to be allocated such land without any fraud or outside influence, but simply on the merits.

In the instant case, there is evidence that John Mea, the former proprietor of the lease in relation to the subject property, was not informed that his lease was going to be forfeited. In other words, he was not served a notice to show cause why his lease should not be forfeited. The State went ahead and forfeited his lease and then granted a new lease to the plaintiff. Given the situation that John Mea was not given a chance to defend the continuation of his lease, I am of the view that the failure to give him notice was a fundamental breach by the State officers. In my view, it would amount to a breach of John Mea's rights under category 4, as I have outlined.

Another factor that needs to be given serious consideration is that an unsuccessful applicant had lodged an appeal under s 12(2)(a) of the Land Act, appealing against the granting of the lease to the appellant in this case. While that appeal was on foot, the lease was registered in the name of the appellants. The registration of the lease at that stage in the name of the appellants would fall under category 2 of my list of exceptions.

It is basically for those reasons that I do not think the appellant has a properly acquired title to the subject property.

Appeal dismissed.

Questions

1 Which one of these statements more accurately represents the *ratio* of this case?:

(i) The principle of indefeasibility did not apply because the grant was made in breach of the provisions of the Land Act.

(ii) The principle of indefeasibility did not apply because of the 'highly irregular and tantamount to fraud' manner the matter was handled subsequent to the forfeiture.

(iii) The principle of indefeasibility did not apply because, on the facts of the case, its application was unsuitable for the circumstances of PNG.

2 If none of the above statements, in your view, represents the *ratio* of the case, formulate what you consider to be its *ratio* and why.

3 Does the case of *Emas Estate Development Pty Ltd v John Mea and Another* overrule *Mudge v Secretary For Lands* or distinguish it? Can you distinguish the two cases?

4 Justice Amet said in his judgment that the principle of indefeasibility is not necessarily suitable for the PNG circumstances. Do you agree? Why? Compare with Platt J in *Mudge, supra,* p 432.

The National Court in *Steamship Trading Company Ltd v Minister of Lands and Physical Planning and Others* (unreported, N1959, OS 552 of 1999), and *Hi Lift Company Pty Ltd v Secretary for Agriculture and The State of Papua New Guinea* (unreported, N2004, OS 329 of 2000), follows the trend set by *Emas'* case. See extracts of the cases below.

STEAMSHIP TRADING COMPANY LTD v MINISTER OF LANDS AND PHYSICAL PLANNING, GARAMUT ENTERPRISES LTD AND GUISE AND OTHER MEMBERS OF THE NATIONAL LAND BOARD
unreported, N1959 PNG National Court of Justice, OS 552 of 1999

[Garamut (the second defendant) were interested in acquiring a State lease over certain open government land. It unsuccessfully applied to the NCD Physical Planning Board for the land to be rezoned commercial. It appealed against the decision to the National Physical Planning Appeal Tribunal. The latter recommended to the Minister to dismiss the appeal. However, the Minister 'having considered all issues' upheld the appeal and the land was rezoned commercial. Soon thereafter Garamut applied for a commercial lease over the subject land. The land was gazetted for public tender pursuant to s 68 of the Land Act 1996. Before the tenders closed the Minister, purporting to act under s 69(2) of the Land Act, exempted the land from public tender. The Lands Department issued a State lease to Garamut and the latter registered the lease in its name under the Land Registration Act. The plaintiffs sought a judicial order to nullify the lease on the ground that the government officers did not follow the prescribed procedure under the Land Act for grant of a State lease.]

SHEEHAN J: Garamut says that notwithstanding all errors or breaches of procedures under the Act that may have occurred, Garamut now holds a registered title. Title that is by s 33 of the Land Registration Act valid for all purposes, a title that is indefeasible. Garamut relies on the Supreme Court decision in *Mudge v Secretary for Lands* [1985] PNGLR 387 that registration is final on all issues and that only the exceptions provided under the Land Registration Act can be invoked to overturn a registered title. Of these, it was submitted only fraud, not specifically pleaded in these proceedings or proved, might have availed the Plaintiff.

Counsel for both the Plaintiff and Garamut also cited *Emas Estate Development Pty Ltd v John Mea and Others* [1993] PNGLR 215 where the Supreme Court took a contrary view of the consequence of breaches of statutory procedures.

In that case, the court, while acknowledging the principles of indefeasibility of title nonetheless did (by a majority) consider irregularities tantamount to fraud as sufficient to overturn a registered title.

In both the *Mudge* and the *Emas Estate* cases there were challenges to the issue of leases and to the subsequent registration of them under Land Registration Act on grounds that irregularities under the Land Act rendered the leases and therefore the registrations void. In the *Mudge* case the court found that the main submission of the Appellant that the Land Registration Act was to be read as subject to the Land Act could not be sustained.

For the Plaintiff it was argued this court should follow *Emas*, while Counsel for Garamut contended that decision was distinguishable on its facts. The essence of the decision he said being to uphold the exception under s 33(c) of the Land Registration Act which provides for a challenge to the register by a proprietor claiming under a prior instrument of title.

In the *Mudge* case the Supreme Court (which followed the Privy Council in *Frazer v Walker* [1967] 1 AC 569) said that notwithstanding there may have been irregularities in the issue of the lease:

> *... it is now settled law that apart from exceptions mentioned in the relevant legislation's once land is under the Torrens system the owner acquires indefeasibility of title.*

It cited *Breskvar v Wall* [1971] 126 CLR 376 where Barwick CJ of the Australian High Court stated the rationale of indefeasibility that arises through that system:

> *... the Torrens system of registered title of which the Act (The Real Property Acts, Queensland 1863) is a form is not a system of registration of title but a system of title by registration.*

Accordingly the court said that in the absence of any explanation or reason why breaches of the Land Act should cause the avoidance of a subsequently registered lease the title must be upheld.

With respect there were significant reasons not put before the court. The stated objects and purposes of the Land Act and the Land Registration Act which differ fundamentally were not raised. Nor was the court asked to consider, if the fundamental element of title were absent at time of registration – that is, if there was no title at all to register – whether registration itself could create it.

The Land Act Part IX provides for the alienation of government land. In s 64(1) it says that '*government land shall not be alienated otherwise than under this Act or another law*'. Parliament thereby clearly prohibits the alienation of government land other than through the processes of the Land Act or another law.

It is very clear too that the Land Registration Act is not 'another law' intended to effect such alienation. The preamble to the Land Registration Act states that it is '*an act to unify the law relating to the Registration of Title to land, and for related purposes*'. The Land Act deals with the issue of title. The Land Registration Act deals with the registration, preservation and strengthening of that title, not the creation of title itself that is described in *Breskvar's* case. There can be no doubt that indefeasibility of registered title exists in PNG. The Land Registration Act provides that. But before that indefeasibility can arise there must first be a title to register.

In neither of the *Mudge* or *Emas Estate* cases did the Supreme Court have argument before it or consider what conclusions should be drawn in the event that the breach of procedures under the Land Act were not just irregularities not going to jurisdiction, but breaches that resulted in a total nullity, such that no lease issued under the Land Act at all; that there was therefore no title to register. Nor was there argument or consideration of why Parliament having stipulated in one Act the only mode of granting of State leases, should by another act grant an indefeasible title by way of lease without any need to follow that process;

whether the obligations to follow the mandates of the Land Act could be wholly ignored and title achieved merely by registration of a document under the Land Registration Act.

For example suppose that on the day following the National Court decisions in either the *Crusoe* or *NCDC* case referred to above; that is the day after the court declared the grant of lease in those cases wholly void, without any process under the Land Act a lease in the same terms was registered through error or negligence. Would that registration create indefeasible title?

It is not to the point to say that the register might be corrected for error. Could registration create a title out of nothing and incidentally defeat a judgment of the court?

Again, under s 99 of the Land Act the Minister may grant a residential or commercial lease over lands on which there are government buildings. In such leases none of the normal processes for grant or forfeiture apply. The Land Registration Act is also said not to apply. If despite that, through error or negligence a commercial lease over the land on which Parliament stands were to be registered under the Land Registration Act in favour of a private company, would the lessee acquire indefeasible title? Would the court in any of these circumstances be obliged to ignore irregularities under the Land Act, would it be precluded from setting aside registration for any ground available under judicial review. In other words are the powers of review under s 155 of the Constitution limited by the rule of indefeasibility of title. The Supreme Court decisions in *Mudge* and *Emas Estate* are not conclusive on these issues.

On the evidence before me I am satisfied that even if the court were to follow the decision in *Mudge*'s case that registration of a document alone creates an indefeasible title, notwithstanding irregularities of process or documentation that would otherwise preclude the grant of title, it is clear from the facts before this court that there has been fraud shown in this case.

It is true that the Plaintiff did not assert fraud in the Statement filed in these proceedings. But the Statement under O 16 is a prayer for relief. It is not the pleading of a cause of action. Pleadings only arise in actions commenced by writ not in any other originating process. (Order 8 R 1 National Court Rules) what the Plaintiff has done however is to assert unreasonableness which includes bad faith, equitable and or constructive fraud.

Counsel for Garamut cited the view of the Privy Council in the decision *Assets Co Ltd v Meri Roihi* [1905] AC 176 that the fraud required to defeat a registered title meant actual fraud – not equitable or constructive fraud – and actual fraud that must be brought home to the registered proprietor whose title is impeached. That view however was based on the Council's reading of the relevant New Zealand Act. Our own Land Registration Act only speaks of fraud and does not limit its meaning nor does it require that fraud be shown in a particular party.

The first and second Defendants failed to follow the zoning laws and have displayed a total disregard for procedures the Land Act provides for the alienation of State land. Instead of the transparent process open to public participation that the Act provides, there has been exclusion and preference shown to the advantage of one only. There has not been just some minor administrative error but rather a subversion of the whole statutory process which the court could not in good conscience support.

But I am satisfied that in this case registration on 23 February 1999 did not grant indefeasible title in favour of Garamut. Because what issued and was registered was no lease, no title able to be registered. It was a nullity.

... It is plain fact that Garamut has now erected a substantial market on the land expending in excess of four million kina in so doing. It was pointed out that such development was carried out on the basis that Garamut believed it had a registered title to land zoned for the development that was carried out.

While it can be said that Garamut did seek the advantage of exclusive access to a commercial lease on grounds it must have known were not valid, there has been no evidence to suggest it otherwise contributed to the gross breaches of the statute that occurred. Counsel for Garamut strenuously argued, grant of any of the relief sought will constitute severe prejudice to the Company. But that prejudice must be balanced with the public interest in good administration as well as the interests of the Plaintiff.

Because of delay in bringing these proceedings I am satisfied that the Plaintiff's applications for injunctions restraining further development or restraint of the conduct of the business should be declined. But to refuse relief as to the issue of the lease itself would be to give court approval to gross mal administration and to publicly condone fraud. In this case, the prejudice to Garamut in striking down the issue and registration of the lease is not necessarily total. Quite apart from rights of action against the first and third Defendants that result from setting aside title, such a decision does not grant title in favour of any other. There is no reason why Garamut cannot institute fresh applications for both zoning and a lease under the appropriate lawful processes for such purposes.

I am satisfied orders should issue sought in the nature of *certiorari* quashing, first the decision of the first Defendant of 15 October 1998 to rezone the land Allotment 23 Section 71 Hohola from open space to commercial; second the decision of first Defendant of 18 February granting a commercial lease of that land to the second Defendant; thirdly the decision of the third Defendant recorded as being made in Land Board Meeting 2004 on 30 September 1999. Finally, there will be an order that the second Defendant that the second Defendant surrender its copy of the registered lease of the said Land to the Land Registrar who shall thereupon cancel the same.

[Application upheld.]

HI LIFT COMPANY v MIRI SATA, MBE, SECRETARY DEPARTMENT OF AGRICULTURE AND LIVESTOCK AND THE INDEPENDENT STATE OF PAPUA NEW GUINEA unreported, N2004, PNG National Court of Justice, OS 329 of 2000

[In 1985 the Department of Agriculture and Livestock (DAL), first defendant, took possession of the disputed land known as 'Portion 2413'. In 1998, the Department of Lands granted the plaintiff a 'Business (Light Industry)' Lease over the said land even though the land was zoned 'Public Institution'. The plaintiff registered the lease under the Land Registration Act. The DAL, which had made infrastructure improvements over the land in excess of half a million kina, refused to vacate the land, whereupon the plaintiffs brought these proceedings for its ejection. In its defence, the DAL claimed that the lease was void because of substantial irregularities in its grant and fraud. The plaintiff claimed that its title was indefeasible.]

SEVUA J: A number of submissions in law have been raised by both counsel, however, I do not propose to canvass all those arguments, even though, I have heard and considered all of them.

The plaintiff argued that it has indefeasible title to the land which cannot be nullified unless there is fraud. Mr Kassman for the plaintiff relied on *Mudge and Mudge v Secretary for Lands*

[1985] PNGLR 382, a decision of the Supreme Court which upheld the principle of indefeasibility of title, protected by s 33 of the Land Registration Act, Ch 191.

The defendants relied on *Emas Estate Development Pty Ltd v John Mea and Others* [1993] PNGLR 215, another decision of the Supreme Court, which also considered and acknowledged the principle of indefeasibility of title, but did not apply the principle for the reasons stated therein.

I do not think that the defendants really dispute the fact that title to Portion 2413 was granted to the plaintiff. So, I am entitled to find as a fact that the title to Portion 2413 was issued to the plaintiff on 8 July 1998.

However, there are several issues that concern this court and it is necessary to address those here because I believe, at the end of the day, the justice of the case will be realised and appreciated.

Firstly, the undisputed evidence is that the lease over Portion 2413 was granted to the plaintiff on 8 July 1998. However there is no evidence at all as to how the plaintiff acquired the land. That is to say, there is no evidence as to whether the land was advertised pursuant to s 68 of the Land Act 1996 or whether the land was exempted from advertisement under s 69(2) of the said Act. All that the plaintiff could say was that it was issued with the title to the land. But what procedure under the Land Act was followed in the allocation of this land?

I consider that this is a crucial issue in the light of the undisputed evidence that the Department of Agriculture and Livestock had occupied the land since 1985, and has improvements valued at half a million kina. Surely, if the land had been advertised, DAL would have taken appropriate measures to protect its interest. If it was not advertised, I would consider the grant to the plaintiff as being quite unfair and irregular because the public interest and more particularly, the interest of DAL was never considered, so it seems.

Secondly, there is also undisputed evidence that Portion 2413 was a Public Institutions zone. The State lease described as Volume 20, Folio 85 and granted to the plaintiff clearly reveals that the lease was a Business (Light Industrial) Lease. In fact, there is undisputed evidence that the land was zoned Public Institutions, not a business lease. The National Capital District Commission Physical Planning Board was requested to rezone Portion 2413 to Commercial Zone except that parcel occupied by DAL. I consider this to be contrary to the zoning requirement under s 67 of the Land Act. The fact that a Business (Light Industrial) Lease was granted over a land zoned as Public Institutions, was contrary to s 67 of the Land Act.

It is my view that the grant of a business lease to the plaintiff was irregular because, Portion 2413 was never a commercial zone, but a Public Institution zone. It was after the lease had been granted to the plaintiff that arrangements for a rezoning were made.

Thirdly, whilst there is no evidence of fraud, I consider that a presumption of fraud exists. Here, the Department of Agriculture and Livestock together with other public institutions like Department of Transport and National Intelligence Organisation occupied Portions 2413 since 1985, until fire destroyed the other offices. DAL has infrastructure improvements valued at K500,000.00 on the land. Was there any investigation carried out by the Lands Department prior to the grant of the lease to the plaintiff on 8 July 1998? If there was an investigation, was the interest of the public held by DAL taken into account? If not, why was the interest of a private legal entity given precedence over the interest of the public? In my view, it must seem quite an irregular and suspicious dealing for the Department of

Lands to grant a lease over Portion 2413 to a private company when the public interest held by the Department of Agriculture and Livestock existed. That is the reason I said that presumption of fraud existed in this case. How could the public interest, be ignored by the Department of Lands? And what is so special about the plaintiff company that its interest seemed to have been given priority over public interest?

It is my view that the decision of *Emas Estate* be preferred to that of *Mudge.* For I consider that the concerns I have highlighted here should invalidate the plaintiff's indefeasible title. I adopt the reasons given by the Chief Justice at p 210 as the basis for which I believe the plaintiff's title to Portion 2413 should not remain indefeasible. The irregularities and illegalities I have referred to here are sufficient, in my view, to invalidate the registration of the plaintiff's title.

Whilst these matters may not strictly amount to fraud, I do not accept that the public interest over this land held by DAL can be easily ignored. I do not believe that the issues I have raised, coupled with possible fraud on the part of officers of the Lands Department ought to prevail to deprive the public of a portion of land which it has held through the Department of Agriculture and Livestock for over 10 years.

I consider that the public through DAL has become the pawn in the sandwich here. The public through the Department of Agriculture and Livestock was an innocent party, deprived of its right and interest to Portion 2413 as a result of the unfair and irregular dealings by the Department of Lands.

In fact, in *Emas'* case, while the Supreme Court acknowledged the principle of indefeasibility of title discussed in *Mudge,* the majority in the latter case concluded that irregularities tantamount to fraud was sufficient to overturn a registered title. That is the position I take in the present case and I apply that principle here. The irregularities in the present case which I have alluded to, are in my view, sufficient to invalidate or nullify the registration of the plaintiff's title because they are tantamount to fraud.

The National Court in the recent case of *Steamship Trading Company Limited v Minister for Lands and Physical Planning, Garamut Enterprises Limited and Ralph Guise and Others,* unreported, N1959, considered that some of the irregular circumstances apparent in that case were tantamount to fraud. The court in that case followed the majority view in *Emas* case.

I agree with Sheehan J's discussions on the purpose of both the Land Act and the Land Registration Act. The Land Act regulates the alienation of State land while the Land Registration Act governs the registration of title to government land after the land is alienated. Section 64(1) of the Land Act specifically provides that *'government land should not be alienated otherwise than under this Act or another law'*. I have already alluded to my views on the lack of evidence as to how Portion 2413 was alienated, ie, lack of evidence of advertisement or exemption of advertisement, etc. I think I am entitled to assume that since there is no evidence of how Portion 2413 was allocated to the plaintiff, there were breaches of statutory procedures, which are sufficient to overturn the plaintiff's indefeasible title.

I reiterate that the plaintiff has not established by credible evidence that there was an open transparency process in the allocation of this land, which open transparency, would include public participation as stipulated by the Act. I say this because, I am sure that, had there been a transparent process, the Department of Agriculture and Livestock would have participated by protecting its right and interest on and over the land. It appears to me that there was exclusion and preference shown, to the advantage of the plaintiff only, and this court could not, in good conscience, support such lack of transparency and preference to one particular corporate citizen.

In my view, it would be morally wrong for this court to sanction such irregularities by the Department of Lands by jumping onto the band wagon of indefeasibility of title and riding it despite the apparent breaches of statutory provisions. Therefore, in my view, whilst these irregularities and breaches may not be fraud, they are sufficient to overturn the indefeasible title of the plaintiff. They must affect the registered title.

The plaintiff has submitted that the defendants (to use the words of Pratt J in *Mudge*) *'are seeking to mount an attack on the principles of indefeasibility of title under the Torrens system'*. The problem with that submission is that, counsel did not appreciate that in *Mudge*, the Supreme Court did not hear arguments or consider what conclusions it should draw in the event that procedural breaches or irregularities were breaches that resulted in a nullity. Sheehan J alluded to this at p 44 of his judgment in *Garamut*'s case. Pratt J was talking about registration of title, not statutory breaches or irregularities. Registration of title, which gives indefeasible title under the Land Registration Act, is one thing, but breaches and or any irregularities under the Land Act, are quite significant that they ought to affect the subsequent registration of title. In my view, such breaches and irregularities under the Land Act, which go to the root of the granting of leases, affect the registration of title so that a title no longer remains indefeasible.

I am therefore of the view that the breaches and irregularities I have alluded to, go to the very root of the granting of the lease or alienating that portion of government land. The plaintiff therefore cannot claim an indefeasible title. I consider that, since the Land Act is primarily the legislation dealing with alienation of government land, the procedures for alienation, must be free from any fraud, breach of statutory provision or irregularities. I believe that good conscience dictate that once there is evidence of, or suspicion of breach of any provision of the Land Act, or irregularities which may not necessarily amount to fraud, the registration of title must be affected so that the registered title holder no longer has a indefeasible title. In other words, the indefeasibility of title remains intact where no breach or irregularity of the Land Act is committed.

Plaintiff's claim dismissed.

Note

The foregoing cases (*Emas Steamship* and *Hi Lift*) also illustrate exceptions to indefeasibility of title created by the judiciary, see below subtitle 'Judicial inroads on the concept of indefeasibility of title'. For a critical discussion of these cases, see Mugambwa J, 'Judicial assault on the citadel of indefeasibility of title under the Papua New Guinean Torrens system of conveyance' (2001) 5 Journal of South Pacific Law (http://www.vanuatu.usp.ac.fj/journal_splaw/Article/Mugambwa1.htm). See extract at p 449.

Exceptions to indefeasibility of title

The principle of indefeasibility is not absolute. There are several exceptions (overriding interests) to this principle within the Land Registration Act and without the Act. Some of the exceptions are obvious and understandable, but some are more difficult to justify in the context of the Torrens system philosophy. As you read these exceptions, it is important to consider the possible policy reasons for a particular exception and whether or not it is justifiable.

Exceptions under the Land Registration Act

The key provision is s 33, which guarantees indefeasibility of a registered title except as provided in this section. The section reads as follows:

Protection of registered proprietor

(1) The registered proprietor of an estate or interest holds it absolutely free from all encumbrances except –

(a) in the case of fraud; and

(b) the encumbrances notified by entry or memorial on the relevant folio of the Register Book; and

(c) the estate or interest of a proprietor claiming the same land under a prior instrument of title; and

(d) in case of the omission or misdescription of any right-of-way or other easement created in or existing on the same land; and

(e) in case of the wrong description of the land or of its boundaries; and

(f) as to a tenancy from year to year or for a term not exceeding three years created either before or after the issue of the instrument of title of the registered proprietor; and

(g) as provided in section 28; and

(h) a lease, licence or other authority granted by the Head of State or a Minister and in respect of which no provision for registration is made; and

(i) any unpaid rates, taxes, or other money which, without reference to registration under this Act, are expressly declared by a law to be a charge on land in favour of the State or of a department or officer of the State or of a public corporate body.

(2) The operation of sub-section (1) is not affected by the existence in any other person of an estate or interest, whether derived by grant from the State or otherwise, which, but for this Act, might be held to be paramount or to have priority.

(i) 'Fraud' (s 33(1)(a) of the LRA)

The term 'fraud' is not defined anywhere in the Land Registration Act. However, s 45(1) makes it clear that the term fraud means more than 'equitable fraud'[9] which is established by simply proving that the purchaser of a legal estate had notice (actual, constructive or imputed) of an earlier equitable interest. Also, s 146(4)(a) makes it clear that fraud under the Act does not refer to the fraud of the person from whom the registered proprietor acquired the interest or the estate. Rather it is the act of the registered proprietor himself or herself. The cases extracted below discuss what constitutes fraud under the Torrens system.

9 See *Assets Company Ltd v Mere Roihi and Others* [1905] AC 176, 210.

ASSETS COMPANY LTD AND OTHERS v MERE ROIHI AND OTHERS [1905] AC 176, Judicial Committee of the Privy Council

[The facts of this case are complicated. Suffice to say for the present purposes that the respondents, members of a Maori community, were the traditional owners of the subject land. Someone called Cooper fraudulently acquired the land from the indigenous community. Ownership of the land changed several times. Assets Co, the appellant, was a subsequent purchaser and was the registered proprietor under the New Zealand Land Transfer Act 1870 (which corresponds with the Land Registration Act). The respondents successfully challenged the appellant's title on grounds, *inter alia*, that its registration as owner was procured by fraud. This is an appeal to the Privy Council against the decision of the New Zealand Court of Appeal.]

LORD LINDLEY: [B]y fraud in [the Land Transfer Act] ... is meant actual fraud, ie, dishonesty of some sort, not what is called constructive or equitable fraud – an unfortunate expression and one very apt to mislead, but often used, for want of a better term, to denote transactions having consequences in equity similar to those which flow from fraud. Further, it appears to their Lordships that the fraud which must be proved in order to invalidate the title of a registered purchaser for value, whether he buys from a prior registered owner or from a person claiming under a title certified under the Native Land Acts, must be brought home to the person whose registered title is impeached or to his agents. Fraud by persons from whom he claims does not affect him unless knowledge of it is brought home to him or his agents. The mere fact that he might have found out fraud if he had been more vigilant, and had made further inquiries which he omitted to make, does not of itself prove fraud on his part. But if it be shewn that his suspicions were aroused, and that he abstained from asking inquiries for fear of learning the truth, the case is very different, and fraud may be properly ascribed to him. A person who presents for registration a document which is forged or has been fraudulently or improperly obtained is not guilty of fraud if he honestly believes it to be a genuine document which can be properly acted upon.

In dealing with Colonial titles depending on the system of registration which they have adopted, it is most important that the foregoing principles should be borne in mind, for if they are lost sight of that system will be rendered unworkable. Their Lordships are keenly alive to the necessity of vigilance to protect natives against unfair and oppressive dealings on the part of Europeans; but on the other hand it is equally important not to disturb registered titles of *bona fide* purchasers, especially when accompanied by long possession and large outlays.

[His Honour discussed allegations of fraud against the defendants' predecessors in title and continued.]

The evidence of fraud by the company breaks down. The evidence shews that in all these cases the agents of the Assets Company in the Colony took to the registrar and got him to register certain documents which according to their purport and effect entitled, and which they believed did in fact entitle, the company to be registered as owners. There is no evidence whatever of any fraudulent statement made by the company's agents to the registrar, nor of any bribery, corruption, or dishonesty in the matter.

Their Lordships cannot help thinking that the equitable doctrines of constructive fraud have weighed too much with the Court of Appeal and have induced it to impute fraud to the Assets Company, although no dishonesty by the company or its agents, or by the liquidators of the City of Glasgow Bank, was really established. Nor is there any proof whatever that the liquidators of the Assets Company dishonestly refrained from making inquiries which an honest purchaser would have made.

The conclusions thus arrived at dispose of all these appeals ... Their Lordships base their judgment on the conclusiveness of the registered title in the absence of fraud.

Questions

1 What sort of facts would assist the court to determine whether a registered proprietor was a party to the fraud?

2 X buys a block of land, which he knows Y has already contracted to buy. X is registered as the proprietor. Advise Y whether the transaction can be set aside on ground of fraud.

3 Bona is the registered proprietor of several high covenant houses in Port Moresby. It is common knowledge in Port Moresby that Bona defrauded his *wantoks* to acquire the land on which the houses are built. Vagi buys one of the houses and has his title registered. Bona's *wantoks* seek your legal advice as to whether they could impeach Vagi's title on ground of fraud.

Notes

In *Steamship Trading Company Ltd v Minister of Lands and Physical Planning and Others* (unreported, N1959 PNG National Court of Justice, OS 552 of 1999), see extract above, at p 440, Sheehan J held refused to follow *Assets* case's interpretation of the term 'fraud'. His Honour said, 'Our own Land Registration Act only speaks of fraud and does not limit its meaning nor does it require that fraud be shown in a particular party'. This view was adopted by Sevua J in *Hi Lift Company Pty Ltd v Miri Sata, MBE, Secretary Department of Agriculture & Livestock and The Independent State of Papua New Guinea* (unreported, N2004, OS 329 of 2000), see extract above, p 443.

In 'Judicial assault on the citadel of indefeasibility of title under the Papua New Guinean Torrens system of conveyance' (2001) 5 Journal of South Pacific Law: http://www.vanuatu.usp.ac.fj/journal_splaw/Article/Mugambwa1.htm, Mugambwa comments on these cases as follows:

> [In *Steamship Trading Company Ltd v Minister of Lands and Physical Planning and Others* (unreported, N1959 PNG National Court of Justice, OS 552 of 1999)] Sheehan J said that even if he was to follow *Mudge and Mudge v Secretary of State for Lands*, on the evidence before him he was satisfied that fraud had been committed. His Honour dismissed Garamut's argument, relying on the Privy Counsel's judgment in *Assets Co Ltd v Meri Roihi*,[10] that fraud required to defeat a registered title meant actual fraud not equitable or constructive fraud, and that the registered proprietor whose title it is desired to impeach must be implicated in the fraud. Sheehan J sought to distinguish *Assets* on the ground that in that the Privy Council based its decision on its interpretation of the New Zealand Transfer of Land Act 1885.[11] His Honour asserted that, 'Our own Land Registration Act only speaks of fraud and does not limit its meaning nor does it require that fraud be shown in a particular party'.

10 [1905] AC 176.

11 This Act was repealed and replaced by the Land Transfer Act 1952 (NZ).

It should be pointed out that the Land Registration Act, as other Torrens statutes in Australia and New Zealand, does not provide any definition of the expression 'fraud'. In all jurisdictions, the meaning of fraud in this context is based on case law. Several cases in various jurisdictions have cited with approval the Privy Council's interpretation of this term. Indeed, that interpretation is regarded as well established.[12] A comparison of the relevant provisions of the Land Registration Act with those of the New Zealand Transfer of Land Act referred to in the *Assets* case, in our view, does not reveal any material difference as to support Sheehan J's argument. For example, s 33 of the Land Registration Act, which is generally regarded as the paramount provision, states that a registered proprietor of an estate or interest holds it absolutely free from all encumbrances except, *inter alia*, 'in case of fraud'. Section 55 of the New Zealand Act had a similar wording.[13]

Fraud is also mentioned in s 146 of the Land Registration Act. The section protects a registered proprietor from action for ejectment except, *inter alia*, by a person deprived of land by fraud against a person registered as proprietor 'through fraud'[14] or a person 'deriving from or through a person registered as proprietor through fraud'.[15] These provisions deal with the outcome in respect to the Register where a person defrauded sues for ejectment of a proprietor registered through fraud.[16] Section 146(3) precludes an action for ejectment against a proprietor who is a *bona fide* purchaser for valuable consideration. Clearly, the object of the latter provision was to except from ejectment an innocent purchaser from a person who procured his or her registration through fraud. The exception would serve no useful purpose if the term 'fraud' were construed to include a *bona fide* purchaser for value. Moreover, if it is accepted that the expression 'fraud' in s 33 of the Land Registration Act, is directed at fraud perpetuated by or on behalf of the registered proprietor, it is most unlikely that the legislature intended to give the term a different meaning in other sections of the Act. As a general rule of construction, terms in a statute are presumed to bear the same meaning throughout unless there is a good reason to the contrary.[17] In this case, there appears to be none.

Section 56 of the Land Transfer Act 1885 (NZ), was materially similar to the foregoing provision of the Land Registration Act. The New Zealand Act, in addition, stated in s 189 that 'except in case of fraud' a potential purchaser from a registered proprietor was not required to inquire or ascertain the circumstances in which the proprietor was registered or acquired the land. The section provided further that such a person 'shall not be affected by notice direct or constructive of any trust or unregistered interest any rule of law or equity to the contrary notwithstanding and the knowledge that such trust or unregistered interest is in existence shall not of itself be imputed as fraud'.[18] This provision reinforced the interpretation in [the] *Assets* case that fraud meant actual fraud and not equitable fraud. There is no such provision in the Land Registration Act, however, s 45(1) of the Act provides that 'notwithstanding any rule of law or equity to the contrary, a transferee ... of land is not, except in case of fraud, affected by actual or constructive notice [of unregistered interest]'.

---

12 See, for example: *Frazer v Walker* [1967] 1 AC 569, at 580; *Breskvar v Wall* (1971) 126 CLR 376, at 384; *Bahr v Nicolay* [No 2] (1988) 164 CLR 604, at 633.

13 See also, for example, s 68 of the Transfer of Land Act 1893 (WA); s 44 of the Real Property Act 1861 (Qld) (repealed).

14 Section 146(2)(d).

15 Section 146(2)(e).

16 *Vassos v State Bank of South Australia* [1993] 2 VR 316, at 327.

17 *Registrar of Titles (WA) v Franzon* (1975) 132 CLR 611, at 618.

18 A similar provision is found most Torrens statutes in Australia.

The Real Property Act 1861 of Queensland contained a similar provision.[19] In the case of *Friedman v Barrett ex p Friedman,*[20] Gibbs J said that the latter provision was inconsistent with the proposition that where there was notice of an unregistered interest and nothing more 'it was fraud to take a transfer that will defeat the interest'. His Honour expressed the opinion that fraud in the Act meant 'actual dishonesty' and not 'constructive fraud'.

Judicial authorities from other Torrens system jurisdictions clearly show that the expression 'fraud' means actual fraud in which the registered proprietor is involved. Although these authorities are merely of persuasive value, it is submitted that in view of the fact that this limited meaning of the term 'fraud' is well established in virtually all Torrens system jurisdictions, the Supreme Court should not depart from it without compelling reasons. With due respect, in our opinion, the reason Sheehan J gave in his judgment that the PNG Torrens statute was different from that of other jurisdictions is not convincing. Admittedly, in the case before his Honour there were serious irregularities and, possibly, fraud on the part of some of the government officials involved. If there was fraud the chances are that the 'beneficiary', Garamut, must have been involved or had notice of it, otherwise why would those officers act fraudulently for the benefit of a total stranger? However, the onus was on the plaintiff to prove not only that there was fraud but also that Garamut was involved. It is suggested that Sheehan J rejected the Privy Council's interpretation of the expression 'fraud' because he was convinced on the facts that the government officers committed fraud. Amazingly, the plaintiffs' lawyers did not even plead fraud against Garamut.[21] Sheehan J attempted to come to their rescue by holding that it was not necessary to assert fraud because the Statement filed in court was a prayer for relief and not the pleading of a cause of action. It is unnecessary for present purposes to take issue with the learned judge on that point. Suffice to say that in any event, allegation of fraud against another is a serious charge and normally a heavy onus of proof lies upon the party alleging it.[22] In the instant case, the plaintiffs did not discharge that onus.

... In *Hi Lift Company Pty Ltd v Miri Sata, MBE, Secretary for Agriculture and the State of Papua New Guinea* [see extract above], Sevua J found that whilst there was no fraud ... the circumstances of the case warranted its presumption 'because it must seem quite an irregular and suspicious dealing for the Department of Lands to grant a lease over Portion 2413 to a private company when the public interest held by the Department of Agriculture and Livestock existed'.

Referring to the two Supreme Court judgments in *Emas* and *Mudge*, Sevua J expressed his preference for the former. He observed that in *Emas* while the Supreme Court acknowledged the principle of indefeasibility espoused in *Mudge*, 'the majority concluded that irregularities tantamount to fraud was sufficient to overturn a registered title'. Accordingly, his Honour concluded that the irregularities in the case before him were 'sufficient to invalidate or nullify the registration of the plaintiff's title because they are tantamount to fraud'.

With due respect, Sevua J seems to confuse 'irregularity' with 'fraud'. The fact that government officials acted irregularly when they granted the plaintiff the lease does not necessarily mean that they acted fraudulently. Fraud entails personal dishonesty or a moral

19 Section 109. The Queensland Act had no provision similar to s 189 of the New Zealand Act.

20 [1962] Qd R 498 at 512.

21 Fraud is a serious allegation and the courts require strict adherence to requirements for pleading and proof in such cases, see *Maki v Pundia & PNG Motors Pty Ltd* [1993] PNGLR 337.

22 *Ibid.*

turpitude on the part of the performer.[23] In this case, the officers might have simply been negligent or incompetent in leasing the land to the plaintiff. Nevertheless, the circumstances of the case raise a strong suspicion of fraud on their part. As has been argued above, fraud does not affect title of a registered proprietor unless they were somehow involved in the fraud. As in *Steamship*'s case, it would be strange that government officers would fraudulently give preferential treatment to the plaintiff without the plaintiff being involved or aware of the fraudulent scheme. However, the defendants had the onus of proving fraud against the plaintiff. It would seem from the facts of the case that they did not. Certainly, his Honour did not make any positive findings of fraud against them.[24] Accordingly, it is submitted that the plaintiff's title was not defeasible on ground of fraud.

Fraudulent registration

LOKE YEW v PORT SWETTENHAM RUBBER CO LTD
[1913] AC 491, Judicial Committee of the Privy Council

[E had a legal title over 322 acres of land, which he agreed to sell to the respondents/plaintiffs. It was the understanding of both parties that out of this land the defendant had an equitable claim over 58 acres which were to be paid for separately by the plaintiffs. The plaintiffs convinced E to sign an instrument of transfer of all 322 acres upon a written assurance that they would negotiate with the defendant for the 58 acres. The respondents/plaintiffs having obtained registration of title over the 322 acres refused to negotiate with the defendants for the 58 acres. They brought these proceedings to eject the defendant from possession. They contended that as registered proprietors they possessed an indefeasible title to the land free from the defendant's unregistered claims. The plaintiff succeeded in the Federate Malay States Court of Appeal. Appeal to the Privy Council.]

LORD MOULTON [Delivering their Lordships' judgment stated that they had come to the conclusion that registration of the respondents' title was obtained through the appellant's fraud. He continued]: So long as the rights of third parties are not implicated a wrong-doer cannot shelter himself under the registration as against the man who has suffered the wrong. Indeed the duty of the court to rectify the register in proper cases is all the more imperative because of the absoluteness of the effect of the registration if the register be not rectified. Take for example the simple case of an agent who has purchased land on behalf of his principal but has taken the conveyance in his own name, and in virtue thereof claims to be the owner of the land whereas in truth he is a bare trustee for his principal. The court can order him to do his duty just as much in a country where registration is compulsory as in any other country, and if that duty includes fresh entries in the register or the correction of existing entries it can order the necessary acts to be done accordingly. It may be laid down as a principle of general application that where the rights of third parties do not intervene no person can better his position by doing that which it is not honest to do, and inasmuch as the registration of this absolute transfer of the whole of the original grants was not an honest act under the circumstances it cannot better the position of the plaintiffs as against the defendant and they cannot rely on it as against him when seeking to enforce rights which formally belong to them only by reason of their own fraud.

Appeal allowed.

---

23 *Butler v Fairclough* (1917) 23 CLR 78, at 90, 97.

24 In the judgment, Sevua J states that there was no evidence of fraud though a 'presumption of fraud existed'.

Questions

1 How would you distinguish *Loke Yew* from *Assets Company*?

2 A was the registered proprietor of a block of land. He mortgaged the land to B as security for a K20,000 loan, but the mortgage was not registered. Later A sold the block to C who had actual notice of B's unregistered mortgage. C had the transfer to him registered without endorsement of B's mortgage. Is C's title subject to B's mortgage?

Further illustration of the meaning of registration 'through fraud'

BAHR AND ANOTHER v NICOLAY AND OTHERS (NO 2)
(1988) 164 CLR 604, High Court of Australia

[The appellants, the Bahrs, facing financial difficulties sold a parcel of land (Lot 340) to the first respondent, Nicolay. The contract was subject to two conditions: that Nicolay would lease the land back to them for three years, and that upon expiration of the lease the Bahrs would have a right to re-purchase the land (clause 6). Nicolay became registered as the proprietor. Before the lease expired, Nicolay sold the land to the second respondents, the Thompsons. The latter's contract contained an express provision by which the Thompsons acknowledged the existence of the right to re-purchase granted to the Bahrs in the earlier contract. After their registration as proprietors of the land, the Thompsons informed the Bahrs that they would honour their right to re-purchase as per the Bahrs' contract with Nicolay. Subsequently, when the Bahrs attempted to exercise the right of purchase, the Thompsons refused to sell the land. The Bahrs sought a vesting order on tender of the agreed price on grounds that the Thompsons' were registered through fraud under the Western Australia Transfer of Land Act 1893, ss 68 and 134 (which correspond with ss 33 and 45 of the LRA). The Thompsons contended that fraud for the purposes of s 68 was confined to dishonesty exhibited by the registered proprietor in securing the transfer of registration of his title. They claimed that up to the time of registration of their title they honestly intended to re-sell the land to the Bahrs but had repudiated their decision sometime after their title was registered. The lower court held that the Thompsons had not committed fraud against the Bahrs. On appeal to the High Court.]

MASON CJ and DAWSON J: [The] point, on which the second respondent heavily relied, emerges from the comments made by Lord Moulton for the Judicial Committee in *Loke Yew* ... Lord Moulton expressed the Judicial Committee's conclusion on the fraud issue by saying ... that, as the transfer had been obtained by fraud, the case fell within the statutory exception to the principle of indefeasibility.

For our part we do not see the illustration given and the statements made in the cases as amounting to definitive pronouncements that fraud is confined to fraud in the obtaining of a transfer or in securing registration. The statements, viewed in their context, merely express the reasons why particular circumstances fall within the statutory exception. Nor do we see anything in the language or the purpose of s 68 which warrants such a restrictive interpretation. Indeed we agree with Higgins J in *Stuart v Kingston* [(1923) 32 CLR 309, at 345] when his Honour said ... that there was much to be said for the view, expressed by Stawell CJ on the equivalent Victorian provision, that the section should be 'construed strictly' and the exception 'liberally'. The section restricts, in the interest of indefeasibility of title, rights which would exist otherwise at law or in equity. And granted that an exception is to be made for fraud why should the exception not embrace fraudulent conduct arising from the dishonest repudiation of a prior interest which the registered proprietor has acknowledged or has agreed to recognise as a basis for obtaining title, as well as fraudulent conduct which enables him to obtain title or registration? In the context of s 68 there is no difference between the false undertaking which induced the execution of the transfer in *Loke Yew* and an undertaking honestly given which induces the execution of a transfer and is subsequently repudiated for the purpose of defeating the prior interest. The repudiation is fraudulent because it has as its object the destruction of the unregistered interest notwithstanding that the preservation of the unregistered interest was the foundation or assumption underlying the execution of the transfer. For the same reason the subsequent repudiation by a transferee of property of a limited beneficial interest in that property is fraudulent, when the transferee took the property on terms that the limited beneficial interest would be retained by the transferor. It is immaterial that the transferee 'may have been innocent of any fraudulent intent in taking the conveyance in absolute form': *Bannister v Bannister* [1948] 2 All ER 133 at 136.

[Their Honours held that the subsequent repudiation of the agreement by the second respondents constituted fraud. They also found against the second respondents on the ground that there was an express trust that the second respondents held the property subject to the rights created in favour of the appellants.]

WILSON and TOOHEY JJ: What then constitutes fraud for the purposes of ss 68 and 134? A convenient starting point is a passage in the judgment of the Privy Council in *Waimiha Sawmilling Co Ltd (In Liq) v Waione Timber Co Ltd* [1926] AC 101 at 106–07:

> If the designed object of a transfer be to cheat a man of a known existing right, that is fraudulent, and so also fraud may be established by a deliberate and dishonest trick causing an interest not to be registered and thus fraudulently keeping the register clear. It is not, however, necessary or wise to give abstract illustrations of what may constitute fraud in hypothetical conditions, for each case must depend upon its own circumstances. The act must be dishonest, and dishonesty must not be assumed solely by reason of knowledge of an unregistered interest.

The most often cited case in which fraud was held to have occurred is *Loke Yew v Port Swettenham Rubber Co Ltd* [1913] AC 491. There a purchaser, with knowledge of the existence of an unregistered interest, represented to the transferor that it would make its own arrangements with the holder of the unregistered interest. It failed to do so, in circumstances where it was held to have been the purchaser's intention to destroy the outstanding interest by registration of its own title. It was the purchaser's fraudulent misrepresentation that persuaded the previous registered proprietor to transfer the land to it.

With this decision may be contrasted *Waimiha Sawmilling Co Ltd (In Liq) v Waione Timber Co Ltd*. The registered proprietor of land, Howe, granted timber rights to the appellant which protected its agreement by caveat. Howe purported to determine the appellant's interest for breach of covenant. The appellant appealed against a judgment upholding Howe's re-entry. While the appeal was pending, Howe sold the land to Wilson who was acting as agent for a company to be formed, the respondent. Howe obtained an order for removal of the caveat (against which the appellant did not appeal) and transfered the land to Wilson. Wilson later transfered the land to the respondent. The appellant's appeal against the judgment upholding Howe's re-entry was itself upheld. Notwithstanding that Wilson knew of the appellant's claim and of the litigation between it and Howe, the Privy Council held that there had been no fraud on the part of the respondent.

Consistently with these authorities, evidence going no further than to show that when the second respondents took a transfer of Lot 340 from the first respondent and became the registered proprietors of the land they were aware of the contents of cl 6, cannot amount to fraud within the meaning of ss 68 and 134. More is needed before the appellants can disturb the second respondents' registered title on that ground.

... Had the second respondents acquired their interest in Lot 340 without knowledge of the existence of the appellants' interest under cl 6 of the earlier agreement, they would, as a matter of priorities, have taken free of that interest. Section 134 would protect them if thereafter they acquired knowledge of the appellants' interest. The position is that they took with knowledge of the contents of cl 6. Again s 134 operates to protect them if they did no more than take with notice. Did they do more?

The second respondents did do more by writing their letter of 6 January 1982. Of course by then they were the registered proprietors of Lot 340; the fraud to which ss 68 and 134 refer is fraud committed in the act of acquiring a registered title: see *Loke Yew v Port Swettenham Rubber Co Ltd* at 503–04 ...

[Their Honours made a finding that the second respondents purchased the land knowing of the appellants' right to re-purchase (which their Honours held constituted an equitable interest) and having agreed to re-sell the land to the appellants, they became subject to a constructive trust in favour of the appellants.]

[Brennan J also allowed the appeal but for different reasons.]

Questions

1 How does this case differ from *Loke Yew*?

2 Do you agree with Wilson and Toohey JJ's reasoning that if before registration a purchaser promises to preserve an unregistered interest (and at the time he honestly intends to do so) but changes his mind after he is registered, he is not acting fraudulently within the meaning of the Act?

3 Suppose after registration of the transfer the second respondents had not reiterated their promise to honour the appellants' right to re-purchase the land, would their refusal to accept the Bahrs' offer have been construed as fraud according to Mason CJ's and Dawson J's definition of fraud?

4 Otto was the registered proprietor of Whiteacre. He entered into a contract to sell the land to Mosbi. In the contract it was disclosed that part of the land was in the possession of Morobe Pty Ltd under an unregistered lease for a term of five years with options for renewal in favour of the lessee. A copy of the lease was annexed to the contract. Mosbi agreed to abide by the terms and conditions of the annexed lease. After the transfer to Mosbi was registered, he sought to evict Morobe Pty Ltd. Advise Morobe Pty Ltd. (See *Snowlong Pty Ltd v Choe and Others* [1991] 23 NSWLR 198.)

Pleading fraud

MAKI v MICHAEL PUNDIA & PNG MOTORS LTD
[1993] PNGLR 337, National Court of Justice

[The first defendant is the registered proprietor of the suit land. The plaintiffs filed a writ of summons claiming ownership of the same land by right of customary law. They alleged that the first defendant unlawfully occupied the said land and fraudulently obtained a tenure conversion under the Land (Tenure Conversion) Act. Then he leased the land to the second defendant. The defendants contended that the pleadings of the plaintiffs were deficient and should be struck out.]

WOODS J: This is a claim challenging the grant of a certificate of title. The claim is that the certificate of title was obtained by fraud. National Court Rules 8 and 30 makes particular reference to pleadings of fraud: 'A party pleading shall give particulars of any fraud, misrepresentation, breach of trust, wilful default or undue influence on which he relies.'

An allegation of fraud is very serious allegation, and the courts have required strict adherence to requirements for pleadings in such cases. Courts have never allowed general allegations of fraud. Courts have required that a person pleading fraud should set out the facts, matters, and circumstances relied on to show that the party charged had or was actuated by a fraudulent intention. The acts alleged to be fraudulent must be stated fully and precisely with full particulars. It is not enough just to say that the person lied or swore a false affidavit. The facts, matters and circumstances which make such statements lies must be particularised. Also, this being a challenge to the procedures under the Land (Tenure Conversion) Act, the fault or fraud in those procedures should be particularised. In such a challenge to a certificate of title to land, the court had traditionally insisted on strict rules for the protection of persons who are in possession of land against attacks from persons who, hoping to find some blot on the title, bring actions against them without any reasonable cause. I am not saying that this action may be [sic] being brought without reasonable cause, but if these rules which protect persons in possession of land from being wrongfully and improperly attacked work hardship on the plaintiffs, that is part of the general purpose of protecting property and persons from being improperly vexed. Surely, the rule is no such hardship. If the plaintiffs know anything, then they can and should plead it.

The amended statement of claim clearly does not plead any facts, matters or circumstances. It merely asserts that the first defendant fraudulently obtained title, without giving any details. However, the plaintiffs have filed a further document called particulars of fraud. Clauses 1 and 2 of those particulars take the allegation of fraud no further, merely alleging that the first defendant told lies without giving the facts and circumstances which may show that he has told lies. Clause 3 refers to the first defendant falsely procuring a statutory declaration. This is a serious allegation, but there are no facts supporting how, or when, or under what circumstances this was done and how this circumvented the procedures under the act under which the certificate of title was granted. An allegation of fraud like this requires more detail. Clause 4, in effect, merely states that the defendant told a lie. It provides no facts to support that allegation. Clause 5 does not really allege anything.

I am satisfied that in this allegation of fraud in the issue of a certificate of title following procedures laid down in an act are not sufficiently particularised to satisfy the requirements of O 8 r 30. I order that the statement of claim and the particulars of fraud pleaded separately be struck out.

Having ordered that the statement of claim and particulars be struck out, does this court then either give judgment for the defendants or strike out the proceedings? Whilst this court has an inherent jurisdiction to control proceedings before it and prevent any abuse of process before it and strike out any proceedings that are an abuse or frivolous and vexatious, and this inherent jurisdiction is a jurisdiction quite apart from the rules of court, such inherent jurisdiction is one that should not be exercised too readily, particularly if the exercise of it effectively puts an end to the action.

In the circumstances, therefore, having struck out the pleadings as not complying with O 8 r 30, I will stay the proceedings generally. Of course, if the plaintiffs take no action within a reasonable time to repair the situation then the defendants can apply to have the proceedings dismissed.

(ii) Encumbrances not on the certificate of title – s 33(1)(b) of the LRA

Except as provided in s 33 of the Land Registration Act, a registered proprietor is not bound by encumbrances[25] or claims not notified[26] on the certificate of title.[27] The following case discusses what constitutes 'notification' for purposes of this provision.

BURSILL ENTERPRISES PTY LTD v BERGER BROS TRADING CO LTD (1971) 124 CLR 73, High Court of Australia

[The plaintiffs (Berger) and the defendants (Bursill) were the registered proprietors in fee simple of adjoining blocks of land. The defendants' predecessor in title had granted to the plaintiffs' predecessors certain rights over the defendants' land. The rights were notified in the Register. The notification stated that title was subject to a right of way created and more fully set out in Transfer No 7922. The defendants had not searched the document referred to (Transfer No 7922). If the defendants had done so they would have realised that it granted the plaintiffs not only the right of way over the defendants' land but also, *inter alia*, ownership of buildings erected over the said passageway and a right to demolish and erect new ones thereon. The defendants contend that for the purposes of s 42 of the Real Property Act 1900 (NSW) (which corresponds with s 33(1)(b) of the LRA) the only notification on the certificate of title was the passage of way. Other rights, which were not expressly mentioned in the Register were not enforceable against their title. On appeal to the High Court.]

BARWICK CJ: It seems to me that it was not intended that the certificate of title alone should provide a purchaser dealing with the registered proprietor with all the information necessary to be known to comprehend the extent or state of that proprietor's title to the land. The dealings once registered became themselves part of the Register Book. It was therefore sufficient that their registration should be by statement of their nature recorded on the certificate of title. Section 42 of the Act of 1862 provided for a memorandum of transfer as the appropriate instrument for the transfer of an estate or interest in land, or for the creation or transfer of any right of way or other easement. Section 49 provided for a memorandum of lease where land is intended to be leased for a life or lives or for any term exceeding those years. Section 54 provided for a memorandum of mortgage when land is to be charged or made security and for a memorandum of encumbrance where annuity, rent charge or sum of money is to be charged on land.

These descriptions in this list indicate, in any opinion, the nature of the various principal instruments which can be registered under the Act. In my opinion, the nature of the instrument to which s 37 refers is its description as a transfer, lease, mortgage, encumbrance, etc. What it achieves in particular is not part of its nature for relevant purposes. It is not necessary, in my opinion, to make a memorial effective as the registration

25 Eg, equitable mortgages, easements, leases, etc.

26 See s 33(1)(f) of the LRA.

27 See below, 'Judicial inroads on the concept of indefeasibility of title', p 481.

of a dealing that the endorsement should particularise to any extent what the instrument does. It is sufficient to state whether it is a transfer or a mortgage etc. Thus, in my opinion, the endorsement of a certificate of title of a statement, 'Memorandum of Transfer No 7922 dated 15 May 1872 produced and entered 15 June 1872 at 12 o'clock noon', would be a sufficient memorial and upon its endorsement on the certificate of title, the memorandum of transfer would be duly registered and form part of the Register Book. There would be no need to state the subject matter of the transfer though the convenient practice is to state on a memorial of a memorandum of transfer, etc, the fact that the whole or part of the land comprised in the certificate of title is the subject of the memorandum. But, in my opinion, the absence of such information will not render the memorial ineffective. Once the memorial is sufficient to effect registration of the instrument then the interest of the registered proprietor becomes subject to the registered instrument because of the words in the body of the grant on certificate of title describing the proprietor's interest.

WINDEYER J: The critical question, as I see the matter, is then whether the interest in respect of buildings that Guy conveyed to Long can be said to have been 'notified on the folium of the register book constituted by ... the certificate of title' within the meaning of s 42 of the Act. If it was, then Bursill holds its land subject to it; and that involves no inroad upon an indefeasible title.

The argument that the interest in the buildings is not notified on the certificate of title proceeded on the assumption that Bursill, when purchasing the land, could safely neglect to search transfer No 7922, which was expressly referred to on the certificate of title. It is contended that this reference to the memorandum of transfer did not amount to constructive notice of its full operation, because it was described as creating an 'Extension of the Right of Way'. Doubtless this description would have been better if it had read 'extension of right of way and rights in buildings above the way'. But it seems to me that what is 'notified' to a prospective purchaser by his vendor's certificate of title is everything that would have come to this knowledge if he had made such searches as ought reasonably to have been made by him as a result of what there appears. I have used the words of s 164 of the Conveyancing Act 1919 (NSW). We are not concerned in this case with s 43, which gives a protection against unregistered instruments, for transfer No 7922 was registered, and is noted on the certificate of title.

It seems to me that, at any time from 1872 till today, a prudent conveyancer acting for a purchaser of the land that is now Bursill's would have ascertained what it was that transfer 7922 referred to on the vendor's certificate of title in law effected. True he might have been surprised to discover all that his search revealed. But surely no prudent person, seeing the reference to a right of way, would neglect to ascertain what exactly was the nature of the right of way, the land subject to it, the person who could avail themselves of it, for what purposes in what manner and at what times. The need to make such a search seems the more obvious if, by an inspection or survey of the land, the intending purchaser had become aware that there was a building over part of the land which was in the occupation of his neighbour. And it seems unlikely that a purchaser of this land in a built-up area of the City of Sydney would not be aware of the existence of the passage way and of the building above it. Whether he was so or not the reference on the certificate of title to transfer No 7922 was I think constructive notice of what it provided, that is that the land was subject not only to a right of way but also to an interest of the adjoining landowner in the building above the way. I think that the registered proprietor of the land that is now Bursill's held his title subject to that interest. Therefore I consider that the owner of the land that is now Berger's has, and has had, in law a right to the exclusive use and occupation of this building.

[Menzies J dissented.]

Appeal dismissed.

Question

Green is the registered proprietor of Greenacre. The land is currently held by X under a five year registered lease with rights to renew the lease for three further five year terms. Before X exercises his first option to renew, Green mortgages Greenacre to the City Credit Bank (CCB). CCB's lawyer searches the Register Book and finds a notification to the effect that the land is subject to a lease for five years in favour of X. The notification does not mention any right of renewal. CCB's lawyer does not read the terms of the lease. The mortgage to CCB is duly registered. Subsequently X purports to exercise his first right of renewal. CCB seeks your advice whether, in the event of future disputes, the renewed terms would be subject to its mortgage (see *Mercantile Credits Ltd v The Shell Company of Australia Ltd* (1976) 136 CLR 326. Also see s 28(3)(A) of the LRA, below).

(iii) The estate of a proprietor claiming the same land under a prior instrument of title – s 33(1)(c)

This is a situation where two or more certificates of title subsist over the same block of land. The situation envisaged could arise from actual blunders in the Lands Department, as the case below illustrates.

KEIMBUN KEINDIP v THE INDEPENDENT STATE OF PAPUA NEW GUINEA AND OTHERS
[1993] PNGLR 28, National Court of Justice

NEWELL AJ: On 5 March 1981 the plaintiff was granted a business lease in respect of allotment, 2, section 5, Wasu government Station, containing an area of 0.1462 hectares. A state lease was granted under volume 91 folio 145. The plaintiff built a trade store on the land and traded until 1984. After that, the building was used for storage purposes. It was stated in evidence that the brother of the plaintiff rented the building and used it as the base for an ice block business. The evidence was rather vague with respect to what usage the land had after 1984.

In 1985, the land was sub-divided into allotments 16, 17 and 18, section 5, Wasu government Station. The plaintiff said in evidence that he was not aware of this occurring, despite there having been a survey, and with relatives supposedly using the land. The plaintiff in 1989 found that the sixth defendant was building a shop on allotment 17, and he refused to stop building when requested by the plaintiff as he thought that he had the title. The manager of the seventh defendant was advised by the plaintiff not to build on allotment 16, and he did not. The land was allotted by notice in the *National Gazette*, and the plaintiff was allotted allotment 18, though he never made any formal application.

There is no notice of a forfeiture by the Minister under s 46 of the Land Act Ch 185, nor does the plaintiff recall being served with any notice that the Minister intended forfeiting allotment 2, section 5.

There was, according to the plaintiff, never any formal gazettal of the entitlement of the sixth defendant to the land, nor did the sixth defendant ever get a title document. The plaintiff states that a search of the title still shows that he is the sole owner of the title to the land. This appears to show a defect in the computer system used by the Department of Lands, which appears not to formally remove old descriptions of land and update them.

The plaintiff submits that he complied with the improvement conditions of the lease and there is no ground for any forfeiture of the lease. He contends that, as he had no notice of any attempt to forfeit the land, any attempt at sub-division of the land was improper and that any title given to the sixth and seventh defendants was improper and should be revoked.

It is alleged that the sixth defendant has irregularly built his shop across the boundary between allotments 17 and 18.

The plaintiff says that he made various approaches to the Lands Department in Lae, but there was no satisfactory resolution of the dispute. It is not clear if the Registrar of Titles was informed at all of the dispute, or whether he has been informed yet. I note that he is not named as a defendant in these proceedings.

Submission by the parties

The plaintiff argues that *Mudge v Secretary for Lands* [1985] PNGLR 387 (hereafter *Mudge*) is a clear statement of the principles of indefeasible title under the Land Registration Act Ch 191 and that, following that decision, I must find in his favour. If I do not find in his favour as to title, he argues that I should award compensation pursuant to ss 84, 87 and 88 of the Land Act Ch 185, together with his costs.

The State contends that, pursuant to s 33 of the Land Registration Act Ch 191, the plaintiff holds an indefeasible title unless one of the clauses in s 33(1) applies, and that the decision in *Mudge* is a clear statement of indefeasibility, but indefeasibility is subject to s 33. Both the plaintiff and the State agree that the decision in *Mudge* is different from the facts in this case.

The State concedes that it cannot contest the indefeasibility of this title, and this prevails over the title of the seventh defendant. It also concedes that the sixth defendant has no legal interest in the land.

The State concedes that I should give the following:

1 a declaration that the plaintiff is the registered proprietor of the land known and described as allotment 2, section 5, Wasu government Station, Morobe Province, containing an area of 0.1462 hectares;

2 a declaration that the purported sub-division of the land by the State and its agents and/or servants, first, second, and third defendants into three new allotments, namely allotments 16, 17 and 18, section 5, Town of Wasu, be declared null, illegal, void and of no effect;

3 a declaration that the re-allocation and grant of the new allotment described as allotment 16, section 5, Wasu government Station, by the Morobe Provincial Land Board and by the agents and/or servants of the third defendant to the Wasu Kabwum Coffee Mill Pty Ltd be declared null, void and of no effect; and

4 a declaration that the grant of allotment 17 to Furewe Isep be declared null, void and of no effect.

It also concedes that costs are discretionary.

The State also contends that, if the sixth and seventh defendants wish to make any claim in the matter against the State, they should bring fresh proceedings.

The sixth and seventh defendants claim that the orders claimed by the plaintiff must fail, but they concede that an order for costs may be made against the first to the fifth defendants. They appear to be making a submission in equity that they have acted in good faith in their dealings with the State and that, on the balance of convenience, the orders should not be granted.

In essence, they argue that the plaintiff's use and occupation of the land is such that compensation for the plaintiff is the appropriate course that should be taken in dealing with this matter.

The seventh defendant says that the decision in *Mudge* is distinguishable and that, as he holds the title latest in time, the prior registration in favour of the plaintiff cannot go unchallenged. He claims his title gets the benefit of indefeasibility, as none of the exceptions apply to it.

The sixth defendant says that, as a matter of public policy, his rights in the land must be acknowledged and that, as he has encroached on the adjoining allotment, he should be given title to that as well.

In effect, the sixth and seventh defendants contend that they have acted in all good faith and that the plaintiff, by his conduct in managing the land, should be held to have lost his title and merely be given an award of compensation for his loss.

The lease of allotment 2, section 5, Wasu government Station, to the plaintiff was issued on 14 November 1984 as State Lease Volume 91 Folio 145. The seventh defendant's lawyer enquired about the status of the land in a letter to the Department of lands dated 7 April 1987. The lawyer acted in the belief that the purchase was from customary landowners. (That lawyer represents the plaintiff in this action, a conflict not brought to my attention during the trial of this matter.)

A lease over allotment 16, section 5, Town of Wasu, was issued to the seventh defendant on 28 February 1989 as State Lease Volume 116 Folio 48. It covered part of the land in the plaintiff's existing lease. There is nothing in the correspondence in any affidavits in the court file to indicate that before this lease was issued the plaintiff was aware of any lease being considered, nor is there any indication that the lawyer for the plaintiff was aware from requisitions (as lawyer for the seventh defendant) that the proposed lease was over land owned under another lease that had not been forfeited.

There are, in fact, discrepancies between the area and allotments shown in the two titles.

Allotments 16, 17 and 18 amount to 0.1991 hectares. Allotment 2 amounts to 0.1462 hectares. It also is apparent that allotment 16 includes part of allotment 5, section 1, as per the plan on State Lease Volume 91 Folio 145.

The sixth and seventh defendants may have title to parts of the land they claim regardless of my decision in this matter, as it is apparent that parts of what was allocated to them are not part of allotment 2, section 6. The plan attached to annexure E on the affidavit of the plaintiff, dated 15 October 1991, appears to indicate that the boundary on the lease to the seventh defendant is incorrect.

My decision is based on the understanding that allotment 2, section 5, Wasu, is virtually the same location as allotments 16, 17 and 18, section 5, Wasu.

Decision

In this matter, we have the result of sloppy practice by the State, but with the State admitting that it has caused the problem.

Whilst I can see that in equity there might be an argument for the contention of the seventh defendant that a person with a later title should have better title than a person with an earlier title, I cannot see how in equity it can be argued that a person with an unregistered title could be given title to land on which he has encroached, though in equity there may be some argument in his favour in respect of title to the land he was granted, even though a title has not issued.

The decision in *Mudge* is authority for the following propositions:

1 registration of leases under the provisions of the Land Registration Act Ch 191 is effective to vest an indefeasible title in the registered proprietor, subject to the exceptions enumerated in s 33 – adopting and applying *Breskvar v Wall* (1971) 126 CLR 376 and the decision of the Privy Council in *Frazer v Walker* [1967] 1 AC 569; and

2 an irregularly issued State lease in breach of the Land Act Ch No 185 registered under the Land Registration Act will confer an indefeasible title.

The facts in this matter are different. There are two titles apparently partly issued over the same block of land. The original title that would be held to be indefeasible when applying the decision in *Mudge* is still extant, but this land was sub-divided, apparently without the plaintiff's knowledge, and a further title issued over part of the sub-division, and two unregistered titles issued over the remainder of the land that was part of the original title.

What I must determine in this matter is whether the second registered title also has indefeasibility and prevails, as to part, over the original title.

Pratt J in *Mudge* at p 395 notes that, 'A divergence of views developed between Australia and New Zealand as to whether there was immediate indefeasibility on registration or whether such indefeasibility was deferred'. He followed Street J in *Mayer v Coe* [1968] 2 NSWR 747 in preferring the view of the Privy Council in *Frazer v Walker*. He notes at p 396 that before the appeal in *Mayer v Coe* could be dealt with, the High Court in *Breskvar v Wall* 'departed from the general interpretation which had heretofore been given to the decision *Clements v Ellis*' (1934) 51 CLR 217 and 'accepted the reasoning and conclusion of the Privy Council in *Frazer v Walker*'.

These cases give no assistance to the parties in this matter except so far as they state that the position on indefeasibility of title in Papua New Guinea is the same as is now the situation in New Zealand and Australia. It should be noted, incidentally that one apparent reason that New Zealand and Australia now have the same situation as Papua New Guinea is that Sir Garfield Barwick sat on both the High Court and Privy Council for their decisions that indefeasibility of title takes effect on registration.

Russell v Registrar General of Land [1906] 26 NZLR 1223 is a case very much on point. It and the even more apposite decision of Richmond J in *Miller v Davy* (1889) 7 NZLR 515, neither of which, I may add, were cited by the parties, deal with two titles registered over the same block of land under the Torrens title system. In *Russell v Registrar General of Land*, we are dealing with a decision of the New Zealand Court of Appeal. A person had received title to land under the Torrens system, part of which had been already granted under the system to another person. Despite his not having searched the title to ascertain the true picture, the court determined that he was entitled to be paid out from the assurance fund. In *Miller v Davy*, the parallel with the matter before me was even more marked. The Registrar General of Land registered two titles over the same block of land, and a finding was made against the Registrar General of Land. Unlike in *Russell v Registrar General of Land*, it was decided that there was contributory negligence of the second party in not searching the register. I do not consider it is for me in this decision to determine whether contributory negligence occurred, or whether there should be any payout to any person from the State or under the Assurance Fund. That is a matter for a separate action by the sixth and seventh defendants.

The two New Zealand decisions of *Russell v Registrar General of Land* and *Miller v Davy* determine that the registered title of the original holder of the land is not affected by any later title issued over the same land. *Mudge* states that title is not obtained until it is registered. As Barwick CJ says in *Breskvar v Wall* at p 385: 'The Torrens system of registered title ... is not a system of registration of title but a system of title by registration.' In this decision, I am building on *Mudge* by extending the indefeasibility principle forward beyond the date of registration, a situation that is supported by *Russell v Registrar General of Land* and *Miller v Davy*. *Mudge* decides that indefeasibility of title subsists from the date of registration for so long as the title has not been removed from the Register of lands. *Russell v Registrar General of Land* and *Miller v Davy* add the condition that, if a later title is issued over the whole or part of land held under a registered title, the earlier title is not affected, and the registration of a later title may, subject to any negligence by the purchaser, lead to a claim on the Assurance Fund. The determination of any question relating to negligence by the later purchaser, or failure by the Registrar of Titles to take prompt action to rectify the error, which may affect the liability of the Assurance Fund, is, as I rule above, a matter for separate proceedings by the sixth and seventh defendants.

With respect to any claim by an unregistered lessee, he has no title superior to that of the plaintiff by reason of the decision in *Mudge*. However, he may still have a claim against the State under the provisions of the Land Act, again subject to any negligence on his part. Negligence is possible in this matter as the plaintiff says that, in 1989, he found that the sixth defendant was building a shop on the land, but the sixth defendant refused to stop building when requested by the plaintiff as he thought that he had title (allotment 17). Because much land is acquired from the State without recourse to independent professional advice from a lawyer, the negligence attributable to a purchaser may vary between whether a lawyer is involved or not.

Perhaps the State should advise all purchasers to get professional legal assistance when purchasing land from it, if what has happened in this matter has occurred before in other matters. Even though it may not be the duty of the Department of Lands and Physical Planning to give such advise [sic], the Minister responsible for consumer protection may need to provide such advice in view of what has occurred in this matter, and the subsequent actions of the sixth defendant.

If there were any suggestion of negligence by the law firm which appears to have acted for the seventh defendant in its purchase from the State (and I do not consider it is for me to make any such finding one way or the other), and if on further investigation there appears to be grounds for such an action, I draw to the attention of the sixth and seventh defendants the decision in *Luxmoore-May v Baverstock* [1990] 1 WLR 1009. This decision appears to suggest that there is a differential duty of care between a firm of lawyers in a small town and one in the National Capital. Could it be, if there were, in fact, any professional negligence that the firm acting for the seventh defendant in Lae did not owe as much of a duty of care to its client as a firm based in the National Capital, which was able to search the original Lands Department files in Waigani? Or were the original files available in 1987 in Lae? Even if they were, were they searchable by a private law firm?

The plaintiff has by registration of title got an indefeasible title, even if there were defects prior to issue, as in *Mudge*, or defects after issue, eg, non-compliance with the improvement covenants. Unless the title were first forfeited, he cannot lose his title.

The plaintiff has the legal title to the land, as conceded by the State, and any later grant cannot prevail against this grant. If there has been a failure to properly follow up alleged breaches of the Land Act by the plaintiff, then this is not a matter that can be taken advantage of by the sixth and seventh defendants. However, the sixth and seventh defendants may have claims against the State, and the seventh defendant may have a claim against the Assurance Fund under the Land Registration Act.

Questions

1 Newell AJ said that the sixth defendant might have been guilty of contributory negligence because when the plaintiff found him building on the land he refused 'to stop building when requested by the plaintiff as he thought that he had title [to] ... allotment 17'. Do you agree?

2 The trial judge apparently accepted the argument of the lawyer for the seventh defendant that 'a person with a later title should have better title than a person with an earlier title ...'. Is this a correct statement of the equitable rule for determining priorities? See *Rice v Rice* (1883) 2 Drew 73; 61 ER 646.

Notes

It is surprising that Newell AJ was at pains to find relevant case law for authority. With respect, he could have decided the case on the basis of s 33(1)(c) of the LRA, which he never referred to in his judgment. Further authority is provided by s 146(2)(g), also not cited in the judgment, which states that a registered proprietor could be ejected by 'a registered proprietor claiming under a prior certificate of title where two certificates are registered under this Act in respect of the same land'. For a correct application of the provision see *Smith v Registrar of Titles, The State and Duna People's Association Inc* (unreported, N1739 PNG National Court of Justice OS 356 of 1996), extracted below.

SMITH v REGISTRAR OF TITLES, THE STATE AND DUNA PEOPLE'S ASSOCIATION INC
unreported, N1739 PNG National Court of Justice OS 356 of 1996

[In 1998, the plaintiff was the registered proprietor of a State lease over certain land known as Portion 1435 Granville. In 1994, the State purported to grant a State lease over certain land referred to as Portion 2269 Granville, to the Duna People's Association Inc (third defendants) and the lease was registered under the Registration of Titles Act (cap 191). It transpired that part of Portion 1435 included land leased to the plaintiff. The plaintiff seeks certain declarations over the status of their State lease.]

WOODS J: The above matters raise directly the question of the indefeasibility of a prior registered title. In the case *Mudge v Secretary for Land & The State* [1985] PNGLR 387 the Supreme Court has agreed with the principle that the registration of leases under the provisions of the Land Registration Act Ch 191 is effective to vest an indefeasible title in the registered proprietor subject only to the exceptions enumerated in section 33.

The plaintiff is asserting that section 33(1)(c) is relevant to his title. That sub-section states:

33(1) The registered proprietor of an estate or interest holds it absolutely free from all encumbrances except ...

(c) the estate or interest of a proprietor claiming the same land under a prior instrument of title.

It is submitted on behalf of the Plaintiff therefore that even if the third defendant was validly issued with a State lease over part of the land in the Plaintiff's own State lease then the third defendant can only hold that State lease subject to the estate of the Plaintiff as he holds the prior interest.

It would seem that there has been a serious error on the part of the Lands Department and the Land Board in that they have considered an application for a lease over land the subject of an existing State lease without there having been any forfeiture proceedings nor any proper sub-division application. The State has produced no evidence as to how this could have happened nor assisted the court with any submissions on the respective rights of the parties in view of the actions of the officers of the State. This should be a matter for an investigation into the operation of the Department of Lands. As to how land could be surveyed whilst it was already the subject of an existing survey and lease and then granted to another party raises serious questions as to the competence and actions of certain Lands Department officers. Further how an area of land could be surveyed and accepted without any access to a properly surveyed and gazetted road access raises questions as to the *bona fides* of the recipient of the later lease.

I find that the land apparently surveyed as Portion 2269 and surveyed under Lands Dept reference number M49/1127 cannot be the subject of a State lease independent of State Lease Volume 119 folio 76 granted to the plaintiff.

I declare that State Lease Volume 11 Folio 148 being Portion 2269 Granville is null and void and I order that the Register of Titles be rectified such that all references to Portion 2269 be removed from the Special Purposes Lease Portion 1435 Granville. I further Order that the Third Defendant its servants and agents are restrained from taking or purporting to take possession of any of the land in Special Purposes Lease Portion 1435 Granville being the land in State Lease Volume 119 folio 76.

Questions

1 Discuss possible remedies available to the Duna People's Association in the above case.

2 A and B were registered as tenants in common of certain land. Each one of them held a separate certificate for their individual shares (s 560 of the LRA). On each certificate there was endorsed a three year lease with several options to renew in favour of K. When later A and B sold their land to S the Registrar destroyed their separate certificates and replaced them with a single fresh certificate, which he issued to S. Inadvertently the Registrar omitted to record on the new certificate K's lease. When K's current lease expired S refused to let him exercise the remainder of the options. S claims that the lease does not bind him because it is not notified on the current certificate. K argues that the lease binds S because it was notified on the 'prior' certificate. Advise S. (See, eg, *Medical Benefits Funds of Australia Ltd v Fisher* [1984] 1 Qd R 606.)

(iv) Wrong description of land or of its boundaries – s 33(1)(e)

This may arise either from mistakes made at the Registrar's Office or from description of the parcel of land made by the parties or their surveyors. An example of this is where a certificate of title issued to X by a series of surveying mistakes includes clan Y's customary land. The effect of this exception is that X's certificate of title is not conclusive as regards land that was wrongly included on the certificate. Y can bring an action for ejectment of X from their land under s 146(2)(f) of the LRA,[28] or rectification of the error.[29] However, this is subject to s 146(3) and (4)(b) which provide as follows:

> (3) This Act does not subject to an action of ejectment a purchaser or mortgagee, acting in good faith and for valuable consideration.
>
> (4) The operation of sub-section (3) is not affected by the fact that the vendor or mortgagor, as the case may be:
>
> (b) derives from or through a person as proprietor through fraud or error, whether by wrong description of land or of its boundaries or otherwise.

Based on these provisions, if X in the above example transfers the land to BP, a *bona fide* purchaser for value, once the transfer to BP is registered Y clan cannot eject him. See the following case of the Full Court of Western Australia for illustration.

WEST AUSTRALIAN FRESH FOODS AND ICE COMPANY v FREECORN (1904) 7 WALR 22, Full Court of Western Australia

[L acquired by possession a block of land, which had a length of 60 feet. The land was not registered under the Transfer of Land Act 1893 (WA). Later when the land was brought under the Act, due to faulty measurements it was recorded as 62 feet which thereby included a two feet wide strip part of the neighbouring block. Ownership of the land changed several times until eventually it was bought by the defendant/respondent. Meanwhile, ownership of the neighbouring block also changed hands several times before it was bought by the plaintiff/appellant. The neighbouring block remained outside the Torrens system. The plaintiff brought this action to evict the defendant from the said two feet wide strip. Section 68 of the TLA (WA) provides, *inter alia*, that a registered proprietor's title is absolutely indefeasible, 'except as regards any potion of land that may by wrong description of parcels or boundaries be included in the certificate of title or instrument evidencing the title of such proprietor, not being a purchaser for valuable consideration, or deriving from or through such a purchaser'. The trial judge held that this exception did not apply to the defendant because he was a *bona fide* purchaser for value. On appeal.]

PARKER ACJ: Then we come to the next ground, wrong description of parcels, and that is the ground that was principally urged before us. But it will be observed that by this 68th section no exception can be taken to any error which appears in the certificate of title, on the ground that some property has been included which ought not to be included owing to a wrong description of boundaries where the land is in the hands and the certificate of title is held by a purchaser for valuable consideration. Is not that the case here? It seems to me perfectly clear that not only the Ice Company and the Emanuels and the present respondents purchased for valuable consideration, but that all the previous purchasers from Harwood downwards purchased for valuable consideration. Mr Burt argues that they never intended to purchase these two feet; that they were purchasers for valuable consideration certainly, but that they never intended to purchase 62 feet, but only 60 feet.

---

28 See *Marsden and Another v McAlister and Others* (1887) 8 LR (NSW) 300.

29 Sections 160 and 161 of the LRA.

Now, are there any grounds for saying that? Take the case of the present respondents. They were shewn a certificate of title being 62 feet, and the Chief Justice finds that they purchased 62 feet, and came to the conclusion that they intended to purchase 62 feet. There is really no ground for saying that they did not intend to purchase 62 feet. Mr Burt argued also before us that the present holders of the land, the respondents, had notice by the certificate of title, and that they ought to have enquired, and then they would have found that two feet of this ground purchased was in the occupation of Freecorn. But the Chief Justice found that there were no facts provided before him which shewed anything which would induce the respondents to make enquiries, and indeed Mr Burt failed to shew us anything here from which we could come to the conclusion that it was necessary for the respondent to make any enquiries. Now, in connection with this point I will refer to the judgment in *Gibbs v Messer*. This judgment was given in respect of the Land Transfer Act of Victoria, but that Act was similar to ours. In giving judgment Lord Watson said: 'The main object of the Act and the legislative scheme for the attainment of that object appear to their Lordships to be equally plain. The object is to save persons dealing with registered proprietors from the trouble and expense of going behind the register in order to investigate the history of their author's title and to satisfy themselves of its validity.' Mr Burt, in fact, argued before us that it was necessary for purchasers to go behind the title. He argued that the purchaser must not be satisfied with the certificate of title, but he must enquire into the vendor's title, and see that everything is right and proper and that the vendor was entitled to the land. Obviously, that is not the view taken by the Privy Council. Continuing, Lord Watson says: 'That end is accomplished by providing that everyone that purchases *bona fide* or for value from a registered proprietor and enters his deed of transfer or mortgage on the register shall thereby acquire an indefeasible right notwithstanding the informity of his author's title.' It is perfectly clear to me that the question of misdescription of boundary can only arise as regards a certificate of title when there has not been a *bona fide* purchase for value. Here the respondents are clearly *bona fide* purchasers for value. They purchased in good faith and for valuable consideration, and in the circumstances, I think that their title to this 62 feet is indefeasible, and that the judgment of the Chief Justice was right.

[McMillan and Burnside JJ agreed.]

Questions

1 Would the outcome of the case have been different if the plaintiff/appellant's title was registered under the Land Registration Act?

2 Can you envisage a possible overlap in some circumstances of the exception to indefeasibility under s 33(1)(c) and s 33(1)(e)? Which exception would prevail and why? See *National Trustees Co v Hassett* [1907] VLR 404.

(v) Omission or misdescription of any right of way or other easement created or existing on the same land – s 33(1)(d) of the LRA

An easement, which is inadvertently omitted from the certificate of title of the servient land, continues to bind the land.

JAMES v REGISTRAR GENERAL [1967] 69 SR (NSW) 361, Supreme Court of New South Wales

[The applicant is the registered proprietor of certain land (the servient land). An easement of way was originally endorsed on the certificate of title of the subject land. When the Registrar replaced the old certificate, he inadvertently omitted to endorse the easement of way. The applicant eventually bought the land and she was registered without any endorsement of the easement on the certificate of title. Subsequently the Registrar ordered the applicant to deliver up her certificate of title so that the omitted right of way could be notified. The applicant declined, arguing that she had an indefeasible title and that the exception in s 42(d) of the Real Property Act 1900 (NSW) (corresponds with s 33(1)(d) of the LRA) did not apply to a *bona fide* purchaser (see also s 135 of the RPA, which corresponds with s 146 of the LRA).]

WALLACE P: The exception contained in s 42(d) is express and unqualified. The subject matter thereof is an easement duly created and registered under the Act, and when so created the totality or bundle of rights which constitute the fee simple of the servient tenement is diminished accordingly. The methods of extinguishing (or modifying) an easement are well known, and I know of no reason why a duly created easement should be extinguished merely because a notification thereof on the certificate of the servient tenement is not made or is omitted as against either the original owner of the dominant tenement or a purchaser for value from such owner ... I can see no reason why ... [the] easement is not valid and subsisting and the unqualified nature of the exception made it proper in my opinion for the Registrar General to correct the certificate of title of the servient tenement ...

JACOBS JA: The question which arises and which must be determined is whether the present applicant, even though a *bona fide* purchaser, nevertheless, takes subject to the omitted right of way which was created in or existing upon the land which she acquired.

The answer to this question seems to me to depend first upon whether the right of way now in question is one to which s 42(b) applies, and secondly, upon whether, even if this be so, s 135 of the Act confers a title on the *bona fide* purchaser free of such a right of way. On the first of these questions, it is my conclusion that the right of way was created in the land the subject of the certificate of title. It was created in a proper manner pursuant to the terms of the Real Property Act. Section 46 provides the manner of creation, and this right of way when it was created complied with the terms of that section. *Jobson v Nankervis* [(1943) 44 SR (NSW) 277] was a different case in that there had been no creation of an easement in the manner prescribed by s 46. The conclusions expressed by Nicholas CJ in Eq must be read in the light of that initial finding. The result was that there could be no right of way by implication. That was a different case, and I think that the decision in *Jobson v Nankervis* in principle rather supports the view that an easement created in accordance with the requirement of s 46 would be within the terms of s 42(b), although there are statements therein which would limit s 42(b) to easements in existence before land is brought under the Act.

So far then the present applicant has no indefeasible title free from this right of way. The second question is whether the terms of s 135 of the Act are wide enough to confer such indefeasibility. Section 135 provides as follows: 'Nothing in this Act contained shall be so interpreted as to leave subject to action for recovery of damages as aforesaid, or to action of ejectment, or to deprivation of the estate or interest in respect to which he is registered as proprietor, any purchaser or mortgagee *bona fide* for valuable consideration of land under the provisions of this Act on the plea that his vendor or mortgagor may have been registered as proprietor, or procured the registration of the transfer to such purchaser or mortgagee through fraud or error, or may have derived from or through a person registered as proprietor through fraud or error, and this whether such fraud or error shall consist in wrong description of the boundaries or of the parcels of any land or otherwise howsoever.' It would be difficult to envisage terms more absolute than appear in this section, and yet it seems to me that one can only fit its terms in with the scheme of s 42 and associated sections if the indefeasibility intended under s 135 is equated with that intended under s 42. I do not doubt that a right of way carved out of a fee simple would deprive the registered proprietor of an interest in the land to the extent of the burden of the right of way. Therefore it becomes necessary to determine whether a *bona fide* purchaser for valuable consideration, although taking absolutely free from all encumbrances, liens, estates or interests not notified on the folium of the register book, nevertheless takes subject to the exceptions stated in paras (a)–(d) inclusive of s 42. There is an indication to me of an intention that this should be so in the fact that in para (c) there is no reference to *bona fides* as there is in s 135, but I do not think that this can be a determining feature.

There is not only the reference to the purchaser for value in para (c) but there is also the fact that para (a) could not operate unless it was outside s 135. If the same land is included in two certificates of title registered under the provisions of the Act, a situation envisaged in para (a), then s 135 could not operate to confer on purchasers *bona fide* for valuable consideration of the same land in the separate certificates of title an indefeasible title in each case. That is an absurdity. Thus there seems to me to be two intrinsic indications in s 42 that s 135 should not operate to confer indefeasibility in the cases excepted in s 42. In addition there is the extrinsic circumstance that tenancies within s 42(d) have been generally accepted as binding upon purchasers of land under the Act. There has never been any real question but that a purchaser of land takes subject to any short term tenancy under s 42(d), even though he may have purchased *bona fide* for valuable consideration.

I thus find a situation where, despite the peremptory language of s 135, it is necessary to regard the four paragraphs of s 42 as exceptions to indefeasibility of title generally. When one reaches that conclusion, and when one also concludes that this easement was undoubtedly created in the land in question, I think that it follows that the land and its registered proprietor are subject to the omitted easement. It also follows that the Registrar General was entitled to supply the omission, and is not now bound to cancel the notification upon the ground that it is an ineffective entry.

[Walsh J dissented.]

Notes

James v Registrar of Titles dealt with an easement, which had been duly registered but subsequently inadvertently left off the Register Book. It has been held that the exception to indefeasibility also extends to unregistered subsisting easements which arose under the general law by prescription or lost modern grant before the land was brought under the

Torrens system (see *Connellan Nominees Pty Ltd v Camerer* [1988] 2 Qd R 248). In addition, it has been held that subsisting implied easements of necessity which existed before the land was brought under the Torrens system (though not recorded in the Register Book) are covered by the exception to indefeasibility (see *Beck v Auerbach* [1986] 6 NSWLR 454). However, it would seem that the exception to indefeasibility does not apply to unregistered easements, which came into existence after the land was registered under the Torrens system. This view is based on the decision of the Full Court of the Supreme Court of Queensland in *Stuy v BC Ronalds Pty Ltd* [1984] 2 Qd R 578. In that case, A and B were the registered proprietors of adjoining lots of land. Each agreed to grant the other a right of way over a common driveway running between their lots. The rights were never registered. Subsequently A sold to TP without any endorsement of the easement on the certificate of title. The Full Court held that while the agreement to grant an easement could have been enforceable as between A and B as a personal obligation, it was not enforceable against TP. The court rejected the argument that the agreement between A and B created an easement which had been 'omitted' within the meaning of s 44 of the Real Property Act (NSW) 1861–1981 (corresponds with s 33(1)(d)). See also *Australian Hi-Fi Publications Pty Ltd v Gehl* [1979] 2 NSWLR 618. However, compare these decisions with the Western Australia Supreme Court decision in *Di Masi v Piromalli* ([1980] WAR 57). X and Y were the registered proprietors of adjoining blocks of land. By prescription, X acquired a right of way over Y's land. Subsequently, X sold his block to the plaintiff and later Y sold his block to the defendant. The court held that the defendant's land was burdened by the right of way even though when they purchased the right of way was not registered against the land and the defendant had no notice of it. (These cases are probably distinguishable because of the slight difference in the wording of the respective statutory provisions. For discussion see Whalan, *The Torrens system, op cit*, note 1, pp 321–24.)

Questions

1 Whalan, in *The Torrens System, op cit*, note 1, p 323, comments that the decision in *James v The Registrar General* resulted in loss to an innocent purchaser for value of land who believed that a clear Register meant that she could safely buy. Do you agree? What are the possible policy justifications for enforcing an 'omitted' easement on the Register book against an innocent subsequent registered proprietor? Is it fair?

2 Is a 'customary' right, for example right of way, enforceable against a registered proprietor as an 'omitted' easement? See also s 98 of the LRA.

(vi) Tenancy from year to year or for a term not exceeding three years[30] created either before or after the issue of the instrument of title of the registered proprietor – s 33(1)(f) of the LRA

A registered proprietor takes the land subject to any unregistered short term lease or tenancy. The exception to indefeasibility does not extend to an option to renew or purchase the land given to the tenant unless s 28 of the LRA is complied with.

30 See also s 49(1) of the LRA, which provides that a lease which does not exceed three years need not be registered.

(vii) The exception under s 28 – s 33(1)(9) of the LRA

Section 28 of the Land Registration Act provides as follows:

Status of registered instrument

(1) In this section –

'interest holder' means a purchaser of the reversion, lessee, mortgagee, chargee or encumbrancee;

'tenancy document' means –

(a) an unregistered lease; or

(b) an agreement for a lease; or

(c) a lease for a term not exceeding three years.

(2) A registered dealing with land is subject to a prior tenancy document where a tenant is in actual occupation under the document.

(3) No right or covenant contained in a tenancy document –

(a) to purchase the freehold the subject of that document; or

(b) for the renewal of the tenancy, the subject of that document,

is valid against a subsequent interest holder, unless the tenancy document is registered or protected by caveat.

(4) An instrument referred to in sub-section (2) imposes the same obligations on the persons signing it, and for the same period of time, as if it had been sealed and delivered.

This exception should be contrasted with s 33(1)(f). The latter only excepts from indefeasibility a short term tenant for a period which does not exceed three years, whereas s 28(2) exception to indefeasibility appears to protect a tenant, provided he is in actual possession under a tenancy document, for any duration stipulated in the tenancy document.[31] The following case illustrates the operation of s 28(3).

OSBORNE PARK CO-OPERATIVE SOCIETY LTD v WILDEN PTY LTD [1989] 2 WAR 77, Supreme Court of Western Australia

[The plaintiffs were tenants of a shop under a three year unregistered lease with an option to renew for a further three years. Before the first term of the plaintiff's lease expired, the landlord sold the land to the defendants and they were registered as proprietors of the freehold. When the plaintiffs purported to exercise their option to renew the lease the defendants declined to renew the lease. The plaintiffs brought these proceedings claiming entitlement to the benefit of the option. The defendants argued that under s 68 of the TLA (WA) they were not bound by the plaintiffs' option to renew. Section 68 provides, *inter alia,* 'no option of purchase or renewal in any ... lease or agreement shall be valid against a subsequent registered interest unless such a lease or agreement is registered or protected by

31 This observation is based on the reasoning of the Victoria Supreme Court in *Downie v Lockwood* [1965] VR 257. The court in that case was discussing the scope of s 42(2)(e) of the Transfer of Land Act 1958 (Victoria), which is similar to s 33(1)(g) of the LRA.

caveat'.[32] The plaintiffs pleaded that the defendants, by their conduct, acknowledged the option and/or were estopped from relying on s 68.]

FRANKLYN J: It seems there are no reported decisions on the meaning and effect of this part of the section which is peculiar to the Western Australian Act. Plaintiff's counsel submits that on its proper interpretation, although an option for renewal granted in an unregistered lease which is not protected by caveat is not enforceable against a subsequent registered proprietor, the option remains 'live' in all other respects and such subsequent registered proprietor may at his option enforce the same against the lessee if the lessee were to purport to exercise the same. His argument proceeds that the lessor in such case is entitled to 'affirm the lease', which I understand to be a reference to the extended term. The submission as I understand it is that it is open to the lessee under the terms of the lease to purport to exercise the option by giving the notice of exercise there provided for, and in such case it is also open to the lessor, being a purchaser subsequent to the grant of such lease, to accept such exercise and to elect to extend the lease, which he may do by recognising the exercise of option. He argues that the effect of the words in the section 'no option shall be valid as against the subsequent registered interests' is that the exercise of the option is voidable at the option of the lessor, and that, notice of exercise having been given, until the expiration of the original term the lessor at his election may either require the lessee to vacate at the end of that term, allow him to remain from the date of expiration as a tenant holding over, or affirm the extended term the subject of the purported exercise of option. As at the date of expiration of the original term, he argues, there are only two choices open, each mutually exclusive of the other, they being either a tenancy by way of holding over, or an affirmation of the renewed term. These choices, being mutually exclusive, give rise to the election on which he relies, it being said to be an application of the common law doctrine of election, the election in this case (to affirm the renewed term) to be inferred from the lessor's conduct. Plaintiff's counsel concedes that the claim based on election must fail unless 'the option' said to be 'live' as against the lessee, gave rise to the obligation on the defendant's part to elect. Specifically he submits that the effect of s 68 on the option is that it is no more than voidable at the option of the subsequent purchaser and remains as:

> ... a species of right which is able to be affirmed by the subsequent purchaser and gives rise – in the event of the tenant having exercised the option to renew, [to] a right of election in the subsequent registered interest to either terminate the estate or affirm.

I have difficulty with this submission although there is nothing objectionable in the proposition that the lessor might willingly grant the renewed term even though by virtue of the section he is not obliged to do so. What is invalid under the section as against the subsequent registered proprietor is the option of renewal. Whether such an option be viewed as an irrevocable offer by the lessor capable of acceptance by the lessee up until the time specified in the lease, or as a conditional contract, that is a contract that the lessor will grant a new lease subject to a condition subsequent to be performed by the lessee, it creates a proprietary right enforceable against the lessor. It is that right which is invalidated by s 68 in the circumstances there provided for and, as a consequence in such case in my opinion no such proprietary right exists as from the date of acquisition of title by the subsequent registered proprietor ...

The need for both a person who has contracted to sell and a person who has contracted to purchase in my opinion is not affected by the nature of a particular option that is whether it

2 This provision is similar to s 28(3) of the LRA.

be an irrevocable offer or a conditional contract. The effect of s 68 is that the subsequent registered purchaser is not a person who has contracted or offered to sell to the optionee. In my opinion the effect of s 68 upon the option provided for in the lease can be seen as follows:

(a) If such option is properly characterised as an offer to grant a further term which the lessor was precluded from withdrawing so long as it remained exercisable then, as from the date that the defendant became the registered proprietor, it was an offer which had no validity as against the defendant and so could not be relied upon by the lessee as an offer open for acceptance or in any way to compel the grant of the extended term. By the operation of the section there was no longer an equitable interest in or proprietary right to the land in favour of the lessee.

(b) If such option is properly characterised as a contract to grant the extended term conditional upon the lessee within the stipulated time binding itself to perform the terms of the offer, then again to give the section effect, as from the date the defendant became the registered proprietor such contract was unenforceable and had not effect as against the lessor. He could not be held to have contacted to sell and the option could not give rise to any interest in or proprietary right to the land in favour of the lessee.

That being so the subsequent giving of a notice by the lessee in terms of the option could be no more than an ineffective gesture giving rise to no contractual obligations and creating no interest in or right to the premises the subject thereof. The contractual purpose of the notice of exercise was (subject to compliance with the other specified terms or conditions) to bring into effect the lessee's acceptance of the irrevocable offer or to make the conditional contract unconditional, as the case might be, a result rendered impossible by the operation by the section. Its giving could not give rise to any obligation on the defendant's part and could not result in it being compelled at law to make any election upon the expiration of the original term. The plaintiff's reliance upon election presupposes that at the expiration of the original term the defendant, because of the giving of the notice, was faced with two alternatives, a holding over or the extended term, one of which it must, as a matter of obligation, choose to the exclusion of the other. The submission however, is not one as to the existence of any obligation and assumes a right on the part of the lessee to give a notice of exercise the giving of which creates a legal relationship resulting in the obligation to make an election. In my view the existence of any such right and/or the notice having such an effect is inconsistent with the provisions of s 68 and would deny the validity of the injunction that the option shall not be valid as against the subsequent registered proprietor. The doctrine of election upon which the plaintiff relies is not appropriate in my opinion to the facts of this case ...

Upon receipt of the notice purporting to exercise the option the defendant was not obliged to do anything. It was not an event which enabled him to exercise alternative and inconsistent rights. The notice created no rights in the plaintiff and imposed no obligation on the defendant to affirm or otherwise. At the expiration of the original term he was in no different position, so far as his rights were concerned, than if no notice had been given. He was not faced with the choice of two or more inconsistent courses of action. There was no question of an alternative right to terminate any existing contract or interest in property. Indeed what the plaintiff seeks to acquire through the doctrine of election is the creation of a new contract granting a fresh term in the sense either that the irrevocable offer has been accepted or alternatively the conditional contract has been made unconditional. The plaintiff's claim based on election fails ...

[His Honour also found that there was not sufficient evidence to support the plaintiff's claim that the defendant was estopped by its conduct from relying on s 68.]

Application dismissed.

In the following case, the High Court of Australia discusses two important issues arising from s 68 of the Transfer of Land Act (WA) (the relevant parts of the section correspond with s 283 of the LRA). The first issue is what constitutes sufficient protection of an option to renew in an unregistered lease. The second issue is whether an option to renew, which does not bind the current proprietor (because the caveat to protect the lease was lodged after registration of the current owner) could spring to life again when the caveat is lodged and bind subsequent purchasers of the freehold.

LEROS PTY LTD v TERARA PTY LTD AND ANOTHER
(1992) 106 ALR 595, High Court of Australia

[On 6 December 1987, Terara (first respondent) obtained from the University of Western Australia (UWA), then the registered proprietor of the subject land, a lease for five years expiring 5 December 1992. The lease contained the option to renew for a further term of seven years. Terara did not then seek to register its lease, or lodge a caveat to protect its interest therein. With the consent of UWA, Terara mortgaged its interest under the lease by way of sub-lease for a term less one day to the second respondent, the National Australia Bank. On 15 July 1988, the Bank lodged a caveat against the title to the land to protect its interest as mortgagee of leasehold by sub-lease. No explicit reference was made in the caveat to the existence of the option. On 28 September 1988, UWA transferred its freehold estate to Jass, which became the registered proprietor. On 31 March 1989, Jass transferred the freehold to Western. The transfer to Jass and Western were expressly stated to be subject to the encumbrance of the Bank but no other encumbrance. On 13 July 1989, Terara lodged a caveat against title to the land claiming an estate or interest in the land in leasehold as lessee for a term expiring on 5 December 1992, with an option for renewal for a further term of seven years. The option forbade registration of any instrument affecting the claimed interest unless the instrument was expressed to be subject to the caveator's claim. On 12 March 1990, Leros (appellant) became the registered proprietor of the land. Leros was aware of Terara's lease and option to renew, and its transfer was registered subject to the Bank and Terara caveats. Terara brought proceedings in the Western Australia Supreme Court for a declaration that its caveat was valid and that Leros' title was subject to the lease and option of renewal. Terara conceded that Jass did not take subject to the option because the lease was not at that time registered or protected by Terara's caveat, but argued that the option had been revived by Terara's caveat lodged shortly before Leros became the proprietor. Alternatively, Terara argued that the Bank's caveat was sufficient to protect Terara's interest and option. The Full Court of Western Australia declared that Terara's caveat was valid as against Leros. Leros appealed to the High Court.

Section 137 of the Transfer of Land Act (1893) (WA) provides: 'Any ... person claiming any estate or interest in land ... may lodge a caveat ... forbidding the registration ... of any instrument affecting such estate or interest either absolutely or ... unless such instrument be expressed to be subject of a claim of the caveator as may be required in such caveat.'

Section 68 of the Act provides that title of a registered proprietor is indefeasible except as against an unregistered lease or agreement for lease for a term not exceeding five years where a tenant is in actual possession. The section provides further that 'but no option of purchase or renewal in any lease or agreement shall be valid as against a subsequent registered interest unless such lease or agreement is registered or protected by caveat'.]

MASON CJ, DAWSON AND McHUGH JJ: This appeal raises important questions concerning the enforceability of interests sought to be protected by caveats lodged under the Transfer of Land Act 1893 (WA) (the Act). The broad question at issue is whether an option of renewal for a further term of seven years of a lease which is to expire on 5 December 1992 is valid and enforceable against the appellant (Leros) which, on 12 March 1990, became and still is the registered proprietor of an estate in fee simple in Lot 10 of Strata Plan 17651, being Shop 34 in the Subiaco Village. The option is said to be protected by two caveats [lodged by the Bank and Terara, respectively.]

The validity of Terara's existing lease, the term of which will expire in 1992, is not in dispute. As a short term tenancy, not exceeding five years to a tenant in actual possession, the existing lease is specifically protected by s 68, notwithstanding that it is not registered. What is in dispute is the enforceability of the option for renewal which is not registered.

The purpose of the last proviso in ... s [68] that which relates to the option of purchase or renewal, is to ensure that no such option should be valid against the person having the benefit of the subsequent dealing unless the instrument creating the lease is registered or a caveat protecting the instrument creating the lease is registered or a caveat protecting the lease is lodged. This proviso was necessary, as Barwick CJ pointed out in *Mercantile Credits Ltd v Shell Co of Australia Ltd* [(1976) 136 CLR 326, at 339] 'because, without it, the effect of the earlier substantive provision of the section would have made the subsequent dealing subject to the right of purchase or of renewal as the case may be'. The assumption was that the prescribed exception to the principle of indefeasibility of the title of the registered proprietor in favour of a prior unregistered lease for a term not exceeding five years would, but for the proviso, extend to an option of renewal ...

The appellant's argument, based on the concluding words of s 68, is that Jass and its successors acquired a title free from that encumbrance from the moment at which Jass was registered as proprietor. The response to that argument, accepted by the majority in the Full Court of the Supreme Court, was expressed by Malcolm CJ in these terms:

> Section 68 does not say that the option of renewal in an unregistered lease is not valid against all subsequent registered interests. It provides only that it shall not be valid against 'a subsequent registered interest unless the said lease is registered or protected by caveat'.

However, this interpretation ignores the fact that, in an appropriate context, the indefinite article 'a' is quite capable of meaning 'any'. And there, when the provision is read in the light of its context and purpose, that is how it would be understood.

The purpose of the last proviso in s 68 is to ensure that the title of the subsequent registered proprietor is indefeasible as against an option of renewal in a prior lease for not more than five years unless the lease was registered or protected by caveat. Section 68 gives expression to the essential principle of the Torrens system, namely, that 'the registered proprietor has the legal property in the land, subject only to equities and such interests as the Act expressly preserves', to quote the words of Windeyer J in *Breskvar v Wall* [(1971) 126 CLR 376, at 400]. A purchaser who takes with notice of an antecedent equitable interest, who becomes registered without fraud takes free from that interest [*Bahr v Nicolay (No 2)* (1988) 78 ALR 1].

To become registered with notice of a prior unregistered interest does not constitute fraud [*Mills v Stokman* (1967) 116 CLR 61, *per* Kitto J at 78].

The Torrens system is, as Barwick CJ noted in *Breskvar* [(1971) 126 CLR, at 385–86]: 'not a system of registration of title but a system of title by registration. That which the certificate of title describes is not the title which the registered proprietor formerly had, or which but for registration would have had. The title it certifies is not historical or derivative. It is the title which registration itself has vested in the proprietor.'

Torrens, in his *Handy Book on the Real Property Act of South Australia* [(1862), p 11], in a passage quoted by Windeyer J in *Breskvar*, described the operation of the legislation as: 'Cutting off the retrospective or derivative character of the title upon each transfer or transmission, so as that each freeholder is in the same position as a grantee direct from the Crown.'

This passage supports the view that the effect of the registration of a subsequent dealing bringing about the registration of proprietorship of an estate or interest in land is to extinguish all prior unregistered estates or interests which, but for that registration, would have conflicted with the proprietor's estate or interest or encumbered that estate or interest, unless the prior unregistered estate or interest falls within the exceptions to indefeasibility of title mentioned in s 68. In other words, a person seeking to preserve an unregistered interest not falling within those exceptions must register that interest in advance of the registration of a subsequent inconsistent dealing or present such registration by caveat or otherwise, and thereby enable registration of the unregistered interest. Once that interest is defeated by registration of a subsequent inconsistent dealing bringing about the registration of a new proprietor, the first interest is extinguished for all purposes and cannot be asserted against any later proprietor. The first interest does not become an inchoate interest capable of being asserted against a later proprietor or an interest which remains in suspension so that it is capable of subsequent revival against such a proprietor. We adopt the comment of Franklyn J in *Osborne Park Co-operative Society Ltd v Wilden Pty Ltd* [[1989] 2 WAR 77, at 84] with respect to the impact of s 68 on an option of renewal in a prior unregistered lease not exceeding five years, namely, that 'no ... proprietary right exists as from the date of acquisition of title by the subsequent registered proprietor'.

It is an incident of the indefeasibility of the title of the registered proprietor not only that he or she holds free from prior unregistered interests, except those specified in s 68, but also that he or she has the capacity to transfer a title to the interest of which he or she is proprietor to a successor, free from such unregistered interests. In this respect, the operation of the Act is similar to the operation under the general law of the doctrine of the *bona fide* purchaser for value who acquires the legal estate without notice of a prior equitable interest. The acquisition of the legal title by such a purchaser in those circumstances defeats the prior equitable interest in the sense that the interest is destroyed. Thus a subsequent purchaser with notice of the equitable interest, who purchases from the first purchaser, is not bound by the interest. If it were otherwise, a *bona fide* purchaser might be unable to deal with his or her property. The sale of the property would be clogged.

The failure of a person entitled to an equitable estate or interest to lodge a caveat against dealing with the land does not necessarily involve any loss of priority which the time of the creation of that interest would otherwise give [*J & H Just (Holdings) Pty Ltd v Bank of New South Wales* (1971) 125 CLR 546, *per* Barwick CJ at 554; and Windeyer J at 558]. That is because the purpose of a caveat against dealings is to operate as an injunction to the Registrar General to prevent registration of dealings forbidden by the caveat until notice is given to the caveator so that he or she has an opportunity to oppose such registration.

Although the failure to lodge a caveat may not result in a loss of priority in a competition between conflicting equitable interests, such a failure will, as previously explained, result in the destruction of the equitable interest as soon as registration of an inconsistent dealing constitutes the registration of a subsequent proprietor who takes free from the prior unregistered equitable interest. In this respect there is a distinction between a competition between unregistered equitable interests and a competition between a prior unregistered equitable interest and a subsequently registered estate or interest in the land. In the second case, the prior unregistered interest is defeated so that the contractual right on which that interest depends, though enforceable against the party who created it, is not enforceable as against the third party who becomes registered as the proprietor of the inconsistent estate or interest ...

The efficacy of the Bank's caveat

The Bank submits that its caveat affords protection for Terara's interest as lessee and option holder, at least to the extent necessary to protect the Bank's subordinate interest as 'mortgage[e] by way of sub-demise'. Provided that the Bank's caveat complies with the statutory requirements with respect to formalities and contents of caveats, the Bank's contention is, in our view, correct ...

The argument for Leros is that every subordinate interest perishes with the superior interest upon which it is dependent, and, therefore, the Bank's caveat perishes with the option. However, it is necessary to distinguish between the validity of a caveat and that of the interest sought to be protected by the caveat. Although a subordinate interest will perish with the destruction of the superior interest upon which it depends, that principle can have no application to a caveat which, as stated earlier, is not a proprietary interest.

Therefore, the first question is whether the caveat sufficiently specifies the Bank's interest as mortgagee by way of sub-demise so as to satisfy the requirements of s 137. It has been said that the purpose of requiring the caveator to 'specify' the estate or interest claimed is to enable the registered proprietor to know, or find out, the claim which he or she will have to meet. It has also been said that another purpose is to enable the Registrar General to determine whether a dealing lodged for registration is inconsistent with the estate or interest claimed by the caveator. But, in evaluating the significance of that purpose, regard must be had to the existence of the Registrar General's power under s 137 to require the caveator to provide a statutory declaration stating the nature of the estate or interest and the title thereto. In the ultimate analysis, it seems to us that 'specify' should be understood in the sense of 'mention definitely or explicitly'. Subject to some qualification, that is the meaning adopted by the Full Court of the Supreme Court of Western Australia in *Kuper v Keywest Constructions Pty Ltd* [[1990] 3 WAR 419].

Two objections are made to the sufficiency of the description of the interest claimed in the caveat: that the caveat does not state the amount of the security and that it does not state the term of the sub-demise. However, in our view, a statement of the amount of the debt is not required as an element in the requisite description of the caveator's interest. And, although the term of the sub-demise does not appear on the face of the caveat, para 6(a) of the annexure reveals to all who examine the caveat that the lessee 'demised to the Caveator all the Lessee's right, title and interest in and to the Lease Premises for the residue of the term of the Lease as renewed or extended from time to time except the last day of the term of the Lease'.

Paragraph 6(b) states that the lessee is to stand possessed of that last day on trust for the Bank. Paragraph 4 states that the term of the existing lease is for a term of five years from 6

December 1987. On reading these paragraphs of the Annexure, a person examining the caveat could be left in no doubt as to the extent and nature of the Bank's claim which he or she would have to meet if he or she proceeded to registration as proprietor subject to that claim.

However, the same cannot be said for the option of renewal, the only reference to which is that made in para 6(a) of the Annexure, as set out above. Accordingly, the option is not sufficiently specified by the Bank's caveat, and the Bank's interest is supported by the caveat only to the extent of the term expiring in December 1992. Thus, the lease, but not the option, is protected by the Bank's caveat to the extent of the dependency.

It should be noted that the observations made previously in *Mercantile Credits Ltd* [(1976) 136 CLR, at 339] do not assist the respondents' case. Even if capable of application to the different question in issue here, they cannot stand in the face of the clear words of s 68.

The question remains whether the caveat lodged by the Bank which, for the purposes of s 137, will protect the lease to the extent necessary to protect the Bank's interest, constitutes protection of the lease itself for the purposes of the concluding words in s 68. There is much to commend the view that the concluding words of that section contemplate a caveat protecting the lease itself as distinct from a dependent and lesser interest. That is the natural reading of the provision and it is supported by the circumstance that protection by caveat is specified as an alternative to registration of the lease itself. In other words, although the tenant's unregistered lease for not more than five years is protected without registration if he or she is in actual occupation, an option for renewal in that lease is not protected unless the lease itself is registered or is itself made the subject of a caveat.

On the other hand, if s 137 permits protection of a superior interest to the extent that such protection may be necessary for the protection of a subordinate and dependent interest claimed by the caveator, why should s 68 be read in the narrow sense that its language might seem to suggest? Is there any discernible purpose to be served by insisting on the stricter requirement? Although the argument is not without force, we favour the stricter interpretation, because the concluding words of s 68 are providing for an exception to indefeasibility of title. As such, the exception should be strictly construed.

For the foregoing reasons we would allow the appeal.

[Deane and Gaudron JJ dissented.]

Note

In *Leros*, the court said that it was not necessary for the Bank to state in its caveat the amount of the debt. This may not be the position under the Land Registration Act. Section 81(3) thereof, provides that a caveat lodged to protect an equitable mortgage must state the amount secured. If the caveat does not state the amount owed the mortgage will not bind the registered proprietor.

(viii) A lease, licence or other authority granted by the Head of State or a Minister and in respect of which no provision for registration is made – s 33(1)(h) of the LRA

An example of this exception is a mining prospecting licence granted by the Minister under s 25 of the Mining Act (Ch No 195). Also s 125 of the Land Act 1996 (Ch 45), gives the Minister power to grant a licence to any person to enter government land for any purpose specified in the section, for example, to graze stock. A licence granted under this section continues for a maximum period of one year.

(ix) Unpaid rates, taxes, or charges – s 33(1)(i) of the LRA

A registered proprietor takes subject to 'overriding statutory rights'. This means that, unless otherwise provided, a proprietor takes the land subject to any outstanding rates or taxes chargeable upon the land, even though at the time he became the owner or occupier there was nothing in the Register Book to alert him of the unpaid charges. See, for example, s 76(6) and (7) of the Local Government Act (Ch No 57).

Questions

1 Do you agree that in all cases statutory charges should prevail over rights of a registered proprietor?

2 Consider the following problem. In 1995 the ABC Bank granted X a loan of K100,000 on security of his State lease. The mortgage was registered. X still owes the Bank K80,000. At the same time he owes the government K20,000 in rates and various other statutory charges over his land accumulated since 1999. The proceeds of sale of X's land are estimated to be less than K50,000. Who, between the government and the Bank has priority over the proceeds and why? (See *The South-Eastern Drainage Board (South Australia) v The Savings Bank of South Australia* (1939) 62 CLR 603.)

Overriding statutory provisions

Therefore, Parliament can override the principle of indefeasibility by simply enacting legislation to that effect. Whether Parliament intended a particular statutory provision to supersede the principle of indefeasibility, is a matter of statutory interpretation. A good example of superseding legislation is the Land Act 1996, discussed in the following extract.

Mugambwa J, 'Judicial assault on the citadel of indefeasibility of title under the Papua New Guinean Torrens system of conveyance' (2001) 5 Journal of South Pacific Law (http://www.vanuatu.usp.ac.fj/journal_splaw/Article/Mugambwa1.htm)

...

Leges posteriores priores contrarias abrogant

It is established rule of statutory interpretation that where there is inconsistency between two statutes, the later statute prevails over the earlier.[33] This rule is summed up in the maxim: *leges posteriores priores contrarias abrogant*. In the High Court of Australia judgment in *Goodwin v Phillips*, Griffith CJ stated the rule thus:[34]

> [W]here the provisions of a particular Act of Parliament dealing with a particular subject matter are wholly inconsistent with the provisions of an earlier Act dealing with the same subject matter, then the earlier Act is repealed by implication ... Another

33 *State v Bonga* [1988–89] PNGLR 360; *State v Tulong* [1995] PNGLR 329.

34 (1908) 7 CLR 1, at 7.

> branch of the same proposition is this, that if the provisions are not wholly inconsistent, but may become inconsistent in their application to particular cases, then to that extent the provisions of the former Act are excepted or their operation is excluded with respect to cases falling within the provisions of the later Act.

The rule is based on the presumption that the legislature in the later enactment impliedly intended to repeal inconsistent provisions in the earlier statute. It is noteworthy that the presumption only applies where the two enactments are so inconsistent that they are incapable of standing side by side.[35] For example, if the retention of the earlier statute would defeat the purpose of the later, it is presumed that the earlier statute was abrogated.[36] It is further emphasised that the rule is just a presumption. For example, it will not apply if the earlier statute specifically deals with the particular topic whilst the later statute only deals with the topic in general terms.[37]

Applying the foregoing rule to the Land Act and the Land Registration Act, the former was enacted in 1996 whilst the latter came into effect in 1981. Hence, the Land Act is the later enactment. It may be argued that the Land Act is largely a consolidation of the 1962 Land Act and the various amendments thereof, in which case its date of enactment should be backdated to 1963 when the original Act came into effect.[38] However, the weight of judicial authority is against such argument. The view generally accepted is that the relevant date for applying the *leges posteriores* maxim is the date the consolidating Act took effect and not that of the original statute. This is so even if it results in reversing the order of the conflicting statutes.[39]

The next question is whether the indefeasibility provisions of the Land Registration Act are so inconsistent with the Land Act that the two cannot stand side by side. Part IX of the Land Act deals with alienation of government land. Section 64(1) provides that 'government land shall not be alienated otherwise than under this Act or another law'. In the case of *Steamship Trading Co Ltd v Minister of Lands and Physical Planning et al*, Sheehan J held that this provision clearly indicates Parliamentary intention to prohibit the alienation of government land other than through the process of the Land Act or another law.[40] His Honour noted that it was obvious that the Land Registration Act was not 'another law' because it has nothing to do with alienation of government land, but rather deals with registration of titles. This writer, with due respect, agrees with Justice Sheehan's interpretation of the provision. The use of the term 'shall' suggests that the procedural requirements are mandatory. Several other provisions of the Land Act reinforce this view. For example, s 65 empowers the Minister to grant State leases of government land as provided by the Act. Section 67 provides that a State lease 'shall not' be granted for a purpose inconsistent with zoning, physical planning law or any other law relating to land use. Section 69 provides that a State lease 'shall not be granted without first being advertised in accordance with s 68'. The latter section prescribes the procedure for advertising available government land for leasing.

---

35 The courts do not readily accept that statutes conflict except where such conclusion is inevitable, see *State v Tulong* [1995] PNGLR 329, at 332.

36 See Pearce, DC and Geddes, RS, *Statutory Interpretation in Australia* (3rd edn, Butterworths, Sydney, 1988), para 7.11.

37 *Goodwin v Phillips*, above, *per* Griffith CJ at p 14.

38 See s 1(1) of the Land Act 1968 (Ch No 185).

39 *Maybury v Plowman* (1913) 16 CLR 468. In any case, with respect to the Land Registration Act, it could also be argued that it is a consolidation of the Real Property Act of 1889 (P) and the Land Registration Ordinance of 1924 (NG).

40 See also Sevua J in *Hi Lift*, above.

> Clearly, in our opinion, the Land Registration Act is inconsistent with the above provisions in that (bar fraud) it confers an indefeasible title upon a registered proprietor notwithstanding that the grant might be void under the Land Act. As Sheehan J observes in *Steamship Trading Co Ltd*, it would seem odd that 'Parliament having stipulated in one Act the only mode of granting of State leases, should by another Act grant an indefeasible title by way of lease without any need to follow that process ...'. The underlying policies of the two statutes appear to cancel each other out. Since the Land Act is the later statute, it impliedly overrides the indefeasibility provisions of the Land Registration Act to the extent of inconsistency.

Note

The writer was in part responding to Sheehan J's judgment in *Steamship Trading Co Ltd*, and Sevua J's judgment in *Hi Lift Company Pty Ltd*. See extracts of both judgments, above.

Judicial inroads on the concept of indefeasibility of title

Section 33(1) of the Land Registration Act states that a registered proprietor's estate or interest is indefeasible except as stated in the section. Notwithstanding this clear prescription, the courts have made additional inroads on the concept of indefeasibility outside the Act. In the Privy Council judgment in *Frazer v Walker*, Lord Wilberforce observed:[41]

> ... their Lordships have accepted the general principle that registration under the ... [Torrens System Acts] confers upon a registered proprietor a title to the interest in respect of which he is registered which is ... immune from adverse claims, other than those specifically excepted. In doing so they wish to make it clear that this principle in no way denies the right of a plaintiff to bring against a registered proprietor a claim *in personam*, founded in law or in equity, for such relief as a court acting *in personam* may grant.

Section 108 of the Land Registration Act, saves the courts' inherent power to enforce equitable claims under the Act. Section 108 provides:

> Saving of jurisdiction
>
> (1) This Act does not take away or affect the legal or equitable jurisdiction of a court to grant relief
>
> (a) on the ground of fraud; or
>
> (b) over contracts or agreements for the sale or other disposition of land; or
>
> (c) over equitable interests generally.
>
> (1) Notwithstanding
>
> (a) the provisions of section 104; or
>
> (b) the powers of disposition or other powers conferred by this Act on proprietors of an estate, interest or security,

41 [1967] 1 AC 569, at p 585, see extract above.

but subject to sub-section (3), the intention of this Act is that equities may be enforced against the title of a subsequent purchaser for valuable consideration duly registered under this Act.

(1) Subject to section 33 no unregistered estate, interest, security, contract or agreement prevails against the title of a subsequent purchaser for valuable consideration duly registered under the Act.

Equitable claims against a registered proprietor may arise out of obligations assumed by him either before or after the registration of his interest. The following case illustrates this point.

BAHR AND ANOTHER v NICOLAY AND OTHERS (NO 2)
(1988) 164 CLR 604, High Court of Australia

[For detailed facts of this case see above, p 453. The issue was whether cl 4 of the Thompsons and Nicolay agreement by which the Thompsons acknowledged the existence of the re-purchase provision of the earlier Bahr and Nicolay contract (cl 6 of that agreement) bound the Thompsons after registration of their title.]

MASON CJ and DAWSON J: What then was the purpose and effect of cl 4 of the agreement between the first and the second respondents? The matrix of circumstances in which the agreement was made throws up three significant factors. First, the making of an agreement between the first and second respondents which would result in the destruction of the appellants' existing rights, or allow the destruction of those rights, by registration of a transfer in favour of the second respondents in circumstances whereby the rights became unenforceable would expose the first respondent to liability for breach of contract ... Secondly, as we have seen, upon registration of such a transfer, the combined effect of ss 68 and 134 would, in the absence of fraud, bring about the destruction of the appellants' rights. Thirdly, at least until registration of such a transfer, the appellants' equitable interest under the 1980 agreement, being first in time, had priority over the interest of the second respondents as purchasers under their agreement with the first respondent.

Viewed in this setting, cl 4 of the later agreement was designed to do more than merely evidence the fact that the second respondents had notice of the appellants' rights. If that were the only purpose to be served by the acknowledgment it would achieve nothing. It would enable the second respondents to destroy the appellants' interest and would leave the first respondent exposed to potential liability for breach of contract at the suit of the appellants. In the circumstances outlined it is evident that the purpose of cl 4 was to provide that the transfer of title to lot 340 was to be subject to the appellants' rights under cl 6 of the 1980 agreement in the sense that those rights were to be enforceable against the second respondents.

At first glance it might seem that the words of cl 4 are inadequate to achieve this purpose. But an acknowledgment of an antecedent agreement in an appropriate context may amount to an agreement or undertaking to recognise rights arising under that antecedent agreement. And here the inferences to be drawn from the matrix of circumstances are so strong that they necessarily influence the interpretation of cl 4. These inferences provide a secure foundation for imputing an intention to the parties and reading cl 4 as a reflection of that intention.

Granted that the purpose of cl 4 is as we have explained it, what is its legal effect? Is it simply an undertaking to perform the 1980 agreement if called upon so to do by the appellants? Contract scarcely seems to give sufficient effect to what the parties had in mind. A trust relationship is a more accurate and appropriate reflection of the parties' intention.

The appellants submitted that cl 4 creates a trust in favour of them as third parties, in accordance with the principles enunciated in cases such as *In Re Schebsman: Official Receiver v Cargo Superintendents (London) Ltd* [1944] (Ch 83) ... However, in the absence of the manifestation of a clear intention to create a trust, the courts have been reluctant to hold that trust exists. Du Parcq LJ elegantly expressed the traditional attitude when he said [[1944] Ch at p 104)]:

> It is true that, by the use possibly of unguarded language, a person may create a trust, as Monsieur Jourdain talked prose, without knowing it, but unless an intention to create a trust is clearly to be collected from the language used and the circumstances of the case, I think that the court ought not to be astute to discover indications of such an intention.

This reluctance to accept that the parties have created an express trust has induced the English courts to impose what has been described as a constructive trust in order to protect a prior interest from destruction on the registration of a later interest: see *Bannister v Bannister* [[1948] 2 All ER 133].

On the other hand Fullagar J stated a contrary view in *Wilson v Darling Island Stevedoring & Lighterage Co Ltd* [(1956) 95 CLR 43, at 67]. 'It is difficult to understand the reluctance which courts have sometimes shown to infer a trust in such cases.' His Honour was referring to contracts whereby a benefit is promised to a third party. We agree with his Honour's comment. If the inference to be drawn is that the parties intended to create or protect an interest in a third party and the trust relationship is the appropriate means of creating or protecting that interest or of giving effect to the intention, then there is no reason why in a given case an intention to create a trust should not be inferred. The present is just such a case. The trust is an express, not a constructive, trust. The effect of the trust is that the second respondents hold lot 340 subject to such rights as were created in favour of the appellants by the 1980 agreement.

Even if we had not reached this conclusion, we would not have regarded the registration of the transfer in favour of the second respondents as destroying the appellants' rights. Having regard to the intention of the parties expressed in cl 4 of the later agreement, the subsequent repudiation of cl 6 of the 1980 agreement constituted fraud. The case therefore fell within the statutory exception with the result that the appellants' prior equitable interest prevails over the second respondents' title, the second respondents taking with notice of that interest ...

BRENNAN J [His Honour made a finding that the parties intention was not only that the Thompsons should have notice of the Bahrs' interest, but that upon acquiring the subject land should be bound by cl 6 of the original contract. He continued]: A registered proprietor who has undertaken that his transfer should be subject to an unregistered interest and who repudiates the unregistered interest when his transfer is registered is, in equity's eye, acting fraudulently and he may be compelled to honour the unregistered interest. A means by which equity prevents the fraud is by imposing a constructive trust on the purchaser when he repudiates the unregistered interest. That is not to say that the registration of the transfer to such a proprietor is affected by such fraud as may defeat the registered title: the fraud which attracts the intervention of equity consists in the unconscionable attempt by the registered proprietor to deny the unregistered interest to which he has undertaken to subject his registered title. The principles are stated in *Bannister v Bannister* [[1948] 2 All ER 133] and *Lyus v Prowsa Developments Ltd* [[1982] 2 All ER 953] ... In *Bannister* [[1948] 2 All ER, at 136] Scott LJ said:

> It is, we think, clearly a mistake to suppose that the equitable principle on which a constructive trust is raised against a person who insists on the absolute character of a conveyance to himself for the purpose of defeating a beneficial interest, which, according to the true bargain, was to belong to another, is confined to cases in which the conveyance itself was fraudulently obtained. The fraud which brings the principle into play arises as soon as the absolute character of the conveyance is set up for the purpose of defeating the beneficial interest, and that is the fraud to cover which the Statute of Frauds or the corresponding provisions of the Law of Property Act 1925, cannot be called in aid in cases in which no written evidence of the real bargain is available. Nor is it, in our opinion, necessary that the bargain on which the absolute conveyance is made should include any express stipulation that the grantee is in so many words to hold as trustee. It is enough that the bargain should have included a stipulation under which some sufficiently defined beneficial interest in the property was to be taken by another.

In *Lyus v Prowsa Developments Ltd* land was sold by a bank, as mortgagee exercising a power of sale, subject to, but with the benefit of, a prior agreement to sell made between the mortgagor and the plaintiffs. The bank had consented to but was not bound by the plaintiffs' contract. The purchaser from the bank (and a sub-purchaser who was subject to the same obligation) was held to take its interest subject to a constructive trust for the plaintiffs. Though a statutory provision similar to s 68 of the Act was relied on, Dillon J found that although there is no fraud merely in relying on legal rights conferred by statute, there was fraud in a purchaser's 'reneging on a positive stipulation in favour of the plaintiffs in the bargain under which the [purchaser] acquired the land'.

Therefore, although a purchaser who secures registration of a transfer of the fee simple merely with notice of a third party's right to purchase acquires on registration of his transfer a title freed of any obligation to the third party which equity would otherwise impose, a purchaser who has undertaken – whether by contract or by collateral undertaking – to hold his title subject to a third party's right to purchase remains bound by his undertaking after registration of his transfer. If he should repudiate the third party's right to purchase, equity imposes a constructive trust so that the registered proprietor holds his title on trust for the third party to the extent of the third party's interest ...

As the Thompsons not only had notice of the Bahrs' interest but had undertaken that their title would be subject to the Bahrs' interest, they cannot rely on the Property Law Act, the Statute of Frauds or the Act to avoid honouring their undertaking. As a contractual undertaking, it can be enforced by Nicolay to whom it was given. As the Bahrs' interest was created by an antecedent agreement pursuant to which Nicolay was bound to enforce the Thompsons' undertaking to honour the Bahrs' interest, there can be no reason for denying the Bahrs' standing to enforce the undertaking against the Thompsons directly in a suit in which Nicolay is a party ... Moreover, the constructive trust on which the Thompsons hold their title is a trust to give effect to the Bahrs' interest. As beneficiaries of that trust, the Bahrs may enforce their interest against their trustee directly ... The Bahrs are therefore entitled to enforce their right of purchase directly against the Thompsons. They do not thereby impeach the registration of the transfer to the Thompsons. Nor does the TLA present a bar to the enforcement of the undertaking though (to adopt what Barwick CJ said in *Breskvar v Wall* (1971) 126 CLR at p 385) the terminal point of a decree enforcing the undertaking might be an order directing the Thompsons to divest themselves wholly of the estate vested in them by that registration.

Appeal allowed.

Note

The Supreme Court judgment in *Emas Estate Development Pty Ltd v John Mea and Another* [1993] PNGLR 215, extracted above, contains additional judicial inroads on the principle of indefeasibility of title, see in particular the judgment of Salika J. See also the National Court judgments in *Steamship Pty Ltd* and in *Hi Lift Company Pty Ltd* (both judgments are extracted above). For a comment on these cases see Mugambwa, 'Judicial assault on the citadel of indefeasibility of title under the Papua New Guinean Torrens system of conveyance', extracted above.

Questions

1 What is the main difference between the exceptions to indefeasibility listed in *Emas Estate Development Pty Ltd* and the *in personam* exception to indefeasibility discussed in *Bahr v Nicolay*?

2 Discuss the advantages and disadvantages of a wider scope for inroads on the concept of indefeasibility.

Overriding 'fundamental' common law principle

ULELIO AND OTHERS v NELULU LAND GROUP AND OTHERS unreported, N1699 PNG National Court of Justice, WS 1113 of 1996

[The defendants claimed customary ownership of over 12,578 hectares of sea known as Aliwo Passage. They lodged with the Land Titles Commission an application to convert their title to freehold under the Land (Tenure Conversion) Act. The Commission granted the title and they were registered as proprietors of the subject sea passage in freehold. The plaintiffs brought these proceedings claiming that the defendants used fraud and duress to influence the decision of the Commission and the Registrar to issue the certificate of title. The defendants denied the allegations and also pleaded indefeasibility of title.]

WOODS J: The general law is clear that the Sea is a public highway, there is a common domain in the seas and in the coastal seas and within what is referred to as the Territorial waters this domain is held by the State. The Plaintiff Land Group must have claimed its ownership of this area of sea by virtue of the fact that the various members of the Land Group are the coastal people of that area who have since time immemorial exercised rights to gather and fish in and over those waters and those waters adjoin their village and traditional land. Unfortunately there is no evidence of the material placed before the Land Titles Commission for this claim. There can be no doubt that coastal peoples have exercised and asserted some form of marine tenure over reefs and coastal waters for the purpose of their livelihood. However there is no evidence how such has been recognised by others. Prior to the advent of the modern legal system in this country any such rights would have been exercised and recognised by either agreement at the time or by force of arms. However when Papua New Guinea became administered by foreign powers as a single country, either in its two parts as Papua and German New Guinea and then as the Administrative unit of Papua and New Guinea then a body of general law was established by way of Orders in Council, ordinances and subordinate enactments and principles of English Common Law and Equity were followed. Generally the Administration of the time ignored any pre-existing customary laws. Of course any pre-existing customary laws were not in any clearly identifiable form such as in writing. However the Administration and the government before Independence did provide for selective recognition of customary laws or rules or practices. However at all times it was clear that any such recognition of custom did not arise from its own force, rather it was only recognised according to modern legal principles and Ordinances ...

With respect to marine resources there was recognition of the rights of owners of adjacent lands to fish and gather from the offshore reefs and in the coastal sea ...

But there was no scheme or framework whereby such rights were to be documented. And at all times there is the underlying or overriding Common Law doctrine of the Crown (and by implication, the State) Prerogative which vests upon the Crown dominion to all sea. There is nothing sinister or selfish over such Crown prerogative it merely recognising a common property in a resource which was never stationary, subject to tides and currents and the general movement of water. And such common property consideration meant that no single individual or community had the exclusive right of access to fisheries resources, instead it would always be open to all fishermen who had the capability to harvest such resource. And this has been the situation accepted by modern States whereby they are able to regulate fisheries and grant access to them supposedly for the benefit of the State as a whole. And the common domain of the sea also recognises the practical aspect of the nature and need for the free passage of people through the sea, the sea being regarded generally as a public highway of all nations subject of course to any right to regulate such a highway for the safety of people and property.

... It may be suggested that the Land Act enables rights to the sea or underwater land to be registered or recognised under the Land Registration Act however there is nothing in that or any other legislation which overrides the fundamental common law principle of the State's dominion over the Sea. One must distinguish the difference between the Common Law principle of the Crown's prerogative over the sea as against its citizens and the administrative nature of the National Seas Act Ch 361 which asserts the State's rights of administration and sovereignty over an area of offshore sea for the purposes of International Law and the international community.

... So where does that leave customary rights to the sea. It is quite clear that ever since Independence the State has recognised that there are some customary rights in individuals and groups to certain marine resources. Thus see the Fisheries Act 1994 which clearly refers to traditional fishing and provides that the Minister responsible for the management of fishing in the coastal waters must have regard to any traditional rights over or in relation to any area of fisheries waters. And both Papua New Guinea and Australia in the Torres Strait Treaty in 1978 recognised the need to preserve the traditional way of life and livelihood of the traditional inhabitants including traditional fishing. However nowhere has there been any recognition of any customary rights to an absolute possessory title or fee simple to the sea, so how did the Certificate of Title purporting to grant a fee simple over the sea be granted.

[His Honour critically discussed the procedure followed by the Land Titles Commission, and continued:] ... The writ alleges that the title was issued as a result of fraud. There are a number of affidavits about what is alleged to have happened between the parties during the period that the matter was being considered so quickly by the Commission. It would appear that there are a number of disputes and disagreements between the peoples in the area. However on the main allegations and without seeing the appropriate files I cannot find that there has been deliberate fraud, perhaps serious misunderstandings and disputes. I am asked to infer fraud from the fact that the official files are missing. Of course the loss of or unavailability of these files does raise serious questions about how the matter was determined and the orders made and about the efficiency and ability of both the Land Titles Commission and the Registrar of Titles especially over such a radical decision. However I am not sure that this court can infer fraud from this loss.

The defendant submits that the principle of the indefeasibility of a Certificate of Title prevents this court from making any Orders to interfere with or otherwise defeat the effect of the Certificate of Title and makes reference to s 33 of the Land Registration Act. Reference is made to the various authorities on indefeasibility of title and in particular to the case of *Mudge v The State and Others* [1985] PNGLR 387. However there is a more fundamental question here, namely [nowhere] under the law can any individual or group have a fee simple over the high sea.

There is no doubt that on the evidence before me the Land Titles Commission acted irregularly and without any clear understanding of the law. Note that the various legislation refers to 'land', and when any legislation refers to the coastal areas it limits land by reference to reefs and banks and structures built on land or over water, see the Land Disputes Settlement Act. So what the Commissioner thought is unknown as there is no file on his deliberations.

... The Certificate of Title Volume 33 Folio 44 before the court in this matter, in so far as it grants a fee simple over an area of sea, is a nullity. The areas of sea referred to in this case as the Aliwo Passage belong to the public domain.

Question

What is the *ratio decidendi* of the above case? Is the case authority for the proposition that the concept of indefeasibility is subject to fundamental principles of the common law?

III PROTECTION OF UNREGISTERED INTERESTS

As already indicated, s 17(1) of the Land Registration Act prescribes that no estate or interest can be created or transferred under the Act until the instrument purporting to create or transfer the same is registered under the Act.[42] Nevertheless, it is established law that the Torrens system recognises equitable interests and, subject to the provisions of the Land Registration Act, are enforceable in accordance with the ordinary principles and rules of law and equity.[43] Unregistered interests may be protected against the operation of the principle of indefeasibility by lodging a caveat against the subject title.

There are two types of caveats: caveats lodged by the Registrar and caveats lodged by private persons.

42 See above. A lease not exceeding three years is an exception to this requirement, see s 17(4).

43 See *Barry v Heider and Another* (1914) 19 CLR 197, at 216, *per* Isaacs J. Several sections of the Land Registration Act also make it clear that unregistered interests are recognised under the Torrens system: ss 17(2), 81, 82, 104 and 108.

Caveats lodged by the Registrar

The Registrar on his own accord may lodge a caveat in certain situations prescribed in s 163 of the Act. The section provides as follows:

163 Caveat by Registrar

The Registrar may –

(a) lodge a caveat on behalf of the State to prohibit dealing with land belonging to or supposed to belong to the State; and

(b) lodge a caveat on behalf of –

(i) a person under the disability of infancy, unsoundness of mind, or absence from the country; or

(ii) a person whose rights in the Registrar's opinion are likely to be endangered by fraud or improper dealing,

to prohibit dealing with land belonging to or supposed to belong to the person; and

(c) lodge a caveat, on behalf of a person whose rights, in the Registrar's opinion, are likely to be endangered or affected by misdescription of land or its boundaries, to prohibit dealing with the land.

Caveats lodged by private persons

Private persons may lodge any of the following caveats as appropriate to protect their claims.

Caveat lodged to protect an option

As we have seen, under s 28(3) of the LRA, an option to purchase land or renew a lease does not bind a subsequent registered proprietor unless the lease is registered or protected by a caveat.[44]

Caveat lodged to protect an equitable mortgage

An equitable mortgagee may lodge a caveat prohibiting dealings in the mortgaged land unless the dealings are subject to his mortgage (s 81(2) of the LRA).[45]

Caveat to protect any caveatable interest

Generally, any unregistered interest may be protected by a caveat under the provisions in Part VIII of the Land Registration Act. The relevant provisions are as follows:

82 Entitlement to lodge a caveat

Subject to section 92, a person claiming an estate or interest may, by a caveat lodged in accordance with the requirements of this Part, forbid –

44 *Leros Pty Ltd v Terara Pty Ltd and Another* (1992) 106 ALR 596.

45 Compare with a caveat lodged under s 82(a), see s 86 of the LRA.

(a) the registration of instruments affecting that estate or interest; or

(b) the amendment of a certificate of title under section 153.

83 Scope of caveat

A caveat under section 82 may be expressed to operate –

(a) absolutely or until after notice of intention to register the instrument has been served in accordance with section 94; or

(b) to forbid one or more instruments or classes of instruments.

86 Restriction on dealings

(1) Subject to sub-section (2), while a caveat under section 82(a) remains in force, the Registrar shall not register an instrument the registration of which is forbidden by the Caveat.

(2) Where an instrument otherwise affected by sub-section (1) is endorsed with the consent of the caveator, that instrument may be registered.

(3) While a caveat under section 82(b) remains in force the Registrar shall not amend the certificate of title to which the caveat relates.

Only a person claiming an 'interest' or 'estate' in the subject land might lodge a caveat. A sufficient interest to support a caveat (ie, 'caveatable interest') partakes 'of the character of an estate or equitable claim upon the land'.[46]

Duration of a caveat

A caveat ceases to be effective in any of the following circumstances: lapse of time; withdrawal by the caveator; cancellation by the Registrar; and cancellation by order of the court. The relevant provisions are reproduced below.

(i) Lapse by effluxion of time

91 Lapse of caveat

(1) Subject to sub-section (2), a caveat lapses after the expiration of three months from the time it came into force.

(2) Where –

(a) a caveat is lodged with the written consent of –

(i) an equitable mortgagee; or

(ii) the registered proprietor of the land affected by the caveat; or

(b) the caveator has, within the period specified in sub-section (1), taken proceedings in the court to establish his title to the estate or interest specified in the caveat and has given written notice of those proceedings to the Registrar,

the caveat does not lapse in accordance with sub-section (1).

46 See Amankwah, Mugambwa and Muroa, *Land Law in Papua New Guinea, op cit*, note 1, pp 207–08.

A person whose caveat has lapsed is prohibited from lodging another caveat on the same grounds (s 92).

(ii) Withdrawal by the caveator

A caveator or his duly authorised agent may at any time before commencement of proceedings in relation to the caveat serve notice to the Registrar to withdraw the caveat (s 93).

(iii) Cancellation by the Registrar

Section 89 gives the Registrar power to cancel a caveat in certain situations:

(1) Where it is proved to the Registrar's satisfaction –

(a) that the estate, interest or claim of the caveator has ceased or been abandoned or withdrawn, or

(b) that the caveator's rights are satisfied or arranged; or

(c) subject to sub-section (2), that the nature of the caveator's estate, interest or claim does not entitle him to forbid the sale or mortgage or other dealing with the land, estate or interest referred to in the caveat,

the Registrar may cancel the caveat.

(2) At least seven days before cancelling a caveat on the ground specified in sub-section (1)(c), the Registrar shall cause notice to be served, in accordance with section 94, on the person who lodged the caveat.

(iv) Removal by order of the court

Any person affected by a caveat may petition the court to order the removal of a caveat or make such order the court deems appropriate. Section 88 reads:

(1) In this section 'affected proprietor', in the case of a caveat –

(a) under section 82(a) – means the proprietor against whose title to deal with an estate or interest a caveat has been lodged and includes a person claiming under a transfer or other instrument signed by the proprietor; and

(b) under section 82(b) – means the person who has made an application under section 153.

(2) Where a caveat has been lodged the affected proprietor may summon the caveator to attend before the court to show cause why he caveat should not be removed.

(3) The court may, on proof that the caveator has been summoned, make such order in the matter and as to costs, either *ex parte* or otherwise, as it deems just.

(4) Without limiting the powers of the court under sub-section (3) the court under that sub-section, may order that the caveat –

(a) continue in force; or

(b) be removed.

(5) The Registrar may make such entries and endorsements as are necessary to give effect to the order of the court.

In determining whether to order the removal of a caveat, the court will look at several factors. These will include whether the caveat complies with the requirements of the Act such as the identification of the interest claimed and the basis of the claim.[47] Most importantly, the caveator must appear to have a sufficient interest to support the caveat. It has been held in several decisions that the courts will not order removal of a caveat in summary proceedings under provisions corresponding with s 88 unless the caveator's claim to the estate or interest appears to be without any foundation or that the interest which justified the caveat no longer exists.[48] The judicial approach is discussed in the following extract.

GENRICH v MAITLAND HOLDINGS PTY LTD [1982] Qd R 58, Full Court of the Supreme Court of Queensland

[The respondents/plaintiffs were the registered proprietors of certain land. They signed a document of sale of the land to the appellants/defendants subject to a formal agreement. Subsequently, a real estate agent drew a formal document of sale which the appellant signed, but which the respondents refused to sign on the ground that it contained terms, which were not in the earlier document. The appellant lodged a caveat against the land under s 98 of the Real Property Act 1861–1980 (Qld). The respondents commenced proceedings under s 99 for the appellants to show cause why the caveat should not be removed (ss 98 and 99 correspond with ss 82 and 88 of the LRA).]

ANDREWS J: The purpose of s 98 ... and s 99 is to preserve the status quo while questions as to title to land or an interest in land are investigated; to protect the rights of any person having or claiming an interest in the land (*Wheeler v Baldwin* (1934–35) 52 CLR 609 at p 622).

It is not essential to support a caveat that the legal right to title to land or interest in land be established when such an application is made.

It was Douglas J who, in *Re Oil Tool Sales Pty Ltd, Classified Pre-Mixed Concrete Pty Ltd, caveator* [1966] QWN II, said that on an application such as this a claim for title to or an interest in land should not be fully litigated; that the effect of a caveat is to prevent any dealing with land, pending the discovery of what the claims of the parties are (*In Re Hitchcock* (1900) 17 WN (NSW) 62); that it is appropriate that matters in issue between the parties be tried otherwise than on such an application.

I think that what Douglas J said there is quite correct.

It does not however mean that the mere fact of making such a claim, even of commencing action to establish it, will support a caveat and entitle such a claimant to prevent a registered proprietor from dealing with the subject land.

In *In Re Caveat No 774 ex p Hodgson* (1873) 3 SCR 142 Cockle CJ held that a caveat ought not to be employed to put a blot on the title, but to establish the right of the caveator. For these reasons one must look at the facts stated in the caveat upon which the caveator's title or interest is said to depend and then at any elaboration of those facts in evidence given upon the application to remove it. Such facts may be subjected to a critical examination to see whether they may support the caveator's claim, without there being any decision upon issues raised by them which would finally dispose of the claim.

47 See *In Re Whalley's Caveat* [1975] Qd R 111.

48 See Whalan, *The Torrens System*, *op cit*, note 1, pp 251–53.

In *In Re Caveat No 773 ex p Hodgson* (1873) 3 SCR 158 at pp 158, 159, Cockle CJ said:

> Now with regard to the question of *onus probandi*, respecting which a great deal was said, I think that in this case, as in every other case, the *onus probandi* rests upon him who takes out the summons. There may be exceptional cases, but in general we know that when a rule is taken out calling upon a person to show cause why he should not do a certain act, the person taking out the rule is obliged to show a case, a *prima facie* case, or a case as strong as he can make it, in favour of his right to have the act done which he calls upon the other person to show cause why he should not do. So far, I think the *onus probandi* is upon those who seek to withdraw the caveat; but then I must qualify that with this remark: we must take care not to confound the *onus probandi* which is thus thrown upon him who takes out the summons to withdraw the caveat with the burden of proving his title, which is a very different matter. The title may incidentally come into question, because the strength of the title may show the weakness of the caveator's claim, and if it comes incidentally into question no doubt this title may be canvassed. I therefore agree with counsel that the *onus probandi* of proving his title is on him who takes out the summons; but whether his title be good or bad, if the caveator's title is displaced, why then the person who takes out the summons must succeed. Now I shall apply that principle here, as I should in all cases. I say that it is sufficient if the person whose caveat is put on shows a colourable title. More than that is not required; less than that will not suffice. There must be a colourable title; that is to say, a fairly arguable title – such a title that the court or a judge will not undertake to dispose of it summarily.

Although the procedure in New South Wales which is discussed in *Wheeler v Baldwin* (*supra*) particularly at pp 622–23 for establishing and disposing of issues in applications under s 27 of the Real Property Act 1900 of New South Wales has not been adopted in Queensland I think that some assistance appears in the following passage from the decision of Dixon J (as he then was) at pp 628 and 629 in *Wheeler v Baldwin* (*supra*) in which he discussed some cases touching upon the burden of proof in an application to remove a caveat:

> In *In Re Marshall* ... the court refused to allow to a caveator setting up a possessory title an issue whether a conveyance made fifty years before was bad as a pretenced title, in the absence of an affidavit that the conveying party was at the date of the conveyance out of possession of the land. In *Brancker v Stewart* ... the court ordered the removal of a caveat setting up a possessory title because, consistently with the facts stated in the caveat, the caveator, who relied upon possession of the previous occupier to make up the full statutory period, might have been an independent trespasser whose possession was not derivative.

Further on p 629 Dixon J said 'That to enable him to lodge a caveat, the caveator must have some right falling within the description, estate, interest, lien or charge, is not open to dispute', and pointed out that an order settling issues might be rescinded upon the ground that it appeared that a caveator had no estate or interest in land. I would hold that the burden of proof upon the respondents to the appeal was a burden of showing that the facts upon which the caveat is said to rest do not support a claim to an estate or interest in the land; that the caveator must then undertake to show that issues exist which so tend to support a colourable title as to justify prevention of dealings with that land until they have been decided in appropriate proceedings – in this case by action.

[His Honour held that on the facts presented there was no concluded contract of sale between the parties. Hence, the appellants had no sufficient interest to support the caveat. Wanstall and Williams JJ agreed.]

Questions

1 What is a 'colourable title'? Why is the caveator only required to put before the court materials sufficient to show 'a colourable title'?

2 X is the registered proprietor of a State lease. He enters into a contract to sell the lease to Y. The sale is subject to Y's bank giving him a loan. While waiting for the Bank's decision, Y receives information that X is planning to mortgage the land. Y's lawyer immediately lodges a caveat against the subject land. X wants the caveat removed. Advise X. (See, eg, *Re Bosca Land Pty Ltd's Caveat* [1976] Qd R 119 (cf *Kuper & Kuper v Keywest Construction Pty Ltd et al* [1990] WAR 419).)

Wrongful lodgment of a caveat

To prevent abuse of the caveat procedure, s 90 of the Land Registration Act provides that any aggrieved person may sue for damages a person who lodges a caveat without a reasonable excuse. In *Young v Rydalmere Credits Pty Ltd*,[49] Macfarlan J explained with reference to corresponding provisions of the New South Wales Act:

> The Real Property Act provides machinery with respect to the use of caveats, and when the machinery is invoked a caveat is said to be lodged. Section 98, as I see it, implies the existence of that machinery and that in accordance with its process a caveat has been lodged but then defines a further field of use of that machinery without reasonable cause. I cannot feel any doubt about the meaning of the phrase 'reasonable cause'. It consist of two words and whether the words are considered separately or together their meaning is, I think, well understood by lawyer and layman, alike. Whether there has been an absence of reasonable cause requires, I think, a consideration of the circumstances existing both before and at the time when the caveat was lodged. In those circumstances, did the defendant lodge the caveat with reasonable cause, or without?

The role of caveats in resolving priorities between competing unregistered claims

Priority over competing unregistered interests of Torrens system title is determined by reference to the underlying law principles, which apply to competing equitable interests.[50] The general rule is that where equities are equal the one who acquired his interest first prevails. Equities are not equal where the one who acquired his interest first is guilty of serious misconduct, which led the subsequent equity holder to act to his prejudice. In such a situation, the court will postpone his earlier equity to that of the latter.[51] For example, if A, the registered proprietor, in 1999 creates an equitable mortgage in favour of B, and in 2000 he creates a second equitable mortgage in favour of C (who is unaware of B's), B's mortgage having been created earlier would have priority over that of C. But if by his conduct B led C to believe on reasonable grounds that B's mortgage had been discharged (for example, where B signed an instrument which indicated that the

49 (1963) 80 WN (NSW) 1463, 1473.

50 *Breskvar v Wall* (1971) 126 CLR 376, at 388, *per* Barwick CJ.

51 *Rice v Rice* (1853) 2 Drew 73; 61 ER 646; *Abigail v Lapin* [1934] AC 491.

secured debt had been fully paid, when in fact it had not) B might lose his first in time priority.[52] The question is whether if B did not lodge a caveat the courts would treat his failure as such a serious omission as to justify postponement of his first in time priority. This is a controversial issue as the materials below illustrate.

BUTLER v FAIRCLOUGH AND ANOTHER [1971] 23 CLR 78, High Court of Australia

[One G was the registered proprietor of a Crown lease under the Transfer of Land Act 1915 (Victoria). The lease was subject to a registered mortgage. On 30 June 1915, G created a second mortgage in favour of the plaintiff (appellant). The mortgage was under seal but it was not registered. On 2 July, G entered into a contract to sell his lease to the respondent/defendant. G represented to the respondent that the land was only subject to the registered mortgage. The respondent searched the register, which confirmed that the land was only subject to one registered mortgage as represented by G. On 7 July, the appellant lodged a caveat claiming an equitable mortgage. On 12 July, the respondent submitted the instruments of transfer to the Registrar, but the instruments were not registered because of the caveat lodged by the appellant. The parties held several meetings. Subsequently, the respondent was registered as proprietor of the lease subject only to the registered mortgage. The appellant brought these proceedings claiming that the respondent fraudulently registered his title in order to defeat the appellant's equitable mortgage.]

GRIFFITH CJ [His Honour dismissed the appellant's allegations that the respondent was registered through fraud. Nonetheless he proceeded to consider whether in any event the appellant's equitable title had priority over the respondent's equitable claim prior to the registration]: [I]t is necessary to consider the question whether the view then taken as to the plaintiff's priority was well founded or ill founded. It must now be taken to be well settled that under the Australian system of registration of titles to land the courts will recognise equitable estates and rights except so far as they are precluded from doing so by the Statutes. This recognition is, indeed, the foundation of the scheme of caveats which enable such rights to be temporarily protected in anticipation of legal proceedings. In dealing with such equitable rights the courts in general act upon the principles which are applicable to equitable interests in land which is not subject to the Acts. In the case of a contest between two equitable claimants the first in time, all other things being equal, is entitled to priority. But all other things must be equal, and the claimant who is first in time may lose his priority by any act or omission which had or might have had the effect of inducing a claimant later in time to act to his prejudice. Thus, if an equitable mortgagee of lands allows the mortgagor to retain possession of the title deeds, a person dealing with the mortgagor on the faith of that possession is entitled to priority in the absence of special circumstances to account for it.

Under the Australian system a clear title on the register is, for some purposes at any rate, equivalent to possession of the title deeds. A person who has an equitable charge upon the land may protect it by lodging a caveat, which in my opinion operates as notice to all the world that the registered proprietor's title is subject to the equitable interest alleged in the caveat. In the present case the plaintiff might, if he had been sufficiently diligent, have registered his charge of 30 June on that day. The defendant, having before parting with the

52 *Rice v Rice* (1853) 2 Drew 73; 61 ER 646.

purchase money to Good found on searching the register that Good had a clear title, and relying on the absence of any notice of defect in Good's title, paid the agreed price.

The question then seems to be: had the plaintiff when the defendant acquired his equitable right taken or failed to take all reasonable steps to prevent Good from dealing with the land without notice of plaintiff's title? ...

It is contended that the holder of an equitable charge is entitled to a longer time than a day before protecting his title by a caveat. If a man having a registrable instrument neither lodges it for registration nor lodges a caveat to protect it, it is clear that a registrable instrument later in date, but lodged before his, will have precedence, notwithstanding notice of the earlier instrument received before lodging his own. That is by reason of the express provisions of the Statute. But why should not the same principle apply in the case of equitable interests? The alternative view would in effect give as great validity to an unregistered equitable assignment unprotected by caveat as to a registrable instrument lodged for registration.

I feel unable to draw any line prescribing the time within which a caveat should be lodged. The person who does not act promptly loses the advantage which he would have gained by promptitude.

For these reasons I come to the conclusion that if a suit had been brought on 3 July [the day after the contract of sale to the defendant] between the plaintiff and defendant raising the question of priority the defendant would have been entitled to succeed ...

ISAACS J: In my opinion, in the absence of some clear explanation justifying or excusing this failure ... [to lodge a caveat] it is one which, at all events in so simple a case as an equitable mortgage, postpones the mortgagee to the person *bona fide* misled by the result of a search as in the present case. The protection given by the Act to an unregistered and, perhaps, unregistrable transaction is coupled with the price of diligence in guarding others against loss arising through ignorance of the transaction.

[Barton J concurred. Other judgments omitted.]

Notes

In the above case, arguably the respondent was 'misled' by the absence of a caveat in believing that there were no unregistered claims against the land. Compare this case with *Lapin and Another v Abigail* [1930] 44 CLR 166. There the Lapins, who had a prior equitable interest, did not lodge a caveat, but Abigail who subsequently acquired an equitable mortgage over the same land did not search the Register before advancing the loan. The High Court of Australia by majority decision held that though the Lapins were negligent in not lodging a caveat, Abigail was not misled by their omission since he did not search the Register before advancing the loan on security of the land. On further appeal, the Privy Council reversed the decision (see *Abigail v Lapin and Another* [1934] AC 491). Lord Wright, at 501–03, observed:

The Full Court of New South Wales regarded the present case as governed in principle by *Butler v Fairclough* [(1917) 23 CLR 78] where there was a conflict of equities between a prior equitable incumbrancer who had lodged no caveat and a subsequent transferee who had, after a search of the register and without notice of the unregistered equitable charge, paid the purchase consideration. It was held that the former was to be postponed ...

Their Lordships think that case was rightly decided ... But the only distinction between *Butler v Fairclough* ... and the present case appears to be that in the present case it was not proved that (though he had no notice of the prior charge) Abigail made any search before lending the money ... The question is whether in such a case as this, where the title on the register was clear, the failure to prove a search by the second incumbrancee can make any difference. There is no reason to think that Heavener [the rogue who fraudulently mortgaged the land] would have ventured to claim that Mrs Heavener [an accomplice to the fraud] was proprietor in fee simple unless she was so registered, and in that sense the grant of the transfer by the respondents to her did cause or contribute to Abigail's lending the money. A search by or on behalf of Abigail's would merely have shown that the transfer purported to be for full consideration, thus excluding any idea of it being by way of security.

In the following case, the High Court of Australia revisited the issue whether failure to lodge a caveat affects the first in time priority.

J & H JUST (HOLDING) PTY LTD v THE BANK OF NEW SOUTH WALES AND OTHERS
[1971] 125 CLR 546, High Court of Australia

[One Josephson was the registered proprietor of the subject land under the Real Property Act 1900–70 (NSW). The Bank (defendant/respondent) lent him money on security of a mortgage created by deposit of the certificate of title with the Bank and a memorandum of mortgage executed by Josephson. The Bank did not register the mortgage nor lodge a caveat. Evidence was given at the trial that it was not an uncommon practice in Sydney for financial institutions to rely on the security of an unregistered memorandum of mortgage accompanied by a deposit of the certificate of title. Subsequently Josephson sought to borrow money from the plaintiffs/appellants on security of the same land. He represented to the appellants that the land was unencumbered and that the certificate of title was merely with the Bank for safekeeping. Before advancing the money, the appellants' solicitor searched the Register and neither found any encumbrances noted on the certificate of title nor any caveat. However, he made no enquiry with the Bank to ascertain the terms on which it kept the certificate of title. Josephson executed a memorandum of mortgage in the appellants' favour. The appellants commenced proceedings for a declaration that its equitable mortgage had priority over that of the Bank even though the latter was first in time. The lower courts held that there were not sufficient grounds for postponement of the Bank's prior equity. On further appeal to the High Court.]

BARWICK CJ: Much has been said in the course of this case about the failure of the Bank to lodge with the Registrar General a caveat against dealings. It is important in this connection to observe the nature and purpose of what is sometimes called an unofficial caveat', distinguishing a caveat lodged by a private person from a caveat lodged by the Registrar General ... It is directed to the Registrar General and may properly be given by a person claiming an estate or interest in the land, against dealings with which it is lodged. It must describe the estate or interest claimed ... Its purpose is to act as an injunction to the Registrar General to prevent registration of dealings with the land until notice has been given to the caveator. This enables the caveator to pursue such remedies as he may have against the person lodging the dealing for registration. The purpose of the caveat is not to give notice to the world or to persons who may consider dealing with the registered proprietor of the caveator's estate or interest though if noted on the certificate of title, it may operate to give such notice. If the caveator does not take proceedings in due time against the person who has lodged a dealing for registration, and the dealing is registered, awareness of the existence of the caveat, and through it, that an estate or interest is claimed by the caveator, will be irrelevant except possibly as an element in establishing fraud in the procurement of the registration. But of itself such awareness will not vitiate of the registration ...

In *Abigail v Lapin* ... husband and wife, the respondents, each the registered proprietor of a separate parcel of land each executed a memorandum of transfer in favour of a nominee of a solicitor. The memoranda were executed as security for certain costs and for the payment of a sum due to a bank. As the matter was ultimately viewed, the respondents in executing and handing over the memoranda of transfer had authorized the solicitor to deal with the property but not for his own benefit or for that of his nominee otherwise than a mortgagee. The transfers were subsequently registered in breach of that authority. The transferee became the registered proprietor of the fee simple in each parcel of land. After other dealings, the appellant lent money on the security of registrable memoranda of mortgage of the land executed by the registered proprietor and of the deposit with him of the duplicate certificate of title. Caveats by the respondents prevented registration of these memoranda of mortgage. The respondents sued the appellant and others claiming that they were entitled to an order that the registered proprietor should transfer the land to them free of encumbrances. Thus the case was one in which the equitable interest of the appellant was derived from a registered proprietor who had come to that place on the register by the misuse of his authority from the respondents and possession of the duplicate certificate of title. That interest was in competition with the equitable interest of the respondents, as mortgagors.

The lodgment of a caveat by the respondents even whilst they were still registered proprietors might well have been thought appropriate, once the duplicate certificates of title and executed memoranda of transfer had been given to the mortgagee. This would be a means of safeguarding themselves against an abuse of the authority which they had given their mortgagee. The respondents in this respect were in a very different situation to that of the Bank. The holder of the executed memoranda of transfer and the duplicate certificate of title was in a position to have the transferee registered as proprietor. Once that person was registered the legal estate in the land would vest in the transferee. But in the case of the Bank no change in the register could properly take place without its concurrence. The difference in the need of the parties for protection against the registration of dealings is thus quite clear.

But it was the respondents' conduct in thus arming the mortgagee with the capacity to become the registered proprietor and able to deal with others as such and not any failure by them to lodge a caveat that was decisive in *Abigail v Lapin* ... Their Lordships' decision was an application of Kindersley VC's judgment in *Rice v Rice* [(1853) 2 Drew 73; 61 ER 646] from which Lord Wright quotes a passage ... adopted as setting out the relevant principles for resolving the competition of the parties' interest in the land. Ultimately 'the case then becomes one of an agent exceeding the limits of his authority but acting within its apparent *indicia' per* Lord Wright ... I emphasize these aspects of the decision *Abigail v Lapin* ... by the Privy Council because, once it is recognized that the respondents' conduct in handing over the memoranda of transfer and the duplicate certificates of title provided the *ratio decidendi*, much of what Lord Wright says about the consequences of a failure by a claimant to an equitable interest to lodge a caveat and particularly his comments on *Butler v Fairclough* ... became, in my opinion, *obiter*.

Whilst it may be true in some instances that 'the register may bear on its face a notice of equitable claims', this is not necessarily so and whilst in some instances a caveat of which the lodgment is noted in the certificate of title may be 'notice to all the world' that the registered proprietor's title is subject to the equitable interest alleged in the caveat this, in my opinion, is not necessarily universally the case. To hold that a failure by a person entitled to an equitable estate or interest in land under the Real Property Act to lodge a caveat against dealings with the land must necessarily involve the loss of priority which the time of the creation of the equitable interest would otherwise give, is not merely in my opinion unwarranted by general principles or by any statutory provision but would in my opinion be subversive of the well recognized ability of parties to create or to maintain equitable interests in such lands. Sir Owen Dixon's remarks in *Lapin v Abigail* ... with which I respectfully agree, point in this direction.

Of course, there may be situations in which such a failure may combine with other circumstances to justify the conclusion that 'the act or omission proved against' the possessor of the prior equity 'has conduced or contributed to a belief on the part of the holder of the subsequent equity, at the time when he acquired it that the prior equity was not in existence' cf *per* Knox CJ in *Lapin v Abigail* ... This is the relevant principle to apply if it is claimed that the priority of a prior equitable interest has been lost in competition with a subsequent equitable interest:

> In general an earlier equity is not to be postponed to later on unless because of some act or neglect of the prior equitable owner. In order to take away any pre-existing admitted title, that which is relied upon for such a purpose must be shown and proved by those upon whom the burden to show and prove it lies, and ... it must amount to something tangible and distinct, something which can have the grave and strong effect to accomplish the purpose for which it is said to have been produced: *per* Lord Cairns LC in *Shropshire Union Railways and Canal Co v The Queen* ... [(1875) LR 7 HL 496, at 507]. The Act or default of the prior equitable owner must be such as to make it inequitable as between him and the subsequent equitable owner that he should retain his initial priority. This in effect means that his act or default must in some way have contributed to the assumption upon which the subsequent legal owner acted when acquiring his equity: *Lapin v Abigail per* Dixon J ...

In my opinion, the failure to lodge a protective caveat cannot properly be said necessarily to be such an act or default. It could not properly be said to be so in the present case.

Mention should now be made of a second reason why in this case the failure to lodge a caveat could not be held to be privative of the Bank's priority. The Bank held the certificate of title and a memorandum of mortgage in registrable form. Whilst there is no express provision of the Act which forbids the registration of a dealing without the production of the duplicate certificate of title, it is the practice of the Registrar General's office to refuse to accept an instrument of transfer or mortgage for registration without production of the duplicate certificate of title, unless the certificate is already in the Registrar General's hands. See Baalman and Wells: *Land Titles Office Practice* (NSW), 3rd edn (1952), at pp 225, 226. Thus a person in the situation of the Bank could reasonably rely upon this practice and his possession of the duplicate certificate of title as a reasonably sufficient protection. Of course, a provisional certificate of title may be issued by the Registrar General if the duplicate is lost, mislaid or destroyed: s 111. The stringency of proof required by the Registrar General before issuing a provisional certificate may be gauged by a perusal of the departmental instructions set out in Baalman and Wells, at p 280. A person in the situation of the Bank in this case does run the remote risk of a fraudulent claim being made to the Registrar General by the borrower in order to obtain a provisional certificate. But, in my opinion, such a person is not to assume such criminal conduct on the part of the registered proprietor.

In any case the failure by such a person to lodge a protective caveat cannot of itself properly be held to be an act fulfilling the requirements to which I have referred of conduct which will deprive a prior equity of its priority. As I have said, the purpose of the caveat is protective: it is not to give notice. The holder of the subsequent equity in my opinion could not properly rely upon the absence of any notification in the register book of the lodgment of a caveat as a representation or as the basis for a conclusion that no equitable interest in the land existed in any person. In my opinion the conclusion and the reasoning of the Court of Appeal Division were correct on this aspect of the case ...

MENZIES J: I agree with the judgment of the Court of Appeal. I would merely add that, in doing so, I am not, I think differing at all from what was said by Griffith CJ in *Butler v Fairclough* ... or by Lord Wright in *Abigail v Lapin* ... about a caveat operating by way of notice to protect the equitable interest therein alleged. Furthermore, I see wisdom in using a caveat for this purpose. It is not to be disregarded that the form of caveat in the 16th Schedule to the Act makes provision for a record to be made thereon of the entry of its particulars in the register book. This statutory form is not only ample warrant for the Registrar General making such an entry; it is an indication from the Act itself that this should be done. The reason for such an entry must be to give notice of the caveat.

WINDEYER J: I agree entirely in the judgment of the Chief Justice. Merely to emphasize my agreement I shall briefly state my view of the effect of the Bank's not lodging a caveat against dealings, the matter in the forefront of the appellant's argument.

Mr Baalman's statement, in his helpful work, *The Torrens System in New South Wales*, at p 170, that 'the price of protection of an unregistered interest is the lodgment of a caveat', would be misleading if it be read as meaning that an equitable interest arising from an unregistered instrument must always succumb unless it be afforded the protection of a caveat. Harvey CJ in Eq, in *Thomson v Richardson* ... [(1928) 29 SR (NSW) 221, at p 223] described the essence of a caveat against dealings – as distinct from a Registrar General's caveat – as follows: 'The caveat is no blot on the title. It is simply a claim by somebody that he shall receive notice before any dealing with the land is carried through.'

Too much has I think been read into the statement by Griffith CJ in *Butler v Fairclough* ... repeated by Lord Wright in the Privy Council in *Abigail v Lapin*:

> A person who has an equitable charge upon the land may protect it by lodging a caveat, which in my opinion operates as notice to all the world that the registered proprietor's title is subject to the equitable interest alleged in the caveat.

It is the practice of the Registrar General to note a caveat upon the relevant folium of the register book, although the Act does not require him to do so and a caveat is not a dealing. A caveat noted in the register book is no doubt a notice, to anyone who searches at the Registrar General's Office, of the caveator's claim. I understand that the Registrar General records all documents as they are lodged and that he lists caveats as if they were dealings and that this record is available for inspection. It is perhaps a register kept under the Act within the meaning of s 43(2). However, the fact that a caveat discoverable by a search of the title is 'notice to all the world' of the interest claimed does not mean that the absence of a caveat is a notice to all and sundry that no interest is claimed. To say that would, it seems, be to equate the noting of a caveat in the register book with the registration of a dealing: it would make competing equitable interests depend not upon priority of creation in time and other equitable considerations, but upon priority of the lodgment of caveats. After all, the primary purpose of a caveat against dealings is not to give notice to the world of an interest. It is to warn the Registrar General of a claim. The word caveat has long been used in law to describe a notice given to an official not to take some step without giving the caveator an opportunity to oppose it. According to the Oxford English Dictionary that sense of the word goes back to 1654. If a person intending to deal with a registered proprietor becomes aware of a caveat, it is notice to him of a claim that an interest is outstanding: and then: caveat emptor; *qui ignorare non debuit quod jus alienum emit*. But a caveat is not the only way in which a purchaser from the registered proprietor can be made aware of the prior equitable claims of another person. It is merely one way, and no doubt a very sure way, in which such a claimant may protect his interest against its subversion by the registered proprietor in favour of another person ...

I can understand that a bank may, for good reasons, not wish to give notice to all the world that it has a charge over a customer's land to secure this overdraft. It may prefer to protect itself by obtaining and retaining possession of the duplicate certificate of title, without producing which no one can register a dealing with the land. I interpolate here that I use the words 'duplicate certificate of title' to denote the deed issued to the registered proprietor in distinction from the corresponding folium of the register book. That is the common usage of the term; and it is I think the sense of the words in s 40; but I am aware that s 32(1) states that 'The Registrar General shall keep a book, to be called the 'register book', and shall bind up therein the duplicates of all grants and certificates of title'.

If, as I see the case, the equitable interest of the Bank is not to be lost or postponed because the Bank did not lodge a caveat, it seems to me irrelevant to enquire whether the appellant was prudent or imprudent in not prosecuting further enquiries before it lent money to the registered proprietor thinking it had the land as security. The conduct of the appellant would only be material if the Bank, by some conduct on its part, had lost the priority in equity which arose from the priority of its transaction in point of time. The Bank did not by not lodging a caveat warning the Registrar General representing to the appellant that it had no claim. It relied upon its possession of a registrable instrument and a clean duplicate certificate of title. It is not to suffer because the registered proprietor made a statement to the appellant that was very far from frank in explanation of the Bank's having his duplicate certificate of title.

I would dismiss the appeal.

[McTiernan J agreed.]

Notes

Whalan, *The Torrens System in Australia, op cit*, footnote 1, p 246, criticises the High Court's decision. He writes:

> Certainly the decision accords with the practice of many banks of holding a mortgage unregistered together with the duplicate certificate of title, but it does give an importance to the duplicate certificate of title that the Torrens system probably never intended ... The decision downgrades the importance of a prospective dealer with land finding a clear Register; he must also find the duplicate certificate of title. It downgrades the importance that has been accorded to the existence of the caveat procedure as being the prime method of protecting rights before registration. The inference from previous decisions has been that the way to prevent the first-in-time priority being lost through negligence was to lodge a

> caveat. It now seems that there are at least two ways to preserve this priority: either lodge a caveat or secure possession of the duplicate certificate of title.

In contrast, Sykes, *The Law of Securities*, p 468, agrees with the High Court's decision. He submits, at 470:

> ... the treatment of failure to lodge a caveat as the sole ground for postponement can only be justified on the footing of actual evidence as to the conveyancing situation in the State concerned, viz, evidence that failure to lodge a caveat by the possessor of an equitable interest is tantamount to negligence on his part.
>
> It may then well be that in Victoria decisions that failure to lodge a caveat may operate as a *sole* ground of postponement are justified on such evidence and that in some other jurisdictions such failure may operate together with other facts of neglect, as auxiliary ground. However, in States where a caveat is of limited duration unless lodged with consent or even in States where it is current practice to take an unregistered interest without caveating, it is submitted that the omission to lodge a caveat has little significance and would hardly amount to a relevant factor.

The High Court of Australia in *Leros Pty Ltd v Terara Pty Ltd and Another* (1992) 106 ALR 595, at 602, citing *J & H Just (Holding) Pty Ltd v The Bank of New South Wales and Others* (1192) 174 CLR 407, at 419, affirmed that failure to lodge a caveat does not necessarily lead to loss of priority.

Questions

1 Do you agree with the reasoning in *J & H Just v The Bank of New South Wales and Others*?

2 Is there any policy reason why failure to lodge a caveat should not by itself be a sufficient ground for postponement of the first-in-time priority?

3 In practice, what significance do lawyers in PNG attach to the absence of a caveat in a title search process? Should the courts consider the legal practice in deciding whether failure to lodge a caveat justifies postponement of the first-in-time priority?

IV REMEDIES FOR WRONGFUL DEPRIVATION OF AN INTEREST IN LAND

Under the Land Registration Act, a person wrongfully deprived of his land may bring an action of ejectment and or damages against the wrongdoer, or in an appropriate case seek compensation from the Registrar. We consider each of these remedies.

Ejectment

Section 146 of the Land Registration Act prescribes circumstances in which an action of ejectment can be brought against a registered proprietor.[53] The section provides as follows:

53 See also ss 11 and 33.

Ejectment against a registered proprietor

(1) Subject to sub-section (2), a certificate of title is an absolute bar and estoppel to an action of ejectment against the person named in the certificate of title as seised of or entitled to the land.

(2) Sub-section (1) does not prevent an action of ejectment against a proprietor if the action is brought by –

(a) a mortgagee against a mortgagor; or

(b) a chargee against a chargor; or

(c) a lessor against a lessee or tenant; or

(d) a person deprived of land by fraud against a person registered as proprietor through fraud; or

(e) a person deprived of land by fraud, subject to sub-section (3), against a person deriving from or through a person registered as proprietor through fraud; or

(f) a person deprived of land by reason of a wrong description of land or of its boundaries; or

(g) a registered proprietor claiming under a prior certificate of title where two certificates are registered under this Act in respect of the same land; or

(h) a registered proprietor claiming under a prior State lease registered under this Act where two State leases are registered under this Act in respect of the same land.

(3) This Act does not subject to an action for ejectment a purchaser or a mortgagee, acting in good faith and for valuable consideration.

(4) The operation of sub-section (3) is not affected by the fact that the vendor or mortgagor, as the case may be –

(a) was registered through fraud or error; or

(b) derives from or through a person registered as proprietor through fraud or error, whether by wrong description of land or of its boundaries or otherwise.

(5) For the purpose of bringing an action of ejectment against a person registered as proprietor, the registration of that person is equivalent to possession by him of the land in respect of which the action is brought.

Note that the combined effect of sub-sections 3 and 4 is to protect a *bona fide* purchaser for value even though he bought from a fraudulent person. Where the action for ejectment is successful, the court has the power to make such order as is necessary to rectify the Register Book.[54]

Compensation of a person deprived of land

Where a person is deprived of an estate or interest in land because of the operation of the system of registration of titles, he may sue for damages under s 150. The section states:

54 Section 149 of the LRA.

150 Damages for deprivation of land

(1) Subject to this section, where a person is deprived of an estate or interest in consequence of –

(a) fraud; or

(b) the issue of a certificate of title to another person; or

(c) an entry, or an error or omission in any entry, in the Register Book; or

(d) an error or omission in a certificate of title,

he may bring an action in the court for the recovery of damages against the person who derived benefit by the fraud or in consequence of a circumstance specified in Paragraph (b), (c) or (d).

(2) Where a person against whom an action may be brought under sub-section (1) –

(a) is dead; or

(b) has been adjudged insolvent; or

(c) has absconded from the jurisdiction of the court,

that action may, subject to this section, be brought against the Registrar as nominal defendant.

(3) An action under sub-section (1) does not lie against –

(a) the Registrar; or

(b) the person who applied to be registered as proprietor in respect of the estate or interest; or

(c) the person certifying an instrument,

unless the action is commenced within the period of six years after the date of the deprivation.

(4) Sub-section (1) does not subject to an action for damages a purchaser or a mortgagee, acting in good faith and for valuable consideration.

(5) The operation of sub-section (4) is not affected by the fact that the vendor or mortgagor, as the case may be –

(a) was registered as proprietor through fraud or error; or

(b) derives from or through a person registered as proprietor through fraud or error, whether by wrong description of land or of its boundaries or otherwise.

(6) For the purpose of bringing an action under sub-section (1) against a person registered as proprietor, the registration of that person is equivalent to possession by him of the estate or interest in respect of which the action is brought.

(7) Where damages are awarded in an action under this section against –

(a) the Registrar; or

(b) any other person,

and the Sheriff or an officer of the Sheriff –

(c) makes a return of *nulla bona*; or

(d) certifies that the full amount with costs awarded cannot be recovered from the judgment debtor,

the judgment creditor may apply to the court for a certificate as to those matters.

For purposes of s 150, a person is not 'deprived' of his title except in circumstances where by virtue of the Act he faces an irrevocable loss or defeat by a superior title. For a good illustration of this rule, see the '*Breskvars* saga' in *Breskvar v Wall* (see extract above) and *Breskvar v White* (extracted below).

Who is liable under s 150?

(i) Wrongdoer

Section 150(1) of the LRA provides that a person deprived of an interest in land can bring an action for damages against the 'person who derived benefit by the fraud' or in consequence of one of the circumstances specified in sub-section (1)(b), (c) or (d).

(ii) Registrar

If the 'wrongdoer' is dead, or insolvent, or has absconded the jurisdiction, the action for damages may be brought against the Registrar as nominal defendant. Damages awarded against the Registrar are payable out of the Assurance fund.[55] An action for damages may also be brought against the Registrar where a person suffers loss or damages through an omission, mistake or misfeasance of the Registrar or other officers in the exercise of their duty (s 151). As under s 150, damages and costs awarded against the Registrar are payable out of the Assurance Fund (s 151(5) and (6)).

Assurance fund

This is a fund established under s 138 of the Land Registration Act, built up by contributions and fees levied against persons on registration of interests (s 137). An action to recover damages against the Registrar must be brought within a period of six years from the date of deprivation (s 150(3)(a)). This case illustrates the practical difficulties of complying with this requirement.

BRESKVAR v WHITE [1978] Qd R 187, Supreme Court of Queensland

[This is a continuation of the *Breskvars* saga.[56] On 15 October 1968, Wall, through fraud committed by his agent (Petrie), became the registered proprietor of the Breskvars' land. On 31 October 1968, Wall sold the land to A Pty Ltd, an innocent party, which thereby acquired an equitable interest. Before A Pty Ltd registered their title, the Breskvars lodged a caveat to prevent registration. Hence A Pty Ltd's title was not registered. In subsequent proceedings, the Supreme Court held, on 18 March 1971, that A Pty Ltd's equitable interest prevailed over that of the Breskvars and ordered the Registrar to remove the caveat. In the same judgment, the court awarded damages to the Breskvars against Petrie and Wall under s 126 of the Real Property Act (which corresponds with s 150(1) of the LRA). The High Court subsequently upheld this decision.[57] In February 1977, the Breskvars unsuccessfully

55 Section 150(7)–(9), see below.

56 (1972) 126 CLR 76, see extract above.

57 *Breskvar v Wall* (1972) 126 CLR 76.

attempted to execute the judgment against Wall (Petrie having died). On 8 March 1977, the Sheriff issued a certificate to the effect that Wall had not sufficient funds to cover all the costs and damages. On 14 March 1977, they petitioned the Governor for payment out of the Assurance Fund (procedure similar to s 150(7)). The issue was whether their petition for payment was time-barred.]

CONNOLLY J: It was agreed by the parties that the specific question I am to decide is whether the period of six years mentioned in the proviso to s 127 [this corresponds with s 150(3) of the LRA] ... had run when the Governor was asked for his warrant on March 14 last ... [I]t is the Crown's contention that the cause of action referred to in the proviso is in this case the cause of action which is the subject of s 126 [this corresponds with s 151 of the LRA].

To understand the argument of the applicants it is necessary to examine the first limb of s 127 [corresponds with s 150(2) of the LRA]. It provides that in case the person against whom 'such action for damages' (and this must mean the action for the recovery of damages which is the subject of s 126) is directed to be set out in s 126: 'shall be dead or shall have been adjudged insolvent or shall have absconded out of the jurisdiction of the Supreme Court then in such case it shall be lawful to bring an action for damages against the Registrar General as Nominal Defendant for the purposes of recovering the amount of the said damages and costs against the assurance fund hereinbefore described.' It will be seen that the first limb of s 127 itself creates a statutory cause of action against the Registrar General as Nominal Defendant. It is argued that the natural way to read the phrase 'the cause of action' in the first proviso to s 127 is to treat it as referring to the first antecedent to which it can naturally be referred and that is to the newly created statutory cause of action which is the subject of the earlier part of the section itself. Section 126 contains its own period of limitation in its own first proviso. The argument is that the first proviso to s 127 has nothing to say in relation to judgments recovered under s 126.

Mr Moynihan for the Crown, however, says that the language of the first proviso to s 127 is quite general and that it applies whenever payment of any damages is sought from the assurance fund.

I should say first that in my opinion the first limb of s 127 creates a fresh statutory cause of action which is related to, but not the same as, that which is created by s 126. The arising of the cause of action under the first limb of s 127 requires a concurrence of the existence of a cause of action under s 126 and either the death, insolvency or absconding of the person benefited ... The Crown contends that the cause of action under the first limb of s 127 is alternative to that which is created by s 126 and I incline to think this is correct although it is unnecessary to express a concluded opinion on the point.

Now the Crown's reading of these provisions certainly results in an anomalous situation in that, in a case in which it is necessary to obtain payment of the judgment from the assurance fund, the applicant can never avail himself of the full period of limitation allowed by the first proviso to s 126. In many cases a plaintiff under s 126 would have no way of knowing that the defendant might prove to be insolvent when after litigating his claim and possibly conducting an appeal or appeals he ultimately came to execute his judgment. Bearing in mind that litigants have only a limited degree of control over the time which may be involved between issue of proceedings and the execution of judgment, it is obvious that a litigant who ultimately needs payments from the assurance fund should commence his proceedings early rather than late in the six year period. This means that for him the six year period of limitation is really illusory. If, therefore, s 127 were open to a construction which would avoid this anomaly I should adopt it.

Unfortunately, I do not think that it is. The second limb of s 127 deals with all of the situations in which judgments fall to be satisfied out of the fund. The causes of action upon which these judgments are recovered are those created by ss 126 and 127. The first proviso to s 127 does not in truth limit the time within which actions may be brought and to treat it as confining payment out of the fund to cases in which the judgment is brought on the cause of action created by the first limb of s 127 is to give it a restricted application for which, as it seems to me, there is no warrant in the language. If it had been intended to provide a limitation period in respect of actions under the first limb it would I think have been more natural to have used the form of words employed in the first proviso to s 126 and to provide that no such action should lie or be sustained after the chosen period.

The conclusion to which I have come accepts the anomalous situation to which I have referred above in relation to causes of action under s 126. But the situation under the first limb of s 127 is really not very different. The claimant must still not merely initiate his proceedings but carry them to the point at which he can perfect a judgment which entitles him to present payment from the fund and obtain the Governor's warrant within six years of the death, insolvency or absconding of the person benefited. The provision is stringent but in my view no other reading is open.

The earliest date on which the Treasurer could have been asked for payment against the assurance fund was 14 March 1977 when the Governor's warrant was sought. I have already expressed the view that the Breskvars were deprived of their land on 31 October 1968 when Wall created in favour of Alban Pty Ltd the equitable interest in that land which proved to be superior to their equity against Wall. The judgment of Hart J was delivered on 18 March 1971 and if their cause of action under s 126 arose on that date the period of six years would still not have elapsed. But it was not the court which deprived the Breskvars of their land it was the act of Wall in selling to Alban Pty Ltd and I must therefore, although with regret, declare that the assurance fund is not liable for the payment of the damages, the subject of the certificate of Williams J of 10 March 1977.

[Connolly J held that the Breskvars were nevertheless entitled to be paid their costs out of the Assurance Fund as the bar created by the proviso to s 127 was silent as to costs.]

Questions

1 Can the traditional owners of land in the case such as, *The Administrator of the Territory of Papua and New Guinea v Blasius Tirupia and Others* [1971–72] PNGLR 229, sue for compensation under s 150 or s 151?

3 Assume that two years ago the National government acquired land by purchase from clan X. The land was leased to Paul Pty Ltd which had the lease registered under the Land Registration Act. Paul Pty Ltd later sold to Sanyu Pty Ltd. The latter is currently the registered proprietor of the subject leasehold. It has recently transpired that the subject land includes a portion of land, which belongs to members of clan Y. Advise the elders of clan Y of all possible legal causes of action (including names of potential defendants) and available remedies.

Note

In *Keimbun Keindip v The Independent State of Papua New Guinea and Others* [1993] PNGLR 28, at 33–34 (extracted above, p 459), Newell AJ expressed a view that compensation from the Assurance Fund under s 151 of the LRA was not payable or may be reduced if the claimant's negligence contributed to his or her loss. For example, the court may order reduction of the compensation payable where the claimant failed to carry out a proper title search, which could have revealed error in the registry.

V NATIONAL LANDS REGISTRATION

The Commission of Inquiry into Land Matters (CILM) in its report recommended that government land should be declared 'National land' and registered in a special National Land Register.[58] This proposal was prompted by numerous cases in which the traditional landowners disputed the State's title to land, especially, in urban areas. The CILM felt that the State's title over land required for public purposes should be protected against dispute in any court of law.[59] Following its recommendations, in 1977 the National Parliament enacted the National Land Registration Act (Ch No 357). The preamble declares the objectives of this Act:

> Being an Act to –
>
> (a) establish a Register of National land; and
>
> (b) make provision for the registration in the Register of National Land of all land acquired or to be acquired by the State on or after Independence Day; and
>
> (c) make provision for the registration in the Register of National Land acquired before Independence Day by a pre-Independence Administration in Papua New Guinea and which is now required for a public purpose; and
>
> (d) give effect to section 54(a) (*special provision in respect of certain lands*) of the Constitution by providing for the recognition of the title of the State to certain land that is required for public purposes, the title to which may be, or may appear to be, in doubt; and
>
> (e) settle grievances in relation to the land described in Paragraph (d) by providing for certain settlement payments; and
>
> (f) declare and describe, for the purposes of section 53(1) (*protection from unjust deprivation of property*) of the Constitution, certain matters as public purposes and justified reasons for the acquisition of property,
>
> and make provision for those and related purposes.

For purposes of the Act, State land is grouped into two categories: land acquired by a pre-Independence administration[60] and land acquired by the government after Papua New Guinea's Independence Day.

---

58 Recommendation 51, Report of the CILM, Port Moresby, October 1973.

59 John Mugambwa, 'Land disputes in PNG: a colonial legacy and post-Independence solutions' (1987) 15 Melanesian Law Journal 94, p 110.

60 See s 1 of the National Land Registration Act, for definition of 'pre-independence administration'.

Land acquired before Independence Day

Land acquired before Independence Day may be declared National land by following the procedure stipulated in the following sections:

Section 7 Notice of intention to declare National land where land was acquired before Independence Day

1 Where, in the opinion of the Minister –

(a) any land was acquired before Independence Day by a pre-Independence Administration in Papua New Guinea; and

(b) the land is required for a purpose or a reason that is declared or described by section 3 or by an Organic Law or another Act to be –

(i) a public purpose; or

(ii) a reason that is reasonably justified in a democratic society that has a proper regard for the rights and dignity of mankind,

and that is specified in the notice,

the Minister may, by notice in the *National Gazette*, intimate his intention to declare, not earlier than the expiry of three months following the date of publication of the notice, that the land is National land.

2 A notice under sub-section (1) shall –

(a) contain a description of the land; and

(b) where the Minister is of the opinion that there may be a genuine dispute as to whether the land was acquired validly, or at all, from the customary owners – refer to the fact that there may be a genuine dispute as to the acquisition of the land, but the omission of such a reference shall not be deemed to imply that such a genuine dispute does not exist; and

(c) state that any person aggrieved by the notice may make representation to the Minister within 60 days of –

(i) the date of publication of the notice in the *National Gazette*; and

(ii) compliance by the Minister with the requirements of section 52; and

(d) specify the estate acquired in the land.

Section 8 Person aggrieved by notice may make representation to the Minister

Any person aggrieved by a notice under section 7(1) may, within 60 days of –

(a) the date of publication of the notice in the *National Gazette*; and

(b) compliance by the Minister with the requirements of section 52, make representation to the minister.

Section 9 Declaration of National land acquired before Independence Day

Where the Minister has published a notice under section 7(1) in respect of any land, he may –

(a) after the expiry of three months following –

(i) the date of publication of the notice in the *National Gazette*; and

(ii) compliance by him with the requirements of section 52; and

(b) after consideration of any representations made to him under section 8, declare, by notice in the *National Gazette*, that the land, or any part of the land, is National land.

2 A declaration made under sub-section (1) shall –

(a) contain a description of the land; and

(b) specify the estate in the land acquired by the State.

Note that land acquired before Independence Day can only be declared 'National land' where the land is required for a 'public purpose' or for 'a reason that is reasonably justified in a democratic society that has a proper regard for the rights and dignity of mankind'. Purposes, which constitute 'public purposes' within meaning of the Act are declared in s 3:

For the purposes of section 53 (*protection from unjust deprivation of property*) of the Constitution and of this Act, and of any other law –

(a) the following purposes are public purposes:

(i) the purposes defined as public purposes in section 1 of the Land Act; and

(ii) the purpose expressed in section 1 of the Lands Acquisition (Development Purposes Act; and

(iii) a purpose of –

(A) urban development, being development within a town; or

(B) land settlement, including the maintenance of existing land settlement schemes, and declared schemes as defined in the Land Settlement Schemes (Prevention of Disruption) Act and any settlement for the provision of land for land short Papua New Guineans; and

(b) the acquisition of land or of anything on land for a purpose or reason connected with a purpose referred to in Paragraph (a) is an acquisition for a purpose that is reasonably justified and reasonably justifiable in a democratic society that has a proper regard for the rights and dignity of mankind.

Land acquired on or after Independence Day

Any land acquired by the government after Independence Day, may be declared 'National land'. In this regard it is important to note that it is not a requisite that the subject land is required for a public purpose. The procedure to be followed by the Minister is stated in the following sections:

Section 11 Notice of intention to declare National land where land acquired after Independence Day

(1) Where for any purpose the State has acquired land on or after Independence Day, the Minister shall, by notice in the *National Gazette*, intimate his intention to declare, not earlier than the expiry of three months following the date of publication of the notice, that the land is National land.

(2) A notice under sub-section (1) shall –

(a) contain a description of the land; and

(b) state that any person aggrieved by the notice may make representation to the Minister within 60 days of –
    (i) the date of publication of the notice in the *National Gazette*; and
    (ii) compliance by the Minister with the requirements of section 52; and
(c) specify the estate acquired in the land.

Section 13 Declaration of National land acquired on or after Independence Day

(1) Where the Minister has published a notice under section 11 in respect of any land he may –
    (a) after the expiry of three months following –
        (i) the date of publication of the notice in the *National Gazette*; and
        (ii) the compliance by him with the requirements of section 52; and
    (b) after consideration of any representations made to him under section 12,

declare, by notice in the *National Gazette*, that the land, or any part of the land, is National land.

(2) A declaration made under sub-section (1) shall –
    (a) contain a description of the land; and
    (b) specify the estate in the land acquired by the State.

Registration of title to National land

National land declared under ss 9 or 13 vests in the State to the extent of the estate declared and, subject to any rights granted by the government prior to its declaration, may be dealt with as other land the property of the State.[61] The National Land Registration Act makes provision for the registration of National land under a Register known as the 'Register of National Land'.[62] Registration under this Act has the same effect as registration under the Land Registration Act. It is conclusive evidence that the State has title to the land, and the certificate of title issued by the Registrar is deemed to be conclusive evidence of registration and the particulars contained in it.[63]

Remedies of aggrieved claimants

Persons aggrieved by the Minister's decision under the National Land Registration Act, have various remedies open to them as outlined below.

---

61 Section 14 of the National Land Registration Act.

62 Section 15.

63 See ss 19, 22 and 23 of the National Land Registration Act.

(i) Judicial proceedings against declaration of National land

Section 10 Appeals against declarations of National land

(1) Subject to sections 57 (*enforcement of guaranteed rights and freedoms*) and 155 (the *National Judicial System*) of the Constitution, and to section 6 –

(a) a declaration under section 9 is not subject to appeal or review, and shall not be called in question in any legal proceedings; and

(b) compensation is not payable in respect of or arising out of any such declaration,

except as provided in this section.

The scope of this section was considered by the Supreme Court in *The Independent State of Papua New Guinea and Boyamo Sali v Lohia Sisia*.[64] In that case, the Minister in 1979 declared under s 8 of the National Land Registration Act, certain land acquired prior to Independence Day to be National land. Five and a half years later, the respondent, claiming to be acting on behalf of the traditional owners of the land, sought and obtained a judicial declaration that the Minister's declaration was invalid. On appeal to the Supreme Court the decision was reversed. Bredmeyer J, in his leading judgment, made the following observations:[65]

> The learned trial judge granted the declaration sought that the Minister's declaration of National land was invalid. As I have said, he did so on two bases: that the Minister had not complied with s 52 of the National Land Registration Act and that his action was harsh and oppressive under s 41 of the Constitution. The trial judge did not discuss the time lapse of five and a half years between the Minister's declaration of December 1979 and the writ of summons challenging its validity issued in June 1985. The matter is important and needs to be discussed.
>
> Section 155(4) of the Constitution which reads:
>
> (4) Both the Supreme Court and the National Court have an inherent power to make, in such circumstances as seem to them proper, orders in the nature of prerogative writs and such other orders as are necessary to do justice, in the circumstances of a particular case.
>
> In particular the power comes from the latter words of that sub-section 'such other orders as are necessary'. The Constitution is a superior law to a statute, and any statute must be read subject to the Constitution – see s 10 of the Constitution. Thus s 155(4) of the Constitution overrides s 9 [sic, s 10] of the National Land Registration Act which provides that the Minister's declaration under s 8 shall not be subject to appeal or review nor called in question in any legal proceeding, and s 19 of the Act which states that registration is conclusive evidence of the State's title to the land.
>
> I consider that this power under s 155(4) of the Constitution to invalidate a Minister's declaration of National land should be used sparingly. The courts should give some weight and some respect to Parliament's view expressed in s 9 and s 19 that the Minister's decision is not appealable or reviewable and that registration is conclusive evidence of the State's title. The way to do that is to say that the Minister's decision is reviewable by the courts but

64 [1987] PNGLR 102.

65 *Ibid*, at 107–08.

> will only be reviewed in special cases or in exceptional circumstances. I consider that that is the proper way we should exercise our powers under s 155. The courts have enormous power under s 155 to review the decision of any minister, tribunal or court. In exercising that power we can ignore any time limits imposed on appeal or review by statute, and any statutory 'ouster' provisions excluding review or appeal, of which there are many, such as s 9 [sic, s 10] of the National Land Registration Act. I consider that in all these cases it is the public interest that unreasonable delay should be a bar to review under s 155. Ministers, officials and tribunals should make their decisions fairly and in accordance with the law, and if they go wrong that can be corrected by the courts, but good government would be frustrated if decisions could be challenged *ad infinitum* in the courts.

The Supreme Court found that the delay of five and a half years was unreasonable and that the respondent had not shown special circumstances for the long delay. The court also held that the declaration of the subject land as National land was not 'harsh and oppressive' within meaning of s 41 of the Constitution.[66]

(ii) Settlement payment

Persons aggrieved by a declaration of land as National land under s 9, are entitled to claim for 'settlement' payment from the National Land Commission established under the Act.[67] The criteria and the procedure to be followed for making claims is summarised in the following extract:[68]

> Before any compensation is paid claimants must comply with certain conditions. In the first place, the subject land must have been declared National land and registered in the National Land Register. Secondly, the claim must be made within six months of the declaration in the *Gazette*. Thirdly, the claimants must prove that before independence a previous claim to the land was made under a law by virtue of which a claim to the land might have been made. Finally, they must not have received any payment (including *ex-gratia* payment) whether in cash or not by a pre-independence administration [s 40]. These provisions were intended to deter fresh claims from springing up, and to ensure that those which had previously been settled, however imperfectly, were not brought up again. Nevertheless, apart from the first condition the rest are flexible. The Commission at its discretion may allow claims which do not comply with these requirements. For example, if there are special reasons for not lodging a claim prior to independence and the Commission is of the opinion that non enforcement would be unfair, it may admit the claim. Also if the purchase price which was originally paid was, in its view, insignificant, it may allow the claim.

In its proceedings the Commission is not bound by technical rules of procedure and evidence. Section 34(4) of the Act states that the Commission shall investigate and inform itself on any matter before it in such manner as it thinks proper and admit and consider such relevant information as is available for purposes of determining the matter. Its only obligation is to comply with the rules of natural justice. Where the Commission is satisfied that the claimants are the owners of a customary right in the subject land, if it

66 It is not clear whether s 41 of the Constitution can be invoked against the exercise of any statutory powers or whether its application is limited to the exercise of qualified and basic rights set out in the Constitution. See *In the Matter of an Application by Rose Tarere et al v Australia and New Zealand Banking Group* (PNG) Ltd [1988] PNGLR 201 (extracted above, p 240).

67 Section 39.

68 John Mugambwa, 'Land disputes in PNG: a colonial legacy and post-Independence solutions', *op cit*, note 59, pp 112–13.

had not been acquired by the colonial administration, it must make an order for the payment by the state of a settlement payment. The amount of compensation payable is limited as prescribed in the schedule to the Act [ss 44 and 45].[69] Unlike proceedings before the Land Titles Commission, there is no right of appeal to the court except on the grounds of denial of natural justice.[70]

Note

The National Land Registration Act has no special provision for compensation of persons aggrieved by a declaration of National land under s 13 (land acquired on or after Independence Day). Presumably, aggrieved persons may challenge a declaration by way of review under the ordinary rules of law. However, once a declaration is registered it is conclusive of the State's title (ss 19 and 23).

Questions

1. What are the possible policy reasons for the requirement that State land acquired by a pre-Independence administration may be declared National land only if required for a public purpose, but that there is no such requirement where the subject land was acquired after Independence Day?
2. Assume that the State claims title over a small block of land fronting the sea. A nearby traditional community has for a long time disputed the State's title. Recently, the Minister declared the land to be 'National land' and plans to lease the land to an expatriate company to construct a block of luxury flats. Advise the traditional community of its legal options, if any.
3. Assume that in 1988, the government granted your client, A Pty Ltd, a special purpose lease for a period of 21 years. A Pty Ltd informs you that it has received a letter from a law firm representing a certain community claiming that the subject land is its customary land. The community threatens legal action unless A Pty Ltd vacates the land. You investigate and find that the lease is registered under the Land Registration Act, but the land has not been declared National land. You informally discuss with the relevant Minister the possibility of declaring the land 'National land' but the Minister makes it clear to you that a declaration is completely out of question because it might have adverse political repercussions against the government. What legal advice you would give your clients?

69 Schedule 2. The scale ranges from a minimum of 500 to a maximum of 28,300 kina for urban areas and between 100 and 750 kina (plus 10 kina per hectare in excess of 30 hectares) for rural areas. The Minister may at his discretion increase the payment in individual cases by up to 50% – s 45(4).

70 *Toare Karakara v The Independent State of Papua New Guinea* [1986] PNGLR 186.

INDEX

Accounting for profits,
  co-owners' liability 173–75

Acquiescence 141, 142

Acquisition of land,
  agreement, by 38
  compulsory process, by 271–74
  generally 1–4
  German New Guinea 18–27
  waste and vacant land 8, 9–11, 38

Airspace,
  ownership of 103–07

Alien enemy property,
  expropriation of 33

Alienated land,
  development of 11–16
  generally 78, 117–19
  Papua New Guinea 1962–73 37–38

Allodial title,
  British New Guinea 7
  generally 128–33
  German New Guinea 27, 32
  Mandated New Guinea 32

Annexation of territory,
  effect on customary or
    indigenous land rights 6–7
  generally 1–4

Australia,
  military administration 31–32
  See also Mandated New Guinea
    1921–45

Bodies corporate,
  joint tenants, as 153–54

British New Guinea 1884–1906 1–18
  acquisition of native land by
    individuals before annexation 1–4
  alienated land, development of 11–16
  allodial title, and 7
  common law, reception of 4–6
  customary land,
    allodial title 7
    annexation, effect of 6–7
    improving 16
    private dealings in 7–8
    public dealings in 8–9
  indigenous land rights,
    effect of annexation 6–7
  waste and vacant land,
    acquisition of 8, 9–11, 38

Chattels,
  fixtures distinguished 113–15

CILM Report 54–58, 67–68,
  89, 92, 93–94,
  97–98

Classification of land 117–19

Co-ownership of land,
  accounting for profits 173–75
  determination of 176–96
  enjoyment, rights of 165–76
  eviction of co-owner 171–72
  generally 151
  improvements and repairs,
    adjustments and
      allowance for 173, 175–76
    no compensation for 167–68
  joint tenancy
    See Joint tenancy
  no liability rule,
    exceptions 171–76
    improvements and repairs 167–68
    occupation rent 166–67
    trespass 169–71
  occupation rent,
    express or implied
      agreement to pay 173
    no liability for 166–67
  ouster of co-owner 171–72
  partition 196
  severance 176–96
  tenancy in common,
    creation of 155–65
    determination of 196
    joint tenancy
      distinguished 151, 158, 159
    meaning 151
    money advanced
      on mortgage 162
    partition 196
    partnership assets 159–61
    presumption in equity 158–64
    property purchased
      with funds contributed
      in unequal shares 158
    sale 196

words of severance 155–58
trespass, no liability for 169–71
types of 151–55
Commission of Inquiry into
Land Matters (CILM) 53–54
CILM Report 54–58, 67–68, 89, 92, 93–94, 97–98
Common law,
joint tenancy 155
land, conception of 103
reception of 4–6
Companies,
joint tenants, as 153–54
Compensation,
damages for deprivation
of land 502–04
assurance fund 504
liability 504
improvements and
repairs, for,
co-ownership of land 167–68, 173, 175–76
fixtures 108–13
State lease 396–98
termination of lease, on 355–57
land compensation claims 77–78
Covenants,
assignment 323–27, 333
reversion, of 331–32
enforcement,
assignment of reversion 331–32
generally 327
Land Registration Act,
under 333–34
neither privity of contract
nor of estate, where 332–33
privity of contract 328
privity of estate 328
express 312
generally 311–12
'good and tenantable repairs' 319–23
implied covenants,
fitness for human habitation 316–17
generally 312
landlord, against 312–17
not to derogate from grant 315–16
quiet enjoyment, for 312–15, 334
statute, implied by 318–19
usual covenants 318
remedies for breach,
distress 339
forfeiture
See Leases, forfeiture
landlord 339–52
tenant 334–38
restrictive covenants,
discharge of 418
enforcement 413–14
generally 399, 413–15
nature of 413, 415
requirements for 415
scheme of development 416–18
Torrens system, and 418–19
sublease 323–27, 333–34
usual covenants 318
Crown ownership,
absolute 119–21
minerals 107
Customary land,
alienability of interests in 73
British New Guinea,
allodial title 7
annexation, effect of 6–7
improving customary land 16
private dealings 7–8
public dealings 8–9
government monopoly
over land deals 79–86
Mandated New Guinea 34–35
Papua New Guinea,
1906–45 29
1945–62 36–37
1962–73 39–52
registration of 39
security of title 75
tenure,
conversion 39–40
economic development, and 41–51
Customary law,
allodial title 128–33
definition of land at 116–17
interests at 128–33
usufruct 108, 128–33

Damages
  See Compensation
Death,
  joint tenancy, and 154–55
Distress 339

Easements,
  abandonment 410
  certificate of title as
    evidence as to 410
  creation of 406–09
  definition 399
  essential features 399–405
  extinguishment 410, 413
  generally 399
  implied grant 406–07
  intended easement 408–09
  Land Registration Act, under 410–13
  merger 410
  modification 413
  registration 410–13
  way of necessity, of 407–08
Economic use of land 71–86
Ejectment 501–02
  summary 59, 340–43
Enemy property,
  expropriation of 33
Equitable estoppel 141
Estate,
  doctrine of 119–28
Estoppel,
  equitable 141
Eviction,
  co-owner, of 171–72

Fixtures,
  chattels distinguished 113–15
  compensation claims 108–13
  generally 108
  right to remove 116
Foreclosure
  See Mortgage

German missions 33–34
German New Guinea 1885–1914,
  administration and judicial
    application of regulations 27
  allodial title 27, 32
  generally 18
  imperial land legislations 18–27
Government monopoly in
  customary land deals 79–86

Homicide,
  severance by 193–96

Illegal occupation of land 59–60
Improvements and repairs,
  compensation 355–57
    co-ownership of land 167–68, 173, 175–76
    State lease 396–98
  covenants as to 319–23
Indigenous land rights,
  annexation, effect of 6–7
Indigenous peoples,
  restoration of land to 59–68
Interests in land 133–49

Joint tenancy,
  common law 155
  companies as joint tenants 153–54
  creation of 155–65
  determination of tenancy 196
  four unities 151–53
  meaning 151
  mortgage, money advanced on 161
  partition 196
  partnership assets 159–61
  property purchased with funds
    contributed in unequal shares 158
  sale 196
  severance,
    act of one joint tenant, by 177–89
    course of dealing, by 191–93
    generally 176–77
    homicide, by 193–96
    mutual agreement, by 189–91
    partial transfer of interest, by 186–89
    transfer to each other 180–85

transfer to third party 177–80
unilateral declaration 185–86
words of 155–58
simultaneous deaths 154–55
survivorship, right of 153–55
tenancy in common
See also Co-ownership of land
distinguished 151, 158, 159

Laches,
generally 142
res judicata 142–49

Land,
classification 117–19
common law conception 103
definition,
customary law, at. 116–17
statutory 103
interests in. 133–49
rights to,
above surface 103–07
below surface 107
fixtures. 108–16

Land Board. 360–64

Land registers,
restoration of 36

Large-scale farming,
economic development, and 45–46

Leases,
assignment 323–27, 333
reversion, of 331–32
certainty of duration. 277–80
classification,
private lease 359–60
significance of 359–60
State lease 359–60
compensation for
improvements 355–57
State lease 396–98
conditions 311–12
forfeiture for breach 339
covenants
See Covenants
creation of 296–311
distress. 339
duration, certainty of 277–80
essential features 277–96
exclusive possession 281–96
forfeiture,
condition, breach of. 339
definition. 339
duration of breach. 339
enforcement 339–43
equity. 348–50
generally 339
judicial proceedings 340–43
non-payment of rent 343–45, 351–52
relief against 348
self-help. 340
State lease,
appeals. 392–95
fine in lieu 395
judicial review 388–92
relief from forfeiture 396
statutory provisions 387–88
statutory relief against 351–52
summary ejectment. 340–43
waiver of right to enforce. 345–47
intention to create 281–96
licences distinguished. 275–77
merger 355
Minister, approval of. 303–11
nature of 275
non-payment of rent 343–45, 351–52
notice to quit. 352–54
private lease 359–60
registration requirement 297–98
effect of failure to register 298
equity, in 301–03
law, in. 298–301
rent, non-payment of. 343–45, 351–52
restrictive covenants
See Restrictive covenants
State leases
See State leases
sub-lease. 323–27, 333–34
surrender. 355
State lease, of 396
termination,
compensation for
improvements 355–57

effluxion of time . . . 352
merger . . . 355
notice to quit . . . 352–54
State lease . . . 387–98
surrender . . . 355
tenant, by . . . 334
vesting function for . . . 74

Licences,
leases distinguished . . . 275–77

Mandated New Guinea 1921–45,
allodial title . . . 32
customary rights in land,
protection of . . . 34–35
expropriation of alien
enemy property . . . 33
generally . . . 32
German missions . . . 33–34
land ownership as at 1942 . . . 32–33
restoration of civil
administration . . . 32
security of tenure . . . 32
uniform land policy . . . 34

Minerals,
ownership of . . . 107, 386

Mortgage,
collateral advantages . . . 260
continuing after redemption . . . 262–71
expiring with mortgage . . . 260–62
common law and statutory
mortgage distinguished . . . 197–98
compulsory process,
land acquired by . . . 271–74
creation of . . . 200–01
discharge by payment . . . 253–54
effect of . . . 197–200
equitable . . . 200–01
foreclosure,
action on a personal
covenant . . . 207–10
effect of . . . 204–10
generally . . . 202–04
re-opening . . . 205–07
sale in lieu . . . 211–12
title vests in mortgagee . . . 204
generally . . . 197
intention to create . . . 254
irredeemableness . . . 255–57
mortgagee,
nature of interest . . . 198–200
rights and remedies of . . . 201–54
special statutory provisions . . . 271–74
mortgagor, rights of . . . 254–74
nature of . . . 197–200
option to purchase . . . 255–57
payment, discharge by . . . 253–54
possession . . . 212–13
liability of mortgagee in . . . 213–15
receiver, appointment of . . . 216–18
redemption,
attempt to exclude right to . . . 255–57
equity of . . . 255–57
illusory right to redeem . . . 258–60
postponement of
redemption date . . . 257–58
registered . . . 200
sale,
application of proceeds of . . . 251–52
duties of seller . . . 220–26
duty of care . . . 226–39
effect of . . . 253
equitable mortgagee's
power of sale . . . 253
good faith, duty to act in . . . 223–26
harsh and oppressive acts . . . 239–44
in lieu of foreclosure . . . 211–12
manner of . . . 220
protection of purchaser . . . 244–50
statutory power of . . . 219–20
tenancy in common, and . . . 162
unregistered . . . 200–01

National land registration,
appeal against declaration . . . 511–12
generally . . . 69–71, 507
land acquired on or after
Independence Day . . . 509–10
land acquired before
Independence Day . . . 508–09
registration of title . . . 510
remedies of aggrieved
claimants . . . 510–13
settlement payment . . . 512–13

Native land
 See Customary land

New Guinea 1914–21,
 Australian military
  administration 31–32
 generally 29–31

Notice to quit 352–54

Occupation rent,
 co-ownership, and. 166–67, 173
 express or implied
  agreement to pay. 173

Ouster,
 co-owner, of 171–72

Papua New Guinea 1906–45,
 customary land,
  judicial system, and. 29
 native agriculture and economy. 29
 new constitution 28
 security of tenure. 28–29

Papua New Guinea 1945–62,
 customary land 36–37
 economic and social
  development 36–37
 generally 36
 restoration of land registers. 36
 security of title 36–37

Papua New Guinea 1962–73,
 alienated land. 37–38
 customary land, registration of. 39
 customary tenure, economic
  development, and 41–51
 tenure conversion 39–40
 unalienated land 38

Partition. 196

Plantation Redistribution Scheme 67–68

Plantations,
 redistribution of. 59–68

Privity of contract 328

Privity of estate 328

Receiver,
 appointment of 216–18

Registration of titles,
 caveats,
  cancellation by registrar 490
  duration of 489–92
  generally 487–89
  lapse by effluxion of time. 489–90
  removal by order of court 490
  resolving priorities between
   competing unregistered
   claims. 493–501
  withdrawal by caveator 490
  wrongful lodgment. 493
 customary land 39
 essential characteristics 421–87
 forged instrument of transfer 428–31
 fraudulent registration. 447–57
 generally 421
 indefeasibility of title 423–28
  easements, omission or
   misdescription of. 468–70
  encumbrances not on
   certificate of title 457–59
  exceptions. 446–87
  fraud 447–57
  judicial inroads on
   concept of 481–87
  lease or licence granted
   by Minister 478–79
  overriding statutory
   provisions 479–81
  prior instrument of title,
   claim under. 459–65
  tenancy document,
   possession under 471–78
  unpaid rates,
   taxes or charges 479
  unregistered short term
   lease or tenancy 470
  wrong description of land
   or boundaries 465–67
 National land registration 510
 protection of unregistered
  interests. 487–501
 restoration of land registers. 36
 State lease issued in breach of
  prescribed statutory
   procedure 431–46
 title by registration 421–23
 void instrument of transfer,
  under 427–28

Repairs
See Improvements and repairs
Res judicata 142–49
Restoration of land to
indigenous peoples 59–68
Restrictive covenants,
discharge of 418
enforcement 413–14
generally 399, 413–15
nature of 413, 415
requirements for 415
scheme of development 416–18
Torrens system, and 418–19

Security of tenure,
Mandated New Guinea 32
Papua New Guinea 1906–45 28–29
Security of title,
customary land 75
Papua New Guinea 1945–62 36–37
Smallholder farming,
economic development, and 43–45, 46, 47–51
State land,
definition 68
securing 68–71
State leases,
business lease 364
compensation for
improvements 396–98
forfeiture,
appeal against 392–95
fine in lieu 395
judicial review 388–92
relief from 396
statutory provisions 387–88
generally 359–60
grant of,
appeal against 365
judicial review 366–72
appeal distinguished 373–78
procedure 360–64
grant in breach of 431–46
purposes for 378–87
judicial review,
forfeiture 388–92
grant of State lease 366–78
Land Board 360–64
mineral rights 386
residence purpose lease 364
special purposes lease 364
surrender 396
termination 387–98
urban development lease 364
Sub-lease 323–27, 333–34
Summary ejectment 59, 340–43
Surrender of lease 355
State lease 396
Survivorship,
companies as joint tenants 153–54
joint tenancy, and 153–55
right of 153–55
simultaneous deaths 154–55

Tenancy in common
See also Co-ownership of land
creation of 155–65
determination of 196
joint tenancy distinguished 151, 158, 159
meaning 151
money advanced on mortgage 162
partition 196
partnership assets 159–61
presumption in equity 158–64
property purchased with funds
contributed in unequal shares 158
sale 196
severance
See Joint tenancy
Tenure,
doctrine of 119–28
security of
See Security of tenure
Tenure conversion 39–40
Title
See Registration of titles;
Security of title
Trespass,
airspace, to 103–07
co-ownership, and 169–71
summary ejectment 59

Unalienated land 38, 117–19
Usufruct 108, 128–33

Vacant land,
acquisition of 8, 9–11, 38

Waste land,
acquisition of 8, 9–11, 38